The
Economist

# DICTIONARY OF
# POLITICAL
# BIOGRAPHY

The
Economist

# DICTIONARY OF POLITICAL BIOGRAPHY

The
Economist
Books

First published in Great Britain by Business Books Ltd, an imprint of Random Century Ltd, Random Century House, 20 Vauxhall Bridge Road, London SW1V 2SA, in association with The Economist Books Ltd.

Research and compilation by Cambridge International Reference on Current Affairs Ltd (CIRCA), for The Economist Books Ltd.

*Editor* Jane Carroll
*Assistant Editor* Angela Brown
*Sub-editor* Miles Smith-Morris
*Copy editors* Elizabeth Clark, Isla MacLean, Roger Thomas
*Production Assistants* Alan Duff, Sara Harper

*Editorial Director* Stephen Brough
*Art Director* Douglas Wilson
*Production Manager* Robert Gray

**Editorial panel**
Hilary Barnes, Patrick Blum, Jim Bodgener, Paddy Bowie, Keith Boyfield, Derek Brooke-Wavell, Sir Mervyn Brown, Tom Burns, David Butter, Duncan Campbell-Smith, Jonathan Carr, Jonathan Crusoe, Chris Cviic, Daniel de Roulet, John Earle, Simon Edge, Stephen Ellis, Vaudine England, Teresa English, Granville Fletcher, Daniel Franklin, Jeremy Gaunt, Phil Gunson, Simon Henderson, Angus Hindley, Diana Hubbard, Derek Ingram, Shaun Johnson, Tim Judah, David Lane, Barry Langridge, Dick Leonard, Simon Long, W. L. Luetkens, Gill Lusk, Paul Maidment, Jon Marks, Richard Mayne, James Miles, Mario Modiano, Vahe Petrossian, David Pike, Kevin Rafferty, Vladimir Sobell, Peter Spinks, Judy Stowe, Frederick Studemann-Schulenburg, Richard Synge, Mary Ellen Synon, Elizabeth Teague, David Usborne, Louisa Vinton, Philip Wearne, Elizabeth Wright, Dick Wilson.

Special thanks are also due to Roger East and Martin Wright of CIRCA.

The greatest care has been taken in compiling this book. However, no responsibility can be accepted by the publishers or contributors for the accuracy of the information presented. Where opinion is expressed it is that of the author and does not necessarily coincide with the editorial views of *The Economist* newspaper.

Any correspondence regarding this publication should be addressed to: The Editorial Director, The Economist Books, Axe and Bottle Court, 70 Newcomen Street, London SE1 1YT

A catalogue record for this book is available from the British Library.

ISBN 0-09-174847-X

Typeset by TPS, London
Printed in Great Britain by Butler and Tanner, Frome, England.

# INTRODUCTION

In this first edition of *The Economist Dictionary of Political Biography* our aim has been to provide succinct portraits of those who most influence the world of politics today. The following categories of people have been included: heads of state, heads and members of government, political party leaders, leading parliamentarians, prominent regional or state governors, other key figures in local government, influential public servants, leading trade unionists, heads of professional and non-governmental bodies, leaders of dissident groups, lobbyists and campaigners, international public servants and Euro-politicians.

We made our selection of names from among people who were *alive and active in politics and exercising significant influence on the national or international political scene.* The cut-off date was 31 December 1990, but a *Stop Press* section lists major political events between then and going to press.

We are very grateful for the invaluable specialist assistance given by members of the editorial panel, who are listed on the facing page, and we welcome any comments that will help in the preparation of future editions.

# CONTENTS

## January

**1st.** *Jordan:* Taher al-Masri was appointed foreign minister, replacing **Marwan al-Qasem**.

*Switzerland:* **Flavio Cotti** became president and **René Felber** vice-president for one-year terms under Switzerland's rotating presidential system.

**4th.** *Poland:* **Jan Krzysztof Bielecki** was sworn in as prime minister, following his nomination by President **Lech Wałęsa** on December 29. The split among Solidarity deputies in Poland's parliament was formalized with the formation of the Democratic Union, led by **Bronisław Geremek**.

**5th.** *Bangladesh:* Charges of illegal possession of firearms and embezzlement of public funds were filed against former president **Hussein Mohammed Ershad**.

**6th.** *Guatemala:* **Jorge Serrano Elias** emerged as the clear winner in the second round of the presidential elections. His opponent, **Jorge Carpio Nicolle**, conceded defeat the following day and promised to act as a loyal but watchful opposition. Serrano was sworn in on January 8 and announced a multi-party "national unity" cabinet, including **Alvaro Arzú**, who came fourth in the first round of the presidential elections, as foreign minister.

**7th.** *India:* Murli Manohar Joshi was elected president of the Bharatiya Janata Party, replacing **Lal Krishna Advani**.

*USA:* Agriculture Secretary **Clayton Yeutter** was chosen by President **George Bush** as new chairman of the Republican National Committee. **Edward Madigan** was nominated as new agriculture secretary.

**8th.** *Argentina:* **Mohammed Alí Seineldin** and six other officers were sentenced to indefinite imprisonment for their involvement in the rebellion of December 3, 1990.

*USSR:* Lithuania's prime minister, **Kazimiera Prunskiene**, resigned. Albertas Shiminas was chosen on January 10 to succeed her.

**9th.** *Gulf:* Talks between US Secretary of State **James Baker** and his Iraqi counterpart **Tariq Aziz** in Geneva failed to make any progress in reaching a peaceful solution to the Gulf crisis.

*Lebanon:* The newly formed Lebanese "government of national unity" won a vote of confidence in the National Assembly, but Druse leader **Walid Jumblatt** resigned from it the following day.

**12th.** *Hungary:* **Ferenc József Nagy** was replaced as agriculture minister by Elemer Gergatz; Nagy became a minister without portfolio.

*India:* Leaders of three factions of the Akali Dal announced they would merge to form Shiromani Akali Dal, under **Simranjit Singh Mann**.

*Poland:* Parliament voted to accept the cabinet proposed by the new prime minister **Jan Krzysztof Bielecki**. Three members of the previous government retained their posts: **Leszek Balcerowicz** (deputy prime minister and finance minister), **Krzysztof Skubiszewski** (foreign affairs) and Vice-Admiral **Piotr Kołodziejczyk** (defence). **Wiesław Chrzanowski** was appointed justice minister. **Zdzisław Najder** joined a committee of advisers to President **Lech Wałęsa**.

*Spain:* **Alfonso Guerra González** resigned as deputy prime minister.

**13th.** *Cape Verde:* In the first multi-party legislative elections, the newly formed Movement for Democracy (MPD), led by **Carlos Veiga**, defeated the ruling African Party for the Independence of Cape Verde (PAICV).

*Germany:* **Lothar Späth** resigned as premier of Baden-Württemberg but denied allegations that he had accepted benefits in the form of free holidays. He was succeeded by Erwin Teufel, the Christian Democratic Union leader in the Baden-Württemberg parliament.

*Portugal:* **Mário Soares** was re-elected for a second five-year term as president.

**14th.** *USSR:* **Valentin Pavlov** was appointed prime minister, replacing the ailing **Nikolai Ryzhkov**, with **Vitaly Doguzhiyev** and Vladimir Velichko as first deputy premiers and **Yury Maslyukov** and **Nikolai Laverov** as deputy premiers.

**15th.** *USSR:* **Alecsander Bessmertnykh** and **Boris Pugo** were confirmed as new foreign affairs and interior minister, replacing **Eduard Shevardnadze** and **Vadim Bakatin**.

**16th.** *Gulf:* Hostilities began with US and British air raids shortly before midnight on the first day on which military action could be taken under UN Security Council resolution 678.

*Albania:* The first multi-party elections were postponed from February 10 to March 31.

*Argentina:* Public works minister **Roberto Dromi** was dropped from the cabinet.

*Germany:* Chancellor **Helmut Kohl** announced agreement on a government programme and on the distribution of cabinet portfolios. Most principal portfolios remained unchanged. Former education minister **Jürgen Möllemann** became economy minister, replacing **Jürgen Warnke.** **Irmgard Adam-Schwätzer** was appointed construction minister. **Hans Engelhard** was replaced as justice minister by an independent, Klaus Kinkel. The portfolio for youth, family, women and health, formerly held by **Ursula-Maria Lehr** was split up, with the health component going to **Gerda Hasselfeldt**, Angela Merkel taking responsibility for women and youth and Hannelore Rönsch for family and the elderly. **Günther Krause** took over the transport portfolio from **Friedrich Zimmermann.** Only three members of the new cabinet were from the former East Germany: Merkel, Krause and the new education minister, Rainer Ortleb.

**17th.** *Norway:* **King Olav V** died after a long illness. His son **Harald** was sworn in as Harald V on January 21.

**20th.** *São Tomé and Príncipe:* The ruling Movement for the Liberation of São Tomé and Príncipe – Social Democratic Party was defeated by the opposition Democratic Convergence Party – Reflection Group (PCD – GR) in the islands' first multi-party elections. PCD – GR general secretary Daniel Lima dos Santos Daio was named to form an interim government.

**22nd.** *Uganda:* George Cosmas Adyebo, 43, former principal of the Uganda College of Commerce, was named prime minister. His predecessor, **Samson Kisekka**, was appointed vice-president.

**28th.** *Argentina:* **Domingo Cavallo** moved to the economy ministry, to replace **Antonio Erman González**, who had resigned. González was appointed defence minister, replacing Guido di Tella, who moved to the foreign ministry.

**29th.** *France:* Defence minister **Pierre Chevènement** resigned after arguing unsuccessfully that the Gulf war should be restricted to Kuwait; he was replaced by **Pierre Joxe**, the former interior minister. Philippe Marchand became interior minister.

*Somalia:* Ali Mahdi Mohammed of the rebel United Somali Congress (USC) was sworn in as interim president; his predecessor **Mohammad**

**Siyad Barre** had fled Mogadishu three days earlier, after more than a month of fierce fighting between government and rebel forces. Umar Arteh Ghalib, who had been appointed prime minister by Siyad Barre on January 20, was asked to head the interim government.

*South Africa:* African National Congress deputy president **Nelson Mandela** met Inkatha leader **Mangosuthu Buthelezi** in Durban in an effort to end the violence between supporters of their two organizations and announced that they had agreed on a peace strategy.

## February

**1st.** *UK:* **Brian Griffiths,** former head of the Downing Street policy unit, was appointed chairman of the Centre for Policy Studies.

**2nd.** *South Africa:* In a speech to parliament, President **F. W. de Klerk** promised to repeal the remaining apartheid legislation.

**3rd.** *France:* Gaullist rebel **Michel Noir** was re-elected to the National Assembly.

*Italy:* Delegates to the Italian Communist Party's 20th congress voted to accept the party's new name: Democratic Party of the Left (PDS).

**4th.** *South Africa:* The trial of **Winnie Mandela** on charges of kidnapping and assault began in Johannesburg.

**5th.** *Ireland:* Brendan Daly was named defence minister, the post formerly held by **Brian Lenihan**.

**7th.** *Haiti:* **Jean-Bertrand Aristide** was sworn in as president; he named agronomist and baker Réné Préval as prime minister.

**8th.** *Czechoslovakia:* The split in Civic Forum was formalized, with chairman **Václav Klaus** leading the free-market faction and the liberal group around **Jiří Dientsbier** pursuing a more social democratic orientation. But the two groups agreed to operate under the Civic Forum banner until the next general election.

**9th.** *Italy:* **Achille Occhetto** was elected to head the new Democratic Party of the Left, the former Communist Party.

*Malaysia:* The resignation of finance minister **Daim Zainuddin** was announced. He was replaced by former education minister **Anwar Ibrahim**. **Abdullah Ahmad Badawi** returned to the cabinet as foreign minister, replacing **Abu Hassan Omar**, who moved to the portfolio of domestic trade and consumer affairs. New education minister was Suleiman Daud. The reshuffle was due to take effect on March 15.

*Suriname:* The military regime announced elections would be held on May 25.

**17th.** *Benin:* Twenty-four parties contested the first multi-party elections; seventeen of the parties won seats in the National Assembly but none obtained an overall majority.

*Cape Verde:* Former Supreme Court judge Antonio Mascarenhas Monteiro of the Movement for Democracy was elected president, defeating the incumbent, **Arístides Pereira**.

**19th.** *India:* Five ministers, including foreign minister **Vidya Charan Shukla**, resigned from the government following their disqualification as MPs in January.

**20th.** *Albania:* After widespread unrest, President **Ramiz Alia** announced the formation of a new government, headed by Fatos Nano.

*UK:* Dame **Shirley Porter** (her new title was announced in the New Years honours list) announced she would stand down in April.

**23rd.** *Gulf:* Forces of the US-led coalition began the ground assault to recapture Kuwait.

**24th.** *Thailand:* The government of prime minister **Chartchai Chunhawan** was overthrown in a bloodless military coup.

**25th.** *Gulf:* Iraqi president **Saddam Hussain** ordered the withdrawal of Iraqi forces from Kuwait.

**26th.** *Gulf:* Kuwaiti and Saudi forces entered Kuwait City following the Iraqi withdrawal.

*Greece:* A hardliner, Aleka Papariga, was elected secretary-general of the Greek Communist Party (KKE), replacing **Grigoris Farakos**.

*Pakistan:* Foreign minister **Sahabzada Yaqub Khan** resigned, following criticism from within the ruling Islamic Democratic Alliance of Pakistan's support for the US-led coalition in the war against Iraq.

**27th.** *Gulf:* President **George Bush** announced the suspension of fighting in the Gulf war, subject to Iraq's acceptance of all UN Security Council resolutions on the occupation of Kuwait and the immediate return of prisoners of war.

*Bangladesh:* General elections result in a victory for the Bangladesh Nationalist Party (BNP) led by **Begum Khaleda Zia**, which fell just short of winning an overall majority in parliament.

*USA:* A Senate committee cleared four senators, including **John Glenn** and **Don Riegle**, of

intervening with federal regulators on behalf of savings and loan executive Charles Keating. It found, however, "substantial credible evidence" that Senator **Alan Cranston** committed ethical violations in his relationship with Keating.

**28th.** *El Salvador:* Former presidential candidate **Guillermo Manuel Ungo** died.

*Mongolia:* Budragchaa Dashiyondon was elected general secretary of the Mongolian People's Revolutionary Party by the party congress, replacing **Gombojavyn Ochirbat**.

**March**

**1st.** *Sri Lanka:* Minister of state for defence **Ranjan Wijeratne** was killed in a car bomb explosion in Colombo.

**3rd.** *São Tomé and Príncipe:* **Miguel Trovoada**, the sole candidate, won 81% of the vote in the presidential election.

*Thailand:* Industrialist and former diplomat Anand Panyarachun was appointed interim prime minister by the military junta.

**4th** *Kuwait:* Crown Prince **Shaikh Saad al-Abdullah al-Sabah** and other members of the government returned from exile.

**6th.** *India:* Prime minister **Chandra Shekhar** resigned following a boycott of parliament by the Congress (I) party.

**7th.** *Austria:* The environment, youth and family affairs minister, **Marilies Flemming**, resigned.

*South Africa:* **Enos Mabuza** announced his resignation as chief minister of the KaNgwane "homeland".

*International:* **Barber Conable** announced his decision to step down as president of the World Bank at the end of June 1991. He was to be replaced by Lewis Preston.

**10th.** *Benin:* Prime minister **Nicéphore Soglo** failed to secure an overall majority in the presidential election. He was to face a run-off on March 24 against President **Mathieu Kérékou**.

*El Salvador:* The Nationalist Republican Alliance (Arena) claimed victory in national and municipal elections, although the left-wing Democratic Convergence made gains.

**11th.** *Spain:* Former defence minister **Narcís Serra** was appointed deputy prime minister. **Julián García**, the former health minister, took over the defence portfolio. Agriculture minister **Carlos Romero** was replaced by Pedro Solbes.

# A

**ABALKIN, Leonid.** *USSR.* Former deputy prime minister, responsible for economic reform. A Russian, born in 1930, his long academic career culminated in his appointment in 1986 as director of the Institute of Economics at the Academy of Sciences. From 1976 he was also an economic adviser to the Communist Party of the Soviet Union central committee. He was brought into the government in July 1989, and given the unenviable task of producing a workable rescue plan for the crisis-ridden economy. His programme of market reforms presented in May 1990 was criticized as incoherent and too heavily reliant on price rises, and was returned by parliament for reworking. Resubmitted in September 1990, the plan came under renewed fire before the eventual adoption of **Abel Aganbegyan**'s compromise version.

**ABBOTT, Diane.** *UK.* Labour politician. Born in 1953 and educated at Cambridge University, she worked in television, the union movement and local government before being elected to parliament in 1987, its first black woman member.

**ABDELAZIZ, Mohammed.** *Western Sahara.* Secretary-general of Polisario. Educated in Morocco, he became a supporter of the movement to secure independence for the Spanish colony of Western Sahara during his student days in Rabat in the early 1970s. He helped to found the Polisario Front in 1973 and became its most important leader. He was elected its secretary-general in 1976 and is effective head of state of the Polisario-proclaimed Sahrawi Arab Democratic Republic.

**ABDEL-MEGUID, Ahmed Esmat.** *Egypt.* Foreign minister and deputy prime minister. Born in 1923, a lawyer by training, he served as an attaché at Egypt's London embassy from 1950–54, returning to head the UK desk at the foreign ministry. A series of diplomatic appointments followed, including ambassador to France from 1970–72 and to the UN from 1972–82. He was appointed foreign minister in 1984 and deputy prime minister the following

year. A cautious and skilful diplomat, he has presided over Egypt's reintegration into the Arab world after its years in the wilderness following the Camp David treaty with Israel.

**ABDEL-RAHMAN, Sheikh Omar.** *Egypt.* A blind theologian, he teaches Islamic principles at the University of Assiut, which has a reputation as a hotbed of fundamentalism; he is allegedly the spiritual leader of the outlawed Al-Jihad (Holy War) organization. Acquitted of complicity in the assassination of President Anwar Sadat in 1981, he was repeatedly rearrested on charges of incitement to riot in the 1980s. The government, aware of his popularity among the poor of Cairo and the industrial towns of the Delta, appears reluctant to make a martyr of him through lengthy imprisonment.

**ABDULLAH, Farooq.** *India.* Former chief minister of Kashmir and Jammu. Born in Srinagar in 1937, a medical doctor by profession, he became leader of the Kashmir National Conference (KNC) and chief minister of Kashmir after the death in 1982 of his father, Sheikh Mohammed Abdullah. His government was destabilized in 1983, when Congress encouraged a minority faction in the KNC to break away. The dissident group entered a coalition with the state Congress (I) party and displaced Abdullah. His supporters responded with a campaign of mass civil disobedience which paralysed the state administration and forced the imposition of central rule in 1986. Shortly after the collapse of the Kashmir government **Rajiv Gandhi** reached an agreement with Abdullah which provided for a KNC-Congress (I) coalition with Abdullah as chief minister. The coalition won the 1987 election in the Muslim Kashmir valley, but amid widespread accusations of corruption and vote-rigging. It was highly unpopular and was seen as a betrayal of Kashmiri autonomy and tarnished with allegations of corruption. Militant separatist groups gained increasing support. Unable to contain the ensuing disorder, Abdullah's government was finally dismissed by the National Front government in 1990 and the state again placed under central government control.

**ABDULLAH AHMAD BADAWI, Datuk.** *Malaysia.* United Malays National Organization (UMNO) vice-president. An influential figure within UMNO despite his absence from the cabinet in recent years, Abdullah was born in 1939 and educated at the University of Malaya before joining the civil service. His first government post was as minister without portfolio in the prime minister's office in 1982. He subsequently served as education minister from 1984–86 and defence minister until 1987 when he backed **Mahathir Mohamad**'s rival **Razaleigh Hamzah** in the divisive elections for the UMNO presidency. Abdullah remained popular within UMNO and held on to his position as one of its three vice-presidents at the party's November 1990 general assembly; he is regarded as a likely rival to **Anwar Ibrahim** to succeed Mahathir.

**ABDULLAH IBN ABDUL-AZIZ, Prince.** *Saudi Arabia.* First deputy prime minister. Born in Riyadh in 1923, the 13th son of King Abdul-Aziz, he represents the traditionalists within the Saudi royal family. Since 1963 he has headed the 40,000-strong National Guard, which is recruited exclusively from the leading Saudi tribes and acts as a counterweight to the army. Abdullah does not appear to have had a formal education, official sources stating that he was taught by "noted scholars and intellectuals". Most of his early years were spent in the desert and he remains a bedouin at heart, enjoying strong ties with tribal leaders. After King Faisal's assassination in 1975 he was appointed first deputy prime minister.

**ABE, Shintaro.** *Japan.* Liberal Democratic Party (LDP) politician and faction leader. Born in 1924 in Tokyo, he moved to Yamaguchi prefecture after his parents' divorce. His father, Kan, was a politician during the pre-war period. Abe graduated from the law faculty of Tokyo Imperial University (now Tokyo University) and joined the *Mainichi Shimbun* newspaper. While a political reporter he married the daughter of Nobusuke Kishi, a former prime minister and a very influential LDP politician. Abe became his father-in-law's secretary in 1956, when Kishi was appointed foreign minister. Under Kishi's experienced eye, he was elected to the House of Representatives (lower house) in 1958. He first entered the cabinet as chief cabinet secretary under **Takeo Fukuda** in 1977, successively holding various important posts such as

chairman of the Policy Research Council, international trade and industry minister and foreign minister. After an unsuccessful challenge for the LDP leadership in the 1982 party elections, he was again appointed foreign minister under **Yasuhiro Nakasone**. In 1986, Abe became a faction leader, and chairman of the LDP general council, again unsuccessfully contesting the party presidency in 1987. Defeated by **Noboru Takeshita**, who had the blessing of Nakasone, Abe gained the post of secretary-general. Despite being tainted by the Recruit corruption scandal, he remains a powerful party figure. Thanks to his extensive tenure at foreign affairs, Abe has a diplomat's sixth sense for international issues. His health is not good, however, and his chances of acquiring the leadership of the party and, indeed, maintaining control of his faction, seem to be receding.

**ABRAHAM, Hérard.** *Haiti.* Army commander. Abraham, a career soldier, first entered politics as information minister in the cabinet appointed after the fall of former president Jean-Claude Duvalier in 1986. He was later transferred to foreign affairs. As army commander after the overthrow of General Henri Namphy in September 1988, he supported Prosper Avril and then Ertha Pascal-Trouillot as president while avoiding the presidential office himself. Promoted to the rank of major-general in 1990, he is often seen as one of the few forces for stability in Haitian politics.

**ABU GHAZALA, Field-Marshal Mohammed Abdel-Halim.** *Egypt.* Assistant to the president. Born in 1930, he received military training in the USA and served in the Middle East wars of 1948, 1956, 1967 and 1973. From 1976–80 he was defence attaché at the Egyptian embassy in Washington, establishing valuable contacts that he was later to exploit in strengthening Egypt's strategic alliance with the USA. Appointed chief of staff in 1980, he was brought into the cabinet by Anwar Sadat in March 1981 as defence and military production minister. He was wounded during Sadat's assassination in October that year. In 1982 President **Hosni Mubarak** awarded him the additional post of deputy prime minister. Long regarded as a rival and potential successor to Mubarak, he is said to have refused the premiership in March 1989 because he would not have been allowed to retain the defence portfolio, which he had used to establish a power base within the armed forces as well as to build up Egypt's defence capabilities. In

August 1989, however, in what was seen as a demotion, he was removed from his post and appointed an assistant to the president, a position without specific responsibilities. This followed reports that he had been implicated in attempts to smuggle classified US missile technology to Egypt. In 1990 he was put in charge of co-ordinating the government's controversial privatization programme.

**ABU NIDAL (Sabri Khalil al-Banna).** *Palestinian.* Leader of the "Revolutionary Council of Fatah", more commonly known as the "Abu Nidal Group", a notorious terrorist faction responsible for attacks on Israelis, Westerners and "moderate" Palestinians. Born in the 1930s in Jaffa, Abu Nidal joined **Yasser Arafat's** Fatah guerrilla group in the late 1950s. Dissatisfied with its relatively moderate stance, he broke away to form his own organization in 1973, based in Iraq and later in Syria. The Abu Nidal Group's attempted assassination of the Israeli ambassador in London, Shlomo Argov, in June 1982 gave Israel a pretext to invade Lebanon. The group specialized in attacks on Arab figures whom it viewed as traitors to the Palestinian cause, killing the moderate Palestine Liberation Organization (PLO) member, Issam Sartawi, in August 1983, and the Israeli-appointed mayor of Nablus, in the West Bank, in March 1986. In their most notorious operation, in December 1985, Abu Nidal Group guerrillas carried out particularly brutal attacks on passengers at Rome and Vienna airports. Abu Nidal's activities have been repeatedly condemned by the PLO, which sentenced him to death in 1974. By 1988, under intense pressure from Arab states and a re-united PLO, Abu Nidal had reportedly agreed to rein in his guerrillas, and to abide by the decisions, including the ban on terrorism, made by the mainstream PLO. According to reports, he has been back in his Baghdad base since late 1989.

**ACHEIKH IBN OUMAR.** *Chad.* Presidential councillor. Formerly leader of the Libyan-based opposition Revolutionary Democratic Committee (CDR), he returned to Chad in November 1988, leaving most of his former followers in exile. He was appointed foreign minister five months later and used his contacts in Libya to negotiate an agreement to take the Aozou strip territorial dispute to international arbitration. After the overthrow of **Hissène Habré** in December 1990 he was appointed a special councillor to new President **Idriss Déby**.

**ADAM-SCHWÄTZER, Irmgard.** *Germany.* Minister of state in the foreign ministry. One of the younger and brighter faces in the Free Democratic Party (FDP), she was born in Münster in 1942. She studied pharmacy, gained her doctorate in 1971 and worked in industry, spending two years with her pharmacist husband in Brussels. She was first elected to parliament in 1980, having joined the FDP in 1975 when she claimed she needed a hobby. A strong supporter of the FDP's decision to switch coalition partners from the Social Democrats to the Christian Democrats, she was rewarded by election as party secretary-general, and in 1984 took over the difficult post of treasurer. After the FDP's election success in 1987 she joined her leader, **Hans-Dietrich Genscher**, in the foreign ministry as minister of state.

**ADAMS, Gerry.** *UK and Ireland.* Irish nationalist politician. Born in 1948, he has been active in the civil rights movement and nationalist politics since his youth. He was interned in 1972 and again in 1973 on suspicion of belonging to the Irish Republican Army (IRA). He was released in 1977. In 1983 he was elected president of Sinn Féin, often described as the "political wing" of the IRA. It marked a watershed in the party's history: control shifted from a Dublin-based old guard to a new generation of militants based in Northern Ireland, and a new set of left-wing "Irish republican socialist" principles was adopted. He has been the brains behind Sinn Féin's transformation into a populist movement intent on seeking social as well as political change. The new emphasis on electoral politics – complementing the "bullet" with the "ballot" – has brought the party considerable electoral gains in Northern Ireland (although its support in the Irish republic has collapsed). He was elected to the House of Commons in 1983, as MP for West Belfast, but has refused to take his seat at Westminster.

**ADEDEJI, Adebayo.** *Nigeria.* Executive secretary of UN Economic Commission for Africa (ECA). Born in 1930, he studied economics in Nigeria, the UK and USA and taught public administration in Nigeria. He was economic development minister from 1971 until his appointment as ECA executive secretary in 1975.

**ADHIKARI, Man Mohan.** *Nepal.* Communist Party leader. Identified in 1987 as a leading left-winger associated with the banned Nepali Congress Party opposition, he opposed participation in the non-party local elections arranged by the regime of **King Birendra** that year. By late 1989 he had become vocal in demanding the abolition of the *panchayat* system and the formation of a national government. Imprisoned briefly in December 1989, he was released and contributed to the success of the period of agitation known as the "stir", which by April 1990 had forced the king to accept the need for fundamental reforms. Now identified as leader of the Communist Party of Nepal, he became the most trenchant critic of subsequent attempts by Birendra to evade the pledges of change wrung from him by the "stir".

**ADVANI, Lal Krishna.** *India.* Bharatiya Janata Party (BJP) leader. Born in Karachi in 1914, he joined the militant Hindu association, the Rashtriya Swayamsevak Sangh (RSS), in 1942 and helped to found its political wing, the Bharatiya Jan Sangh, in 1951. After a career in Delhi municipal politics, he became a member of the Rajya Sabha (upper house) in 1970. He was imprisoned by Indira Gandhi's administration during the emergency of 1975–77. The Jan Sangh merged with other opposition parties to form the Janata Party in 1977 and Advani became information minister in the Janata government (1977–79). After the break-up of the Janata coalition, the Jan Sangh re-formed as the BJP with Advani as its first general secretary. In 1986 he was elected its president. The government formed by **V.P. Singh** after the November 1989 elections depended on BJP support for its parliamentary majority. The withdrawal of this support, with Advani riding the tide of Hindu intransigence over the Ayodhya mosque dispute, was enough to bring down Singh's government a year later. When the **Chandra Shekhar** government took office with Congress (I) support in November 1990, Advani became opposition leader.

**AFANASYEV, Yury.** *USSR.* Leading radical politician. A historian and government critic, he is best known for demanding that the USSR fully admit its crimes and failures. In July 1989 he joined **Boris Yeltsin**, **Gavriil Popov** and the late Andrei Sakharov in the leadership of the Inter-Regional Group, the first opposition faction in the USSR Congress of People's Deputies. He was a leading member of the "Democratic Platform" faction formed by Communist Party radicals in January 1990, but in April he resigned from the party, declaring it "beyond redemption".

**AGA KHAN, Prince Sadruddin.** *Iran.* Personal representative of the UN secretary-general for humanitarian assistance relating to the Gulf crisis. Born in 1933, a son of the (immensely wealthy) third Aga Khan, the spiritual leader of the Ismaili Muslim sect, he was educated at Harvard University. Since 1958 he has spent much of his time acting as a consultant to the UN and UN bodies and has become one of the organization's most experienced servants. Among his main interests has been the plight of refugees; he was UN high commissioner for refugees from 1965–77. His most recent assignments have been to co-ordinate assistance for refugees in Afghanistan (until December 1990), Iraq and Kuwait. In the 1980s he co-chaired an independent commission on international humanitarian issues, whose report *Famine: A Man-made Disaster?* was much admired for its level-headedness and absence of fashionable polemic – qualities that also characterize his proposals for reform of the UN as a whole. He is regarded as a possible candidate for the post of UN secretary-general when **Javier Pérez de Cuéllar's** term of office ends in 1991.

**AGANBEGYAN, Abel.** *USSR.* Refomist economist. An Armenian, born in 1932 in Tbilisi, Georgia, he has been professor of economics at Novosibirsk State University since 1985 and head of the economics department of the USSR Academy of Sciences since 1986. He was one of the earliest and most vocal proponents of the kind of economic reforms that constituted the first phase of **Mikhail Gorbachev's** *perestroika* programme. In 1990 he returned to the public eye when he was commissioned to work out a synthesis of rival economic reform programmes – a task he eventually acknowledged to be impossible, insofar as his compromise, adopted in October, was conspicuously short on detail.

**AGNOS, Art.** *USA.* Mayor of San Francisco. Born in Massachusetts in 1938, he took office in 1988, defeating the incumbent **Dianne Feinstein** by a large majority. His attempt to cope with a $172.4m budget deficit resulted in lay-offs, reduced services and increased transport fares. The damage caused by the 1989 earthquake caused further strain, as has increased immigration and the growth of Los Angeles as a trading centre. Agnos has a mix of conservative and liberal policies: he is a vehement opponent of drugs legalization but has supported the extension of city health benefits to unmarried and homosexual couples.

**AHMAR, Abdullah al-.** *Syria.* Assistant secretary-general of the ruling Ba'th Party. Ahmar is one of the large number of Sunni

Muslims who hold senior posts under the leadership of the quasi-Shia Alawi President **Hafez al-Assad**. In 1985, he replaced the president's disgraced brother, Rifaat, as vice-president for security affairs. The following year, he was briefly detained by the Israelis when the Libyan executive jet in which he was travelling was forced down in Israel.

**AHMED, Kazi Zafar**. *Bangladesh.* Former prime minister. Born in 1940, he was a student activist in Dhaka (and imprisoned on several occasions in the mid-1960s), and an active participant in the independence struggle in 1971. He led the left-wing dissidents who split from the National Awami Party to form the United People's Party, and held office as education minister under Ziaur Rahman in 1978; the UPP merged into president **Hussein Mohammed Ershad**'s National Party (Jatiya Dal) before the 1986 elections. Ahmed was appointed prime minister in August 1989 after three years in the government. He was deposed after Ershad's downfall and fled the country.

**AHMED, Moudud**. *Bangladesh.* Former vice-president. Appointed to this position by former president **Hussein Mohammed Ershad** in August 1989, he retained the industry portfolio which he had previously held during a year in office as prime minister, and also took on the responsibility for law and justice. He was born in 1940, trained as a lawyer, and worked from exile in India in 1971 to organize publicity for Bangladesh as the new country was being created through the defeat of Pakistan. He was arrested following Ershad's overthrow in December 1990.

**AHMED, Shehabuddin**. *Bangladesh.* Acting president. Formerly chief justice, he was nominated to act as president by the three main opposition alliances after the resignation of president **Hussein Mohammed Ershad** in early December 1990. He was expected to hand over power to an elected government after the February 1991 parliamentary elections.

**AHN EUNG MO.** *South Korea.* Home affairs minister. Born in 1930, he headed the national police headquarters from 1982–83 before resigning after the death of a businessman in custody. In 1984 he became governor of South Chungchong province and was deputy director of the National Security Planning Agency from 1988–89.

**AIKHOMU, Augustus**. *Nigeria.* Vice-president and retired vice-admiral. Born in 1939 in Bendel state, he joined the navy in 1958, receiving training in the UK. At the time of the military coup of 1983 he was chief of naval operations and became chief of naval staff under president **Muhammadu Buhari**. A member of the Armed Forces Ruling Council under President **Ibrahim Babangida**, he was promoted to chief of general staff in 1987, effectively Babangida's number two. In August 1990 he was appointed to the new post of vice-president and simultaneously retired from the navy as part of a bid to "civilianize" the higher echelons of the Babangida government in the run-up to the return to civilian rule planned for 1992.

**AÏT AHMED, Hocine**. *Algeria.* Leader of Socialist Forces Front (FFS). A leader of the independence struggle, Aït Ahmed has been one of the regime's most outspoken critics since going into opposition in 1963. Imprisoned after the unsuccessful "FFS revolt" of 1964, he escaped abroad two years later. He returned from exile in December 1989 to a rapturous reception from his supporters. His party has strong support among the Kabyle (Berber) population.

**AITKEN, Jonathan**. *UK.* Conservative politician, journalist and broadcaster. Born in 1942, the grandson of newspaper publisher Lord Beaverbrook, he studied law and then worked as a foreign correspondent from 1966–71. Elected to parliament in 1974 – and MP for Thanet South since 1983 – he is a maverick Tory: anti-European but strongly supporting more open government (the latter preoccupation moulded by the experience of having been tried and acquitted under the Official Secrets Act in 1971). From 1981–88 he was also a director and shareholder of a major television franchise, TV-am. He hosts meetings of the Conservative Philosophy Group, a clutch of Tory intellectuals.

**AKAYEV, Askar**. *USSR.* President of Kirghizia. A leading scientist and a member of the Communist Party, he was president of the republic's academy of sciences before his election to the executive presidency in October 1990. He emerged as a compromise candidate after a party power struggle, and was regarded as effectively unconnected with the hitherto dominant Kirghiz party machine, since he had been away in Leningrad pursuing his academic career for the past 15 years. In common with other rising stars in the republic, Akayev combines a cautious willingness to reform with continuing loyalty to the general concept of the Soviet Union. One of his first acts was to preside over Kirghizia's declaration of sovereignty.

**AKBULUT, Yıldırım**. *Turkey.* Prime minister. Born in 1935, he practised law until his election to parliament in 1983. He rose very rapidly to positions of influence, as interior minister from 1984–87, then as speaker of parliament. In October 1989 he became prime minister, when **Turgut Özal** moved up to the presidency. A moderate right-winger with a low political profile, Akbulut's surprise appointment was seen by many as a sign that Özal was preparing to transfer key executive powers to the presidency in accordance with the 1982 Constitution. Since he took over the reins, the ruling Motherland Party (ANAP) has performed disappointingly in the polls and suffered a severe loss of popular support, although it did surprisingly well in local elections in June 1990.

**AKHMEDOV, Khan.** *USSR*. Prime minister of Turkmenia. Born in 1936, he was promoted from first deputy premier of the Central Asian republic in late 1989 after the incumbent was sacked for failing to combat corruption. The republic's Supreme Soviet reappointed him as prime minister in November 1990.

**AKIHITO, Tsugu no Miya.** *Japan*. Emperor. Born in 1933, the eldest son of Emperor Hirohito, he became Japan's 125th emperor following his father's death in January 1989 and was formally enthroned in November 1990; the new era commencing with his accession was to be known as Heisei. His education included four years spent studying English under an American tutor, and six months abroad in 1953. Such influences, his enjoyment of sports, and his visits abroad as crown prince, helped to mould him as a monarch for Japan's modern and more internationally open society. His marriage in 1959 to Michiko Shoda, the daughter of a prominent industrialist, was a clear break with tradition in that she was neither royal nor from a noble family line, but she is held in great affection among ordinary Japanese people and has contributed to the popularity of the monarchy.

**ALAOUI, Moulay Ahmed.** *Morocco*. Minister of state and director of the daily *Le Matin du Sahara et du Maghreb*, Alaoui often acts as the mouthpiece of the regime.

**ALATAS, Ali.** *Indonesia*. Foreign minister. Born in 1932, Alatas joined the foreign service in the mid-1950s and after spells in Washington and Geneva returned to Jakarta in the late 1970s to work in the office of vice-president Adam Malik. After Malik's retirement in 1983, Alatas was appointed ambassador to the UN where he successfully kept the sticky subject of Jakarta's annexation of East Timor off the General Assembly agenda. In March 1988 he replaced Mochtar Kusumaatmadja as foreign minister, becoming the first career diplomat to hold the post.

**ALBRECHT, Ernst.** *Germany*. Christian Democratic Union (CDU) politician and former premier of Lower Saxony. A polished politician, he was premier of Lower Saxony for 14 years until the CDU's bitter defeat in the May 1990 elections, but was frustrated in his ambition to become his party's candidate for the chancellorship. Born in 1930 in Heidelberg, he studied law and economics before embarking on a career with the European Commission, where he was director-general for competition from 1967–70. In 1959 he was awarded a doctorate in political science and went into politics. In Lower Saxony he pursued an active foreign policy, building up the Land (state) parliament's links with many foreign countries, including China, but was dogged by a series of scandals in the latter years of his premiership.

**ALDERS, Hans.** *Netherlands*. Housing, physical planning and environment minister. Born in 1952, he worked in local government before being elected to the Staten Generaal (parliament) in 1982. A tireless worker, he became secretary of the Labour Party (PvdA) parliamentary group in 1987 and is said to be particularly close to party leader **Wim Kok**. When the PvdA returned to government in coalition with the Christian Democrats in November 1989, Alders was put in charge of the housing, physical planning and environment ministry, a particularly sensitive portfolio in an increasingly ecologically obsessed country.

**ALEKSII II.** *USSR*. Patriarch of Moscow and All Russia (head of the Russian Orthodox Church). Although tainted (like most senior clergymen) by a history of compromise with the state, Aleksii was elected in June 1990 on the strength of a reformist reputation (and despite being not a Russian but an Estonian, born Aleksii Ridiger in Tallinn in 1923). Known for his energy and administrative skill, he had been running two dioceses simultaneously while also chairing the Conference of European Churches. Aleksii is expected to capitalize on religious freedoms introduced since 1988 and to seek a more assertive role for the church in society.

**ALEXANDER, Lamar.** *USA*. Nominated by **George Bush** in December 1990 to succeed **Lauro Cavazos** as education secretary. Elected governor of Tennessee at the age of 38, he served two terms from 1979–87, and was chairman of the National Governors' Association in 1985–86. He is an energetic proponent of changes such as merit pay for teachers and has direct experience of educational administration as president of the University of Tennessee from 1986–90.

**ALGABID, Hamid.** *Niger.* Secretary-general of the Organization of the Islamic Conference. An able administrator, Algabid held a number of junior ministerial posts in the early 1980s, successfully negotiating the rescheduling of Niger's debt before being appointed prime minister in the wake of an unsuccessful coup attempt against President Seyni Kountché in 1983. He became secretary-general of the Islamic Conference in 1988.

**ALHAJI, Alhaji Abubakar.** *Nigeria.* Finance and economic planning minister. A key ally of President **Ibrahim Babangida** and architect of the government's structural adjustment programme, he joined the civil service in 1964 and served as permanent secretary in a series of ministries after 1975. After Babangida took power in 1985, he was responsible, as permanent secretary in the ministry of finance and, from mid-1988, as minister of state for budget and planning, for negotiations with Nigeria's international creditors. In August 1990 he was appointed finance and economic planning minister on the departure from the cabinet of his rival **Olu Falae**. A northern Muslim aristocrat, the nephew of **Alhaji Ibrahim Dasuki**, the Sultan of Sokoto, Alhaji is rumoured to be favoured by Babangida for appointment as Sardauna of Sokoto, a key position in the Muslim hierarchy that has been vacant since the 1966 assassination of Sir Ahmadu Bello, the first prime minister of northern Nigeria.

**ALIA, Ramiz.** *Albania.* Head of state. Born in 1925 in Shkodër to poor Muslim parents, he joined the Communist Party (in 1948 renamed the Party of Labour of Albania) in 1943, and by the age of 19 was carrying out important political and military responsibilities within the National Liberation Army. He was a youth movement leader for many years before moving on to build a career in the party. Since 1961 he has been a full member of the politburo and in 1982, after holding many senior party posts, he became head of state. Since the death in 1985 of Enver Hoxha, Albania's leader for over 40 years, Alia has introduced a degree of reform. The reform process has been speeded up noticeably in the face of growing popular discontent; in December 1990 Alia allowed opposition parties

to form and he scheduled elections for early 1991.

**ALMUNIA AMANN, Joaquín.** *Spain.* Public administration minister. Born in 1948 in Bilbao and trained as an economist, he joined the Spanish Socialist Workers' Party (PSOE) in 1974, was an economic adviser to the socialist General Workers' Union (UGT) from 1976–79, and has been a deputy for Madrid since 1979. He was labour and social security minister from 1982 until 1986, when he was appointed to head the new public administration ministry, charged with overhauling the structure and staffing of government departments.

**ALONI, Shulamit.** *Israel.* Citizens' Rights Party (CRP) leader. Born in 1929 in Tel Aviv, Aloni is a lawyer. She became a Labour MP in 1965, but left the party in 1973 to found the CRP, championing liberal causes and women's issues, and trying to counter the political power of religious groups.

**ALPTEMOÇİN, Ahmet Kurtcebe.** *Turkey.* Foreign minister. Born in 1940, he trained as a mechanical engineer and pursued a business career before being brought into politics in the "technocrat" cabinet appointed by the ruling Motherland Party (ANAP) under **Turgut Özal** in 1983. A loyal supporter of Özal, he became finance and customs minister in 1984, but increasingly had to take a back seat in the government after the 1987 elections, and was dropped in the March 1989 cabinet reshuffle. He regained political favour in October 1990 when he was appointed, to general surprise, as foreign minister after the sudden resignation of **Ali Bozer**.

**ALTISSIMO, Renato.** *Italy.* Italian Liberal Party (PLI) secretary. Born in 1940, in the province of Venice, he graduated in political science from Turin University and went into industrial management, rising to become vice-president of the employers' association Confindustria from 1970–74. He entered the Chamber of Deputies in 1972, served as health minister in 1979–80 and again from 1981–1983, then became industry minister in the first administration of **Bettino Craxi**. In May 1986 he was elected secretary of the PLI in succession to Alfredo Biondi; he left the cabinet soon after.

**ALVÁREZ ALVÁREZ, Luís Héctor.** *Mexico.* Opposition leader. Born in 1919, Alvárez studied engineering in the USA. A successful businessman and former mayor of Chihuahua, he was the National Action Party (PAN) presidential candidate in 1958. In 1986 he achieved national prominence by undertaking a 40-day hunger strike in protest at the lack of electoral reform. In 1987 he was elected president of PAN.

**AMATO, Giuliano.** *Italy.* Italian Socialist Party (PSI) deputy secretary. Born in 1938 in Turin, he became professor of constitutional law at Rome University. He entered the Chamber of Deputies in 1983 and from 1983–87 served as chief political counsellor to prime minister **Bettino Craxi**. In July 1987 he was appointed deputy prime minister and treasury minister in **Giovanni Goria**'s cabinet, and remained at the treasury when **Ciriaco De Mita** took over as prime minister. As treasury minister, he sponsored a banking reform – the "Amato law" – passed in 1990, to allow the partial privatization of public-sector banks.

**AMBROZIAK, Jacek.** *Poland.* Head of the office of the council of ministers. A lawyer, born in 1941, he was legal adviser in 1980–81 to the Solidarity newspaper *Tygodnik Solidarność* (of which **Tadeusz Mazowiecki** was editor-in-chief), and then to the Polish episcopate. He took part in the 1989 round-table talks on the Solidarity side, and was briefly deputy editor of *Tygodnik Solidarność* before Mazowiecki brought him into the government with ministerial rank in September 1989.

**AMINU, Jibril.** *Nigeria.* Oil minister. Born in 1939 in Gongola, he trained as a cardiologist and was a lecturer and medical consultant until his appointment as vice-chancellor of Maiduguri University in 1980. In 1985 he joined **Ibrahim Babangida**'s first government as national education minister. A northern Muslim, he was unpopular as education minister because of policies considered by many to be anti-Christian. In December 1989 he was moved to the key post of oil minister.

**AMOUR, Salmin.** *Tanzania.* President of Zanzibar. Born in 1942, he trained as an economist and worked as principal secretary in the Zanzibar ministries of finance and trade and industry. In 1990 he was selected by the ruling Chama Cha Mapinduzi (CCM) as the sole candidate for the presidency of Zanzibar in the October elections. A member of the CCM national executive committee and its secretary for economic affairs and planning, he is credited with a significant role in the formulation of the party's recent economic policies. Replacing the unpopular Idriss Abdul-Wakil, he faces increasing secessionist pressures in the islands.

**ANANIEVA, Nora.** *Bulgaria.* Parliamentary leader of Bulgarian Socialist Party (BSP). A deputy director of the Institute on Contemporary Theories, she is sociology and political science specialist. Ananieva is a long-standing member of the Bulgarian Communist Party, renamed the BSP in 1990. In February 1990 he was appointed a deputy premier in the Socialist government of **Andrei Lukanov**, partly on the basis of her record as an outstanding figure in the country's women's movement. She was not included, however, in the transitional coalition formed by **Dimitur Popov** ten months layer.

**ANDERSSON, Sten.** *Sweden.* Foreign minister. Born in 1923, he taught at the Workers' Educational Association and was a local councillor in Stockholm until 1962. On the strength of his performance as secretary of the influential Stockholm branch of the Social Democratic Labour Party (SAP) he was appointed party general secretary in 1963, a post he held for 19 years, proving himself one of the craftiest operators in Swedish politics. When the SAP returned to government in 1982, he was appointed health and social affairs minister. In 1985 he switched to the foreign ministry, succeeding Lennart Bodström who had come under heavy criticism over the presence of foreign submarines in Swedish territorial waters.

**ANDRÉ, Harvie.** *Canada.* Minister of state and government leader in the House of Commons. Born in 1940 in Edmonton, Alberta, he was educated at the University of Alberta and the California Institute of Technology, and was formerly a consultant engineer. First elected to the House of Commons in 1972 for the Progressive Conservative Party of Canada, André is known to his colleagues as the "Pit Bull" because of the manner with which he pushes legislation through. In February 1990 he became minister of state and government leader in the lower house.

**ANDREOTTI, Giulio.** *Italy.* Prime minister and Christian Democrat Party (DC) politician. Born in Rome in 1919, he took a law degree at Rome University in 1941 and in 1946 was elected a member of the constituent assembly which drafted the new republican constitution. In the April 1948 general elections, the first held under the new constitution, he was elected to the Chamber of Deputies for Lazio, the constituency he has represented ever since. He held junior positions under Alcide De Gasperi and Giuseppe Pella, attained cabinet rank as interior minister in Amintore Fanfani's short-lived government of 1954, and went on to hold at various times the major portfolios of finance, treasury and defence. In February 1972 he became prime minister and served until June 1973. He headed four successive governments in the crucial period between July 1976 and August 1979. Thus, although before 1962 he had opposed the DC's *apertura a sinistra* (opening to the left), he was head of government during the whole of the *compromesso storico* (historic compromise) experiment, when the Italian Communist Party (PCI) supported DC-led governments. In 1978 his government was shaken when the left-wing Red Brigades kidnapped and murdered former prime minister Aldo Moro. He was unable to form a new coalition in 1979, but returned to government in August 1983 as foreign minister in **Bettino Craxi**'s cabinet and retained that post for six years under the successive premierships of Fanfani, **Giovanni Goria** and **Ciriaco De Mita**. Two months after the resignation of the De Mita government in May 1989, Andreotti formed a new administration, his sixth. A five-party coalition, it was weakened by his rivalry with De Mita within his own party, leading to a cabinet crisis in July 1990 which he weathered despite the resignation of five leftist DC ministers. Andreotti has served in more governments over a longer period of time than any other Italian politician – a tribute both to his political skills, which have earned him the nickname of *il volpone* (old fox), and to his influence. He heads his own faction within the DC, and has supporters throughout Italian political and economic life. Tough and imperturbable, he combines typical Roman cynicism with Anglo-Saxon understatement and a sometimes cutting sense of humour.

**ANDRIESSEN, Frans.** *Netherlands.* European Commission vice-president and commissioner for external relations and trade policy. Born in 1929, he studied law and then worked for some years at the Catholic Housing Institute. Elected to parliament for the Catholic People's Party (KVP, a precursor of the Christian Democratic Appeal, CDA) in 1967, he was the party's floor leader from 1971–77 and finance minister from 1977–80. He was appointed an EC commissioner in 1981, responsible for competition policy (1981–84), agriculture (1984–89) and external relations and trade (since 1989). In the latter position he has been at the centre of the troubled negotiations on the General Agreement on Tariffs and Trade (Gatt)

in 1990. Deprived of the post he clearly felt should have been his, president of the European Commission, his relations with **Jacques Delors** are often strained.

**ANDRIESSEN, Koos.** *Netherlands.* Economics affairs minister. Born in 1928 and an economist by training, he held various academic posts until his appointment as economics minister in 1963. After the fall of Victor Marijnen's government two years later he joined the board of the Van Leer packaging group, becoming its chairman in 1980. After retiring in 1987 he was elected president of the Dutch Christian Employers' Federation (NCW). Despite his trenchant criticisms of the industrial policies pursued under the prime minister, **Ruud Lubbers**, he ended a 24-year break from government in November 1989, accepting an offer to head the economic affairs ministry in Lubbers's new centre–left coalition.

**ANDRUS, Cecil.** *USA.* Democratic governor of Idaho. Born in 1931, he was a state legislator, and then served as governor in the early 1970s, becoming secretary of the interior in **Jimmy Carter**'s administration. A strong environmentalist, his leadership was decisive in 1980 in pushing through controversial restrictions to protect wide areas of Alaska from commercial exploitation. As governor since election in 1986, he has placed a priority on improving state public education.

**ANGELOZ, Eduardo César.** *Argentina.* Opposition politician. Born in 1931 and educated at Córdoba University, Angeloz rose to become governor of Córdoba. In 1988 he was chosen as presidential candidate for the Radical Civic Union (UCR) but, although well respected, he lacked the mass popular appeal of his principal opponent, **Carlos Menem**. In 1990 he rejected an offer to join Menem's cabinet.

**ANGUITA GONZÁLEZ, Julio.** *Spain.* Communist Party leader. Born in Fuengirola in 1941, he was Communist mayor of Córdoba from 1983–87, earning the nickname "Red Caliph", and was president of the Andalusian branch of the Communist Party of Spain (PCE) until 1988. In February of that year the PCE turned to him for more charismatic leadership, in the light of its continuing decline under Gerardo Iglesias. As PCE national secretary-general he achieved some early successes in rebuilding the fragmented party. It was largely his influence, in coaxing his comrades to accept greater prominence for non-communists, that enabled the United Left (IU) coalition to perform creditably in the 1989 elections.

**ANNAN, Justice D.F.** *Ghana.* Vice-chairman of Provisional National Defence Council (PNDC). A retired appeals court judge and former president of the Ghanaian national Olympic committee, he was appointed a member of the ruling PNDC in May 1984. He was simultaneously appointed to chair the newly formed National Commission for Democracy (NCD), which has presided over the formation of new political structures at local level but done little to meet demands for more democracy in national politics. Later that year he was also appointed chairman of the National Economic Commission, charged with overseeing government economic reforms.

**ANNUNZIO, Frank.** *USA.* Democratic congressman from Illinois. Born in Chicago in 1915, he was a product of the **Richard Daley** political machine but has adapted successfully to new-style issue politics. Formerly a union official, he was elected to the House of Representatives in 1964. As financial institutions subcommittee chairman, he has been a strong supporter of the now beleaguered savings and loan sector, and has promoted legislation to control debt collection malpractices.

**ANSTEE, Margaret Joan.** *UK.* Director-general of the UN Vienna office. Born in 1926, she graduated in modern languages at Cambridge University and has a degree in economics from London University. After four years in the diplomatic service, she began working for UN organizations in 1952, primarily the UN Development Programme (UNDP). In 1986–87 she was entrusted with the delicate task of overseeing much-needed administrative reforms within the UN system. In 1987 she became the first woman under-secretary-general, and head of the Vienna Centre for Social Development and Humanitarian Affairs, and co-ordinator for all the UN's drug-related activities.

**ANTALL, József.** *Hungary.* Prime minister. Born in 1932, the man who was to become leader of post-communist Hungary had a political upbringing. His father helped to found the original Independent Smallholders' Party, held ministerial office in post-war coalitions until the communists forced the party out of existence in 1947, and supported Imre Nagy's short-lived multi-party coalition as Soviet tanks were massing for the 1956 invasion. Antall became active in youth organizations supporting the uprising, and in consequence was banned

from pursuing his career as a history teacher. He took up archive work, rising to become director of the Semmelweis museum in 1974. By his own definition a patriotic liberal democrat, he was a founder-member of the Hungarian Democratic Forum (MDF) in September 1987, and worked to deflect the movement's more radical populist nationalists and consolidate its position on the centre-right as the tide flowed towards multi-party politics. His quiet effectiveness and skill in building contacts was rewarded by his emergence as MDF president in October 1989. He exuded gravitas, suiting the public mood at the spring 1990 elections with the promise of fundamental change pursued without panic. The MDF's strong showing gave him the chance to form a government; his family contacts helped to bring the new independent Smallholders' Party into coalition; and his conciliatory style helped to ensure workable relations in with the opposition Alliance of Free Democrats. In December 1990 he was re-elected over-whelmingly as MDF president, although in the preceding weeks he had been incapacitated by illness and was undergoing treatment for cancer.

**ANTHONY, Beryl.** *USA.* Democratic congressman from Arkansas. Born in 1938, he was a lawyer and prosecuting attorney before being elected to Congress in 1978. A Southern moderate, he chairs the Democratic congressional campaign committee which funds House candidates, but failed to gain promotion in the 1989 leadership contests.

**ANWAR IBRAHIM, Datuk Seri Encik.** *Malaysia.* Education minister. Born in 1947, Anwar is regarded by many observers as a future prime minister. He rose to prominence as leader of the Islamic youth movement, Abim. In 1982, he was elected president of the influential United Malays National Organization (UMNO) youth movement. The following year he entered the cabinet as sport, youth and culture minister; he was moved to agriculture in 1984 and two years later he was promoted to the difficult education portfolio. An Islamic scholar of international repute, he has moderated his fundamentalist views since entering mainstream politics. In late 1990 he emerged from party elections as the most senior of UMNO's three vice-presidents and thus next in line of succession to **Mahathir Mohamad**.

**ANYAOKU, Emeka.** *Nigeria.* Commonwealth secretary-general. Born in 1933, he studied in Nigeria, the UK and France before joining the Nigerian diplomatic service in 1962. He was seconded on several occasions to the Commonwealth Secretariat, and joined it permanently as deputy secretary-general in 1978. A more cautious, less flamboyant man than his predecessor, Sir Shridath (Sonny) Ramphal, he became secretary-general in 1990.

**AQAZADEH, Gholamreza.** *Iran.* Oil minister. Born in Khoy, Azerbaijan province in 1948, Aqazadeh has been oil minister since October 1985. A graduate in mathematics and computer technology, he worked for the Bandar Abbas steel industry until 1979. After the 1979 revolution, his Islamic credentials secured for him the posts of manager of the daily *Jomhuri Islami* newspaper and of deputy prime minister for administration and finance.

**AQUINO, Maria Corazon (Cory).** *Philippines.* President. Born Maria Corazon Cojuangco in 1933, she comes from a wealthy Chinese-Filipino sugar plantation family in Tarlac province on Luzon Island and was educated in New York. Her husband, Benigno Aquino, a leading figure in the liberal political opposition to the Ferdinand Marcos regime, was assassinated – many believe on Marcos's orders – on his return in 1983 after three years in exile. His widow was the initially reluctant inheritor of Benigno's mantle as opposition figurehead. She agreed to stand as opposition candidate (for the Lakas ng Bayan alliance) in the "snap" presidential election of February 1986, narrowly defeating Marcos, whose attempt to cling to power was swept aside by the demonstration of "people power" on the streets of Manila, and by a marked lack of support from the USA. Originally simply the guardian of her husband's memory and policies, she came to enjoy substantial support in her own right, and is credited with having restored democracy. After the initial honeymoon, however, her capacity to exert authority over the country's disparate centres of power has seemed increasingly in doubt. A series of open rebellions by disaffected right-wing military leaders has seriously weakened the government's credibility, while electoral undertakings to address the desperate plight of the Filipino poor, notably through land reform, have for the most part remained unfulfilled, fuelling support for communist and Muslim separatist insurgents. She is a devout Catholic and few doubt her sincerity in wishing to bring some form of stability and prosperity to the country, but many question her ability to impose reform on conservative vested interests who retain considerable influence within her

government. Her post-revolutionary status as the darling of the American liberal conscience was encapsulated by her being chosen as *Time* magazine's Woman of the Year in 1986. But some impatience with the weakness of her government now colours official American views of her.

**ARAFAT, Yasser.** *Palestinian.* Chairman of the Palestine Liberation Organization (PLO). Born in Cairo in 1929, by the age of 17 he was involved in gun-running from Egypt to Palestine. He studied civil engineering in Cairo in 1950, becoming a student activist; in 1952 he was elected president of the Palestinian Students' Union, which he helped to found. He started work as an engineer in 1957, but became increasingly involved in Palestinian guerrilla activities. In the early 1960s he helped establish the Palestinian commando group Fatah (Victory), and in 1969 he was elected chairman of the PLO executive committee. After their expulsion from Jordan in the "Black September" fighting of 1970, Arafat's forces took refuge in Lebanon, carving out a semi-autonomous "Fatahland" in the south and taking an active part in the Lebanese civil war. Repeated raids on Israel provoked the "Peace for Galilee" invasion of 1982, culminating in the Sabra and Chatila massacres and PLO withdrawal from Lebanon. Arafat has since been based at PLO headquarters in Tunis, although he spends much time in Baghdad. After the withdrawal from Lebanon, Arafat's supremacy within the PLO was challenged by a Syrian-backed rebel movement. The bulk of Palestinian civilians refused to be swayed from their long-standing loyalty to Arafat, and by the late 1980s the PLO was effectively re-united under his leadership, although policy divisions remained. Arafat has always held open the possibility of a peaceful settlement, as in his famous speech to the UN General Assembly in 1974, when he declared that he bore "an olive branch in one hand and a freedom-fighter's gun in the other". The *intifada,* which broke out dramatically in the West Bank and Gaza in 1988, paved the way for his dramatic recognition of Israel's right to exist and renunciation of terrorism. This started discussions with the USA but little of substance resulted, and Arafat grew increasingly frustrated with the US–Egyptian efforts to promote dialogue between Israel and the Palestinians, from which the PLO was to be excluded. Arafat relished the tougher line taken by **Saddam Hussain** in early 1990, seeing Baghdad's position as a strategic asset for the Palestinians. The PLO's failure quickly to condemn Iraq's invasion of Kuwait in August 1990 did Arafat great damage.

**ARANZADI MARTÍNEZ, Claudio.** *Spain.* Industry and energy minister. Born in 1946 in Bilbao. An industrial engineer and economist and member of the Spanish Socialist Workers' Party (PSOE), he headed the National Institute of Industry (INI) before becoming industry and energy minister in 1988.

**ARAYA MONGE, Rolando.** *Costa Rica.* National Liberation Party leader. A chemical engineer by training, Araya was elected secretary-general of the National Liberation Party (PLN) in 1984. He is a leader of the younger generation within the party, but as two of his brothers have links with the extreme left, he is sometimes viewed with suspicion by senior party members.

**ARBATOV, Georgy.** *USSR.* Senior policy adviser, leading Soviet expert on the USA. Born in 1923 in the Ukraine, he worked first as a journalist and editor, and subsequently as an international affairs researcher in the central committee of the Communist Party of the Soviet Union. He was appointed director of the Institute of US and Canadian Studies at the Academy of Sciences in 1967. Although a personal adviser to **Mikhail Gorbachev** from 1985–90, he is regarded with suspicion in some quarters, standing accused of being too closely identified with the discredited policies of Leonid Brezhnev. In December 1990 he was appointed to **Boris Yeltsin's** advisory council. His son, Aleksei Arbatov, is an influential civilian arms control specialist.

**ARDANZA GARRO, José Antonio.** *Spain.* Basque region premier. Born in 1941 in Elorrio, he was sympathetic to the ETA Basque separatist movement as a teenager, but joined the moderate Basque Nationalist Party (PNV) in the 1960s. For most of his professional career he was a legal adviser to the Caja Laboral Popular savings bank, the financial arm of the Mondragón co-operativist movement. In January 1985 he became leader of the PNV after the party had passed a vote of no-confidence in his predecessor, **Carlos Garaikoetxea Urriza.** At the same time he became *lendakari* (premier) of the Basque government. A moderate, Ardanza has worked closely with the Madrid government to limit tensions in the region, and has remained in office as a result of coalition agreements with the Basque Socialist Party (PSE-PSOE), the most

recent of which followed the regional elections of October 1990, which left the PNV as the largest single party in the parliament.

**ARENS, Moshe.** *Israel.* Defence minister. Born in Lithuania in 1925, he left in 1939 for the USA where he studied aeronautical engineering, a training he later used as vice-president of Israel Aircraft Industries and as a visiting professor at the Haifa Technion (Israel Institute of Technology). A lifelong right-wing Zionist, Arens was elected a Herut MP in 1974, sitting on the Knesset (parliament) foreign affairs and defence committee. In 1978 he criticized Menachem Begin for being too soft during the Camp David peace negotiations. Arens became ambassador to the USA in 1982 and his ability to get on with Americans proved a valuable asset to a Likud government unpopular in Washington. He returned to the cabinet in 1983, taking over the defence portfolio from **Ariel Sharon.** He resigned as minister without portfolio in the first Labour Likud coalition in 1987 in protest at the cancellation of the Lavi jet fighter project. Arens joined **Yitzhak Shamir's** inner cabinet as foreign minister in 1988, becoming defence minister again in June 1990. Noted for his pragmatism, Arens continues to seek dialogue with moderate Palestinians from the occupied territories.

**ARGYROS, Stelios.** *Greece.* President of the Federation of Greek Industries. Born in Athens in 1945 into a family of industrialists, he gained a doctorate in mechanical engineering at MIT while working as a consultant to the World Bank. He was a staff member of the UN Industrial Development Organization in Vienna from 1974–76 and in 1978 he joined the family spinning business, where he remains a member of the board. From 1981–84, he managed the state-owned Phosphoric Fertilizers Industry, overseeing a modernization and expansion programme. Frustrated by bureaucracy, he returned to the private sector, where he became associated with a number of venture-capital businesses. He was elected president of the Federation of Greek Industries in 1988.

**ARIAS CALDERÓN, Ricardo.** *Panama.* First vice-president, government and justice minister. As president of the Christian Democrat Party (PDC), Arias joined the Democratic Civic Opposition Alliance (ADOC) and was its first vice-presidential candidate in May 1989. He was appointed government (interior) minister in **Guillermo Endara's** cabinet, a position which gave him responsibility for the new Public Force.

**ARIAS SÁNCHEZ, Oscar.** *Costa Rica.* Former president. Born in 1941 into a wealthy land-owning family, Arias was educated at the London School of Economics and Essex University in the UK. He served as director of the National University and central bank. In 1972 he was appointed national planning and economic policy minister. In 1978 he became secretary-general of the centre-left National Liberation Party (PLN) and in 1986 was elected the youngest president in the country's history. He gained international respect for his vigorous search for new solutions to conflict in the region (the "Arias plan"), for which he received the Nobel peace prize in 1987.

**ARISTIDE, Jean-Bertrand.** *Haiti.* President-elect. A charismatic left-wing priest, born in 1953, he made the cause of the poor the basis of his successful campaign for the presidency, under the banner of the National Front for Change and Democracy, winning a 70% vote in the December 1990 elections. Due to take office in February 1991, he remained under threat from a Duvalierist backlash.

**ARMITAGE, Richard.** *USA.* Special negotiator and formerly assistant secretary of state for East Asian and Pacific affairs, a post to which he moved in 1989 after serving as assistant secretary of defence for international security. In 1990 he led the US delegation that negotiated the future of US military bases in the Philippines.

**ARONSON, Bernard.** *USA.* Assistant secretary of state for inter-American affairs. A Democrat with a commitment to human rights, he served as a speechwriter for **Jimmy Carter** from 1977–81. In 1986 he played a major role in building congressional support for the **Reagan** administration's military aid to the Contra rebels in Nicaragua, and in 1989 was appointed to his current post by **George Bush**.

**ARPAILLANGE, Pierre.** *France.* Lawyer and former cabinet minister. Born in 1924, and decorated after the war for resistance activity, he has made the law his career, combining his steady progress in this field with the role of adviser in various ministerial cabinets. He was appointed to the Court of Appeal in 1974, and became its procurator-general in 1981. **Michel Rocard** brought him into government in 1986, as justice minister and keeper of the seals. Following the October 1990 cabinet reshuffle, he moved to the Court of Accounts.

**ARRATE, Jorge.** *Chile.* Socialist Party (PSCh) leader. Born in 1941, Arrate was vice-president of the state copper company and a minister during Salvador Allende's administration. Forced to leave the country after the 1973 coup, he returned after the ban against him had been lifted in 1987. In December 1989 he was elected secretary-general of the newly unified PSCh.

**ARTHIT KAMLANG-EK, General.** *Thailand.* Deputy prime minister. Born in 1925, Arthit was a powerful force in Thai politics as army commander-in-chief from 1983–86. During his period in command he came into conflict with prime minister Prem Tinsulanonda, who removed him from the post in 1986. Prior to the 1988 elections Arthit took over the leadership of the Thai People's Party (Puangchon Chao Thai), which campaigned against Prem and won 17 seats. **Chartchai Chunhawan** brought Arthit, whose political support base lies in the poor north-east, into the cabinet as a deputy prime minister in August 1990.

**ARTHIT URAIRAT.** *Thailand.* Foreign minister. A member of the Ekkaparb Party, second in dominance to the Chart Thai in the ruling coalition, he was appointed foreign minister in December 1990 in place of Subin Pinkayan.

**ARZALLUS ANTIA, Xabier.** *Spain.* Basque Nationalist Party (PNV) president. Born in 1932 in Azcoitia and a former Jesuit, he joined the PNV in 1964, was its president from 1980–84, and again from January 1989, when he set about the task of modernizing the party.

**ARZÚ, Alvaro.** *Guatemala.* Conservative politician. Mayor of Guatemala City until 1989, Arzú was the candidate for the National Advancement Party (PAN) in the November 1990 presidential election. Although representing one of the strongest conservative hopes, with support from the business sector, he finished in fourth place in the first round.

**ASHAGRE YIGLETU.** *Ethiopia.* Deputy prime minister. A former commerce minister and principal Ethiopian negotiator in peace talks with the Eritrean People's Liberation Front (EPLF), he was appointed deputy prime minister in charge of social affairs in November 1989.

**ASHCROFT, John.** *USA.* Republican governor of Missouri. Born in 1942, he was a lawyer and law professor, then successively state auditor and attorney-general, and in 1984 he was elected governor. A conservative, he has emphasized economic development, educational reform and stricter eligibility requirements for welfare recipients.

**ASHDOWN, Paddy.** *UK.* Liberal Democrat leader, MP for Yeovil. Born in 1941, he joined the Royal Marines after leaving school in 1959. In a 12-year military career he rose to the rank of captain, commander of a special forces unit. He switched careers in 1971 to become first secretary with the British mission to the UN in Geneva. In a further major switch he joined the Westland aerospace company in 1976 and the Morlands wool company in 1978, and worked briefly in local government before being elected in 1983 to parliament for the Liberals. His unusual background for a politician helped to bring him prominence within the small contingent of Liberal MPs, and he proved a capable spokesman on trade and industry and then on education and science for the Liberal–Social Democrat Alliance. When **David Steel** announced his resignation as party leader after the Alliance's disappointing performance in the 1987 elections, Ashdown defeated the more right-wing **Alan Beith** for the leadership of the newly merged Social and Liberal Democrats 1988. He threw himself into the daunting task of rebuilding centre-party support with customary vigour, and has had some success at ensuring the survival of the Liberal Democrats. But, despite having made some impressive speeches in the House of Commons, he has not managed to regain the ground the party has lost since the heady Alliance days of the mid-1980s.

**ASPE ARMELLA, Pedro.** *Mexico.* Finance and public credit minister. Born in 1950, Aspe trained as an economist at the Mexican Autonomous Institute of Technology and at MIT in the USA. He was professor at the Centre of Latin American Monetary Studies from 1978 until 1982, when he joined **Carlos Salinas**'s team as under-secretary at the planning and budget ministry, succeeding Salinas as minister in 1987. He was appointed finance minister in 1988 to help implement further economic reforms.

**ASPIN, Les.** *USA.* Democratic congressman from Wisconsin. He was born in 1938, educated at Yale and Oxford universities and MIT, and was an economics professor before his election to the House of Representatives in 1970. Formerly a critic of big military budgets, Aspin has surprised liberals in his role as armed services committee chairman since 1985 by supporting aid to the Contras and the MX missile programme. Nevertheless, he has adapted rapidly to the Cold War's passing and has disputed the need for the planned B-2 bomber.

**ASSAD, Lieutenant-General Hafez al-.** *Syria.* President. Born in Qardaha in north-west Syria

in 1930, a member of the quasi-Shia Alawi sect of Islam, which has long dominated the Syrian military, he was defence minister at the time of the abortive Syrian intervention in support of the Palestinians in Jordan in 1970. Its failure led him to oust the civilian administration in November 1970 and take over the premiership, becoming president the following year. He has maintained his position through a combination of ruthlessness and political skill; his real instruments of power are the military and the security services. Close relatives, heading militias which acted as counterweights to the army, formed the inner circle of power until Assad's brother, Rifaat, staged a bid for the leadership in the wake of the president's massive heart attack, brought on by diabetes, in 1983. Since the showdown with Rifaat, Assad has ruled through an informal grouping of a dozen associates, each heading a separate cell structure. A new constitution introduced in 1973 proclaimed Syria a "democratic, popular and socialist state" but Assad has sometimes faced opposition from religious forces, notably the rebellion in the Sunni-dominated city of Hama in 1982, which was suppressed at a cost of up to 10,000 lives. Generally regarded as a radical within the Arab world, Assad for long enjoyed Soviet support, supported Iran in the war with Iraq and backed rebels within the Palestine Liberation Organization. However, his awareness of Iraqi ambitions led him to renew diplomatic relations with Egypt and deploy substantial forces in Saudi Arabia after the invasion of Kuwait in August 1990. In return, he appears to have been allowed a relatively free hand to impose a *pax syriana* on Lebanon.

**ATHULATHMUDALI, Lalith.** *Sri Lanka.* Education minister. An able young lawyer from the Sinhalese professional elite, he rose under the United National Party regime of Junius Jayawardene, joining his cabinet at the outset in 1977. He headed the national security ministry from its creation in March 1984, an increasingly high-profile post as the island slipped deeper into violence and war. His hopes of succeeding as president were disappointed when the party chose prime minister **Ranasinghe Premadasa** in late 1988. In the new government he has less the air of the *dauphin*; in the March 1990 reshuffle he was moved sideways from agriculture to education.

**ATKINS, Robert.** *UK.* Minister for sport since July 1990 and MP since 1979. Born in 1946, he is a keen cricketer who was previously minister of state for transport. His principal tasks at sport were to control football hooliganism and rationalize the complexities of sports administration. In November 1990, he became under-secretary of state for education and science, retaining the sport portflios.

**ATTALI, Jacques.** *France.* President of the European Bank for Reconstruction and Development. Born in 1943 in Algeria, he graduated from France's key educational institutions, the Ecole Polytechnique, Ecole Nationale d'Administration and the Institut d'Etudes Politiques de Paris, and from the Ecole des Mines de Paris. He started his career as a mining engineer in 1968, but later taught economics at the Ecole d'Etudes Politiques. Auditor at the prestigious Council of State in the 1970s, and a socialist activist since 1967, he established from 1973 a relationship with **François Mitterrand** which marked him out as a man to watch. He has earned an unequalled and envied reputation as the president's intellectual confidant and special adviser. In 1990, when Attali was appointed president-designate of the new, London-based European bank, there were mutterings in some smaller EC countries about the preponderance of Frenchmen in top community posts. His 15 published works include books on politics, economics and a novel, *La vie éternelle.*

**ATTAS, Haider Abu Bakr al-.** *Yemen.* Prime minister. A former construction minister, he was South Yemen's prime minister from 1985–86 and, following the overthrow of the government of Ali Nasser Mohammed, was president from February 1986. When the two Yemens united in May 1990, he became prime minister.

**AUKEN, Svend.** *Denmark.* Leader of the Social Democratic Party. Born in 1943, he taught political science at Aarhus University for eight years from 1969, entering the Folketing (parliament) in 1971. He rose rapidly through the ranks of the Social Democrats to become deputy leader of the parliamentary group in 1975 and of the party itself in 1985. He was labour minister from 1977 until the collapse of the minority Social Democratic administration in 1982. After succeeding Anker Jørgensen as party leader in 1987, he steered the party on a more left-wing course, in particular with regard to defence policy. He led the Social Democrats to a good electoral performance in December 1990, gaining 14 more seats, and called (unsuccessfully) for **Poul Schlüter**'s resignation as prime minister.

**AUNG SAN SUU KYI.** *Myanmar (Burma).* Opposition leader. The daughter of independence hero Aung San, she returned to Burma from her home in the UK just before the massive anti-government demonstrations of 1988. She quickly emerged as a leader of the opposition. Although she was by then under house arrest, her image was very much in the public mind when her party, the National League for Democracy (NLD) won a stunning victory in the May 1990 elections. Since the elections, however, the military junta has made no effort to transfer power to the NLD and Aung San Suu Kyi remains under house arrest.

**AVICE, Edwige.** *France.* Government minister. Born in 1945 and a graduate in law and politics from the Institut d'Etudes Politiques, she took up a career in hospital administration and banking. In 1972, she joined the Socialist Party (PS) and was elected to the executive in 1977. Identified with the left of the PS, she was first elected as a National Assembly deputy in 1981, and was brought into the left government immediately, first as a junior minister for leisure (youth and sport), then in 1984–86 as junior minister for defence. In 1988 she moved another rung up the ladder to become deputy minister for foreign affairs.

**AYLWIN AZÓCAR, Patricio.** *Chile.* President. Born in 1918, Aylwin studied law at the University of Chile, returning as a lecturer there and at the Catholic University. He was elected a senator for the Christian Democratic Party (PDC) in 1965, also serving as party president. He was president of the Senate from 1970–73, and initially welcomed the military coup, believing that there would be a rapid return to democracy. He was elected president of the newly legalized PDC in 1987 and in 1989 was chosen as the presidential candidate of the opposition Coalition for Democracy (CPD). He easily defeated his conservative opponent in the presidential elections and took over power from President **Augusto Pinochet** in March 1990. Although a figure from the political past, Aylwin has striven to consolidate Chile's return to democracy by stressing the co-operation between the wide range of political groupings making up the ruling coalition. His relations with Pinochet have been tense, particularly over the commission set up to investigate human rights abuses during the military regime.

**AZIKIWE, Nnamdi.** *Nigeria.* Former president. The chief architect of Nigerian independence, he was born in 1904 in northern

Nigeria, where his father, an Ibo from the south, was working as a clerk. The young Azikiwe stowed away on a ship to the USA, where he worked his way through college, then worked as a newspaper editor in the Gold Coast (now Ghana) before returning to Nigeria in 1937. Setting up a chain of newspapers, he was soon in the forefront of the campaign for self-rule. In 1946 he founded the National Council for Nigeria and the Cameroons (NCNC), which had its power base among the Ibo in eastern Nigeria but nevertheless argued for a centralized form of government. Azikiwe was prime minister of eastern Nigeria from 1954–59 and took the NCNC into coalition with the Northern People's Congress after the 1959 elections to form the first government of independent Nigeria. With Sir Abubakar Tafawa Balewa as prime minister, Azikiwe took the largely ceremonial post of governor-general. He became president on proclamation of the republic in 1963 but was removed in 1966 when the assassination of Balewa was followed by a military takeover. His opposition to his fellow Ibos' disastrous attempt to create the independent state of Biafra went unheeded as the country plunged into civil war in 1967. Azikiwe remained a respected national figure, serving as chancellor of Lagos University from 1972–76 and returning to active politics again in preparation for the return to civilian rule in 1979, standing unsuccessfully in the presidential elections that year (won by **Shehu Shagari**) as candidate of the Nigerian People's Party. His final retirement from politics came in 1986 with the ban by **Ibrahim Babangida**'s government on former politicians. Reports of his death in November 1989 were, as he said, "greatly exaggerated".

**AZIZ, Tariq.** *Iraq.* Foreign minister. Born into a Chaldean Christian family in Mosul in 1936, Aziz studied at Baghdad University before going into journalism. He first worked on *Al-Jumhuriyah*, before becoming chief editor of *Al-Jamaheer* in 1963. He held various journalistic and government posts until he was appointed information minister in 1974. He became a member of the Arab Ba'th Socialist Party regional leadership in 1977, deputy prime minister in 1979, and foreign minister in 1983. In the summer of 1990 Aziz led Iraq's campaign of intimidation against its erstwhile Arab allies in the summer of 1990 which culminated in the invasion of Kuwait in August.

**AZLAN MUHIBUDDIN SHAH, Raja.** *Malaysia.* Supreme head of state. Born in 1928, Azlan served a two-year term as Lord President of the Judiciary before becoming sultan of the western state of Perak in 1984. He was elected in 1989 for a five-year term as Yang di-Pertuan Agong (supreme head of state) by the hereditary rulers of nine of Malaysia's 13 states.

**AZNAR LÓPEZ, José María.** *Spain.* Popular Party (PP) leader. Born in 1953 in Madrid, and a former tax inspector, he was premier of the Castile-León regional government from 1987–89. Although only a vice-president of the PP at the time of the 1989 general election (when the veteran **Manuel Fraga** was still party leader), Aznar headed the PP list, and won Galicia for the PP, overturning a Spanish Socialist Workers' Party (PSOE) majority. He became PP leader in April 1990.

# B

BABANGIDA, Major-General Ibrahim.
*Nigeria*. President. Born in 1941 in what is now
Niger state in Nigeria's middle belt, he received
military training in northern Nigeria and in
India and was commissioned in 1963. After the
civil war he became an instructor at the Nigerian
defence academy and rose to the rank of
lieutenant-colonel in the armoured corps. In
1976 he helped to put down the coup attempt in
which head of state General Murtala Muhammed
was killed. In December 1983, as army chief of
staff, he masterminded the military coup that
removed **Shehu Shagari**'s government and
installed Major-General **Muhammadu Buhari**
as head of state, but dissatisfaction with Buhari's
austere and repressive rule led him to take over
in August 1985, breaking with the precedent set
by past military rulers by taking the title of
president. Babangida projected a more easy-
going and affable image than his predecessor and
quickly moved to undo some of Buhari's more
unpopular policies, releasing political detainees
and appointing a cabinet that aimed to achieve a
regional balance and restore links with
disaffected groups in society. He pushed ahead
with economic adjustment policies that the
Buhari government had dithered over and he
won the respect and support of Nigeria's
international creditors. His popularity at home
has waned, however, against a background of
worsening economic conditions. The open style
of government of his early months has been
replaced by a more repressive approach. He has
shown ruthlessness in dealing with challenges to
his rule: many of those involved in coup
attempts in December 1985 and April 1990
were executed. The fast political footwork that
earned him the nickname of the "Maradona" of
Nigerian politics will be needed in large measure
if he is to manage the promised transfer to
civilian rule by 1992. His attempts to create a
new, cleaner brand of politics have already been
marred by the resurgence of old regional and
religious interest groups, leading to his decision
in September 1989 to set up two custom-built

political parties, "one a little to the right, one a
little to the left" with manifestos prepared by
government officials, to contest the forthcoming
elections. His opponents accuse him of being
reluctant to hand over power and of planning to
transform himself into a civilian president.

BADRAN, Mudar. *Jordan*. Prime minister.
Born in Jerash in 1934, he was educated at
Damascus University. He headed Jordan's
military and general intelligence before entering
the cabinet, rising to the post of prime minister
in 1976–84. In late 1989 he returned to the
post, replacing Zaid ibn Shaker, whose position
had been weakened by price rise riots in April
and the subsequent electoral success of the
Muslim Brotherhood. Although feared for his
intelligence work in the past, Badran is also a
pragmatist. He was responsible in late 1989 for a
radical reform of the feared *mukhabarat* secret
police. His critics attacked him, nevertheless, for
encouraging fundamentalism as a counterweight
to Jordan's Palestinian and leftist groups.

BAFYAU, Pascal. *Nigeria*. Trade unionist. The
former general secretary of the Nigerian Union
of Railwaymen, he was elected president of the
national trade union federation, the Nigerian
Labour Congress, in 1988. His election was seen
as representing a compromise between radical
left-wing and moderate factions within the
union movement.

BAHNINI, Haj Mohammed. *Morocco*. Minister
of state. Born in 1916 in Fez, he served as
secretary-general to the cabinet from 1954–72
under both King Mohammed V and his son,
**King Hassan**. Often an important link between
the palace and politicians, he has held a series of
ministerial posts, and is now one of two senior
ministers of state.

BAKATIN, Vadim. *USSR*. Former interior
minister and Presidential Council member. A
Russian, born in 1937, he worked as a
construction engineer in West Siberia before
becoming a full-time Communist Party of Soviet
Union official in 1973, holding posts in regional
administration and the central party apparatus.

Named interior minister in 1988, he had one of the toughest jobs in central government as the country experienced soaring crime rates and inter-ethnic strife. Criticized for failing to measure up to these daunting challenges, he was dismissed in December 1990 and replaced by **Boris Pugo**.

**BAKER, James, III**. *USA*. Secretary of state. As the long-time friend and campaign manager of **George Bush** (with whom he shares a passion for hunting), Baker is unquestionably the closest of the tightly knit group of advisers surrounding the president. This, even more than the importance of his office, makes Baker the administration's most powerful figure and a likely Republican Party contender in the 1996 presidential election. Born in Texas in 1930, he was educated at Princeton University and the University of Texas Law School. After serving in the US Marines from 1952–54, he practised law until 1975 when he became President Gerald Ford's under-secretary of commerce. In 1976 he managed Ford's unsuccessful presidential campaign and, in 1980, Bush's contest for the Republican nomination. Both men eventually backed **Ronald Reagan** and, following his 1980 election victory, Baker was appointed White House chief of staff. A moderate conservative, Baker was one of the few non-Californians in Reagan's inner circle and soon became the effective manager of the administration. In February 1985 he arranged a highly unusual exchange of posts with Treasury secretary Donald Regan at a time when economic recession was predicted to be imminent. His use of the Group of Five (subsequently Group of Seven) industrialized countries to manage a smooth devaluation of the dollar and a shift in emphasis from floating to more managed exchange rates was widely perceived to have been crucial to the revival of US manufacturing output and exports. Known for his skill at negotiating with Congress, Baker made no secret of his interest in applying his talents to the world stage as secretary of state, and in August 1988 he resigned from the Treasury in order to chair Bush's presidential campaign. Baker's skills played a significant part in enabling the vice-president, who was trailing his Democratic opponent by a substantial margin in the polls, to secure a comprehensive victory in an often nasty campaign. In 1989 Baker was appointed secretary of state and, although generally considered to possess abundant intellectual reserves and political acumen, he has been criticized for not keeping career officials in his department fully informed of his strategy. He has also been accused of reacting to the dramatic world events of 1989–90, rather than seeking to shape them through the initiation of clear policy objectives. The Gulf crisis that blew up in 1990 gave him a high-profile role as a key architect of the US diplomatic response, but exposed his department to the charge of having underestimated the danger of Iraqi ambition in the area.

**BAKER, Kenneth**. *UK*. Home secretary since 1990. Born in 1934, he became an MP in 1970 after an active career in the Conservative student movement. He was parliamentary private secretary to **Edward Heath** from 1974–75 and joined **Margaret Thatcher**'s government in 1981. In 1984 he became minister for local government and began the research into local rates reform that produced the poll tax. After a spell as environment secretary, he succeeded **Keith Joseph** at education in 1986, laying the groundwork for sweeping educational reforms that included a national curriculum and the right of schools to opt out of local authority control. Appointment as party chairman followed, a position in which his apparently limitless self-confidence was severely tested by the Tories' poor showing in a long run of opinion polls through the period of turmoil that preceded Margaret Thatcher's defeat as party leader. In **John Major**'s reshuffle he was made home secretary.

**BAKLANOV, Oleg**. *USSR*. Senior Communist Party official. Born in 1932 and an engineer by profession, he was named deputy minister of general machine building (with special responsibility for the defence industry) in 1981, rising to minister in 1986. He was transferred to take responsibility for the defence industry within the Communist Party of the Soviet Union (CPSU) secretariat in 1988. Although Soviet defence spending is being cut as the economic crisis deepens, and military industries are being switched to producing consumer goods, Baklanov and his portfolio were left untouched by the sweeping leadership changes approved at the July 1990 CPSU Congress.

**BALAGUER RICARDO, Joaquín**. *Dominican Republic*. President. Born in 1906 and educated at the University of Santo Domingo and at the Sorbonne, Balaguer served under the dictatorship of Rafael Trujillo, being titular president at the time of Trujillo's assassination in 1961. He returned from exile after founding the conservative Reformist Party (PR – later the Social Christian Reformist Party – PRSC) and was elected president in 1966. Defeated in 1978, he was returned to power in 1986, although by then almost blind, and was narrowly re-elected in 1990.

**BALCEROWICZ, Leszek.** *Poland.* Deputy prime minister and finance minister. Born in 1947 and educated in Warsaw and New York, he began working as an economist in 1970, for a time at the Warsaw Central School of Planning and Statistics. He quit the ruling communist Polish United Workers' Party in 1981, becoming a consultant to Solidarity, and was part of the Solidarity-led government from its formation in September 1989. He is the author of the January 1990 Balcerowicz plan, which seeks to control inflation and lay the foundations of a market economy.

**BALLADUR, Edouard.** *France.* Gaullist politician. Born in 1929 in Smyrna, Turkey, he trained as a lawyer and entered the diplomatic service. A member of the Gaullist Rally for the Republic (RPR), he was closely associated at the start of his political career with Georges Pompidou, acting as technical adviser while Pompidou was prime minister under the presidency of Charles de Gaulle. In 1969, when Pompidou became president, Balladur was appointed secretary-general to the presidency. He subsequently pursued a career in industry, becoming chairman of two subsidiaries of the state-owned electricity company. A councillor of state from 1984–88, he acted as chief political adviser to **Jacques Chirac** shortly before the latter became prime minister in 1986. Despite his lack of parliamentary or Treasury experience, Chirac named him minister of state for economy, finance and privatization, a post he held until 1988, when he was elected to the National Assembly as deputy for Paris. Active in European affairs, he made his mark in 1987 with proposals for a single European currency and central bank, playing a key role in meetings with West German leaders on developing a common policy in this area.

**BALLIN, Ernst Hirsch.** *Netherlands.* Justice minister. Born in 1950, he studied law and, at the age of 31, was appointed professor of constitutional and administrative law at Tilburg University. A Christian Democrat, he was put in charge of the justice ministry in 1989.

**BALSAI, István.** *Hungary.* Justice minister. Born in 1947, he was active in the Hungarian Democratic Forum (MDF), entering the

government in the spring of 1990 when his party colleague **József Antall** formed his conservative-led government after the first elections of the post-communist period.

**BANDA, Hastings Kamuzu.** *Malawi.* President for life. Banda is generally considered to have been born in about 1898, but his official birthdate is 1906. Autocratic and conservative by nature, he brought his country to independence and has run it as a personal fief ever since, brooking neither opposition nor the emergence of any likely successor from within his own Malawi Congress Party (MCP). Trained in medicine, he practised as a doctor in the USA, UK and Ghana before returning home in 1958 to take up leadership of the MCP. An arch-opponent of the Central African Federation, he was detained by the British during 1959. He became prime minister in 1963 after the break-up of the federation and president after independence in 1966. In 1971 he was named president for life and has also retained the key ministerial portfolios of external affairs, justice, works and agriculture. He has always followed a highly individual path, notably towards South Africa; until recently Malawi was the only Organization of African Unity member to have diplomatic relations with Pretoria. Recently, however, he has improved with some of his neighbours, notably Zimbabwe and Mozambique, and has also been obliged to rethink some of his social policies to improve health and education. He is an elder of the Church of Scotland.

**BANDARANAIKE, Sirimavo.** *Sri Lanka.* Opposition leader. Born in 1916 and convent-educated in Colombo, she was married in 1940 to Solomon Bandaranaike, who was prime minister from 1956 until his assassination in 1959. Taking over his political mantle as president of the Sri Lanka Freedom Party (SLFP), she headed left-wing coalition governments in 1960–65 and 1970–77, and on both occasions also held the defence and foreign affairs portfolios. An implacable and formidable opponent of the Junius Jayawardene regime which followed her annihilation at the polls in 1977, she was debarred from active politics from 1980–85, on the grounds of alleged abuse of power while in office; she had to leave the parliamentary leadership of the SLFP to her son Anura, while keeping its future firmly in her thrall. In line with her challenge to the legitimacy of the government when it extended the term of parliament in 1982, she held the

SLFP aloof from talks on the increasingly critical Tamil issue, at the risk of being marginalized. Her daughter Chandrika Kumaranatunga led a breakaway from the SLFP in 1984. In December 1988 Sirimavo proved her durability by running **Ranasinghe Premadasa** close in the presidential elections, campaigning on a platform of ending the Indian involvement but granting limited devolution to the Tamil north and east. Her erstwhile links with leftists long discarded, she remains a critic of the all-out free-market stance of the ruling United National Party. Drawing heavily on the sympathy she had won from being banned, she also campaigns to condemn the government for its oppressive use of power and to secure a bill of rights and essential freedoms.

**BANGEMANN, Martin.** *Germany.* European Commission vice-president and commissioner for the internal market and industrial affairs. Born in 1934, he studied and practised law until his election to parliament for the liberal Free Democratic Party (FDP) in 1973. Although not an economics expert, he was put in charge of that department in 1984. The following year he also became party chairman (although **Hans-Dietrich Genscher** nevertheless remained the party's real leader). In 1989 he became an EC commissioner, primarily responsible for managing the complex path to a single European market. Known for his diplomatic skill but dislike of technical details, Bangemann's reputation has waned since he came to Brussels with hopes of succeeding **Jacques Delors** as commission president in 1993.

**BANGERTER, Norman.** *USA.* Republican governor of Utah. Born in 1933, he was a building contractor, who was speaker of the state legislature before being elected governor in 1984. Although he had promised not to do so, he increased taxes in 1987 to prevent a state deficit and ensure adequate educational funding, and therefore sank in the polls. But he was able to regain support, and was elected as governor in 1988.

**BANHAM, John.** *UK.* Business leader. Born in 1940, he studied natural sciences and worked briefly as a civil servant and marketing director before joining the McKinsey management consultancy group in 1969, becoming a director in 1980. He left in 1983 to become controller of the Audit Commission (the body which oversees local government) and was elected director-general of the Confederation of British Industry (CBI) in 1987.

**BANHARN SILPA-ARCHA.** *Thailand.* Finance minister. The "strongman" of the right-wing Thai Nation Party (Chart Thai), Banharn, born in 1932, was elected as an MP in 1976 and briefly served as agriculture minister in the early 1980s. He acquired a controversial image during his 1986–88 spell as communications minister, against a background of mounting unease over allegations of high-level corruption. After two years as industry minister he was moved to head the interior ministry in early 1990 and to the finance ministry in December that year.

**BANKS, Tony.** *UK.* Labour politician. Born in 1937, he studied at York University and the London School of Economics, and then worked as a full-time official for two unions from 1969–83. A flamboyant member and chairman of the Greater London Council until its abolition in 1986, he was elected to parliament for his east London seat in 1983, and has since made the most of opportunities to exercise his wry wit.

**BANNON, John.** *Australia.* Premier of South Australia. Born in 1944, he was elected as a Labor member of South Australia's legislative assembly in 1977. He became state premier after the Australian Labor Party's return to power in Adelaide in 1982 and is identified with its centre right. Opinion polls often show him to be the most popular state premier.

**BÁNZER SUÁREZ, Hugo.** *Bolivia.* National Democratic Action (ADN) leader. Born in 1926, Bánzer pursued a conventional military career until the 1964 coup, when he was appointed education minister. He was dismissed as head of the military college for attempting a coup, but returned from exile to stage a successful coup in 1971. His right-wing regime was uniquely long-lasting by Bolivian standards, as well as notoriously repressive. An economic boom fuelled by foreign investment could not be sustained, however, and economic crisis and industrial unrest led to his overthrow in 1978. Returning to civilian politics, he founded the right-wing ADN, which has grown steadily in influence, allowing Bánzer to play an increasingly important role. In 1985 he forged a pact with President Víctor Paz Estenssoro, and after coming second in the 1989 elections he led his ADN into a ruling alliance with his old enemy **Jaime Paz Zamora**. Bánzer became head of the National Political Council (Conapo), charged with defining overall policy goals.

**BARCO VARGAS, Virgilio.** *Colombia.* Former president. Born in 1921, he trained as a civil engineer at Columbia University and MIT, and worked in public administration before entering politics as a local councillor. He became involved in national politics when elected to the House of Representatives and then the Senate. He served as a minister from 1958–64 and also held senior diplomatic posts, including those of ambassador to the UK and the USA. His popularity at home derives in part from his term as mayor of Bogotá from 1966–69. As Liberal Party candidate he won the 1986 presidential elections, gaining a strong mandate for social reform. However, his presidency was soon overshadowed by conflict with left-wing guerrillas and then the "Medellín cartel" drug barons; Barco at first took a low profile in this conflict, declaring "war" on the drug traffickers only shortly before the end of his presidency in August 1989.

**BARNALA, Surjit Singh.** *India.* Akali Dal leader and former chief minister of Punjab. Born in 1925, Barnala was union agriculture and irrigation minister in the Janata government (1975–77). He assumed leadership of the Sikh regionalist Akali Dal in 1985 after the assassination of his patron, Sant Longowal, becoming chief minister of the Punjab. Faced with the nearly impossible task of finding a balance between the pressures of New Delhi and Sikh militants, his authority foundered. In June 1987 he was dismissed as chief minister and the state was placed under president's rule.

**BARNIER, Michel.** *France.* Gaullist politician. Born in 1951 and a graduate in commercial studies, he began his career in politics and public administration, winning county council elections aged only 22 and a seat in the National Assembly five years later for the Gaullist Rally for the Republic (RPR). In the 1970s and 1980s, he was an attaché to various ministers, ranging from youth and leisure questions to industrial affairs. In the environmental arena he is generally seen – alongside **Alain Carignon** – as the "greenest" Gaullist deputy, with a strong interest also in humanitarian issues.

**BARÓN CRESPO, Enrique.** *Spain.* President of the European Parliament. Born in 1944, Barón Crespo studied in Spain and France and was a leading figure in the anti-Franco student movement in the early 1970s. He ran a legal and economic consultancy until his election to parliament for the Spanish Socialist Workers' Party (PSOE). Initially the party's spokesman on economic affairs, he was appointed transport and tourism minister in 1982. He became a member of the European Parliament in 1986 and was elected its president in 1989, but has disappointed many by his failure to argue strongly for an increase in the parliament's powers in the constitutional reform due in 1991.

**BARRANTES LINGÁN, Alfonso.** *Peru.* Left-wing politician. Born in 1928, Barrantes studied law at the National University of San Marcos. He joined the Peruvian Communist Party in 1960, but resigned in 1972 to become an independent. He helped to form United Left (IU) in 1980 and was elected mayor of Lima in 1983. He came second to **Alan García** in the 1985 presidential contest. He lost his position as mayor of Lima in 1986 and was forced by internal politicking to resign as leader of IU in 1987, but remains the most popular figure on the left.

**BARRE, Raymond.** *France.* Right-wing politician. Born in Réunion in 1924, he graduated in law and politics at the Institut d'Etudes Politiques and built himself an academic career, combining this with the role of government economic adviser after 1959. He was chosen by Charles de Gaulle in 1967 to be a senior EC Commission member, serving from 1968–72 as Commission vice-president with responsibility for economic and financial affairs. In 1975 he was one of the team of experts involved in preparing for the Rambouillet international economic summit. Early the following year he was brought into the government as foreign trade minister and, in August 1976, he replaced **Jacques Chirac** as prime minister, a post he kept until 1981. Acting also as his own economy and finance minister, he dispensed the strong dose of austerity that became known as the "Barre plan". He proved surprisingly popular, partly because he won a reputation for telling unpalatable truths, and partly because of his reassuringly roly-poly appearance. In 1978 he was elected for the first time to the National Assembly, where he sits as a Union for French Democracy (UDF) deputy for Lyon. In the 1980s he emerged temporarily as France's most popular politician, making a virtue of his "boffin" image, but made a serious miscalculation in his opposition to the 1986–88 power-sharing "cohabitation" exercise. In the 1988 presidential election he finished a poor third behind **François Mitterrand** and Jacques Chirac, but he remains an influential figure on the centre-right and has kept alive the possibility of forming a new centre-right movement.

**BARRIONUEVO PEÑA, José.** *Spain.* Transport and communications minister. Born in

1942 in Berja, Almeria province, and educated in law and journalism, he became professor of labour law at Madrid University. As interior minister in the Socialist government from 1982–88, a time of intensive activity by the Basque nationalist ETA, he was regarded as a hardliner on law and order. He became transport and communications minster in 1988 after allegations that his ministry and the police had been involved in setting up anti-terrorist "death squads".

**BARRIOS, Gonzalo.** *Venezuela.* Democratic Action (AD) leader. Born in 1902, he is the elder statesman of the social democratic AD, which he helped to found in 1941. From 1945–46, he was a member of the seven-man junta installed after the 1945 pro-AD coup. He was secretary of the presidency under president Romulo Gallegos, but was imprisoned after Gallegos's overthrow and later exiled. He was elected to Congress in 1958, soon after his return to Venezuela and was AD's presidential candidate in 1986, losing by a very narrow margin to Rafael Caldera. He has been AD president since then.

**BARROT, Jacques.** *France.* Centrist politician. Born in 1937 and a graduate in law and in politics from the Institut d'Etudes Politiques, he won election to the National Assembly on a centrist platform in 1967. During the 1970s he held several ministerial portfolios, including housing, trade, artisan affairs, health and social security. In 1986, he became president of the National Assembly's committee on cultural, family and social affairs. Since 1984 he has been secretary-general of the centrist Centre of Social Democrats (CDS).

**BARROW, Dame Nita.** *Barbados.* Governor-general. Born in 1916, the sister of Errol Barrow, Barbados's first prime minister, she trained as a nurse, serving in senior nursing positions in Barbados, Canada and Jamaica. She has an international reputation as a health professional, serving as director of the Christian Medical Commission from 1975–80 and as a consultant to the World Health Organization from 1981–86. In 1986 she became permanent representative to the UN and in June 1990 governor-general.

**BARTONČÍK, Josef.** *Czechoslovakia.* Chairman of the Czechoslovak People's Party. Representing a party which had formerly been a junior partner of the communists, Bartončík was a deputy chairman of the Federal Assembly before the June 1990 elections. In that first free election his party formed part of the Czech Christian

Democrat Union, which performed notably less well than its Slovak counterpart. The discrepancy was attributed in part to controversy over allegations that he had been a police informer. He resisted demands that he should withdraw from the election, but kept a low profile and was also undergoing hospital treatment for heart trouble. His party, propounding Christian values and conservatism in a free-market economy, came third in local elections in the Czech Lands in November 1990.

**BARTOSZCZE, Roman.** *Poland.* Polish Peasant Party leader. A member of a famous family of opposition peasant activists, he became a Solidarity parliamentary deputy. In May 1990, however, he was elected Peasant Party chairman at a special congress, when the revived Polish Peasant Party (banned since 1947) joined up with the United Peasants' Party (a junior government coalition partner throughout communist rule) and defectors from Rural Solidarity. Although outstripped in the May 1990 local elections by the Solidarity-backed Citizens' Committees, Bartoszcze's party performed best of the national political parties, winning 6% of the seats in the first completely free elections for more than half a century. He was a presidential candidate in the November 1990 elections, finishing fifth in the first round with just over 7% of the vote.

**BASHIR, Lieutenant-General Omar Hassan Ahmed al-.** *Sudan.* Head of state. Born in 1934, a northerner and a career soldier, he received military training in Egypt, Malaysia, the USA and Pakistan, and fought with the Sudanese brigade in the 1973 Arab–Israeli war. From 1975–79 he served as military adviser in the United Arab Emirates. In February 1989 he was one of 150 officers who signed an ultimatum calling for an end to the civil war in the south, where he had served for two years as a garrison commander. At the time of the June 1989 coup that brought him to power Al-Bashir was head of an armoured brigade stationed near Khartoum. A devout Muslim, Al-Bashir has links with the Islamic fundamentalists, whose grip on the government has become steadily stronger. The new government claimed that it would tackle corruption but has caused widespread discontent by banning political parties and imprisoning and torturing opponents. Efforts to bring the civil war to a peaceful end have been abandoned. Two alleged coup attempts, in March and April 1990, provoked brutal repression.

**BASRI, Driss.** *Morocco.* Interior and information minister. A lawyer, born in 1938, he joined the government in 1974 as secretary of state for internal affairs. He has come to dominate the security apparatus and has also overseen the devolution of power to local authorities, a major trend of recent years.

**BASU, Jyoti.** *India.* Chief minister of West Bengal, member of the politburo and the central executive committee of Communist Party of India (Marxist). Born in Calcutta in 1914, an English-trained barrister, he has been a communist member of the West Bengal state assembly since 1947. He was deputy chief minister in the United Front governments of 1968–70, also serving first as finance minister and subsequently as home minister. In 1977 he became chief minister at the head of a "Left Front" government, a position he has held ever since. When the Communist Party split in 1964 Basu supported the left-wing CPI(M). As chief minister, however, he has advocated a pragmatic course for the party, concentrating on its power bases in West Bengal and Kerala and co-operating with wider anti-Congress forces on a national level. Under Basu's influence, CPI(M) dominates both state and federal politics in West Bengal, although it maintains the "Left Front" together with several small left-wing parties. Widely popular within the state, with a reputation for effectiveness and honesty, Basu has pushed through important reforms in areas such as housing and tenants' rights.

**BATALLA, Hugo.** *Uruguay.* Opposition leader. Born in 1927, Batalla was a human rights lawyer during the period of military rule. In 1985 he was elected a senator for the Broad Front (FA), but in 1989 his Party for the Government of the People (PGP), broke away as a more moderate grouping. In the November 1989 presidential election he campaigned unsuccessfully on the New Space (NE) ticket.

**BATLLE IBAÑEZ, Jorge.** *Uruguay.* Opposition politician. Born in 1927 into Uruguay's foremost political family – both his father and great-uncle had been president – Batlle led his own faction within the Colorado Party. He was a journalist and member of the Chamber of Deputies during the 1960s. On the return to civilian rule in 1984, he gained a seat in the Senate. Widely regarded as a "neo-liberal", he was an unsuccessful presidential candidate of the Colorados in 1989.

**BATTAGLIA, Adolfo.** *Italy.* Industry minister and Italian Republican Party (PRI) politician.

Born in 1930 in Viterbo, he obtained a law degree and became a journalist. He entered the Chamber of Deputies in 1972, and has been industry minister since July 1987. In this post, which also carries responsibility for energy, he has pressed for the lifting of the *de facto* ban on nuclear power.

**BAUDOUIN I.** *Belgium.* King. Born in 1930, he was educated privately and succeeded to the throne in 1951 after his father, Leopold III, abdicated. The most unenviable of Europe's monarchs, he has had to juggle the diverse interests of his Dutch-speaking Flemish and French-speaking Walloon subjects. His evenhandedness, low-key style and symbolically important fluency in both Dutch and French have earned him the respect of most Belgians, and he is widely seen as an essential unifying force in a country with few others. He married a Spanish princess, Fabiola of Aragon, in 1960. They have no children, and the succession will pass through his brother to his nephew, Philippe.

**BAUM, Gerhart Rudolf.** *Germany.* Free Democratic Party (FDP) politician. Born in Dresden in 1932, he joined the FDP at Cologne University. He qualified as a lawyer and was a leading member of the West German employers' organization before becoming a junior minister in the federal interior ministry and then, from 1978–82, interior minister. His left–liberal and green-inclined attitudes sit ill with his party's current orientation towards the Christian Democrats, but like others in his party he could return to the limelight if a new centre–left coalition were in prospect.

**BAVADRA, Adi Kuini.** *Fiji.* Labour Party leader. The electoral success of Adi Kuini Bavadra's husband Timoci Bavadra in April 1987 brought into office his multi-racial, but primarily Indian, democratic socialist government, whose challenge to ethnic Fijian dominance sparked the coup led by Major-General **Sitiveni Rabuka** the following month. The death of Timoci Bavadra from cancer in November 1989 was followed by the election of his widow to lead the coalition, now condemned to apparently permanent opposition. Adi Kuini is of noble birth and related to **Kamisese Mara** and **Penaia Ganilau**, and her links with the traditional Fijian power system made her possibly more acceptable than her late husband, a commoner. She marked her assumption of the opposition leadership by calling for compromise and realism. Indignant over the continuing manipulation of power by the regime, however, latterly she has supported a boycott of elections, which are to be arranged on the basis of constitutional changes pushed through in July 1990 to entrench ethnic Fijian control.

**BAYH, Evan**. *USA*. Democratic governor of Indiana. Born in 1955, he is the son of former US senator Birch Bayh and practised law before being elected Indiana secretary of state in 1986. In 1988 he ran on a platform of fiscal conservatism and social liberalism to become the nation's youngest governor, breaking a 20-year Republican grip. A skilled media performer, he is a rising star who is likely to seek elevation to national politics.

**BAYKAL, Deniz**. *Turkey*. Opposition politician. Secretary-general of the Social Democratic Populist Party since 1988, Baykal was regarded as its strong man until the failure of his attempt to oust **Erdal İnönü** from the leadership in September 1990 led to his replacement. He has been a particularly vigorous critic of President **Turgut Özal**, whose behaviour he has described as despotic. He has government experience – as a minister of finance and of energy in two social democratic governments of the 1970s – but now looks set to spend some time in the political wilderness.

**BAYLET, Jean-Michel**. *France*. Government minister. Born in 1946 and a law graduate, he became a journalist and newspaper manager. Politically, he identified with the Movement of Left-wing Radicals (MRG), which he co-founded; he became MRG national secretary in 1973, vice-president in 1978, and president in 1983. He has also been an MRG mayor, deputy and senator in the 1980s. From 1984–86 he was junior minister for foreign affairs; in 1988 he was appointed junior minister for local government, and in the October 1990 reshuffle he became minister-delegate in charge of tourism.

**BAZARGAN, Mehdi**. *Iran*. Opposition leader. Born in 1907 in Tehran, Bazargan was a deputy minister in Mohammad Mossadeq's government from 1951–53 and co-founded the Freedom Movement of Iran in 1961. Arrested and imprisoned several times under the Shah, he co-founded the Human Rights Association in 1977 and was appointed by Ayatollah Khomeini to control the anti-Shah strike of oil workers. He became Iran's first post-revolutionary prime minister, assuming office in February 1979 after the overthrow of Shapour Bakhtiar's government. A committed moderate, he

resigned over the student takeover of the US embassy, and served as a member of parliament for Tehran from 1980–84. His subsequent career has been one of uncompromising opposition to the regime's excesses. He operates on the limits of official tolerance, and has frequently encountered harassment from radical militants, notably over his outspoken opposition to the 1980–88 war with Iraq. He co-founded the Association for Defence of the Freedom and Sovereignty of the Iranian Nation in 1987. He continues to enjoy something of a charmed life as one of Iran's few dissenting voices, openly accusing the regime of corruption, cruelty and incompetence. Some of his colleagues, however, were arrested in June 1990 in an apparent warning that he is no longer immune.

**BAZIN, Marc**. *Haiti*. Party leader. Born in 1932 and educated in law in Paris, Bazin worked for the World Bank in West Africa and the USA. In 1982 he was appointed finance minister, but was dismissed after only five months when he attempted to introduce reforms and halt corruption. He returned to Haiti in 1986 to found the Movement for the Installation of Democracy in Haiti (MIDH). Widely regarded as the US choice for president, he derives his support mainly from the middle classes, but his popularity with them has been in decline, and he finished a poor second in the December 1990 elections.

**BEATRIX**. *Netherlands*. Queen. She succeeded to the throne in 1980, when her mother Queen Juliana abdicated. Born in 1938, she graduated in law from Leiden University in 1961. Regarded as headstrong, she married the German diplomat Claus von Amsberg in 1966 against considerable opposition, largely because of his nationality. Nominally above politics, she takes considerable interest in political and social issues, and has at times revealed left-leaning tendencies. Increasingly self-confident, in her Christmas message of 1988 she deplored the deterioration of the country's environment, directly contradicting the upbeat assessment given by the government a few months earlier. The approval of an ambitious environmental clean-up plan was a major national issue the following year.

**BEAZLEY, Kim**. *Australia*. Transport and communications minister and leader of the House of Representatives. One of the brightest and most combative of Labor politicians, Beazley is regarded as a possible successor to **Bob Hawke** as leader of the Australian Labor Party

(ALP). Born into a well-known Western Australian Labor family, he was educated at the University of Western Australia and at Oxford University. He then taught political science at Murdoch University before his election to the House of Representatives as member for Swan in 1980. While in opposition he concentrated on foreign affairs and defence issues, and after the Labor victory of 1983 was appointed aviation minister and then, in 1984, defence minister. He remained in this post until after the 1990 election, when he was appointed transport and communications minister to oversee the rationalization of the fragmented, state-owned telecommunications industry. Like his main rival for the succession, **Paul Keating**, and Bob Hawke, Beazley belongs to the "Labor Unity" (right-wing) faction of the ALP.

**BECKERS, Ria**. *Netherlands*. Left-wing politician. Born in 1938, she was elected chairwoman of the small Radical Political Party (PPR) in 1974 and a member of the Staten Generaal (parliament) in 1977. In 1989 she was returned as the PPR member of the new Green Left (Groen Links) coalition of small left-of-centre parties which place environmental issues at the centre of their policies.

**BECKETT, Margaret**. *UK*. Labour politician. Born in 1943, she worked as an experimental officer in a university metallurgy department and as a researcher for the Labour Party and then for Granada Television before being elected to parliament for Lincoln in 1974. Initially on the extreme left of the party, she lost her seat five years later but re-entered parliament (for Derby South) in 1983, adopting a more moderate line. She joined the opposition Treasury team in 1989, and is seen as a potentially important ally of **John Smith** if he should become chancellor in a future Labour government.

**BEECHAM, Jeremy**. *UK*. Labour politician. Born in 1944, he has practised as a solicitor since 1968. He was elected to the city council of Newcastle upon Tyne in 1967, becoming its leader in 1977. One of Labour's younger generation of local government leaders, he has been pragmatic in his efforts to regenerate a city whose heavy industry base collapsed in the 1980s.

**BEIBA, Mahfoud Laroussi Ali**. *Western Sahara*. Prime minister of Sahrawi Arab Democratic Republic. Born in about 1953 near El-Ayoun, he moved to Mauritania in the early 1970s to join the movement for independence from Spanish, and subsequently Moroccan, rule. He was elected

assistant secretary-general of the Polisario Front in 1974 and briefly held the leadership of the movement in 1976 after the death in action of El-Ouali Mustapha Sayed before being replaced by **Mohammed Abdelaziz**. Beiba was appointed prime minister, and interior and justice minister in May 1989.

**BEILENSON, Anthony**. *USA*. Democratic congressman from California. Born in 1932, he practised law before his election to the House of Representatives in 1976. A liberal of independent outlook, he supports tax increases to reduce the federal budget deficit. He has been intelligence committee chairman since 1987.

**BEITH, Alan**. *UK*. Liberal Democrat politician. Born in 1943, he studied politics at Oxford University and then lectured in politics from 1966 until his election as Liberal Party member of parliament for Berwick-on-Tweed in 1973. A solid, undemonstrative figure (and a Methodist lay preacher) on the right wing of the party, he was elected chief whip in 1976 and was also its spokesman on education (1977–83), constitutional affairs (1983–87 – important in a party campaigning for electoral reform), and foreign affairs (1985–87). He was elected deputy leader in 1985 and in 1988 stood for the leadership of the new Social and Liberal Democratic Party, but was heavily defeated by **Paddy Ashdown**.

**BELCHEV, Belcho**. *Bulgaria*. Former deputy premier and finance minister. Born into a poor peasant family in Krastinetsi in 1932, Belchev joined the Communist Youth League in 1947. He graduated from the Karl Marx Higher Economics Institute in Sofia in 1957 and then went on to hold a series of civil service posts. He has been a member of the National Assembly since 1976, holding the post of finance minister from 1976–87 and again from November 1989. He added the post of deputy premier in the Socialist government formed by **Andrei Lukanov** in February 1990, retained his posts in September but lost them in December, when a transitional coalition government was formed by **Dimitur Popov**.

**BELHADJ, Ali**. *Algeria*. Opposition leader. A militant Islamic preacher who leads the radical wing of the Islamic Salvation Front (FIS), he was convicted in 1987 of collaborating with the fundamentalist rebel Mustapha Bouiali. Belhadj played an important role in co-ordinating the anti-government demonstrations of 1988.

**BELOUSOV, Igor**. *USSR*. Former deputy prime minister. Born in 1928, he worked in shipbuilding, becoming deputy minister of shipbuilding in 1969, first deputy minister in 1976 and minister in 1984. In 1989 he was appointed deputy premier and chairman of the Bureau for the Military Industrial Complex, in which capacity he had to contend with a shrinking defence budget and the reassignment of military industries to consumer goods production.

**BELSTEAD, Lord.** *UK.* Minister of state at the Northern Ireland office since 1990. Educated at Eton College and Oxford University, Belstead was born John Ganzoni in 1932 and succeeded to his family's title in 1958. Since 1970 he has held ministerial posts in education, industry, home and foreign affairs, agriculture and environment. Before being appointed to his current position, he was leader of the House of Lords.

**BEN ALI, Zine el-Abidine.** *Tunisia.* President. Born in 1936, he joined the army in 1958 and rose to the rank of general, specializing in intelligence and security. He was director-general of national security from 1977–80 and again in 1984, after a spell as ambassador to Poland. He joined the cabinet as national security minister in 1985, becoming interior minister two years later. In October 1987, he was appointed prime minister and one month later replaced the ageing president, Habib Bourguiba. Viewed as a hardliner before taking power, Ben Ali soon surprised his compatriots by ushering in an unprecedented period of reform and democratization, opening a dialogue with the opposition, releasing political prisoners and encouraging exiles to return. A number of political parties have been legalized, although Ben Ali has drawn the line at recognizing the Islamic fundamentalist opposition, stating that politics and religion do not mix.

**BEN BELLA, Ahmed.** *Algeria.* Former president and now leader of the Movement for Democracy in Algeria (MDA). Born in 1916, Ben Bella served in a Moroccan regiment in World War II and was a founder-member of the Algerian independence movement in the late 1940s, directing the movement from exile in Cairo between periods of detention during the 1950s. He was Algeria's first prime minister at independence in 1962 and president from 1963 until his overthrow by his defence minister, Houari Boumedienne, in 1965. After 16 years in detention he was allowed to go into exile in 1981. He returned in September 1990 to participate in multi-party politics, promoting

himself as a symbol of the country's original revolutionary aspirations.

**BENFLIS, Ali.** *Algeria.* Justice minister. A reformer, he was appointed to the National Liberation Front (FLN) politburo at the November 1989 party congress, but resigned from it in July 1990 to help open the party leadership to younger politicians.

**BENKOW, Jo.** *Norway.* Conservative politician. Born in 1924, Benkow is a photographer and writer. A member of the Storting (parliament) since 1965, he became vice-chairman of the Conservatives (Høyre) in 1973, chairman from 1980–84 and led the parliamentary party from 1981–85. After the 1985 elections he was elected speaker of the Storting.

**BENN, Tony.** *UK.* Labour politician. Born in 1925, he studied at Oxford University and was elected to parliament (for a Bristol seat) as a Labour member in 1950. In 1960 he came to national prominence because of his struggle to renounce the title – Viscount Stansgate – he had inherited from his father (and which barred him from serving in the House of Commons). An act passed in 1963 allowed peers to renounce their titles, and he was elected to parliament the following year, becoming postmaster-general (1964–66) and subsequently technology minister (1966–70), party spokesman on trade and industry (1970–74) and secretary of state for industry (1974–75) and energy (1975–79). During the 1970s he shifted steadily to the left, emerging after the Labour defeat in 1979 as a powerful champion of the left wing of the party. He became increasingly scornful of the Labour governments of the 1960s and 1970s (though he had served in them all) and called repeatedly for Labour to embrace a full-blooded socialism, involving a big rise in public spending, widespread nationalization, withdrawal from Nato and the EC and much greater commitment to open government. In 1981 he lost an election for the deputy leadership by the narrowest of margins. Thereafter, and particularly in the wake of Labour's election defeat in 1983 (when he lost his own seat, before returning to parliament as member for Chesterfield in a by-election the following year), his power base in the party shrank rapidly. The successful modernization of Labour under **Neil Kinnock** left him on the margin of British politics, but he remains a key figure in the demonology of the right,.

**BENNETT, William.** *USA.* Former director of the Office of National Drug Control Policy. Born in Brooklyn in 1943, he served as an administrator at the National Humanities Center in North Carolina from 1976–81, before being appointed as president of the National Endowment for the Humanities in 1981. A right-wing Democrat who became a Republican in 1986, he served as secretary of education in the administration of **Ronald Reagan** from 1985 until his resignation in 1988. In 1989 he was appointed "drugs czar", a new post created by **George Bush**, who had singled out the eradication of drug abuse as a key objective of his administration. Although both Bennett and Bush announced major anti-drug initiatives during 1989, these concentrated resources on law enforcement and against drug-trafficking, and appeared to have little impact on the widespread use of illegal drugs within the USA. Resigning his drug control post in November 1990, he was Bush's choice to be Republican National Committee chairman, but could not afford to take up the role as it would preclude him pursuing consultancy work.

**BENTKOWSKI, Aleksander.** *Poland.* Justice minister. A lawyer, born in 1941, he joined the United Peasants' Party (ZSL) in 1962 and defended opposition figures in political trials. This led to his endorsement by Solidarity in the partly free Sejm (parliament) elections of June 1989, after which he led the ZSL parliamentary group. He then championed the ZSL's defection from the communist-led coalition government to one led by Solidarity and was rewarded with the justice portfolio in September 1989.

**BENTSEN, Lloyd.** *USA.* Democratic senator from Texas. Born in 1921, he attended the University of Texas, was a bomber pilot in World War II, and served four terms in the House of Representatives from 1947–55. After a career in corporate law and finance, he became a senator in 1970. Pro-business on economic issues, he has defended Texan oil and natural gas interests and has been a prominent advocate of tough trade policies, particularly towards Japan. His record on social and racial issues is more liberal. His career flagged after the Republicans gained control of the Senate in 1981 but revived when he became finance committee chairman in 1987. His selection as vice-presidential nominee in 1988 disappointed some liberals who wanted **Michael Dukakis** to choose **Jesse Jackson**, but Bentsen, a Washington insider with appeal to business and the South, gave the Democratic ticket better balance. He campaigned effectively and easily outshone **Dan Quayle** in the televised vice-presidential debate. His crushing dismissal

of his youthful rival's leadership qualities – "Senator, you're no Jack Kennedy" – was a campaign highlight. Although some see him as too old for a presidential bid in 1992, he is recognized as a top Democratic senator with substantial influence in national party circles.

**BÉRÉGOVOY, Pierre.** *France.* Minister of state for economy, finance and budget. Born in 1924, he worked as a fitter and railwayman and graduated in labour law. A member first of the old socialist party (SFIO), then of the Unified Socialist Party (PSU), he became a leading figure in the new Socialist Party (PS) after 1969, initially within the national committee and executive, then (from 1973) within the secretariat, where he was responsible for relations with the Communist Party (PCF). Adviser to **François Mitterrand** in 1981–82 as Elysée secretary-general, he then became social affairs and social security minister until 1984. In 1984 he was promoted to economy, finance and budget minister, and returned to this portfolio (with the rank of minister of state) when the left came back into government in 1988, having earned himself a reputation for sound management and for hard-headed realism about the need for deflationary austerity measures.

**BÉRENGER, Paul.** *Mauritius.* Mauritian Militant Movement (MMM) secretary-general. Born in 1945 and educated at the University of Wales and at the Sorbonne in Paris, where his radicalism was forged in the turbulence of the late 1960s. Returning to Mauritius he helped to form MMM with **Aneerood Jugnauth** in 1969, mobilizing an urban power base among the trade unions. Industrial unrest reached a peak in the dock strike of 1971, which led to the declaration of a state of emergency and the brief detention of Bérenger and other MMM leaders. The collapse of sugar prices in the late 1970s brought an economic crisis and the MMM was swept to power in a landslide victory in the 1982 elections, when Jugnauth became prime minister and Bérenger finance minister. The severity of the economic crisis forced the radical socialist Bérenger to seek assistance from the IMF and World Bank; attacks on his policies led to his departure from the government the following year. He remained a potent force in opposition, but stepped down as party leader in favour of **Prem Nababsingh** before the 1987 elections, in an attempt to broaden the MMM's appeal with the Hindu population. The MMM returned to government in 1990 in a new alliance with Jugnauth, centring on plans to transform

Mauritius into a republic within the Commonwealth, of which Bérenger would become president.

**BERGÉ, Pierre.** *France.* Artistic promoter and administrator. Born in 1930, he has been occupied with the arts and culture throughout his career, initially as editor and director of the artistic journal, *La Patrie Mondiale,* from 1949–61. Subsequently, he founded, managed or presided over various bodies devoted to fashion, music, art and design, and has been president of the Yves Saint Laurent Society (America) since 1971. In 1985, he became president of the French Institute of Fashion and is president of the Paris Opéra. He is editor of *Globe* magazine and is politically close to **Laurent Fabius.**

**BERMAN, Howard.** *USA.* Democratic congressman from California. Born in 1941, he is a lawyer and served in the state legislature before his election to the House of Representatives in 1982. He has been active in pursuing tighter regulation of arms sales and anti-apartheid legislation, and is a major political force in California politics.

**BERNINI, Carlo.** *Italy.* Transport minister, and Christian Democrat party (DC) politician. Formerly premier of the Veneto regional government, he first attained cabinet rank as transport minister in July 1989. He aroused criticism in 1990 for banning the entry of Austrian trucks in a dispute over transport rights, later referred to the European Court of Justice.

**BERON, Petar.** *Bulgaria.* Leading opposition politician. Born into a non-party family in Sofia in 1940, Beron's parents were economists. He trained as a biologist and zoologist, specializing in the study and exploration of caves, for which he travelled the world. He was a founder-member of the environmental group, Ecoglasnost, which was one of the first opposition groups to become active in Bulgaria, and the first to be recognised after president Todor Zhivkov was ousted in 1989. A member of the National Assembly, he succeeded **Zhelyu Zhelev** as chairman of the main opposition coalition, the Union of Democratic Forces (UDF), in August 1990. Beron is a respected politician of liberal views. He resigned the UDF chairmanship four months later, however, amid allegations that he had acted as a police informer under the former communist regime; he was replaced by **Filip Dimitrov.**

**BERRADA, Mohammed.** *Morocco.* Finance minister. Born in 1933 and educated in France,

he was a university lecturer before joining the government. Berrada has overseen Morocco's structural adjustment programme and the liberalization of large areas of the economy.

**BERRI, Nabih.** *Lebanon.* Amal leader. Born in 1939 in the Lebanese town of Tibnin, Berri was a lawyer before becoming leader of the Movement of the Deprived, better known as Amal (Hope), when its founder, Musa Sadr, disappeared (presumed killed) in 1978 during a trip to Libya. Amal gained in strength in the early 1980s, and fought hard against the Israeli invaders in 1982, although it later clashed bitterly with the Palestine Liberation Organization. Under Berri, Amal became the mainstream Shia organization, but has lost considerable support to the more militant, and better-financed, Hezbollah.

**BERRÍOS MARTÍNEZ, Rubén.** *USA (Puerto Rico).* Puerto Rico Independence Party (PIP) president. One of Puerto Rico's most dynamic politicians, he is president of the PIP, the main proponent of a vote for full independence in the referendum on Puerto Rico's future status scheduled for September 1991. Berríos ran as his party's candidate for governor in 1972, but finished a distant third. He has since gradually made an impression on the electorate, improving his share of the vote by the time of the 1980 gubernatorials, and winning election four years later as his party's first member of the Puerto Rico Senate.

**BESSMERTNYKH, Aleksandr.** *USSR.* Ambassador to the USA. Born in 1933 and a graduate of the Moscow State Institute of International Relations, he joined the diplomatic service in 1957. He served in the Washington embassy (1970–83), headed the foreign ministry US department (1983–86), and was then appointed successively deputy and first deputy foreign minister. He has participated in nearly all Soviet–US summit and foreign ministerial meetings since 1983. Appointed ambassador to Washington in May 1990, he is considered a more incisive analyst of US politics than his predecessor, Yury Dubinin.

**BETETA, Mario Ramón.** *Mexico.* Governor of Mexico state. Born in 1925, Beteta studied law at the National Autonomous University of Mexico, where he later pursued an academic and teaching career. He then joined the Treasury, as under-secretary from 1970–75 and as minister in 1975–76. In 1982 he was appointed to the important position of head of Pemex, the state petroleum enterprise. In 1987 he was elected governor of Mexico state.

**BHATTARAI, Krishna Prasad.** *Nepal.* Prime minister and Nepali Congress Party president. Briefly speaker of parliament, in 1959–60, before the abolition of party politics under the *panchayat* system of royal despotism, he spent the following three decades in opposition activity, with years in prison, prolonged campaigning from exile in India, and brief periods of detention in Nepal whenever there was a civil disobedience campaign (May 1986, January 1988, February 1990). After the success of the "stir" agitation which forced **King Birendra** to introduce multi-party democracy he was appointed prime minister in April 1990. His administration is responsible for the running of a country in the economic doldrums – an exacting task for the elderly sage of Nepali politics.

**BHUMIBOL ADULYADEJ (RAMA IX).** *Thailand.* King. Born in 1927, Bhumibol was formally crowned as the ninth Chakri king in 1950 after his elder brother, Ananda Mahidol, had died four years earlier. During his long reign King Bhumibol has served as a powerful force for national unity; his authority is such that no government can survive without his support.

**BHUTTO, Begum Nusrat.** *Pakistan.* Former Pakistan People's Party (PPP) leader. Born in 1934, widow of Zulfiqar Ali Bhutto and mother of **Benazir Bhutto**, she chaired the PPP after her husband was hanged in 1979, but had passed the reins almost entirely to her daughter before the end of the Zia regime, having been released to go abroad for medical treatment. She had a seat in Benazir's cabinet in 1988–90, but went back to London soon after she was ousted, and was still abroad at the time of the October 1990 elections.

**BHUTTO, Benazir.** *Pakistan.* Former prime minister and Pakistan People's Party (PPP) leader. Born in 1953 to a Sindhi landowning family, she is the daughter of PPP leader and prime minister Zulfiqar Ali Bhutto, who was overthrown in 1977 by General Zia ul-Haq and hanged in February 1979. Educated at Harvard and Oxford universities and seemingly marked out for glittering prizes, she enjoyed prominence as president of the Oxford Union, but returned to Pakistan to face prolonged periods of house arrest after her father's fall. Released to go to London in 1985 and join her mother **Begum Nusrat Bhutto**, with whom she shared the PPP leadership, she returned to Pakistan the following year, assuming a high profile in the Movement for the Restoration of Democracy, a

broad alliance where some resented her presumption of leadership. Her opponents in the party criticized her for taking part in local elections in November 1987, in which PPP candidates made a poor showing; they also claimed she was abandoning the party's socialist principles. Nevertheless, she had her hour of triumph in the post-Zia elections of 1988, leading the PPP back to power, and taking office that December as the Islamic world's first woman prime minister. If campaigning suited her talent for wooing crowds, she proved a poor administrator. In seeking to reach beyond the army and the narrow Punjabi establishment, she fuelled the hostility of the army hierarchy. Her vulnerability was compounded by accusations of haughtiness, poor judgement in choosing advisers, and vindictiveness towards opponents; and by her paradoxical role as both premier and newly-wed obedient Muslim wife and mother. The charge of corruption, aimed particularly at her businessman husband Asif Ali Zardari, enabled her enemies to engineer her downfall in August 1990 and her dismissal by President **Ghulam Ishaq Khan**. Criminal charges were brought against her husband and associates, and she herself faced the prospect of prison after the hurriedly called October 1990 elections, which confirmed her loss of popularity and returned instead a government more acceptable to the military establishment.

**BICHAI RATTAKUL.** *Thailand.* Democrat Party leader. Born in 1926, Bichai resigned as deputy prime minister in late 1989 after six years in the post. He remained leader of the troubled Democrat Party, which was the third largest component of the six-party ruling coalition until its departure from government after the controversial December 1990 reshuffle.

**BICKERSTAFFE, Rodney.** *UK.* Trade unionist. Born in 1945, he joined the National Union of Public Employees (NUPE), one of the country's largest unions, after completing a sociology degree in 1966. He became a national officer in 1977 and general secretary in 1982. His uncompromising position on the left of the union movement made him one of the harshest critics of the government of **Margaret Thatcher** in the early 1980s. But he has been eclipsed in recent years by younger colleagues espousing a less dogmatic approach.

**BID, Ali Salim al-.** *Yemen.* Vice-president. After rising to the post of deputy prime minister in pre-unity South Yemen, he was dismissed in 1981 for "breaking the family law". Re-entering the cabinet in 1985, he played a key role in the overthrow of President Ali Nasser Mohammed the following year. Taking over as secretary-general of the ruling Yemen Socialist Party, he worked hard to unite moderates and hardliners during the period leading up to unity with North Yemen, and was rewarded with the post of vice-president of the new state on its formation in May 1990.

**BIDEN, Joseph (Joe)**. *USA*. Democratic senator from Delaware. Born in 1942, he practised law before his election to the Senate in 1972. A liberal, he combines brashness with legislative skills. He opposed the Central American policy of **Ronald Reagan**'s administration and strongly supports arms reduction. Judiciary committee chairman since 1987, he has taken special interest in criminal law reform and anti-drug policy. Revelations of plagiaristic speeches (including homilies borrowed from UK Labour Party leader **Neil Kinnock**) destroyed his 1988 presidential nomination bid but, health permitting (he had major brain surgery in 1988), he may try again for national office.

**BIEBER, Owen**. *USA*. President of the United Auto Workers (UAW). Born in Michigan in 1929, he has been involved in the Democratic Party and the UAW for most of his adult life. First elected as the union's president in 1983, he was re-elected for a third term in 1989, soundly defeating a rival faction known as "New Directions". They opposed Bieber's strategy of co-operation with management, which he has adopted in the face of job losses and foreign competition, adapting to changes in areas such as health care and profit sharing. One of his main planks is opposition to the steady influx of Japanese automobiles.

**BIEDENKOPF, Kurt**. *Germany*. Saxony premier. A Christian Democratic Union (CDU) leader of the 1970s in West Germany, his political career was unexpectedly revived when he was chosen at the age of 60 to lead the CDU in the Saxony elections after unification in October 1990. An expert in commercial law, he had seen his role in the party in the 1970s as the promotion of analysis and ideas; he held the key post of party general secretary (1973–77), but was never a skilled tactician in party manoeuvrings, and was ousted after coming into conflict with his arch-rival **Helmut Kohl**.

**BIELECKI, Jan Krzysztof**. *Poland*. Prime minister-designate. Born in 1951, he trained and worked as an economist. A strong supporter of the government's economic reform programme,

he was nominated for the premiership by **Lech Wałęsa** following the latter's election victory in December 1990.

**BIFFEN, John**. *UK*. Conservative politician. Born in 1930, he studied at Cambridge University and then worked for Tube Investments from 1953–60, followed by a brief period with The Economist Intelligence Unit. Elected to parliament in 1961 (for Oswestry, later Shropshire North), he was appointed secretary for trade in 1981 and leader of the House of Commons in 1982. Intelligent and urbane, he was a popular and successful leader of the house for five years. But he grew steadily more critical of Thatcherism and emerged as a leading campaigner for a "period of consolidation" in the late 1980s. He left the government in 1987 and has been one of its shrewdest backbench critics in recent years.

**BILDT, Carl**. *Sweden*. Leader of the Moderate Unity Party. Born in 1949, he became a political secretary at the headquarters of the conservative Moderate Unity Party immediately after completing his studies. Elected to the Riksdag (parliament) in 1979, he took over as party leader from the abrasive Ulf Adelsohn in 1986, after the party's setback in the previous year's election. He has been more subtle than his predecessor in challenging Sweden's left-dominated consensus.

**BIRD, Lester**. *Antigua and Barbuda*. Deputy prime minister. Born in 1940, the son of the prime minister, **Vere Bird**, he rose to become deputy prime minister and is favourite to succeed his father, especially since his elder brother, Vere Jr, was barred from holding public office in November 1990.

**BIRD, Vere C**. *Antigua and Barbuda*. Prime minister. Regarded as "father of the nation", he has dominated politics in Antigua, serving successively as chief minister, premier and (after independence) prime minister, with only five years, 1967–71, spent in opposition. Born in 1910, he trained with the Salvation Army before becoming involved in trade unionism. A conservative by nature, in recent years he has been accused of being too indulgent towards his sons; the eldest, Vere Bird Jr, was barred from holding public office in November 1990 by a commission of inquiry investigating the country's involvement in the shipping of Israeli arms to Colombian drug barons.

**BIRENDRA BIR BIKRAM SHAH DEV**. *Nepal*. King. Head of state since the death in 1972 of his father Mahendra, he was crowned in

1975. Born in 1945 and educated at Eton College in the UK and at Tokyo and Harvard universities, he came to power as an absolute ruler, with no political activity allowed outside the non-party advisory *panchayat* system devised by his father. A referendum in 1980 narrowly approved the continuation of this state of affairs, but an upsurge of opposition activity in 1990 compelled him to accept real reforms. Despite signs that he wanted to drag his feet over concessions granted, the framing of a new dispensation – formalized in the new constitution proclaimed in November 1990 – relegated him to the role of constitutional monarch in a multi-party democracy. He is still revered in the remoter areas as a god-like figure and must be accounted a potent political force.

**BÎRLADEANU, Alexandru.** *Romania*. President of the Senate and former first deputy prime minister. Born in Tighina county in 1911, he was educated at the University of Iaşi where he later taught law. Bîrladeanu moved to Bucharest in 1944 and held the chair of political economy at the Academy of Economic Studies. In 1955 he was elected a full member of the Romanian Academy, of which he is now the vice-president. A life-long member of the Romanian Communist Party, he was elected a senator for the National Salvation Front in the May 1990 elections.

**BIWOTT, Nicholas K.** *Kenya*. Energy minister. A former secretary to President **Daniel arap Moi**, he was brought into the cabinet as a minister of state in 1979 and appointed to the new portfolio of regional development, science and technology in 1982. The following year he combined responsibility for energy with that for regional development, but has held the energy portfolio alone since 1988. One of the most infuential members of the cabinet, he is a key ally of the president and, like him, a member of the small Kalenjin ethnic group.

**BIYA, Paul.** *Cameroon*. President. A loyal but low-profile prime minister to Cameroon's first president, Ahmadou Ahidjo, Biya was a surprise choice as successor when Ahidjo stepped down in 1982. Born in 1933, Biya studied law and politics in Paris, joining the Cameroon civil service in 1962. After a period at the education ministry he held a series of posts at the presidency after 1968, until appointed prime minister in 1975, a position in which he exercised little influence. A Catholic from Sangmelima in the south, Biya's accession to the presidency challenged the previous hegemony of

Muslim northerners, some of whom were involved in attempts to overthrow him in 1983 and 1984. Although Biya initially promised increased democracy – within the framework of a one-party state – progress has been scant and slow. Faced with the agitation for multi-party democracy sweeping francophone Africa in 1990, he agreed to some political liberalization. Biya, who has a reputation for indecisiveness, remains prey to competing factions, notably in the army. The death of Ahidjo in exile in 1989, however, removed from the scene a credible rival who had shown signs of revived interest in Cameroonian politics.

**BJERREGAARD, Ritt.** *Denmark*. Social Democratic politician. Born in 1941, she worked as a teacher and was active in the teachers' union before election to the Folketing (parliament) in 1971. Gaining ministerial experience at education and at social affairs, she became deputy leader of the Social Democratic parliamentary group in 1982, and was fancied to succeed Anker Jørgensen as party leader in 1987, but lost out to **Svend Auken**.

**BLACKMUN, Harry A.** *USA*. Supreme Court associate justice. Born in Illinois in 1908, he became a federal appeals court judge in 1959, a position he held until 1970 when he was appointed to the Supreme Court. His appointment was in accordance with Richard Nixon's stated aim of creating a conservative majority on the nine-member court. He has subsequently gained a reputation as something of a liberal.

**BLACKSTONE, Baroness (Tessa Blackstone).** *UK*. Academic and socialist activist. Born in 1942, she studied sociology, then lectured in social and educational administration, and worked for the Inner London Education Authority from 1983–87. In the 1970s and 1980s she made influential contributions to left-wing thinking on educational and social issues in particular. A member of Lord Rothschild's Central Policy Review Staff in the 1970s, she was one of the authors of a highly critical report on the diplomatic service. She was appointed master of Birkbeck College in London in 1987 and also became head of a new left-wing think-tank, the Institute for Public Policy Research, in 1988. She was created a life peer in 1987 and sits as a Labour member of the House of Lords.

**BLAIR, Tony.** *UK*. Labour politician. Born in 1953, he studied law and practised from 1976. Elected to parliament in 1983, he soon earned his spurs as a junior spokesman on trade and industry, attacking the government on complicated financial matters with skill and panache. His standing among fellow MPs thus enhanced, he was elected to the shadow cabinet in 1988, and entrusted with the shadow energy and then employment portfolios – both high-profile jobs.

**BLANCHARD, James**. *USA*. Former Democratic governor of Michigan. Born in 1942, he was a lawyer before his election to the House of Representatives in 1974. As a congressman he helped promote the Chrysler Corporation bail-out of 1980, the foundation for his election as governor in 1982. He presided over the "Michigan economic miracle" of the 1980s, after the depressed 1970s, but lost the governorship to **John Engler** in the 1990 gubernatorial election.

**BLEWETT, Neal**. *Australia*. Trade negotiations minister. Born in Sydney in 1933, he was educated at the University of Tasmania before undertaking postgraduate research at Oxford University where he was a Rhodes Scholar. He then pursued an academic career, becoming professor of political theory and institutions at Flinders University in 1974. In 1977 he was elected to the House of Representatives as Australian Labor Party (ALP) member for the South Australian seat of Bonython and became health minister in **Bob Hawke**'s government in 1983. He was given additional responsibility for community services and continued as minister until the dissolution of 1990. In the new administration he moved to trade negotiations. Although a member of the centre–left faction of the ALP, Blewett has a reputation for independence in the internal politics of the Labor parliamentary caucus.

**BLIN, Maurice**. *France*. Centrist senator. Born in 1922 and a philosophy graduate, he was a teacher and researcher before first winning elective office as a centrist politician. From 1958–62 he sat as a deputy for the Catholic centre-left Popular Republican Movement (MRP), and has been a senator since 1971, specializing in budgetary and financial matters. In 1986, he was appointed to the watchdog committee for the state-owned bank, the Caisse des Dépôts et Consignations.

**BLIX, Hans**. *Sweden*. Director-general of International Atomic Energy Agency (IAEA). Born in 1928, he studied law and then lectured in international law, also acting as an adviser to the Swedish foreign ministry from 1963–76. He

then held several junior ministerial posts, and was briefly foreign minister in a centre-right government in 1978. He was appointed head of the IAEA in 1981; the previous year Sweden had become the first country to vote to phase out nuclear energy.

**BLONDEL, Marc**. *France*. Trade union leader. Born in 1938, he joined the Force Ouvrière (CGT-FO) trade union in 1958, thereafter winning various posts representing white-collar workers, mainly in the Paris region. In 1989, he succeeded **André Bergeron** as secretary-general of the FO, also becoming vice-president of the European Trade Union Confederation and the International Confederation of Free Trade Unions.

**BLÜM, Norbert**. *Germany*. Labour and social policy minister and Christian Democratic Union (CDU) deputy chairman. One of the few postwar German politicians who started his career as a factory worker, he was born in 1935 and gained his educational qualifications at evening school while working as a toolmaker by day. He later studied at Cologne and Bonn, gaining his doctorate in 1967. A Catholic, he made his way in the CDU through its trade union wing, and held office in the government of West Berlin before being appointed labour and social policy minister, a post he has held since 1982.

**BLUNKETT, David**. *UK*. Labour politician. Born in 1947 and blind from birth, he was educated at various tertiary colleges and Sheffield University, and taught industrial relations from 1974–87. Elected to Sheffield council in 1969, he was its leader from 1980–87, gaining a nationwide reputation as an innovative, pragmatic and effective "municipal socialist". He was elected to parliament in 1987. Widely respected in the House of Commons, he has become one of Labour's leading thinkers on local government issues and sits on the national executive committee.

**BOAHEN, Adu**. *Ghana*. Movement for Freedom and Justice (MFJ) chairman. A respected historian, he was named interim chairman of the MFJ, an umbrella grouping set up to campaign for multi-party democracy, on its formation in August 1990. The MFJ, which questions the legitimacy of the government's experiments in democracy at local level, has representatives from a wide political spectrum, including disillusioned former members of the **Jerry Rawlings** government.

**BOATENG, Paul**. *UK*. Labour politician. Born in 1951, he trained as a solicitor and practised until 1987. Elected to parliament in that year as one of four new black Labour members, he refused to join the others in the informal black caucus, arguing that he preferred to be considered "an MP who is black" rather than a "black MP".

**BOD, Péter Ákos.** *Hungary.* Economist, and trade and industry minister. Born in 1951, he was a department head in the state planning office and gained international experience with UN missions in Africa and Vietnam, and as visiting lecturer at several US universities. He rose to political prominence as the lone economics expert in the Hungarian Democratic Forum (MDF), entering the National Assembly after the spring 1990 elections. Taking on his ministerial portfolio in May 1990, he began to seek ways of engineering gradual transformation to a market economy, with the emphasis on attracting foreign capital and promoting small-business development. The October 1990 strike by taxi and lorry drivers over fuel price increases left his popularity badly shaken.

**BOESAK, Reverend Allan.** *South Africa.* Anti-apartheid churchman. Born in 1946, he trained as a minister of the (coloured) Dutch Reformed Mission Church. His anti-apartheid stance gained political weight from his election as president of the World Alliance of Reformed Churches in 1982. In the same year he helped to set up the United Democratic Front (UDF), embodying its commitment to non-violent action; from 1984–87 he was also president of the South African Council of Churches. Boesak's articulate and forthright style earned him an increasingly high international profile during the mid-1980s. He took part in various symbolic acts of defiance against apartheid, such as the February 1989 hunger strike and, with fellow churchman Archbishop **Desmond Tutu**, the "march for peace" protest in Cape Town on the day before **F. W. de Klerk**'s election to the state presidency in September 1989. De Klerk's reforms, however, allowed wider political action, and churchmen became less prominent in public protest. The forthright Boesak's appeal to coloured radicals was overtaken by that of young African National Congress figures like Cheryl Carolus. In July 1990 he resigned his ministry, and the post he had held as church moderator, after admitting an extra-marital affair.

**BOGIĆEVIĆ, Bogić.** *Yugoslavia.* Bosnia and Hercegovina's member of the collective state presidency. An ethnic Serb, he was born in 1953. In January 1989 he was elected to the central

committee of the Bosnia and Hercegovina communist party, and in June of the same year he was endorsed by popular referendum as the youngest member of the collective state presidency, for a five-year term. He favours pluralism, but as part of a co-operative system of "socialist self-management".

**BOHLEY, Bärbel.** *Germany.* Politician and former East German dissident. Born in 1945, a painter from Berlin and co-founder with biologist Jens Reich of East Germany's dissident New Forum movement, she is still known to some as "mother of the revolution", and was once again active in trying to mediate in the city authorities' bitter confrontation with squatters in the autumn of 1990. In the heady days of 1989 she had demonstrated with the people but became identified with out-of-touch intellectuals. The group around her, left stranded by the tide of opinion even in New Forum itself, had wanted to change East Germany, while fearing that unification would make it just an "appendage" of the capitalist and materialist west. She became a member of the all-Berlin city parliament in December 1990, elected on the Alliance '90 list.

**BOLDIN, Valery.** *USSR.* Senior Communist Party administrator, former Presidential Council member. A Russian, born in 1935, and formerly an economic journalist with *Pravda*, Boldin was named as an assistant to **Mikhail Gorbachev** in 1985, headed the Communist Party of the Soviet Union central committee's general department from 1987–90, and was appointed to the short-lived Presidential Council on its formation in March 1990.

**BOLGER, James.** *New Zealand.* Prime minister and National Party leader. Born in 1935, he became a successful sheep and cattle farmer, and was elected as an MP in 1972, later holding a series of posts in the cabinet of Robert Muldoon from 1977–84. As leader of the opposition from March 1986, he was an effective political manager with a homespun style, making a virtue of being a down-to-earth farmer rather than a university-educated intellectual. Despite his lack of charisma and his limitations in debate, he led the party to a convincing electoral victory in October 1990 against the demoralized Labour Party, capitalizing on his comforting image. He held out the promise of a healing process, new investment to reduce unemployment, and the promotion of exports.

**BOLKESTEIN, Frits.** *Netherlands.* Right-wing politician. Born in 1933, he worked for the Shell group before being elected to the Staten Generaal (parliament) for the People's Party for Freedom and Democracy (VVD) in 1977. He served as defence minister from 1988 until the VVD left the coalition government a year later. In 1990 he took over from Joris Voorhoeve as parliamentary leader of the VVD.

**BOLKIAH, Sultan Sir Hassanal.** *Brunei.* Sultan. Born in 1946. Income from Brunei's large oil and gas reserves have made the Sultan one of the world's richest men. He was educated in Malaysia and at the Royal Military Academy, Sandhurst, UK. His father, Sir Omar Ali Saifuddin III, appointed him as crown prince and heir apparent in 1961. Sir Omar abdicated in 1967 and the following year Sir Hassanal officially replaced him as Sultan. When Brunei became fully independent in 1984, Sir Hassanal assumed the office of prime minister at the head of a new cabinet liberally sprinkled with his closest relatives.

**BONDEVIK, Kjell Magne.** *Norway.* Leader of the Christian People's Party (KrF) and former foreign affairs minister. Born in 1947, he studied theology and was ordained a Lutheran pastor in 1977. Elected a member of the Storting (parliament) for the KrF in 1973, he became party leader in 1983. Known for his strong anti-abortionist views, he tried to insist on a change in the liberal abortion law, as the price for joining a centre–right coalition, but was overruled by the party. He held the education and religious affairs portfolio in 1983–86, and was foreign affairs minister in the centre–right coalition that held power from 1989–90.

**BONGO, (Albert-Bernard) Omar.** *Gabon.* President. Born in 1935, he served in the air force for two years before joining the civil service in 1960, becoming director of President Léon M'ba's private office two years later. During the 1960s he held the information, defence and tourism portfolios before being appointed vice-president in March 1967, succeeding to the presidency on M'ba's death in November. Bongo consolidated his power by instituting a one-party state and has been re-elected three times as sole candidate, most recently for seven years in 1986. A skilled politician, he has made careful use of the country's oil wealth to dispense patronage to potential opponents and was quick to recognize that the unrest of early 1990 demanded political liberalization. A member of the small Batéké ethnic group, he has devoted special attention to the development of his home region, in the south-east, and has based his power on a coalition of smaller ethnic groups. Bongo has maintained close links with the former colonial power, France, and has also cultivated relations with his conservative Arab partners in Opec, converting to Islam and adopting the name Omar in 1973.

**BONIOR, David.** *USA.* Democratic congressman from Michigan. Born in 1945, he served in Vietnam and was a probation officer before his election to the House of Representatives in 1976. He leapt to prominence in 1987 when speaker Jim Wright, seeking to improve relations with liberal Democrats, selected him as chief deputy whip, an office he retains despite Wright's downfall in 1989.

**BONNER, Yelena.** *USSR.* Human rights activist. Born in 1924, Bonner is the widow of Andrei Sakharov. In 1986 she was released with her husband from internal exile in Gorky where they had been sent – he sentenced in 1980, she formally exiled in 1984 – for allegedly slandering the state. Bonner continues to monitor and report on the Soviet human rights record.

**BOODHOO, Harish.** *Mauritius.* Mauritius Socialist Party (PSM) leader. Leader of a dissident group in the Mauritius Labour Party in the 1970s, he formed the Mauritius Socialist Party (PSM) in 1980. He was appointed information minister in the coalition government that came to power in 1982, dissolving his party to join the prime minister, **Aneerood Jugnauth**'s Mauritius Socialist Movement and masterminding the election campaign that secured the position of the new coalition government the following year. He resigned as government chief whip in 1986 after criticizing its handling of a drug-trafficking scandal, and revived the PSM two years later. Allegations in his party newspaper that government members were involved in selling Mauritian passports abroad brought him into renewed conflict with the government in early 1989.

**BOREN, David.** *USA.* Democratic senator from Oklahoma. Born in 1941, he practised law after education at Yale, Oxford (as a Rhodes scholar) and Oklahoma universities. Elected in 1978, he gained prominence as chairman of the select committee on intelligence during the "Irangate" controversy in 1987. Constituency interests make him a strong ally of the oil and natural gas industries. He is also a keen fighter for campaign-finance reform, refusing money from political action committees.

**BORGE MARTÍNEZ, Tomás.** *Nicaragua.* Sandinista politician. Born in 1930, he is the sole survivor of the group that founded the Sandinista National Liberation Front (FSLN) in 1961. An implacable Marxist ideologue, he fought against the regime of Anastasio Somoza and was captured, imprisoned and tortured in 1976–78. He was made interior minister in the Sandinista administration in 1979 and effective commander of the internal security apparatus. Since the Sandinistas' election defeat in February 1990 he has become a focus for the front's more radical members.

**BORJA CEVALLOS, Rodrigo.** *Ecuador.* President. Born in 1935, Borja studied political science and law at the Central University of Ecuador, where he later also taught as a professor. First elected as a deputy in 1962, he founded the Democratic Left (ID) in 1970. He entered the presidential contests in 1978 and 1984, winning the first round of voting in 1984, but losing to **Léon Febres Cordero** in the second. Elected president in 1988, he promised to reverse the pro-USA, free-market policies of his predecessor and reach a consensus on tackling the country's economic problems, but elections in June 1990 left Congress dominated by his opponents.

**BOROSS, Péter.** *Hungary.* Interior minister. Born in 1928, he was brought into **József Antall**'s 1990 government as a non-party technocrat, serving initially as minister without portfolio before his promotion in the December reshuffle to interior minister.

**BOSCH GAVIÑO, Juan.** *Dominican Republic.* Opposition party leader. Born in 1909, Bosch combined a career as a notable writer with opposition in exile to the Trujillo dictatorship. As leader of the Dominican Revolutionary Party (PRD) he was elected president in 1962 but was overthrown by a military coup in September 1963, only seven months after he took office. An attempt by his supporters in the military to restore him in 1965 led to the US invasion. He quarrelled with the PRD in 1974 and formed his own left-wing party, the Dominican Liberation Party (PLD), remaining a trenchant critic of both other major parties. In 1990 he just failed to win the presidency for a second time.

**BOSKIN, Michael.** *USA.* Economic adviser. A distinguished economist, born in New York in 1945 and educated at the University of California, he held numerous academic posts before his appointment to chair **George Bush**'s Council of Economic Advisers in 1989. He has

counselled against accepting too drastic a programme of cuts in spending to reduce the budget deficit, fearing the recessionary impact on the economy. He also warned bluntly in April 1990 that measures to stop global warming could cost "trillions". He earned opprobrium from the environmental lobby when he went on – before co-chairing the Washington global warming conference – to suggest that a temperature increase could benefit US agriculture and that technology such as air conditioning could help combat the adverse effects.

**BOSSANO, Joe.** *UK (Gibraltar).* Chief minister. Born in 1939, he had worked in a factory, on a ship, as a health inspector and in the building trade, and had studied economics by the time he was elected leader of the Gibraltar branch of the Transport and General Workers' Union (TGWU), the rock's only industrial union, in 1974. As such, he succeeded in securing pay parity with British workers for shipyard employees. He became leader of the Gibraltar Socialist Labour Party (GSLP) in 1984. His popularity enhanced by an uncompromisingly nationalist stance on the issue of Spanish claims to sovereignty over Gibraltar, he led the party to a record election victory in 1988, ending four decades of almost uninterrupted right-wing rule.

**BOSSI, Umberto.** *Italy.* Lombard League secretary. Born in 1941 in the province of Varese, he co-founded the Lombard League (Lega Lombarda) in 1979, taking on the post of party secretary. He set up the newspaper *Lombardia Autonomista* three years later, to promote the populist, anti-centralist and anti-immigrant programme (aimed at both southern Italians and foreigners) with which the league made a breakthrough in the May 1990 regional elections. He has set up a "Lega Nord" out of the various northern political leagues, but there is likely to be some opposition to any attempt by him to dominate the proposed grouping. Bossi, an effective, if demagogic, speaker, was elected to the Senate in 1987.

**BOTCHWEY, Kwesi.** *Ghana.* Finance and economic planning minister. A former law lecturer at the University of Legon, he has been the architect of Ghana's economic reform programme since his appointment as finance and economic planning minister by **Jerry Rawlings** in May 1982. An efficient technocrat, he has promoted market-oriented reforms and a drive for foreign investment, sometimes in the face of opposition from more socialist-minded members of the government.

**BOTERO RESTREPO, Oscar.** *Colombia.* Defence minister. Born in 1933, he followed a military career. During Belisario Betancur's presidency (1982–86) he was head of the palace military barracks. He was then appointed military attaché to Spain before returning to become head of the army general staff and army inspector-general, with the rank of major-general. He was made defence minister in 1989 and assumed an important role in the struggle against the drug barons.

**BOTHA, Roelof Frederik "Pik".** *South Africa.* Foreign minister. Born in 1932, he was a career diplomat for over 25 years before entering parliament as a National Party MP in 1970. A diplomat again from 1974 to 1977, as ambassador to the UN and the USA, he then re-entered parliamentary politics and immediately became foreign minister, a job he has held ever since (with additional responsibility for information from 1980–86). Forceful and dynamic, a stylish if sometimes brusque performer who comes over well on television, he has won sometimes grudging international acknowledgement of his role as one of the architects of reform. His string of successes in white South Africa's strategic retreat have not endeared him to his party, however; many mark him down as a lover of the high life. He finished last of four in the February 1989 contest to succeed P.W. Botha as party leader.

**BOTTOMLEY, Virginia.** *UK.* An MP since 1984, and minister for health since 1989. Born in 1948, Bottomley was a psychiatric social worker and researcher into child poverty before entering politics. She is married to MP Peter Bottomley, a former junior minister at transport and at the Northern Ireland Office.

**BOUABID, Abderrahmane.** *Morocco.* Opposition politician. Born in 1920 and trained as a lawyer in France, he was an early member of the Independence Party (Istiqlal). After independence in 1956 he served as finance minister and deputy prime minister until he left Istiqlal in 1959 to join the National Union of Popular Forces (UNFP), which he led from 1962–73. He has remained a leading figure on the left wing of Moroccan politics as leader of the Socialist Union of Popular Forces (USFP), formed after the UNFP split in 1973.

**BOUABID, Maati.** *Morocco.* Leader of the Constitutional Union (CU). Born in 1927, he practised as a lawyer in Casablanca and Tangier

before joining the government as labour and social affairs minister in 1958. He was chairman of Casablanca city council from 1963–65, returning to national politics in 1977 as justice minister and prime minister from 1979–84. The UC, which he founded in 1983, is a member of the governing coalition and the largest party in parliament.

**BOUCETTA, Mohammed.** *Morocco.* Opposition leader. Born in Marrakech in 1925, he studied philosophy and law in Paris and practised law on his return, entering politics as a member of the Independence Party (Istiqlal), whose newspaper he edited. He became party leader in 1974 on the death of Allal el-Fassi. He served as minister of state for foreign affairs from 1977–84, but took his party into opposition after its poor showing in the 1984 elections.

**BOULARES, Habib.** *Tunisia.* Foreign minister. A former culture minister and ambassador to Egypt and a close aide to President **Zine el-Abidine Ben Ali**, he moved from the president's office to the foreign ministry in August 1990. The appointment reflected Ben Ali's concern to maintain close contacts with Arab states in the wake of the Iraqi invasion of Kuwait.

**BOURASSA, Robert.** *Canada.* Premier of Quebec. Born in Mercier in 1933, he was educated at Oxford and Harvard universities after receiving a law degree from the University of Montreal. He was elected to Quebec's national assembly in 1966 after a short career as a lawyer and professor. In 1970 Bourassa became Quebec's youngest-ever premier. He was re-elected in 1973, but defeated in 1976 at the height of the Quebec Party's (PQ's) popularity. Bourassa returned to Quebec politics in 1983 as leader of the Liberal Party of Canada (Quebec), and was re-elected premier in 1985. A cold, pragmatic politician, Bourassa has forged a close relationship with the prime minister, **Brian Mulroney**, who has made concessions to Quebec. Bourassa has written three books: *La Bai James*, *L'Énergie du Nord: La force du Québec* and *Le défi technologique.*

**BOUSSENA, Sadek.** *Algeria.* Industry and mines minister. Born in 1948, Boussena is one of the younger generation of Algerian technocrats. A former university teacher, he has spent much of his career since 1973 in the energy sector. In November 1988 he was appointed energy minister in the new government of **Kasdi Merbah**, becoming mines minister in the reshuffle of September 1989, and taking on the industry portfolio as well, in August 1990.

**BOUTERSE, Désiré (Desi).** *Suriname.* Army commander. An army sergeant, Bouterse participated in the overthrow of the civilian government in 1980, emerging as effective leader with the rank of lieutenant-colonel. The crushing of unrest in 1982 strengthened his position but also led to condemnation of the regime and the withholding of development aid by international donors. After a flirtation with left-wing groups, he initiated a return to civilian rule, but his military-backed political party was overwhelmingly defeated at the 1987 elections. He retained an influential position as military council chairman and army commander, but resigned the latter post in December 1990, after claiming that President Ramsewak Shankar had collaborated with the Dutch government to humiliate him by denying him access to the Netherlands while in transit through Amsterdam. His deep-seated resentment with the Shankar government's willingness to search for a peaceful solution to the revolt led by **Ronnie Brunswijk** had simmered for some time. Several days later, Shankar was toppled in a bloodless military coup widely seen as being carried out on Bouterse's instructions by the new commander-in-chief, Commander Iwan Grangoost. The new interim president, **Johan Kraag,** speedily re-appointed Bouterse as army commander.

**BOWSHER, Charles Arthur.** *USA.* Comptroller-general of the USA. Born in Indiana in 1931, he received his MBA from the University of Chicago, and went on to become a partner with Arthur Andersen & Co. He replaced Elmer B. Staats in 1981 as the head of the government's General Accounting Office and has been involved in the Herculean tasks of reducing the budget deficit and bailing out the savings and loan sector. Something of a gadfly at congressional hearings, he is given to highlighting serious management problems in nearly every government agency, and offering politically embarrassing estimates of the cost of rescuing the savings and loan industry.

**BOYER SALVADOR, Miguel.** *Spain.* Socialist politician. Born in 1939 in France, he has been active within the Spanish Socialist Workers' Party (PSOE) since 1960, and was once imprisoned for political activity. As economy and finance minister from 1982–85, he was the architect of the tough monetarist policies that prepared Spain for EC membership. He left the cabinet to become chairman of the state-controlled Banco Exterior and then joined the private sector as chief executive of the Grucycsa holding company in 1988.

**BOZER, Ali.** *Turkey.* Former foreign minister. Born in 1925, he pursued a legal career which included a spell at the European Court of Human Rights in 1974–76, before being appointed customs and monopolies minister by the military junta in 1981. The civilian government of **Turgut Özal** put him in charge of relations with the EC in 1986, and made him a deputy prime minister. Bozer is now regarded as a liberal despite his past association with a nationalist group; his appointment in March 1990 to replace **Mesut Yılmaz** as foreign minister was an attempt to counter a growing trend towards conservatism and Islamic influence in government circles. He resigned suddenly in October – apparently in protest at President Özal's failure to consult him over official policy on the Gulf crisis. He was replaced by **Ahmet Kurtcebe Alptemoçin.**

**BRADLEY, Bill.** *USA.* Democratic senator from New Jersey. Born in 1943, he was educated at Princeton and at Oxford universities (where he was a Rhodes scholar), and was a star basketball player for the New York Knicks. Elected in 1978, he specialized in financial issues. Having opposed **Ronald Reagan**'s 1981 tax cut as a giveaway to the wealthy, he was instrumental in enacting the 1986 tax bill which had "fair tax" provisions. Since 1987, his main interest has been third world debt. As chairman of the international debt subcommittee he favours interest rate reductions and selective forgiveness for debtor nations. Bradley also has a strongly liberal record on aid to the needy at home. A possible contender for the 1992 presidential nomination, he may prove too interested in policy detail (and too dull a speaker) to be an effective campaigner in the popularity contests that primaries have become. His stand on taxes has also antagonized powerful lobbies.

**BRADLEY, Tom.** *USA.* Mayor of Los Angeles. Born in 1917, he was a police officer, lawyer and city councillor before becoming the first black mayor of a big city in 1973. His five-term tenure in office was initially built on the traditional Democratic constituency's votes, but his pro-business policies and strong law-and-order stance gained broad support. He was twice Democratic candidate for the governorship of California, losing narrowly in 1982 and heavily in 1986.

**BRADY, Nicholas.** *USA.* Secretary of the Treasury. Born in 1930, he grew up on his family's 4,000-acre estate in New Jersey, and was educated at Yale and Harvard universities. From 1954–88 he worked for Dillon, Read & Co, a Wall Street investment company, eventually becoming co-chairman. He became a close friend of **George Bush** after they met at a tennis match in 1975, and in 1979 he assisted Bush's campaign for the Republican presidential nomination. He served for a brief spell in the US Senate in 1982 after being appointed by Governor **Tom Kean** – a friend of both Brady and Bush – to fill a vacated seat. In 1988 Brady assembled and organized the team for Bush's presidential campaign, and when **James Baker** resigned from the cabinet to chair the campaign in August 1988, Brady replaced him as secretary of the Treasury. He retained the post after Bush's election as president, but his performance has been compared unfavourably with Baker's. Whereas Baker was orderly, precise and instinctively political, Brady was accused by some of projecting an over-casual image, an abhorrence of detail and a political awkwardness that frequently made for difficult relations with the press.

**BRAINE, Sir Bernard**. *UK*. MP since 1950 and "Father" (doyen) of the House since 1987. The staunchly Catholic Braine, born in the London suburb of Ealing in 1914, holds strong opinions on drug and alcohol abuse and is a leading anti-abortionist. He also has a strong interest in human rights issues and third-world development. He served as a junior minister in the 1960s.

**BRAITHWAITE, Nicholas**. *Grenada*. Prime minister. Born in 1929, he was an educationalist and former head of the Commonwealth's youth programme in the Caribbean. He was chairman of the non-partisan interim administration in 1983–84. In 1988 he joined the National Democratic Congress and was elected unopposed to the leadership.

**BRANDSTAD, Terry**. *USA*. Republican governor of Iowa. Born in 1946, he was a lawyer, state legislator and lieutenant governor before being elected the conservative governor of a relatively liberal state in 1982. Revitalizing the ailing farm economy has been his priority.

**BRANDT, Willy**. *Germany*. Socialist politician and "elder statesman" figure who as foreign minister (1966–69) and chancellor (1969–74) played a major role in overcoming the division of Europe and ending the cold war. The son of an unmarried shop assistant, he was born Herbert Karl Frahm in Lübeck in 1913. As a youthful

Social Democrat he fled Germany for Norway when Hitler gained power in 1933. He worked as a journalist in Scandinavia, using the pseudonym Willy Brandt, and devoted himself to the anti-Nazi cause, adopting Norwegian citizenship. After his return to Germany in 1945, and the return of his German citizenship in 1948, he rose quickly in the Social Democratic Party (SPD) as a modernizer and anti-communist. He was one of the authors of the non-Marxist Bad Godesberg Programme adopted by the SPD in 1959. Between 1957 and 1966 he was governing mayor of West Berlin and gained stature in 1961, to the detriment of Chancellor Konrad Adenauer, by becoming identified as a symbol of the city's refusal to be cowed by Soviet threats. He stood unsuccessfully for the federal chancellorship in 1961 and 1965, and then took a risk by taking the SPD, whose chairman he became in 1964, into the "grand coalition" in 1966. This move succeeded in ending the party's political isolation, and allowed him, as foreign minister, to begin the "Ostpolitik" with which he was to be identified in his subsequent period as chancellor (1969–74). Forced to resign the chancellorship in 1974 when an East German spy was discovered among his staff, he remained SPD chairman until 1987, working for East–West and North–South dialogue (on which he chaired the influential Brandt Commission). He was a member of the European Parliament from 1979–83 and chairman of the Socialist International from 1976 onwards. In 1990, he pushed the SPD to accept German unity despite the misgivings of their candidate for chancellor, **Oskar Lafontaine**. Brandt has been married three times and has four children; his present wife, Brigitte Seebacher-Brandt, is well known as an historian of the SPD.

**BRANG SENG**. *Myanmar (Burma)*. Kachin leader. Brang Seng, the former headmaster of a Methodist school, presides over the Kachin Independence Organization, arguably the most effective and best organized of Burma's non-communist insurgent forces. Under his leadership, it has remained a potent force despite the efforts of Burma's ruling military.

**BRAUN, Théo**. *France*. Former government minister. Born in 1920 and a building technician by training, he emerged as a post-war leader of Christian trade unionism, and as a social security expert. From 1951–62 he sat on the national Economic and Social Council, and subsequently presided over various co-operative and mutual credit and banking organizations, at national and European level. Having made a name for himself as a lobbyist for the elderly, he was a popular choice as minister-delegate for the elderly in 1988–90, but in the October 1990 reshuffle he left the government, moving to local and regional political activities.

**BRAZAUSKAS, Algirdas.** *USSR.* Leader of the Lithuanian Democratic Labour Party and a deputy premier in the separatist Lithuanian government. Born in 1932, he held senior republican government posts from the mid-1960s. He was named party first secretary in October 1988, and in December 1989, in an effort to keep abreast of the upsurge in Lithuanian nationalism, he led the party in declaring independence from the Communist Party of the Soviet Union. This earned him huge personal popularity. He served briefly as Lithuania's president at the beginning of 1990, but after the February election victory of the nationalist Popular Front (Sajudis), with which he sympathizes, he was defeated for the presidency by **Vytautas Landsbergis**. He refused the vice-presidency, but accepted a role in the government of **Kazimiera Prunskiene**. In December 1990 the Lithuanian Communist Party reorganized itself as the Lithuanian Democratic Labour Party and elected him as chairman.

**BREEDEN, Richard.** *USA.* Securities and Exchange Commission (SEC) chairman. Born in 1950, he was appointed to his present post in August 1989. Breeden favours further deregulation of financial markets, is opposed to restricting hostile takeovers and leveraged buy-outs, and supports the global co-ordination of securities trading, arguing that US traders should not be put at a disadvantage by having to work within stricter rules than those applied elsewhere. He has played a major role in the plan to bail out the country's savings and loans institutions, supervized government policy on the Alaskan oil-spill, and advocated a stiff prison sentence for Michael Milken when the SEC succeeded in bringing the "junk-bond king" to book.

**BREIT, Ernst.** *Germany.* Trade union leader. Chairman of the German Trade Union Federation (DGB) from 1982–90, Breit was born in north Germany in 1924. He made his career in the post office and the postal trade union, whose chairman he became in 1971.

**BRITTAN, Sir Leon.** *UK.* European Commission vice-president and commissioner for competition policy and financial institutions. Born in 1939, he trained and practised as a barrister until his election to parliament for the Conservative Party in 1974. Although not on the right wing of the party, he gained the confidence of **Margaret Thatcher** and was given junior ministerial office in 1979. He became home secretary in 1983 and trade and industry secretary in 1985. The following year he accepted responsibility in the Westland affair (involving the leak of a confidential letter by government officials) and resigned. In 1989 he was appointed an EC commissioner, responsible for competition policy and for the single market in financial services. He quickly acquired a high reputation in Brussels for his ability to master his portfolio and for challenging the scepticism about closer European union among his former colleagues. He was knighted in 1989.

**BRIZOLA, Leonel da Moura.** *Brazil.* Governor of Rio de Janeiro. Born in 1922, Brizola has been a constant champion of democracy. As governor of Rio Grande do Sul in the early 1960s he led the campaign to prevent the military toppling President João Goulart. He was federal deputy for Rio de Janeiro until he was exiled after the military coup in 1964. He returned in 1979 to found the Democratic Labour Party (PDT) and was elected governor of Rio de Janeiro state in 1982. Despite his populist image, his centre-left campaign for the presidency in 1989 was overtaken by that of "Lula" da Silva. In 1990, he was re-elected governor of Rio.

**BROMLEY, (David) Allan.** *USA.* Office of Science and Technology Policy director. Born in Canada in 1926, a former Yale University physics professor and past president of the American Association for the Advancement of Science, he is one of the world's leading nuclear physicists. He replaced William Graham in his current post in 1989, and is set to play an unprecedented role in the administration of **George Bush**, drafting speeches and participating in cabinet meetings. Bush made him chairman in 1990 of his new President's Council of Advisers on Science and Technology. He is both pragmatic and persuasive, and has worked to convince the administration of the reality of global climate change.

**BROOKE, Peter.** *UK.* Secretary of state for Northern Ireland since 1989. Born in 1939, Brooke was educated at Oxford University and at Harvard Business School. He worked as a management consultant before becoming an MP in 1977. Succeeding **Norman Tebbit** as

Conservative party chairman in 1987, he caught some flak for his party's poor showing in the 1989 Euro-elections, but proved surprisingly bold in the testing Northern Ireland posting, declaring his determination to restore some kind of basis for local politicians to resume genuine political activity in the province. He drew sharp criticism from some quarters for his suggestion in 1990 that Britain could not defeat the IRA by purely military means; but as a good listener he has won friends on both sides of the Irish border.

**BROOKS, Jack.** *USA.* Democratic congressman from Texas. Born in 1922, he practised law before his election to the House of Representatives in 1952. He proved an unrelenting inquisitor during the "Watergate" and "Irangate" investigations. Judiciary committee chairman since 1989, he is liberal on constitutional issues and pro-business on commercial law. He revels in partisan politics and has the reputation of a hatchet-man. He is noted also for his occasional insensitive remarks about women.

**BROUWER, Ina.** *Netherlands.* Left-wing politician. Born in 1950, a lawyer and lecturer in law before being elected to the Staten Generaal (parliament) for the small Communist Party of the Netherlands (CPN) in 1981. A reformist, she was elected party leader the following year. In 1989 she was returned as the CPN member of the new Green Left (Groen Links) coalition of small left-of-centre parties which place environmental issues at the centre of their policies.

**BROWN, Gordon.** *UK.* Labour politician. Born in 1951, he studied economics at Edinburgh University, played a radical role in student politics, lectured at a Glasgow tertiary college from 1976–80 and then worked for Scottish Television as a journalist until 1983. Elected to parliament in that year, his sharp intelligence impressed colleagues, who placed him at the top of the poll for the shadow cabinet in 1987. One of Labour's influential "Scottish mafia" and a quick-witted economics expert, he rose to national prominence in 1988 when he stood in for the temporarily incapacitated **John Smith** as shadow chancellor and proved a match for the then chancellor **Nigel Lawson**. He did his reputation no harm after taking over the shadow trade and industry portfolio in 1989, and has been mentioned as a possible future Labour leader.

**BROWN, Willie.** *USA.* Speaker, California State Assembly. Born in Texas in 1934, he was elected speaker in 1980, and has since become expert at maintaining a bipartisan coalition in the assembly. This coalition was threatened by dissident Democrats, known as the "Gang of Five", who sought to curb the speaker's influence and opposed him on a number of key issues. Despite this, he survived two leadership challenges in 1989 to become the longest serving assembly speaker in California history and one of the most senior black legislators in the USA. **Jesse Jackson**'s national campaign chairman in the 1988 presidential election, Brown supports health and automobile insurance reforms, limited gun control, and bilingual education.

**BRUCAN, Silviu.** *Romania.* Retired diplomat, former editor of the Romanian Communist Party newspaper *Scînteia*. Born in 1928, he served as ambassador to the USA and the UN. A critic of the Ceauşescu regime following the Braşov riots in 1987, he visited Moscow in December 1988 where he received a cordial, high-level welcome. In March 1989 he signed an open letter to Ceauşescu attacking his policies and was placed under house arrest. After the revolution he became chief spokesman for the National Salvation Front (NSF) and foreign affairs adviser on the provisional executive council until February 1990. He parted company with the NSF before the May 1990 elections; since then he has frequently written articles for newspapers and is regularly interviewed on television.

**BRUNDTLAND, Gro Harlem.** *Norway.* Prime minister. Born in 1939, she qualified as a medical doctor in 1963 and went on to study public health at Harvard University. From 1965 until her first ministerial appointment she worked in the national health service. A member of the Norwegian Labour Party (DNA) since her school days, she was appointed environment minister in 1974, elected deputy party leader the following year and elected a member of the *Storting* (parliament) in 1977. She took over as party leader and prime minister when Odvar Nordli resigned in 1981, but was forced to resign after an election setback later that year. In opposition she won international recognition for her energetic work as chair of the World Commission on Environment and Development, which launched the concept of "sustainable development" in its 1987 report *Our Common Future*. She also learned to temper her tendency to lecture people. When the centre–right coalition was defeated in the *Storting* on a tax issue in 1986, she returned as prime minister at as prime minister at the head of a minority Labour government, which – unprecedented even in emancipated Norway – had eight women in a cabinet of 18. Proving that she could take difficult decisions, she forced austerity on the Norwegians and got the economy back on course after the collapse in oil prices in 1985–86. Voters did not reward her, and the 1989 elections brought a new centre–right coalition to power. When that coalition collapsed in October 1990, she was able to put together a minority Labour government once again, this time with nine women in a cabinet of 19.

**BRUNSWIJK, Ronnie.** *Suriname.* Of *bosneger* (maroon) descent, Brunswijk was dismissed as a presidential bodyguard to **Désiré Bouterse** in 1986 in a dispute over pay. With others he then formed the Surinamese Liberation Army, or Jungle Commando, in the interior to conduct an anti-government guerrilla campaign that eventually posed a serious threat to the stability of the country. An outline peace accord was reached in 1989, but its implementation and the future of Brunswijk remain unclear, particularly in view of Désiré Bouterse's opposition to a peaceful settlement.

**BRUTON, John.** *Ireland.* Fine Gael leader. Born in Dublin in 1947, he was elected to parliament in 1969 and held a number of junior government posts before entering the cabinet as finance minister in 1981. After a spell at industry, trade, commerce and tourism in 1982–86, he returned to finance, and in 1987 was elected deputy leader of Fine Gael. Out of office, he served as spokesman on industry and commerce (1987–89), and education (1989). In November 1990 he was elected leader of Fine Gael, succeeding Alan Dukes.

**BUCARAM ORTIZ, Abdalá.** *Ecuador.* Opposition politician. A flamboyant and often controversial populist, Bucaram in 1980 founded the Ecuadorian Roldosista Party (PRE) – named after his brother-in-law, President Jaimé Roldós, who died the following year. He was elected mayor of Guayaquil in 1985, but fled to Panama after being accused of insulting the honour of the military. He returned to contest the 1988 presidential election, coming second to **Rodrigo Borja**, but fled abroad again soon afterwards to avoid charges, later dropped, of alleged misappropriation of funds during his term as Guayaquil's mayor.

**BUCHANAN, John.** *Canada.* Former premier of Nova Scotia and Conservative senator. He was born in 1931 in Sydney, Nova Scotia, and was educated at Mount Allison and Dalhousie universities. He practised law before election to Nova Scotia's legislature in 1967. He was appointed leader of the provincial Progressive Conservative Party of Canada in 1971, elected premier in 1978, and was the longest-serving premier until his resignation in September 1990 amid allegations of corruption in his administration. His appointment to the Senate by the prime minister, **Brian Mulroney**, was controversial, as Mulroney sought to dilute the Liberal domination of the upper house.

**BUĆIN, Nenad.** *Yugoslavia.* Montenegro's member of the collective state presidency. Born in Kotor in 1934, he graduated in philosophy and went on to become a university professor. He joined the communist party in 1953 and has held senior posts in the party and its umbrella organization, the Socialist Alliance. In April 1989 he was elected for a five-year term in Montenegro's first western-style election as its member of the collective state presidency.

**BUJAK, Zbigniew.** *Poland.* Solidarity activist. Born in 1955, he became involved with Solidarity in 1980 as an organizer of strikes in Warsaw's Ursus tractor factory. Elected to the Solidarity leadership, he went into hiding when martial law was imposed in December 1981 and headed the Warsaw Solidarity underground. He was captured in May 1986 but released soon afterwards in an amnesty. He is proprietor of *Gazeta Wyborcza*, an influential daily newspaper set up in May 1989. With fellow Solidarity veterans **Władysław Frasyniuk** and **Adam Michnik** he broke with Solidarity chairman **Lech Wałęsa** in July 1990, siding instead with Prime Minister **Tadeusz Mazowiecki** and setting up the Citizens' Movement for Democratic Action (ROAD) to back Mazowiecki in the November 1990 presidential elections.

**BUKMAN, Piet.** *Netherlands.* Agriculture and fisheries minister. Born in 1934, he served under the second **Ruud Lubbers** government as development co-operation minister in November 1986 and state secretary for economic affairs in the third Lubbers government in November 1989. In September 1990 the Christian Democrats appointed Bukman to replace Gerrit Braks as agriculture and fisheries minister after a no confidence motion following a scandal concerning overfishing by the Dutch fishing fleet.

**BUMPERS, Dale.** *USA.* Democratic senator from Arkansas. Born in 1925, he had a varied career in law, management and farming. Elected in 1974, he is a liberal southerner, often mentioned as a possible presidential nominee but always refusing to run. A fervent environmentalist, he has battled with the oil companies from his position as second-ranking Democrat on the energy committee. In 1989 he was instrumental in killing a bill that would have opened the Arctic National Wildlife Region to exploration and drilling. He is also a critic of nuclear energy.

**BUREŠOVÁ, Dagmar.** *Czechoslovakia.* Chairwoman of the Czech National Committee (parliament of the Czech republic). Born in 1929 in Kladno, she studied law at Charles University in Prague. After 1952 she worked as a lawyer and was active in professional legal organizations. Before her election as chairwoman of the national committee in June 1990 she held the post of justice minister, to which she was appointed following the November 1989 revolution.

**BURNHAM, Viola.** *Guyana.* Vice-president. The widow of former President Forbes Burnham, she was chairwoman of the Women's Revolutionary Socialist Movement of the People's National Congress. Made a vice-president on the death of her husband in 1985, she has latterly lost much of her earlier influence over decision-making.

**BURNS, Sir Terry.** *UK.* Economist. Born in 1944, he studied economics and then lectured at the London Business School, becoming a professor in 1979. A monetarist, appointed chief economic adviser to the Treasury in 1980, he has been at the centre of the Conservative government's economic policy-making. He was knighted in 1983.

**BUROKEVICIUS, Mikolas.** *USSR.* Leader of Lithuania's pro-Soviet communists. An historian born in 1926, he was among a small number of old-guard Lithuanian communists who, together with larger numbers of ethnic Russians and Poles, defied the decision of a Lithuanian Communist Party congress in December 1989 to declare independence from the Communist Party of the Soviet Union (CPSU), and instead set up a rival party. With about 40,000 members, the "Lithuanian Communist Party on the CPSU Platform" is dwarfed by the independent party led by **Algirdas Brazauskas**. Nevertheless, Burokevicius's office entitled him to membership of the CPSU politburo in July 1990.

**BURT, Richard.** *USA.* Ambassador to Germany and arms negotiator. Born in 1947, his early career in journalism included a stint on *The New York Times*. After a spell as military adviser during **Ronald Reagan**'s presidency, he became assistant secretary of state for European and Canadian affairs in 1983 and ambassador to West Germany two years later. He effectively replaced the hawkish Max Kampelman as the chief strategic (long-range) arms negotiator in 1989. Politically conservative but moderate on arms control, his other priorities include the reorganization of the Stealth bomber and Midgetman, MX and land-based missile programmes.

**BUSEK, Erhard.** *Austria.* Science and research minister. Born in Vienna in 1941, he studied at Vienna University. From 1964–68 he held the post of second secretary of the parliamentary Austrian People's Party (ÖVP). In 1968 he joined the federal executive committee of the Austrian Economic Federation, a subsidiary of the ÖVP. In 1969 he became deputy secretary-general of the federation and served as its secretary-general from 1972–75. In 1975–76 he was also general secretary of the ÖVP and sat in parliament from 1975–78. He was deputy mayor of Vienna from 1978–87 and joined the government in April 1989 as science and research minister. Busek has make his mark by his advocacy of environmental protection and by occasionally straying from party orthodoxy.

**BUSER, Walter.** *Switzerland.* Chancellor. Born in 1926, he studied law and economics, became a legal consultant, and from 1977 lectured in law at Basle University. From 1965–81 he headed the legal and information service of the federal interior department. A Social Democrat Party (SPS) member, his legal expertise made him a natural choice as vice-chancellor (from 1968–81) and chancellor since 1981.

**BUSH, Barbara.** *USA.* First lady. Known widely as "the Silver Fox", she was born in New York City in 1925, the daughter of a publishing executive, and married **George Bush** in 1945. Her own sphere of public action has been in charitable work; some have attributed her motivation to her own experience of personal tragedy and the early death of her daughter. After her husband became president, she established the Barbara Bush Foundation for Family Literacy and has written a book, *C. Fred's Story: A Dog's Life*, in aid of the anti-illiteracy cause. Her homely, approachable style has made her widely popular.

**BUSH, George.** *USA.* President. Born in 1924 in Massachusetts, he was educated at the prestigious Phillips Academy and at Yale University, before serving with distinction as a naval pilot in the Pacific from 1942–45. He entered politics in 1967 as a member of the legislature in his adopted state of Texas, where he had founded the Zapata Petroleum Corporation in the 1950s. Thereafter, he was permanent representative to the UN from 1971–72, chairman of the Republican National Committee from 1973–74, head of the US Liaison Office in Beijing from 1974–75, and director of the CIA from 1976–77. In 1980 he withdrew from the contest for the Republican Party presidential nomination after the Oregon primary in late May, and was then chosen at the party convention to be the running mate of **Ronald Reagan**; thereafter he served consecutive terms as vice-president between 1981 and 1989. He secured the Republican nomination for the presidency in 1988 after a bitter contest, in the early stages of which he struggled to shake off the image of a privileged background and a reputation for weakness and indecision – the so-called "wimp factor". There followed a robust presidential campaign in which the Bush camp was widely criticized for using negative tactics to destroy the reputation of **Michael Dukakis**, the Democratic Party nominee. Although Bush defeated Dukakis in the November 1988 election, the Democrats made gains in the simultaneous legislative elections and secured control of both chambers of Congress. After the election Bush attempted to mollify the legacy of ill-feeling caused by the campaign by using his inaugural speech as an opportunity to appeal for a bipartisan working relationship with the new Congress. In sharp contrast with the West Coast style of the Reagans, Bush and his wife, Barbara, have sought to project the more homely image of an ordinary family. In June 1990, in the face of the country's growing budget deficit, he accepted the need to increase taxes, thereby reneging on one of the few firm pledges he had made during the presidential campaign. Later that year he faced his two toughest tests yet. On the Gulf crisis he was accused of wavering but by the end of the year as his resolve to take military action against Iraq had hardened, he had steadily recovered public support. The budget deficit shambles had done most to drag his popularity down to the point that many Republicans felt the need to distance themselves from him in the November 1990 mid-term elections.

**BUTHELEZI, Chief Mangosuthu Gatsha**. *South Africa*. Inkatha leader. Born in 1928 in a royal Zulu family, a tribal chief from the age of 25 and assistant to King Cyprian for 15 years, he became leader of the Zululand territorial authority under the "homeland system" in 1970 and has been chief minister of KwaZulu since 1976. Setting himself steadfastly against the false promise of "independent" status, he cultivated his power base within the Zulu people, the country's largest ethnic constituency, founding the Inkatha organization in 1976, but clashing increasingly with young militants who were turning to the African National Congress (ANC). The ANC had supported him from exile as a black leader of substance within the country, but from the mid-1980s there was open conflict between the two organizations in Inkatha's Natal heartland. The release of **Nelson Mandela** and the growing toleration of ANC activity from early 1990 brought Buthelezi up sharply, as his rivals took centre stage. Effusive praise from anti-ANC western leaders, such as **Margaret Thatcher**, did little to endear him to non-Zulu radicals. The growing "black-on-black" ethnic violence taught the ANC that Buthelezi could not just be wished away, even while the killings cemented hatred on the ground. An intensely proud man who brooks no opposition within Inkatha, and a colourful celebrant of Zulu identity, he still sees his leadership ambitions in national rather than tribal terms, and has won backing from some prominent business leaders.

**BUTLER, Sir Robin**. *UK*. Head of the civil service. Born in 1938, he joined the civil service on graduating from Oxford University in 1961. He rose swiftly within the Treasury, and was private secretary to three prime ministers (**Edward Heath** in 1972–74, Harold Wilson in 1974–75 and **Margaret Thatcher** in 1982–85). In 1988 he was appointed to the immensely powerful job of cabinet secretary and head of the civil service. He was knighted in the same year.

**BUTTON, John**. *Australia*. Industry, technology and commerce minister and government leader in the Senate. Born in Ballarat, Victoria, in 1933, he was educated at Melbourne University. After a short spell with the British TUC he followed a legal career until his election to the Senate as an Australian Labor Party (ALP) member in 1974. He has been industry minister since 1983. Although not formally identified with any ALP faction, he is close to the centre–left grouping.

**BUYOYA, Major Pierre**. *Burundi*. President. Born in 1949 and educated at the Royal Military Academy in Brussels, Buyoya was brought to power in the bloodless coup of September 1987. He was formerly head of logistics for the armed forces and a close colleague of ousted president Jean-Baptiste Bagaza, serving on the central committee of the ruling Union for National Progress. Buyoya has attempted to end the bitter conflict between the country's Tutsi and Hutu communities, which resurfaced in the massacres of August 1988. This policy has so far failed to win the acceptance of the Tutsi military elite that brought Buyoya to power.

**BYAMBASUREN, Dashiyn.** *Mongolia.* Prime minister. Born in 1942, he joined the Mongolian People's Revolutionary Party (MPRP) in 1963, becoming a member of its central committee in 1990 before being elected prime minister of the new coalition government in September 1990. Previously first deputy chairman of the former council of ministers, he was trained in Moscow as an economist and statistician, has worked on several state economic committees, and is committed to introducing a market economy.

**BYLIŃSKI, Janusz.** *Poland.* Agriculture minister. A farmer and activist in the peasant movement, he was one of the founders in 1980 of the Rural Solidarity farmers' union which, in Poland's new pluralist conditions, has become a highly efficient nationwide organization. He became chairman of the Sejm (parliament) agricultural commission following the partly free June 1989 elections, and was appointed agriculture and food economy minister in September 1990, taking over this crucial job from his party's political rival, the Polish Peasant Party.

**BYRD, Robert.** *USA.* Democratic senator from West Virginia. Born in 1917, he was elected to the House of Representatives in 1952 and, unusually for a US politician, it was only after this that he gained his law degree. He entered the Senate in 1959 and was appointed Democratic whip in 1971 becoming Democratic leader in 1978. His relations with **Jimmy Carter**, whom he considered a political amateur, were uneasy. However, his own political style has been deemed too old-fashioned for the television age. Originally on the Democratic right (he was once a member of the Ku Klux Klan), he moved to the centre in the mid-1960s, apparently to gain party advancement, but his relationship with liberals was always wary. Promoting his state's interests, particularly its coal industry (he is a coalminer's son), has been one of his fortes. Since 1982 he has almost single-handedly killed efforts to strengthen the Clean Air Act against urban smog and acid rain. He resigned his leadership post in 1989 in a deal that took him to the chair of the powerful appropriations committee. He is also president pro tempore of the Senate, which gives him the occasional chance to wield a partisan gavel over the Senate chamber.

# C

**CABANNES, Jean.** *France.* Constitutional councillor. Born in 1925 and a law graduate, he entered the legal profession, initially as a lawyer and government adviser. In 1976 he was appointed to the highest appeal court, and in 1989 to the watchdog Constitutional Council.

**CABRAL, Bernardo.** *Brazil.* Former justice minister. Born in 1932, Cabral trained and practised as a lawyer, and first became involved in politics in Amazonas state. He was a federal deputy when his political rights were suspended in 1968. He then pursued his legal career, becoming president of the bar association. He won a deputy's seat in 1986 and became president of the constituent assembly. In 1989, he deserted the Brazilian Democratic Movement (PMDB) to support **Fernando Collor de Mello** after the second round of voting and was subsequently appointed justice minister. He resigned in October 1990, following the revelation of his affair with the finance minister, **Zelia Cardoso de Mello.**

**CABRERA HIDALGO, Alfonso.** *Guatemala.* Special affairs minister. A member of the Guatemalan Christian Democratic Party (PDCG), Cabrera was president of Congress and then foreign minister in 1987. He was made special affairs minister after he had been chosen as PDCG candidate for the 1990 presidential elections, in which he finished third.

**CAFIERO, Antonio Francisco.** *Argentina.* Governor of Buenos Aires. Born in 1922, Cafiero was educated at Buenos Aires University. He joined the Peronist party and was foreign trade minister in the 1950s, and treasury minister from 1975–76. He became leader of the reformist faction within the Peronist movement and was elected governor of Buenos Aires in 1987. His bid to become the Peronist presidential candidate was defeated by his rival, **Carlos Menem.**

**CAGLIARI, Gabriele.** *Italy.* Industrial manager. Born in 1926 in the province of Reggio Emilia, he took a degree in industrial engineering and has made his career in the state-owned oil conglomerate ENI (Ente Nazionale Idrocarburi), on whose board he has sat since 1983. In November 1989 he succeeded **Franco Reviglio** as ENI chairman. Cagliari is a friend of Socialist leader **Bettino Craxi.**

**CAITHNESS, The Earl of.** *UK.* Minister of state at the Foreign and Commonwealth Office since July 1990. Born Malcolm Sinclair in 1948, he succeeded his father as the 20th Earl in 1965. He has served in the House of Lords as whip, social services and Scottish spokesman, transport, home office and environment minister, and paymaster-general, all since 1984.

**CALDERÓN FOURNIER, Rafael Angel.** *Costa Rica.* President. Born in 1949, the son of President Rafael Calderón Guardia, Calderón was elected to the National Assembly in 1974 and was foreign minister from 1978–80. He helped to form the conservative United Social Christian Party (PUSC) and was the conservative presidential candidate in 1982 and 1986. He won the 1990 elections on the promise of political and economic reform.

**ČALFA, Marián.** *Czechoslovakia.* Prime minister. A Slovak former communist turned reformist, and federal premier since December 1989, he is the most prominent of the small handful of politicians who have successfully cast off the taint of a communist past to play a leading role in building the new democratic Czechoslovakia. Born in 1946 in East Slovakia into a railway worker's family, he worked as a legal official for the federal government from 1972–88. He was appointed federal minister without portfolio in April 1988, and emerged as a pivotal figure in the negotiations with the opposition during the "velvet revolution" of late 1989. His appointment as federal premier in December that year heralded the creation of the first Czechoslovak government since 1948 with a non-communist majority. Resigning from the Communist Party of Czechoslovakia (KSČ) in January 1990, he was elected to the Federal Assembly as a candidate for Civic Forum/Public against Violence in the June general elections.

As a Slovak of real political stature, his continuing role as premier was seen as counterbalancing the presidency of **Václav Havel**, a Czech. He enjoys a reputation for efficiency, and for an ability to find compromise solutions.

**CALLAGHAN, Lord (James Callaghan).** *UK.* Labour politician. Born in 1912, he entered the civil service as a tax officer after leaving school in 1929 and was the assistant general secretary of the Inland Revenue Staff Federation from 1936–47. He was elected to parliament for a Cardiff seat in 1945. In a ministerial career spanning 33 years, he held, uniquely, all senior government offices: chancellor of the exchequer (1964–67), home secretary (1967–70), foreign secretary (1974–76) and finally prime minister (1976–79). Although widely experienced, he was persistently accused of indecision and lack of vision: he almost single-handedly destroyed attempts to reform the trade union laws in the late 1960s, for example. But during his last years in office he attacked many sacred cows of British socialism – notably over public spending and the limits on effective demand management in the economy – and hinted at the need for many profound changes, later enacted by **Margaret Thatcher**. Created a life peer in 1987, he sits as a Labour member of the House of Lords.

**CALLEJAS ROMERO, Rafael Leonardo.** *Honduras.* President. Born in 1943, Callejas was educated as an agricultural economist at Mississippi University, USA. He worked in agricultural planning for the government and was natural resources minister in the 1970s before developing a successful career as a banker, heading Banco Mercantil from 1980–83. He formed his own faction within the National Party (PN), becoming party president and its presidential candidate in 1985, winning the presidency at his second attempt in 1989.

**CAMACHO SOLÍS, Víctor Manuel.** *Mexico.* Governor of the Federal district. Born in 1946, and trained as an economist, he served in a variety of bureaucratic posts before joining **Carlos Salinas**'s planning and budget ministry as under-secretary for regional development in 1982. In 1988 he was appointed urbanization and ecology minister. In the same year he was elected secretary-general of the ruling Institutional Revolutionary Party (PRI). A close friend of Salinas, whose 1988 election campaign he managed, he was rewarded with the important and delicate job of running the Mexico City district.

**CAMDESSUS, Michel.** *France.* Managing director of the International Monetary Fund (IMF). Born in 1933, he studied economics and gained a postgraduate degree from the prestigious Ecole Nationale d'Administration (ENA). He joined the civil service in 1960, rising swiftly to become deputy director of the Treasury in 1974 and director in 1982. From 1978–84 he also chaired the Paris Club of Western creditor countries. He was appointed governor of the French central bank in 1984 and became managing director of the IMF in 1987. Unlike his predecessors, he has encouraged a much more open atmosphere at the organization. At the personal level, he has not shied away from publicly criticizing US policy-makers for failing to deal with huge trade and budget deficits and the commercial banks for their reluctance to reschedule third-world debt.

**ÇAMI, Foto.** *Albania.* Chief ideologist of the Party of Labour of Albania. Born in 1925 in Labovë, he was active as a partisan during World War II. He worked his way up through the Communist Party of Albania (in 1948 renamed the Party of Labour of Albania) to become a full member of the central committee in 1971, and of the politburo in 1986. He studied philosophy at Enver Hoxha University in Tirana, and has been a member of the Albanian Academy of Sciences since 1972 and its president since 1984. Although a noted reformist and secretary of the party central committee, he was omitted from the politburo in the December 1990 reorganization.

**CAMPBELL, Carroll, Jr.** *USA.* Republican governor of South Carolina. Born in 1940, he was a real estate agent, state legislator and US congressman before being elected South Carolina's second Republican governor of the twentieth century in 1987. Conservative in national politics, he supports state activism in education and social programmes.

**CÂMPEANU, Radu.** *Romania.* Vice-president of the Senate and leader of the National Liberal Party (NLP). Born in Bucharest in 1922, he studied law and economics. Leader of the Liberal Party's student organization, he was imprisoned for his political activities in 1947 when the communists came to power. Freed in 1956, he later went into exile in Paris. Following the overthrow of Nicolae Ceaușescu, he returned to Romania to became NLP leader and its presidential candidate. He was heavily defeated by **Ion Iliescu**, but was assured a seat on his party's list for the Senate.

**CAP, Josef.** *Austria.* Socialist Party of Austria (SPÖ) joint secretary. Born in Vienna in 1952, he studied politics, law and education and served as chairman of the socialist youth movement. He was appointed joint secretary of the SPÖ in November 1988.

**CAPERTON, Gaston.** *USA.* Democratic governor of West Virginia, Born in 1940, he was a wealthy insurance executive before winning the governorship in 1988 from a Republican incumbent whose efforts to deal with the state's declining economy had failed. His priority is attracting new industry to the state.

**ÇARÇANI, Adil.** *Albania.* Prime minister. Born in 1922, he joined the Communist Party of Albania (in 1948 renamed the Party of Labour of Albania) during World War II. A member of the People's Assembly since 1950, and of the politburo since 1961, he ranks as a veteran member of the government, having held ministerial posts since 1959, and the premiership since 1982. He was entrusted by President **Ramiz Alia** with the task of forming a reformist government in December 1990.

**CÁRDENAS SOLÓRZANO, Cuauhtémoc.** *Mexico.* Opposition leader. Born in 1934, the son of former president Lázaro Cárdenas, he pursued a political career within the ruling Institutional Revolutionary Party (PRI), serving as a senator, deputy agriculture minister and, from 1980, as governor of Michoacán state. In 1987 he formed a dissident faction within the party, Democratic Current (CD). He left to form his own grouping after the failure of the PRI to hold an open selection contest for its presidential candidate. In 1988 he brought five opposition parties together to form the leftist National Democratic Front (FDN). Using the appeal of his father's name and populist politics, Cárdenas campaigned strongly against the ruling party and came second in the presidential contest; his supporters claimed he was denied victory only because of government fraud. He then formed a new party, the Party of the Democratic Revolution (PRD).

**CARDOSO DE MELLO, Zelia.** *Brazil.* Economy minister. Born in 1954, Cardoso studied economics at São Paulo University. After working for a state company in São Paulo, she joined the team of advisers to finance minister Dilson Funaro for the "cruzado plan". She was subsequently hired by **Fernando Collor de Mello** as a consultant when he was governor of Alagoas state and became his finance adviser. In 1990 she was appointed to head a new economics "super-ministry" to implement the *"plano Collor"*

to deal with Brazil's mounting economic problems. In October 1990 she survived the scandal that followed the revelation of her affair with justice minister **Bernardo Cabral**, who resigned his post.

**CARIGLIA, Antonio.** *Italy.* Italian Democratic Socialist Party (PSDI) secretary. Born in 1924 in the province of Foggia, he gained a degree in political and social sciences and became a journalist. He served as a member of the Chamber of Deputies from 1968–76 and was elected to the European Parliament in 1979 and 1989. In 1987 he was elected to the Senate and became secretary of the PSDI in March 1988.

**CARIGNON, Alain.** *France.* Gaullist politician. Born in 1949 and a graduate in company administration, he followed a civil service career. Since 1983 he has gained something of a green image as the environment-conscious mayor of Grenoble, and he was elected first to the European Parliament (in 1984), then to the National Assembly (in 1986). As a prominent member of the Gaullist Rally for the Republic (RPR), and its national secretary since 1984, he was given a role in **Jacques Chirac**'s 1986–88 government as infrastructure, housing, regional planning and transport minister. Since the defeat of the right in 1988, he has pursued a semi-independent path, emphasizing consensual politics and the need for political party reforms, but suffering ostracism from the right as a consequence.

**CARL XVI GUSTAF.** *Sweden.* King. Born in 1946, he gained a reputation as a playboy with an interest in fast cars and sports. He became king on the death of his grandfather, Gustaf VI Adolf, in 1973. Constitutional amendments passed two years later removed all remaining powers from the monarch, who now has even less influence on the political process than his European counterparts. Since his marriage to a German interpreter, Silvia Sommerlath, in 1976, he has concentrated on the more traditional role of the constitutional monarch as ambassador for his country and its social conscience, thereby all but silencing the republican lobby.

**CARLI, Guido.** *Italy.* Treasury minister. Born in 1914 in Brescia, he gained a law degree at Padua University and began a long career which has spanned industry, banking and politics. After helping to draft the Vanoni 10-year development plan for Italy, he first held ministerial office in 1957–58, as a non-party extra-parliamentary expert in charge of foreign trade. In 1959, he was appointed general manager of the Banca d'Italia (central bank) and was governor from 1960–75. From 1976–80 he was president of Confindustria, the private sector industrialists' organization; in 1983 he became a senator on the Christian Democrat party (DC) list. In 1989 he returned to government as treasury minister, a post that enables him to continue the campaign for financial stringency that he pursued as central bank governor. Although highly respected, he is inclined to be rigid in his views.

**CARLSON, Arne.** *USA.* Republican governor of Minnesota. Born in 1934 and formerly state auditor, he was drafted in at the last moment in 1990 to contest the governorship for the Republicans; the man who beat him in the primary was forced to withdraw amid allegations of sexual impropriety. Pro-choice on the abortion issue, he succeeded in defeating the incumbent Rudy Perpich.

**CARLSSON, Ingvar.** *Sweden.* Prime minister. Born in 1934, his career followed the trusted pattern employed by the Social Democratic Labour Party (SAP) of grooming prospective leaders from an early age. The assassination of Olof Palme in 1986 brought his rise to party leader – he is only the fifth in the SAP's century-long history – and to prime minister earlier than expected. Carlsson graduated in politics and economics in 1958, did two stints in the prime minister's office under Tage Erlander (1958–60 and 1967–69), and led the SAP youth wing from 1961–67. He entered the Riksdag (parliament) in 1964, and held ministerial posts at education and culture from 1969–73 and at housing and planning from 1973–76. When the party returned to government in 1982, his status as heir apparent was confirmed by his appointment as deputy prime minister. His succession to long-time colleague and close friend Palme brought little change in policy but a definite change in style. While Palme was middle class, flamboyant, intellectual and arrogant, Carlsson's background is working class and he has gained a reputation as a drier, more consensual politician, short on dogma and long on common sense.

**CARLSSON, Roine.** *Sweden.* Defence minister. Born in 1937, he worked in a paper mill and became a trade union organizer, rising through the ranks to become leader of the pulp and paper workers' union in 1962 and a deputy leader of the powerful Swedish Trade Union Confederation (LO) in 1973. Benefiting from the strong institutional and personal links between the LO and the Social Democratic Labour Party

(SAP), he became junior minister in the industry ministry when the SAP returned to government in 1982. Elected to the Riksdag (parliament) in 1985, he was appointed defence minister the same year.

**ČARNOGURSKÝ, Ján.** *Czechoslovakia.* Leading Slovak politician and former dissident. Born in 1944 in Bratislava, he studied law at Charles University, Prague, and practised as a lawyer in Bratislava until 1981, when he was dismissed from the Bar for defending a teacher charged with sedition. He then worked as an enterprise lawyer, and also defended human rights activists, but from 1987 was without work. Detained in August 1989 and charged with incitement, he was acquitted in November 1989, but detained pending appeal by the prosecution, until his release was ordered by president Gustav Husak two days later. He was named deputy federal premier in the government of national accord in December 1989, and became a founder-member of the Christian Democratic Movement (CDM) in Slovakia early in 1990. After the June elections, Civic Forum wanted him to join the federal coalition government, but he chose instead to concentrate on the Slovak republic, where his CDM had emerged as the second strongest force, and he was brought into the government there as first deputy premier.

**CARPIO NICOLLE, Jorge.** *Guatemala.* National Centrist Union (UCN) leader. The UCN's candidate for the presidency in the November 1990 elections, he topped the poll with over one quarter of the votes and went forward for the January 1991 run-off against **Jorge Serrano.** A self-made millionaire and publisher, he is deferential towards the power of the army.

**CARR, Shirley.** *Canada.* President of Canadian Labor Congress. Born in Niagara Falls, Ontario, she is a graduate of Stamford Collegiate Vocational Institute and the Niagara College of Applied Arts and Technology. She became executive vice-president of the Canadian Labor Congress in 1974 and was elected president in 1986, the first woman leader of Canada's labour federation. Carr was a member of the governing body of the International Labour Organisation from 1980–85, and is vice-president of the International Confederation of Free Trade Unions and chairwoman of the Commonwealth Trade Union Council.

**CARRARO, Franco.** *Italy.* Mayor of Rome, tourism minister and Italian Socialist Party (PSI) politician. Born in 1939 in Padua, he became a champion water skier, then pursued a career in sports administration, serving from 1978–87 as president of the national Olympic committee and from 1982–87 as a member of the International Olympic Committee. He is also a former president of the Italian Football Federation and in 1990 was chairman of the organizing committee for the World Cup football competition. In July 1989 he was appointed tourism minister; five months later he was also elected as Rome's first socialist mayor.

**CARRILLO, Santiago.** *Spain.* Communist politician. Born in 1916 in Gijon, he was secretary-general of the Communist Party of Spain (PCE) from 1960–82. Carrillo played a prominent role in the civil war and, returning to Spain after nearly 40 years in exile, he was briefly arrested in December 1976 before the party won its campaign for legalization. Under his leadership the PCE formally abandoned Leninism in 1978, played an important part in the transition to democracy and followed a Euro-communist line, but lost much of its support in the 1982 elections. Carrillo, replaced as secretary-general in 1985, was expelled from the central committee in 1985 and responded by forming a misleadingly named dissident group, Communist Unity, in 1985 and then the Workers' Party of Spain – Communist Unity (PTE–UC) in 1986.

**CARRINGTON, Lord.** *UK.* Conservative politician. Born in 1918, Peter Carington succeeded as 6th baron in 1938. Trained at the Royal Military College Sandhurst, he first held government office in 1954. He was the Conservative leader in the House of Lords from 1963–70 and 1974–79 and secretary of defence from 1970–74. He was influential in advising **Edward Heath** to go to the country in February 1974 – advice for which he was later criticized. Affluent, affable and witty (in short, the diplomat par excellence), he was appointed foreign secretary in 1979, but resigned after the Argentine invasion of the Falkland Islands in 1982. After a brief stint with GEC, he served as secretary-general of Nato, from 1984–88. He is now chairman of fine art auctioneers Christie's.

**CARTER, Jimmy.** *USA.* Former president. Born in Plains, Georgia, in 1924, he graduated from the US Naval Academy at Annapolis in 1946. In 1951 he was senior officer on the *Sea Wolf*, the second nuclear submarine built in the USA. He subsequently followed his father into business and held a seat in the Georgia state

senate from 1963–66. A religious experience in 1967 confirmed his "liberal" social views. From 1971 he served four years as Georgia governor, adopting forward-thinking policies on environmental controls and social welfare. His election to the presidency in 1976 was viewed with great hope, following the scandals surrounding Richard Nixon. Capitalizing on the image of a plain-speaking southern peanut farmer, he set out with a "populist" political agenda, and made human rights a major policy objective for the first time. His mediation between Egypt and Israel, leading to the Camp David peace accords of 1977, is widely regarded as his major foreign policy success, despite its failure to achieve peace in the region. However, by 1980 he was blamed for what he himself described as America's "malaise", its economic stagnation, and his administration's growing frustration in foreign policy, epitomized by the Tehran hostage debacle. Since leaving office he has recovered substantial international stature, working through the Carter Presidential Center to resolve conflicts. Encouraged by the administration of **George Bush**, Carter has acted as a mediator in Nicaragua, Somalia, Panama, Ethiopia, and elsewhere. Historians have also begun to re-evaluate his presidency, noting important successes.

**CARVALHAS, Carlos.** *Portugal.* Communist party official. Born in 1942, he is an economist and a member of the European Parliament. He was elected to the new post of deputy secretary-general of the Portuguese Communist Party (PCP) in 1990, in belated recognition of the need to put a fresher face on a party notorious for its sclerotic Stalinism under the veteran **Alvaro Cunhal**.

**CASEY, Robert.** *USA.* Democratic governor of Pennsylvania. Born in 1932, the son of a coalminer, he was a lawyer and state legislator whose record as a cost-effective and scandal-free state auditor helped his election as governor in 1986. His main policy concerns have been economic development, environmental protection and education.

**CASTILLO MORALES, Carlos Manuel.** *Costa Rica.* Former Legislative Assembly president. Born in 1928, Castillo trained as an economist and served as minister of the presidency and finance minister in the 1970s and president of the central bank (until 1984) during National Liberation Party (PLN) administrations. Widely regarded as a "neo-liberal", he opposed **Oscar Arias** for the PLN presidential candidature in

1986, but was then appointed president of the Legislative Assembly. In 1990 he was the PLN's unsuccessful presidential candidate.

**CASTLE, Michael.** *USA.* Republican governor of Delaware. Born in 1935, he was a lawyer, state official, state legislator, and lieutenant governor before being elected governor in 1984. Presiding over a booming state economy, he has maintained the policies of his predecessor, Pierre DuPont, particularly in attracting business firms to relocate in Delaware.

**CASTRO RUZ, Fidel.** *Cuba.* Head of state. Born in 1927 of prosperous middle-class parents, Castro studied law at Havana University. He used his legal training in his first challenge to the regime of Fulgencio Batista, an attempt to have the 1952 coup declared illegal in the courts. His military campaign against Batista began with the disastrous attack on the Moncada barracks in Santiago in 1953. After being imprisoned and then granted amnesty, he returned secretly from exile in 1956 to start a guerrilla campaign in the Sierra Maestra. Growing support led to his final overthrow of Batista in 1959. Appointed prime minister, he soon started to reform Cuban society, nationalizing foreign-owned land and assets. The failure of the US-backed "Bay of Pigs" invasion strengthened Castro's position and in December 1961 he was able to pronounce himself a Marxist-Leninist and Cuba a socialist state. In 1976, upon the adoption of a new constitution, Castro became president of the Council of State and effective head of state. Castro has ruled Cuba with an iron grip, but at the same time tried to improve the conditions for the majority of the population, especially in education and health. His penchant for cigars, military fatigues and long speeches have become hallmarks of a political style in which he has also portrayed himself as the friend of the third world and the bogeyman of the USA. As a leader of the non-aligned movement, Castro has pursued an active foreign policy, both in the region and in Africa. His latest defiant slogan, "socialism or death", may, however, mask some of the adjustments that will gradually take place as the regime faces up to the collapse of communism elsewhere.

**CASTRO RUZ, Raúl.** *Cuba.* Vice-president. Born in 1931, the younger brother of **Fidel Castro**, Raúl has stood alongside his brother since 1953 and acted as his deputy, a position formalized in the offices he holds within the party and government. Often regarded as more radical than Fidel, as head of the armed forces,

with the rank of general, he wields considerable influence. His wife, Vilma Espin, is also an important senior party figure.

**CAVACO SILVA, Aníbal Antonio.** *Portugal.* Prime minister. Born in 1939 in Loule, he followed a career as an economist and was finance minister during 1980 and president of the national planning council from 1981–84. He became prime minister in 1985, as leader of the centre-right Social Democratic Party (PSD). In 1987, after refusing to patch up a coalition government, he sought a mandate for stable government. Adopting a more popular rhetorical style in his election campaign, he spoke of a "patriotic duty" to support the PSD, which espoused free-market economic policies. A surge of support, in particular among the young, won him the first overall majority since the 1974 revolution. Using this support to launch constitutional reforms as well as a determined privatization programme, Cavaco Silva has latterly seen his government's popularity diminished by charges that it is technocratic and averse to consultation.

**CAVALLO, Domingo.** *Argentina.* Foreign minister. Born in 1946, he studied economics at Harvard University and headed the Central Bank during the military regime in the late 1970s. Elected to Congress in 1987, he was appointed foreign minister in 1989, illustrating the importance to **Carlos Menem** of a foreign minister able to conduct negotiations over debt and economic policy with foreign countries and organizations.

**CAVAZOS, Lauro.** *USA.* Former secretary of education. The first Hispanic ever to serve in a US cabinet, he was born in 1927 and is bilingual in Spanish and English. He studied zoology at Texas Tech, and obtained his doctorate from Iowa State University. He had a distinguished academic career and was professor of anatomy and dean of medicine at Tufts University, Boston, from 1975–80, and president of the Health Sciences Center at Texas Tech from 1980–88. During his tenure at Texas Tech, Cavazos was generally regarded as a personable, apolitical administrator who was prepared to delegate responsibility and search for consensus, but in 1984 he was severely criticized by his colleagues for his handling of a bitter dispute over staff tenure rules. Although Cavazos had no national reputation in education policy, he was appointed education secretary by **Ronald Reagan** in August 1988 in what was widely seen as an attempt by the Republicans to bolster electoral support in the key state of Texas and among the country's Hispanic population. **George Bush** kept him on when he took office in 1989, but he remained a low-profile cabinet member. He resigned in December 1990, after criticism of his effectiveness by fellow Republicans at a time when education was becoming the subject of national debate.

**CEREZO ARÉVALO, Mario Vinicio.** *Guatemala.* Former president. Born in 1942, Cerezo studied law at San Carlos University. He became involved in politics early, in support of the Guatemalan Christian Democratic Party (PDCG), rising to become its secretary-general in 1976. Elected president in 1986, he attempted to consolidate civilian rule after a period of military dictatorship. His popularity, however, was gradually tarnished by his accommodation with the military and his failure to deal with the country's economic problems; the PDCG candidate, **Alfonso Cabrera**, finished a poor third in the November 1990 presidential elections.

**CÉSAIRE, Aimé.** *France (Martinique).* Poet and left-wing politician. Born in 1913 and educated in Paris at the Ecole Normale Supérieure, Césaire has pursued a dual career in politics and literature, dominating the post-war scene in French Martinique as president of the Martinique Progressive Party, member of the National Assembly since 1946, mayor of Fort-de-France and left-wing figurehead. In literature and politics alike, he emerged as a distinguished critic of colonialism, helping to establish the concept of *négritude* as a positive, identifying value.

**CÉSAR AGUIRRE, Alfredo.** *Nicaragua.* Presidential adviser. Born in 1951, he studied engineering, before joining the Sandinistas. He became internal development minister and president of the central bank in the early Sandinista regime. Disillusioned by the move towards the left, he broke away to become a "contra" leader in Costa Rica, co-founding the Nicaraguan Resistance (RN) in 1987. He later became a close adviser to President **Violeta Chamorro**.

**ÇETİN, Hikmet.** *Turkey.* Opposition politician. A veteran politician, his career stretches back over 30 years to the now proscribed Republican People's Party (RPP). He was an obvious choice to succeed Deniz Baykal as secretary-general of the Social Democratic Populist Party (SHP) in September 1990. He had held this post in the RPP under **Bülent Ecevit**, but stood aloof from the group of ex-RPP members surrounding Baykal.

**CHADLI BENDJEDID.** *Algeria.* President. Born in 1929, he joined the resistance to French colonial rule in 1955. After independence he was military commander of the Oran region from 1963–79, being appointed acting chief of staff in 1978. With the backing of the army in the power struggle that followed President Houari Boumedienne's death in December 1978 he was elected secretary-general of the ruling National Liberation Front (FLN) and president in February 1979. Chadli has pursued gradual liberalization after the austerity of the Boumedienne years, especially since the rioting of October 1988. He has pushed ahead with economic reforms and the introduction of a multi-party system against fierce resistance from the old guard of the FLN.

**CHALFONT, Lord (Alun Jones).** *UK.* Politician, journalist and broadcaster. Born in 1919, he served in the army from 1940–61. Since then he has written and broadcast on foreign affairs and defence issues. He was a junior Labour foreign minister from 1964 – the year he was created a life peer – until 1970, but has since moved sharply to the right. He was appointed vice-chairman of the Independent Broadcasting Authority (IBA) in 1989, giving up that post at the end of 1990 when he became chairman of the new Radio Authority.

**CHALKER, Lynda.** *UK.* Minister for overseas development since 1989, and MP since 1974. Born in 1942, and on the liberal wing of the Conservative Party, Chalker is known for her tough stance on South Africa, and was seen as fighting a rearguard action against **Margaret Thatcher**'s enthusiasm for lifting sanctions. She faces the competing demands of aid to the third world and assistance to Eastern Europe. Many were surprised that she was not given a place in **John Major**'s first cabinet in 1990.

**CHAMLONG SRIMAUNG, Major-General.** *Thailand.* Mayor of Bangkok. Chamlong, born in 1935, was one of the leading members of the "Young Turk" group of officers which emerged as a powerful army faction in the 1970s. However, he distanced himself from the group before its abortive 1981 coup attempt and in 1985 retired from the army and was elected mayor of Bangkok. His austere traditional Buddhist lifestyle appealed to the citizens of Bangkok and he quickly emerged as one of the most popular of Thai politicians. He formed a political party, Righteous Force (Palang

Dharma), to contest the 1988 elections and won 14 seats; in early 1990 he was re-elected for another term as mayor.

**CHAMORRO, Violeta Barrios de.** *Nicaragua.* President. Born in 1929, in 1950 she married Pedro Joaquín Chamorro, editor of the influential family-owned newspaper, *La Prensa.* Her political life did not begin until after the assassination of her husband in January 1978, an action which helped contribute to the overthrow of the regime the following year. She joined the junta set up by the Sandinistas just before Somoza's departure, but left it in 1980. She then acquired ownership of *La Prensa*, making her son, Pedro Joaquín, the editor and confirming its position as the organ of conservative opposition to the Sandinistas until its closure by the government in 1986. Politics soon divided the family, with one son running the Sandinista paper, *Barricada*, one daughter a Sandinista diplomat, another taking over editorship of *La Prensa*, and Pedro Joaquín himself joining the "contras" in exile. In 1989 the popular appeal of the Chamorro name made her an ideal candidate as presidential nominee of the 14-party anti-Sandinista coalition, the National Opposition Union (UNO), although she belonged to none of the parties. She was elected president after decisively winning the February 1990 elections and immediately negotiated with **Daniel Ortega** for a smooth transfer of power. Strongly backed by the US administration, Chamorro needs US aid and investment to deal with Nicaragua's weakened economy.

**CHAN, Sir Julius.** *Papua New Guinea.* Former prime minister and leader of conservative People's Progress Party (PPP). Born in 1939 and educated in Australia, he first entered the House of Assembly in 1968, formed his business-oriented PPP with other north coast conservatives two years later, and exercised a powerful voice in government economic policy in coalition under **Michael Somare** until 1978. He then took the party into opposition, and became prime minister himself when Somare lost a vote of no confidence in March 1980. The electoral reverse of 1982 took him back into opposition until late 1985, when Somare's administration was again brought down by the loss of its majority and Chan began two years as deputy prime minister under **Paius Wingti**. A prominent advocate of privatization, he has been the opposition deputy leader and finance spokesman since **Rabbie Namaliu** took office in 1988.

**CHANDRA SHEKHAR, N.L.** *India.* Prime minister, defence, home affairs and information and broadcasting minister. An influential Janata Dal member of the Lok Sabha (lower house) before the successful manoeuvre by which he became premier in November 1990, he was born in 1927 in Ibrahimpatti, Uttar Pradesh. He was an early *habitué* of the "Young Turk" circle that gathered around Indira Gandhi after she became Congress leader. A member of the Rajya Sabha (upper house) from 1962–77, he was among the top Congress leadership in the early 1970s. Alarmed by Gandhi's increasingly authoritarian style during the emergency of 1975–77, he became increasingly critical, and was briefly imprisoned. On his release in 1977, he joined the opposition Janata Party and was elected to the Lok Sabha in 1977. After the break-up of the Janata coalition he became president of the rump Janata Party. He joined Janata Dal when the Janata Party was merged with it in 1988, but remained opposed to **V.P. Singh**'s leadership and led a band of party dissidents in forming a government with Congress support when Singh's government fell in November 1990.

**CHAOVALIT YONGCHAIYUT, General.** *Thailand.* Armed forces adviser. Born in 1932. A graduate of Chulachomklao Royal Military Academy, the bespectacled general succeeded **Arthit Kamlang-Ek** as army commander-in-chief in 1986. As a self-styled "soldier for democracy", Chaovalit's championing of a "peaceful revolution" in Thailand led to accusations that he had been influenced by communism. He resigned his post in March 1990 and immediately joined **Chartchai Chunhawan**'s cabinet as deputy prime minister and defence minister. After three months he resigned, a move seen by some as part of his plan to succeed Chartchai. In October he formed his own party, New Aspiration.

**CHAPUIS, Robert.** *France.* Minister of state for technical education. Born in 1933, he played a prominent role in student politics. After graduating he became a high school teacher. Like many of his political contemporaries, he moved from the Unified Socialist Party (PSU) to the Socialist Party (PS), specializing in research and technology and joining the executive in 1979. Since 1981 he has held a seat in the National Assembly and was appointed minister of state for technical education in 1988. He is a close supporter of **Michel Rocard**.

**CHARASSE, Michel.** *France.* Government minister. Born in 1941 and a student of law and politics at the Institut d'Etudes Politiques, he began a career in the civil service. In the 1970s he won local and regional elections as a Socialist Party (PS) candidate and sat in the Senate for most of the 1980s. In 1981–82, he acted as adviser to **François Mitterrand**, and was brought into **Michel Rocard**'s government as minister-delgate for the budget in 1988, with tax reform and economic austerity high on his agenda.

**CHARLES, Eugenia.** *Dominica.* Prime minister. Born in 1919 and educated in the UK, she practised law in the West Indies, becoming involved in politics relatively late in life. As a founder of the conservative Dominica Freedom Party she was actively involved in the opposition to the Patrick John government in the late 1970s and overwhelmingly won the 1980 elections. Her robust anti-communism has earned her the sobriquet of "Iron Lady of the Caribbean". In 1981 she survived two coup plots against her and in 1983 was instrumental in supporting the US intervention in Grenada. She narrowly won a third term in the May 1990 general elections.

**CHARLES, Prince.** *UK.* Heir to the throne. Born in 1948, he was educated at character-building Gordonstoun school in Scotland, which he is reported not to have enjoyed. This was followed by a period of schooling in Australia and three years as an undergraduate at Cambridge. Despite his nickname of "Action Man" because of his love of dangerous sports such as polo, he has often appeared to be something of a Hamlet prince – a thoughtful and restless man, confined within an institutional stereotype. He has used his long period as heir to the throne – his mother is thought unlikely to abdicate – to carve out a niche as an improbable but often effective voice of the people. He has defined his aim as being "to stir things up" and has been, at least by royal standards, remarkably outspoken on issues such as the environment, unemployment, inner-city decay and, perhaps most notoriously, architecture, where his advocacy of traditional classicism and "human scale" buildings has incurred the wrath of many leading modernist architects. He was invested as Prince of Wales (the traditional title for the heir to the British throne) in 1968, and married Lady Diana Spencer, the daughter of an English aristocrat, in 1981.

**CHARTCHAI CHUNHAWAN, General.** *Thailand.* Prime minister. Born in 1922,

Chartchai graduated from the prestigious Chulachomklao Royal Military Academy in the 1940s. He entered politics after the 1947 military coup led by his father Pin Chunhawan, who subsequently became deputy prime minister in Pibul Songkram's government. When Pibul was ousted in 1957 Chartchai left the country and spent 13 years abroad as a diplomat. He was elected as an MP in 1975 and that year was appointed foreign minister in Kukrit Pramoj's government. He became leader of the right-wing Thai Nation Party (Chart Thai – the "businessman's party") in 1986 and was appointed deputy prime minister in Prem Tinsulanonda's government the same year. A cigar-chomping extrovert with a penchant for disco dancing and fast motorbikes, Chartchai has confounded the critics who said his administration would last only three months after its formation in August 1988. His style of leadership has differed markedly from that of his laconic predecessor, Prem Tinsulanonda; aided by a hand-picked group of young advisers, including his son Kraisak, he has guided Thailand into an economic boom. At the same time he has initiated a remarkable foreign policy shift (much to the chagrin of former foreign minister Siddhi Savetsila), dropping Bangkok's traditional hardline approach to Cambodia and calling for the battlefields of Indo-China to be transformed into trading markets. At the end of 1990, however, after three cabinet reshuffles in four months, the latest involving a realignment of parties in the coalition government, Chartchai's position looked increasingly insecure.

**CHAVES GONZÁLEZ, Manuel.** *Spain.* Andalusia premier. Born in 1945 in Ceuta, a Spanish enclave on the North African coast, he gained a doctorate in law, joined the Spanish Socialist Workers' Party (PSOE) in 1968, and has been a member of its executive since 1981; he also sits on the executive of the socialist General Workers' Union (UGT). A deputy for Cádiz since 1977, he was appointed labour and social security minister in 1986. Following elections in Andalusia in 1990 he became head of the regional government.

**CHÁVEZ MENA, Fidel Angel.** *El Salvador.* Opposition politician. A lawyer by profession and a member of the Christian Democratic Party (PDC), Chávez Mena was appointed foreign affairs minister by the military-civilian junta in 1980. He was appointed planning minister in the José Napoleón Duarte government, a post he held until 1988 when he became the PDC's presidential candidate.

**CHEN JIN HUA**. *China*. Minister in charge of the State Commission for Restructuring the Economy. A long-standing Chinese Communist Party activist, he was vice-mayor of Shanghai and also deputy party secretary for the city. He subsequently became head of the China National Petrochemical Corporation. In September 1990, he succeeded **Li Peng** as minister in charge of the state commission. Formed in 1982, the State Commission for Restructuring the Economy had initially played an important role in China's economic reform programme, but had lost much of its authority after the reformists were ousted from power following the Tiananmen massacre of June 1989.

**CHEN JUNSHENG**. *China*. State counsellor. Born in 1927, Chen rose through the party to hold top posts in Heilongjiang, and joined the party Central Committee in 1987. He became secretary-general of the State Council in 1985, and was elevated to the rank of state counsellor in a rejuvenation drive in April 1988.

**CHEN XITONG**. *China*. Mayor of Beijing. Born in 1930, Chen is a hardline ally of **Li Peng** and presided over the implementation of martial law in the capital in May 1989. He has held top party posts in Beijing since 1981, becoming mayor concurrently in 1983. He joined the Central Committee in 1987 and became a state counsellor the following year as part of a rejuvenation drive, taking charge of liaison between Beijing and the central government.

**CHEN YUN**. *China*. Senior conservative leader. Born in 1905 and a Chinese Communist Party member from the age of 20, he is a veteran of the 1934–35 Long March and of three decades in government (as deputy premier continuously from 1949–75 and again from 1978–80). He held a Politburo post until 1987, then "retired upstairs" to become chairman of the Central Advisory Commission. His hardline influence remained much in evidence as the party's internal economic policy debate continued in late 1990.

**CHENEY, Richard (Dick)**. *USA*. Secretary of defence. A native of Wyoming, Cheney is a conservative pragmatist. Born in 1941, he was educated at the University of Wyoming and worked as a financial consultant before becoming Gerald Ford's White House chief of staff in 1974. During his time in the Ford administration Cheney established close ties with **James Baker** and **Brent Scowcroft**, with

whom he was later to serve under **George Bush**. Unlike most others who have held the job, Cheney made few enemies and, after leaving the post in 1976, he eschewed the opportunity to become a Washington lobbyist. He returned to Wyoming and ran for the state's only seat in the House of Representatives. Despite suffering a minor heart attack (the first of three), he was elected in 1978 and immediately began to make his mark as one of the most able Republican legislators of his generation. He became chairman of the Republican policy committee in 1981, progressed to Republican Conference chairman in 1987, served on the House intelligence committee (where he was a leading defender of the White House during the Iran-Contra hearings) and became Republican whip in 1989. His promising congressional career – he made no secret of his ambition to become speaker of the House – was disrupted in 1989 when Bush appointed him as defence secretary after the Senate had rejected Bush's first choice, John Tower. Although quiet and restrained in style, Cheney himself proved an able administrator, capable of responding to policy changes springing from the events in the Soviet Union and Eastern Europe. He responded calmly to calls for a radical reduction in US defence expenditure, suggesting that he would generally accept significant cuts in his department where appropriate. From August 1990 the Gulf crisis dominated his agenda and raised his profile worldwide. He won praise for the military response, and credit for preserving his authority and even his sense of humour under pressure. Cheney's wife, Lynne, chairs the National Endowment for the Humanities. Together they wrote *Kings of the Hill: Power and Personality in the House of Representatives*, a profile of House leaders.

**CHÉRÈQUE, Jacques**. *France*. Government minister. Born in 1928, he was a blue-collar worker in the steel industry and joined the trade union movement in 1959, becoming president of the Lorraine steelworkers in 1965. In 1979 he was elected as deputy general secretary of the French Democratic Confederation of Labour (CFDT), France's second largest union, a post he held until 1984. Subsequently, he became prefect for industrial and regional development and, in 1988, was appointed minister-delegate with responsibility for regional planning and redeployment.

**CHEVÈNEMENT, Jean-Pierre**. *France*. Defence minister. Born in 1939, he graduated in law and politics at the Institut d'Etudes Politiques, and economics and administration from the Ecole Nationale d'Administration. Initial work as a commercial adviser was followed by affiliation to the old socialist party (SFIO) and a key role from 1969 onwards in its successor, the Socialist Party (PS), where he carved out his reputation on the left of the party as programme formulator, author and *contestataire* guru. Elected to the executive in 1971 and a member of parliament since 1973, he held several ministerial portfolios in the 1980s, always controversially. Minister of state for research, technology and industry in 1981–84, then education until 1986, he was appointed defence minister in 1988. He remains nostalgic for the days of the government of left-wing unity, and critical of social democracy and Europeanism within the PS.

**CHEYSSON, Claude**. *France*. Former member of the European Commission. Born in 1920, he was decorated after the war for his resistance activities, and graduated through the prestigious Ecole Polytechnique and Ecole Nationale d'Administration. In 1954 he was *chef de cabinet* for the Socialist prime minister Pierre Mendès France. Subsequently, he occupied technical, commercial and political posts connected with developing countries, and went to Indonesia in 1966 for a three-year stint as French ambassador. As a member of the European Commission from 1973–81, he again concerned himself with development issues and third world co-operation, helping to negotiate the Lomé Convention, which broadened the structure of the EC's relations with developing countries, and earning himself a clear "third-worlder" image, sometimes controversially left-wing. Temporarily moving from the European to the national stage, he was foreign minister from 1981–84, but then went back to Brussels as commissioner with special responsibility for Mediterranean policy and North–South relations. He was elected to the European Parliament in 1989, on the Socialist Party (PS) list. Acting as François Mitterrand's personal representative, Cheysson had talks in Tunis with the Palestine Liberation Organization at the outbreak of the Gulf crisis in August 1990. In the ensuing months he made clear his opposition to Western military intervention in the Gulf crisis, and was reported to have met Iraq's foreign minister **Tariq Aziz** in Amman in October.

**CHIDZERO, Bernard**. *Zimbabwe*. Senior minister of finance, economic planning and development. Born in 1927, he has a doctorate in political science and is a technocrat of formidable intellect and international repute. From 1960–80 he was an international civil servant, ultimately becoming secretary-general of the UN Conference on Trade and Development (Unctad). Returning to Zimbabwe at independence he was appointed to his present post in 1981, initiating the cautious policies that have gained the country the reputation of having one of Africa's best-run economies. Chidzero's weakness has been his lack of a political base; he was not elected to parliament until 1985. Only after his appointment in January 1988 as senior minister and supremo of all economic ministries did he have the power to persuade the cabinet to back the more expansionary policies that he finally unveiled in 1990. Chidzero retains his high international profile: since 1986 he has been chairman of the IMF/World Bank development committee and since 1987 president of Unctad VII. Within the next five years he is expected to respond to efforts to head-hunt him for a top-level post, fulfilling his ambition to return to the international arena full-time.

**CHIEPE, Gaositwe Keagakwa Tibe**. *Botswana*. Foreign minister. One of the government's most able members, she is also one of the few woman African politicians to have held senior ministerial rank. She moved from an early career in education into the diplomatic service, before joining the government as commerce and industry minister in 1974. In 1977 she took over the mines and water resources ministry, where she was responsible for negotiating a highly favourable agreement with South Africa's De Beers for the exploitation of Botswana's vast diamond reserves: the key to its subsequent rapid economic growth. In 1984 she was moved to her present post, taking on the task of dealing with South Africa at a time when it was putting heavy economic, political and military pressure on Botswana.

**CHIKANE, Frank**. *South Africa*. South African Council of Churches general secretary. Born in 1951, he was ordained a minister in 1980 and became a leading church figure in his native Soweto; he has been general secretary since 1987 of the South African Council of Churches. With his brother Iscor in the African National Congress (ANC) security apparatus, and his own prominence in the Mass Democratic Movement, he forms an important bridge between the ANC and anti-apartheid clerics. He is likely to be one arbiter of the difficult decisions for the country's churches, on how much critical distance to put between themselves and the ANC in negotiating South Africa's political future.

**CHILES, Lawton**. *USA*. Democratic governor of Florida. Born in 1930, he practised law after a tour of duty in Korea, and entered the state legislature in 1958, before election to the Senate in 1971. A popular and gentle-mannered politician, he conducted an unconventional campaign for the governorship in 1990, emphasizing his wish to listen to his electorate and relying on small campaign contributions. He defeated the abrasive Republican incumbent **Bob Martinez**, who had become best known for his hardline enthusiasm for capital punishment and opposition to abortion.

**CHIPANDE, Lieutenant-General Alberto Joaquim**. *Mozambique*. Defence minister. A veteran of the independence struggle against the Portuguese, he has been defence minister since independence in 1975. His record in the war against the Mozambique National Resistance (Renamo) has not been without criticism, however; in 1983 President Samora Machel took over active leadership of the war effort and appointed Chipande governor of Cabo Delgado province. Chipande assumed full responsibility for his portfolio again in 1986.

**CHIRAC, Jacques**. *France*. Gaullist leader. Born in 1932, he was educated at France's foremost political and civil service institutions, the Institut d'Etudes Politiques and Ecole Nationale d'Administration. Throughout the 1960s and 1970s he held a number of political offices, initially as adviser to prime minister Georges Pompidou, then as a local councillor and member of parliament, representing the Corrèze. Gaining ministerial experience with brief spells at agriculture (1972–74) and the interior (1974), he supported **Valéry Giscard d'Estaing**'s successful presidential bid in 1974, and was rewarded with the appointment as Giscard's first prime minister. The relationship between the two men proved stormy, and after two years in office Chirac resigned dramatically, complaining that Giscard was too overbearing – in part a reflection of his own temperament. He presided over the creation of a revamped Gaullist party apparatus, the Rally for the Republic (RPR), and was elected in 1977 as mayor of Paris, a post with which he has identified himself powerfully in the public mind on account of various architectural innovations and a clean-up policy under the slogan *Propreté de Paris*. Since 1976,

the rivalry between Chirac and Giscard for leadership of the French right has seen their relationship turn intermittently sweet and sour. Unsuccessful as a right-wing candidate in two presidential elections (1981 and 1988), his hour of triumph came in 1986 when the RPR's success in assembly elections compelled Socialist president **François Mitterrand** to appoint him prime minister. The period of "cohabitation" worked more smoothly than some had predicted, but in 1988 the electorate gave the left back its legislative majority. This defeat put the centre–right and right in some disarray, and Chirac's political future looked uncertain. However, by mid-1990 he had come around to the idea of a reconstituted right-wing confederation, the Union for France (UPF), in an attempt to restore unity and credibility for a fresh challenge to the socialists. As the Gulf crisis developed during late 1990, Chirac showed himself to be less than enthusiastic about French military involvement, and objected in particular to the idea of US-led intervention.

**CHISSANO, Joaquim Alberto**. *Mozambique*. President. A skilled diplomat and able successor to the charismatic Samora Machel, Chissano, born in 1930, was a founder member of the Front for the Liberation of Mozambique (Frelimo) and acted as its head of security during the independence war. From independence in 1975 until 1986 he served as foreign minister and played a key role in winning international support, notably that of the USA, for Frelimo in its fight against the South African-backed Mozambique National Resistance (Renamo) rebel movement. In November 1986 he was elected president by the party's central committee, following the death of Machel in an air crash in South Africa. Chissano has since pursued the economic restructuring begun by Machel and initiated major political reforms, including the abandonment of the single-party system, but his most notable achievement is likely to be a negotiated end to the civil war with Renamo.

**CHITANAVA, Nodar**. *USSR*. Former prime minister of Georgia. Born in 1934 and formerly a senior Communist Party official, he was appointed premier as part of the major leadership upheaval in Georgia that followed the April 1989 massacre of peaceful demonstrators by Soviet troops on the streets of Tbilisi. He was replaced by Tengiz Signa following the nationalist victory in the November 1990 Supreme Soviet election.

**CHOI HO JOONG.** *South Korea.* Second deputy prime minister. Born in 1930, he was a career diplomat serving in the Middle East and Western Europe before joining the trade and industry ministry in 1984. He returned to the foreign ministry a year later and became minister in 1988. In December 1990 he was elevated to the new post of second deputy prime minister, responsible for contacts with North Korea.

**CHRÉTIEN, Jean.** *Canada.* Leader of the Liberal Party of Canada. The son of a mill worker from Shawinigan, Quebec, he was born in 1934 and studied at Laval University. He practised law from 1958, and was director of the bar of Trois-Rivières in 1962–63 before being elected to the House of Commons for the Liberals in 1963. Known widely as "the little guy from Shawinigan" ("*le petit gars de Shawinigan*"), Chrétien is Canada's definitive populist politician. A long-time aspirant to Canada's Liberal Party leadership, he worked his way through various ministerial portfolios and was appointed justice minister and attorney-general in 1980, where he was responsible for the appointment of the first woman supreme-court judge. His first attempt to win the party leadership failed in 1984, and he resigned from the House of Commons in 1986, but remained active in politics and wrote a best-selling book *Straight from the Heart*. In June 1990 Chrétien accomplished his goal of winning the Liberal leadership.

**CHRISTOPHERSEN, Henning.** *Denmark.* European Commission vice-president and commissioner for economic and financial affairs. Born in 1939, he studied economics and then worked at the Danish small-industries federation and as a journalist. Elected to parliament for the Liberals (Venstre) in 1971, he became party leader in 1978 and was briefly foreign minister in 1978–79. In 1985 he was appointed an EC commissioner, responsible for the budget; since 1989 he has been responsible for economic and financial affairs. Once a leading figure on the Commission, he has been increasingly overshadowed by **Jacques Delors**.

**CHRZANOWSKI, Wiesław.** *Poland.* Chairman of the Christian National Union. A veteran Catholic activist, he was imprisoned from 1948–51, having been charged with "attempting to overthrow the system". He was an adviser to Solidarity in 1980–81, and was elected to his present post at the Christian National Union's founding congress in October 1989. Since then the Christian National Union

has become probably the most popular of the emerging Christian Democratic parties, outstripping the rival Christian Democratic Labour Party headed by **Władysław Siła-Nowicki**.

**CHUNG YUNG EUY.** *South Korea.* Finance minister. Born in 1937, he supports expansionist economic measures and headed the Securities Supervisory Board until 1990 when he rose from vice-minister to minister of finance.

**CHURKIN, Vitaly.** *USSR.* Head of information at the foreign ministry and assistant to the foreign minister. Brought in to replace **Gennady Gerasimov** in November 1990 at the age of 38, Churkin was a graduate of the Moscow State Institute of International Relations, had worked in the foreign ministry until 1982 and then spent five years at the Soviet embassy in Washington. He was in the Communist Party of the Soviet Union international affairs department from April 1987 to January 1989 and was then transferred to become adviser to then foreign minister **Eduard Shevardnadze**.

**CIAMPI, Carlo Azeglio.** *Italy.* Central bank governor. Born in 1920 in Livorno, he got a university degree in literature before joining the army in 1941, serving until 1944. After gaining a second degree in law, he joined Banca d'Italia, the central bank, in 1946. Governor of the bank since 1979, he has been a strong defender of its autonomy and a frequent critic of government policies; pressure from Ciampi led to the exposure of the Banco Ambrosiano scandal in 1982. Ciampi and his team have provided an element of consistency in financial policies as governments and ministers come and go. With a sharpness of mind that belies his age, Ciampi shows no inclination to retire and is expected by many to remain in office at least until the bank's centenary in 1993.

**CIENFUEGOS GORRIARÁN, Osmany.** *Cuba.* Vice-president. The elder brother of revolutionary leader Camilo Cienfuegos, he was an active communist in Mexican exile before the revolution. A senior member of the Cuban Communist Party, Cienfuegos has been a vice-president of the Council of State and the Council of Ministers since 1976, as well as secretary of the latter. He was widely regarded as the prime initiator of the Cuban involvement in Angola.

**CIMOSZEWICZ, Włodzimierz.** *Poland.* Chairman of the left-wing parliamentary caucus. A former member of the communist Polish United Workers' Party, he was the left's candidate in the presidential election in

November 1990, finishing fourth with just over 9% of the vote.

**CIRINO POMICINO, Paolo.** *Italy.* Christian Democrat party (DC) politician. Born in 1939 in Naples, he qualified in medicine and surgery, with specialization in neuropsychiatry. He entered the Chamber of Deputies in 1976, and attained cabinet rank as minister without portfolio responsible for public administration in April 1988. In July 1989 he was appointed budget minister. Verbally acid and very adroit, of the three ministers with responsibility for financial matters, he is the closest to prime minister **Giulio Andreotti**.

**CLAES, Willy.** *Belgium.* Deputy prime minister, economics minister. Born in 1938 and elected to parliament for the Flemish Socialist Party (SP) in 1968, he has become one of the country's most influential politicians, particularly as a conciliator between the Flemish and Walloon communities and (as a very pragmatic socialist) between the Christian Democratic and Socialist parties. In the ministerial musical chairs typical of Belgian politics he was twice education minister (1972–73 and 1988–89) and economics minister (1973–74, 1977–82). As *informateur* (a person appointed by the king to investigate coalition options) in 1988 he helped in the formation of a centre–left government in which he served as deputy prime minister and as economics minister for a third time.

**CLARK, Helen.** *New Zealand.* Former deputy prime minister and leading Labour Party left-winger. Born in 1950, and a former university teacher with a strongly academic image, she entered parliament in 1981 and was successively housing and conservation minister, and then health minister, in the David Lange and Geoffrey Palmer cabinets from 1987–90. She proved a powerful voice insisting on the replacement of Palmer as party leader by **Mike Moore**, in an unsuccessful attempt to revive the party's flagging fortunes in the weeks prior to the October 1990 general election.

**CLARK, Joseph (Joe).** *Canada.* Secretary of state for external affairs. Born in 1939 in High River, Alberta, he was educated at the University of Alberta and Dalhousie University. He was a journalist and lecturer at the University of Alberta before standing unsuccessfully for Alberta's legislative assembly in 1967. Clark was elected to the House of Commons for the Progressive Conservative Party of Canada in 1972 and won the party leadership in 1976, despite being considered a long shot.

Largely unknown to many Canadians, he was branded by the media as "Joe Who?". Clark went on to become Canada's youngest prime minister, forming a minority government in 1979. His first budget was defeated in the House of Commons on a vote of no-confidence, and in the 1980 election the Conservatives were defeated by the Liberals under the leadership of Pierre Trudeau. In 1983 Clark resigned as Conservative leader, and was succeeded by **Brian Mulroney**, who appointed him secretary of state for external affairs in 1984.

**CLARKE, Kenneth.** *UK.* Secretary of state for education since 1990, and MP since 1970. Born in 1940 to a family of miners, Clarke was president of the Cambridge University Union before being called to the Bar. Under **Margaret Thatcher** he held junior posts at transport and health; as employment minister until 1987 he took some credit for reducing unemployment, and proposed innovative programmes as inner cities minister in 1988. As health minister, this generally genial man had problems persuading the public that the National Health Service (NHS) reforms would lead to a more flexible and efficient service. Health service professionals were largely antagonistic, while Labour claimed the reform package was a strategy to privatize the health service. Having set in motion the reorganization of this very sensitive part of the welfare state, Clarke was moved to education by **John Major** – another area of acute public concern in the throes of great changes.

**CLARKE, Robert.** *USA.* Comptroller of the currency. Born in Tulsa, Oklahoma, in 1942, he graduated from Harvard Law School in 1966. He has been a prominent fund-raiser in Texas and is an old friend of **James Baker**. He was named comptroller by **Ronald Reagan** in 1985 and was asked to remain in the post by **George Bush** in 1988. Identified as a supporter of bank deregulation, he has seen the pendulum swing back towards stricter supervision in the wake of big bank losses on real estate lending, and became regarded by some as an "over-zealous" regulator. In mid-1990, however, he joined **Alan Greenspan** in opposing stricter rules to stifle credit for qualified borrowers.

**CLAUDE, Sylvio.** *Haiti.* Party leader. A Protestant pastor, he became actively involved in opposition to the regime of Jean-Claude Duvalier in the 1970s and 1980s, forming the Haitian Christian Democratic Party (PDCH) in 1978. Harrassed by the authorities, he eventually went into hiding in 1984. After the fall of Jean-

Claude Duvalier in 1986 he re-emerged to campaign for the presidency. His impassioned preaching has won him a strong following among the urban poor.

**CLINTON, Bill.** *USA.* Democratic governor of Arkansas. Born in 1946, he was a lawyer and law professor, before becoming state attorney-general in 1976 and before being elected the nation's youngest governor in 1978. Defeated in his 1980 re-election bid, he bounced back to regain office in 1983. In 1986 a *Newsweek* poll rated him one of the five best governors. He may seek national office in the future, but refused to run in the 1988 primaries, citing family obligations. However, his reputation was tarnished by his embarrassingly long speech at the 1988 Democratic Convention. His principal achievements as governor include educational improvements, economic development, criminal justice reform and equal opportunity programmes.

**COETSEE, H.J. (Hendrik Jacobus).** *South Africa.* Justice minister. Born in 1931, a barrister and since 1968 an MP, he has led the National Party in his native Orange Free State since 1985. A close adviser to P.W. Botha on security and intelligence issues, "Kobie" Coetsee won the confidence of the military in his first ministerial job, as deputy defence and national security minister from 1978–80, before moving to the justice portfolio. Suggested by some as a successor to President Botha, with "securocrat" credentials but more personable than the defence minister, **Magnus Malan**, he was also the man who initiated the dialogue with **Nelson Mandela** in Pollsmoor prison in 1987. Under **F. W. de Klerk** he has been in the innermost government circle. He chairs the ministers' council in the House of Assembly (white parliament) and ranks, with **Gerrit Viljoen**, as one of the president's closest colleagues. He is extremely publicity-shy and seldom gives interviews.

**COHEN, Herman.** *USA.* Assistant secretary of state for African affairs. Cohen had been senior director for African affairs on the National Security Council staff at the White House before being appointed assistant secretary of state in 1989 and had held several State Department positions before that.

**COJUANGCO, Eduardo (Danding).** *Philippines.* Businessman and politician. Former governor of Tarlac province, where his family are sugar-growers, and the estranged second cousin of **Cory Aquino**, he was reportedly at one time one of the two wealthiest men in the Philippines. A prominent businessman and close associate of Ferdinand Marcos, he fled the country with the deposed president in 1986 but returned in November 1989. Although the government has charged him with misuse of public funds, he is widely expected to stand as a presidential candidate in the 1992 elections.

**COLLINS, Gerard.** *Ireland.* Foreign minister. Born in 1938, he worked as a teacher until his election to parliament for Fianna Fáil in 1967, winning a by-election caused by the death of his father. He was soon appointed to ministerial office, holding the portfolios of justice (1977–81, 1987–89) and foreign affairs (1982 and from 1989).

**COLLOR DE MELLO, Fernando.** *Brazil.* President. Born in 1950 into a political family (his father had been a senator and governor of Alagoas state), Collor studied economics at Brasilia University. His career in politics began in 1979 when he was elected mayor of Maceió. He became federal deputy for Alagoas in 1982 and state governor in 1986. After leaving the Brazilian Democratic Movement (PMDB) in protest at its support for José Sarney's government, he formed the National Renovation Party to support his presidential ambitions. His campaign rapidly gained momentum, helped by his use of advertising on the family-owned television network, itself part of the powerful Globo group. He was able to portray himself as a newcomer, untainted by associations with the past, and committed to tackling corruption and reforming the economy. His opponents attacked him as an opportunist playboy. Support from the middle classes enabled him to defeat **"Lula" da Silva** in the presidential elections, but he lacks political party backing within Congress. Collor will have to rely on his presidential powers if he is to force through his policies without forming a consensus on how to deal with Brazil's economic problems. Within 24 hours of taking office, he announced a radical plan for dealing with inflation, but by late 1990 his economic policies were causing alarm in many sectors of society.

**COMPAORÉ, Captain Blaise.** *Burkina Faso.* President. The former right-hand man of the charismatic Captain Thomas Sankara and one of the group of young officers who brought him to power in 1983, Compaoré headed the October 1987 coup in which Sankara was murdered. His regime has abandoned the more radical elements of Sankara's policies, practising what it calls "state capitalism". His Popular Front government is riven by factionalism, demonstrated most dramatically by the alleged coup attempt of September 1989, after which the two remaining key figures from the Sankara regime were executed.

**COMPTON, John.** *St Lucia.* Prime minister. Born in 1926 on the island of Canouan in the Grenadines, he was educated at the London School of Economics and trained as a barrister. He practised law in St Lucia before entering politics in 1954. In 1961 he left the St Lucia Labour Party (SLP) to form his own party (later the United Workers' Party), winning elections in 1964. Campaigning for greater autonomy from the UK, he became the island's first prime minister on independence in February 1979. He lost the election held soon afterwards, but returned to power in 1982. A conservative, Compton has concentrated on St Lucia's economic development and on regional co-operation; he also holds the finance, home affairs, planning and development portfolios.

**CONABLE, Barber B.** *USA.* World Bank president. Born in 1922, he trained and practised as a lawyer until his election for the Republicans to the House of Representatives in 1964. During his 20 years there he became an influential member of the ways and means committee, and gained a reputation for financial prudence verging on the austere. He retired from Congress in 1985 and worked briefly as a senior fellow at the American Enterprise Institute and as a professor of government at Rochester University before being unexpectedly nominated by **Ronald Reagan** for the senior World Bank post, traditionally held by an American. He carried out a major reorganization of the bank in 1987. His tenure has coincided with pressure for the bank to adopt a more sensitive approach to lending policy in the third world, where the social and environmental impact of many of its projects had been increasingly criticized.

**CONDE GUTIÉRREZ DEL ALAMO, Rosa.** *Spain.* Government spokeswoman. Born in 1947, she studied politics and economics. After working in public administration and as director of the sociological research centre, she became government spokeswoman in July 1988, although she is not a Spanish Socialist Workers' Party (PSOE) member.

**CONNELL, Desmond.** *Ireland.* Roman Catholic archbishop of Dublin and primate of Ireland. Born in 1925, he was ordained a priest in 1951. He lectured in metaphysics at University College Dublin from 1953–88, becoming a professor in 1972 and dean of the faculty of philosophy and sociology in 1983. He was appointed archbishop in 1988.

**CONTÉ, General Lansana.** *Guinea.* President. Conté led the military junta in a successful coup only days after the death of Guinea's first president, Ahmed Sekou Touré, in April 1984. Conté's first few years in power were insecure, marked by an unsuccessful coup attempt by his former prime minister Colonel Diarra Traoré in 1985 and by frequent reshuffles of the ruling Military Committee for National Recovery (CMRN) designed to neutralize potential rivals. By 1989, however, he felt sufficiently secure to publish a timetable for a return to constitutional rule, including a five-year transition to (two-party) democracy.

**CONTE, Silvio.** *USA.* Republican congressman from Massachusetts. Born in 1921, he practised law before election to the House of Representatives in 1958. His voting record, which strongly reflects constituent interests, places him among the small band of liberal Republicans and makes him a natural bridge-builder between the parties in Congress. Conte is known for his humour and wit.

**CONYERS, John, Jr.** *USA.* Democratic congressman from Michigan. Born in 1929, he was a lawyer and civil rights organizer before becoming one of the few black members of the House of Representatives after his election in 1964. Although a persistent rebel against congressional deal-making and compromises, his committee responsibilities, particularly as government operations committee chairman, led to a change of style in the late 1980s. Nevertheless, he remains loyal to his roots and is a strong backer of **Jesse Jackson**'s presidential aspirations.

**COOK, Robin.** *UK.* Labour politician. Born in 1946, he studied English literature and worked in adult education until 1974, when he was elected to parliament as member for Edinburgh Central. He first rose to wider prominence as the informal manager for **Neil Kinnock**'s leadership election campaign in 1983. He became shadow spokesman on European affairs in 1983 and has since made his mark above all as the party's campaign co-ordinator and shadow health secretary, leading an often effective attack on the government's attempts to reform the organization of the national health service. On political reform he is a supporter of proportional representation.

**COORE, David.** *Jamaica.* Foreign minister. Born in 1926, he trained as a barrister. He was deputy prime minister and finance minister from 1972–78, when he resigned to join the Inter-American Development Bank. He was appointed a senator and foreign minister on the People's National Party's return to power in 1989.

**COPOSU, Corneliu.** *Romania.* President of the Christian Democratic National Peasants' Party. He was formerly leader of the National Peasants' Party, one of the historic parties of pre-war Romania, which re-established itself in December 1989 after Nicolae Ceauşescu's downfall. Prior to the May 1990 elections his party merged with the Christian Democratic Party to form the Christian Democratic National Peasants' Party, whose presidential candidate **Ion Ratiu** came a poor third.

**CORCUERA CUESTA, José Luis.** *Spain.* Interior minister. Born in 1945 and trained as an electrician, he was appointed interior minister in 1988, the first blue-collar worker to become a minister since the civil war. He had joined the Spanish Socialist Workers' Party (PSOE) before it was legalized, in 1973, playing an important trade union role in organizing the metal workers within the General Workers' Union (UGT) confederation. He sat on the UGT executive from 1980–85.

**CORNEA, Doina.** *Romania.* Dissident intellectual. Her long-time opposition to the communist regime of Nicolae Ceauşescu led to the loss of her job as a lecturer in French at the University of Cluj and a period of harassment and house arrest. Having initially supported the 1989 revolution and the National Salvation Front, she resigned from the front in January 1990 after it broke its earlier pledge not to contest parliamentary elections.

**CORREA DÍAZ, Enrique.** *Chile.* Secretary-general of the government. Born in 1946 and a member of the Socialist Party (PSCh), he was appointed to his influential position in **Patricio Aylwin**'s cabinet at the beginning of 1990, as the new civilian regime prepared to take over the reins of government.

**COSSÉ, Pierre-Yves.** *France.* Inspector-general of finance. Born in 1934 and a graduate of the Institut d'Etudes Politiques and of the Ecole Nationale d'Administration. He became an inspector of finance in 1964, subsequently advising various state agencies. In 1981, he was attached to the staff of economy and finance minister **Jacques Delors** and in 1982 appointed deputy-director of Banque Nationale de Paris

(BNP). Since 1986, he has been inspector-general of finance.

**COSSIGA, Francesco.** *Italy.* President. Born in Sardinia in 1928, he trained as a lawyer and became a professor of constitutional law. He joined the Christian Democrat party (DC) in 1945, entering parliament in 1958. His friend and fellow Sardinian, prime minister Aldo Moro, brought him into government as defence under-secretary in 1966. Promoted to public administration minister in 1974, he moved to the interior ministry in February 1976, and retained the post when **Giulio Andreotti** became prime minister that July. As interior minister, he was involved in the decision not to negotiate with Moro's Red Brigades kidnappers in 1978. Cossiga resigned after Moro's murder, taking full responsibility for the affair and describing himself as "politically dead". Nevertheless, in 1979, after parliament had rejected several other DC candidates, President Sandro Pertini asked Cossiga to form a government. He served as prime minister until 1980, surviving an attempt to impeach him by Communist deputies over accusations that he had assisted the flight from justice of Marco Donat-Cattin, a wanted terrorist and son of Cossiga's friend **Carlo Donat-Cattin**. The government eventually fell after being defeated on economic reform legislation. Cossiga was elected as a senator and as Senate president in 1983 and became president of the republic in July 1985 – the first president to be elected on the first ballot, even receiving the support of the Communist Party. Cossiga has a reputation for honesty and integrity but in late 1990 he was asked to explain to a parliamentary committee his role as under-secretary for defence in the 1960s, in the light of the "Gladio affair" – revelations about alleged secret anti-communist units set up with Nato involvement. Initially a low-profile president, in contrast to his extrovert predecessor Pertini, he has of late made a series of controversial statements on political issues. Cossiga has said he will not stand again when his present term expires in July 1992.

**COTTI, Flavio.** *Switzerland.* Interior minister. Born in 1939, an Italian-speaker from Tessin, and graduate in law, he has built a successful career in the Christian Democratic People's Party (CVP), the country's leading conservative party. In 1984 he was elected party president. His appointment as interior minister two years later marked his emergence as the leading political figure from the Italian-speaking community. In

1990, under the principle of rotating election of Switzerland's heads of state, he held the office of vice-president.

**COURTER, Jim.** *USA.* Former Republican congressman from New Jersey. Born in 1941, he is a lawyer and was elected to the House of Representatives in 1978, holding his seat until 1990. During the Reagan and Bush administrations, he was a leading Republican spokesman on defence and foreign policy. In 1989 he ran unsuccessfully for governor, failing in part because of his anti-abortion views, but not abandoning his ambition to win this office.

**COVAS, Mario.** *Brazil.* Brazilian Social Democratic Movement (PSDB) leader. Covas was leader of the Brazilian Democratic Movement (PMDB) in the Chamber of Deputies when his political rights were suspended in 1969. He was the party's leader in the constituent assembly and was subsequently elected a senator. In 1988 he formed the PSDB from PMDB dissidents and was its presidential candidate in 1989. He ran for the important governorship of São Paulo in November 1990, but was defeated by Luis Antonio Fleury of the PMDB.

**CRANSTON, Alan.** *USA.* Democratic senator from California. Born in 1914, he was successively a foreign correspondent and realtor before becoming state controller in 1959 and US senator in 1966. In 1977 he became Democratic whip, the number two Senate leadership post. Liberal on civil rights, the environment and welfare, he also zealously protects Californian business interests. On foreign policy, his passions are arms control and aid to Israel. A futile bid for the 1984 presidential nomination extinguished his White House ambitions. He is one of the senators – the "Keating Five" – who came under an ethics cloud connected with the savings and loan debacle. His announcement that he had cancer and would not seek re-election in 1992 has shaken up California politics.

**CRAXI, Bettino.** *Italy.* Italian Socialist Party (PSI) leader. Born in 1934 in Milan, he became a political journalist and in 1968 was elected to the Chamber of Deputies, becoming deputy secretary of the PSI in 1970. Elected as PSI secretary-general in July 1976, Craxi set about healing the splits that had severely weakened the party, and has proved a dynamic party leader. An improved PSI performance in the general elections of June 1983 brought him the chance to form a five-party coalition government. This was to prove the most durable of the post-war period, lasting until June 1986 and surviving the crisis over the hijack of the cruise ship Achille Lauro in October 1985, when defence minister **Giovanni Spadolini** and his fellow Republicans threatened to withdraw and when relations became strained with the USA. A second Craxi administration lasted until 1987, and at the general election in June 1987 his party improved its share of the vote significantly. Craxi has not held a ministerial post since March 1987, but remains an extremely powerful voice. His political relationships are influenced by his intense rivalry with the leading Christian Democrat party (DC) politician **Ciriaco De Mita**, and by his ambition to construct a viable alternative to the DC. His efforts to reconcile differences between the PSI, which he has successfully modernized, and the Italian Democratic Socialist Party (PSDI) have not borne fruit, however, and on the question of accommodation with the Communist Party (PCI) his stance remains ambivalent, coloured by his antipathy towards PCI leader **Achille Occhetto**. Decisive and ambitious, he is accused by his critics of being a socialist in name only. Craxi is a close friend of the powerful media tycoon Silvio Berlusconi. In 1990 he was appointed by UN secretary-general **Javier Pérez de Cuéllar** as his personal representative for third-world debt and development problems; his report, "External debt crisis and development", was published in October 1990.

**CRESSON, Edith.** *France.* Socialist politician. Born in 1934, she gained a doctorate in demography before becoming an adviser to private industry. In the 1970s, she rose through the Socialist Party (PS), becoming a national secretary (for youth), executive member, mayor and member of the European Parliament. In the 1980s, she held a series of ministerial posts: agriculture (1981–83), foreign trade and tourism (1983–84), industrial relocation and foreign trade (1984–86) and European affairs (1988–90). A member of parliament since 1986, she was one of the most conspicuously successful women politicians of the 1980s, but in October 1990 she resigned her government post to return, somewhat disillusioned, to private industry.

**CRISTIANI BURKHARD, Alfredo.** *El Salvador.* President. Born in 1947 into a land-owning family, Cristiani studied business administration at Georgetown University, USA. He became head of the family coffee-growing business and president of the coffee exporters' association. He joined the right-wing Nationalist Republican Alliance (Arena) in 1984 and was elected director of its national executive. He became presidential candidate for the 1988 election after the party's leader, **Roberto d'Aubuisson**, had stepped aside. Cristiani tried to distance himself from Arena's past record, presenting a more moderate image, and he won the election convincingly. In November 1989 he had to face a sustained assault on San Salvador by left-wing guerrillas. Questions about his control of extremist elements in the armed forces were again raised after the murder of six priests at the Central American University in the same month.

**CRITCHLEY, Julian.** *UK.* Conservative politician. Born in 1930, he was educated at the Sorbonne and Oxford University. He was member of parliament for Rochester and Chatham from 1959–64 and was elected member for Aldershot and North Hants (now Aldershot) in 1970. An established writer and broadcaster, his acerbic wit and irreverence have made him one of the sharpest commentators on Westminster politics. He was one of **Margaret Thatcher**'s most trenchant critics from within her own party and was a key supporter of **Michael Heseltine** in the 1990 Conservative leadership elections.

**CROSBIE, John.** *Canada.* International trade minister. He is a Newfoundlander, born in St John's in 1931. Educated at Queen's and Dalhousie universities and the London School of Economics, Crosbie was a lawyer before going into politics. He entered provincial politics as a Liberal, being first elected to Newfoundland's legislature in 1966, where he stayed for nearly a decade. He then ran as a Conservative and won a seat in the House of Commons in 1976. An outspoken minister, Crosbie has occasionally attracted criticism from feminists with his inflammatory remarks about women. He is best known for seeing through the free-trade deal with the USA.

**CUMPLIDIO CERECEDA, Francisco.** *Chile.* Justice minister. Born in 1930, Cumplidio studied law at the University of Chile. He pursued an academic career at the university, becoming a professor in 1962. A member of the Christian Democratic Party (PDC), he was appointed justice minister in 1990.

**CUNHAL, Alvaro Barreirinhas.** *Portugal.* Communist party leader. Born in 1913 in Coímbra, he joined the banned Portuguese Communist Party (PCP) in the early 1930s and by 1934 was organizer of the communist youth movement for the Lisbon region. He was elected secretary-general of the young communists in

1935, and became a member of the party's central committee the following year. His political activities led to repeated terms of imprisonment from 1937–60, until he escaped to spend the next 15 years in East Europe and Moscow. He was elected secretary-general of the party in 1961. He returned to Portugal in 1974, immediately after the April revolution, and was minister without portfolio in the early post-revolutionary governments in 1974–75. He has been repeatedly re-elected as PCP secretary-general, remaining a hardline Stalinist, though he has shown flexibility when the situation has demanded it.

**CUNNINGHAM, John.** *UK.* Labour politician. Born in 1946, he studied chemistry and then worked as a research scientist, teacher and trade-union official before being elected to parliament in 1970. On the right of the party, he held junior ministerial office before Labour's defeat in 1979 and was then shadow industry spokesman. As environment spokesman from 1983, he encountered considerable criticism for his staunch defence of nuclear power, reflecting the fact that the Sellafield nuclear plant employs many of his constituents.

**CUOMO, Mario.** *USA.* Democratic governor of New York. Born in 1932 to Italian immigrant parents, he was educated at St John's University and practised law after briefly playing professional baseball. Appointed New York state's secretary of state in 1975, he was elected lieutenant-governor in 1978 and governor in 1982. In office he established himself as a charismatic, caring liberal, who combined fiscal moderation with social reform. He has been especially innovatory in higher education policy, exemplified by the "Liberty Scholarships" for low-income students. He has a proven capacity to educate public opinion and his electrifying address to the 1984 Democratic national convention, urging the party to stand by its liberal traditions, established him as a national figure. He is vehemently opposed to capital punishment and has vetoed all attempts by the state legislature to impose it. He was expected to run for the 1988 presidential nomination, but ruled himself out for personal reasons. It is generally felt that a Cuomo candidacy would recapture the industrial North for the Democrats, but would have less appeal in the more conservative South and West, where the majority of the population lives.

**CURIEN, Hubert.** *France.* Research and technology minister. Born in 1924, he graduated from the Ecole Normale Supérieure and obtained a doctorate in science, making his career in university teaching and research. His growing eminence, and experience as an administrator, brought him appointments to preside over French, European and international agencies in science, technology, information technology and space exploration; from 1969–73 he headed the National Centre for Scientific Research (CNRS), and in 1979–84 he was president of the European Science Foundation. From 1984–86 he was research and technology minister, and returned to the post in 1988.

**CURRIE, Edwina**. *UK*. Health minister from 1986–88, and an MP since 1983. Born in 1946, Currie quickly earned a reputation in the House of Commons as one of its most energetic self-publicists. This undoubtedly accelerated her rise to ministerial level but soon proved to be counter-productive. She offended many for admonishing northerners for their allegedly unhealthy diet and exhorting pensioners to knit woollies to stave off the winter cold. Frankness finally proved her undoing in 1988 when she took on the powerful farmers' lobby within the agriculture ministry with her now notorious statement that most UK egg production was contaminated with salmonella. She was forced to resign but later scientific reports partly vindicated her.

**CYWIŃSKA, Izabella**. *Poland*. Culture minister. Born in 1935, she became a theatre director in 1966. A Solidarity supporter, she was jailed after the December 1981 imposition of martial law for staging a dramatization of the events surrounding the 1956 killing of strikers by troops in Poznań. Released in 1982, she returned to the Poznań theatre. She became culture minister in the Solidarity-led government formed in September 1989.

# D

DADZIE, Kenneth. *Ghana*. Secretary-general of UN Conference on Trade and Development (Unctad). Born in 1930, he was educated in the UK and in 1952 joined the Ghanaian civil service. He was seconded to the UN secretariat in 1963. One of the most able of African diplomats at the UN headquarters, he was put in charge of restructuring the economic and social sectors of the UN system in 1976–77 and was then given the coveted post of director of development. He was appointed Ghana's high commissioner in the UK in 1982. Unctad secretary-general since 1986, he has tried, with limited success, to minimize friction between industrial and developing countries.

DAHL, Birgitta. *Sweden*. Environment minister. Born in 1937, she worked for various development agencies after completing her studies. Elected to the Riksdag (parliament) as a Social Democrat in 1968, she was appointed to the double portfolio of energy and environment in 1986. This forced her to try to tackle the vexed issue of phasing out nuclear energy, urging caution on the one hand and stressing the government's determination to speed up the process on the other. She was relieved of the energy portfolio and allowed to concentrate on her main interest, the environment, in 1990.

DAILLY, Etienne. *France*. Senator. Born in 1918 and decorated for wartime service, he has successfully married business and politics, becoming president of various banks and companies whilst winning numerous elections as a county, local and regional councillor and senator. Since 1959 he has sat in the Senate on a centre-left platform and regularly won the vice-presidency of the upper chamber, briefly acting as its president in 1974.

DAIM ZAINUDDIN, Datuk Paduka. *Malaysia*. Finance minister. Born in 1938, Daim was appointed finance minister in 1984 by his close friend, prime minister **Mahathir Mohamad**. He had been elected to parliament for the United Malays National Organization (UMNO) in 1982 after a highly successful career

in law and business, during which time he had built up close links with UMNO and its investment arm, Fleet Holdings.

DALAI LAMA (Tenzin Gyatso). *China (Tibet)*. Supreme Buddhist ruler. Born in eastern Tibet in 1935, the fourteenth Dalai Lama reigned as god-king until 1959, when he fled to India after the failed uprising against Chinese rule. From exile in Dharmsala, he provides a focus for the Tibetan independence movement. He has refused Chinese offers to allow him to return from exile on condition that he lives in Beijing. The Chinese in turn rejected his 1988 Strasbourg proposal, to cede control of foreign affairs to China in return for Tibetan internal autonomy. He declared himself the last of the Dalai Lamas, and says that he wishes to return home as a simple monk. He was awarded the Nobel peace prize in 1989.

DALAN, Bedrettin. *Turkey*. Opposition politician. A former mayor of Istanbul, he is an outspoken critic of the government, and in 1990 formed the Democratic Centrist Party.

DALES, Ien. *Netherlands*. Interior minister. Born in 1931, she gained a reputation for a direct, unorthodox and no-nonsense approach while director of Rotterdam's overstretched social services department (1977–81), state secretary (junior minister) for social affairs (1981–82), member of the Staten Generaal (parliament) (1982–87) and mayor of Nijmegen (1987–89). She was appointed interior minister when the Labour Party (PvdA) returned to government in coalition with the Christian Democrats in November 1989.

DALEY, Richard. *USA*. Mayor of Chicago. Born in 1942, the son of Richard Daley Sr, long-term mayor of Chicago, he was a lawyer who became a state senator and state attorney. His defeat in the 1983 mayoral election signified the decline of the once all-powerful Cook County Democratic machine. Nevertheless, he made a personal comeback to become mayor in 1989.

DALY, Right Reverend Cahal. *Ireland and UK (Northern Ireland)*. Bishop of Armagh and

Primate of All Ireland, installed in December 1990 after the death of Cardinal Tomás Ó Fiaich. He is seen as relatively sympathetic to the rights of the Unionist tradition in Northern Ireland and is a long-standing and outspoken critic of IRA violence. He had been Bishop of Down and Connor since 1982, and before that of Ardagh and Clonmacnois. Born in 1917 in County Antrim, he was educated for the priesthood, and taught philosophy at Queen's University in Belfast until 1967, retaining thereafter something of the manner of an academic.

**DAM, Atli.** *Denmark (Faroe Islands).* Chief minister. Born in 1932, he studied at the Danish Academy of Engineering, graduating in 1964, and then joined the engineering firm, Haldor Topsøe. Elected to the Løgting (local parliament) for the Social Democratic Party (Javnaðarflokkurin) in 1970, he has led the party since 1972. Dam served as chief minister in a centre–left coalition government from 1970–80 and from 1984–88. He became chief minister for a third time in 1990, after the November general election. He was one of the two Faroese members of the Folketing (Danish parliament) from 1987–88, and has been a member again since December 1990.

**D'AMATO, Alfonse.** *USA.* Republican senator from New York. Born in 1937, he practised law before a career in county government administration. Narrowly elected in 1980, his assiduous promotion of constituency interests secured a massive 1986 re-election victory, but also a serious ethics investigation in 1990 when he faced accusations of using improper influence on behalf of political contributors in federal housing programmes. His national reputation rests on his tough stance against drug traffickers.

**D'ANCONA, Hedy.** *Netherlands.* Welfare, health and culture minister. Born in 1937, she worked as a broadcaster after obtaining a doctorate in social geography. One of the country's leading feminist campaigners, she was briefly state secretary (junior minister) for women's emancipation from 1981–82. After a stint in the European Parliament she returned to domestic politics, becoming welfare, health and culture minister when the Labour Party (PvdA) returned to government in coalition with the Christian Democrats in November 1989.

**DANDAVATE, Madhu.** *India.* Leading Janata Dal politician. Born in 1924 in Maharashtra, he is a veteran of the nationalist and socialist movements. He became general secretary of the

Socialist Party in 1972 and was one of the opposition leaders imprisoned by Indira Gandhi's administration during the emergency of 1975–77. A member of the Lok Sabha (lower house) since 1979, he was railways minister in the Janata government (1977–79). After the break-up of the Janata coalition he joined the rump Janata Party, becoming the party's leader in the Lok Sabha and one of the principal opposition critics on economic affairs. He was finance minister in the 1989–90 National Front government.

**DANIELS, John.** *USA.* Mayor of New Haven. Born in 1936, he practised law, moving into politics as an alderman and later state senator, and was elected New Haven's first black mayor in 1989. Like **Norman Rice**, mayor of Seattle, he is considered typical of the new breed of black mayors, who seek a broad, multi-racial appeal.

**DANKERT, Piet.** *Netherlands.* State secretary for foreign affairs. Born in 1934 and a teacher by training, he was elected to the Staten Generaal (parliament) in 1968 and to the European Parliament in 1977. Largely on the strength of his record as an adept strategist in the tortuous annual EC budget debates, he was elected president of the European Parliament in 1982 after splitting the right-wing vote by gaining the support of British Conservatives. A division on more traditional left–right lines deprived him of the post two years later. He was appointed a state secretary (junior minister) for foreign affairs, with special responsibility for Europe, when the Labour Party (PvdA) returned to government in coalition with the Christian Democrats in November 1989.

**DARMAN, Richard (Dick).** *USA.* Director of the Office of Management and Budget. Born in 1943 and educated at Harvard, he began his career in government – after a protracted period of graduate studies – as an assistant in several government departments and acquired a reputation as a moderate, traditional Republican with a keen analytical ability. Although distrusted by some of the more radical Republicans associated with **Ronald Reagan**, Darman served as special assistant to the president from 1981–85 and then joined **James Baker** in the Treasury Department as deputy secretary from 1985–87. Although the relationship between Darman and **George Bush** was not close during the Reagan years – it was reported that Bush held Darman responsible for several leaks which reflected poorly on the vice-president – Darman was appointed director of the OMB in December 1988. In presenting Bush's first full budget in January 1990, Darman was criticized by Democrats for attempting to obscure the extent of the deficit. In mid-1990 Darman promoted the bipartisan budget deficit summit which, together with the belief that he was instrumental in persuading Bush to drop his campaign pledge against increased taxes, was interpreted as indicative of a genuine willingness to address the deficit.

**DA SILVA, Luis Inãcio.** *Brazil.* Workers' Party (PT) leader. Born in 1945, da Silva (usually known as Lula) was a metalworker in São Bernardo do Campo and an active trade unionist. In 1980 he founded the left-wing PT and was unofficial head of the Trade Union Confederation (CUT). His union activities, particularly under the military regime, brought him to national prominence and his campaign for the presidency in 1989 achieved unexpected success, deriving support from his working-class origins and his popular blend of Catholicism and socialism. Lula came second in the first round of voting, but narrowly lost the run-off against **Fernando Collor de Mello.**

**DASUKI, Alhaji Ibrahim.** *Nigeria.* Sultan of Sokoto. Born in 1928, he is a former diplomat, businessman and secretary-general of the Council of Islamic Affairs. His appointment as the 18th Sultan of Sokoto in November 1988 provoked riots after rumours that his appointment – in place of the son of the previous incumbent – had been influenced by President **Ibrahim Babangida**'s desire to install a long-standing supporter as head of the northern Muslim hierarchy. Although Dasuki moved to secure his position by appointing one of the sons of his predecessor, Sir Abubakar Siddiq III, as his private secretary, he remains a controversial figure, seen by traditionalists as bringing too secular an approach to his role.

**D'AUBERT, François.** *France.* Right-wing politician. Born in 1943, he studied commerce and law and is also a graduate of the Institut d'Etudes Politiques (IEP) and of the Ecole Nationale d'Administration. He began his career as an *auditeur* at the Court of Accounts and IEP lecturer in the early 1970s, subsequently entering various ministerial teams, including **Raymond Barre**'s in 1977. Since 1978, he has sat in the National Assembly for the Union for French Democracy (UDF) specializing in economic issues.

**DÄUBLER-GMELIN, Herta.** *Germany.* Social Democratic Party (SPD) politician. Born in 1943 in Pressburg, she became a lawyer in Stuttgart. An evangelical Christian, she joined the SPD in 1965, was first elected to the Bundestag in 1972, and sits on the presidium of the SPD executive committee, as well as being a deputy chairman of its parliamentary group.

**D'AUBUISSON ARRIETA, Roberto.** *El Salvador.* Right-wing politician. Born in 1944, d'Aubuisson joined the army, reaching the rank of major and the post of assistant chief of intelligence. As an alleged organizer of right-wing death squads, he was linked with the murder of Archbishop Oscar Romero in 1980. Already involved in politics as leader of the Broad National Front (FAN), he founded the extreme right-wing Nationalist Republican Alliance (Arena) in 1981. He was president of the constituent assembly between 1982 and 1984 and Arena's presidential candidate in 1984. Since 1985 he has served as a deputy in the legislative assembly, allowing **Alfredo Cristiani** the more public role as president.

**DAVIES, Howard.** *UK.* Public sector chief executive. Born in 1951, he studied history and French at Oxford University before joining the Foreign and Commonwealth Office in 1973. After working as private secretary to the British ambassador in Paris, he left the diplomatic service in 1976 to work at the Treasury and later moved, via Stanford business school, to management consultants McKinsey. He was seconded from McKinsey to work as special adviser to **Nigel Lawson**, the chancellor of the exchequer. In 1987 he was appointed controller of the Audit Commission, the independent watchdog body set up by the government in 1983 to monitor the auditing of local authorities. Under his direction the commission has extended its activities to monitoring the National Health Service.

**DEAN, Brenda.** *UK.* Trade unionist. Born in 1943, she has worked for the Society of Graphical and Allied Trades (Sogat) printing union since the age of 16. She worked her way up to branch secretary in 1976 and was elected president in 1983 – becoming the most senior of the few women in positions of power in the union movement. She rose to national prominence during the printing unions' dispute with Rupert Murdoch's News International over new technology in the mid-1980s.

**DE BEAUCÉ, Thierry.** *France.* Government minister. Born in 1943 and a graduate of the

Institut d'Etudes Politiques and of the Ecole Nationale d'Administration (ENA), he became a civil servant, specializing in foreign and cultural affairs. From 1971–77 he was a deputy mayor in greater Paris and in 1986–87 was responsible for cultural, scientific and technical relations at the foreign ministry. In 1988 he responded to **Michel Rocard**'s "opening" to non-socialists, becoming secretary of state for international cultural relations.

**DE BEER, Zach**. *South Africa*. Democratic Party leader and business executive. A qualified doctor, he was born in Cape Province in 1928, sat as an opposition liberal MP from 1953–61 and again in 1977–80, and has been on the board of Anglo American Corporation since 1974. He epitomizes the surprisingly strong liberal tendency within South African business. He briefly led the Progressive Party before its merger into the Democratic Party, which was founded in February 1989 with De Beer, **Denis Worrall** and Wynand Malan as its leading triumvirate. De Beer became the party's sole leader at its September 1990 congress.

**DEBRÉ, Michel**. *France*. Gaullist politician. Born in 1912 and a graduate in law and politics, he was decorated for his war record in the Gaullist resistance. He played a significant role in France's reconstruction and stabilization after World War II, notably in creating the Ecole Nationale d'Administration and in drafting the current constitution in 1958. Subsequently, he became Charles de Gaulle's prime minister, from 1959–62, and held a series of ministerial posts at economy and finance, foreign affairs and defence, over the next decade. A member of the Council of State and a prolific author on political matters, Debré has won numerous elections since 1948, principally as a deputy or senator. In 1979, he and **Jacques Chirac** led the Gaullist list in the European elections and, two years later, he stood unsuccessfully (winning less than 2% of the vote) for the French presidency. Throughout the 1980s, he remained politically active, always vehemently championing French national interests against moves towards European integration, and pouring scorn on talk of "supranationality". In 1988 he was elected to the French Academy.

**DÉBY, Idriss**. *Chad*. President. One of the key military figures in **Hissène Habré**'s regime, Déby was army chief of staff from 1982–85 and associated with many of the successes against Libyan intervention. Subsequently security adviser to the president, he helped to forge the ethnic alliance that kept Habré in power. Apparently alienated by the president's policy of accommodation with former opponents, he went into exile following the abortive rebellion of April 1989, becoming effective leader of the armed opposition to Habré, operating across the border with Sudan. He was swept to power in December 1990, when his Patriotic Salvation Movement mounted an offensive that drove Habré's government from office with minimal resistance. Déby called for national unity and promised to respect human rights and hold free elections.

**DECAUX, Alain**. *France*. Historian and government minister. Born in 1925 and a law graduate, he pursued an extremely productive literary career, crowned by election to the French Academy in 1979. Also a journalist and broadcaster, in 1985 he was appointed member of the Haut Conseil de la Francophonie, which served as a stepping stone to his appointment in 1988 as minister-delegate for francophone affairs.

**DEETMAN, Wim**. *Netherlands*. Centre politician. Born in 1945, he worked in the education service before being elected to the Staten Generaal (parliament) for the Christian Democratic Appeal (CDA) in 1978. He was appointed education and science minister in 1981, a post he held until his election as speaker of the Second Chamber (lower house of parliament) in 1989.

**DEHAENE, Jean-Luc**. *Belgium*. Deputy prime minister, communications and institutional reform minister. Born in 1940, he has a background in Christian social work administration and was a senior adviser to various ministers from 1972–81 before being appointed social affairs minister. He was elected to parliament for the Christian People's Party (CVP) in 1987, having previously been a co-opted member of the senate. He played a major role as *informateur* (a person appointed by the king to investigate coalition options) in the formation of the new centre-left government in 1988, when he became a deputy prime minister and communications and institutional reform minister.

**DE KLERK, F.W. (Frederik Willem)**. *South Africa*. State president. Born in 1936, son of Jan de Klerk, whose long cabinet career ended in 1969, he practised law from 1961–72 before entering parliament himself. Holder of various ministerial posts from 1978 onwards, he was internal affairs minister by 1982, the year in which he became the National Party's (NP's) Transvaal leader. By the time of P.W. Botha's resignation as NP leader in 1989 he had emerged as favourite for the succession, with five solid years behind him as national education and planning minister, and a reputation for caution and prudence to set against the more liberal *verligte* image of the slightly younger **Barend du Plessis**. Since then, and especially since his succession to the state presidency in September 1989, his recognition of the need for change has led him to launch a process of far-reaching reform. One historic de Klerk speech, on February 2, 1990, announced the release of **Nelson Mandela** and the unbanning of the African National Congress (ANC) and other organizations. The logic of the process has taken him on to the progressive repeal of apartheid laws, as well as the dismantling of his predecessor's "securocrat" system and the lifting of emergency powers. Reviled on the right as a traitor to the Afrikaner *volk*, he has won his country greater acceptance in the West, and now finds himself repeatedly urging his own deeply conservative party to face the inevitability of "one man, one vote" and has staked his now very considerable reputation on the success of negotiations.

**DE KLERK, Willem.** *South Africa.* Presidential adviser. Younger brother of the president, and a leading member of the secretive Afrikaner elite society, the Broederbond, "Wimpie" was associated with the February 1989 formation of the liberal opposition Democratic Party, and was part of a delegation which met **Thabo Mbeki** and other African National Congress leaders in London in October that year. He is now increasingly seen as one of the Afrikaner intelligentsia advising his brother on the path of future reform and negotiation.

**DE LA CUADRA SALCEDO Y FERNÁNDEZ DEL CASTILLO, Tomás.** *Spain.* President of Council of State. Born in 1946 in Madrid. A university professor of law, he was secretary of state for regional and local government from 1982–85 and was appointed president of the Council of State in 1985.

**DE LA GARZA, Kika.** *USA.* Democratic congressman from Texas. Born of Mexican-American parents in 1927, he practised law before election to the House of Representatives in 1964. As agricultural committee chairman since 1981 he has been instrumental in reorganizing the farm credit system and preventing deep cuts in farm aid.

**DELAMURAZ, Jean-Pascal.** *Switzerland.* Economics minister. Born in Vevey in 1936, he studied law and made a name for himself as a student leader. He subsequently entered local politics, serving as mayor of Lausanne from 1974–81. Known as an effective administrator (he is a former head of SBB, the Swiss railways), he represents the liberal Radical Democratic Party in the government coalition where he has been economics minister since 1984. Under the rotation principle he held the office of president of the Swiss Confederation in 1989.

**DELEBARRE, Michel.** *France.* Minister of state for urban affairs. Born in 1946 and a geography graduate, he began as a civil servant, rising to prominence in the Socialist Party (PS) in the Nord/Pas-de-Calais region under the wing of **Pierre Mauroy.** He worked as Mauroy's adviser when the latter was prime minister in 1981–82, and was labour, employment and vocational training minister from 1984–86. Elected to parliament in 1986, he resumed his ministerial career in 1988 with (briefly) the social affairs and employment portfolio, then as minister of infrastructure, housing, transport and the sea. He is regarded by many as a potential successor to Mauroy as head of the PS.

**DELLUMS, Ronald.** *USA.* Democratic congressman from California. Born in 1935, he was a student activist at the University of California (Berkeley) in the 1960s. He pursued idealistic causes after his 1970 election to the House of Representatives, usually without success – apart from promoting tough South African sanctions legislation, in spite of presidential opposition, in 1986. Since the mid-1980s, however, chairmanship responsibilities, particularly on the subcommittee that oversees new weaponry, induced him to work more within the system. He is a member of the Congressional Black Caucus.

**DE LORENZO, Francesco.** *Italy.* Health minister and Italian Liberal Party (PLI) politician. Born in 1938, he studied medicine in his native Naples, which he has represented in the Chamber of Deputies since 1983. His first cabinet appointment was as ecology minister in August 1986. He was appointed health minister in July 1989.

**DELORS, Jacques.** *France.* President of the European Commission. Born in 1925, he studied economics at the University of Paris and in 1945 joined the Banque de France. From 1962 he held a number of senior civil service and advisory posts, dealing particularly with professional education and social affairs. He became the Socialist Party (PS) spokesman on international economic affairs in 1976, and when the PS came to power in 1981 became economy and finance minister. A controversial figure within the party for his unorthodox economic views, he was closely associated with the U-turn in government policy and the introduction of an austerity programme in 1983. In 1985 he was appointed president of the European Commission. He has successfully heightened the profile of his office – much diminished under his two immediate predecessors – by moving the Commission into the centre of policy-making, directly involving himself in many of its activities, and using his considerable personal authority to keep his fellow commissioners in line (more or less). He has pursued the creation of the single market and the realization of economic and political union with characteristic energy and eloquence. His ultimate aim is seen by many to be the presidency of France. A lover of jazz and sport, his favourite newspaper is the French sports daily *L'Equipe*.

**DELPINO, Juan José**. *Venezuela*. Trade union leader. As leader of the Workers' Confederation of Venezuela (CTV), the trade union affiliate of Democratic Action (AD), Delpino has been a close ally of President **Carlos Andrés Pérez**.

**DE MAIZIÈRE, Lothar**. *Germany*. Christian Democratic Union (CDU) politician. The Christian Democrat who emerged as prime minister after East Germany's first multi-party elections in March 1990, he became deputy leader of the merged CDU in the unified Germany six months later. Born in 1940 near Erfurt, he played the viola professionally, was active in the Evangelical church, and worked as a lawyer, defending conscientious objectors and other dissidents on occasion. Soft-spoken and a little-known figure in politics before 1989, De Maizière appeared scarcely tainted by the CDU's co-operation with the communist regime, and was elected in November 1989 as party leader, entering the **Hans Modrow** government with responsibility for church affairs. Swept into office by the pro-unification tide at the March 1990 elections, the CDU and its Alliance for Germany partners turned to him as their most obvious leader, although he seemed at first hesitant to take on the mantle of prime minister. Overshadowed in every sense by Chancellor **Helmut Kohl**, he nevertheless proved adept in promoting the material interests of East Germans in the unification process. When

Germany was unified in October he was one of five East Germans brought into the federal cabinet, as ministers without portfolio. He resigned in December 1990 from both his cabinet and CDU posts after allegations that he had worked for the Stasi, the East German secret police.

**DEMAREST, David**. *USA*. Republican adviser. Born in 1952, he is a long-time Republican political strategist who served in the labour department and in the Office of Public and Intergovernmental Affairs under **Ronald Reagan**. He was the communications director for **George Bush**'s 1988 presidential campaign. Like other members of the Bush administration's "inner circle", Demarest appears to have been chosen at least in part for his low profile.

**DEMENTEI, Nikolai**. *USSR*. President of Byelorussia. Born in 1931, he was a career Communist Party official before his 1989 election as Supreme Soviet presidium chairman of one of the most conservatively-led Soviet republics. He was narrowly re-elected to the post (restyled as chairman of the Byelorussian Supreme Soviet) in May 1990. An increasing tendency to radicalism reflects the influence of rapid developments in Russia and the Ukraine.

**DE MICHELIS, Gianni**. *Italy*. Foreign minister and Italian Socialist Party (PSI) politician. Born in 1940, he gained a degree in chemistry and has held teaching posts at Padua and Venice universities. He was elected to the Chamber of Deputies in 1976, representing his native Venice. In April 1980 he entered **Francesco Cossiga**'s second cabinet as minister for state-owned industries, retaining this position in the governments of **Arnaldo Forlani**, **Giovanni Spadolini** and Amintore Fanfani. He was labour minister from 1983–87. Subsequently, he served as deputy prime minister in the government of **Ciriaco De Mita** from 1988–89 and was appointed foreign minister in the government formed by **Giulio Andreotti** in July 1989. De Michelis is an ardent Europhile, eager to promote faster integration within the EC, but has also been instrumental in constructing the informal *pentagonale* economic grouping of Italy, Austria, Czechoslovakia, Hungary and Yugoslavia. Long-haired and flamboyant, he published a guide to disco-dancing in 1988.

**DEMİREL, Süleyman**. *Turkey*. Opposition leader and former prime minister. Born in 1924, he worked as an engineer before becoming president of the centre-right Justice Party in 1964. Known for his confrontational political style, he headed six governments during the 1960s and 1970s, and was prime minister at the time of the 1980 military coup. After the coup, Demirel was interned for three years and was banned from politics until 1987; this did not stop him building up the newly formed centre-right True Path Party, with which he won a fifth of the vote in the December 1987 elections. Demirel uses his extensive business contacts to great effect, and he is a strong contender for the premiership. Although softening with age, he has still promised if he becomes prime minister again to impeach his arch-rival, President **Turgut Özal**, for abusing presidential powers; any coalition partners are likely to come from the right.

**DE MITA, (Luigi) Ciriaco.** *Italy.* Christian Democrat party (DC) politician. Born in 1928 in Nusco, not far from Naples, he gained a law degree at the Catholic University of Milan and entered the Chamber of Deputies in 1963. Appointed trade and industry minister in 1973, De Mita was subsequently foreign trade minister and minister without portfolio, with responsibility for the Mezzogiorno (southern Italy). In March 1979, he became deputy secretary of the DC and in May 1982 succeeded Flaminio Piccoli as secretary-general. From April 1988–May 1989, he headed a five-party coalition government. As prime minister, one of his most important achievements was to secure, in late 1988, the passage of legislation virtually abolishing the secret vote in parliament, a procedure which had contributed to the instability of Italian governments, because it enabled deputies covertly to vote against their own parties in pursuit of factional rivalries or other interests. In February 1989, facing opposition within the party to the concentration of power in his hands, he was pressurized into standing down as secretary-general, making way for **Arnaldo Forlani**. He took the honorary post of party president, but resigned in February 1990, leading a pull-out from leadership posts by DC leftists. De Mita's political stance is influenced by an intense rivalry with socialist leader **Bettino Craxi**. With his strong provincial accent, his bald head and convoluted forms of speech, he is an easy butt for critics and cartoonists, but opponents have learned that his staying power is not to be under-rated.

**DEMSZKY, Gábor.** *Hungary.* Mayor of Budapest. A lawyer and former dissident who had emerged as a prominent member of the Alliance of Free Democrats (SzDSz), he became mayor of the capital in late 1990 at the age of 38, elected as the candidate of his party's centre-left opposition alliance with the Young Democrats (FIDESz).

**DENG XIAOPING.** *China.* Even though he has relinquished all leadership posts, Deng remains the paramount figure in Chinese politics. Born in 1904, the son of a Sichuan landowner, Deng joined the Chinese Communist Party (CCP) at the age of 20 after a period as a worker-student in France, and took part in the 1934–35 Long March. After the CCP victory in 1949, he soon rose to become vice-premier in 1952, secretary-general of the Central Committee in 1954, and a member of the Politburo in 1955. Deng's pragmatic approach brought him into conflict with Mao Zedong over agricultural policy after the disastrous Great Leap Forward of 1957–59 when he supported a return to private plots and small-scale free markets. His famous dictum "It doesn't matter whether it's a black cat or a white cat, as long as it catches mice it's a good cat" dates from this time. Labelled "No 2 capitalist-roader in the party" during the Cultural Revolution (1966–76), he was stripped of his posts only to re-emerge in 1973 in senior state and military positions. In 1976 Deng was again accused of rightism and dismissed from office. After the fall of the Gang of Four in 1976, he returned to power in June 1977 as vice-premier, a member of the Politburo Standing Committee and vice-chairman of the party's Central Military Commission. Best known as the architect of China's modernization programme which has introduced market reforms, Deng's reformist tendencies do not extend to tolerating organized dissent. A supporter of Mao's purge of intellectuals in 1957 and responsible for crushing the 1978–79 democracy movement, Deng is widely believed to have ordered the ruthless military crackdown on the pro-democracy movement in June 1989. In 1987 Deng took the lead in the campaign to rejuvenate the leadership by retiring from the Politburo, the Central Committee and the Central Advisory Commission. He retained his positions as head of the party and state Central Military Commissions, until November 1989 and April 1990 respectively, ultimately handing over both these posts to **Jiang Zemin**, the third in a line of chosen successors (after Hu Yaobang, disgraced in 1987, and **Zhao Ziyang**). Since his retirement from public life, Deng's writings have become required reading for party cadres, even though Deng himself claims to be an "ordinary citizen".

**DENHAM, Lord.** *UK.* Conservative politician. Born in 1927 and educated at Cambridge University, he succeeded to the barony in 1948. He was appointed the party's deputy chief whip in the House of Lords in 1974 and chief whip in 1978. In the late 1980s he successfully marshalled support in the upper house to push through some of the Conservative government's more controversial measures.

**DENIAU, Jean-François.** *France.* Centre-right politician. Born in 1928 and trained as an economist, he graduated in 1952 from the elite Ecole Nationale d'Administration. He began his career as a finance ministry official, specializing in European integration issues. After serving on the staff of the European Commission, and then for three years as ambassador to Mauritania in the mid-1960s, he became one of the French members of the European Commission, overseeing the Community's development aid programme (1969–73) before returning to Paris as junior minister for foreign affairs, then for agriculture. In 1975 he joined the Independent Republicans, led by the then president **Valéry Giscard d'Estaing** and subsequently merged into the Union for French Democracy (UDF). He was ambassador to Spain in 1976–77, then returned to the government, successively in charge of foreign trade and then administrative reform. In 1981 he lost his seat in the National Assembly, but was re-elected in 1986 and became vice-president of the assembly's foreign affairs committee in 1988.

**DENKTAS, Rauf.** *Cyprus.* Turkish Cypriot leader. Born in 1924, he studied as a lawyer and was called to the Bar in London. When Greek Cypriot agitation for self-determination looked likely to lead to union with Greece, he helped to organize the armed Turkish Resistance Movement (TMT). At independence in 1960 he was elected president of the Turkish Cypriot communal chamber. After the inter-communal fighting in 1963–64, he was expelled to Turkey, returning in 1968 as the Turkish Cypriot representative of negotiations between the two communities. After the Turkish invasion and occupation of the northern third of Cyprus in 1974, Denktas became president of the new "federated" state. In 1983, he declared the area to be the independent Turkish Republic of Northern Cyprus, which is recognized only by Turkey. He has since twice been elected its president, most recently in April 1990.

**DER'I, Arie.** *Israel.* Interior minister and general secretary of Shas (Sephardic Guardians of the Torah). Moroccan-born Der'i was trained as a rabbi and in 1988 became, at 29, Israel's youngest-ever minister. His star may wane, however, if allegations that he misappropriated public funds are proved to be true.

**DE ROBIEN, Gilles.** *France.* Right-wing politician. Born in 1941, he began his career as an insurance agent and credit broker in the 1960s. A member of the Republican Party (UDF-PR), he became a deputy in 1986 and secretary of the National Assembly.

**DERTLIEV, Petar.** *Bulgaria.* Leader of the Social Democratic Party (SDP) and one of the most powerful leaders of the opposition alliance, the Union of Democratic Forces (UDF). Born in 1916 in the village of Pisarovo, near Pleven. His father was leader of the national teachers' union. Dertliev was a medical student; he graduated in 1940. An active anti-fascist, he was arrested several times during his student years. After the war he became leader of the Social Democrats' youth wing. He was also elected to parliament. A vigorous opponent of the communists, he was also arrested in 1948 and spent ten years in prisons and labour camps. After his release, he went back to medicine. After the collapse of orthodox communism in November 1989, Dertliev was instrumental in the re-founding of the SDP and became its leader. The UDF candidate for president in July 1990, Dertliev eventually withdrew and **Zhelyu Zhelev** was adopted as a compromise candidate.

**DERWINSKI, Edward.** *USA.* Secretary of veterans' affairs. Born in 1926, he was a Republican representative from Illinois in the House from 1959–83. He worked in the Department of State from 1983–87, and became an under-secretary of state in **Ronald Reagan**'s administration from 1987–88, before being chosen by **George Bush** to head the new Department of Veterans' Affairs.

**DE SARKOZY, Nicolas.** *France.* Gaullist politician. Born in 1955 and a graduate in law and in politics from the Institut d'Etudes Politiques, he became a lawyer. He joined the Gaullist movement in 1974, sat on its central committee from 1977, and became its deputy secretary-general in 1990. Mayor of Neuilly-sur-Seine since 1983 and elected to the National Assembly in 1988, de Sarkozy is close to **Jacques Chirac** and is seen as a potential candidate for higher office.

**DEVINE, Grant.** *Canada.* Premier of
Saskatchewan. Born into a farming family in
Regina in 1944, he taught agricultural
economics at the universities of Ohio and
Saskatchewan. He is the author of numerous
papers on agriculture. Chosen leader of the
Progressive Conservative Party of Saskatchewan
in 1979, Devine was first elected to the
provincial legislative assembly, and became
premier, in 1982.

**DE VRIES, Bert.** *Netherlands.* Social affairs and
employment minister. Born in 1938, he studied
economics and worked for the tax service, the
Philips electronics company and as a lecturer
before being elected to the Staten Generaal
(parliament) in 1978. Still virtually unknown
outside the party, he was elected as
parliamentary leader of the Christian Democratic
Appeal (CDA) in 1982. His quiet but
determined style earned him respect, and he used
his position – an influential one in Dutch
politics – to champion more centrist policies
within the CDA. He was appointed social affairs
and employment minister in **Ruud Lubbers's**
third administration in November 1989.

**DHLAKAMA, Afonso.** *Mozambique.* Guerrilla
leader. A shadowy figure, he is president and
commander-in-chief of the Mozambique
National Resistance (Renamo). Initially set up
by the Rhodesian government to attack
Zimbabwean nationalist bases in Mozambique
during the independence war of the late 1970s,
Renamo was taken over by the South Africans at
Zimbabwean independence in 1980 to act as a
destabilizing force against the Front for the
Liberation of Mozambique (Frelimo)
government. Although achieving considerable
military success in its campaign to overthrow the
government, Renamo has received little
international recognition. Since 1989, the
government has been negotiating with Renamo
to end the civil war; its willingness to push
ahead with rapid political reform may have
outdistanced Renamo, which might have
difficulty transforming itself into a legitimate
political party.

**DIENSTBIER, Jiří.** *Czechoslovakia.* Foreign
minister. Born in 1937, he worked as a reporter
for Czechoslovak radio from 1959–70, and was a
prominent foreign correspondent in many parts
of the world in the 1960s. Dismissed in 1970, he
worked as an archivist and later as a boilerman.
He signed the dissident Charter 77, and was its
spokesman in 1979 and 1985, receiving a three-
year prison sentence in October 1979 as a result

of his dissident activities. He was a founder-
member of Civic Forum in November 1989, was
named foreign minister in the federal
government of national accord in December
1989, and reappointed after the June elections.
He is a close friend of **Václav Havel** and a fellow
playwright.

**DIEPGEN, Eberhard.** *Germany.* Mayor of
Berlin. The first person to have charge of
running a unified Berlin since World War II, he
gained this distinction by virtue of the crushing
victory of his Christian Democratic Union
(CDU) over the outgoing socialist/Alternative
List (AL) administration in the city's elections in
December 1990. He was born in 1941 in Berlin
and studied law there. He joined the CDU in
1962 and sat in the West Berlin parliament from
1971–81, before spending a year as one of its
representatives in the Bundestag. From 1984–89
he was mayor of West Berlin, and has developed
a strong rivalry with **Walter Momper,** who
wrested the mayorship from him in 1989 only to
lost it again after unification.

**DIESTEL, Peter-Michael.** *Germany.* Christian
Democratic Union (CDU) politician. A young
lawyer, he was general secretary of the right-
wing German Social Union (DSU) at the March
1990 Volkskammer (East German parliament)
elections. His pragmatic attitude towards the
prospect of a grand coalition, ranging from the
DSU to the Social Democrats, contrasted with
the stance of DSU chairman **Hans-Wilhelm
Ebeling** who had tried to smear the Social
Democrats as crypto-communists. Diestel's
pragmatism on this occasion was credited with
making **Lothar de Maizière's** broad coalition
possible. In July he left the DSU for the CDU.
In office as East German deputy prime minister
and interior minister, he suffered a serious loss of
political credibility, condemned for failing to
eliminate former communists from positions of
influence and for dragging his feet in
investigations into the secret police, the Stasi,
many of whose former members he employed.
He subsequently headed the CDU campaign in
the post-unification Land (state) election in
Brandenburg in October, but, alone among the
CDU candidates in the five former East German
Länder, he was defeated in a contest with the
SPD led by **Manfred Stolpe.**

**DIMITROV, Filip.** *Bulgaria.* Chairman of the
main opposition coalition, the Union of
Democratic Forces (UDF), and leader of the
Greens. Born in 1955 into an intellectual and
professional family, Dimitrov studied and then

practised law. Not a member of any political group before the collapse of orthodox communism in November 1989, Dimitrov was relatively unknown until chosen as a compromise candidate to lead the UDF after the resignation of **Petar Beron**. Unlike his predecessor, Dimitrov, who is not an MP, has a calm and unconfrontational manner and approach.

**DING GUANGEN**. *China*. Alternate member of the Politburo. Born in 1930, Ding was railways minister from 1985–88 before resigning in the wake of three major train accidents. A close associate of **Deng Xiaoping**, he immediately became a vice-minister of the State Planning Commission and head of the government's Taiwan Affairs Office. Elected to the Central Committee in 1985, he joined the Politburo in 1987, and subsequently the Secretariat after the crackdown on the pro-democracy movement in June 1989.

**DINGELL, John**. *USA*. Democratic congressman from Michigan. The son of a congressman, he was born in 1926 and practised law before election to the House of Representatives in 1955. In 1981 he became energy and commerce committee chairman, whose wide-ranging jurisdiction covers about 40% of all House bills. The desire to protect Michigan's car industry shapes his approach to environmental issues and trade policy.

**DINKINS, David**. *USA*. Mayor of New York. Born in 1927, he was a lawyer and state legislator. He became New York's first black mayor in 1989, after serving as city clerk and borough president. He ran as a clean-government candidate after the scandals of Edward Koch's administration, but almost lost because of splits between the once politically allied black and Jewish communities. Healing this divide and combating crime and drug problems are his mayoral priorities, but he has already been criticized for the paucity of his early achievements.

**DIOP, Serigne Lamine**. *Senegal*. Justice minister. Born in 1931, he trained as a hydraulic engineer, and was director of statistics and director of customs before joining the government in 1978 as secretary of state for the budget. He later served as industrial development minister and was appointed economy and finance minister in 1988. He took on the justice portfolio in March 1990.

**DIOUF, Abdou**. *Senegal*. President. Born in 1935 at Louga in northern Senegal, he studied law and political science in Dakar and Paris before joining the civil service. He first made his mark as secretary-general to the government during the 1960s, joining the cabinet as planning and industry minister in 1968. Two years later he was the surprise choice of president Léopold Senghor for the revived post of prime minister, in which he proved an able and efficient administrator. On Senghor's retirement in 1981, Diouf succeeded to the presidency and the post of secretary-general of the ruling Socialist Party (PS) in what was then one of Africa's few multi-party democracies. Diouf has permitted a gradual political and economic liberalization, allowing opposition parties relatively free rein, although his victories in the presidential elections of 1983 and 1988 were hotly disputed by the opposition.

**DISCUA, Brigadier-General Luis Alonso**. *Honduras*. Commander-in-chief of the armed forces. A military intelligence specialist and commander of the small Honduran navy, General Discua became head of the armed forces in December 1990 after the controversial removal of his predecessor, General Arnulfo Cantanero. He was born in 1946, and received military training including a parachute course in Germany, a military intelligence course in Argentina and courses in the US-run School of the Americas in Panama. His military career has included a spell in charge of the notorious Batallion 3-16, allegedly responsible for human rights violations. In contrast to Cantanero, he is seen as a hardliner who will maintain at all costs the autonomy of the military and their ascendancy over the civilian authorities, but unrest among some officers suggest that his tenure might be brief.

**DISSANAYAKE, Gamini**. *Sri Lanka*. Politician. A lawyer from the Sinhalese professional elite, he was long considered the main rival of **Lalith Athulathmudali** for the succession to United National Party leader and president Junius Jayawardene, but his star has waned since the top job went instead to **Ranasinghe Premadasa** in late 1988. Dissanayake had been irrigation minister throughout Jayawardene's rule from 1977, with responsibility for overseeing the massive Mahaweli project, the centrepiece of the government's development strategy. Premadasa moved him sideways to the plantation industries portfolio in early 1989, and his claims for the (largely ceremonial) job as prime minister were again overlooked in the March 1990 reshuffle, when he left the government.

**DIXON, Julian.** *USA.* Democratic congressman from California. Born in 1934, he practised law and served in the state assembly before election to the House of Representatives in 1978. Chairman of the Congressional Black Caucus from 1983–84, he generally works within the system to advance black interests. He chaired the ethics committee whose investigation ultimately led to speaker Jim Wright's 1989 resignation.

**DJOHAR, Saïd Mohammed.** *Comoros.* President. The former president of the supreme court, Djohar served as interim president after the assassination of Ahmed Abdallah by his own praetorian guard, a band of foreign mercenaries led by Frenchman Bob Denard, in November 1989. In March 1990, the first free presidential elections since independence in 1975 confirmed him in this position, despite accusations of vote-rigging by his opponents. Djohar appears to have the support of France, the former colonial power and major aid donor, in his attempt to restore stability and democracy.

**DLAMINI, Obed Mfanyana.** *Swaziland.* Prime minister. A former trade unionist, he was appointed prime minister in July 1989 after his predecessor Sotsha Dlamini had been sacked by **King Mswati III** for "disobedience". He enjoys little real power, with virtually all decision-making in the hands of the king. Dlamini was founder and secretary-general of the Swaziland Federation of Trade Unions before working in personnel management.

**DLOUHÝ, Vladimír.** *Czechoslovakia.* Economy minister. Born in 1953, he studied in Prague and Louvain (Belgium), then worked as a lecturer at the Prague School of Economics, from 1983 as a scientific worker at the Czechoslovak Academy of Sciences, and in 1984 at the prognostic institute of the Academy of Sciences, where he became deputy director in 1988. He was appointed deputy premier in the federal government of national accord in December 1989, as a member of the Communist Party of Czechoslovakia (KSČ) but proposed by Civic Forum; by the year's end he had left the KSČ, and was elected as a Civic Forum candidate in the June 1990 elections. He became federal minister in charge of the economy ministry in the new coalition government, charged with guiding the country's transition to a market economy.

**DO MUOI.** *Vietnam.* Prime minister. Born in 1917, Do Muoi joined the Communist Party in the 1930s and held government posts in North Vietnam before travelling to the newly communist South in 1976 to supervise the initial socialist transformation effort. Elected prime minister in 1988 after beating off a challenge from **Vo Van Kiet**, he makes the correct "reformist" noises, but is widely regarded as a conservative member of the northern "old guard".

**DOBROVSKÝ, Luboš.** *Czechoslovakia.* Defence minister. Born in 1930, he attended a secondary military school but decided not to pursue a military career, studying Czech and Russian at university instead. He served as Czechoslovak radio correspondent in Moscow in 1968 and after leaving this post joined the staff of the outspoken weekly *Listy*. After *Listy* was closed down in 1969 Dobrovský was active as a dissident and was a signatory of Charter 77. Following the "velvet revolution" of November 1989 he joined the foreign ministry and became spokesman for the foreign minister, **Jiří Dienstbier**, and deputy foreign minister. He played a major role in talks with the USSR on the withdrawal of Soviet forces. He was appointed national defence minister in October 1990 after the dismissal of his predecessor General Miroslav Vaček for his high profile under the communist regime.

**DOBSON, Frank.** *UK.* Labour politician. Born in 1940, he studied economics and then worked in the electricity industry and in local government. Elected to his inner London seat in 1979, he has been the party's spokesman on education (1982–83), health (1983–87), and energy (since 1989).

**DODD, Christopher.** *USA.* Democratic senator for Connecticut. Born in 1944, he became a lawyer after service in the Peace Corps. He sat for three terms in the House of Representatives before winning election in 1980 to the Senate. A liberal, he promotes "the family agenda" as chairman of the subcommittee on children, families, drugs and alcoholism. He is also a powerful defender of insurance companies (many of which are Connecticut-based) as the Senate securities subcommittee chairman. He also chairs the Senate foreign relations subcommittee on western hemisphere affairs, and made a name as a critic of government policy in Central America, opposing support for the "contras", backing increased aid to Nicaragua, and introducing a measure to cut aid to El Salvador unless its government showed a serious commitment to peace and human rights. In May 1990 he joined seven other senators in supporting the **Howard Metzenbaum** initiative to launch a Coalition for

Democratic Values, speaking out for defence cuts and progressive tax policies.

**DOǦAN, Ahmed.** *Bulgaria.* Leader of the Movement for Rights and Freedoms and effective political voice of Bulgaria's ethnic Turkish minority. A philosopher and academic, he promoted the rights of ethnic Turks in the face of the Bulgarian nationalist feeling whipped up in the latter years of communist rule. In June 1989 he was arrested and sentenced to ten years' imprisonment for founding an "anti-state" organization. He was granted an amnesty in December 1989. At the age of only 36, he led his organization to a strong showing in the June 1990 elections, while vociferously rejecting the claim of the main opposition coalition, the Union of Democratic Forces (UDF), that his movement should be debarred as an ethnic-based body.

**DOǦAN, Hüsnü.** *Turkey.* Defence minister. A nephew of President **Turgut Özal**, Doǧan was born in 1944 at Malatya. He rose rapidly in the early 1980s, from his position as head of the foreign investment branch at the state planning office, becoming agriculture minister in Özal's first government of 1983, and acquiring considerable experience in international affairs in the following years. A deputy for İzmir since 1987, he was dropped from the government in March 1989 after criticism of Özal's political favouritism toward family members. His appointment to replace **Safa Giray** as defence minister in late October 1990 seemed likely to heighten the political infighting inside the ruling Motherland Party (ANAP) about Özal's leadership style.

**DOGUZHIYEV, Vitaly.** *USSR.* Deputy prime minister. Born in 1935, an ethnic Adygey, he was responsible in the government for the development of space technologies and was general machine building minister for a year prior to his appointment in July 1989 as a deputy premier. He was put in charge of a new State Commission for Emergency Situations, set up after recent major disasters exposed the inadequacies of Soviet civil defence and emergency relief.

**DOI, Takako.** *Japan.* Japan Socialist Party (JSP) leader. Born in 1928 in Hyogo prefecture, she studied law and took up an academic post at Doshisha University, becoming active in the JSP and entering the House of Representatives (lower house) in 1969. Deputy leader of the party from 1983, she became leader after the crushing electoral defeat of 1986 and has rallied the party's fortunes, shedding some of its ideological baggage and moving it gradually to the right, while working especially hard to involve more women in political activity. She took much of the credit for the dramatic JSP success when half the seats in the House of Councillors (upper house) came up for re-election in 1989 – an upset which raised exaggerated hopes for the House of Representatives election in February 1990. In the event the JSP won 53 more seats, but the Liberal Democratic Party kept a firm hold on power. Without a substantial faction of her own in the JSP, Doi must manoeuvre with caution as she confronts some intractable obstacles to opposition unity, notably whether the JSP can afford its controversial anti-nuclear stance and its commitment to revise the security treaty with the USA.

**DOLE, Elizabeth.** *USA.* Former secretary of labour. Born in 1936 in North Carolina, "Liddy" studied at Harvard and Oxford universities before practising law in Washington DC in the mid-1960s. She held a variety of minor government posts before her appointment as transport secretary by **Ronald Reagan** in 1983. The only woman in Reagan's cabinet, she resigned in 1987 in order to assist her husband, **Robert Dole**, in his unsuccessful campaign for the 1988 Republican presidential nomination. Following her husband's defeat, Dole returned to the government in January 1989 as secretary of labour in the new administration of **George Bush**. In early 1990 a nine-month dispute between the Pittston Coal Company and the United Mine Workers' Union was brought to an end after the intervention of Dole. Her willingness to mediate was in marked contrast to the laissez-faire attitude to labour disputes which had been a hallmark of the Reagan administration. In October 1990 she announced her resignation, the first cabinet member to leave the Bush administration; she was to be president of the American Red Cross from January 1991, but was widely expected to return to active politics and seek elective office in 1992.

**DOLE, Robert (Bob).** *USA.* Republican senator from Kansas. Born in 1923, he was driven in his early career by a determination to overcome the disability of a virtually useless right arm and an impaired left one, the result of World War II wounds. After attending Kansas and Washburn universities, he practised law and was elected senator in 1968. National prominence followed in 1976 when Gerald Ford surprisingly chose him as running mate, but a robust, argumentative style made him an unattractive campaigner and probably lost crucial votes in a close election. He has tried since to sound less strident, but his career bears testimony to the truth that congressional success cannot be easily translated into a successful presidential bid. Dole was a forceful majority leader from 1985–86, willing to use his power to overcome opponents, and was very supportive of **Ronald Reagan**'s administration. Senate leadership responsibilities hampered his 1988 primary campaign preparations, however, and he failed to endow his campaign with appealing general themes. Deficit reduction, the issue dearest to him, did not figure prominently in the 1988 election agenda because economies and tax increases were unpopular with voters. Although Dole won the Iowa caucuses, where his farm-state background was advantageous, he could not repeat this success in the New Hampshire primary. An ill-tempered remark on election night that **George Bush** should "stop lying about my record" made him appear a sore loser. His lack of appeal in the South was cruelly exposed on "Super Tuesday", when defeat in all 17 primaries (and also in some primaries outside the South) effectively ended his campaign. Despite personal coolness towards Bush, he has been a loyal Senate minority leader. The realization that his hopes for national office are dead probably makes it easier to subordinate himself to the president who, by appointing Bob's wife **Elizabeth Dole** as labour secretary, signalled his own desire for reconciliation.

**DOMENICI, Peter (Pete)**. *USA*. Republican senator from New Mexico. Born in 1932, he practised law before his election in 1972. Budget committee chairman from 1981–86, he remains the principal Republican spokesman on Capitol Hill for fiscal affairs and favours a bipartisan offensive to reduce the deficit.

**DOMOKOŞ, Géza**. *Romania*. Leader of the Hungarian Democratic Union of Romania and member of the Assembly of Deputies. A writer and director of the Bucharest publishing house, Kriterion, he was founder-member and chairman of the Hungarian Democratic Union of Romania, a Transylvanian-based party, formed in December 1989, that champions the rights of Romania's ethnic Hungarians.

**DONALDSON, Lord (John Donaldson)**. *UK*. Lawyer and judge. Born in 1920, he practised as a barrister until being appointed a high-court judge in 1966, an appeal court judge in 1979 and master of the rolls (England's senior civil

judge) in 1982. He was knighted in 1966 and created a life peer in 1988. He has not escaped political controversy, notably over his role in the industrial relations tribunal and in the imprisonment of the "Guildford Four". His talents are more of a skilled administrator than a great jurist. He has been a keen critic of the plans for reform of the legal profession.

**DO NASCIMENTO, Lopo Fortunato Ferreira**. *Angola*. Politician. Born in 1940, a veteran member of the ruling Angolan People's Liberation Movement (MPLA), Do Nascimento was prime minister from independence in 1975 until 1978. From 1975 he was also successively minister of internal trade and planning. He held the latter post from 1979 to 1986, when he was made commissioner of Huíla province in the south, where he has been resonsible for implementing a successful economic liberalization strategy, the blueprint for the goverment's plans at national level.

**DONAT-CATTIN, Carlo**. *Italy*. Labour minister and Christian Democrat party (DC) politician. Born in 1919 in Liguria, he pursued a career as a journalist and served as a regional trade union leader. He entered the Chamber of Deputies in 1958 and became leader of the party's Forza Nuova (New Force) faction, which although nominally left-wing has sometimes supported conservative positions. In August 1969 he was appointed labour and social security minister, where he was credited with mediating a settlement with the metal workers that ended the "hot autumn" of 1969, and subsequently held various other portfolios before becoming deputy secretary of the DC in October 1978. In 1979 he was elected to the Senate. In May 1980 he resigned his party post when it emerged that he had advised his son Marco to flee to avoid arrest on terrorism charges. He returned to cabinet office in August 1986, as health minister, retaining this post until July 1989, when he moved to the job of labour minister.

**DORLHAC, Hélène**. *France*. Government minister. Born in 1935, she graduated in medicine and worked as a doctor. President of the Federation of Independent Republicans in the Gard *département* in 1973, she was brought into the government as minister of state for prisons attached to the justice minister from 1974–76. Subsequently, while retaining membership of the Giscardian Union for French Democracy (UDF), she responded to socialist overtures to serve as adviser to the government in 1984 and became identified as a supporter of

**François Mitterrand**. She was appointed as minister of state for the family in 1988, taking on the extra responsibility for the elderly in October 1990.

**DOS SANTOS, José Eduardo**. *Angola*. President. Born in 1942, he trained as a petroleum engineer in the Soviet oil fields before returning home in 1970 to participate in the war against the Portuguese. After independence in 1975 he held several senior posts in the ruling Angolan People's Liberation Movement (MPLA) central committee before being appointed planning minister in 1978. After the death of Agostinho Neto in 1979 he was elected to succeed as state president by the central committee. As chairman of the council of ministers he also effectively acts as prime minister. His power has increased considerably over the last decade, particularly since the formation of the defence and security council in 1984. The council, which he chairs, is the most powerful organ of government, determining overall economic, political and military strategy. Since the late 1980s, he has overseen moves to reach a negotiated end to the civil war, liberalize the economy and, most recently, democratize the political system.

**DOUBIN, François**. *France*. Government minister. Born in 1933 and a graduate of the Institut d'Etudes Politiques and of the Ecole Nationale d'Administration, he was a manager in the nationalized car industry, becoming secretary-general of Renault in 1984. He belongs to the Movement of Left-wing Radicals (MRG) and was elected its president in 1985 and 1987. In 1988, he was appointed minister-delegate attached to the industry and regional planning minister, with special responsibility for trade and the artisan industries.

**DOURDA, Abu Zaid Omar**. *Libya*. General People's Committee (GPC) secretary. Appointed secretary of the GPC – effectively prime minister – in October 1990, Dourda is a close adviser of **Muammar Qaddafi** and has also held the agriculture, economy, information and foreign affairs portfolios.

**DOWIYOGO, Bernard**. *Nauru*. President. Born in 1946, and trained as a lawyer in Australia, he has been an MP in Nauru since 1973. As leader of a loosely knit opposition group calling itself the Nauru Party, he succeeded in ousting the long-standing head chief and president, Hammer DeRoburt, and becoming president himself from 1976–78. DeRoburt then returned to office, dominating a

political structure based primarily on family ties, and Dowiyogo served as his justice minister from 1983 until DeRoburt's fall in 1989 over a vote of no confidence. Dowiyogo emerged victorious in a presidential contest against the veteran former leader in December 1989. He has shown himself to be a radical in South Pacific politics over the issue of demilitarization.

**DRACH, Ivan**. *USSR*. Ukrainian nationalist leader. Born in 1936 near Kiev, he was elected in September 1989 as chairman of the Ukrainian People's Movement (Rukh). The largest nationalist group in the republic, Rukh commands substantial support, especially in western Ukraine, and forms an influential minority in the Ukrainian parliament; in October 1990 it adopted complete independence for the Ukraine as its main policy objective. A quiet, deliberate anti-demagogue, Drach is a distinguished author and poet.

**DRAPER, William H., III**. *USA*. Administrator of UN Development Programme (UNDP). Born in 1928, he studied law and then worked for a steel corporation and a number of investment companies (including his own). A close associate of **George Bush**, he was president of the US Export-Import Bank (Eximbank) from 1982 until 1986 when he was appointed administrator of UNDP, which finances development projects in the third world. A low-profile figure, he has not sought personal recognition, unlike a number of his UN colleagues.

**DRASKOVIĆ, Vuk**. *Yugoslavia*. Leader of the hard-line right-wing Serbian National Renewal Party. A fiery nationalist, he notoriously called for a "declaration of war" in October 1990 against Croatia because of the treatment of ethnic Serbs. Such extremism may have frightened away support, especially with Serbia's president **Slobodan Milošević** himself so ready to play the nationalist card, and Drasković and his party were seen as the main losers in the Serbian elections at the end of 1990. He finished a distant second with 20% in the presidential poll.

**DRENTCHEV, Milan**. *Bulgaria*. Leader of the Nikola Petrov Agrarians, who broke away from the Bulgarian Agrarian People's Union (BZNS) in 1945, and refounded their party in 1989. The Petrov Agrarians are one of the largest constituent parts of the opposition coalition, the Union of Democratic Forces. Born in 1916, Drentchev spent three years in prison for his anti-fascist activities and then a further 14 years in communist jails and labour camps.

**DREYFUS, Tony.** *France.* Government minister. Born in 1939, he became a lawyer at the Paris Court of Appeal after playing an active role in student politics. Politically, he moved with **Michel Rocard** from the Unified Socialist Party (PSU) to the Socialist Party (PS) whilst, professionally, establishing close working relations with **Jacques Chérèque**. In 1981, he advised **Pierre Mauroy**'s government on nationalization policy, subsequently sitting on the board of Crédit Commercial de France (1982–86). He became a junior minister (without portfolio) attached to the office of the prime minister in 1988 when Rocard became premier.

**DRNOVŠEK, Janez.** *Yugoslavia.* Slovenia's member of the collective state presidency. Born in 1950, he holds a doctorate in economics and is a deputy in the federal assembly. He has worked in industry, banking and the diplomatic service. A liberal technocrat, he stood as an independent candidate in Slovenia's first democratic presidential poll in May 1989, and defeated the communist party's nominee. He advocates economic liberalism and closer links with the EC. In October 1990 he announced his withdrawal from the collective state presidency in protest against its systematic manipulation by **Borisav Jović**, Serbia's member who took over as president for one year in May 1990.

**DROMI, Roberto.** *Argentina.* Public works and services minister. Born in 1945, Dromi studied law at Mendoza University and practised as a lawyer. He was appointed a minister by **Carlos Menem** in 1989.

**DRUK, Mircha.** *USSR.* Prime minister of Moldavia. Born in 1940, he worked in academic research and subsequently as director-general of the Moldavian national centre for co-operation with foreign countries before his election as premier in April 1990. His government programme demonstrates strong market reformist credentials.

**DUBA, Ali.** *Syria.* Special forces commander. Formerly military intelligence chief, Duba took on the key post of commander of the army's special forces after the retirement of Ali Haidar in September 1988. Duba is from the same Mutawirah Alawi clan as President **Hafez al-Assad**. He is considered one of the regime's rising stars and some see him as a potential rival to the president.

**DUBČEK, Alexander.** *Czechoslovakia.* Federal Assembly chairman. The personification of his country's experiment with "socialism with a human face" in the Prague spring of 1968, Dubček's return to the public arena after the years of enforced obscurity provided one of the emotional highlights of the "velvet revolution" in late 1989. The welcome given to him as he addressed the demonstrators in Bratislava and Prague raised the suggestion that he might again play a leadership role. In the event it was the younger generation who provided the country's new leaders, with Dubček taking the largely ceremonial role of Federal Assembly chairman. Born in 1921, he rose through the Communist Party in Slovakia, where he became party leader, but was a little-known figure before his election in January 1968 as first secretary of the party at national level. His popular and daring programme of liberal reforms ended as the tanks of the Warsaw Pact countries rolled into Prague in August; Dubček was arrested and taken to the USSR that same night. He could do nothing to prevent the occupation of his country, and in October signed a protocol amounting to capitulation on his policies. He resisted Soviet pressure for his resignation but eventually stood down as first secretary in April 1969. He was sidelined to chair the assembly, then went as ambassador to Turkey, before being thrown out of the party as the purge took hold in mid-1970. He was then packed off to obscurity with the forestry administration in Bratislava.

**DUCHAC, Josef.** *Germany.* Thuringia premier. Elected in October 1990 to head the government in the smallest Land (state) in east Germany, he appeared unassuming in the campaign, overshadowed by the political heavyweights from the west who dominated the party's rallies. A qualified chemical engineer, he has made industrial regeneration a clear priority for his administration. Born in 1938, he first joined the Christian Democratic Union (CDU) under the communist regime in 1957, but did not emerge in the leadership at all until the convulsions of late 1989, when he joined the party national executive.

**DUISENBERG, Wim.** *Netherlands.* Economist, Labour politician and banker. Born in 1935, he was professor of economics at the University of Amsterdam from 1970–73 and then finance minister in the 1973–77 centre–left coalition. He was elected to the Staten Generaal (parliament) for the Labour Party, PvdA, but in 1977, left politics the following year to go into banking, becoming president of the central bank in 1982.

**DUKAKIS, Michael**. *USA*. Former Democratic governor of Massachusetts and 1988 Democratic presidential nominee. Born in 1933 to Greek immigrant parents, he was educated at Swarthmore College and Harvard University. A lawyer and state legislator, he became governor in 1974 but the unpopularity of his economic policies lost him renomination in 1978. After teaching government at Harvard he was elected to a second gubernatorial term in 1982. This was distinguished by promotion of the "economic miracle" of Massachusetts through the encouragement of high-tech industries, higher education and new business investment. He surprisingly won the Democratic presidential nomination in 1988 with a campaign in which he was depicted as a centrist technocrat and proven executive leader. In the presidential election, this strategy fell apart when **George Bush**'s "l-word" attacks saddled him with a liberal image. His failure to make a clearcut stand for or against liberalism left voters confused about his position, and his huge opinion poll lead was transformed into a landslide defeat. The outcome virtually ensured that Dukakis's career in national politics was over. Increasingly unpopular as the economic boom in Massachusetts collapsed, he did not seek a fourth gubernatorial term in 1990.

**DUMAS, Roland**. *France*. Minister of state for foreign affairs. Born in 1922 and decorated for wartime activity, he graduated in law, politics and languages before taking up a career as a lawyer, journalist and politician. As a long-standing colleague and friend of **François Mitterrand**, he was first elected to the National Assembly in 1945 and has been a deputy in numerous subsequent parliaments, holding a seat continuously since 1981. An expert in foreign affairs, he was appointed European affairs minister in 1983, then foreign minister in 1984–86, and since 1988 has been minister of state for foreign affairs. Well-respected and diplomatic, he works well with Mitterrand, the two of them effectively running French foreign policy together.

**DUNKEL, Arthur**. *Switzerland*. Director-general of General Agreement on Tariffs and Trade (Gatt). Born in 1932, he studied economics and in 1956 joined the federal office for external economic affairs, where over the years he represented Switzerland in multilateral and bilateral negotiations on trade and development issues. Appointed director-general of Gatt in 1980, he has had the unenviable task of trying to find a worldwide consensus on trade issues within the Uruguay Round of negotiations. His considerable diplomatic skills kept the show on the road, but the imperatives of impartiality, combined with budgetary constraints, have limited the secretariat's ability to take on a more active role.

**DUNN, Dame Lydia**. *Hong Kong*. Politician and businesswoman. Born in 1940, she rose in the Swire Group, becoming executive director of Swire Pacific in 1982. She is also a director of Cathay Pacific Airways, and The Hongkong and Shanghai Banking Corporation. She became a member of the Legislative Council in 1975, and of the policy-making Executive Council in 1982. In 1990 she lobbied unsuccessfully for full British nationality for Hong Kong residents, and is a supporter of greater democracy in the colony. Tipped as a possible future governor, she is married to Michael Thomas, the attorney-general.

**DU PLESSIS, Barend**. *South Africa*. Finance minister. Born in 1940, he qualified as a teacher and subsequently worked in broadcasting. After local government experience in Roodepoort, he was elected an MP in 1974. After a brief spell as minister in charge of black education, he became finance minister in 1984, and emerged as a relatively liberal *verligte* to run **F. W. de Klerk** a close second in the 1989 National Party leadership contest. Although thereby becoming the nominal heir apparent, he has hardly emerged as a credible national leader, and does not feature among the president's closest confidants. He might, however, be a reassuring face for white business if he were to retain his post in any future ANC-led government.

**DURAFOUR, Michel**. *France*. Civil service and administrative reform minister. Born in 1920 and a graduate in law and politics, he has had a long and active political career since 1944, notably as a government adviser and as a centrist member of the National Assembly. In the centre-right government under President **Valéry Giscard d'Estaing** he was labour minister from 1974–76, but found himself ill at ease with the more radical right-wing interventionism of the neo-Gaullist prime minister, **Jacques Chirac**. His own leanings were better suited to the Union for French Democracy (UDF), formed in 1978, on which he served as a national council member. In 1983 he became a senator. Five years later, in the face of the criticism from his erstwhile colleagues, he responded to overtures from the moderate left by accepting the post of civil service and administrative reform minister, subsequently becoming minister of state, and the highest-ranking non-socialist in **Michel Rocard**'s government.

**DURIEUX, Bruno.** *France.* Government minister. Born in 1944 and a graduate of the Ecole Polytechnique, he followed a civil service career, specializing in economics and planning. In the 1970s he acted as adviser to the prime minister, **Raymond Barre**, and since 1986 has been a member of the National Assembly, representing the Centre of Social Democrats (CDS). In October 1990 he accepted **Michel Rocard**'s invitation to become minister-delegate for health.

**DURNWALDER, Luis.** *Italy.* South Tyrol People's Party (SVP) politician. Born in 1941 in Pfalzen, in the mainly German-speaking Alto Adige (South Tyrol), he studied agricultural sciences and law and became a teacher. He entered politics in 1969, when he was elected mayor of Pfalzen. Four years later he joined the prominent Council of Alto Adige, with responsibility for agriculture and forestry. In 1984 he was elected first deputy chairman of the SVP and in March 1989 succeeded SVP president, **Silvius Magnago**, as leader of the Alto Adige Provincial Council. He represents the younger generation of South Tyrol nationalism, which has become less militant in recent years as a greater degree of regional autonomy has been granted.

**DUVAL, Sir Gaëtan.** *Mauritius.* Leader of Mauritius Social Democratic Party (PMSD). Born in 1930, a barrister by training, he has been a controversial figure in Mauritian politics since colonial days. Representing the island's creole community, he initially opposed independence but has since played an active part in the shifting coalitions of Mauritius's turbulent democracy. He served as deputy prime minister in the **Aneerood Jugnauth** administration from 1983–88 but the partnership was not a happy one. Duval's arrest and trial the following year on charges of conspiracy in the murder of a political activist 18 years earlier threatened to revive intercommunal tensions, although the charges were later dropped.

**DYREMOSE, Henning.** *Denmark.* Finance minister. Born in 1945, he graduated as a chemical engineer in 1969 and worked as a lecturer and a management consultant before accepting a senior position at the NOVO pharmaceuticals company. Elected to the Folketing (parliament) for the Conservative People's Party (KF) in 1979, he resigned five years later to return to NOVO. In 1986 he re-entered politics as labour minister and in 1989 he became finance minister.

**DZASOKHOV, Aleksandr.** *USSR.* Senior Communist Party official. An ethnic Ossete born in 1934, he began his career as Komsomol leader in North Ossetia (an autonomous republic in the Caucasus) in 1957. After serving as chief of Soviet specialists in Cuba, he worked from the late 1960s in the USSR committee for solidarity with African and Asian nations. Appointed ambassador to Syria in 1986, he returned to North Ossetia in late 1988 as local Communist Party leader. In mid-1989 he was appointed chairman of the USSR Supreme Soviet's foreign affairs commission. After the 1990 Communist Party of the Soviet Union congress he was elected a politburo member and took over the secretariat portfolio for ideology from Vadim Medvedev.

**DZHUMAGULOV, Apas.** *USSR.* Kirghiz prime minister. A regional Communist Party official prior to his 1986 election as premier of his Central Asian republic, he was re-elected in April 1990. He was prominent in negotiations to end the inter-ethnic violence between Kirghizes and Uzbeks in mid-1990. In October 1990 he stood unsuccessfully for the republic's executive presidency, won by **Aksar Akayev**.

**DZORIG, Sanjaasurengiyn.** *Mongolia.* Mongolian Democratic Union (MDU) leader. Born in 1962, the former lecturer in scientific communism at the Mongolian State University launched the MDU, the first opposition party, in December 1989. He was elected the first chairman of the parliamentary group of the People's Little Hural (lower house) in September 1990. A shrewd politician, but at something of a disadvantage as an urban intellectual without a rural base, he was defeated in the September 1990 election for the vice-presidency by the Social Democratic Party's **Radnaasumbereliyn Gonchigdorj**. Although he is in opposition, his views are similar to those of reformists in the ruling Mongolian People's Revolutionary Party, including support for multi-party democracy and private enterprise.

# E

EAGLEBURGER, Lawrence. *USA*. Deputy secretary, state department. Born in 1930, he entered the foreign service in 1957, and was ambassador to Yugoslavia from 1977–81. Something of a survivor from the **Reagan** years, and part of a close-knit foreign policy team, he is considered a policy heavyweight in **George Bush**'s administration. His involvement with Kissinger Associates, a consultancy firm founded by **Henry Kissinger**, led to conflict-of-interest charges at his confirmation hearings. Though he holds the traditional post-war US view on foreign relations, he plays an active role in Bush's more tolerant attitude toward China.

ECEVİT, Bülent. *Turkey*. Opposition leader and former prime minister. Born in 1925, he worked as a journalist until 1961, when he became labour minister in a social democratic government. He went on to head three governments in the 1970s; but, stymied by obstructionist parliamentary tactics, he failed to deal effectively with the country's growing economic crisis, or with its mounting internal security problems. The military coup of 1980 brought three years' internment and a seven-year ban from politics; he nevertheless continued working with the fledgling Democratic Left Party (DSP), for which he was tried and acquitted in 1986. On being allowed back into politics in 1987, he became chairman of the DSP, but has been unable to shake off allegations of inconsistency. In 1987 he publicly announced his retirement from politics; he is still there.

EDA, Satsuki. *Japan*. United Social Democratic Federation (USDF) leader. Born in 1941, he is the son of Saburo Eda, a former Japan Socialist Party secretary-general and founder of the USDF. Satsuki studied law and became an assistant judge. Politically he followed in his father's footsteps, entering the House of Councillors (upper house) after his father's death in 1977 (and later moving to the House of Representatives), and taking on his party's leadership in 1985. An advocate of unity among the various social democratic parties, he has attempted, so far unsuccessfully, to realize this objective by putting his own small party forward as a mediating force.

EDGAR, Jim. *USA*. Republican governor of Illinois. Born in 1946, he became governor in 1990. In his campaign he attracted the liberal support which traditionally went to the Democrats, notably by his advocacy of increased taxation on high income earners to finance education expenditure.

EDMONDS, John. *UK*. Trade unionist. Born in 1944, he gained a scholarship to Oxford University. He joined the General and Municipal Workers' Union (GMWU, now known as GMB) in 1966, working as a research officer and industrial officer for many years. He became general secretary in 1986 and has promoted a pragmatic line, adapting the union to the new economic realities and quietly promoting more mainstream policies within the Labour Party.

EDWARDS, Mickey. *USA*. Republican congressman from Oklahoma. Born in 1937, he practised law before his election to the House of Representatives in 1976. He chairs the Republican policy committee, which helps to shape the party agenda, and is a leading advocate of tougher penalties for drug users.

EGGAR, Timothy. *UK*. Minister of state for education since July 1990 and MP since 1979. Born in 1951, Eggar trained as a lawyer and worked in banking. He was a junior foreign minister from 1985–89 before moving on to employment where he specialized in small business development.

ELGORRIAGA GOYENECHE, Julén. *Spain*. Socialist politician. Born in 1950 in Irun in the Basque region, he is prominent among the younger generation of Basque members of the Spanish Socialist Workers' Party (PSOE), which he joined in 1973. He played a key role in negotiations with the nationalist movement ETA in the late 1980s as the government's delegate in the Basque region until November 1989. His local and regional government experience is substantial, including terms as mayor of Irun and governor of Guipuzcoa province.

**ELIZABETH II.** *UK.* Queen and head of the Commonwealth since 1952, when she succeeded to the throne on the death of her father, George VI. Born in 1926, her upbringing was constrained by rigid protocol. Immensely scrupulous about her position as the impartial head of state, she is considered remarkably astute and has avoided controversy (unlike her husband, Philip, Duke of Edinburgh, and her eldest son, **Prince Charles**).

**ELLEMANN-JENSEN, Uffe.** *Denmark.* Leader of the Liberals. Born in 1941, he graduated in economics and then turned to newspaper and television journalism. Elected to the Folketing (parliament) for the Liberals (Venstre) in 1977, he was appointed foreign minister when a centre–right coalition took power in 1982 and was elected party leader in 1984. He is tipped as a likely future prime minister.

**ENDARA GALIMANY, Guillermo.** *Panama.* President. Born in 1937, Endara trained as a lawyer. He joined the Authentic Panameñista Party (PPA) and was an adviser to President Arnulfo Arias. He became secretary-general of the anti-**Manuel Noriega** faction of the PPA and was the presidential candidate of the Democratic Civic Opposition Alliance (ADOC) in May 1989 when the election results were annulled. He was installed as president after the US invasion in December 1989.

**ENGELEITER, Susan.** *USA.* Small Business Administration (SBA) administrator. Born in Milwaukee in 1952, she was the Republican leader in the Wisconsin state senate for four years. She was the youngest woman in the country to take a seat in a state legislature, and the first woman in Wisconsin history to be elected to a major leadership post. She ran unsuccessfully for the US Senate in 1988, before her appointment to the SBA in January 1989.

**ENGELHARD, Hans.** *Germany.* Justice minister since 1982. Born in Munich in 1934, he studied law and was elected in 1972 to the Bundestag, where he became deputy chairman of the Free Democratic Party parliamentary group (1977–82).

**ENGELL, Hans.** *Denmark.* Justice minister. Born in 1948, he came through newspaper journalism to become director of information at the Conservative People's Party (KF) and editor of the party paper in 1978. In 1982 he was appointed defence minister in **Poul Schlüter**'s first administration, a difficult post in a government that did not command a parliamentary majority on defence issues. Elected to the Folketing (parliament) in 1984, he left the cabinet for the leadership of the KF parliamentary group in 1987 but returned as justice minister two years later. He is tipped as a likely successor to Schlüter as party leader.

**ENGHOLM, Björn.** *Germany.* Social Democratic Party (SPD) politician and Schleswig-Holstein premier. Born in Lübeck in 1939, he left grammar school to become a printer, and later studied politics at Hamburg University. From 1969–82 he was an SPD member of the Bundestag and served as education and science minister in 1981–82. He was then elected chairman of the SPD group in the Land (state) parliament of Schleswig-Holstein, where he became premier in 1988. In December 1990 he was nominated by the party presidium to succeed **Hans Jochen Vogel** as SPD chairman in May 1991.

**ENGLER, John.** *USA.* Republican governor of Michigan. Born in 1948, he was on the right of the party, and had been majority leader in the state senate, before his unexpected victory in the 1990 gubernatorial election against incumbent **James Blanchard**.

**ENGSTRÖM, Odd.** *Sweden.* Deputy prime minister. Born in 1941, he worked as a civil servant before becoming secretary to the parliamentary group of the Social Democratic Labour Party (SAP) in 1977. From 1982 he held further senior posts in local and central government, becoming junior minister at the finance ministry in 1988. In 1990 he was appointed deputy prime minister, which put him in a strong position to succeed **Ingvar Carlsson** as party leader.

**ENRILE, Juan Ponce (Johnny).** *Philippines.* Veteran politician and opposition leader. Born in 1924, he was educated at Harvard Law School and specialized in taxation before entering politics. Appointed justice secretary under Ferdinand Marcos in 1968, he subsequently served as defence secretary from 1970–78, when he was promoted to defence minister. He switched his allegiance to **Cory Aquino** at a critical point in the 1986 revolution, and was rewarded by being re-appointed as defence minister when Aquino took office. He soon became distanced from Aquino, however, and resigned from the cabinet in November 1986 after being increasingly identified with right-wing sections of the military opposed to Aquino.

After offering tacit support to several military revolts, he was accused by government prosecutors of being behind the December 1989 coup attempt and of harbouring the coup leader, **Gregorio Honasan**. He was subsequently charged with rebellion and murder and also asked about his "unexplained wealth". Charges were dropped in June 1990, however, in a court decision that was seen as a further weakening of Aquino's authority. Enrile has declared his intention of standing for the presidency in 1992.

**ERSHAD, Lieutenant-General Hussein Mohammed.** *Bangladesh.* Former president and armed forces commander-in-chief. Born in 1930 and trained in the East Bengal Regiments, he was stationed in West Pakistan in 1971 and could take no part in the creation of Bangladesh, but was repatriated there in 1973 and continued his rise through the senior officer corps in the newly independent state. He became chief of army staff in 1978, and led a bloodless military takeover in March 1982, pledging himself to eradicate corruption and foster economic development on a commercial basis. His regime faced a sustained if not always coherent mass campaign for the restoration of democracy. In December 1990, the popular campaign against him reached a peak, and Ershad, having lost the support of the army, stepped down and was placed under house arrest. He nevertheless announced plans to contest the February 1991 elections.

**ESCHEIKH, Abdelhamid.** *Tunisia.* Interior minister. Formerly ambassador to Algeria, Escheikh was brought into the cabinet as youth and sports minister by President **Zine el-Abidine Ben Ali** in April 1988. He was promoted to the foreign ministry in 1989, and in March 1990 became interior minister. His military background – he was chief of staff from 1975–81 – signalled a hardening of the government's line against Islamic militants, particularly in the universities.

**ESQUIVEL, Manuel.** *Belize.* Opposition leader. Born in 1940, he taught physics before helping to found the opposition United Democratic Party (UDP) in 1973. He was appointed a senator in 1979 and became UDP leader in 1982. After the party's election victory in 1984 he served as prime minister until 1989. His premiership was marked by the opening of negotiations over Guatemala's territorial claims to Belize.

**ESTANISLAO, Jesus.** *Philippines.* Finance secretary. Estanislao was appointed to **Cory** Aquino's cabinet in 1989, with the task of pushing through economic reform, notably changes in tariff regulations, in the face of opposition from the business community. Despite determined expressions of intent, he has had only limited success, with the economy increasingly hampered by mounting inflation and diminishing investment. Conflict with **Jose Concepcion**, the trade and industry secretary, has further reduced his effectiveness, as has a lack of political will for reform, from both the president and Congress.

**ETXTEBESTE, Eugenio.** *Spain.* Basque nationalist. A leading ETA figure (known in the organization as Antxon), he was ETA's political chief until his arrest in 1984. Deported to Ecuador, he was brought to Algeria in 1987, identifying himself as a moderate by his willingness to enter talks with the Spanish government. The Algiers negotiations were abandoned in early 1988, however, and in April Etxtebeste was deported again, to the Dominican Republic.

**EVANS, Gareth.** *Australia.* Foreign minister. One of the most able of **Bob Hawke**'s senior ministers, and one of Australia's most effective foreign ministers, Evans was born in Melbourne in 1944. He studied law at Melbourne University before going to the UK, where he got a first-class degree in PPE (philosophy, politics and economics) at Oxford University. He returned to lecture in Melbourne until elected to the Senate as an Australian Labor Party (ALP) member for Victoria in 1980. With the Labor victory of 1983 he became attorney-general, and the following year resources and energy minister. In the second Hawke government from 1987 he was initially transport and communications minister, and then he moved in 1988 to the foreign affairs portfolio vacated by **Bill Hayden** before the latter's investiture as governor-general. Evans remained foreign minister after the 1990 election. He has consistently emphasized the importance of regionalism in Australian foreign policy and given greater attention to relations with South-east Asia and the South Pacific. Despite his obvious abilities there has been little talk of him as a potential leadership contender. Unlike Hawke and the "declared" candidates for his job, **Paul Keating** and **Kim Beazley**, who are on the right of the ALP, Evans belongs to its centre–left faction.

**EVERT, Miltiades.** *Greece.* New Democracy (ND) politician. He was born in 1939, and his father served as Athens chief of police during the

Nazi occupation but was later revealed to have been a British double agent. An economist by training, Evert was an ND MP from 1974–86, and was re-elected in 1989. He held junior cabinet posts from 1976, rising to become finance minister in 1980. In 1986 he was elected mayor of Athens and raised the profile of local government by borrowing funds for projects that central government would not finance. As mayor he also broke the state monopoly on the mass media by defiantly setting up a municipal radio station. A hefty, ebullient man, Evert "the bulldozer" is tipped as one of the prime contenders to succeed **Constantine Mitsotakis** as ND leader. He was appointed minister to the prime minister after the April 1990 elections.

**EVIN, Claude.** *France.* Solidarity and social security minister. Born in 1949, he moved from the Unified Socialist Party (PSU) to the Socialist Party (PS), becoming a member of the National Assembly in 1978 and, in 1986, one of its vice-presidents. Within the PS, he has specialized in social and family questions. In 1988 he became solidarity, health and social security minister, combining this portfolio with the role of official government spokesman in 1988–89, but delegating the health portfolio to **Bruno Durieux** in October 1990.

**EYADÉMA, General Gnassingbe (Etienne).** *Togo.* President. Born in 1937 in the politically isolated and economically underdeveloped north of Togo, Eyadéma was in the French army from 1953–61, seeing service in Indochina, Algeria and French West Africa, and reaching the rank of company sergeant-major. After Togo's independence he took part in the 1963 coup that overthrew President Sylvanus Olympio. By 1967 he was chief of the general staff of the Togo armed forces and in January of that year seized power from Nicolas Grunitsky. In 1969 he abolished multi-party politics, setting up one-party rule under the Togolese People's Rally (RPT). A skilful authoritarian, Eyadéma governed through a coterie of trusted advisers, carefully cultivating his image as the "father" of the nation. In October 1990, however, faced with widening unrest, he announced plans for a return to multi-party democracy. His economic policies, allowing the private sector a free rein, have so far done more to benefit a small number of foreign investors than the mass of the population.

**EYSKENS, Mark.** *Belgium.* Foreign minister. Born in 1933, he studied law, economics and philosophy in Belgium and the USA and became a lecturer at Leuven University. Elected to parliament for the Christian People's Party (CVP) in 1977, he became development co-operation minister in 1979 and finance minister in 1980. In 1981 he became prime minister of a centre-left coalition after his party colleague **Wilfried Martens** failed to secure support for drastic austerity measures. Elections later that year brought back Martens as prime minister; Eyskens remained in government as, successively, economics, finance and foreign minister.

# F

**FABIUS, Laurent**. *France*. National Assembly president. Born in 1946, he graduated through France's elite educational institutions, the Ecole Normale Supérieure, Institut d'Etudes Politiques and Ecole Nationale d'Administration before becoming an *auditeur* at the Council of State. Since 1978 he has held a seat in the National Assembly as a Socialist Party (PS) deputy. Between 1981 and 1983 he was minister-delegate for economy and finance, with budgetary responsibility; he was then promoted to become industry and research minister. In 1984, when he was only 38, **François Mitterrand** chose him to be prime minister, symbolizing the PS's swing from left-wing politics to "economic realism". Fabius was widely seen as Mitterrand's chosen *dauphin*. The two years out of government from 1986–88, however, saw his star wane; he failed to regain the premiership, and lost to **Pierre Mauroy** in the contest for the party leadership in 1988, settling for leadership of the party's 1989 Euro-election campaign and the presidency of the National Assembly.

**FADLALLAH, Shaikh Mohammed Hussein**. *Lebanon*. Hezbollah leader. With Shaikh Ibrahim al-Amin, Shaikh Fadlallah is one of the best-known leaders of the Hezbollah (Party of God), a shadowy umbrella organization of radical Shias with Iranian links. Based in South Beirut, it aims to set up an Islamic state in Lebanon, and is believed to be behind some of the seizures of Western hostages.

**FAHD IBN ABDUL-AZIZ**. *Saudi Arabia*. King. Born in 1923, he is the eldest of the seven sons (the "Sudairi Seven") of King Abdul-Aziz's favourite wife, Hassa bint Ahmad al-Sudairi. In 1953, he joined the kingdom's first council of ministers as education minister. Effective ruler after the assassination of his older half-brother King Faisal in 1975, he became king on the death of his other half-brother, King Khaled, in June 1982. Since the Iranian revolution in 1979 and the siege by Islamic fundamentalists in Mecca the same year, King Fahd has made efforts to neutralize the militants who accuse the regime of decadence. His adoption of the title "Custodian of the Two Holy Shrines" in 1986 was aimed at inoculating the Saudi regime from further militant anger. In August 1990, however, he inflamed radical Arab opinion by inviting US forces to defend the kingdom after the Iraqi invasion of neighbouring Kuwait.

**FALAE, Chief Olu**. *Nigeria*. Finance and economic development minister and former secretary to the government. Appointed to his present post in December 1989, he took a hardline approach to negotiations with Nigeria's creditors, which brought him into conflict with the powerful budget and planning minister **Alhaji Abubakar Alhaji**. Dropped from the cabinet in the August 1990 reshuffle, he was tipped to become the presidential candidate of the Social Democratic Party, one of the two political parties set up by the government in 1989.

**FALIN, Valentin**. *USSR*. Senior Communist Party official, leading Soviet expert on German affairs. A Russian, born in 1926, he was originally a career diplomat, rising to serve as ambassador in Bonn from 1970–78. Returning to Moscow as deputy head of the Communist Party of the Soviet Union (CPSU) central committee's international information department, he became political observer of the newspaper *Izvestia* in 1983, and in 1986 director of the Novosti press agency. He was appointed in October 1988 as head of the central committee international department and, after scraping through the central committee elections at the July 1990 CPSU congress, he was named a party secretary, sharing responsibility for international ties with **Gennady Yanayev**.

**FALL, Médoune**. *Senegal*. Defence minister. Born in 1919 in Saint-Louis, he began his career in the civil service and was governor of the Djourbel region from 1961–63. He held a series of ambassadorial posts in the 1960s and 1970s, representing Senegal at the UN from 1971–79, before being appointed interior minister in

1980. He moved to the defence ministry in 1983, where he was a key figure in the confrontation with neighbouring Mauritania in 1989.

**FANG LIZHI.** *China.* Astrophysicist and dissident. Born in 1936, Fang is known as "China's Sakharov". Physics professor at the University of Science and Technology in Hefei from 1978, and also university vice-president from 1984, he was removed from both posts and expelled from the Chinese Communist Party in 1987 for attacks on party leadership and involvement in student protests in December 1986. Fang and his wife Li Shuxian, a physicist active in local politics, were later accused of being the "black hand" behind the 1989 pro-democracy movement. After the crackdown, they took refuge in the US embassy in Beijing until June 1990, when they were quietly permitted to leave for the UK. Fang took up a research post at Cambridge University for a few months before moving to the USA.

**FARAKOS, Grigoris.** *Greece.* Secretary-general of the Communist Party of Greece (KKE). Born in 1923, he trained as an electrical engineer before joining the communist-led partisans during the Nazi occupation. During the civil war (1946–49) he fought with the communist Democratic Army, retreating to Eastern Europe after the uprising was crushed. He had become a member of the central committee of the KKE by 1968 when he secretly returned to Greece to organize clandestine resistance to the military dictatorship. He was arrested and in May 1969 sentenced to life imprisonment for sedition. When the KKE was legalized in 1974, he stood for parliament and has been a deputy in every assembly since then. For a number of years he served as editor of the party newspaper *Rizospastis*. In 1990, he was elected secretary-general of KKE.

**FARRAKHAN, Louis.** *USA.* Black religious leader. Born Louis Eugene Walcott in New York city in 1933, he was a calypso singer before joining the Nation of Islam movement in 1965. This is a Chicago-based group which believes that Allah appeared in the form of Master Fard Muhammed in 1930, and follows the black-supremacy teachings of Elijah Muhammed. Farrakhan soon rose to become captain of The Fruits of Islam, the movement's security force. After the death of Malcolm X, he became minister of the Harlem Temple, where he stayed until 1975. A charismatic speaker, he is often reviled for his militant anti-white and anti-semitic stance. He came to national prominence when he supported **Jesse Jackson**'s bid for the presidency in 1984, although Jackson soon found Farrakhan's outspoken militancy a liability and disowned him. Since 1987, Farrakhan has tried to move closer to the mainstream, endorsing the entrepreneurial spirit of black capitalists. He has also found limited acceptance among some orthodox Muslims and black Christian clergy, who wonder whether he may play a role in defusing gang violence in American cities.

**FASCELL, Dante.** *USA.* Democratic congressman for Florida. Born in 1917, Fascell practised law before election to the House of Representatives in 1954. A foreign policy specialist, he drafted the 1973 War Powers Resolution restricting presidential war-making and has been the foreign relations committee chairman since 1984. Constituency interests led him to back the policy of **Ronald Reagan**'s administration on Central America and Cuba but he strongly supports arms control.

**FATAFEHI TU'IPELEHAKE, Prince.** *Tonga.* Prime minister. Brother of **King Tupou IV Taufa'ahau**, born in 1922, he has served as prime minister since his brother's accession to the throne in 1965. He also holds the agriculture, forestry and fisheries and marine affairs portfolios.

**FAURE, Maurice.** *France.* Left-wing Radical politician. Born in 1922, he studied literature and law and worked as a teacher before becoming adviser to government and a junior minister. A fervent European, he was one of the signatories of the Rome treaties establishing the EEC and Euratom. In 1958, briefly, he was the interior and European affairs minister. From 1951–83, almost without a break, he sat in the National Assembly as a centre-left radical and subsequently in the Senate for the Movement of Left-wing Radicals (MRG). In 1988 he became minister of state for infrastructure and housing, ranking as the highest-placed non-socialist in **Michel Rocard**'s government. In 1989 he moved to the Constitutional Council.

**FAUROUX, Roger.** *France.* Industry and regional planning minister. Born in 1926 and a graduate of the Ecole Normale Supérieure and Ecole Nationale d'Administration (ENA), he worked as a civil servant and financial director in the 1950s and 1960s, moving on to occupy top jobs in industry, with major firms Pont-à-Mousson, Saint Gobain and Honeywell-Bull. In 1986 he was appointed director of ENA, and in

1988 joined the government, putting his experience to use as industry and regional planning minister. Politically, he identifies with the centrist "United France" movement led by **Jean-Pierre Soisson**.

**FEBRES CORDERO RIVADENEIRO, León.** *Ecuador*. Former president. Born in 1931, Febres Cordero studied mechanical engineering in the USA, returning to pursue a career as an engineer and industrialist. He was first elected a member of the National Assembly in 1966. In 1979 he was re-elected a senator for the Social Christian Party (PSC). Elected president in 1984, he pursued a policy of free-market economics and alignment with the USA. At a time when his popularity was declining in the face of growing economic hardship, he was kidnapped and held for several days in 1987 by rebellious air force commandos.

**FEINSTEIN, Dianne.** *USA*. Democratic politician from California. Born in 1933, she was mayor of San Francisco from 1978–87, taking office after George Moscone's assassination. She handled the gay issue by balancing sympathy with her opposition to the ordinance allowing marriage between homosexuals. In 1989 she won the Democratic gubernatorial nomination with a strategy that blended social liberalism, fiscal prudence and support for the death penalty. Ultimately unsuccessful against the republican **Pete Wilson**, she gained wider national exposure from the contest and is a likely candidate for elective office in the future.

**FELBER, René.** *Switzerland*. Foreign minister. Born in Bienne in 1933, he trained as a teacher but soon abandoned the profession in favour of politics. He was elected to the national parliament as a Social Democratic Party (SPS) member in 1967, but his governmental experience was confined to the canton of Neuchâtel until 1988, when he was brought in to replace his party colleague Pierre Aubert as foreign minister.

**FENECH ADAMI, Edward (Eddie).** *Malta*. Prime minister and Nationalist Party (NP) leader. Born in 1934 and a lawyer by training, he edited the weekly *Il Poplu* prior to entering parliament in 1969, and rose through a succession of party posts to become leader of the centre-right NP in 1977. He was regarded as being on the left of his party, but quickly proved to be a combative opponent of the Labour government, particularly in the early 1980s when he led a boycott of parliament over alleged gerrymandering. Since becoming prime minister

in 1987, he has emphasized a greater willingness to negotiate and compromise. On taking office he committed his government to national reconciliation, making domestic issues his main concern. He also sought rapprochement with Western countries and closer involvement with the EC (which Malta applied formally to join in July 1990), thus confirming Malta's shift from the non-aligned posture of the Dom Mintoff years.

**FERNANDES, George.** *India*. Leading Janata Dal politician. Born in 1930 in Mangalore, Karnataka, he became involved in socialist politics in his late teens. He rose through the ranks of the Socialist Party to become general secretary from 1969–77, also holding the presidency of the powerful All-India Railwaymen's Federation from 1973–75. He led a national strike of railway workers in 1974 which was suppressed by the government, and was imprisoned by Indira Gandhi's administration during the emergency of 1975–77. Active in Bombay municipal politics from 1961 onwards, he was first elected to the Lok Sabha (lower house) in 1967. He was industry minister in the Janata government of 1977–79, gaining a reputation for the tough line he took with foreign companies operating in India – most notably Coca-Cola, which withdrew from the country rather than agree to a technology-sharing plan. After the breakup of the Janata coalition he joined Lok Dal, and then crossed over to the rump Janata Party. He became a member of Janata Dal when the Janata Party merged with it in 1988. He was railways minister in the 1989–90 National Front government.

**FERNÁNDEZ, Eduardo.** *Venezuela*. Opposition politician. Born in 1946, he rose to become secretary-general of the Christian democratic Organizing Committee for Independent Electoral Policy (COPEI). He stood as its presidential candidate in the 1988 elections, but only after a damaging contest and disagreements with the faction in the party led by former president Rafael Caldera. Fernández lacks the popularist flair of **Carlos Andrés Pérez** and was defeated in the election, but he remains the leader of the younger generation within COPEI.

**FERNÁNDEZ ORDÓÑEZ, Francisco.** *Spain*. Foreign minister. Born in 1930 in Madrid, and a founder member of the Union of the Democratic Centre (UCD), he was finance minister from 1977–79 and justice minister from 1980–81 in successive UCD governments. As justice minister he steered a controversial divorce law through the Cortes (parliament). A social democrat within the UCD, he resigned from the cabinet in 1981 because of the party's rightward drift, and early the following year set up the Democratic Action Party (PAD). He was elected as a deputy in 1982 on the Spanish Socialist Workers' Party (PSOE) platform, but gave up his seat in 1983 to head the state-controlled Banco Exterior. In 1985 he returned to government as foreign minister, and has particularly promoted Spain's commitment to Latin America.

**FERNÁNDEZ SANZ, Matilde.** *Spain.* Social affairs minister. Born in 1950 and trained as a psychologist, she rose through the union movement to become general secretary of the chemical industries and energy branch of the socialist General Workers' Union (UGT). She joined the Spanish Socialist Workers' Party (PSOE) in 1973 and became its executive secretary with responsibility for women's affairs in 1984. She was appointed social affairs minister in 1989.

**FERRE, Luis.** *USA (Puerto Rico).* National Republican Party chairman. Born in Puerto Rico in 1904, Ferre is the son of Antonio Ferre, a Cuban immigrant who became a prominent local industrialist. Ferre was educated at MIT and continued in his father's business. Originally, he stood on the platform of the Statehood Republican Party. In 1967, after three unsuccessful bids for governor, he helped organize the pro-statehood New Progressive Party (PNP), became its first president, and won the governorship in 1968 on the tide of its electoral success. Defeated in the 1972 gubernatorial election by **Rafaél Hernández Colón**, he was a senator in the legislature from 1976–85, and now chairs the National Republican Party. An elder statesman, he is a leading proponent of the "statehood" option favoured by **George Bush**'s administration for the 1991 referendum on Puerto Rico's status.

**FIELD, Frank.** *UK.* Labour politician. Born in 1942, he studied economics and taught at two tertiary colleges before becoming director of the Child Poverty Action Group (1969–79) and the Low Pay Unit (1974–80), proving himself an effective campaigner on poverty and unemployment issues. He was elected to parliament for Birkenhead in 1979, and has recently faced reselection threats from the radical left in his local Labour Party. Field is held in high esteem on all sides of the house. He is a

member of the Church of England synod.

**FIELD, Michael.** *Australia.* Premier of Tasmania. He was born in 1948 and educated in Tasmania where he was a teacher and community development officer before entering Tasmania's legislative assembly as an Australian Labor Party member in 1976. In 1988 he became leader of the opposition and, following the indecisive election of the following year, Labor premier in an often uneasy coalition with the Green Independents who held the balance of power.

**FIGUEREDO PLANCHART, Reinaldo.** *Venezuela.* Foreign minister. Born in 1938, Figueredo is a former president of the foreign trade institute. A close associate of President **Carlos Andrés Pérez**, he was appointed secretary-general of the presidency in January 1989 and transferred to the foreign ministry in August of that year.

**FILALI, Abdellatif.** *Morocco.* Foreign minister. An experienced diplomat, he held a series of key ambassadorial posts before being appointed foreign minister in 1985, a portfolio he had held briefly in 1971–72. He also served as higher education minister from 1968–70. Filali's son, Foued Filali, is **King Hassan**'s son-in-law, and has extensive business interests.

**FILMON, Gary.** *Canada.* Premier of Manitoba. Filmon was born in Winnipeg in 1942 and was educated at the University of Manitoba. First elected to Manitoba's legislative assembly in 1979, he became provincial leader of the Progressive Party of Canada in 1983 and formed a minority government in 1988. A pivotal force in the Meech Lake constitutional discussions, Filmon worked with the two opposition parties in Manitoba to oppose the accord, which was rejected in June 1990. He held on to power in the September 1990 elections, despite a growing challenge from the New Democratic Party.

**FINI, Gianfranco.** *Italy.* Italian Social Movement–National Right (MSI–DN) politician. Born in 1952 in Bologna, he got a degree in education at Rome University and became a journalist. He was first elected to the Chamber of Deputies in June 1983. He led the right-wing party's youth wing, and in December 1987 was chosen by Giorgio Almirante to succeed him as party secretary, narrowly defeating **Pino Rauti** and becoming the first MSI–DN leader not to have served under Mussolini. He lost the post to Rauti in 1990.

**FINNBOGADÓTTIR, Vigdís.** *Iceland.* President. Born in 1930, she studied literature and French drama, and worked as a teacher and tourist guide. She became a public figure as director of the Reykjavík theatre company from 1972 and as presenter of a television series on French language and literature. Supported by the right-wing and centrist parties, she was elected to the non-executive post of president in 1980, thus becoming the world's first popularly elected woman head of state. She was re-elected in 1984 and 1988.

**FINNEY, Joan.** *USA.* Democratic governor of Kansas. A former state treasurer and vocal opponent of abortion, she was born in 1925 and was elected as governor in 1990.

**FISCHER, Tim.** *Australia.* Leader of the National Party and shadow minister for energy and resources. A member of the federal parliament since 1984, he emerged from relative obscurity in April 1990 to take over the leadership of the conservative, rural-based National Party of Australia.

**FISH, Hamilton.** *USA.* Republican congressman for New York. Born in 1926, he practised law before following in his father's and grandfather's footsteps by winning election to the House of Representatives in 1968. A respected senior political figure, he generally favours pragmatic bipartisan co-operation. He opposed federal involvement in the Eastern Airlines labour dispute in 1989–90, voting to uphold the president's veto of a commission on the matter and arguing that the courts should not be fettered by legislative interference.

**FISSEHA DESTA, Lieutenant-Colonel.** *Ethiopia.* Vice-president. One of the group of army officers involved in the overthrow of Emperor Haile Selassie in 1974, Fisseha was assistant secretary-general of the ruling Dergue from 1977 until its dissolution in 1987, when he was appointed vice-president. **Mengistu Haile Mariam**'s deputy and loyal ally, he has been closely involved with the establishment of the Worker's Party of Ethiopia and the introduction of "civilian" rule. A Tigrayan, he was appointed in November 1989 to co-ordinate the campaign against the Tigray People's Liberation Front (TPLF).

**FISZBACH, Tadeusz.** *Poland.* Polish Social Democratic Union (PUS) leader. Born in 1935, he worked in the ruling Polish United Workers' Party (PZPR) apparatus from 1963, notably as Gdansk regional party leader at the time of Solidarity's emergence there in 1980. A candidate PZPR politburo member in 1980–81, he was then transferred to the diplomatic service,

an indication of a fall from favour. After the partly free June 1989 elections he was elected a deputy Sejm (parliament) speaker. When the PZPR disbanded at a January 1990 congress to reform itself as the Social Democracy of the Polish Republic, Fiszbach led a walkout of those who wanted a cleaner break with the communist past, and became chairman of the rival PUS.

**FITZGERALD, Garret.** *Ireland.* Social democrat politician and opposition leader. Born in 1926, he trained as an economist and a lawyer, and was called to the Bar in 1947. Until 1958 he worked for Aer Lingus, the national airline, and then lectured in political economy at University College Dublin until 1973. During this time he also wrote extensively on economic issues for Irish and overseas newspapers. He was elected to parliament for Fine Gael in 1969, and was appointed foreign minister four years later. He became party leader in 1977 and prime minister in 1981 at the head of a coalition with the Labour Party. This was defeated in early 1982 but regained power in another election later that year. He resigned as party leader after Fine Gael lost power in the 1987 election. While in power he sought to come to grips with Ireland's great intractable problems: a weak economy, the dominance of the Roman Catholic church in the social field, and the Northern Ireland question. He achieved limited, if controversial, success in the latter with the signing of the Anglo-Irish Agreement in 1985, which gave Ireland a say in the affairs of the North. On the other two issues he had to admit failure. Voters rejected reforms of restrictive laws on divorce and abortion, and disappointing results on the economic front brought electoral defeat in 1987. Despite the bruising he has received in the political arena, he has gained wide respect for his honesty and intellect.

**FIVE, Kaci Kullmann.** *Norway.* Conservative politician. Born in 1951, she studied politics and then worked for the Norwegian Employers' Federation (NAF) on women's rights issues. A life-long member of the Conservatives (Høyre), she was chairwoman of its youth wing from 1977–79. Elected a member of the Storting (parliament) in 1981, she was trade and shipping minister in the centre–right coalition that held power from 1989–90.

**FLEMMING, Marilies.** *Austria.* Environment minister. Born in 1933, she has a doctorate in law, and served as secretary-general of the women's movement of the Austrian People's Party (ÖVP) from 1977–84, becoming its leader in 1984. Appointed environment, youth and families minister in 1987, she has proved to be a well-liked, lively national figure. A long list of environmental laws was presented and passed under her stewardship.

**FLETCHER, Arthur.** *USA.* Chairman of the US Commission on Civil Rights since 1990. He is considered a fair-minded, moderate Republican who promises to restore credibility to the commission, which suffered major cutbacks and fell into disrepute during the 1980s. As Richard Nixon's assistant labour secretary in 1969, he was the first to develop guidelines for private industry on hiring people from minority groups.

**FLORAKIS, Charilaos.** *Greece.* Communist politician. Born in 1914, he trained as a telegraphist and became an active union organizer in the 1930s. During the Nazi occupation he joined the Communist Party, organized strikes in Athens and eventually fled to the mountains where he joined the communist-led partisan army, ELAS. During the civil war of 1946–49 he was an officer in the insurgent army. Florakis has spent 17 years either in prison or in concentration camps as a political detainee. He was elected first secretary of the Communist Party of Greece (KKE) in 1972, and was confirmed in that post with the title of general secretary in 1978. He was elected MP for Athens B in 1974 when the KKE was legalized. In 1989 he became president of the Alliance of Left and Progressive Forces (Synaspismos), in which the KKE is the principal partner. He took the communists into government for the first time in a brief Synaspismos–New Democracy (ND) coalition during the summer of that year.

**FLORIO, James.** *USA.* Democratic governor of New Jersey. Born in 1937, he was a lawyer and state legislator before being elected to the House of Representatives in 1974. In Congress he drew up legislation to finance the clean-up of hazardous waste, a key issue in New Jersey. His 1989 election as governor owed much to his congressional record on environmental and consumer issues and to his liberal stand on abortion. He has since introduced a package of tax rises and spending programmes that have proved exceedingly unpopular.

**FLYNN, Raymond.** *USA.* Mayor of Boston, Massachusetts. Flynn first became mayor in 1983, after serving on the Boston city council for five years. He was born in 1939, holds a PhD from Northeastern University, and was a state representative from 1971–78. He was an active

antagonist of former governor **Michael Dukakis**, and as such was seen as a possible gubernatorial candidate.

**FOGH RASMUSSEN, Anders.** *Denmark.* Economic and fiscal affairs minister. Born in 1953, he was politically active from an early age, founding a Liberal (Venstre) youth group in his school at the age of 17, and chairing the Liberal youth organization at 21. After graduating in economics from Aarhus University, he was elected a member of the Folketing (parliament) in 1978, and his party's vice-chairman in 1986. He was appointed fiscal affairs minister the following year, adding the economic affairs portfolio in December 1990.

**FOKIN, Vitold.** *USSR.* Prime minister of the Ukraine. Regarded as being on the liberal wing of the Communist Party in the Ukraine, he was elected as a compromise candidate to the chair of the republic's council of ministers, in November 1990, after the hardliner Aleksandr Bulyanda had been persuaded to step down. He succeeded Vitaly Masol, whose resignation had been announced the previous month. Fokin, aged 58 when he became premier, had been one of the compilers of the plan put forward in the name of the republics for a transition to a market economic system.

**FOLEY, Thomas (Tom).** *USA.* Democratic congressman for Washington and speaker of the House of Representatives. Born in 1929, Foley was educated at the University of Washington and practised law before being elected to the House of Representatives in 1964. He chaired the agricultural committee from 1975–81 but made his reputation through his rapid rise to party leadership in the 1980s. In recognition of his parliamentary skills, he was elected Democratic whip in 1981, then majority leader in 1987 and became speaker in 1989. Taking office amid the bitterest inter-party feuding in Congress for many years, following the enforced resignation of the speaker, Jim Wright, on financial malpractice charges, Foley sought an end to rancour but was immediately confronted with a Republican National Committee press release alleging that he was homosexual. To widespread praise, he defused the situation, accepted **George Bush**'s condemnation of the smear and set about restoring good party relations in Congress. Foley is neither an inspiring orator nor a legislative activist; his strength as party leader rests on his skills as a consensus builder and tactician.

FORD, Guillermo. *Panama*. Second vice-president and planning and economy minister. As leader of the National Republican Liberal Movement (Molirena), Ford joined the Democratic Civic Opposition Alliance (ADOC) and was its second vice-presidential candidate in May 1989. He was badly beaten by supporters of **Manuel Noriega** after the annulment of the election results. When the **Guillermo Endara** government was installed after the US invasion in December 1989 he was appointed planning and economy minister.

FORD, William. *USA*. Democratic congressman for Michigan. Born in 1927, he practised law before his election to the House of Representatives in 1964. A liberal, whose main interests are industrial relations and education policy, Ford is in line to become education and labour committee chairman.

FORLANI, Arnaldo. *Italy*. Christian Democrat party (DC) politician. Born in Pesaro in 1925, he gained a law degree at Urbino University and was first elected to the Chamber of Deputies in 1958. Between 1969 and 1979 he held a number of cabinet posts, including the portfolios of defence and foreign affairs. In October 1980 he formed a four-party coalition government, and held office as prime minister until revelations concerning the Propaganda Due (P2) secret masonic lodge precipitated his resignation in May 1981. From 1983–87, he was deputy prime minister in the two successive administrations headed by **Bettino Craxi**. Forlani became secretary-general of the DC in February 1989, in succession to **Ciriaco De Mita**. He is known for his ability to keep the party machine running and to smooth the rough edges between contending parties without adopting a definite stance himself.

FORMICA, Rino. *Italy*. Finance minister and Italian Socialist Party (PSI) politician. Born in 1927, he was elected to the Senate in 1979 and since 1983 has represented his native Bari in the Chamber of Deputies. He first attained cabinet rank as transport minister in April 1980. As finance minister in the cabinets led by **Giovanni Spadolini**, Formica's differences with the Christian Democrat treasury minister, Beniamino Andreatta, over economic policy contributed to the fall of the government in November 1982. In later cabinets he held the portfolios of foreign trade and labour, returning to the finance ministry in July 1989. A hard-nosed operator, Formica is regarded as a typical southern Socialist politician, more interested in ideas than in their implementation; his introduction of a capital gains tax on share dealings was widely criticized as misconceived.

FORSYTH, Michael. *UK*. Conservative politician. Born in 1954, he was active in Tory student politics while at St Andrew's University. Soon to become the leading young Thatcherite radical in Scotland, he was elected to parliament in 1983, and was appointed a junior Scottish office minister in 1987. He was also an abrasive chairman of the beleaguered Scottish Conservatives for just over a year in 1989–90; his resignation from this post was widely seen as a victory for the more moderate politics espoused by the then Scottish secretary **Malcolm Rifkind** with whom he had repeatedly clashed. His simultaneous promotion to minister of state, however, indicated his high standing with **Margaret Thatcher**, although he was seen as somewhat isolated after **John Major** became prime minister.

FOXLEY RIOSECO, Alejandro. *Chile*. Finance minister. Born in 1939, Foxley studied economics at Wisconsin and Harvard universities in the USA and the Catholic University in Valparaiso. He pursued an academic career in Chile and abroad, including periods as professor at the Catholic University from 1970–76 and as president of Corporation for American Economic Research from 1976–90. A member of the executive committee of the Christian Democratic Party (PDC), he became **Patricio Aylwin**'s adviser on economic affairs and was appointed finance minister in 1990.

FRAGA IRIBARNE, Manuel. *Spain*. Galicia premier. Born in 1922 in Villalba, Galicia. A lawyer with a distinguished academic record, he pursued a career within the National Movement, then Spain's only legal party. Under General Franco he promoted a limited liberalization of the censorship laws as information and tourism minister from 1962–66. He had little political influence during the last years of the Franco regime, serving as ambassador to the UK in 1973–75. He returned to political prominence as deputy prime minister and interior minister in the first post-Franco cabinet in December 1975. Fraga left the government when **Adolfo Suárez** was picked by King **Juan Carlos** to lead a reformist government in July 1976. He founded Popular Alliance as an umbrella for former Franco supporters and was widely credited with reconciling the Spanish right to democracy. Fraga gradually moved the party, which was renamed the Popular Party (PP) in 1988, towards the political centre. After the demise of the Union of the Democratic Centre (UCD) in 1982, Fraga's party became the main opposition to **Felipe González**'s governing Spanish Socialist Workers' Party (PSOE). In 1990 Fraga retired from national politics after he won elections to head the regional government in his home state of Galicia.

**FRANK, Barney.** *USA*. Democratic congressman for Massachusetts. Born in 1940, Frank was a lawyer and state assemblyman before his election to the House of Representatives in 1980. A liberal, with a strong record on housing policy and civil liberties, in 1987 he became the first congressman to announce publicly that he is a homosexual. In 1989–90, he was embroiled in a messy scandal involving a male prostitute, but he has so far weathered the storm.

**FRASER, Malcolm.** *Australia*. Former prime minister. He was born in 1930 into the "old money" grazier "squatocracy" and was educated at Oxford University and in the USA before moving into Liberal Party politics. He entered the House of Representatives in 1955, representing the Victoria seat of Wannon. As leader of the opposition in 1975 he was the beneficiary of the constitutional "coup" that unseated Gough Whitlam's Labor government. Assuming power, he remained at the head of a distinctly conservative administration until defeat at the hands of **Bob Hawke**'s Labor Party in the 1983 election. Fraser resigned from parliament immediately after this defeat and became something of an activist elder statesman. From 1985–86 he was co-chairman of the Commonwealth Eminent Persons Group that reported on South Africa. This brought out his deeply held anti-apartheid feelings, which had always been somewhat at odds with his right-wing reputation on domestic affairs. In 1989 the Hawke government sponsored his (ultimately unsuccessful) candidature for the post of Commonwealth secretary-general.

**FRASYNIUK, Władysław.** *Poland.* Solidarity activist. A Solidarity organizer in 1980 in Silesia, he joined the union's national leadership in 1981. Under martial law he led the Solidarity underground in Wrocław until he was arrested in October 1982 and sentenced to six years' imprisonment for organizing demonstrations. He was granted amnesty in July 1984 but re-arrested in June 1985 and sentenced to three-and-a-half years' imprisonment for fomenting unrest. He was again granted amnesty in mid-1986. With **Adam Michnik** and **Zbigniew**

**Bujak** he broke with Solidarity chairman **Lech Wałęsa** in July 1990, backing **Tadeusz Mazowiecki** and helping to set up the pro-Mazowiecki Citizens' Movement for Democratic Action (ROAD). In September 1990 he resigned as Solidarity leader in Lower Silesia.

**FREIVALDS, Laila.** *Sweden.* Justice minister. Born in 1942 in Latvia, she graduated in law in 1970 and practised it until 1975, after which she worked at the Board for Consumer Policies, becoming its director and consumer ombudsman in 1983. She was appointed justice minister in 1988.

**FROLOV, Ivan.** *USSR.* Communist Party theoretician, now editor of *Pravda*. A Russian born in 1929, he is one of the closest political advisers to **Mikhail Gorbachev**. His appointment in October 1989 as editor-in-chief of *Pravda* appeared to be a move to wrest the main Communist Party of the Soviet Union (CPSU) newspaper from the party's conservative wing. However, his own very conservative editorial policy has been blamed for *Pravda*'s loss of readers. He was appointed to the CPSU secretariat in December 1989, and transferred to the politburo in July 1990.

**FUCHS, Anke.** *Germany.* Social Democratic Party (SPD) politician. The daughter of an SPD mayor of Hamburg, she was born in 1937. She qualified as a lawyer and worked as an official in the trade union IG Metall before taking up a parliamentary career in 1977. She was appointed state secretary in the labour and social policy ministry, and was briefly youth, family and health minister in 1982, before the fall of Helmut Schmidt's SPD-led government later that year. She has been seen as a potential candidate for the post of chancellor.

**FUJIMORI, Alberto.** *Peru.* President. Born in 1939 of Japanese immigrant parents, Fujimori trained as an agricultural engineer. He rose to become rector of the Agrarian University of La Molina. A political novice, he entered the 1990 presidential contest as the candidate of the independent group Cambio 90 and rapidly built up support, winning the second-round contest. His lack of a political record, his racial origins, and his promises of change without hardship appealed to the predominantly mixed-race poor. On assuming power, however, he imposed a severe austerity programme in an attempt to deal with Peru's rampant inflation, mounting debt and weak economy.

**FUJINAMI, Takao.** *Japan.* Liberal politician. Born in 1932, he graduated from Waseda

University and was active in local politics in his native Mie prefecture before entering the House of Representatives (lower house) on the Liberal Democratic Party (LDP) list in 1967. With government experience as labour minister under Masayoshi Ohira in 1979, he was identified as a rising force in the party and a possible successor to the **Yasuhiro Nakasone** faction leadership. However, he suffered a serious setback as a result of his involvement in the Recruit share scandal and left the LDP formally (without severing his political connections within the party) in May 1989.

**FUKIDA, Akira.** *Japan.* Home affairs minister. Born in 1927, he was appointed to his present position in the December 1990 cabinet reshuffle.

**FÜR, Lajos.** *Hungary.* Defence minister. Born in 1930, Für, like his Hungarian Democratic Forum (MDF) party leader **József Antall**, was a professional historian who represented the centre-right moderate nationalist strand in the party rather than its more populist wing. They emerged together as leaders at the MDF conference of October 1989, with Für chosen as candidate for the presidency of the republic. The presidential contest was postponed, however, leaving the way open for Antall to bring his colleague into his cabinet as defence minister in May 1990. Für was returned to the 20-member MDF presidium at the party conference in December 1990.

# G

**GÁL, Fedor.** *Czechoslovakia.* Chairman of Public Against Violence. Born in 1945 in Terezin, he studied chemical technology to postgraduate level and subsequently worked as a researcher at several institutes including the Institute for the Standard of Living in Bratislava and the Slovak Academy of Sciences. He has published about 100 scholarly articles and monographs. He is chairman of Public Against Violence, the Slovak counterpart of Civic Forum.

**GAMSAKHURDIA, Zviad.** *USSR.* Chairman of Georgia's Supreme Soviet (*de facto* president). The son of a famous writer, Gamsakhurdia, born in 1939, was from the age of 17 frequently detained for his nationalist and anti-communist views; the most recent occasion was after the April 1989 Tbilisi massacre of nationalist demonstrators by Soviet troops. Considered the doyen of Georgian dissidents, he is also one of the most radical and outspoken, advocating Georgia's immediate independence, while his personal following gives him considerable influence with Georgia's communist leaders. In November 1990 the decisive nationalist victory in Georgia's elections was followed by his almost unanimous election as chairman of the republic's Supreme Soviet.

**GANDHI, Maneka.** *India.* Environment and forests minister. Born in 1956 in the Punjab, she is a former fashion model who married Indira Gandhi's younger son, Sanjay, in 1974. After the death of her husband in 1980, she fell out with Gandhi and left Congress to form the Sanjay Vichar Manch. In 1988 her party merged with the Janata Party, which in turn fused with the Janata Dal; the following year she was made minister of state for environment and forests in the National Front government. She left the **V.P. Singh** government in October 1990, the month before its collapse, but returned to her old post in its successor. Articulate and photogenic, she is an effective advocate of third world concerns at international environmental conferences. Within India, she undertakes well-publicized swoops on polluting industrial sites, dishing out humiliating reprimands to factory owners.

**GANDHI, Rajiv.** *India.* President of Congress (I). Born in 1944 in Bombay, the elder of Indira Gandhi's two sons, he pursued a career as a pilot with Indian Airlines until the death of his brother Sanjay in 1980. Under strong pressure from his mother and the Congress rank-and-file he reluctantly agreed to enter politics. He was elected to the Lok Sabha (lower house) in 1981 and became a general secretary of Congress (I) in 1983. He played a central role in reorganizing the party machine and as an adviser to his mother. After her assassination in 1984, a small group of party leaders chose him as successor, and he was promptly sworn in as prime minister. Committing himself to eradicating corruption from both the party and public life, he began his term of office on a wave of popularity. After a promising start, in which he defused the regional crises by reaching agreements with the main regionalist parties in Kashmir, Assam and the Punjab, he found it increasingly difficult to implement his political promises. His administration lost its dynamism and became increasingly faction-ridden. A scandal involving allegations of corruption connected with a multi-million-dollar defence contract with the Swedish firm Bofors cast into doubt his administration's reputation for probity. A number of critics of the administration, including the effective finance minister **V.P. Singh**, joined the opposition. In the November 1989 election his party lost its majority, although it remained the single largest party in parliament. Despite the defeat Gandhi was re-elected party president and became leader of the opposition. Within a year he was back at centre-stage, lending his indispensable backing to the dissidents under **Chandra Shekhar** who brought down the Singh government in November 1990.

**GANILAU, Ratu Sir Penaia.** *Fiji.* President. Born in 1918 of noble parents, Ganilau was an international rugby player and became a colonial administrator, then had a long career as a government minister both before and after independence in 1970, in the successive Alliance Party governments of **Kamisese Mara**. He became governor-general in 1983 and was embroiled in the political manoeuvring after the first coup led by Major-General **Sitiveni Rabuka** in May 1987, controversially dissolving parliament, forming his own interim administration until the second Rabuka coup in September. He exchanged the title of governor-general for that of president of the republic in December 1987, after Fiji had ceased to be a member of the Commonwealth. He remains an active participant in the continuing power play between the ambitions of Rabuka and the prime minister, Mara. His son, Brigadier Epeli Ganilau, is Rabuka's chief of staff and likely successor as army commander.

**GARAIKOETXEA URRIZA, Carlos.** *Spain.* Moderate Basque politician. Born in 1938 in Pamplona (Navarra), he became president of the Basque Nationalist Party (PNV) and was elected to the Navarra parliament in 1979. In the first elections to a Basque parliament the following year, he was elected as *lendakari* (premier) of the Basque government, a post he held until 1984. In 1986 he broke with the PNV, which shifted its support to **José Antonio Ardanza**, and he founded a rival nationalist party called Basque Solidarity (EA). He was elected to the European Parliament in 1986.

**GARANG, Colonel John.** *Sudan.* Leader of Sudan People's Liberation Army. Born in 1943 in Jonglei, southern Sudan, he studied in the USA, receiving a PhD in agricultural economics from Iowa State University. He joined the Sudanese army in 1969 and returned to the USA for military training before working at the Military Research Centre in Khartoum. In May 1983, alienated by the attempts of President Jaafar Nimeiri's government to impose Islamic law on the country and the belief that northerners were exploiting southern Sudan's resources, Garang formed the Sudanese People's Liberation Movement from defectors from the army and police and began a guerrilla campaign in southern Sudan, backed by Ethiopia. Driven by a vision of a tolerant, non-sectarian state, he claims to oppose the secession of the south and denies he is fighting to become president. His relentless campaign has, however, been pursued with apparent indifference to its immense cost for the people of southern Sudan.

**GARBA, Joseph Nanven.** *Nigeria.* Politician and retired army officer. Born in Langtang in 1943, he underwent military training at Aldershot and Camberley in the UK and obtained a master's degree in public administration in 1983 from Harvard University. He was commander of the Brigade of Guards from 1968–75 and a member of the Supreme Military Council (SMC) from 1975–79. Appointed permanent representative to the UN in 1984, he was president of the UN General Assembly in 1989–90, and won praise as a brisk and efficient chairman. Although designated Nigeria's first ambassador to independent Namibia in 1990, he never took up the post, instead becoming a foreign affairs adviser to the Nigerian government. He is regarded as a potential candidate for the post of UN secretary-general when **Javier Pérez de Cuéllar**'s term of office ends in 1991.

**GARCÍA DAMBORENEA, Ricardo.** *Spain.* Socialist politician. Born in 1940 in Madrid. A doctor, Spanish Socialist Workers' Party (PSOE) deputy for Vizcaya and member of the PSOE federal committee, he created in 1989 a dissenting faction within the PSOE known as Socialist Democracy, and was subsequently expelled from the party.

**GARCÍA PÉREZ, Alan.** *Peru.* Former president. Born in 1949 and trained as a lawyer, García's rise to power was rapid. He first won a seat to the lower house of Congress in 1980 and in 1982 was chosen as secretary-general of the American Popular Revolutionary Alliance (APRA). He was elected president in 1985 amid hopes that his youth and dynamism could help solve Peru's problems. The initial optimism rapidly dissolved as García failed to tackle the economic crisis or deal with the attacks by Sendero Luminoso (Shining Path) guerrillas; by the end of his five-year term he had become deeply unpopular.

**GARCÍA VARGAS, Julián.** *Spain.* Health and consumer affairs minister. Born in 1946 in Madrid, he studied economics and rose to become president of the Official Credit Institute in 1982. One of the architects of the Spanish Socialist Workers' Party's (PSOE's) 1982 economic programme, he has been health and consumer affairs minister since July 1986.

**GARDNER, Booth.** *USA.* Democratic governor of Washington. Born in 1936, he was a business executive and state legislator before being elected governor in 1984. His priorities are administrative efficiency, economic redevelopment and educational programme expansion.

**GAREL-JONES, Tristan.** *UK.* Minister of state at the Foreign and Commonwealth Office and MP since 1979. Born in 1941, Garel-Jones was deputy chief whip until he was transferred to the Foreign and Commonwealth Office in July 1990. In the whips' office, he had a reputation as one of the most accomplished political "fixers" in the Tory administration. During the Conservative leadership election he was alleged to have played an influential role in persuading cabinet ministers that **Margaret Thatcher** could not win. He is one of the most outspoken advocates of closer co-operation with the UK's partners in the EC.

**GARN, Edwin Jacob (Jake).** *USA.* Republican senator for Utah. Born in 1932, he was an insurance executive, and mayor of Salt Lake City from 1972 until his election to the Senate in 1974. A conservative, his advocacy of federal deregulation has been directed particularly at the banking industry, but extends as far as opposition to the 1990 clean air bill, and to the plans to "throw money at" the drugs problem during the administration of **George Bush**. He is an enthusiastic supporter of the US space programme, and won fame when he took a trip on board the shuttle *Discovery* in April 1985, casting the first ever proxy vote from space.

**GARRETT, Peter.** *Australia.* Singer and political activist. Born in 1953, he is lead singer in the rock group Midnight Oil and president of the Australian Conservation Foundation. He stood and lost narrowly as Nuclear Disarmament candidate in the Senate elections of 1984.

**GASANOV, Gasan.** *USSR.* Prime minister of Azerbaijan. Formerly a senior Communist Party official, Gasanov was appointed premier in January 1990. His appointment formed part of the shake-up of Azerbaijan's leadership that followed an upsurge of nationalist violence and the temporary collapse of Soviet rule in the face of support for the nationalist Popular Front. He succeeded **Ayaz Mutalibov**, who beat him in an election for the post of Azerbaijani Communist Party leader.

**GASPARI, Remo.** *Italy.* Public administration minister and Christian Democrat party (DC) politician. Born in 1921 in the province of Chieti, he has sat in the Chamber of Deputies since 1953; he first attained cabinet rank in August 1969, as transport and civil aviation minister. Since then he has held various portfolios, including health, posts and telecommunications, civil defence, and, since July 1989, public administration. His power base is in his home region of Abruzzo, which benefited from his period as minister for the Mezzogiorno.

**GAUCK, Joachim.** *Germany.* Cleric and political campaigner. A Protestant pastor from Rostock with credentials as a dissident under the communist regime, he was elected to the East German Volkskammer in early 1990, at the age of 50, as a member of Alliance '90. Within the parliament he led efforts to ensure that former members of the Stasi secret police were brought to justice. Before re-unification the Volkskammer chose him as overseer of the Stasi files, thereby ensuring that control of investigations did not pass to someone appointed from Bonn.

**GAVIRIA TRUJILLO, César.** *Colombia.* President. Born in 1947 and trained as an economist, he was elected president in 1990 as the Liberal Party candidate. He had previously served as finance and interior minister in **Virgilio Barco**'s administration (1986–89). He represents a younger generation, removed from the traditional "old guard" of Colombian politics. In returning to the practice of including opposition politicians in his cabinet, he hopes to achieve consensus in dealing with the drug barons and in reforming the political system. The Liberals suffered a setback in the December 1990 elections, barely winning the poll with their lowest turnout since 1930.

**GAYOOM, Maumoun Abdul.** *Maldives.* President. Born in 1937 and educated in Cairo, he became a teacher, a government official and a diplomat before entering the government in 1976. In 1978 he became president, an office which he has retained at successive single-candidate elections, and in the face of the intrigues of his predecessor Ibrahim Nasir, who is believed to have been the influence behind the 1988 mercenary coup attempt when Gayoom had to be rescued by Indian military intervention.

**GBAGBO, Laurent.** *Côte d'Ivoire.* Opposition leader. Born in 1945, he is a lecturer in modern history at Abidjan University, and the most trenchant and effective critic of the regime of President **Félix Houphouët-Boigny**. Detained for two years in the early 1970s, he was forced into exile in France in 1982 soon after he founded the Ivorian Popular Front (FPI), a loose coalition of six socialist parties, which functioned underground until its legalization in 1990. Since his return in 1988 he has been able to voice his criticisms of the president with relative impunity, suggesting that the government is nervous about the extent of his support. Nevertheless, in the October 1990 presidential elections Houphouët-Boigny swept back to power with over 80% of the vote, a victory which provoked claims from Gbagbo of widespread electoral malpractice and intimidation of FPI candidates and supporters. Gbagbo won a seat in the national assembly in parliamentary elections the following month, one of only nine FPI members in the 175-seat assembly.

**GEAGEA, Samir.** *Lebanon.* Christian leader. Geagea emerged as a hard-line Christian Phalangist leader in the mid-1980s. In January 1986, he seized control of the Phalangist Lebanese Forces militia after their commander, Elie Hobeika, had agreed to a Syrian-sponsored peace accord. His forces survived a bruising bout of internecine fighting with General Michel Aoun's army units in early 1990, and in April he announced his recognition of the Syrian-backed government of **Elias Hrawi.**

**GEINGOB, Hage Gottfried.** *Namibia.* Prime minister. Born in 1941, he is a long-standing member of the South West Africa People's Organization (Swapo) and has been a member of its politburo since 1975. He played a key role, as petitioner to the UN from 1964–71, in gaining international recognition for Swapo. In 1975 he was appointed founding director of the UN Institute for Namibia in Lusaka. He became first prime minister of independent Namibia in March 1990.

**GEISSLER, Heiner.** *Germany.* Christian Democratic Union (CDU) politician. Born in Munich in 1930, he studied philosophy and law, and worked briefly as a judge before taking up politics in 1962. He was elected to the Bundestag in 1965, leaving two years later to join the CDU government of Rheinland-Palatinate, and then returning to the Bundestag in 1977. He served as youth, family and health minister from 1982–85. The left-leaning Geissler was CDU secretary-general for 12 years from 1977, but lost out to **Volker Rühe** in July 1989 when Chancellor **Helmut Kohl** wanted a more robust ally in the post.

**GENSCHER, Hans-Dietrich.** *Germany.* Foreign minister and deputy chancellor. Genscher ranks with **Willy Brandt** and **Helmut Kohl** among the most influential postwar German politicians. There is affectionate irony in his portrayal as the strip cartoon superhero "Genschman", but his undoubted stature as a world statesman belies

his unassuming, somewhat avuncular manner. Born in 1927, he went to school in Halle and studied law at Leipzig University after brief war service. He made the crucial decision to leave East Germany in 1952. He had been a Liberal Party member there, and automatically became a member of the Free Democratic Party (FDP) in the west. In 1965 he was elected to the Bundestag and was already a leading figure in the FDP, having become its vice-chairman in 1958. In 1969 he was appointed interior minister in Brandt's government. Since 1974 (when he became FDP leader) he has been foreign minister and deputy chancellor, leading his party out of the coalition with the Social Democrats and into alliance with the Christian Democrats in 1982. His powerful influence in foreign policy, with a record 16 years at the helm, has ensured continuity, above all in relations with the Soviet bloc. He played a leading role in 1989–90 in negotiating German unification, an issue particularly close to his heart as a native of what had become East Germany, but there was public alarm when he was hospitalized with heart trouble as this process moved towards fulfilment. Despite his health problems he showed every sign that he would sustain the momentum, assuming the role of chief architect in the task of creating a European home large enough to accommodate the USSR. Genscher has concentrated latterly more on his government role than on his party, and he stepped down from the party chairmanship in 1985 in favour of **Martin Bangemann.** His party's strong showing in the December 1990 elections reflected his popularity throughout united Germany.

**GEPHARDT, Richard.** *USA.* Democratic congressman for Missouri. Born in 1941, Gephardt attended Northwestern and Michigan universities and practised as a lawyer before being elected to the House of Representatives in 1976. His legislative specialities are tax and trade policies. In 1985 he played a major role in negotiating terms for the Gramm-Rudman-Hollings anti-deficit law and is currently second-ranking Democrat on the budget committee. Politically a moderate, in 1984 he was instrumental in forming the Democratic Leadership Council whose aim is to give the party a centrist image. In 1988 Gephardt ran for the presidential nomination on a populist protectionist platform which appealed to farmers and blue-collar workers, particularly in calling for retaliatory measures against countries whose trade barriers enabled them to run a large trade surplus with the USA. He proved an effective public speaker and started well by winning the Iowa caucuses. However, lack of money bedevilled his campaign, and in the "Super Tuesday" Southern primaries, he carried only Missouri. In 1989 he was elected majority leader, which led some observers to believe that his presidential ambitions have been shelved in favour of congressional leadership.

**GERASHCHENKO, Viktor.** *USSR.* President of the USSR State Bank (Gosbank). Born in 1937, he served in the USSR Bank for Foreign Trade before his election by the USSR Supreme Soviet as Gosbank president in August 1989. The introduction of market economic reforms should see him presiding over major changes in Gosbank's functions as a new lower tier of commercial banks is established.

**GERASIMOV, Gennady.** *USSR.* Former foreign ministry spokesman. A Russian, born in 1930, he worked as a journalist for the Novosti press agency, rising to the post of agency deputy chairman and editor-in-chief of the newspaper *Moscow News* in 1984. His appointment as head of the foreign ministry information department by **Eduard Shevardnadze** in 1986 made him a familiar figure on the international scene as the USSR conducted its worldwide diplomatic offensive. As the principal Soviet public voice abroad, Gerasimov was renowned for his mastery of press conferences, his perfect English and his fine line in wise-cracking humour: in October 1989 he invented the "Sinatra doctrine" ("they can do it their way") to describe the Soviet Union's new non-interventionist relationship with its East European allies. In November 1990 he was replaced as foreign ministry spokesman by **Vitaly Churkin**, and was to be given an ambassadorial post.

**GEREMEK, Dr Bronisław.** *Poland.* Former Solidarity parliamentary leader. Born in 1932, he became a medieval historian, working mostly at the Polish Academy of Sciences, but also at the Sorbonne in Paris (1960–65). A member of the ruling communist Polish United Workers Party (PZPR) from 1950–68, he joined the dissident movement after 1976, and became an adviser to Solidarity in 1980. He was interned for a year following the December 1981 imposition of martial law, and was briefly detained again in 1983, having resumed working with Solidarity. He led the opposition side in negotiations on "political reform" during the round-table talks of early 1989. Following Solidarity's victory in the

partly free June 1989 elections he was chosen to chair the Citizens' Parliamentary Club, uniting the Solidarity Sejm and Senate deputies. A supporter of prime minister **Tadeusz Mazowiecki** in November 1990, he was replaced as Solidarity's parliamentary leader by Mieczyslaw Gil, a supporter of **Lech Wałęsa**.

**GETTY, Donald.** *Canada.* Premier of Alberta. Born in Westmount, Quebec in 1933, he was educated at the University of Western Ontario. He played professional football for ten years before being elected to Alberta's legislative assembly in 1967. Getty was until 1975 a prominent minister in the government of Peter Lougheed. He worked as an investment counsellor and oil consultant for ten years before returning to politics as provincial leader of the Progressive Conservatives and premier of Alberta in 1985.

**GHAFAR BABA, Encik Abdul.** *Malaysia.* Deputy prime minister and rural development minister. Born in 1925, Ghafar Baba served in a wide variety of political posts before retiring from active politics in 1976 to pursue business interests. Prime Minister **Mahathir Mohamad** persuaded him to return to the cabinet in 1986 to replace outgoing deputy prime minister **Musa Hitam**. He has since proved himself to be one of Mahathir's most trusted allies.

**GHANNOUCHI, Mohammed.** *Tunisia.* Economy and finance minister. One of the key proponents in government of the IMF-backed austerity programme, he was planning and economics minister until March 1990, when he took charge of an expanded economy and finance ministry.

**GHANNOUCHI, Rashid.** *Tunisia.* Islamic fundamentalist leader. Born in 1942, he first became involved with Islamic fundamentalist politics while studying in Damascus. Returning to Tunisia in 1968, he worked as a secondary school teacher and set up Islamic study groups and a newspaper, quickly gaining a following among students. In 1981 he set up the clandestine Islamic Tendency Movement (MTI) and in the same year was imprisoned for his criticism of the government. Released in 1984, Ghannouchi was sentenced to life imprisonment in 1987 after a government crackdown on the MTI at a time of mounting public unrest. He was released in 1988 as part of President **Zine el-Abidine Ben Ali**'s reforms. However, the government has so far refused to grant formal recognition to the MTI – renamed the Party of Renewal (Hizb el-Nahda) in 1989 – as a political party. Ghannouchi has spent much of his time since his release in self-imposed exile, leaving the internal direction of the party to his deputy, Abdelfattah Mourou.

**GHIZ, Joseph.** *Canada.* Premier of Prince Edward Island (PEI). Born in 1945 in Charlottetown, PEI, he was educated at Dalhousie University and Harvard Law School. He was a lecturer in business law at the University of PEI before becoming leader of the Liberal Party of PEI in 1981. He was elected to the provincial legislative assembly in 1982 and has been PEI premier since 1986.

**GHOZALI, Sid Ahmed.** *Algeria.* Foreign minister. A French-trained economist, born in 1937, Ghozali was briefly public works minister in 1964–65, leaving the cabinet after Houari Boumedienne's coup to chair the state hydrocarbons giant Sonatrach, a position he held until 1984. After being minister of energy, and of irrigation and water affairs, and ambassador to Belgium, he was appointed finance minister in **Kasdi Merbah**'s government in November 1988, and was responsible for negotiating the first agreement with the IMF. He became foreign minister in September 1989, a post for which he is well suited because of his pragmatism and experience in international negotiations.

**GIDASPOV, Boris.** *USSR.* Senior Communist Party official. Born in 1933, he managed a Leningrad chemical enterprise before being named as local Communist Party leader in Leningrad in 1989. Initially thought to be in the reformist mould of **Mikhail Gorbachev**, he has subsequently established his credentials as one of the leading "neo-conservatives", combining populism with calls for party discipline and ideological purity. He was appointed to the Communist Party of the Soviet Union secretariat at the watershed July 1990 congress.

**GIES, Gerd.** *Germany.* Saxony-Anhalt premier. Relatively unknown before the October 1990 elections for Land (state) governments in what had been East Germany, Gies, a 47-year-old veterinary surgeon, was chosen as a local candidate to head the Christian Democratic Union list, having been a party member since 1970 and for some time a party leader at local level in Stendal. He was elected to the Volkskammer (East German parliament) in March 1990 and is also active in Protestant church affairs.

**GILLES, Serge.** *Haiti.* Party leader. Born in 1936, he is the founder of the social-democrat

Progressive Nationalist Revolutionary Party (Panpra), which has emerged as one of the main centrist parties.

**GILMOUR, Sir Ian.** *UK.* Conservative politician. Born in 1926, he studied law and practised briefly before becoming editor and owner of *The Spectator* magazine in 1954. Elected to parliament in 1962 (for Norfolk Central until 1974 and for Chesham and Amersham since), he held various junior ministerial appointments in the defence ministry and was secretary of state for defence from 1970–74. Appointed to the government as Lord Privy Seal in 1979, he was sacked two years later and has since been one of the most consistent Tory opponents of radical Thatcherism, advocating a return to the more traditional conservatism of the Tory party. His *Inside Right*, published in 1977, is an erudite work of Conservative political theory.

**GINGRICH, Newt.** *USA.* Republican congressman for Georgia. Born in 1943, Gingrich was educated at Emory and Tulane universities and was a professor of history before his election in 1978 to the House of Representatives. He gained prominence instead as an advocate of confrontational politics. In the mid-1980s he launched the Conservative Opportunity Society, a group of junior Republican congressmen dedicated to partisan activism. Capitalizing on Republicans' frustration with their long-standing minority status, he gained election as whip in 1989, effectively becoming the party's number two in the House. It was he who led the attack that eventually brought about the resignation of the speaker, Jim Wright, over financial malpractice charges. Gingrich hopes to capitalize on the ethics issue to portray the Democrats as the party of corruption, the Republicans as the party of reform. Inevitably he has become the target of Democratic counter-attacks and has ridden out two charges relating to ethics in 1989–90. His success as whip will be judged not on conventional legislative criteria, but on whether his party will increase its congressional strength in the early 1990s as a result of the new confrontational style of politics.

**GIRAY, Safa.** *Turkey.* Former defence minister. Born in 1931, Giray worked as a civil engineer until taking up his first cabinet post as public works and housing minister in 1983. Regarded as a technical specialist rather than a politician, he was nevertheless offered the politically sensitive post of national defence minister in 1989. He resigned in October 1990, however, after an apparent rift with the prime minister, **Yildirim Akbulut** over policy toward the country's increasingly fraught relations with neighbouring Iraq; his replacement was **Hüsnü Dogan**. Giray is a close ally of **Mesut Yılmaz**, a fierce rival of Akbulut and former foreign minister who was forced out of the government in March 1990.

**GIRENKO, Andrei.** *USSR.* Senior Communist Party official. A Ukrainian, born in 1936, and a mine mechanic by profession, he was a regional party leader in the Ukraine prior to being appointed to the Communist Party of the Soviet Union (CPSU) secretariat in 1989. After the July 1990 CPSU congress he was given the difficult secretariat portfolio with responsibility for inter-ethnic problems.

**GISCARD D'ESTAING, Valéry.** *France.* Former president. Born in 1926 and a graduate of the Ecole Polytechnique and Ecole Nationale d'Administration, he briefly pursued a civil service career, but won his first parliamentary seat in 1956 as a member of the National Centre of Independents and Peasants (CNIP). To many at that time he seemed a glamorously youthful high-flier. In the 1960s he led his own party, the Independent Republicans (RI), and subsequently formed and led the Union for French Democracy-Republican Party (UDF-PR). A junior finance minister in 1959, Giscard became finance and economic affairs minister in 1962–66 but clashed with Charles de Gaulle. Georges Pompidou recalled him in 1969, making him economy and finance minister. When Pompidou died in 1974, Giscard was well placed to succeed him and defeated **François Mitterrand** in the presidential election in May, having seen off the official Gaullist contender Jacques Chaban-Delmas in the first round. He could claim some successes for the liberal social and economic reforms pioneered at the beginning of his term; he then sought re-election in 1981 on the promise of further "reform within the established order". However, running against Mitterrand, he suffered from his new image of aristocratic aloofness, a contrast with his earlier reputation for travelling by *métro* in a roll-neck sweater, and his difficulty in adjusting to the politics of opposition after his defeat. He nevertheless worked assiduously in the 1980s to build up a coherent and unified political structure on the right, a process leading in 1990 to the creation of the Union for France (UPF). The revival of Giscard's own political status was marked by his leadership of the successful united

right-wing campaign in the 1989 elections to the European Parliament.

**GJESTEBY, Kari.** *Norway.* Justice minister. Born in 1947, she studied at the Norwegian School of Economics and Business Administration and served as state secretary for education and religious affairs and then for finance, before becoming the first woman in the country to be given the important post of minister of trade and shipping, in **Gro Harlem Brundtland**'s first Labour government in 1981. Gjesteby was deputy general secretary of the Nordic Council from 1983–86, state secretary for foreign affairs from 1986–88 and a director of the central bank from 1989 until 1990 when she returned to government, as justice minister, in Brundtland's minority Labour government.

**GLEMP, Archbishop Józef.** *Poland.* Roman Catholic primate. Born in 1929, he was ordained a priest in 1956, studied in Rome from 1958–64, and joined the secretariat of the Polish Primate in 1967. He was appointed Archbishop-Metropolitan of Gniezno and Warsaw and Primate of Poland in July 1981, and was elevated to cardinal in 1983. His actions and comments have often caused controversy: under martial law (1981–83) he was criticized for appearing to seek an accommodation with the military authorities, while in 1989 he was accused of anti-semitism when he supported the establishment of a convent at the former Auschwitz concentration camp.

**GLENN, John.** *USA.* Democratic senator for Ohio. Born in 1921, Glenn was the first American astronaut to orbit the earth. Elected in 1974, he is a moderate of technocratic bent. A master of detail, he has difficulty articulating broad themes and is an uninspiring speaker; these weaknesses undermined his bid for the 1984 presidential nomination. As chairman of the government affairs committee, he was instrumental in the creation of a new cabinet department of veterans' affairs. His current priority is the clear-up of nuclear weapons plants. In 1990 he was facing ethics charges stemming from the collapse of the savings and loans associations in the late 1980s.

**GLISTRUP, Mogens.** *Denmark.* Right-wing politician. Born in 1926, he turned his specialist skills as an income tax lawyer to account when he launched the Progress Party (FP) in 1972 with a platform that included the abolition of income tax, huge cuts in public spending and the restriction of immigration. The party became the second largest in the Folketing (parliament) at the first attempt, in the 1973 elections, and Glistrup was confirmed as the bogeyman of national politics. He was accused of tax evasion and fraud in 1974 and finally convicted and imprisoned in 1983 after the longest trial in Danish history. By this time his increasingly erratic behaviour had lost him the support of most of his party colleagues. He was eased out as party leader by **Pia Kjærsgaard** in 1986, but retained a strong popular following on the far right. Expelled from the party in November 1990, he concocted a bizarre arrangement to run under the far-left Common Course (FK) banner, in an attempt to re-enter parliament the following month.

**GODMANIS, Ivars**. *USSR*. Prime minister of Latvia. Born in 1940, a university mathematics lecturer, Godmanis is deputy chairman of the pro-independence Latvian Popular Front, formed in 1988, which won a sizeable majority in the March 1990 elections to Latvia's parliament. This body elected him as premier of the republic in May 1990.

**GODOY SALAZAR, Virgilio**. *Nicaragua*. Vice-president. Born in 1934, he was a professor at Nicaragua University between 1966 and 1979. As leader of the Independent Liberal Party (PLI), he joined the Sandinista-led Patriotic Revolutionary Front (FPR) as labour minister. He contested the 1984 presidential elections, but withdrew just before the voting.

**GOH CHOK TONG**. *Singapore*. Prime minister. Born in 1941. A trained economist and former shipping executive, Goh entered parliament in 1976 as a member for the ruling People's Action Party. By the 1980s he had risen to become the leading figure in the so-called "second generation" of politicians. Appointed first deputy prime minister in 1985, he was subsequently chosen by the cabinet as **Lee Kuan Yew**'s successor, taking over at the end of November 1990. Goh lacks Lee's charisma and the indications are that he will adopt a more participatory and accommodating style of government.

**GOL, Jean**. *Belgium*. Walloon right-wing Liberal politician. Born in 1941, he practised law and was first elected to parliament for the Liberal Reform Party (PRL) in 1971, rising to party president from 1979–81. As deputy prime minister and justice and institutional reform minister from 1981–88, he was embroiled in much controversy, not least over his handling of an outbreak of urban terrorism.

**GOMES, General Carlos Tinoco Ribeiro**.

*Brazil*. Army minister. A career soldier, he was involved in the period of military rule during the 1960s and 1970s but, unlike some other serving officers, did not oppose the return to civilian rule. Widely trusted by the civilian administration, he was appointed army minister by **Fernando Collor de Mello**.

**GÓMEZ HURTADO, Alvaro**. *Colombia*. National Salvation Movement (MSN) leader. Born in 1918, the son of President Laureano Gómez Castro, he was presidential candidate for the Conservative Party (now the Social Conservative Party) in 1974. He subsequently led a right-wing breakaway faction which was not re-united with the party until 1981. He was first designate (vice-president) between 1982 and 1984 and the unsuccessful Conservative presidential candidate in 1986. In 1988 he was kidnapped and held by April 19 Movement (M-19) guerrillas for two months. Two years later he split the Conservative vote again by forming his own party, the MSN, coming second in the 1990 presidential election.

**GOMOLKA, Alfred**. *Germany*. Mecklenburg-Pomerania premier. Born in Breslau and a long-time Christian Democratic Union (CDU) member under the communist regime, he left the party in 1968, when he was 26, in protest over the invasion of Czechoslovakia, but later resumed his membership and was a city councillor in Greifswald for the first part of the 1980s. A scientist, less forceful in manner than many politicians, he won approval for his calm and composed attitude on the campaign trail after his unexpected selection to lead the CDU list in the October 1990 Land (state) election.

**GONCHIGDORJ, Radnaasumbereliyn**. *Mongolia*. Vice-president. Born in 1954, and a former head of the mathematics institute of the Mongolian Academy of Sciences, he left the Mongolian People's Revolutionary Party (MPRP) in April 1990 to found a second opposition party, the Social Democratic Party. He was replaced as party leader in October following his election as vice-president and ex-officio chairman of the People's Little Hural (lower house). He represents a constituency in central Mongolia, his rural base being seen as a factor in securing his election to the vice-presidency in preference to urban intellectual **Sanjaasurengiyn Dzorig**.

**GÖNCZ, Árpad**. *Hungary*. President. Born in 1922 and a lawyer by profession, he was personal secretary to one of the original Independent Smallholders' Party leaders before 1947, but under communist rule had to work as a welder. He joined the 1956 uprising and was arrested and sentenced to life imprisonment. He served six years in prison, teaching himself English and afterwards working as a literary translator and playwright. As a dissident intellectual, he gravitated to the Budapest "democratic opposition" from which the Alliance of Free Democrats (SzDSz) ultimately emerged in late 1988. He was elected the following year as president of the writers' union, and won a seat in the National Assembly for the Free Democrats in the spring 1990 elections. His dissident credentials, and his friendship with Hungarian Democratic Forum (MDF) leader and prime minister-designate **József Antall**, made him an obvious choice as speaker and interim president, and the MDF did not oppose his candidacy for the post. A referendum in late July 1990 failed to muster enough interest in the idea of a direct presidential election, leaving the choice to the National Assembly, and Göncz – the only candidate –was duly returned in August.

**GONZÁLEZ, Antonio Erman**. *Argentina*. Finance minister. A member of the Christian Democratic Party (PDC), González was appointed health minister in 1989, but transferred to the finance ministry in December to deal with Argentina's collapsing currency. He had previously been a vice-president of the central bank, and is a close associate of **Carlos Menem**, serving as treasury minister in La Rioja state when Menem was governor.

**GONZALEZ, Henry**. *USA*. Democratic congressman for Texas. Born of Mexican-American parents in 1916, Gonzalez practised law before being elected to the House of Representatives in 1961. A passionate populist, his particular interest is low-income housing. In 1989 he became chairman of the banking, finance and urban affairs committee and was instrumental in enacting the bail-out of the savings and loans sector, in particular adding amendments that tightened federal regulation of the industry. He is a colourful character who has been known to throw the occasional punch.

**GONZÁLEZ MÁRQUEZ, Felipe**. *Spain*. Prime minister. Born in 1942 in Seville, he began his career as a labour lawyer in Andalusia and joined the then clandestine Spanish Socialist Workers' Party (PSOE) in the early 1960s, serving from 1964–70 on the party's provincial committee and then on its national committee. He became the leader of the party's "renovators", mostly young professionals living in Spain, who

challenged the ageing PSOE leadership based in France and Mexico. González was elected secretary-general of the PSOE at a congress in France in 1974 (the PSOE was not legalized in Spain until 1977). He resigned in 1979 over the question of party orientation, but was re-elected at an extraordinary congress in September 1979, which endorsed his decision to drop the party's Marxist label. He led the party to a landslide electoral victory in 1982 and formed the first left-wing government in Spain since the civil war. He was returned to power, with reduced majorities, in 1986 and in 1989, to become the longest-serving prime minister in modern Spanish history. Styling himself an "unorthodox" socialist, he is a skilled and pragmatic politician who has embraced Nato, the EC and a market economy. He has played a major part in the consolidation of democracy in post-Franco Spain.

**GORBACHEV, Mikhail**. *USSR*. President and Communist Party of the Soviet Union (CPSU) leader. A Russian, born in 1931 into a peasant family in the Stavropol territory of the north Caucasus, he started work aged 14 as a tractor driver. He went on to study law at Moscow University (where he joined the CPSU in 1952). On graduation in 1955 he returned to Stavropol as a Komsomol official and then (from 1962) was a CPSU official, rising to regional first secretary in 1970. During this time he completed a correspondence course in agriculture – which, together with his law degree, makes him the best-educated Soviet leader since Lenin. He was elected to the CPSU central committee in 1971 and was brought to Moscow in November 1978 as central committee secretary for agriculture. He joined the politburo as a candidate member in November 1979 and a full member in October 1980; his rise through the party ranks was sponsored successively by politburo patrons Fyodor Kulakov and Mikhail Suslov (both former Stavropol party leaders). Gorbachev's true mentor, however, was Yury Andropov (also a native of the north Caucasus); after Andropov's November 1982 election as CPSU general secretary, Gorbachev began to emerge as a likely future leader. He was elected CPSU general secretary in March 1985 but, unlike his predecessor, he did not immediately also assume the office of chairman of the USSR Supreme Soviet Presidium (at that time, titular head of state); for that position he had to wait until October 1988. Under Gorbachev the USSR has been transformed in many important ways, although his attempts at economic reform have signally failed to reverse stagnation and have in many respects worsened the crisis. More positive results have emerged from *glasnost* and the consequent freeing of the media and public expression. His democratic reforms have centred on increasing popular participation in government through the introduction of multi-candidate elections, ending the Communist Party's constitutional guarantee of power, and on shifting authority from the CPSU to the state, seen most clearly in new legislative structures set up in early 1989. Simultaneously his state post was restyled as chairman of the Supreme Soviet, and in March 1990 he was elected to the new executive office of president of the USSR, endowed with broad powers. Since then, mounting political and economic crises have prompted Gorbachev twice to seek further increases in the powers of the president. He is a consummate political tactician and in his early years as party chief used personnel changes to strengthen his support in the highest leadership, balancing between radical and conservative forces. More recently he has kept himself at the helm to guide the new democratic process by sheer energy and force of personality. But his failure to revitalize the economy has led to a sharp drop in popularity and he is far less well regarded at home than abroad, as was demonstrated by the reactions to the award to Gorbachev of the 1990 Nobel peace prize. Despite growing criticism of his style of government, he won approval at the end of the year for constitutional amendments to give himself unprecedented executive powers. By this time, however, he was widely believed to be reliant on the forces of conservatism in the country, as he struggled to grapple with the increasingly dire economic situation and to hold the Soviet Union together in the face of the nationalist challenge. His frequent foreign visits (accompanied by his stylish wife Raisa) have constituted an unparalleled diplomatic offensive (cynics have called it a "charm offensive") and his abandonment of the "Brezhnev doctrine" hastened the collapse of communist rule in Eastern Europe and hastened the end of the Cold War. However, by the end of 1990 Western regard for Gorbachev was cooling as a result of fears raised by **Eduard Shevardnadze**'s warning that "dictatorship is coming" and the hard line being pursued against nationalists in the republics.

**GORBUNOVS, Anatolijs**. *USSR*. Chairman of the Latvian Supreme Soviet (*de facto* president).

An advocate of full independence for his Baltic republic, he had been a speaker at the October 1988 founding congress of the Latvian Popular Front. However, he was himself a member of the republic's Communist Party, and had not joined the pro-independence minority which split off to form a separate party at the April 1990 congress. He had shown his support for Latvian nationalism as president of the presidium of the republic's Supreme Soviet from October 1988, and had won with the front's endorsement when he contested a Latvian constituency in the landmark Congress of Deputies election of March 1989. The front, the dominant group in the Supreme Soviet after the March-April 1990 elections, also supported his election to the post of chairman of the Latvian Supreme Soviet (*de facto* president) in May 1990.

**GORE, Albert, Jr**. *USA*. Democratic senator from Tennessee. Born in 1948, he was educated at Harvard and at Vanderbilt Law School, went to Vietnam as an army reporter and later worked as a journalist in Tennessee. His political career progressed rapidly, with election to the House of Representatives in 1976 and to the Senate – where his father once held office – in 1984. In 1988 he made a creditable presidential nomination bid, effectively gaining third place in the Democratic race. Although known as a liberal, Gore changed his stance to that of a Southern moderate in order to profit from the huge number of delegates on offer in the South's "Super Tuesday" primaries. His campaign floundered because he lacked appeal in the North. However, he is well placed for another White House bid in the 1990s and is currently developing issues to give himself national appeal. The rightward orientation of US politics and the Democrats' need to recapture the loyalties of the South favour Gore. He is also something of a forward thinker, having been among the first US politicians to draw attention to depletion of the ozone layer, and he is a prominent spokesman on environmental issues. A member of the Armed Services Committee, his other major interest is arms control. His wife, "Tipper" Gore, is a passionate opponent of rock-music lyrics about sex and drugs.

**GORIA, Giovanni**. *Italy*. Christian Democrat party (DC) politician. Born in 1943 in Asti, in the north-west, he studied economics and went into banking. He was elected to the Chamber of Deputies in 1976 for the constituency of Cuneo–Asti and held junior ministerial positions between 1978 and 1982. In December 1982 he was appointed treasury minister and held the post until June 1987. After the June 1987 general election, he became (at almost 44) the youngest prime minister in Italian history, at the head of a five-party coalition. His administration encountered considerable difficulties over the passage of the 1988 budget, but a crisis relating to nuclear energy policy precipitated his resignation in March 1988. As prime minister he was popular with the public but subject to attacks from both the right and the left.

He has not held ministerial office since but has been quietly cultivating the left of the DC in the hope of building the power base he has so far lacked.

**GORMAN, Teresa.** *UK.* Conservative politician. Born in 1931, she studied science and subsequently set up her own company making teaching equipment. A prime example of the Thatcherite "enterprise culture" before the term was coined, she set up the Alliance of Small Firms and Self-Employed People in 1974. Elected to parliament (for Billericay) in 1987, she has strongly championed small businesses and women's rights and is one of the most vocal Tory backbenchers. She was one of **Margaret Thatcher**'s most forthright champions during the Tory leadership crisis in November 1990.

**GOSS, Wayne.** *Australia.* Premier of Queensland. Born in 1951 and educated at the University of Queensland, he was a lawyer before entering Queensland's legislative asssembly as an Australian Labor Party (ALP) member in 1983. He became leader of the Queensland Labor Party in 1988 and led his party to victory in the 1989 state election. His achievement was to unite the chronically divided and demoralized Queensland ALP following the exposure of national ALP wrongdoing by the Royal Commission headed by barrister Tony Fitzgerald.

**GOTODA, Masaharu.** *Japan.* Liberal Democratic Party politician. Born in 1914 and a graduate in law, he worked in the home affairs ministry and rose to become director-general of the National Police Agency in 1969. First elected to the House of Representatives (lower house) in 1976, he held senior ministerial office at home affairs, and later as chief cabinet secretary. His command of the workings of government, and access to information, helped make him a force to be reckoned with among the members of the Diet (parliament), although latterly his power has waned with that of former prime ministers Kakuei Tanaka and **Yasuhiro Nakasone**.

**GOUKOUNI OUEDDEI.** *Chad.* Former president and exiled opposition leader. Born in 1944, Goukouni was a leader of Frolinat, the Libyan-backed group involved in the northern-based rebellion against the governments of presidents François Tombalbaye and Félix Malloum in the 1970s. The power struggle within Frolinat in 1980 between Goukouni and **Hissène Habré** led to the first Libyan intervention, resulting in the installation of Goukouni as head of the Transitional Government of National Unity (GUNT). Since Habré's triumph in 1982, Goukouni has lived in exile, resisting attempts to persuade him to return home, with his leadership of the pro-Libyan opposition challenged by younger figures.

**GOULD, Bryan.** *UK.* Labour politician. Born in New Zealand in 1939, he studied law at Auckland and Oxford universities. He entered the foreign service in 1964 before becoming a lecturer in law at Oxford in 1968. Elected to parliament (for Southampton Test) in 1974, he lost his seat in 1979 and then embarked on a third career as a reporter and presenter of a television current affairs programme. In 1983 he returned to parliament, this time for the safe seat of Dagenham in London. He has been a member of the shadow cabinet since 1986, first as spokesman for trade and industry until 1989 and then for environment. Clever and telegenic, he was an important supporter for Labour leader **Neil Kinnock**, presenting the genial face of the "new" modernized Labour party, particularly during the 1987 election. More recently, his influence has waned within the inner circle of colleagues around the Labour leader, though he remains a likely member of any future Labour government.

**GOULDING, Marrack.** *UK.* UN under-secretary-general. Born in 1936, he studied at Oxford University and in 1959 joined the diplomatic service, first becoming an ambassador (to Angola) in 1983. From 1979–83 he had been counsellor at the British mission at the UN, and in 1986 he was appointed an under-secretary-general, responsible for special political affairs. Known for his hands-on approach, patience and personal style, he is in overall charge of the UN's peace-keeping forces in such troublespots as Lebanon, Kashmir, Central America and Cyprus. He has also tried to negotiate the release of hostages in the Middle East.

**GOULED APTIDON, Hassan.** *Djibouti.* President. Born in 1916, he is a veteran Issa politician, who represented French Somaliland in the French government from 1952–58, when he became vice-president of the territorial assembly, later serving as education minister. He became president on independence in 1977, and has since been re-elected twice as the sole candidate. He has attempted to create a balance between the country's Issa and Afar ethnic groups, emphasizing common Islamic allegiances and distributing government posts evenly between the two communities, but there is still Afar disaffection. With the president rumoured to be in poor health, the succession is increasingly at issue.

**GOWON, General Yakubu.** *Nigeria.* Former head of state. Born in 1934 in Jos, central Nigeria, the son of a Christian missionary, he enlisted in the army in 1954, receiving training at the UK's Sandhurst Military Academy from 1955–57. He served with the UN peacekeeping forces in the Congo in 1960–61 and in 1963 was appointed adjutant-general of the Nigerian army. In 1966 he emerged as leader of the military government – at the time Africa's youngest head of state – but was unable to prevent the breach with the Ibo-dominated Eastern region which led to the secession of Biafra in 1967. After nearly three years of civil war, Biafra was defeated but Gowon proved less effective as a peacetime leader than as a military commander and in 1975 was overthrown in a bloodless coup led by General Murtala Muhammed. Gowon has since spent much time abroad, studying political science at Warwick University in the UK from 1975–83, but he maintains business interests in Nigeria.

**GRAČANIN, Colonel-General Petar.** *Yugoslavia.* Internal affairs minister. Born in Serbia in 1923, he joined Tito's partisans in 1941 and went on to build a career in the army, serving as chief of staff from 1982–85. Now retired, he was elected president of the presidency of Serbia in 1987. In April 1989 he was appointed federal internal affairs minister. A close ally of Serbian hardliner **Slobodan Milošević**, he is opposed to pluralism. His appointment was seen as a concession by **Ante Marković**, the federal prime minister, to Serbia and to the army.

**GRAHAM, Robert (Bob).** *USA.* Democratic senator from Florida. Born in 1936, he was a developer and cattleman who served in the state assembly and for two terms as governor before his 1986 election to the Senate. He is a moderate with a particular interest in budget reduction

and arms control.

**GRAMM, Phil.** *USA.* Republican senator from Texas. Born in 1942, he was educated at the University of Georgia and later taught economics. Elected to the House of Representatives as a Democratic congressman in 1978, he co-operated with Republican colleagues on the budget committee to support the Reagan administration's expenditure reductions and tax cuts. In revenge the House Democratic leadership rescinded his committee appointment in 1983, provoking him to change parties. After winning a special election, he regained his committee seat as a Republican. Elected senator in 1984, he was the driving force behind the 1985 Gramm-Rudman-Hollings proposal to timetable mandatory budget reductions with a view to eliminating the mammoth federal deficit by 1991. Initially an independent operator in the Senate, where his legislative triumphs owed much to a shrewd sense of timing, Gramm has become more of a team-man in order to gain important committee assignments. He still pursues cost-cutting concerns from his budget committee seat, gained in 1989, and advocates deregulation of the banks from his banking committee seat.

**GRANT, James.** *USA.* Executive director of the UN Children's Fund (Unicef). Born in 1922, he studied law and after war service practised until 1954. He has since held a range of positions in the US administration and agencies primarily concerned with overseas development programmes. He was president of the Overseas Development Council for 11 years before his appointment as Unicef executive director in 1980.

**GRAY, C. Boyden.** *USA.* Counsel to the president. Born in 1944, he graduated with distinction from Harvard University and the University of North Carolina, and became a prominent lawyer in Washington, DC. He is a member of **George Bush**'s "inner circle" of advisers, and has been his personal lawyer since 1981. He also holds the role of watchdog on ethics, an issue Bush has been eager to promote.

**GRAY, Herb.** *Canada.* Liberal leader in the House of Commons. Born in 1931 in Windsor, Ontario, he was educated at McGill University, Montreal, and Osgoode Hall Law School, Toronto. A veteran of federal politics, Gray was first elected for the Liberal Party of Canada in 1962 and is known by his colleagues as "Dean" of the House of Commons. He was named opposition leader in the House in February 1990 when John Turner announced he was leaving politics, and re-appointed later that year by **Jean Chrétien** who won the Liberal leadership but had no parliamentary seat.

**GRAY, William, III**. *USA*. Democratic congressman from Pennsylvania. Born in 1941, he was educated at Franklin and Marshall College, Drew Theological Seminary and Princeton University. He was a Baptist minister in a black Philadelphia church before his election to the House of Representatives in 1978. He rose rapidly in the House because of his consensus-building expertise and was an effective budget committee chairman from 1985–88, doing much to improve Democratic unity on budget issues after the disharmony during **Ronald Reagan**'s first term. He was active in the 1986 legislative battle for tougher sanctions against South Africa, using his personal prestige to good effect, and, from his seat on the foreign operations subcommittee, he is a vigorous advocate of generous aid to black Africa. In 1989 he was appointed majority whip and became chairman of the Congressional Black Caucus. Although sensitive to criticisms that he is the white establishment's preferred alternative to **Jesse Jackson**, Gray has benefited from his ability to operate outside the traditional style and agenda of black politics. Despite Justice Department investigations of payroll padding by his staff in 1989, seasoned observers believe that he may become the first black speaker of the House or a vice-presidential nominee.

**GREEN, Hamilton**. *Guyana*. Prime minister. Born in 1934, he became a staunch party activist in the People's National Congress and was considered the favourite to succeed President Forbes Burnham, rising to vice-president for labour and public welfare, and then for agriculture. He became prime minister after Burnham's death in 1985, when his rival **Desmond Hoyte** became president.

**GREENSPAN, Alan**. *USA*. Chairman, Federal Reserve Board. Born in 1926, the son of a stockbroker, he is deeply influenced by the economist philosopher Ayn Rand's "rational selfishness" and is a firm believer in the morality of capitalism. He was nominated to the Fed by **Ronald Reagan** in 1987, and since then has tried to achieve "steady, maximum growth" without inflation. He managed to save the social security system from bankruptcy in the early 1980s as chairman of the National Commission on Social Security Reform and re-established confidence in the stock market after Black

Monday. Greenspan's style is one of legality and consensus, and he is widely respected.

**GREGG, Judd**. *USA*. Republican governor of New Hampshire. Born in 1947, he is the son of a former governor and is a former US congressman. His 1988 election as governor benefited from New Hampshire's thriving economy. Environmental issues are high on his agenda but on many issues he takes a more traditional conservative line, and on abortion he has a "pro-life" stance. He was re-elected in 1990.

**GREINER, Nick**. *Australia*. Premier of New South Wales. As state Liberal Party leader, he defeated the increasingly creaky New South Wales Labor machine in the state elections of 1987. Part of the "yuppie" rather than the "squatocracy" wing of his party, Greiner was born in Hungary in 1947. His Australian nationalist tendencies, expressed for example in his opposition to imperial honours, have raised eyebrows in the more socially conservative sections of the party. He was educated at Sydney University and Harvard Business School and has extensive domestic and US commercial interests ranging from publishing to building. First elected to the New South Wales parliament in 1980, he was opposition leader in the state from 1983 until the Labor defeat in 1987. His political and social style has much in common with that of the federal Liberal leader **John Hewson**.

**GRIFFITHS, Brian**. *UK*. Economist. Born in 1941, he studied economics and lectured at various universities and business schools from 1965–85. A leading monetarist and free-marketeer (and a keen evangelist), he was appointed head of the Downing Street policy unit, **Margaret Thatcher**'s own think-tank, in 1985. He was replaced by **Sarah Hogg** when **John Major** became prime minister and received a life peerage in Thatcher's resignation honours list.

**GRIGORYANTS, Sergei**. *USSR*. Dissident editor. Born in 1941, his publishing activities in 1983 gained him a sentence of 10 years in labour camp and internal exile, but he was released (like most other dissidents) and pardoned in 1986. In July 1987 he set up the unofficial *Glasnost* bulletin which, after initial hindrance from the authorities, has grown into an international publishing venture.

**GRÍMSSON, Ólafur Ragnar**. *Iceland*. Finance minister. Born in 1940, he studied and taught sociology before being elected to the Althingi (parliament) for the People's Alliance (Althýdubandalag) in 1979. A reformer intent on shedding the party's orthodox communist heritage, he became its leader in 1987. In 1988 he became finance minister in a centre–left coalition.

**GUBENKO, Nikolai.** *USSR.* Culture minister. Born in 1941, he made his name as an actor and as a theatrical and film director. He was artistic director at the Taganka theatre from March 1987 until **Mikhail Gorbachev**'s imaginative decision to bring him into the government in November 1989. In 1990 he was appointed to the Presidential Council shortly before it was swept away in the December 1990 constitutional changes.

**GUEBUZA, Armando Emilio.** *Mozambique.* Transport and communications minister. Born in 1943, he was interior minister from 1975–77 and from 1983 until June 1984, when he was dismissed by President Samora Machel because of his controversial policing policies and hardline attitude towards the war against the Mozambique National Resistance (Renamo) rebels. He retained his number five position in the ruling Front for the Liberation of Mozambique (Frelimo) central committee but was out of the cabinet until January 1987, when he was appointed transport and communications minister. Guebuza's stance on the war has moderated and in 1990 he became one of the leaders of the government team in peace negotiations with Renamo.

**GUERRA GONZÁLEZ, Alfonso.** *Spain.* Deputy prime minister. Born in 1940 in Seville, a former bookseller and amateur theatre director, he has been a close friend of **Felipe González** since their youth, and his unfailing political ally. He joined the then clandestine Spanish Socialist Workers' Party (PSOE) in 1962 and, with González, was responsible for transforming it into a major political organization uniting the diverse components of Spanish socialism. As deputy secretary-general of the PSOE since 1979 and deputy prime minister since 1982 he has maintained strong centralized discipline and acted as a link between the prime minister's office and ministerial departments. He has a reputation for administrative skill but is also dubbed ruthless and demagogic. In 1990 a simmering scandal boiled over in which his brother Juan was accused of using political influence for financial gain. Alfonso Guerra was subjected to much adverse publicity; he denied any knowledge of his brother's business affairs,

and throughout the year resisted calls for his resignation, with the staunch support of Felipe González, but his reputation was badly dented.

**GUICHARD, Baron Olivier.** *France.* Gaullist politician. Born in 1920 and a graduate in law and politics, he began his career in public administration. From 1951–58 he was head of Charles de Gaulle's political staff (*chef de cabinet*) and remained a prominent adviser to the Gaullist state. In the 1960s he formulated the "Guichard Plan", a benchmark in regional planning, and from 1967–77 was minister for several departments including education, industry, regional planning and justice. Elected to the National Assembly in 1968, he sits with the Gaullist Rally for the Republic (RPR), specializing in local and regional government.

**GUIGOU, Elisabeth.** *France.* Minister-delegate attached to the minister of foreign affairs, responsible for European affairs. Born in Morocco in 1946 and daughter of a settler family, she graduated from the elite Ecole Nationale d'Administration in 1974 and worked as a Treasury official. A fluent English-speaker, she was financial attaché at the embassy in London from 1979–81. In 1982, on leaving **Jacques Delors**'s office at the economy and finance ministry, she established herself as a protégé of **François Mitterrand** and from 1984 onwards was responsible for European affairs within his team of presidential advisers. She played a key role in supporting the president's handling of the "cohabitation" with a centre-right government from 1986–88, and during this period she headed the secretariat of the inter-ministerial committee on European economic co-operation. A member of the Socialist Party (PS), she was increasingly identified as a potential future minister, despite her low public profile. In 1990, before her appointment to the government in October, she was given the additional responsibility within the Elysée team for policy towards central and Eastern Europe.

**GUJRAL, I.K.** *India.* Leading Janata Dal politician. Born in 1919 in Jhelum, in what is now Pakistan, he was imprisoned for his nationalist activities in the 1930s and during the Quit India movement in 1942 and moved to India after partition in 1947. He began his political career in Delhi municipal politics, serving as vice-president of the New Delhi Municipal Committee from 1959–64. He was elected to the Lok Sabha (lower house) in 1964 and to the Rajya Sabha (upper house) in 1970.

He held ministerial office under Indira Gandhi from 1964–76, including the information and broadcasting portfolio. Mrs Gandhi appointed him ambassador to the USSR in 1976, a post he held until 1980. In 1987 he left Congress and joined the Jan Morcha of **V.P. Singh**, and was elected as a Janata Dal MP in the 1989 election, joining the new National Front government as external affairs minister but resigned in 1990.

**GUMBARIDZE, Givi**. *USSR*. Former president of Georgia. Born in 1945 and previously a full-time Communist Party official, he was named Georgian KGB chief in December 1988. Four months later he took over as Georgian Communist Party leader, and in November 1989 as chairman of the presidium of the Georgian Supreme Soviet in the overhaul of Georgia's leadership that followed the April 1989 massacre of demonstrators by troops in Tbilisi. Gumbaridze came under pressure to meet the demands of Georgia's burgeoning nationalist movement, although he was reputedly on friendly terms with senior nationalist leader **Zviad Gamsakhurdia**. Gamsakhurdia succeeded him as president after the nationalist election victory in November 1990, and the following month the Georgian Communist Party held a congress, announced its secession from the CPSU, and replaced him with Avtandil Margiani as first secretary.

**GUMMER, John Selwyn**. *UK*. Agriculture, fisheries and food minister since 1989. Born in 1939, educated at Cambridge University and an MP since 1970, Gummer was junior employment minister, paymaster-general and, from 1983–85, Conservative Party chairman, before joining the cabinet. As a Church of England synod member he was the government's perfect choice to denounce the church's critical *Faith in the City* report. As agriculture minister, the youthful-looking MP for Suffolk Coastal has on several occasions found himself caught between the hammer and the anvil of embattled farmers and consumers anxious about food safety, notably over the "mad cow disease", BSE.

**GURENKO (HURENKO), Stanislav**. *USSR*. Ukrainian Communist Party leader. Born in 1936, he worked as an engineering plant manager in Donetsk before joining the party administration there in 1976. He was a deputy premier of the Ukraine from 1980–87, became first secretary of the Ukrainian Communist Party in June 1990, and thus joined the Communist Party of the Soviet Union politburo the following month.

**GURIRAB, Theo-Ben**. *Namibia*. Foreign minister. Born in 1938 he was the South West Africa People's Organization (Swapo) representative for North America until appointed head of its mission to the UN in 1972. In this position he was senior adviser to Swapo president **Sam Nujoma** in the negotiations leading to the adoption of UN resolution 435 on Namibian independence in 1978. Appointed foreign affairs secretary on Swapo's politburo in 1986, Gurirab became independent Namibia's first foreign minister in March 1990.

**GUSEV, Vladimir**. *USSR*. Former deputy prime minister. A Russian born in 1932, and a chemical engineer by profession, he was a regional Communist Party official before being made a first deputy premier of the Russian Federation government in 1985. He was appointed as a USSR deputy premier in 1986, when one of his first tasks was to supervise the clean-up operation after the Chernobyl nuclear accident. In July 1989 he was made chairman of the Bureau for the Chemical and Timber Sectors.

**GUTIÉRREZ BARRIOS, Fernando**. *Mexico*. Government (interior) minister. Born in 1927, he joined the army, reaching the rank of captain before joining the political police. He rose to become its deputy director and then its head between 1964 and 1982; he was reponsible for the suppression of student unrest in 1968. He subsequently served as governor of Veracruz state from 1984–89, before being appointed to the cabinet by **Carlos Salinas**.

**GUZMÁN RENOSO, Manuel Abimael**. *Peru*. Left-wing guerrilla leader. Guzmán (known as President Gonzalo to his followers) was born in 1934 and studied philosophy. Deeply involved in Marxist politics, in the 1970s he formed Sendero Luminoso (Shining Path) as a splinter group of the Maoist Communist Party of Peru–Red Flag. A shadowy and elusive figure, Guzmán has led Sendero Luminoso in an increasingly bitter and violent anti-government campaign based in the Peruvian Andes.

**GYOTEN, Toyoo**. *Japan*. Financial administrator. Born in 1931 in Kanagawa prefecture, he graduated from the economics faculty of Tokyo University and entered the finance ministry in 1955. After serving as deputy director-general of the International Finance Bureau in 1980, he was appointed to the same post in the Banking Bureau in 1983. He became vice-minister of finance for international affairs in 1986. Since retiring, Gyoten has served as adviser to the finance ministry since 1989 and he became a guest professor at Columbia University in the USA in 1990. With a good command of English and high international reputation, he has been tipped for top international posts.

**GYSI, Gregor.** *Germany.* Party of Democratic Socialism (PDS) leader. Leader, at its demise, of what had been the ruling Socialist Unity Party (SED), and the man who upheld the fortunes of its successor, the PDS, as it avoided electoral extinction in 1990, Gysi was born in Berlin in 1948 into a partly-Jewish family with a long tradition in communist politics. His father Klaus, a journalist and diplomat, was culture minister and then state secretary for religious affairs until 1988. Gregor, a lawyer, joined the SED in 1967, but was noted for defending dissidents and found his natural home on the reform wing of the party. In the convulsions of late 1989 he helped to bring down Egon Krenz, and took on the party chairmanship in December, but repeatedly stressed the need for a clear break with the past, epitomized in the change of name. The unexpected measure of PDS success at the March 1990 elections reflected in part the charisma of Gysi as its leader, but the party faced fresh difficulties in October over the investigation of illegal transfers of funds abroad. Aided by his sharp sense of humour and debating skills, he could still strike some chords in a united Germany with reminders of unfashionable social values; the relative success of the PDS in the December 1990 all-German elections was as much a personal triumph for Gysi as for his party's policies.

# H

HABASH, George. *Palestinian.* Head of the Popular Front for the Liberation of Palestine (PFLP). Habash, a Christian expelled from his home in Lydda by the advancing Jewish forces in 1948, studied medicine at the American University of Beirut, where he first became involved with the Palestinian cause. After a campus demonstration by his Arab Nationalist Movement, Habash and his followers were offered places at Cairo University by Egypt's President Gamal Abdel Nasser, and formed the PFLP in 1967. It was responsible for much of the Palestinian "terrorism" in the next few years, and from the mid-1970s, Habash was the effective leader of the hardline "rejectionist front" in the Palestine Liberation Organization. After initially siding with the Fatah "rebels" in the mid-1980s, Habash eventually became reconciled with **Yasser Arafat**, while maintaining his scepticism of the latter's willingness to negotiate with Israel. He gave full backing to Iraq in the Gulf crisis in 1990, a move that resulted in improved ties with Jordan and tension with Syria.

HABIBI, Hassan Ebrahim. *Iran.* First vice-president. Born in 1937, Habibi was a member of the Freedom Movement of Iran in the early 1960s and became active in the anti-Shah movement while studying law in France. After the 1979 revolution he helped to draft the constitution of the Islamic republic and became culture and higher education minister in its provisional government. He was the dominant Islamic Republican Party's unsuccessful candidate for the first presidential election in 1980 and became a member of the republic's first parliament. His political stance is relatively moderate. He was appointed justice minister in 1984 and first vice-president in 1989.

HABIMANA, Bonaventure. *Rwanda.* Secretary-general of National Revolutionary Movement for Development (MRND). He was appointed secretary-general of the MRND, the new party set up by President **Juvénal Habyarimana**, on its foundation in 1975, continuing to hold his earlier post of justice minister until 1977. As MRND secretary-general, Habimana is constitutional successor to the president.

HABRÉ, Hissène. *Chad.* Former president. A leader of northern opposition to the southern-dominated government of President François Tombalbaye in the early 1970s, Habré served briefly as prime minister in 1978–79 in the ill-fated coalition government of Félix Malloum. His power struggle with fellow northerner **Goukouni Oueddei** led to the first large-scale Libyan intervention and establishment of the short-lived Transitional Government of National Unity (GUNT) in 1979 under Goukouni. Habré fought back with French and US backing, recapturing Ndjamena in 1982 and inflicting a series of crushing defeats on the Libyans. He had recovered the bulk of Chadian territory by the time of the 1987 ceasefire and has brought relative stability to Chad after years of conflict. In December 1990, having lost the support of France, he was swiftly overthrown by former aide **Idriss Déby** and fled to exile in Cameroon.

HABYARIMANA, Major-General Juvénal. *Rwanda.* President. Born in 1937, he was educated in Zaïre before returning home to receive military training. He joined the national guard, whose chief of staff he became in 1963. Two years later he was appointed national guard minister and chief of staff of the police and in 1973, soon after his promotion to the rank of major-general, he ousted President Grégoire Kayibanda in a bloodless coup. A member of the Hutu ethnic group, he dissolved the ethnically based political parties soon after he came to power. He established the National Revolutionary Movement for Development in 1975 as the sole party with the declared purpose of ending ethnic conflict and forging national unity. Rwanda has enjoyed relative stability under Habyarimana's rule, but the invasion by Tutsi exiles from Uganda in October 1990 was a reminder that the old divisions still linger.

HADI AWANG, Ustaz Abdul. *Malaysia.* Fundamentalist leader. Born in 1947, Hadi

Awang was, during the 1980s, a member of the Trengganu state assembly, emerging as one of the most controversial politicians in Malaysia. As the dominant figure in the fundamentalist Parti Islam SeMalaysia, Hadi is treated with suspicion by the government, but his passionate oratory in support of an Islamic Malaysia attracts consistently large crowds.

**HAGEN, Carl.** *Norway.* Right-wing politician. Born in 1944, he studied business and marketing and headed the Norwegian subsidiary of the Tate & Lyle sugar conglomerate from 1970–74. He cut his political teeth as secretary of the anti-tax Anders Lange's Party in 1973–74 and was elected leader of the renamed Progress Party (FP) in 1978. A smooth performer with a talent for exploiting television to get his anti-tax, anti-big-government and anti-immigrant message across with considerably more subtlety than most of his party colleagues, he quickly rose to nationwide prominence. This did not translate into votes in 1981 or 1985, but brought a spectacular quadrupling of support in the 1989 elections.

**HAIDER, Jörg.** *Austria.* Freedom Party of Austria (FPÖ) leader. Born in Bad Goisern in 1950, he has a doctorate in law from Vienna University. He worked as an academic from 1972–76 and has been active in the nationalist wing of the FPÖ since his student days. He was elected to parliament in 1979 for the Kärnten (Carinthia) region, where he was the FPÖ secretary. Elected head of the FPÖ in 1986, he has been provincial premier since 1989 in Kärnten, the heartland of support for nationalism. His personal charisma has greatly increased his party's capacity to attract votes, exploiting fears of immigration, and appealing to protest voters and those dissatisfied with the political establishment and the consensual system of economic management. The October 1990 elections confirmed his achievement in raising the FPÖ from the status of a fringe party to a serious claimant for a share in power at national level. His confrontational style is unusual in Austrian politics.

**HAILSHAM, Lord (Quintin Hogg).** *UK.* Conservative politician. Born Quintin Hogg in 1907, he was an MP until 1950 when he succeeded his father as Viscount Hailsham. In the 1950s and early 1960s he held several senior posts, including those of Conservative party chairman and education secretary, displaying his contrasting sides – the thoughtful intellectual and the irrepressible showman. He renounced his hereditary peerage in 1963 in an unsuccessful bid to succeed Harold Macmillan as prime minister. Created a life peer in 1970, he was appointed Lord Chancellor in 1979, a position he held until 1987. At that time he was the last surviving member of Churchill's wartime cabinet to remain in office.

**HALL, Aleksander.** *Poland.* Democratic Right Forum chairman. Born in 1953 in Gdansk, he worked as a history teacher and became active in the human rights movement in the late 1970s. He helped to found the "Young Poland Movement" in 1979 and is regarded as an acute independent theorist with right-wing views. He joined Solidarity in 1980, and spent nearly three years in hiding following the December 1981 imposition of martial law. He became a journalist in the early 1980s, took part in the 1989 round-table talks on the Solidarity side, and was appointed minister without portfolio, responsible for co-operation with political organizations and associations in the Solidarity-led coalition government formed in September 1989. In October 1990 he resigned to support the prime minister, **Tadeusz Mazowiecki,** in the presidential campaign. The following month he was elected chairman of the Democratic Right Forum, a pro-government group committed to liberal economics.

**HALL, Gus.** *USA.* Chairman of the Communist Party USA. Born in 1911, he has been a party member since 1927 and leader for over 30 years. The changes in Eastern Europe and within his own party have slightly outpaced him, but he still believes "communism is the next stage of human society". He began as a lumberjack and a steelworker, and remains a tireless campaigner.

**HALL, Wes.** *Barbados.* Sports and tourism minister. Born in 1937, he enjoyed a glittering cricket career as a fast bowler, playing in 48 test matches for the West Indies in the late 1950s and 1960s. Appointed a Democratic Labour Party senator, he became employment and labour relations minister in 1986, moving to his present portfolio two years later.

**HAMDI, Mahmoud Abdel-Rahim.** *Sudan.* Finance minister. A member of the National Islamic Front, he was appointed finance minister in the April 1990 cabinet reshuffle. Previously a banker, he had helped to set up one of Sudan's leading Islamic banks and has good connections with international financiers, particularly in Saudi Arabia.

**HAMILTON, Lee.** *USA.* Democratic congressman from Indiana. Born in 1931, he practised law and was elected to the House of Representatives in 1964. Formerly intelligence committee chairman, he also chaired the special House committee investigating the arms sales to Iran by the administration of **Ronald Reagan**. He is influential on the foreign affairs committee and is its probable future chairman, and chairs its Europe and Middle East subcommittee. Unlike many Democrats, he supports arms sales to moderate Arab nations as a means of promoting US influence.

**HAMMADI, Sa'adoun.** *Iraq.* Deputy prime minister. Born in Kerbala in 1930, he studied in Lebanon and the USA before returning to Baghdad as professor of economics. He held various economic posts before becoming chairman of the Iraq National Oil Company in 1968, oil and minerals minister from 1969–74 and foreign minister from 1974–83. In mid-1986 **Saddam Hussain** strengthened his hand in a purge in which Hammadi, by now chairman of the National Assembly, was elected to the pivotal Revolutionary Command Council, replacing Naim Haddad. In 1989 Hammadi replaced Adnan Khairallah, Saddam's brother-in-law, as deputy premier after the latter's death in a mysterious helicopter crash. He advocated compromise during the 1980–88 war with Iran and later became the leading proponent of political and economic reforms.

**HAMMER, Zevulun.** *Israel.* A leading light in the National Religious Party and education minister. Born in 1936 in Haifa, he entered the cabinet in 1977 as education minister, revising the national syllabus. He replaced the veteran Josef Burg at religious affairs in 1986, before returning to education in 1990. An early supporter of Gush Emunim settlers, he now seems more moderate.

**HAMMOND, Eric.** *UK.* Trade unionist. Born in 1929, he was a shop steward for (what is now) the Electrical, Electronic, Telecommunications and Plumbing Union (EETPU) for ten years before becoming a full-time EETPU official in 1958. He was elected to the union executive in 1963, and in 1984 succeeded his mentor Frank (now Lord) Chapple as general secretary. Less brash and more cautious than his predecessor, he staked his union's future on a new approach to industrial relations involving "single-union" agreements whose stated intention is to avoid disruption. The union was suspended from the Trades Union Congress (TUC) for flouting its rules in 1988, and has drawn fierce criticism from more traditional leftist union leaders.

**HAMROUCHE, Mouloud.** *Algeria.* Prime minister. A close aide of President **Chadli Bendjedid**, Hamrouche had no previous ministerial experience when appointed prime minister in September 1989, with a brief to speed up reform. Secretary-general of the president's office since 1986 and a member of the National Liberation Front (FLN) central committee since 1983, Hamrouche had been active in drawing up reform policies and has committed himself to economic liberalization and multi-party politics.

**HAMUTENYA, Hidipo.** *Namibia.* Information and broadcasting minister. Born in 1939, he entered politics in 1960 in the footsteps of his father, a founder member of the South West Africa People's Organization (Swapo). He was elected to the Swapo central committee and politburo in 1976 and made information and publicity secretary in 1981, taking on the ministerial portfolio in the first Namibian government in March 1990. He has particular influence among former Swapo guerrillas and security officers.

**HANDAL, Shafik.** *El Salvador.* Guerrilla leader. Handal is secretary-general of the Communist Party of El Salvador (PCS) and of its armed wing, the Armed Forces of Liberation. In 1980 he became one of the leaders of the left-wing front, the Farabundo Martí National Liberation Front (FMLN).

**HANI, Chris.** *South Africa.* Militant leader within the African National Congress (ANC). Discouraged from the priesthood by his father, he studied Latin and English, but by his mid-20s had become embroiled in the ANC's ill-fated military expedition with **Joshua Nkomo's** guerrillas into white-run Rhodesia in 1967. An exile for the next two decades, he fell foul of the ANC's military leadership when he attacked them for incompetence and abuse of office, but gained a romantic aura as the survivor of several South African assassination attempts, and built up his own position to become political commissar in the armed wing, Umkhonto we Sizwe (Spear of the Nation), in 1982. Regarded in ideological terms as a Marxist-Leninist and closely linked with hardline South African Communist Party (SACP) leader **Joe Slovo** in Maputo, he is thought to have been a member of the SACP politburo since 1981, and was named as a senior SACP leader at the party's re-launch in Soweto in 1990. In his long-standing rivalry with Umkhonto leader Joe Modise, he has gradually established himself as the coming man. The balance of power tipped in his favour with the influx of Xhosa-speaking radicals from the Cape townships in the mid-1980s. He ranks as the man who was able to talk down, and then suppress, the 1984 mutiny among ANC guerrillas based in Angola, who were reluctant to devote themselves to the war against **Jonas Savimbi**'s National Union for the Total Liberation of Angola (Unita). In 1987 he took over as Umkhonto number two, replacing Slovo as chief of staff, and the following year persuaded the ANC to take the guerrilla war into white South Africa. He has a powerful appeal among militant youth, with his tough stance, guerrilla credibility, and flamboyant stylishness. Left out of the ANC team for the pre-negotiations of mid-1990, he based himself in Transkei and cultivated the Xhosa-speaking constituency in the townships of the eastern Cape; among the younger generation he ranks as the most likely future rival to **Thabo Mbeki** for the ANC leadership.

**HANK GONZÁLEZ, Carlos.** *Mexico.* Agriculture minister. Born in 1927 of a German father, he began his career as a schoolteacher. He became involved in politics as mayor of Toluca in 1955, subsequently serving as a federal deputy between 1958 and 1961. From 1964–69, he was an official of the state agency responsible for selling food and basic commodities to the poor, which helped boost his populist image. He was a close associate of President José López-Portillo, during whose administration he served as governor of Mexico state and mayor of Mexico City. The following years were spent in the political wilderness until he was brought back into government by **Carlos Salinas**.

**HANNIBALSSON, Jón Baldvin.** *Iceland.* Foreign affairs and foreign trade minister. Born in 1939, he studied economics before becoming a teacher and journalist. He was editor of a daily newspaper from 1979–82. Elected to the Althingi (parliament) for the Social Democratic Party (Althýduflokkurinn) in 1982, he became leader two years later and revived its fortunes, not least by advocating market-oriented economic policies. He became minister of finance in 1987 and of foreign affairs and foreign trade in 1988.

**HANS ADAM II.** *Liechtenstein.* Prince and head of state. Born in 1945, he studied economics and, to prepare him for his high office, worked in a range of locations, from a bank in London to a farm in Texas. In 1984 his ageing father, Franz Josef II, named him regent and transferred the extensive executive powers of the head of state; he succeeded on his father's death in 1989. Very much a new broom, he advocates a more active foreign role for the tiny principality, which joined the UN in 1990.

**HANSENNE, Michel.** *Belgium.* Director-general of the International Labour Organisation (ILO). Born in 1940, he trained as a lawyer and practised briefly until his election to parliament for the centrist Walloon Social Christian Party (PSC) in 1974. He was labour and employment minister from 1981–88 and sponsored some imaginative measures on job creation and working practices. The entry of socialists into the coalition government in 1988 thwarted his chances of advancement, and after a brief stint as public affairs minister he was appointed ILO director-general in 1989.

**HAPPART, José.** *Belgium.* Walloon Socialist politician. A farmer, born in 1947, he has been at the centre of a long-standing language dispute in the small eastern commune of Fourons (Voeren) which brought down the government in 1987. Ridiculed abroad as a Ruritanian farce, the affair in fact provided a sharp reminder of Belgium's unresolved language question. After local electoral success, he became mayor of Fourons in 1982 but was removed from office a year later when he refused to sit an obligatory Dutch language test. There followed a sequence of crises and messy compromises at national level, with political parties lining up on linguistic rather than ideological lines. The dispute appeared to have been resolved in 1989 when, in return for standing down as mayor, he secured a top place on the Walloon Socialist Party (PS) list for elections to the European Parliament and an enhancement of the status of French in Voeren.

**HARA, Kenzaburo.** *Japan.* Veteran parliamentarian and Liberal Democratic Party member. Born in 1907, his education included a spell at university in Oregon, after which he went into the publishing business. He was first elected to the House of Representatives (lower house) in 1946, and has held a variety of ministerial posts, notably as labour minister under Eisaku Sato in the 1960s and early 1970s. Under Zenko Suzuki's government in 1980 he was brought back into the cabinet as director-general of the National Land Agency and Hokkaido development agency. Speaker of the House of Representatives between 1986 and 1989, he is the longest-serving member of the Diet (parliament).

**HARALD, Prince.** *Norway.* Crown prince, the third child and only son of **King Olav V**. Born in 1937, he was the first prince to have been born in Norway for nearly 600 years. He lived in exile in the USA during World War II and was then educated in Norway at Smestad School and Katedralen, before taking up a military career. His marriage in 1968 to a commoner, Sonja Haraldsen, was highly controversial.

**HARMAN, Harriet.** *UK.* Labour politician. Born in 1950, she trained as a solicitor and worked at a law centre before becoming the legal officer of the National Council for Civil Liberties (NCCL) in 1978. She was elected to parliament for Peckham in London in 1982, and subsequently became a Labour spokeswoman on health issues.

**HARRIS, Lord (Ralph Harris).** *UK.* Economist. Born in 1924, he studied and then lectured in economics at St Andrews University. He played a key role in setting up the Institute of Economic Affairs (IEA) in 1957, the think-tank that championed free-market economics well before it became politically fashionable as the new-right Thatcherite orthodoxy. He became IEA chairman in 1987 after 30 years as general director, and was created a life peer in 1979.

**HASHIMOTO, Ryutaro.** *Japan.* Finance minister. Born in 1937, he graduated from the law faculty of Keio University. Following his father, Ryogo, Hashimoto was elected to the House of Representatives (lower house) in 1963. He first entered the cabinet as health and welfare minister under Masayoshi Ohira in 1978. Later, he became transport minister under **Yasuhiro Nakasone** in 1986, where he was instrumental in the privatization of Japan National Railways. As a member of the **Noboru Takeshita** faction, he served as secretary-general of the Liberal Democratic Party (LDP) in 1989 and led the party during the House of Councillors (upper house) election campaign. In spite of the LDP's crushing defeat, his substantial personal charisma continued to attract public attention. Initially hopeful of succeeding Sosuke Uno as LDP president, he was compelled to withdraw when it became clear that he would not enjoy the support of his own faction; some continue to see him as a possible future party president, however. He was appointed finance minister by **Toshiki Kaifu** in 1989.

**HASSAN IBN TALAL.** *Jordan.* Crown prince. Born in Amman in 1947, educated at Harrow and Oxford University, Hassan is his brother **King Hussein**'s intellectual voice, and is deeply involved with organizations such as the Royal Scientific Society, of which he is president. Nevertheless, he takes the helm when the king is away and did so with courage during the food riots of 1989. He is passionately involved in the cause of Palestine, despite Palestinian misgivings about his role during the 1970–71 civil war.

**HASSAN II.** *Morocco.* King. The 17th monarch of the Alaouite dynasty, he was born in 1929 and educated at Bordeaux University. Forced into exile after the 1954 abdication of his father, Mohammed V, Hassan returned with Mohammed's restoration to the throne to be installed as crown prince and commander-in-chief of the armed forces in 1957. Appointed defence minister and vice-premier in 1960, he succeeded to the throne on his father's death the following year. A consummate politician, Hassan has balanced ruthless suppression of dissent with a parliamentary system that permits limited opposition. He has survived two coup attempts, in 1971 and 1972, and exploited his position as a loyal ally of the west to continue the long-running battle for control of the Western Sahara on his southern border. His role as a religious leader – commander of the faithful – has helped him to neutralize Islamic fundamentalist pressures.

**HASSAN, Brigadier-General Hussain Kamel.** *Iraq.* Oil, industry and military industrialization minister. He was acting industry and minerals minister until July 1988 when he was given the key post of industry and military industrialization. As **Saddam Hussain**'s son-in-law he enjoys considerable influence, which has increased since the death in a mysterious helicopter crash in 1989 of Adnan Khairallah, Saddam's brother-in-law. Of late he has been tipped as the man to replace **Taha Yassin Ramadhan** as Saddam's number two, and in October 1990 he added oil to his list of responsibilities.

**HASSANALI, Noor Mohammed.** *Trinidad and Tobago.* President. Born in 1918, he trained in law and rose to become an appeal court judge. He was elected as non-executive president in 1987, the first "East Indian" to hold the post.

**HASSELFELDT, Gerda.** *Germany.* Regional planning, building and urban development minister. Born in Lower Bavaria in 1950, she studied economics before working in the labour ministry as a careers advisory specialist. She joined the Christian Social Union (CSU) in 1969 and filled the vacancy in the Bundestag created by the death of Franz Josef Strauss in 1987. She was appointed regional planning, building and urban development minister in 1989.

**HATFIELD, Mark**. *USA*. Republican senator from Oregon. Born in 1922, he was a political science professor who served as state legislator and governor (1959–67) before being elected senator in 1966. Liberal in outlook, except on abortion, he has often criticized big defence budgets and considers US Middle East policy too pro-Israel. He is ranking Republican on the appropriations committee, which he chaired from 1981–87.

**HATTERSLEY, Roy**. *UK*. Labour politician and journalist. Born in 1932, he graduated in economics from the University of Hull, and then worked for the health service, took up journalism and became a local councillor in Sheffield before being elected to parliament in 1964. He held a number of junior ministerial posts before being appointed secretary of state for prices and consumer protection in 1976. Since Labour lost power in 1979 he has been opposition spokesman on the environment (1979–80), home affairs (1980–83 and again since 1987) and economic affairs (1983–87). On the right of the party, he was elected deputy leader to **Neil Kinnock** in 1983 – one half of the "dream ticket" to which he brought gravitas and experience, in contrast to what was seen at the time as Kinnock's dynamic radicalism. He is one of only two members (the other is **John Smith**) of the shadow cabinet who have held senior ministerial office. He is a keen advocate of constitutional reforms – and of the need for a written constitution – but has emerged as a leading opponent of proportional representation, at a time when many of his colleagues have begun to look more favourably at possible changes to the electoral system. A busy columnist – and recently novelist – he has sometimes been criticized for devoting too much time to his writing career.

**HAU PEI-TSUN, General**. *Taiwan*. Prime minister. Born in about 1918 on the Chinese mainland, Hau is a staunch anti-communist and anti-independence conservative, and has been a member of the Kuomintang (KMT) central standing committee since 1984. A career soldier, he was chief of general staff until he resigned from the army in November 1985 to become defence minister. His nomination as prime minister in March 1990 was seen as a retrograde step towards militarization, with his alleged readiness to call out the troops to maintain law and order causing concern to civil libertarians.

His energy and decisiveness have nevertheless won him considerable popularity and earned the grudging respect of his critics.

**HAUFF, Volker**. *Germany*. Social Democratic Party (SPD) politician. Born in 1940, he studied economics and social science at the Free University of Berlin. He worked for IBM before serving (1972–78) as state secretary in the research and technology ministry in Helmut Schmidt's SPD-led government. Promoted to minister in 1978, he was moved to the transport portfolio in 1980, a post which he held until 1982.

**HAUGHEY, Charles**. *Ireland*. Taoiseach (prime minister). Born in 1925, he studied commerce, trained as a lawyer and founded what became one of the country's major accountancy firms. Elected to parliament for Fianna Fáil in 1957, he quickly rose to prominence, not least because he was the son-in-law of Seán Lemass (prime minister from 1959–66). He was appointed minister of justice in 1961, agriculture in 1964 and finance in 1966. A self-styled man of the people, he seemed a foregone choice for the party leadership, but his career took a nosedive in 1970 when he was accused of gun-running for the Irish Republican Army (IRA) in Northern Ireland. He was acquitted of the charge, but nevertheless had to leave the government. Rehabilitated as health minister in 1977, he completed a remarkable comeback two years later with his election as party leader and prime minister. Under his leadership Fianna Fáil lost the 1981 election, won in early 1982, lost later that year and finally returned to power in 1987. "The Great Survivor" gave further proof of his skill as a political operator two years later, when he succeeded in forming a coalition with the Progressive Democrats after having failed to gain an absolute majority in the elections.

**HAUSSMANN, Helmut**. *Germany*. Free Democratic Party (FDP) politician. Born in 1943 in Tübingen, he studied economics and social science, then worked in industry while studying for a doctorate. He was elected to the Bundestag in 1976, and served as FDP secretary-general from 1984–88, but was still little known until his appointment to the highly influential post of economics minister in 1988. Criticism of his lack of leadership on the economics of unification prompted his resignation from the cabinet in December 1990.

**HAVEL, Václav**. *Czechoslovakia*. President. Born in 1936 into a prosperous business family in Prague, he was debarred from receiving further education in the 1950s by the communist authorities because of his bourgeois origins. He found work as a laboratory technician, studied in evening classes, and entered the Prague theatre world in 1959 as a stage-hand, subsequently filling various increasingly prominent posts at the Theatre on the Balustrade. He began to establish his international reputation as a playwright with his first play, *The Garden Party*, published in 1963, and won several international and other awards from 1969–89. Politically active for democratic change in 1968, and banned from public life soon after the Warsaw Pact invasion of Czechoslovakia, he was forced out of the theatre and thereafter worked in various menial jobs (including one in a brewery). In 1977 he was one of the founders of Charter 77 (and its spokesman in 1977, 1978–79 and 1989), and in 1978 he helped set up the Committee for the Defence of the Unjustly Persecuted (VONS). Detained without trial from January to May 1977, he was sentenced in October to 14 months' imprisonment, suspended for three years, for "anti-state" activities. From 1979–83 he was imprisoned for "sedition", and was again imprisoned in February 1989 for "incitement and obstruction", but his detention attracted international attention and he was released in May after the charge against him was reduced to a misdemeanour. In November 1989 he became a founder-member of Civic Forum, swiftly emerging as its undeclared leader and, for all his expressions of reluctance about political involvement, as the prime mover in the "velvet revolution" which brought down the communist regime. Elected president of the republic in December 1989, for an interim six-month period, he was the only person considered to have the moral stature to lead the country into the first free elections since 1946. In July 1990 he was re-elected with overwhelming majority support for a further two-year term. Unassuming and informal in manner, he retains the appearance of something of a "philosopher-king" but nevertheless, as head of state, plays a very active role in shaping government policy.

**HAWATMEH, Naif.** *Palestinian.* Head of the Democratic Front for the Liberation of Palestine (DFLP). Born in 1935 to a Christian family near the Jordanian town of Salt. He formed the DFLP after splitting from **George Habash**'s Popular Front for the Liberation of Palestine in 1969. Although he shares Fatah's goal of a democratic Palestinian state in which Jews, Muslims and Christians live in equality, he believes in the preservation of Arab and Jewish identities within the state. Based in Damascus, the DFLP plays the role of loyal opposition to Fatah and has well-developed contacts with left-wing Israelis. In this sense, at least, Hawatmeh is seen as a moderate leader.

**HAWKE, Bob.** *Australia.* Prime minister. Born in South Australia in 1929, he later moved with his family to Western Australia. His political power base, however, is in the formidable Victoria state Labor Party. Educated at the University of Western Australia and Oxford University (where he was a Rhodes Scholar), he joined the Australian Council of Trades Unions in 1958 as a research officer and industrial negotiator, eventually becoming the union federation's president. Meanwhile, he had also been cultivating his position in the Australian Labor Party (ALP). He became president of the ALP in 1973, resigning when he was elected to the House of Representatives in 1980. In parliament he moved immediately to the opposition front bench as shadow employment minister. In February 1983, a month before the federal general election, Hawke replaced **Bill Hayden** as leader of the opposition, supposedly in order to enhance the ALP chances in the poll. Labor won the March 1983 election under Hawke, as it has all others since. Throughout his period in power, and irrespective of the performance of his government, Hawke has enjoyed extraordinarily high personal levels of public approval, a considerable achievement in a political culture devoted to lopping the "tall poppies". This is partly the result of assiduous attention to his public relations, which has carefully fostered the image of reformed "larrikin" (hooligan) whose drinking and womanizing, though now firmly in the past, supposedly qualify him to speak to and for the ordinary Australian male. Hawke belongs to the right-wing "Labor Unity" faction of the ALP and has pursued the interests of this grouping with a resolve that has at times made him more enemies within his own party than in the country as a whole. (Among the more significant party figures who have been immune to the Hawke magic is the previous Labor prime minister, Gough Whitlam.) While few would argue with the power of his charisma, there has been an underlying dissatisfaction among sections of the ALP at his evident lack of a clear political doctrine.

**HAWKINS, Augustus (Gus).** *USA.* Democratic congressman from California. Born in 1907, he was a real estate agent and long-serving state assemblyman, before being elected in 1962 as first black member of the House of Representatives from a western state. Chairman of the education and labour committee since 1984, his old-style liberalism is somewhat out of touch with deficit-conscious younger Democrats. As a result, some committee-backed bills have suffered defeat, but the 1988 education bill authorizing higher funds for many programmes was a personal triumph.

**HAYATOU, Sadou.** *Cameroon.* Secretary-general to the presidency. A northern aristocrat (son of the Lamido of Garoua), born in 1942, he studied economics in France, joining the Cameroon civil service in 1968. A former banker, he held the agriculture and planning portfolios before being appointed finance minister in 1987. A proponent of market-oriented economic reforms when holding the finance portfolio, he was appointed to his present post in September 1990, effectively becoming number two to President **Paul Biya**.

**HAYDEN, Bill.** *Australia.* Governor-general. Born in Brisbane, Queensland in 1933, he was a policeman for eight years before his election in 1961 to the House of Representatives for the Queensland seat of Oxley. Between 1972 and the constitutional "coup" of 1975 he was social security minister and then treasurer in Gough Whitlam's government. Succeeding Whitlam as leader of the parliamentary Australian Labor Party (ALP), he was in turn succeeded by **Bob Hawke** on the eve of the 1983 general election. Hayden held the foreign affairs portfolio until his resignation in 1988 in preparation for his investiture as governor-general at the beginning of 1989. One of his major achievements as foreign minister was to limit the damage caused by New Zealand's *de facto* departure from the Anzus alliance, managing to maintain good relations with both Wellington and Washington. Before he became governor-general, Hayden's long-held republican views were felt by many to sit uncomfortably with the office's role; he was on the centre-left of the ALP.

**HEALEY, Denis.** *UK.* Labour politician. Born in 1917, he graduated from Oxford University and after distinguished wartime service became international secretary of the Labour Party in 1945. Elected to parliament in 1952, he was first appointed to the shadow cabinet in 1959, and was defence secretary (1964–70) and chancellor of the exchequer (1974–79). As chancellor, he began by threatening "to squeeze the rich until

the pips squeak" but ended as the *bête noire* of Labour's left for his accommodation with the IMF during and after the sterling crisis of 1976. A robust operator on the right of the party with a knowledge of international affairs probably unparalleled within parliament, he will be remembered as the best leader that Labour never had: he was narrowly denied the leadership in 1981, largely by moderates within the party who feared that Healey as leader would alienate the left and split the party. He developed a reputation for the acid parliamentary put-down, once comparing an attack by **Geoffrey Howe** to being "savaged by a dead sheep". But in his political twilight, he has taken on the mantle of an entertaining elder statesman, with friends on both sides of the house.

**HEATH, Edward.** *UK.* Conservative politician. Born in 1916, he gained a scholarship to Oxford University. After wartime service, he briefly worked as a civil servant, journalist and banker before being elected to parliament in 1950. He became chief government whip in 1955, labour minister in 1959, lord privy seal (with foreign office responsibilities) in 1960, and secretary of state for industry and trade in 1963. A year after the Conservative defeat in 1964 he was elected party leader – marking the advent of a new generation and, more importantly, the first stage in ending the party's domination by the traditional gentry (a process completed by his successor as party leader, **Margaret Thatcher**). Somewhat stiff and lacking the popular touch, he nevertheless led the party to a surprise election victory in 1970 on a programme of reform that in many ways foreshadowed Thatcher's policies. In 1973 he achieved his greatest political ambition, the accession of the UK to the EC. Domestically, his government clung for two years to its convictions, shunning direct intervention in the economy and accepting that higher unemployment would have to be the price of pay rises not linked to productivity gains. But widespread strikes and a steep rise in unemployment prompted a reversal of policy – the famous U-turn subsequently abhorred by all Thatcherites. A period of reflation (the "Barber boom") ended with more strikes and the stand-off battle with the miners that brought electoral defeat in 1974. A year later he was unseated as leader by Thatcher. His personal persistent bitterness towards her lost him many friends but he has remained influential. Many in government got their first taste of power when he was prime minister and his never dimming enthusiasm for Europe has given him a special political platform in recent years.

**HEKMATYAR, Gulbuddin.** *Afghanistan. Mujaheddin* commander and fundamentalist Hizb-e Islami leader. The most determined exponent of the original *mujaheddin* aim of expunging the communist regime, his reputation was tarnished by his support for the abortive March 1990 coup attempt, launched from within the Kabul regime by General Shanawaz Tanai. Closely in tune with Pakistani military intelligence, he came under pressure in October 1990 to soften his hostility to his bitter rival **Ahmed Massud**, and was isolated in his desire to launch an all-out assault on Kabul before US military support dried up. His unremitting determination to maintain a protracted and often bloody guerrilla struggle has increasingly distanced him from Western support.

**HELMS, Jesse.** *USA.* Republican senator from North Carolina. Born in 1921, he was a newspaperman (city editor) and broadcasting commentator and executive, before being elected senator in 1972. A fervent right-winger, the extent of conservative change in the Reagan era disappointed him, particularly as he had to defend administration compromises as a senior senator. Despite his free-market faith, he sought to protect his state's tobacco industry as agriculture committee chairman from 1981–86. The controversial permanent authorization for tobacco price supports, won in 1986, reinforced his position. Combined with the Democratic recapture of the Senate in 1986 and a lack of personal ties to **George Bush**, this has allowed Helms to voice more extreme views on social issues and foreign policy, his main interests. He is hostile to gay rights and once advocated the quarantine of AIDS sufferers. As ranking Republican on the foreign relations committee, he tends to play an obstructionist role on issues relating to Soviet-American rapprochement and nearly delayed ratification of the 1988 INF treaty. He has also been accused of over-friendly relations with Latin American dictators. The cornerstone of his political base is the National Congressional Club, a direct-mail fund-raising body.

**HENDRICKSE, Reverend (H.J.) Allan.** *South Africa.* Minister and chairman of the ministers' council of the House of Representatives (coloured parliament). Born in 1927, he became a teacher after studying at Fort Hare, and was then ordained a congregationalist minister,

rising to head the United Congregational Church of Southern Africa in 1972. Regarded as an able, if politically cautious, operator, he has been the dominant figure in the representative institutions for coloured voters for over a decade, leading the Labour Party since 1978. In his previous spell as chairman of the ministers' council in the coloured chamber, when the tri-racial chamber idea was first introduced, he was one of two token non-whites in the South African cabinet, as minister without portfolio from 1984–87. His acquiescence earned him the vilification of radicals in both the black and coloured communities. He was restored to his present post by **F. W. de Klerk** after the September 1989 elections.

**HENG SAMRIN.** *Cambodia.* State president and party leader. Born in 1934, he took up the revolutionary cause in the late 1950s. He served as a military commander under the Khmer Rouge regime (1975–78) but fled to Vietnam in mid-1978 when **Pol Pot** purged the eastern provinces. He was installed as state president in Phnom Penh by the Vietnamese in 1979 and became party leader two years later. Regarded as a Vietnamese puppet, he has been increasingly overshadowed in public by **Hun Sen** but still heads a hardline faction within the party.

**HERMANNSSON, Steingrímur.** *Iceland.* Prime minister. Born in 1928, he studied engineering in the USA and then worked as an engineer. Elected to the Althingi (parliament) for the Progressive Party (Framsóknarflokkurinn) in 1971, he became its secretary in the same year and leader in 1979. He has established himself as one of the country's leading political figures and held numerous ministerial posts, becoming prime minister from 1983–87, and again since 1988, this time at the head of a centre–left coalition.

**HERNANDEZ COLÓN, Rafael.** *USA (Puerto Rico).* Popular Democrat governor of Puerto Rico. Born in 1936, he was a lawyer and law professor who won a single gubernatorial term in 1972 and regained office in 1984. A belief that the trade policies of **Ronald Reagan**'s administration ignored Puerto Rico's interests has made him favour greater economic autonomy from the mainland, but not independence.

**HERNÁNDEZ GIL, Antonio.** *Spain.* Supreme Court president. Born in 1915 in the Badajoz area, a lawyer and professor of civil law at Madrid's Complutense University, he was president of the Cortes (parliament) and of the Council of the Realm in 1977–78. He was president of the Council of State from 1982 until his appointment in 1985 as president of the General Council of Judicial Power and of the Supreme Court of Justice.

**HERVÉ, Edmond.** *France.* Socialist politician. Born in 1942 and a graduate in law and politics, Hervé began as a teacher, became a university professor of law, gained prominence in the Socialist Party (PS) as a dynamic mayor of Rennes from 1977, and has been a member of parliament since 1981. Between 1981 and 1986 he held various junior ministerial appointments in industry, energy, health and social affairs. Within the party he continues to be identified as a close supporter of **Pierre Mauroy**.

**HERZOG, Chaim.** *Israel.* President. Born in Belfast in Northern Ireland in 1918, the son of a rabbi, Herzog studied law at Cambridge and London universities and in Jerusalem. He served in the British army in Egypt during World War II. He fought with the Israeli defence forces in 1948–49, and later headed military intelligence. A radio commentator in the 1967 and 1973 wars, he was ambassador to the UN (1974–78), and later a Labour MP. In 1983 he became a popular choice as president (a post with little real political power) and was re-elected in 1988.

**HESELTINE, Michael.** *UK.* Secretary of state for the environment. Ambitious, talented and wealthy, Heseltine was born in Swansea, Wales in 1933. He studied law at Oxford University, built a successful publishing career and a personal fortune at the helm of the Haymarket Press empire, entered parliament in 1964 and held several ministerial posts under **Edward Heath**. A strong advocate of selective intervention by government in key areas of the economy, he served as environment secretary in **Margaret Thatcher**'s first government. He favoured urban renewal to eradicate the causes of inner-city riots, but in seeking to use public funds he upset cabinet hardliners. After the Falklands war Heseltine became defence secretary until 1986, when he walked out of a cabinet meeting to resign over what he saw as gross misrepresentation of his role in the Westland helicopter affair. An impassioned public speaker, Heseltine – whose nickname is Tarzan – then worked hard at espousing an alternative platform to Thatcherism and was long thought of as the principal Tory rival to Margaret Thatcher. His eventual challenge precipitated her resignation in November 1990, although Heseltine withdrew from the subsequent leadership battle when it became

clear he could not win. In **John Major**'s cabinet he was given the post of environment minister with responsibility for reforming the politically disastrous poll tax – a tax he had criticized from its inception.

**HEWSON, John.** *Australia.* Leader of the Liberal Party of Australia and the federal opposition. Born in 1946 and educated at Sydney University, and the University of Saskatchewan in Canada, he took a doctorate at Johns Hopkins University in the USA. In the early 1970s he worked as an economist with the IMF before taking up a post with the Reserve Bank of Australia. In 1978 he was appointed professor of economics at the University of New South Wales, a position he held until his 1987 election to the House of Representatives for the New South Wales seat of Wentworth. In 1988 he became shadow finance minister and then shadow treasurer from 1989 until the 1990 election, when he was elected Liberal Party leader. The appointment of this relatively inexperienced political newcomer was seen by the party managers as a means of ending the manoeuvrings of the "leapfrogging" former leaders Andrew Peacock (who had led the Liberals in the election) and John Howard which had, in their view, damaged the party's electoral performance since the mid-1980s. Regarded as a technocrat (or "political yuppie" to the less well disposed), Hewson enjoys considerable independence of manoeuvre in policy matters, but his lack of a clear power base could prove a weakness in the internal party politics of prolonged opposition.

**HICKEL, Walter.** *USA.* Independent governor of Alaska. Born in 1919, he served in the late 1960s and early 1970s as the state's Republican governor, first elected in 1966. In 1978 he came close to winning the Republican primary again, standing as the candidate who would promote a development boom. (A wealthy investor and developer himself, he is also a former US secretary of the interior.) In 1990 he campaigned on an independent ticket, rejecting appeals not to split the Republican vote, and made political capital from his anti-abortion stance.

**HILLS, Carla.** *USA.* US trade representative in the Executive Office of the President. Born in 1934, she was educated at Stanford and Oxford universities before attending law school at Yale. After working as a lawyer until 1974, she served as assistant attorney-general in the Department of Justice from 1974–75, and as secretary of housing and urban development from 1975–77.

She resumed her law career in 1977, but rejoined the government in 1989 when **George Bush** chose her as his trade representative, one of only two women in his cabinet. Despite conflict-of-interest allegations arising from her past legal representation of foreign companies, Hills's appointment was confirmed by the Senate and she promised to root out unfair trade practices "with a crowbar if necessary". Combining an astute grasp of the relevant issues with toughness and personal charm, Hills was a key participant in negotiations on fair trade with Brazil, India and, notably, Japan. She was particularly involved in the series of Structural Impediments Initiative (SII) talks between the USA and Japan which, in mid-1990, produced agreements in a number of areas, raising hopes that Japan's trading surplus with the USA would be reduced. She played a key role in the 1990 General Agreement on Tariffs and Trade (Gatt) talks which became deadlocked, having little sympathy with the protectionism of European farmers.

**HNATYSHYN, Ramon.** *Canada.* Governor-general. Born in Saskatoon, Saskatchewan, in 1934, of Ukrainian descent, he is the son of a senator, and began his association with politics as a page in the Senate. Educated at the University of Saskatchewan, where he later lectured in law, Hnatyshyn was first elected to the House of Commons in 1974. He was energy minister in **Joe Clark**'s short-lived government in 1979 and also served as justice minister and attorney-general in **Brian Mulroney**'s cabinet from 1986 until he lost his seat in the 1988 general election. His appointment as governor-general in January 1990 was considered controversial because of his inability to speak French.

**HODGE, Margaret.** *UK.* Labour politician. Born in 1944, she was elected to Islington local council in central London in 1973 and became its leader in 1982. Since 1985 she has been chairman of the Labour-dominated Association of London Authorities, one of the local government bodies that have struggled to sustain a political voice for London in the aftermath of abolition of the Greater London Council in 1986.

**HODOUL, Jacques.** *Seychelles.* Tourism and transport minister. A key ally of President **Albert René**, Hodoul is a potential rival to **James Michel** in the succession stakes. He moved to the tourism ministry from national development in the June 1989 cabinet reshuffle;

given the importance of tourism to the islands' economy, this is not necessarily a demotion. Like his rival, Hodoul has begun to soften his previous hardline socialist stance.

**HOGG, Douglas.** *UK.* Minister of state at the Foreign and Commonwealth Office since November 1990, and MP since 1979. Born in 1945, the son of **Lord Hailsham** and husband of **Sarah Hogg**, he was educated at Oxford University and was called to the bar in 1968. He has held several junior government posts.

**HOGG, Sarah.** *UK.* Adviser to **John Major**. Born in 1946, she got an honours degree from Oxford University before embarking on a career in journalism. She has built a reputation as an outstanding writer on economics, starting at *The Economist* and working later for most of the quality press. Her appointment as head of Major's policy unit countered criticism of him for appointing an all-male cabinet.

**HOLKERI, Harri.** *Finland.* Prime minister. Born in 1937, he studied political science and immediately joined the conservative National Coalition Party (Kokoomus) as a full-time official, completing a rapid rise to the top when he became secretary-general in 1966 and leader in 1971. His less confrontational attitudes towards the USSR, and more consensual domestic policy stance, paved the way for the party's eventual return to government. Far more popular than his party, not least because of his amateur athletics and skiing exploits, he was appointed governor of the Bank of Finland in 1979, traditionally a stepping-stone to the presidency. He stood for that office in 1982 and 1988, but was defeated on both occasions by **Mauno Koivisto**. After the 1987 elections, in which Kokoomus made significant gains, Koivisto chose Holkeri rather than the man who had taken over from him in 1979 as party leader, **Ilkka Suominen**, to lead a four-party left–right coalition including the Social Democrats.

**HOLLANDE, François.** *France.* Socialist politician. Born in 1954 and a graduate of the Institut d'Etudes Politiques and the Ecole Nationale d'Administration, he worked in public administration, in particular at the Court of Accounts, and was a notable representative of the rising young generation as adviser to **François Mitterrand** and **Roland Dumas** in the 1980s. In 1983, he became a Socialist Party (PS) local councillor and in 1988 he was elected to the National Assembly, where he is secretary of the important finance committee.

**HOLOMISA, General Bantu.** *South Africa.*
Military ruler of Transkei "homeland". Head of
the Transkei defence force, he assumed power in
a military coup at the end of 1987. A product of
South Africa's military staff college, he is
distantly related to **Nelson Mandela,** and in late
1989 came out openly in support of the African
National Congress (ANC), following the lead of
**Enos Mabuza** in KaNgwane. No political
sophisticate, he lectured the visiting **F. W. de
Klerk** in January 1990 on the "winds of change"
in the region. He then moved forward with the
idea of a referendum, to pave the way for re-
integrating the nominally "independent"
Transkei into a unitary South African state.
Thanks to South African concerns to preserve the
fiction of homeland independence, his
formidable personality could be given some rein,
although he detected the hand of the South
African security services behind an attempt to
unseat him by a coup in November 1990.
**HOLST, Johan Jorgen.** *Norway.* Defence
minister. Born in 1937, he studied at Columbia
University in the USA and at Oslo University,
and worked at the Norwegian Institute of
International Affairs (NUPI). He was state
secretary for defence from 1976–79 and then for
foreign affairs from 1979–81, before holding the
defence portfolio in **Gro Harlem Brundtland**'s
Labour government of 1986–89. He was director
of NUPI when he was recalled to ministerial
office in Brundtland's minority Labour
government in November 1990.
**HONASAN, Gregorio.** *Philippines.* Rebel
leader. Born in 1947, he enjoyed a spectacularly
successful army career, rising to the rank of
colonel in his late thirties. One of a number of
young officers disillusioned with Ferdinand
Marcos, "Gringo", as he is known, lent active
support to the "people power" revolution that
brought **Cory Aquino** to power in 1986. He
subsequently turned against the regime,
however, ostensibly disappointed at Aquino's
failure to prosecute the struggle against the
communist insurgents with sufficient vigour. As
a leading light in the Reform the Armed Forces
Movement (RAM), he led the August 1987
uprising, escaping from custody in early 1988
with the connivance of his guards. Believed to be
behind several subsequent coup attempts, he has
close connections with **Juan Ponce Enrile,**
whose security chief he was immediately after
the 1986 revolution. His popularity with the
military continues to pose a serious threat to the
administration.

**HORN, Gyula.** *Hungary.* Hungarian Socialist
Party (MSP) leader. Born in 1932 and trained as
an economist, Horn worked in government in
Budapest and in the diplomatic service, then
spent 16 years in the international department of
the ruling communist Hungarian Socialist
Workers' Party (MSM), before going to the
foreign ministry first as state secretary
(1985–89), then as foreign minister. An expert
on European security issues and firmly identified
with the reformists, he has been persuasive as
Hungary's voice in the new Eastern bloc politics.
Domestically, he helped promote the burial of
the MSM and the emergence of the MSP, its
social democratic successor, but was not spared
his share of the rebuff when the voters turned
away from yesterday's men in the spring 1990
elections. Defeated in his constituency, he
nevertheless entered the National Assembly on
the MSP list, and took over in late May 1990 as
party chairman. Horn is most noted in the
outside world (especially Germany) for his part
in the decision to let East Germans across the
"green" border with Austria in the summer of
1989, thus allowing a process which ultimately
led to the dismantling of the Berlin Wall.
**HORNER, Constance.** *USA.* Director, US
Office of Personnel Management. Born in New
Jersey in 1942, she was a high school teacher
before serving on the boards of several
government agencies. She joined the Office of
Management and Budget in 1983 and took on
her present post in 1985. She has advocated
drugs screening of federal employees but is
opposed to random testing.
**HORVAT, Franc.** *Yugoslavia.* Foreign
economic relations minister. Born in 1942, he is
a liberal economist from Slovenia. A federal
minister from July 1988 until he resigned in
December 1988, he was appointed federal
foreign economic relations minister in March
1989.
**HORVÁTH, Balazs.** *Hungary.* Deputy leader of
the Hungarian Democratic Forum (MDF) and
minister without portfolio. Born in 1942, he is a
lawyer by profession and an MDF member for
Veszprém. Appointed interior minister in May
1990, he set himself the task of creating a
modernized apolitical police force for the post-
communist period. Deputizing for **József Antall**
during the prime minister's illness in late 1990,
he was criticized for his handling of the fuel
crisis, and in December 1990 Antall moved him
from the interior ministry, while evidently
continuing to regard him as a probable successor;

he was given the post of minister without portfolio, responsible for relations with parliament and for Hungarians abroad. On Antall's recommendation the MDF conference that same month elected Horváth as party vice-president.

**HOSS, Dr Selim al-.** *Lebanon.* Former prime minister. Born in 1930, Hoss was a professor of economics before entering politics. A Sunni Muslim, he was labour and education minister in September 1986 when given the task of drawing up a new national accord to replace the bitterly controversial 1943 covenant, which divided political power on sectarian lines. Hoss became prime minister in June 1987, after Rashid Karami's death in a helicopter crash. His authority was apparently increased under the new constitutional accord signed by President **Elias Hrawi** in September 1990, but in December 1990 he resigned and left **Umar Karami** with the task of forming a new government.

**HOUPHOUËT-BOIGNY, Félix.** *Côte d'Ivoire.* President. Africa's senior conservative statesman, Houphouët-Boigny had a distinguished political career even before independence. Born in 1905 (officially – other sources place his birth before the turn of the century), the son of a prosperous cocoa planter, he qualified as a doctor and practised for 15 years, but his early political activity stemmed from his agricultural roots. In 1944, he helped to form an association of African farmers to fight unfair assistance to European planters. This formed the nucleus of the Ivorian Democratic Party (PDCI), which was set up a year later as a focus for radical debate and in 1990 is still the ruling party. Elected a member of the French national assembly in 1946, he celebrated by adding the word "boigny" (irresistible force) to his name. Houphouët-Boigny remained a member of the assembly until 1959, severing his initial alliance with the French Communist party in 1950; from 1956 he held a series of ministerial posts in the French government, resigning in 1959 to pursue politics at home. Opposed to French efforts to create a West African Federation, he opted for independence for his country in 1960. Since then his personal control over both state and party have been virtually unchallenged; opposition has been neutralized by the distribution of patronage and occasional repression. Mounting unrest in early 1990 forced him to permit the legalization of opposition parties. Eccentricities such as the construction of a new capital at his birthplace,

Yamoussoukro, complete with massive Catholic basilica, have increased concern that Houphouët is losing his grasp of reality. But he retains his grip on the political system. In the October 1990 presidential elections he swept home with over 80% of the vote, a result that his principal opponent, **Laurent Gbagbo**, claimed was attained by widespread intimidation.

**HOWARD, Michael.** *UK.* Secretary of state for employment since 1990, and MP since 1983. Born in 1941, he studied law and became a QC before securing a Commons seat. He was a junior environment minister when Norman Fowler's resignation led to his sudden promotion to the cabinet.

**HOWE, Sir Geoffrey.** *UK.* Conservative politician. Born in 1926, he studied law at Cambridge University and was elected MP in 1964. A former chairman of the Tory Bow Group and a forthright critic of Labour's conduct in the Treasury, Howe was **Margaret Thatcher**'s natural choice as chancellor of the exchequer from 1979–83. In successive budgets he laid the groundwork for a Tory regime of fiscal frugality, cutting taxes and public spending. Shadow chancellor **Denis Healey** quipped that being attacked by Howe was like being "savaged by a dead sheep"; but to others his new steadfastness was surprising for one who had expressed clear social concerns in the late 1960s. Succeeded at the Treasury by **Nigel Lawson** in 1983, Howe became foreign secretary. He overcame inexperience in this field to excel as the UK's representative abroad when the country had to reassess its European role. In 1989 he was replaced at the Foreign and Commonwealth Office and given the grand-sounding position of deputy prime minister. But the post represented an effective political sidelining, and the antipathy between him and Thatcher became steadily more marked. His eventual resignation in 1990 led to **Michael Heseltine**'s challenge for the leadership and the downfall of Thatcher.

**HOYER, Stenny.** *USA.* Democratic congressman from Maryland. Born in 1939, he practised law and was state senator before entering the House of Representatives in 1981. A consensus-builder of liberal persuasion rather than an issue politician, his chairmanship of the Democratic caucus since 1989 has focused on promoting party unity.

**HOYTE, Desmond.** *Guyana.* President. Born in 1929, he trained as a barrister in the UK and started practising in Guyana in 1960. He became a People's National Congress member of parliament in 1968 and a minister in 1970. He was made a vice-president in 1980 and first vice-president and prime minister in 1984, on the resignation of Ptolemy Reid. As such he became president after the sudden death in August 1985 of Forbes Burnham, and was confirmed in the post at elections in December that year. A pragmatist, Hoyte has attempted to move away from some of Burnham's socialist policies and to improve relations with the USA and other Western countries to help alleviate Guyana's economic crisis.

**HRAWI, Elias.** *Lebanon.* President. Born in 1930 into an old Maronite Christian family in Zahle, in the Bekaa Valley, he was active in drawing up the 1989 Taif peace agreement, and he enjoys good relations with both Syria and the Maronite leadership. He was elected president after the assassination of his predecessor President René Mu'awwad in November 1989. His position was strengthened by the Syrian defeat of General Michel Aoun in October 1990 and the implementation of a security plan involving the expulsion of rival militias from Beirut.

**HU, Richard.** *Singapore.* Finance minister. Born in 1926. In early 1985 Hu entered the cabinet as trade and industry minister taking with him a stack of sound credentials earned in the private sector, as first Singaporean chairman of Shell Singapore, and as managing director of the Monetary Authority of Singapore and of the Government of Singapore Investment Corporation. After less than six months at trade and industry he was promoted to the finance ministry.

**HUANG HSIN-CHIEH.** *Taiwan.* Chairman of the opposition Democratic Progress Party (DPP). Huang heads the Formosan faction of the DPP, which campaigns for increased democracy and renunciation of claims to the Chinese mainland. A former political prisoner, Huang was elected to his present position in November 1988, two months before the DPP was officially recognized.

**HUBER, Erwin.** *Germany.* Christian Social Union (CSU) secretary-general. Born in 1946, he studied economics at Münster. He was elected to the Bavarian parliament in 1978 and succeeded Gerold Tandler as secretary-general of the CSU in 1988.

**HUCHON, Jean-Paul.** *France.* Political adviser. Born in 1946, he graduated from the Institut d'Etudes Politiques and from the Ecole Nationale d'Administration and built his career in the civil service and in politics. Closely identified with **Michel Rocard**, whom he has served as an adviser since 1977 and as *chef de cabinet* since 1988, he has won plaudits for his skills in seeking and building a consensus on key issues.

**HU JINTAO.** *China.* Party secretary in Tibet. Born in 1934, Hu held senior party posts in Gansu and Guizhou until 1988 when he became party secretary in Tibet. A moderate reform-minded leader, he was expected to reduce tensions in the region in the wake of protests against Chinese rule in 1987 and 1988, but police action against demonstrators intensified, and martial law was imposed in Lhasa in March 1989. Hu saw the lifting of martial law in May 1990 as the beginning of another phase in the struggle against separatism, not the end of it.

**HUME, John.** *UK.* Socialist and Irish nationalist politician. Born in 1937 in Northern Ireland, he studied politics and international relations. President of the Credit Union League of Ireland from 1964–68, he began his political life as a civil rights activist in the 1960s, was elected to the Northern Ireland parliament in 1969 and to the abortive assemblies that followed its abolition in 1973. One of the co-founders of the Social Democratic and Labour Party (SDLP), seeking equality for the Catholic community through constitutional rather than violent means, he became leader of the SDLP in 1979 and has been MP for Foyle since 1983. A noted creative thinker on the Northern Irish question and an inspiration behind an Anglo-Irish Agreement of 1985, his proposals for co-operation with the Unionist majority have caused tension with the more nationalist wing within his own party (led by deputy leader **Seamus Mallon**).

**HUN SEN.** *Cambodia.* Prime minister. Born in 1951, Hun Sen served as a courier during the Khmer Rouge attack on Phnom Penh in 1975 when he lost an eye. After fleeing to Vietnam to escape **Pol Pot**'s purges, he returned in 1979, and at the age of 28 and with scant experience, he took on the exacting role of foreign minister in the new pro-Hanoi regime founded in 1979. He became prime minister in 1985 and has gained respect as Phnom Penh's chief negotiator on the international scene, but is considered too liberal by party hardliners.

**HUNT, David.** *UK.* Secretary of state for Wales since 1990, and MP for Wirral since 1983. Born in 1942, Hunt moved to the Welsh Office after the sudden resignation in March 1990 of Peter

Walker, last survivor of **Margaret Thatcher**'s 1979 cabinet. Previously, Hunt had been the minister responsible for urban development, and proved his party loyalty as deputy chief whip from 1987–89.

**HUNT, Guy.** *USA.* Republican governor of Alabama. Born in 1933, he was a farmer, probate judge, and US Department of Agriculture official, before his election in 1986 as Alabama's first Republican governor since 1874. A conservative enthusiast for tax and expenditure cuts, he has been criticized for the absence of blacks in his administration.

**HUNTE, Julian.** *St Lucia.* Opposition leader. A businessman and former United Workers' Party member, he was elected leader of the St Lucia Labour Party in 1984.

**HURD, Douglas.** *UK.* Foreign secretary since 1989, Conservative MP since 1974. Hurd's career has in a sense been one long preparation for his current position. He worked in the diplomatic service from 1952–66, and was a junior foreign minister from 1979–83. Born in 1930, and educated at Eton College and Cambridge University, his tenure as political secretary to **Edward Heath** from 1970–74 was not the ideal platform for a ministerial career under **Margaret Thatcher**. After a stint as Northern Ireland secretary, Hurd took over the Home Office in 1985. His non-confrontational style proved an asset to a government saddled with a rising crime rate, though his endorsement of tighter official secrets laws in 1988 – after the *Spycatcher* affair – and his restrictions on broadcast interviews with IRA supporters angered many on the left. As foreign secretary Hurd has played a key role in redefining the UK's role in the new Europe and he has won widespread respect for his handling of the Gulf crisis. Essentially moderate, he has contradicted Tory hardliners such as **Norman Tebbit** (on Hong Kong) and **Nicholas Ridley** (on Germany). His carefully maintained statesman-like exterior belies the fact that he has written ten thriller novels in his spare time. He entered the leadership contest in 1990 as somewhat of a reluctant candidate and came a poor third. He was swiftly confirmed as foreign secretary by **John Major**.

**HURTADO LARREA, Oswaldo.** *Ecuador.* Former president. Born in 1939, he was educated at the Catholic University in Quito, where he later became a professor. In 1964, he founded the Christian Democrat Party (PDC), which merged with People's Democracy (DP) in 1978. In 1979 he was elected vice-president, assuming the presidency on the death of President Jaimé Roldós in 1981 until the end of the presidential term in 1984.

**HUSSEIN IBN TALAL.** *Jordan.* King. Born in Amman in 1935 and educated in the UK at Harrow school and Sandhurst Military Academy, Hussein succeeded to the throne in 1952 when his father Talal abdicated because of ill-health. He married his fourth wife Elizabeth (Lisa) Halabi, the present Queen Noor in 1978. Urbane and westernized, King Hussein has represented the moderates in the Arab camp, although his army has taken much of the brunt of the wars fought with Israel. Despite periods of unrest, he has been largely successful in absorbing the Palestinians who make up about 65% of Jordan's population. In the wake of a short, bloody civil war in 1970–71, the Palestine Liberation Organization leadership fled abroad, mostly to Lebanon. Since then relations between the king and the Palestinians within Jordan have improved. In recent years he has come under increasing pressure from Islamic fundamentalists, who have benefited from political liberalization to achieve electoral success and popular appeal. His perceived pro-Iraqi stance on the Gulf crisis earned him unprecedented popularity at home, but caused friction with his Western allies.

**HUSSEINI, Faisal.** *Palestinian.* Leading activist. One of the alleged chief co-ordinators of the *intifada* (uprising) in the West Bank and Gaza, he was freed by the Israelis in January 1989 after 21 months in prison. He favours "free and democratic elections" in the West Bank.

**HYDE, Henry.** *USA.* Republican congressman from Illinois. Born in 1924, he is a lawyer and was elected to the House of Representatives in 1974. Formerly a single-issue conservative, being fervently anti-abortion, he became a key Republican spokesman on defence and foreign policy in the 1980s and was **Ronald Reagan**'s foremost congressional defender over the Iran-Contra affair.

# I

IACOVOU, Georgios. *Cyprus*. Foreign minister. Born in 1938 near Famagusta, he studied engineering, economics and industrial psychology in the UK and USA before returning to work in Cyprus for the three years following independence in 1960. After the first round of inter-communal fighting he went to work in the UK, returning in 1972. After the Turkish invasion in 1974, he was put in charge of refugee relief and rehabilitation, later being seconded to the office of the UN High Commissioner for Refugees (1976–79). Following a series of postings as ambassador in Europe, and a spell as director-general of the foreign ministry, he was appointed foreign minister in 1983.

IBRAHIM, Alhaji Waziri. *Nigeria*. Former minister. Born in 1921 and educated at Kaduna College, he joined the United Africa Company, a Unilever subsidiary, in 1948 and rose to become general manager for the Kaduna district before joining the federal government in 1959 as health minister. He served as economic development minister from 1961–65 before returning to private business. He returned to active politics in the late 1970s and, after failing to be adopted as presidential candidate of the Nigerian People's Party, set up his own party, the Greater Nigeria People's Party, in 1979. His presidential ambitions were thwarted when he came last of the five candidates in the presidential elections that year. He again stood unsuccessfully for the presidency in 1983. In May 1989 he was arrested on charges of breaching the ban on party politics by setting up the Brotherhood Club of Nigeria. He continues to hanker after active political involvement, although his prospects of leading his own party seem dimmed in the light of the decision by President Ibrahim Babangida's government to set up its own parties as a prelude to a return to civilian rule.

ICHIKAWA, Yuichi. *Japan*. Clean Government Party (Komeito) secretary-general. Born in 1935, he graduated from Waseda University's commerce department, joined the centre-left Buddhist-inspired Komeito, and worked as a journalist on the party newspaper before being elected to the House of Representatives (lower house) on the tide of increased support for Komeito in 1976. He chaired the party's Diet strategy committee prior to his selection to replace Katsuya Ikeda as Komeito secretary-general in 1988, advocating the formation of a centre-left coalition to challenge the dominance of the ruling Liberal Democratic Party (LDP). The failure to form a coalition and the embarrassment of seeing several Komeito leaders embroiled in the Recruit shares scandal allowed the LDP a further clear victory in the February 1990 general election, when support for Komeito fell back to 8%. The party remained the second largest opposition force, but lost votes to the Japan Socialist Party.

IDIGORAS, Jon. *Spain*. Basque nationalist and spokesman for United People (HB), the political wing of ETA. He was one of the HB members elected to the Cortes (parliament) in 1989, and the first to speak in parliament in September 1990 when the HB members were finally allowed to take their seats without swearing the standard oath of acceptance of the constitution.

IENG SARY. *Cambodia*. Khmer Rouge number two. Born in 1930, he was educated in Paris where he helped to establish the core of the Khmers Rouges. As foreign minister in Pol Pot's regime, he was, together with his wife Ieng Thirith, the most internationally prominent of the Khmers Rouges. He and his wife disappeared from the public eye in 1979, although reputedly remaining influential behind the scenes.

IKEDA, Yukihiko. *Japan*. Defence Agency director-general (minister of state). Born in 1937, he worked as an official in the finance ministry, and represented a Hiroshima constituency in the House of Representatives (lower house). He was briefly director-general of the Management and Co-ordination Agency in 1989 under the premiership of Sosuke Uno, and returned to government in the December 1990 reshuffle. Taking charge of defence policy at a time of radical change, he stated that Japan should work within the existing structure of a strictly limited and domestic role for its self-defence force.

**IKIMI, Chief Tom.** *Nigeria.* National Republican Convention (NRC) chairman. An architect from Bendel state, he was elected in August 1990 to chair the NRC, one of the two political parties set up by the government in 1989 to participate in the planned return to civilian rule in 1992.

**ILIESCU, Ion.** *Romania.* President. Born in Olteniţa in 1930, the son of a communist railway worker, he was educated in Bucharest at secondary school and then the polytechnic before completing his training in water engineering at the Power Engineering Institute in Moscow. A member of the Union of Communist Youth from 1944 (he was its first secretary from 1956–60 and later youth affairs minister), he was elected a member of the Romanian Communist Party (PCR) central committee in 1968, becoming its propaganda secretary in 1971. Conflict over the launching of a "cultural revolution", and the growth in Nicolae Ceauşescu's personality cult saw Iliescu removed from national politics in 1971 and sent to Timişoara as chief of party propaganda. In 1974 he was named first secretary of the PCR county organization in Iaşi. The downward slide of his career continued in 1979, when he was appointed head of the National Water Council, and in 1984, when he was effectively demoted to director of a technical and scientific publishing house in Bucharest. At the outbreak of the revolution, Iliescu was one of the first leaders to emerge, heading the National Salvation Front (NSF) and becoming president of the Provisional Council of National Unity in February 1990. He won an overwhelming victory in the presidential elections in May, despite earlier controversy over his support for strong-arm tactics against anti-government demonstrators. Allegations of electoral irregularities, combined with mounting fears that former communists within the NSF had effectively hijacked the revolution, made his position seem less than secure when demonstrators returned to the streets.

**INGRAM, James.** *Australia.* Executive director of the World Food Programme (WFP). Born in 1928, he studied international relations and then joined the foreign service. He gained his first ambassadorship in 1970, and served in the Philippines and Canada until he became director of the Australian Development Assistance Bureau in 1977. Appointed WFP director in 1982, he has led the programme energetically at a time when it has had to deal with ever-growing demands for emergency food aid for developing countries and the ever-increasing millions of refugees.

**INGRAO, Pietro.** *Italy.* Italian Communist Party (PCI) politician. Born in 1915 in the province of Latina, he graduated in letters, philosophy and law at Rome University and joined the PCI in 1940, working under cover during the war. From 1947–57 he was manager of the party newspaper *L'Unità*. He sat in the Chamber of Deputies for the Rome constituency from 1948, serving as president of the chamber from 1976–79. A hardliner, he was at the head of the significant minority at the March 1990 extraordinary party congress which opposed **Achille Occhetto**'s proposals to open the party to the non-communist left.

**İNÖNÜ, Erdal.** *Turkey.* Opposition leader. A professor of atomic physics, he is the son of İsmet İnönü, a former Turkish president and prime minister from 1961–65. In 1983 he founded the Social Democratic group, in the frustrated hope of being allowed to contest the 1983 elections. In 1985 he led the group into a merger with the left-wing People's Party to form the Social Democratic Populist Party (SHP), which he has continued to lead.

**INOUYE, Daniel.** *USA.* Democratic senator from Hawaii. Born of Japanese descent in 1924, he lost his right arm during World War II. A lawyer, he was elected to the House of Representatives in 1959 and to the Senate in 1964. His chairmanship of the special committee investigating the Iran-Contra affair, though competent, did not live up to his earlier performance as a Watergate select committee member. As defence appropriations subcommittee chairman he generally supports large military budgets, and as Indian affairs subcommittee chairman he is a passionate advocate of native American rights.

**IRIANI, Abdel-Karim al-.** *Yemen.* Foreign minister. Essentially a technocrat, he studied in the USA and first entered the North Yemeni cabinet in 1976. He was appointed prime minister in 1980, but was relieved of the post three years later. In 1984, however, he returned as deputy prime minister and foreign minister, retaining the latter post after unification with South Yemen in May 1990.

**ISAYAS AFEWORKI.** *Ethiopia.* Founder and leader of the Eritrean People's Liberation Front (EPLF). Born in 1944, he left university in Addis

Ababa in 1966 without completing his engineering studies to join the Eritrean Liberation Front (ELF). In 1967 he became one of the movement's first members to be sent to China for training. On his return he became a leader of a radical Christian faction that split from the ELF in 1971 to form the nucleus of the EPLF. Under his leadership the EPLF has developed into a formidable military and political organization, scoring a string of successes against government forces that left it by 1990 in control of all of Eritrea except the capital Asmara.

**ISHIDA, Koshiro.** *Japan.* Clean Government Party (Komeito) chairman. Born in 1930, he graduated from Meiji University's commerce department, worked as a journalist on the newspaper *Seikyo Shimbun,* and then was sent to Aichi prefecture to build up the regional organization of the centre-left Buddhist-inspired Komeito party. He entered the House of Representatives in 1967, the first lower house elections in which Komeito took part. As one of the party's senior members he replaced Junya Yano as Komeito chairman in May 1989, a change made necessary by the involvement of leading Komeito figures in the Recruit shares scandal. Under Ishida's leadership the party conducted a defensive campaign to limit its losses in the February 1990 general election, when its support fell back to 8%, although it remained the second largest opposition force.

**ISHIHARA, Takashi.** *Japan.* Industrial leader. Born in 1912, he graduated from Tohoku University and joined Nissan Motor Company in 1937. He became president of the company in 1977 and chairman in 1985; his great achievement was to turn Nissan around when it looked as if it were about to lose its position as number two carmaker to Honda in the mid-1980s and to spearhead its international expansion. Ishihara also serves as the influential chairman of the Japan Association of Corporate Executives (Keizai Doyukai), one of the four major business lobbies.

**IVANS, Dainis.** *USSR.* Latvian nationalist leader. A journalist born in 1955, he was named chairman of the Latvian Popular Front on its formation in 1988. He faced a difficult re-election battle in October 1989, when radical nationalists opposed him for being too cautious in pressing for independence, and for being a Communist Party member. In May 1990 the new Latvian parliament, with a Popular Front majority, elected Ivans as first deputy chairman

(*de facto* Latvia's vice-president). In October 1990 he was replaced as Latvian Popular Front chairman by Romualdas Razukas.

**IVASHKO, Volodymyr (Vladimir).** *USSR.* Deputy leader of the Communist Party of the Soviet Union (CPSU). A Ukrainian born in 1932, he trained as a mining engineer, and spent his early career as a lecturer in Kharkov. He joined the Ukrainian Communist Party apparatus in 1973, becoming regional party leader in Dnepropetrovsk in 1978 and a central committee secretary in 1986 (after a stint in the early 1980s as a political adviser to Afghan leader Babrak Karmal). He was elected first secretary of the Ukrainian Communist Party in September 1989, after a year as second secretary. In June 1990 a new Ukrainian Supreme Soviet elected him as its chairman (*de facto* Ukrainian head of state). This was despite fierce protests from the strong nationalist opposition lobby, which argued that he was too closely identified with the arch-conservative Vladimir Shcherbitsky (his predecessor as party leader); in answer to one of the opposition objections, Ivashko stood down as party leader soon afterwards. Ivashko has been described variously as a "cautious centrist" and a "pragmatic neo-conservative", and he is identified as a compliant supporter of **Mikhail Gorbachev,** who nominated him at the watershed July 1990 CPSU congress for the new post of deputy general secretary. His victory over the conservative Yegor Ligachev allowed Gorbachev safely to abdicate responsibility for the routine running of the party to concentrate on the presidency. Immediately after the congress, Ivashko resigned as Ukrainian head of state.

**IZAGUIRRE ANGELI, Alejandro.** *Venezuela.* Interior minister. A social democratic politician, he was secretary-general of Democratic Action (AD) before being brought into the government by his party leader, newly elected President **Carlos Andrés Pérez,** in February 1989.

**IZETBEGOVIĆ, Alija.** *Yugoslavia.* President of Bosnia and Hercegovina. A devout Muslim and a former political prisoner, he led the main Muslim party, the Party of Democratic Action (SDA), in the republic's first multi-party elections in late 1990. The SDA, emerging as the largest single party, proceeded to pioneer a power-sharing arrangement with the republic's other nationalist groups, the Serbs and Croats, putting the communists in an unfamiliar role as the opposition.

# J

**JABURI, Major-General Saadi Tu'ma Abbas al-.** *Iraq.* Defence minister. A career soldier, he was appointed defence minister by President **Saddam Hussain** in December 1990. His elderly predecessor, General Abdel-Jabbar Khalil Shanshal, had been appointed in 1989 with the promise that he would not need to serve for more than one year. Reported to be a strong supporter of Saddam and of his stance on Kuwait, Al-Jaburi was formerly inspector-general of the armed forces, and prior to that, a deputy chief of staff. During the Iran-Iraq war, he was decorated for his achievements as commander of the First Army Special Corps.

**JACKSON, Reverend Jesse.** *USA.* Civil rights leader and politician. The pre-eminent black US politician, he represents both traditional and radical elements in the political spectrum; since the 1988 presidential election, he has proven his legitimacy as a national leader. Born in Greenville in North Carolina in 1941, he was brought up in the city's black ghetto, making his mark as an excellent student and a promising athlete. He became involved in the civil rights movement in 1963, when still a student, organizing a sit-down strike in Greensboro, North Carolina. He entered the Chicago Theological Seminary in 1965 and became a close associate of Reverend Dr Martin Luther King. By 1967, Jackson was national director of Operation Breadbasket, a programme devised by King's Southern Christian Leadership Conference (SCLC) to force businesses to hire more black workers. Jackson was highly successful with this and by the time of King's murder in 1968 – the year Jackson became a Baptist minister – was seen as one of the inheritors of his mantle. However, a dispute with the SCLC leaders led to his dismissal as director of Operation Breadbasket in 1971. He went on to found Operation Push (People United to Save Humanity), which he led until 1983. As a presidential candidate in 1984, he made several tactical errors, such as challenging the party system and making what were perceived as anti-semitic remarks. His campaign in the 1988 election reflected his greater political maturity and he made a major impact in the Democratic primaries, capturing 7m votes. He now works with the Democratic leadership on the formation of party policy. Although he is the undisputed national leader of the poor, particularly the black poor, a new generation of black politicians threatens to dilute his supremacy. His high media profile has also given rise to charges of opportunism.

**JAGAN, Cheddi.** *Guyana.* Opposition politician. Born in 1918 and trained as a dentist, Jagan entered politics as a member of the Legislative Council in 1947. His leftist politics led the British to dismiss him as chief minister in 1953, but he resumed the post in 1957, going on to become premier of British Guiana from 1961–64. His People's Progressive Party has been in opposition since and he remains a committed Marxist-Leninist.

**JALLOUD, Major Abdel-Salam.** *Libya.* The regime's number two. The practical man behind **Muammar Qaddafi** the visionary, Jalloud has been the key figure in day-to-day government for the past 20 years. Born in 1944, he went through secondary school and military training with Qaddafi, and was one of the architects of the 1969 coup. A skilled negotiator and the most widely travelled of the Libyan leadership, Jalloud secured the evacuation of UK and US forces after the revolution. He served as deputy prime minister and finance minister from 1970–72, prime minister from 1972–77 and general secretary of the General People's Congress from 1977–79. Although he is now effectively Qaddafi's deputy, he holds no official title.

**JAMES, Edison.** *Dominica.* Founder of Dominica United Workers Party. Formerly general manager of the Dominica Banana Marketing Corporation, he established the Dominica United Workers' Party (DUWP) in 1988 as a vehicle for opposition to the ruling Dominica Freedom Party of **Eugenia Charles**. In the May

1990 elections, the DUWP took six of the 21 parliamentary seats, replacing the Labour Party as the main opposition.

**JANOWSKI, Professor Jan Stanisław.** *Poland.* Deputy prime minister. Born in 1928, he joined the staff at Kraków's University of Mining and Metallurgy in 1954, rising to the office of rector in 1987. He was suspended from the leadership of the Democratic Party (junior coalition partner of the ruling communist Polish United Workers' Party) in 1982 after voting in the Sejm (parliament) against legislation outlawing Solidarity, but was reinstated in 1985. He was the most senior Democratic Party member in the Solidarity-led coalition government formed in September 1989, combining his deputy premiership with the post of minister-head of the Office for Advancement and Applications of Science and Technology.

**JARUZELSKI, General Wojciech.** *Poland.* Outgoing president. Born in 1923 into the Polish gentry, he was deported to the USSR following the September 1939 Soviet annexation of eastern Poland. He served in the communist-controlled (Berling) Polish Army in the USSR from 1943–45, subsequently becoming a career soldier. He rose through the ranks to become deputy defence minister in 1962 and minister in 1968. From 1960–65 he headed the army's central political board, and joined the politburo of the ruling communist Polish United Workers' Party (PZPR) in 1970. During the national leadership crisis that followed Solidarity's emergence he was named prime minister in February 1981 and PZPR first secretary in October. With the regime fearing Solidarity's power, he introduced martial law in December 1981, heading the military junta that ran the country for the next two years. He resigned the premiership in November 1985 but remained PZPR first secretary and head of state. Following strikes in 1988, he supported round-table negotiations with Solidarity. After the partly free parliamentary elections in June 1989 he initially confounded general expectation by declining to stand for the presidency, an office tailored for him at the round-table talks. He changed his mind, but only narrowly scraped through the vote in parliament (he was sole candidate) thanks to support from Solidarity deputies who feared destabilization if he lost. Since then he has loyally co-operated with the Solidarity government and tried to improve his image, appearing without military uniform and the ubiquitous dark glasses. But he remains widely resented for having introduced martial law, and cannot overcome the perception that he is an anachronistic communist relic in Poland's new democracy. In September 1990 he bowed to protests by agreeing to step down as president by the end of the year, opening the way for the election of **Lech Wałęsa** in December.

**JATOI, Ghulam Mustapha.** *Pakistan.* Former prime minister. A former chairman of the Pakistan People's Party (PPP) in Sind province, he was a close associate of fellow Sindhi landlord Zulfiqar Ali Bhutto, but later crossed swords with **Benazir Bhutto**, setting up the centrist National People's Party in 1986. He advocated negotiation with General Zia ul-Haq, but held out for the restoration of democratic government, only to be swamped by the PPP tide, failing to win his own seat in Sind in the November 1988 elections. He showed his durability by rebuilding his position, and was appointed caretaker prime minister after the dismissal of Benazir Bhutto in August 1990. After the October elections, which he contested within the successful conservative Islamic Democratic Alliance (IDA), some top army leaders saw in the amiable Jatoi the potential to be a conciliatory prime minister. Ultimately, however, he lacked the power base of his rival **Nawaz Sharif.**

**JAWARA, Sir Dawda Kairaba.** *The Gambia.* President. Born in 1924, Jawara, who trained as a veterinary surgeon in Glasgow, became The Gambia's first prime minister at independence in 1965. Five years later, after a referendum, The Gambia became a republic, with Jawara as executive president. His rule has not gone unchallenged; in 1981 a bloody coup attempt was only put down with the help of troops from Senegal. But, in one of Africa's few multi-party democracies, Jawara and his People's Progressive Party have maintained their lead over a fragmented opposition. The Senegalese intervention brought the two countries together in the Senegambian Confederation, but this was dissolved in 1989, a victim of Gambian distrust of the intentions of its larger francophone neighbour. The breach has soured relations with Senegal, but appears to have strengthened Jawara's popular support.

**JAYAKUMAR, Professor Shunmugam.** *Singapore.* Home affairs and law minister. Born in 1939, Jayakumar served as dean of Singapore University's law faculty during the 1970s. He entered parliament in 1980 and the cabinet in 1983. He was appointed home affairs minister in

1985 and two years later he took over the law portfolio from "old guard" veteran Ernest Barker.

**JAYALALITHA, Jayaram.** *India.* General secretary of Tamil regionalist All-India Anna Dravida Munnetra Kazhagam (AIADMK). A popular classical dancer and Tamil film star, she rose to political prominence as a close associate of M.G. Ramachandran, founder of the AIADMK and former chief minister of Tamil Nadu. After Ramachandran's death in December 1987, Jayalalitha's supporters emerged victorious over a rival faction led by his widow. The party was defeated by the rival Dravida Munnetra Kazhagam (DMK) in the January 1989 state elections, but in alliance with Congress (I) made a strong come-back in the 1989 union elections.

**JEAN, Grand Duke.** *Luxembourg.* Head of state. Born in 1921, his education involved the usual European male royals' mix of university and military training. Having left the country with his family after the German invasion in 1940, he returned as an officer in the Allied landings. He acted as lieutenant-representative for his ailing mother, Charlotte, from 1961 and succeeded on her abdication in 1964.

**JELVED, Marianne.** *Denmark.* Leader of the Radical Liberals. Born in 1943, she studied in Copenhagen and worked as a teacher. She was elected to the Folketing (parliament) for the Radical Liberals (RV) in 1987, and succeeded **Niels Helveg Petersen** as party leader the following year.

**JENKINS, Ed.** *USA.* Democratic congressman from Georgia. Born in 1933, Jenkins practised law and was elected to the House of Representatives in 1976. A quiet conservative, his 1988 bid to become majority leader lacked multi-regional support, but he is influential as a bridge-builder between the House leadership and southerners. A defender of the ailing textile industry, he promoted protectionist trade legislation, which **Ronald Reagan** vetoed.

**JENKINS, Lord (Roy Jenkins).** *UK.* Liberal Democrat politician, historian and author of distinguished political biographies. Born in 1920, he studied at Oxford University, and was elected to parliament for the Labour Party in 1948 (for a London seat until 1950 and a Birmingham seat until 1976). Recognized as one of Labour's brightest stars, he was immediately given senior office when the party came to power in 1964. As home secretary (1965–67) he oversaw the abolition of capital punishment and reformed the laws on theatre censorship, divorce

and homosexuality. As chancellor of the exchequer (1967–70) he turned a balance-of-payments deficit into a surplus. At this time he was one of Britain's most admired politicians and widely seen as a future prime minister. But his growing disillusionment with Labour's drift to the left came into the open over the question of British membership of the EC, which he strongly supported. Having failed to gain the party leadership after the resignation of Harold Wilson, he left domestic politics in 1976 to become president of the European Commission. In 1981 he joined three prominent Labour right-wingers (in the so-called "Gang of Four") to form the Social Democratic Party (SDP) and was re-elected to parliament for Glasgow Hillhead in 1982. The party's first leader, he stood down after the party failed to achieve its much-vaunted breakthrough in the 1983 election, and lost his seat to Labour in 1987. Later the same year, he was created a life peer and now leads the Liberal Democrats in the House of Lords.

**JERVOLINO RUSSO, Rosa.** *Italy.* Minister without portfolio and Christian Democrat party (DC) politician. Born in 1936 in Naples, she obtained a law degree at Rome University. In 1979 she was elected to the Senate. One of the few women in government, her first cabinet post was as minister without portfolio responsible for special affairs in the government formed by **Giovanni Goria** in July 1987 and she retained this post in the administrations of **Ciriaco De Mita** and **Giulio Andreotti**.

**JESZENSZKY, Géza.** *Hungary.* Foreign minister. Born in 1941, he trained as an historian, specializing in international relations and modern diplomatic history and becoming a firm anglophile (he speaks excellent English). He headed the Hungarian Democratic Forum's (MDF's) foreign affairs committee and after the successful party campaign in the spring 1990 elections, his father-in-law **József Antall** rewarded him in May with the sensitive post of foreign affairs minister. Here he was initially cautious over demands for rapid disentanglement from the legacy of Soviet domination, but was somewhat steamrollered into accepting a government statement explicitly opposing the Warsaw Pact. One of his most sensitive jobs is to deal with neighbouring countries where there are Hungarian minorities. He was elected to the 20-member MDF presidium at the party's December 1990 conference.

**JEYARETNAM, J.B.** *Singapore.* Opposition leader. Born in Ceylon (now Sri Lanka) in 1926.

A lawyer by profession, Jeyaretnam remains the principal opposition figure in Singapore despite being banned from parliament in 1986 after he was fined and imprisoned for alleged perjury. He was elected secretary-general of the left-wing Workers' Party in 1971 and a decade later he became Singapore's first opposition MP after winning a famous victory in Anson constituency.

**JIANG ZEMIN.** *China.* General secretary of the Chinese Communist Party (CCP). Jiang's unexpected rise to power, after the fall of **Zhao Ziyang** and the crushing of the pro-democracy movement in June 1989, can be attributed to his close involvement with the "open-door" reform policy and his conviction that "the more reform develops, the more political-ideological work must be strengthened". Born in 1926 and trained as an electrical engineer, Jiang worked in the machine-building ministry for 26 years. In 1980 he became vice-chairman of the State Council's commissions on imports and exports and foreign investment, before moving to the electronic industry ministry in 1982, where he was minister from 1983–85. He then moved to Shanghai as mayor until 1988, holding top party posts in the municipality at the same time. As mayor, his tactical approach defused the student protests of December 1986 and he was able to retain control of the city without military help by using worker pickets to patrol the streets and dismantle barricades. He was also the first provincial leader to indicate his support for martial law in Beijing. As the new "core of the leadership", Jiang was also elevated to the Politburo Standing Committee and the Secretariat in June 1989. His position was further bolstered when he succeeded **Deng Xiaoping** as chairman of both the powerful state and party Central Military Commissions in November 1989 and April 1990 respectively.

**JOBERT, Michel.** *France.* Former cabinet minister. Born in 1921 and a graduate of the Ecole Nationale d'Administration, he worked as a civil servant, notably at the Court of Accounts. In the 1950s and 1960s he was adviser in several ministerial offices and secretary-general to the president in 1969–73. In 1973–74 he was foreign minister under Georges Pompidou, showing his colours as an outspoken Gaullist, although more "European" than his late master. Despite this political identity, he was invited to join the socialist-led government in 1981, serving for two years as foreign trade minister. He leads his own small party, the Movement of Democrats (MD), and has a reputation for his reservations about fully free trade within the EC.

**JODA, Ahmed.** *Nigeria.* Former civil servant. Born in 1930 in Gongola state, he worked for Nigerian broadcasting from 1956–60 and in the northern Nigeria public service until 1967 when he was appointed permanent secretary to the federal government. He held this key post until he retired in 1978, to pursue a business career. He was appointed chairman of the state-controlled Nigerian liquefied natural gas company in April 1990.

**JOHANSSON, Olof.** *Sweden.* Leader of the Centre Party. Born in 1937, he worked as a farmer, journalist, teacher and farmers' representative until 1966, when he became secretary of the parliamentary group of the Centre Party. Elected to the Riksdag (parliament) in 1970, he held two junior ministerial posts from 1976–82. He was elected deputy party leader in 1986 and leader in succession to Thorbjörn Fälldin the following year.

**JOHN PAUL II (Karol Wojtyła).** *Vatican.* Pope and Vatican head of state. Born in 1920 in Wadowice, Poland, he worked briefly in a factory and was ordained as a priest in 1946. He obtained degrees in theology and philosophy at the Jagiellonian University of Kraków and the Angelicum Academy in Rome. From 1953–58, he was a professor of ethics and of moral theology at Lublin and Kraków universities. He was archbishop of Kraków from 1963–78 and was created a cardinal by Pope Paul VI in 1967. He was elected pope on October 16, 1978, on the third day and eighth ballot of the secret conclave of cardinals, the first non-Italian to hold the post since 1523, and the first Polish pope. His tenure has been characterized by high-profile overseas travel, with scarcely any part of the world left unvisited, and by a greater willingness than many of his recent predecessors to comment on political developments and to seek to influence events in many parts of the world. Nevertheless, his strenuous efforts to sway the Italian electorate during the campaign leading up to the May 1981 referendum on abortion failed, with more than two-thirds voting in favour of retaining the abortion option. On two occasions, in May 1981 and May 1982, attempts were made on his life. The first, in St Peter's Square, was the more serious, for he was wounded by bullets fired at close range by a Turk, Mehmet Ali Agça, and had to undergo emergency surgery. On the second occasion, at Fatima, in Portugal, a Spanish priest was prevented from attacking him with a bayonet. In terms of formal relationships with Catholic states, major developments of his papacy include new concordats with Spain and Italy, replacing those concluded with previous fascist regimes. Many have been disappointed by his strict adherence to Catholic orthodoxy on matters such as birth control and by his apparent reluctance to encourage the movement towards ecumenism initiated by John XXIII.

**JOHNSEN, Sigbørn.** *Norway.* Finance minister. Born in 1950, he studied at the Norwegian School of Management and worked as a bank cashier and accountant. He was vice-chairman of the Norwegian Labour Party (DNA) youth wing from 1975–77, and has been an elected Labour member of the Storting (parliament) since 1977. He has served on several parliamentary committees, and in 1985 became a delegate to the Council of Europe's parliamentary assembly. He is an expert on financial affairs and took on his present portfolio when **Gro Harlem Brundtland** formed her minority government in November 1990.

**JOHNSON-SIRLEAF, Ellen.** *Liberia.* Politician and banker. Born in 1939, she was educated at Harvard University and served as finance minister in the government of President William Tolbert before the 1980 coup. She went on to work for the World Bank and in commercial banking, serving as Citibank's vice-president for Africa, based in Nairobi, in the mid-1980s. She returned to Liberia in 1985 to help set up the Liberian Action Party to oppose President Samuel Doe in the presidential elections that October, in which she was elected to the Senate. She was among those who alleged the poll had been rigged and was detained after the coup attempt led by General Thomas Quiwonkpa the following month. She was released into house arrest in June 1986 and went into exile four months later, returning to banking in the USA, where she was granted political asylum. In August 1990 she joined the interim government formed in exile under the leadership of **Amos Sawyer.**

**JONES, Walter.** *USA.* Democratic congressman from North Carolina. Born in 1913, he was a business executive and state legislator who was elected to the House of Representatives in 1966. Chairman of the merchant marine and fisheries committee since 1981, he is the ailing maritime industry's foremost ally. Also supportive of the oil industry, he is in favour of drilling in Alaska's protected coastal wilderness.

**JORDAN, Bill.** *UK.* Trade unionist. Born in 1936, he became a convener of shop stewards at the Guest Keen & Nettlefolds (now GKN) engineering firm in 1966 and a full-time divisional organizer of (what is now) the Amalgamated Engineering Union (AEU) in 1976. He was elected union president in 1986, and has become one of the leading right-wingers among union leaders, endorsing aspects of the Conservative government's industrial relations legislation which have provoked vitriolic opposition from other union leaders.

**JOSEPH, Lord (Keith Joseph).** *UK.* Conservative politician. Born in 1918, he was MP from 1956 until he became a life peer in 1987. After cabinet service under **Edward Heath,** he founded the right-wing think-tank, the Centre for Policy Studies and in 1975 wrote *Reversing the Trend,* an important statement of the tenets of Thatcherite Conservatism. In the same year he made way for **Margaret Thatcher** in the Tory leadership contest and went on to serve in the cabinet as industry and later education and science secretary until 1986.

**JOSPIN, Lionel.** *France.* Minister of state for education, youth and sport. Born in 1937 and a graduate of the Institut d'Etudes Politiques and of the Ecole Nationale d'Administration, he followed a civil service and university teaching career before rising through the Socialist Party (PS) to become, in 1981, a member of the National Assembly and **François Mitterrand**'s ally and successor as party first secretary. As such, Jospin consolidated his political base with skill. Since 1988, having resigned the party leadership, he has been minister of state for education, youth and sport. Experienced, and highly intelligent, he remains a key contender for high office.

**JOTTI, Leonilde (Nilde).** *Italy.* President of Chamber of Deputies and Italian Communist Party (PCI) politician. Born in 1920, she obtained a degree in letters and philosophy at Milan University and became a teacher in her native Reggio Emilia. In 1946 she was a member of the Constituent Assembly which drafted the new republican constitution. A veteran PCI stalwart, the *compagna* of post-war Communist leader Palmiro Togliatti, and a central committee member since 1956, she has held her seat in the Chamber of Deputies since April 1948 and became vice-president of the chamber in May 1972. As president of the chamber since 1979, she is the foremost woman in politics.

**JOVIĆ, Borisav.** *Yugoslavia.* President and Serbia's member of the collective state presidency. Born in Batočina in 1928, he is an ethnic Serb and holds a doctorate in economics. He joined the communist party in 1951 and after a series of party appointments served as a federal minister from 1971–75. He spent the next five years as ambassador to Italy. He was president of the presidency of Serbia from 1988–89 and in May 1989 was elected for a five-year term as Serbia's member of the collective state presidency. Federal vice-president from May 1989 to May 1990, he then took over as federal president for a one-year term. He is a hardliner and a close ally of **Slobodan Milošević**.

**JOXE, Pierre.** *France.* Interior minister. Born in 1934 and educated in law and administration at the Ecole Nationale d'Administration, he is the son of the ex-Gaullist minister and diplomat, Louis Joxe. His own career took him via the civil service and university teaching. He has moved from the Unified Socialist Party (PSU) to the Socialist Party (PS), and was first elected to parliament in 1973. Industry minister briefly in 1981 and interior minister from 1984–86, he returned to the latter post in 1988. Associated closely with **François Mitterrand**, he has a reputation for toughness, intellect, and strong organizational ability.

**JUAN CARLOS I.** *Spain.* King. Born in 1938 in exile in Italy, he was brought up there and in Switzerland and Portugal by his father, Don Juan de Borbón (the pretender to the Spanish throne). He was summoned home by General Franco in the early 1950s to be educated and groomed as his successor, Franco having declared Spain a monarchy in 1948, while reserving for himself the right of choosing who would be king. After education at military academies and at university in Madrid, he was officially designated Franco's successor in 1969, and assumed power on Franco's death in 1975. Once installed, he defied those who thought he would follow doggedly in the dictator's footsteps, and began helping to implement plans for a transition to democracy, with a keen political acumen whose real extent has emerged only with hindsight. In particular, he assumed responsibility in 1976 for appointing **Adolfo Suárez** as prime minister to replace Carlos Arias Navarro, a diehard from the Franco era, and supported him at critical moments. He also supported the process of devolving limited powers to the regions. At a crisis for Spanish democracy in February 1981, when dissident members of the military tried to stage a coup, his commitment to liberal democracy, his skill as a political operator of integrity, and his popularity with and involvement in the armed forces, were decisive factors in the successful thwarting of the coup attempt. As Spanish democracy became more firmly established during the 1980s he began to play a more conventional role as a constitutional monarch, while continuing to exercise considerable influence.

**JUGNAUTH, Sir Aneerood.** *Mauritius.* Prime minister. Born in 1930 in Majorca, he is a London-trained lawyer who held ministerial office in the first post-independence government in the mid-1960s. In 1971 he joined the Mauritian Militant Movement (MMM), which mobilized grassroots opposition to the Mauritian elite. He became prime minister after the MMM's landslide election victory in 1982, but differences over economic policy soon split the party and he emerged heading a new, largely Hindu-based grouping, the Mauritian Socialist Movement (MSM). This allied with the Mauritius Labour Party (MLP) and Mauritius Social Democratic Party against his former colleagues in the 1983 elections. The Social Democrats left the government in 1988 and Jugnauth's fragile alliance with the MLP finally collapsed in July 1990, after the revelation that he had formed an electoral pact with the MMM. Jugnauth formed a new government with MMM support in September.

**JUMA, Omar Ali.** *Tanzania.* Chief minister of Zanzibar. A qualified veterinary surgeon and senior government official, he was appointed chief minister in January 1988 after the dismissal of the popular Seif Sharrif Hamad. Juma was elected to the central committee of the ruling Chama Cha Mapinduzi in October 1989. His considerable political skill will be fully tested by continuing demands for secession from the mainland.

**JUMBLATT, Walid.** *Lebanon.* Druse leader. As the head of the Jumblatt family, he is effectively the traditional leader of the Druse community, an ethno-religious group whose origins date back to a heretical Muslim sect in the Middle Ages, and whose heartland is the Chouf mountains, east of Beirut. Jumblatt's institutional authority lies in his role as president of the Progressive Socialist Party (PSP), which, despite its name, was founded as the main Druse political body by Walid's father, Kamal, in 1949. A garrulous man with a fiery temper, Jumblatt succeeded as PSP president after Kamal's assassination in 1977. As such, he has played a leading role in Lebanese affairs, his politics backed up by the guns of the PSP militiamen. With a penchant for denim jeans, leather jackets and fast motorbikes, he has an accessible, westernized personality, which sets him apart from some of the country's other Muslim leaders and which is reinforced by his readiness to talk to journalists. Essentially, he has but a single policy: to defend the semi-autonomous Druse enclave. This has seen the PSP allied with other Muslim forces, most notably the moderate Shia Amal militia of **Nabih Berri**, and the Syrian army, against Christian forces. Alliances have fluctuated, however; the arrival of the Syrian army in Beirut in early 1987 was triggered by ferocious clashes between Amal and the PSP, after Jumblatt had reacted against Amal's attacks on the Palestinian camps. His cabinet post as transport and tourism minister, gained under an agreement to allow opposition forces into government after a swingeing Druse–Amal victory in 1984, has been all but an irrelevance. So long as there is no incursion into the Druse fief, Jumblatt is likely to be happy to accept *pax syriana*.

**JUPPÉ, Alain**. *France*. Secretary-general of the Gaullist RPR. Born in 1945, he graduated through the prestigious educational institutions, the Ecole Normale Supérieure, Institut d'Etudes Politiques and Ecole Nationale d'Administration, emerging as a financial specialist and becoming inspector of finance. Taking a more political line from the time of his 1976 appointment as financial adviser to **Jacques Chirac**, he rose within Chirac's Rally for the Republic (RPR), won a European Parliament seat in 1984, and entered the National Assembly in 1986. As Chirac's right-hand man he was government spokesman from 1986–88, then worked as his mentor's presidential campaign spokesman, but moved over immediately after the elections to become party secretary-general. In this role he led the party's Euro-election campaign, adopted a tough line against those who advocated contacts with the extremist National Front, and emerged as a potential successor to Chirac.

**JUQUIN, Pierre**. *France*. Left-wing politician. Born in 1930, he was educated at the Ecole Normale Supérieure and went on to a career in teaching. As a Communist Party (PCF) activist, he joined the central committee in 1964, the French National Assembly in 1967 and the party politburo in 1979. Since 1984, however, he has been openly critical of the PCF line and withdrew in 1987 after declaring an interest in standing in the 1988 presidential election. Running as an alternative "red-green" candidate, he polled only 2%, and since then has seen his future in terms of moving further away from his communist roots and joining forces with the small but rising green movement.

**JUSU-SHERIFF, Salia**. *Sierra Leone*. Second vice-president. Born in 1929 and trained as a chartered accountant in the UK, Jusu-Sheriff was elected to parliament in 1962 and held a series of ministerial posts in the Albert Margai government until its defeat in 1967. He remained active in opposition until appointed finance minister by President Siaka Stevens after the first one-party election in 1982, becoming economic planning minister two years later and second vice-president soon after **Joseph Momoh**'s accession to the presidency in 1985.

# K

**KACZYŃSKI, Jarosław.** *Poland.* Leading Solidarity activist. A senator, like his twin brother **Lech Kaczyński**, he has been chief political adviser since 1989 to Solidarity chairman **Lech Wałęsa**; he engineered the Solidarity coalition with the United Peasants' Party and the Democratic Party that made possible the formation of the **Tadeusz Mazowiecki** government in August 1989. In 1989 Kaczyński succeeded Mazowiecki as editor of *Tygodnik Solidarność*, an influential Solidarity newspaper. In May 1990 he founded the new Centre Alliance, a right-of-centre political grouping formed principally by Solidarity activists. This supported Wałęsa in Solidarity's factional disputes, championing his bid for the presidency and the political programme of "acceleration". At the end of 1990 Wałęsa appointed him head of the presidential chancellery, with the rank of minister of state.

**KACZYŃSKI, Lech.** *Poland.* Leading Solidarity activist and specialist in labour law. Like his twin brother **Jarosław Kaczyński**, he is a senator. Second-in-command to **Lech Wałęsa** in the Solidarity trade union, Lech Kaczyński was regarded a likely successor as Solidarity chairman; in December 1990 he became one of two interim co-chairmen, with Stefan Jurczak.

**KÁDÁR, Béla.** *Hungary.* International economic relations minister. Born in 1934, he rose through the academic world to become research director of Budapest's World Economy Institute, an economic adviser to the communist government and well-known lecturer abroad. In May 1990 he was one of two non-party academic experts (the other being **Ferenc Rabár**) brought in to strengthen the **József Antall**'s government for the key task of transforming the economy.

**KADDOUMI, Farouk al-.** *Palestinian.* Head of the Palestine Liberation Organization (PLO) political department. He was elected Palestine's foreign minister at the key meeting of the PLO's 60-member central council in Tunis in April 1989. The meeting followed the Palestine National Council's November 1988 decision to declare the existence of an independent Palestinian state.

**KADIJEVIĆ, Colonel-General Veljko.** *Yugoslavia.* Defence minister. An ethnic Serb from Croatia, he was born in 1925 and joined Tito's partisans and the communist party in 1943. After the war he received a formal army education and went on to become managing editor of the armed forces' theoretical journal, *Vojno Delo* (Military Matters). As army deputy chief of staff, he was chiefly responsible for reshaping the national defence system in 1975. Since 1981, he has served in the defence ministry, becoming federal national defence minister in May 1988. Kadijević is not an outspoken politician, having built his reputation on his management skills. However, in the Serbian elections at the end of 1990 he publicly endorsed the campaign of **Slobodan Milošević**.

**KADZAMIRA, Mama Cecilia Tamanda.** *Malawi.* Official state hostess. The niece of **John Tembo**, she has performed many of the functions of a spouse in the household of President **Hastings Banda** since the late 1950s. Her efforts since early 1986 to raise her own political profile by founding and patronizing Chitukoko Cha Amayi m'Malawi (CCAM), a women's development organization, have given rise to speculation that – like her uncle – she harbours presidential ambitions. However, she is deeply unpopular and Banda's conservatism makes it unlikely that he would support her. In 1987 he made a public statement ridiculing allegations about her political ambitions.

**KAFAROVA, Elmira.** *USSR.* Azerbaijani official. As chair of the Azerbaijani Supreme Soviet Presidium from June 1989 Kafarova was in effect the republic's head of state. She was vocal in support of the nationalist Popular Front in Azerbaijan's conflict with neighbouring Armenia, and in criticizing Soviet security operations against Azerbaijani militants. She was effectively demoted in a restructuring of the republican leadership in May 1990, her responsibilities being more narrowly defined as parliamentary speaker.

**KAHVECİ, Adnan.** *Turkey.* Finance minister. Regarded as a liberal, his appointment as finance and customs minister in March 1990 was seen as a blow against the rise of conservatism and Islamic fundamentalism in the ruling Motherland Party (ANAP). A former economic policy adviser to the government (sometimes described as a "one-man think-tank"), he had been without a post since being dropped from his post as minister of state in a cabinet reshuffle in the spring of 1989.

**KAIFU, Toshiki.** *Japan.* Prime minister. Born in 1931, he graduated from the law faculty of Waseda University in 1954, where he was known as a good orator. He was secretary to Kinsho Kono, a very close confidant of Takeo Miki (prime minister from 1974–76) and quickly developed a strong bond with the powerful politician. Following Kono's death, his wife successfully stood for election but was persuaded to stand down in favour of Kaifu in 1960. At 29, Kaifu was the youngest successful candidate in the country. He served as deputy chief cabinet secretary in the Miki cabinet and only pressure from senior politicians dissuaded Miki from appointing him chief cabinet secretary. Kaifu's relationship with Miki, who was on the left of the Liberal Democratic Party (LDP), enabled him to develop a keen political sense and rise steadily in the party. His personal charm and charisma ensured him ample media attention. After serving twice as education minister, under Takeo Fukuda and **Yasuhiro Nakasone**, Kaifu unexpectedly came to the fore following the successive resignations of prime ministers **Noboru Takeshita** and Sosuke Uno. Untainted by the scandal that brought them down, he benefited from a close relationship with Takeshita, who still wielded power in the LDP. This helped to balance the relatively small size of his party faction (led by **Toshio Komoto** in succession to Miki) which left him dependent on the goodwill of power-brokers in the party, even as party leader. In August 1989 Kaifu became prime minister but was quickly seen to have relatively little power, with **Shintaro Abe** and **Shin Kanemaru** in particular well placed to restrict his freedom of movement. Kaifu's position both within the LDP and at the centre of Japanese government was strengthened unexpectedly in February 1990 when, contrary to most predictions and following the heavy defeat in the 1989 House of Councillors (upper house) election, the LDP emerged as comfortable

victor in the general election. He continued to balance the LDP factions successfully in his December 1990 cabinet reshuffle.

**KAJDOMAJ, Hisen.** *Yugoslavia.* Former president of Kosovo. An ethnic Albanian, he was executive secretary of the Kosovo communist party presidium from April 1986 to November 1989. In June 1989, he was elected president of Kosovo, a post from which he resigned in July 1990 in protest at the controversial constitutional changes restoring full Serbian control over the autonomous province of Kosovo, which it had lost in the late 1960s. Ethnic Albanians form 90% of the province's population.

**KALUGIN, Major-General Oleg.** *USSR.* Former KGB officer. Born in 1934, he was a KGB counter-intelligence officer for 32 years before being forced to retire in March 1990. He came to international prominence three months later when he made allegations of KGB abuses of power (some in collusion with the Communist Party of the Soviet Union) in interviews first with the USA and then with the Soviet press. He was officially denounced, stripped of his rank and pension, and threatened with criminal charges. His revelations earned him massive public support, however, leading to his victory in September 1990 in a by-election for the USSR Congress of People's Deputies.

**KAMANGA, Reuben Chitandika.** *Zambia.* Politician. Born in 1929, he has been close to President **Kenneth Kaunda** throughout his long political life and remains a member of his inner circle of confidants. He was vice-president from independence in 1964 until he moved in 1967 to the foreign ministry, where he expressed bitter criticism of the UK's handling of Rhodesia's unilateral declaration of independence. His unswerving loyalty to Kaunda has ensured his place in the top echelons of the ruling United National Independence Party (Unip). He is currently chairman of the party central committee's rural development committee.

**KAMARA, Alhaji Abu Bakar.** *Sierra Leone.* First vice-president. Born in 1929, Kamara is a London-trained lawyer and was formerly finance minister and justice minister. He was appointed first vice-president after the implication of his predecessor, Francis Mishek Minah, in a plot to overthrow President **Joseph Momoh** in 1986.

**KANEKO, Mitsuhiro.** *Japan.* Japan Communist Party (JCP) politician. Born in 1921 and a graduate of Tokyo's school for railway workers, he rose through the railway union, joined the JCP in 1946, and first entered the House of Representatives (lower house) when the party achieved its unexpectedly good electoral showing in 1972. Party secretary-general from 1982 and elected as vice-chairman of its presidium in 1990, he is the author of several books dealing with, in particular, his party's criticisms of nuclear power policy and of the controversial consumption tax.

**KANEMARU, Shin.** *Japan.* Senior Liberal Democratic Party (LDP) politician. Born in 1914 in Yamanashi prefecture, he graduated from Tokyo Agricultural University and was first elected to the House of Representatives (lower house) for the LDP in 1958. He served as construction minister under Kakuei Tanaka in 1972, and later as director-general of the Defence Agency under Takeo Fukuda in 1977. Within the LDP, he played a key role in setting up the Soseikai group (the vehicle by which **Noburo Takeshita** took over the Tanaka faction) and served as secretary-general of the LDP for two years under **Yasuhiro Nakasone**. Deputy prime minister from 1986–87, he is a powerful figure within the LDP, with a particularly strong base in party administration, and gives his influential backing to current secretary-general **Ichiro Ozawa**.

**KARAMANLIS, Constantine.** *Greece.* President. Born in 1907, he practised law in the Macedonian town of Serres before entering politics for the conservative Populist Party in 1935. He was a successful junior minister in the conservative Greek Rally government when, on the death of its leader in 1955, he was unexpectedly named prime minister by King Paul. Karamanlis formed the National Radical Union (ERE) and in 1956 was elected prime minister in his own right, holding the post for eight years and providing one of the longest periods of stable government in contemporary Greece. In 1963, after a defeat in a general election and a previous dispute with the monarch, he went into self-imposed exile in Paris where, during the colonels' dictatorship (1967–74), he became the focus of conservative opposition to the military regime. Recalled in July 1974 to head the restored civilian government he launched the centre-right New Democracy party (ND) and won a landslide victory in the first free elections, remaining as prime minister until 1980 when he was elected by parliament as president of the republic. An accomplished statesman who was the architect of

Greece's accession to the EC, he resigned in 1985 after the socialist government withdrew support for his re-election. He was re-elected, however, in May 1990 after ND was returned to government.

**KARAMANOV, Uzabakay.** *USSR.* Prime minister of Kazakhstan. Born in 1937, he trained as a construction engineer. Before his election as the republic's premier in mid-1989 he served as the republic's deputy construction minister and (from 1987) chairman of Kazakhstan's State Committee for Material and Technical Supply. In those capacities his most lauded achievement was largely to rid Kazakhstan of the severe housing shortages that are increasingly at the root of social and inter-ethnic unrest elsewhere in Soviet Central Asia.

**KARAMI, Umar.** *Lebanon.* Prime minister. A Sunni Muslim from a long-established Lebanese family, he is the brother of former prime minister Rashid Karami, assassinated in 1987. He was education minister until the resignation of the prime minister, **Selim al-Hoss** in December 1990. He was then charged with the Herculean task of presiding over a cabinet whose authority was questioned by rival militia leaders, and which was responsible for implementing the *pax syriana* in the war-ravaged country.

**KARIMOV, Islam.** *USSR.* President of Uzbekistan. Born in 1938, he worked first as a mechanical engineer, and then from 1966 in government economic planning, reaching the post of deputy premier. He was appointed a regional Communist Party leader in 1986, at the height of the purge of party officials for corruption which, since the 1970s at least, had been endemic in Uzbekistan. He took over as Uzbek Communist Party leader from **Rafik Nishanov** in 1989, and became Uzbek Supreme Soviet chairman (effectively Uzbekistan's president) in March 1990. His party post earned him Communist Party of the Soviet Union politburo membership in July 1990. Generally seen as an old-style conservative, he took an unexpected stand alongside **Boris Yeltsin** in December 1990, arguing that the republics rather than the centre should determine the distribution of powers under a new union treaty.

**KARRUBI, Hojatoleslam Mehdi.** *Iran.* Speaker of parliament. Born in 1937, Karrubi was imprisoned several times under the Shah's regime, for leading mass prayer meetings. A member of parliament for Tehran, he was deputy Majlis (parliament) speaker until 1989 when he replaced **Ali Akbar Hashemi Rafsanjani** as speaker. A hardliner who believes in the export of the Islamic revolution, he has tended to side with **Ali Akbar Mohtashami** in opposition to Rafsanjani's pragmatism. He was re-elected speaker for a further year in May 1990.

**KARUNANIDHI, M.** *India.* Chief minister of Tamil Nadu and leader of Dravida Munnetra Kazhagam (DMK). Born in 1924 in Tirukuvalai, Tamil Nadu, a popular playwright and film scriptwriter, he became a founder-member of the DMK in 1949, was elected to the state assembly in 1957 and served as deputy leader of the party in 1962–67. Two years later, he became party president and was chief minister of the state from 1969–76. The party split in 1972, and from 1977 onwards it was eclipsed by the rival All-India Anna Dravida Munnetra Kazhagam (AIADMK) led by M.G. Ramachandran. Ramachandran died in 1987 and the DMK, now allied with Janata Dal, won the 1989 state elections.

**KASPAR, Jean.** *France.* Trade union leader. Born in 1941 and a potash miner, he joined the French Democratic Confederation of Workers (CFDT) in 1958, and rose through the trade union hierarchy. Elected to the executive committee of the CFDT in 1982, he became secretary-general in November 1988 of a more unified trade union movement.

**KASSEBAUM, Nancy.** *USA.* Republican senator from Kansas. Born in 1932, the daughter of 1936 Republican presidential candidate governor Alf Landon, she was a broadcasting executive with no experience of political office when she became the lone woman in the Senate in 1978. Widely respected, she is more a "citizen-legislator" than a partisan. Budget reduction and foreign policy are her main interests.

**KATEGAYA, Eriya Tukahiirwa.** *Uganda.* First deputy prime minister. Born in 1945 and trained as a lawyer in Tanzania, he worked in private legal practice and as a state attorney before joining Milton Obote's government in 1980 as commerce minister. He later joined **Yoweri Museveni** in the guerrilla struggle to overthrow Obote, becoming and remaining his most trusted lieutenant. He was appointed to the newly created post of first deputy prime minister in February 1988.

**KATO, Mutsuki.** *Japan.* Liberal Democratic Party (LDP) policy affairs research council chairman. Born in 1926 in Okayama prefecture, he graduated from Himeji high school (now Kobe University) and became a school teacher.

After serving as secretary to the late Niro Hoshijima, speaker of the House of Representatives (lower house), Kato entered parliament in 1967. Implication in the Lockheed scandal did not prevent him from being appointed director-general of the National Land Agency in 1982 and agriculture, forestry and fisheries minister in 1986, both under **Yasuhiro Nakasone.** Kato is an expert on the tax system and transport administration. He was involved in the Recruit scandal, but returned to prominence on being appointed chairman of the LDP policy affairs research council in 1990. His elder brother, Takenori, is a member of the House of Councillors (upper house).

**KAUFMAN, Gerald.** *UK.* Labour politician. Born in 1930, he graduated from Oxford University and after a short stint as assistant general secretary of the Fabian Society, the venerable think-tank of the British left, he began a journalistic career that took him from the *Daily Mirror* newspaper and the *New Statesman* magazine to the House of Commons, where he became Labour parliamentary press liaison officer. Elected to parliament for a Manchester seat in 1970, he held two junior ministerial posts from 1974 until Labour's defeat in 1979. He gained a reputation for his aggressive and effective parliamentary style, and was elected to the shadow cabinet for the first time in 1983. He was given the key portfolio of spokesman on home affairs and then, in 1987, on foreign affairs. On the centre-right of the party, he memorably described Labour's left-wing 1983 election manifesto as the "longest suicide note in history".

**KAUNDA, Kenneth David.** *Zambia.* President. Born in 1924, his political career began in the 1950s when, with Malawi's **Hastings Banda**, he led a campaign to dissolve the Central African Federation. On the break-up of the federation in 1962 he became prime minister of the first black majority government and in 1964 president of newly independent Zambia. He has held the post ever since, presiding over a one-party state since 1972 through the ruling United National Independence Party (Unip). He rose to international prominence after he closed Zambia's borders with Rhodesia in 1973 and has continued to play a central role in the search for solutions to southern Africa's problems. Chairman of the Organization of African Unity in 1970–71 and 1987–88 and head of the Non-Aligned Movement from 1970–73, he is current chairman of the Front-Line States. His style of government, influenced by his philosophy of "humanism" (a mixture of socialism and Christianity) and his early career as a schoolteacher, has been paternalistic and moralistic. An emotional man, he is also a populist who has made effective use of the mass media to bolster his reputation as "KK", the man of the people. Until recently this enabled him largely to escape growing popular criticism of his party's political and economic record. Events since 1988, however, culminating in the riots and coup attempt of June 1990, have confirmed his fall from grace. He has been forced to agree to implementation of a multi-party constitution. It is clear that belated reform of Unip, including a limit on the number of presidential terms, means that his political career is nearing its end.

**KAWAWA, Rashidi.** *Tanzania*. Chama Cha Mapinduzi (CCM) vice-chairman. A tough and able administrator, he was the right-hand man of **Julius Nyerere** for more than a quarter of a century. Born in 1929, he began his career in the government film service, starring in three locally made comedy films in the early 1950s. Active in trade unionism, he helped to found the Tanganyika Federation of Labour, whose president he became, and in 1959 was elected to the Tanganyika Legislative Council. He was local government and housing minister from 1960–61 and was generally recognized as Nyerere's deputy with his appointment as minister without portfolio in April 1961. In the following year he took over as prime minister when Nyerere stepped down to concentrate on party work. Following the declaration of the republic in December 1962 he was appointed first vice-president, becoming second vice-president on the union with Zanzibar in 1964, a post he held until 1977, combining it with the premiership after 1972. In 1977 he was made defence minister and in 1980 minister without portfolio in the president's office. In 1982 he was elected secretary-general of the ruling CCM, becoming vice-chairman on Nyerere's retirement as chairman in August 1990, but he is an old-guard politician whose ideals are not in harmony with Tanzania's new pragmatism.

**KAYSONE PHOMVIHANE.** *Laos*. Prime minister and party leader. Born in 1920, he was sent by his Vietnamese father in the 1940s to study in Hanoi, where he became involved in the anti-French struggle. Returning to Laos after the Japanese surrender, he went underground and became leader of the Lao People's Revolutionary Party on its formation in 1955. He emerged in public only after the communist victory in 1975.

**KEATING, Paul.** *Australia*. Treasurer and deputy prime minister. Born in Sydney in 1944, he is an exception in his generation of Labor ministers in not having had a university education. He is, however, one of the most intellectually able figures in contemporary Australian politics. After joining the Australian Labor Party at the age of 15, he followed a familiar path into the trade union movement, becoming a full-time official in the mid-1960s. In 1969 he was elected to the House of Representatives for the New South Wales seat of Blaxland, and had a short career on the front bench as minister for Northern Australia in the last months of the Whitlam government in 1975. In opposition, he held a number of posts, culminating in treasury spokesman just before the 1983 election. He was immediately appointed treasurer in **Bob Hawke's** government and has retained this post since then. Perhaps inevitably for a hard-headed financial manager in a fundamentally hedonisitic society (or incipient "banana republic" as he himself has characterized it), Keating is regarded with grudging respect rather than affection. He has made no secret of his intention to succeed to the leadership, an ambition towards which Hawke appears ambivalent.

**KEBICH, Vyacheslav.** *USSR*. Prime minister of Byelorussia. Born in 1936, he trained as a mechanical engineer, but was a career party official for many years before being named in 1985 as chairman of Byelorussia's state planning committee. In that capacity he acquired a reputation as a maverick economic reformer, and is credited with Byelorussia's relative economic success compared with other republics. He was elected premier in April 1990.

**KEÇECILER, Mehmet.** *Turkey*. Minister of state. He leads the right-wing "Holy Alliance" a religious grouping within the ruling Motherland Party (ANAP). He is a former critic of President **Turgut Özal**, who once used a veto to keep him out of the government. Since joining the **Yıldırım Akbulut** government, he has campaigned energetically for a more religious emphasis: in 1989 he forced through the trebling of the religious spending budget, and in 1990 he succeeded in getting a court judgment revoked, so that Muslim women in the universities could wear their headscarves (even though in theory these are banned under the

Turkish constitution).

**KELLY, John.** *USA.* Assistant secretary of state for Near East and South Asian affairs. Born in 1939, he was ambassador to Lebanon from 1986–88 before his current appointment in 1989.

**KELTY, Bill.** *Australia.* Secretary of the Australian Council of Trades Unions. Born in Melbourne in 1948, he moved directly from university to a full-time trade union career. He joined the ACTU as a research officer in 1974 and became secretary in 1983.

**KEMP, Jack.** *USA.* Secretary of housing and urban development. Born in 1935 and educated at Long Beach State University in California, Kemp, an ebullient former professional football star, worked in public relations before becoming a full-time politician. A conservative Republican, he served as assistant to Californian governor **Ronald Reagan** in 1967 and as chairman of the Republican National Committee in 1969. In 1971 he was elected to the House of Representatives for Buffalo (NY) district. He campaigned for the Republican presidential nomination in 1987–88, but withdrew from the contest in March 1988 when **George Bush** established an unassailable lead. In 1989 he was appointed to the Bush cabinet – one of the few real ideologues to achieve this – as secretary of housing and urban development (HUD). Within months an extensive series of scandals emerged involving misuse of HUD funds. By exposing years of mismanagement, these presented Kemp with an unexpected congressional mandate to reform the department along his own conservative lines. Despite this, however, the continuing corruption investigation (and its attendant prosecutions) meant that a disproportionate amount of HUD resources were spent on damage control. This, together with Kemp's sometimes abrasive management style (which included a fondness for hyperbole, lengthy oratory and desk-pounding enthusiasm), caused several senior aides to resign from the HUD within the first 20 months of the new administration.

**KENGO WA DONDO.** *Zaïre.* Former prime minister. Born Léon Lobitsh in 1935, of half-Polish parentage, he trained as a lawyer in Zaïre and Belgium. In 1968 he was appointed legal and political adviser to the president and then attorney general of the republic. He also had appointments in the political bureau and the central committee of the ruling Popular Revolutionary Movement (MPR) party. From 1980–82 he was ambassador to Belgium before being recalled in November and named as prime minister. Having earned a reputation as a strict disciplinarian, he had been appointed by President **Mobutu Sese Seko** to carry through tough economic reforms recommended by the IMF. When Mobutu abruptly broke off relations with the IMF in 1986, Kengo was dismissed but was later brought back into government, first as foreign minister and then as prime minister again in November 1988. Kengo left the government in April 1990, when Mobutu bowed to pressures for a transitional government to oversee the introduction of multi-party politics. With his mixed parentage, Kengo is one of a powerful clique of *métis* surrounding Mobutu but, while sometimes tipped as a possible president, he is disqualified since he is not of wholly Zaïrian origin.

**KENNEDY, Anthony.** *USA.* Supreme Court associate justice. Born in California in 1936, he was educated at Stanford and Harvard universities and the London School of Economics. After practising and teaching law, he was appointed as a federal appeals court judge in 1976. Kennedy was, under the administration of **Ronald Reagan**, third choice to fill the Supreme Court vacancy arising from the resignation of Lewis Powell in 1987. Since his appointment in 1988, Kennedy has voted consistently with the court's conservatives.

**KENNEDY, Charles.** *UK.* Liberal Democrat politician. Born in 1959, he studied philosophy and politics, winning a Fulbright scholarship to Indiana University. He then briefly worked as a journalist in the Scottish Highlands before unexpectedly being elected to parliament for the Social Democratic Party (SDP) in 1983. Although one of the youngest MPs, his manner is heavyweight (modelled, it is said, on **Roy Jenkins**). He was a strong supporter of the proposed merger between the SDP and the Liberal Party in 1988, and was elected president of the new Social and Liberal Democratic Party (SLD – now the Liberal Democrats) in 1990.

**KENNEDY, Edward.** *USA.* Democratic senator from Massachusetts. Born in 1932, he was educated at Harvard and the University of Virginia, trained as a lawyer and was elected senator in 1962. After his brother Robert's assassination in 1968, he became heir to the family presidential tradition and the beacon of American liberalism, but the Chappaquiddick tragedy of 1969 blighted his career. In 1980 he made an inept bid to wrest the presidential nomination from **Jimmy Carter**. His 1985 announcement that he would not seek the 1988 nomination effectively signified the end of these ambitions. "The pursuit of the presidency is not my life," he avowed, "public service is". This decision probably enhanced his Senate influence, because his actions and statements are now taken at face value rather than as manoeuvres for the presidency. While the Senate was Republican-controlled from 1981 to 1986, Kennedy's aim was to keep liberal issues in the media spotlight. He continues to articulate ideas, such as his 1988 call for a "Marshall Plan" for American youth, but he has put his priorities on promoting specific legislation since becoming labour and human resources committee chairman in 1987. This necessitates political compromise and acceptance of budget constraints. In 1988 he steered into law the two most important civil rights advances in two decades. In 1989 he devised the first comprehensive AIDS-care bill and began building support for a comprehensive national health insurance programme jointly funded by employers and government.

**KENNEDY, Joseph, III.** *USA.* Democratic congressman from Massachusetts. Born in 1952, the son of Robert Kennedy, he was an executive of a non-profit organization that supported the energy needs of the old and the poor before becoming the first of the third Kennedy generation to enter Congress after his election in 1986. Though viewed by many House colleagues as a brash newcomer ambitious for higher office, he has worked effectively on the banking, finance and urban affairs committee, particularly on third-world debt issues.

**KÉRÉKOU, Brigadier-General Mathieu (Ahmed).** *Benin.* President. Born in 1933. An army major brought to power in a coup in the former French colony of Dahomey in 1972, Kérékou declared the adoption of Marxist-Leninist principles and changed the country's name to the People's Republic of Benin. He brought some stability to a country that had suffered six coups in nine years, but his popularity evaporated against a background of government incompetence and corruption and economic decline. After a period of growing unrest, the national convention of February 1990, described as a "civilian coup d'état", stripped Kérékou of most of his powers and installed an interim government headed by Nicéphore Soglo. Having apparently lost the army's support, Kérékou broods on the sidelines, with his past record under investigation.

**KERREY, Bob.** *USA.* Democratic senator from Nebraska. Born in 1943, he lost a leg in action in Vietnam, became a restaurateur and won Nebraska's governorship as a political novice in 1982. Elected senator in 1988 by a large majority, he sits on the important appropriations and agriculture committees and has quickly become a Senate force through his consensus-building skills.

**KERRY, John.** *USA.* Democratic senator from Massachusetts. Born in 1943, he served in Vietnam and was one of the organizers of Vietnam Veterans against the War. He then studied law and became lieutenant-governor in 1982. In 1984 he was elected to the Senate. Chairman of the subcommittee on terrorism, he advocates a hard line against international drug traffickers.

**KESSAR, Israel.** *Israel.* General secretary since 1984 of the Histadrut, Israel's powerful labour federation. Born in Yemen in 1931, he made history by becoming the first Sephardic (oriental) Jew to rise so high in what was seen as an Ashkenazi stronghold. A Labour MP since 1988, he is a contender for the party leadership.

**KEZBERS, Ivars.** *USSR.* Independent Latvian Communist Party leader. Previously a secretary of the Latvian Communist Party, he was one of a large minority of party members who walked out of the April 1990 party congress after it rejected a motion to declare independence from the Communist Party of the Soviet Union. Days later, the breakaway independent party elected him as its chairman.

**KHADDAM, Abdel-Halim.** *Syria.* Vice-president. Born in 1932 in Banyas, he studied law at Damascus University. He became governor of Damascus in 1964, and was economy and trade minister from 1969–70, and foreign minister and deputy prime minister from 1970–84. He became vice-president for political and foreign affairs in 1984. A Sunni, he is, unusually for Syria, married to an Alawi woman. He has remained wholly loyal to President **Hafez al-Assad**, and was strongly opposed to Rifaat al-Assad.

**KHALEGHIAR, Fazle-Hagh.** *Afghanistan.* Prime minister. Appointed in May 1990 as prime minister, at the age of 56, he was a former governor-general of the north-west zone and had been a ministerial adviser in the previous cabinet of Sultan Ali Keshtmand. He is not a member of the ruling People's Democratic Party of Afghanistan (PDPA – which in its hardline communist guise had invited Soviet intervention in 1979), and his appointment is taken as an indication of President **Mohammed Najibullah**'s increasing desire to build a broad base of legitimacy for his government.

**KHALIFA, Shaikh Hamed ibn Issa al-.** *Bahrain.* Crown prince. **Shaikh Issa**'s son, he was born in 1950 and educated in Bahrain and later at the UK's Sandhurst Military Academy, the Mons Officer Cadet School and Fort Leavenworth, Kansas, USA.

**KHALIFA, Shaikh Issa ibn Sulman al-.** *Bahrain.* Head of state. Born in 1933, he has been Amir (ruler) since he succeeded his father, Shaikh Sulman, in 1961. Educated in Bahrain, he became heir apparent in 1958, playing a key role in decision-making from 1959 onwards. Despite social tensions, particularly among Bahrain's majority Shia Muslim population since the Iranian revolution in 1979, Shaikh Issa has remained an essentially pro-Western moderate.

**KHAMENEI, Ayatollah Seyed Ali.** *Iran. Vali faqih* – effectively the spiritual leader. Born in 1940, Khamenei entered politics in the 1960s, founding the Council of Militant Clerics in his home town of Mashad. After the 1979 revolution he helped to establish the Islamic Republican Party and was appointed deputy defence minister. In 1981, following the assassination of President Mohammad Ali Raja'i, he was elected as the republic's third president. After Ayatollah Khomeini's death in June 1989, he emerged as the least controversial – even if not the best qualified – candidate for the supreme leadership, resigning the presidency on **Ali Akbar Hashemi Rafsanjani**'s election. Khamenei's politics are difficult to pin down. Although he has assumed Khomeini's radical mantle, he is working closely with the pragmatic Rafsanjani.

**KHAMTAY SIPHANDONE, General.** *Laos.* Defence minister and commander-in-chief. Born in 1926, Khamtay has been politically active since 1946 and has served as commander of the Lao People's Revolutionary Army since 1961. He was therefore the natural choice to become defence minister after the communist victory in 1975.

**KHAN, Ghulam Ishaq.** *Pakistan.* President. Born in 1915, the veteran Punjabi former civil servant was finance minister for seven years under General Zia ul-Haq, then chaired the Senate (1985–88) and became acting president on Zia's death. He held on to the post in December 1988, when **Benazir Bhutto**'s electorally triumphant Pakistan People's Party was constrained to support him to placate the outgoing military regime. In August 1990 it was he who dismissed her, reflecting army impatience with the noisy and untidy workings of democracy. Afterwards he was accused of orchestrating a self-justifying smear campaign against her administration.

**KHAN, Lieutenant-General Sahabzada Yaqub.** *Pakistan.* Foreign minister. Born in 1920, he rose through the army officers' corps before embarking in 1972 on a career as a diplomat in Paris, Washington, Moscow and then Paris again. He returned to Islamabad in 1982 to join General Zia ul-Haq's government as foreign minister, resigning in 1987 but returning the following year, and retaining the post in a notable concession to the right by **Benazir Bhutto**'s incoming government in December 1988. By now he appeared to have made the foreign ministry his fief; he stayed on to ensure continuity through the turbulent period after Benazir's dismissal in August 1990 and joined the new government formed after the October elections.

**KHAN, Sardar Abdul Qayyum.** *Pakistan.* President of the Pakistani-backed government of Azad Kashmir. Part of the Movement for the Restoration of Democracy under the Zia regime, he was bitterly hostile to **Benazir Bhutto**'s Pakistan People's Party (PPP) government, precipitating a crisis in Azad Kashmir just before she was ousted by refusing to swear in a PPP-led regional government. The Azad Kashmir Muslim Conference, which he leads, aligned itself with the Islamic Democratic Alliance in the successful anti-Bhutto coalition for the October 1990 elections.

**KHAROUI, Hamed.** *Tunisia.* Prime minister. Born in 1928, a doctor by profession and a loyal member of the ruling Constitutional Democratic Rally (RCD), he achieved ministerial rank for the first time in 1986 as youth and sports minister. A spell as justice minister followed before he was appointed prime minister and vice-president of the RCD by President **Zine el-Abidine Ben Ali** in September 1989, replacing Hedi Baccouche who had opposed the government's economic reform programme. His reputation as a moderate led to hopes of renewed dialogue at a time of growing polarization in political life. Kharoui promised to give more attention to unemployment and social issues while continuing with the reform programme.

**KHASBULATOV, Ruslan.** *USSR.* First deputy chairman, Supreme Soviet of Russian Federation. A liberal economist from the

Chechen-Ingush autonomous republic in the north Caucasus, he was the favoured candidate of Russian President **Boris Yeltsin** in the May 1990 election for the post of Yeltsin's deputy. A key reason for the choice of Khasbulatov, a non-Russian, was to provide a counterbalance to the ethnic Russian, Yeltsin, in the most ethnically diverse Soviet republic. Before entering the federation parliament, Khasbulatov headed the foreign economics department at Moscow's Plekhanov Institute and was an advocate of the creation of free economic zones in the Soviet Far East and on the Black Sea coast. He is a firm supporter of private ownership and a market economy, as well as of Russian sovereignty.

**KHAYEYEV, Izatullo.** *USSR.* Former prime minister of Tadjikistan. Born in 1936, he was elected Tadjik premier in January 1986. At the height of nationalist riots in Tadjikistan in February 1990 his government survived an attempted "palace coup" by senior officials allied with nationalist leaders. Khayeyev offered to resign, but this was refused by parliament. In December 1990 he was replaced by **Kakhar Makhkamov.**

**KHAYR, Lieutenant-Colonel Tayib Ibrahim Mohammed.** *Sudan.* Presidential affairs minister. A military doctor, he is a hardline Islamic fundamentalist, nicknamed *al-sikha* (iron bar). He was appointed presidential affairs minister after the June 1989 military coup.

**KHELLEF, Abdelaziz.** *Algeria.* Ambassador to Tunisia. A former finance minister and secretary of state for Maghreb affairs, Khellef was appointed ambassador in Tunis in late 1989 in what was seen as a move to give new momentum to the integration efforts of the Arab Maghreb Union (UMA).

**KHIEU SAMPHAN.** *Cambodia.* Khmer Rouge leader. Born in 1932, the son of a judge, he studied in Paris where his doctoral thesis contained many of the fundamental principles of the Khmer Rouge government's future radical social and economic policy. After a spell in the **Sihanouk** government, he joined the Khmer Rouge guerrillas in 1967 and served as head of state in the Democratic Kampuchea regime. Since its removal from power, he has served as chief Khmer Rouge representative in the resistance coalition headed by Sihanouk.

**KHIN NYUNT, Major-General.** *Myanmar (Burma).* Intelligence chief and political leader. During 1990, he emerged as the most prominent member of the State Law and Order Restoration Council (SLORC), Myanmar's ruling junta.

Officially he holds the post of first secretary, but his authority derives from his control of the powerful, and much feared, Directorate of Defence Services Intelligence. He is thought to enjoy the patronage of **Ne Win,** Myanmar's ageing strongman.

**KHOMEINI, Hojatoleslam Ahmad.** *Iran.* Cleric and younger son of the late Ayatollah Khomeini. Born in the holy city of Qom, south of Tehran, in 1946. Overshadowed by his elder brother Mostafa until the latter's death in 1978, he became active in politics after the 1979 revolution. Relatively moderate, he supported President Abolhassan Bani Sadr during the latter's clash with Islamic hardliners in 1981, and lent his weight to **Ali Akbar Hashemi Rafsanjani** when the latter became president in 1989. However, he has retained close links with the hardliners, and in mid-1990 asked both camps to put aside their differences and work for unity. In November 1989 he was appointed a member of the National Security Council. During his father's lifetime, his power lay in his control of access to Khomeini and his only real legacy is a mandate to interpret his father's pronouncements.

**KHUN SA.** *Myanmar (Burma).* Shan warlord. Born in 1933, of Shan and Chinese parents, he has been branded by US drug enforcement officials as one the world's major drug barons. They claim that he uses a private army to control opium production and heroin refining in the Shan state area of the "Golden Triangle". Khun Sa (also known as Chang Shi Fu), who characterizes himself as a guerrilla leader, fighting for the independence of his native Shan state, has offered to switch from drug dealing to drug suppression in return for US financial aid.

**KIBONA, Stephen.** *Tanzania.* Finance and economic planning minister. An able technocrat with a degree in economics from Dar es Salaam University, he began his civil service career in the education ministry in the late 1960s. He was appointed deputy defence minister in 1983, moving to the finance ministry as minister of state the following year, but returning to his defence post in 1987. He joined the cabinet as communications and works minister in March 1989. A year later he was moved to the finance ministry by President **Ali Hassan Mwinyi** as part of a reshuffle seen as intended to consolidate support for a new, more liberal foreign investment code.

**KIECHLE, Ignaz.** *Germany.* Food, agriculture and forestry minister. Born in 1930 in Bavaria, he is a farmer, who received some training in the USA. First elected to the Bundestag in 1969, he is deputy chairman of the joint Christian Democratic Union/Christian Social Union parliamentary group, and has held his ministerial post since 1983, proving to be a redoubtable champion of Germany's farmers.

**KILFEDDER, James.** *UK.* Northern Irish Unionist politician. Born in 1928 and trained as a lawyer, he was Ulster Unionist MP for Belfast West from 1964–66 and was elected MP for North Down in 1970. Ten years later he set up the Ulster Popular Unionist Party (UPUP), standing slightly to the left of the other Unionist parties on social and economic issues.

**KIM CHONG-IL.** *North Korea.* "Dear Leader". The eldest son of **Kim Il-sung**, he was born in 1942 and from the age of 30 has been groomed as his father's successor, initiating the Three Revolutions Movement (in ideology, technology and culture) despite a reputation as a playboy. In 1980 he became first secretary of the Korean Workers' Party and joined the politburo's presidium and the party's military commission. Even with his power base in the politburo and elevation to first vice-chairman of the National Defence Commission in 1990, his position after Kim Il-sung's death does not look secure.

**KIM DAE JUNG.** *South Korea.* Leader of opposition Party for Peace and Democracy (PPD). Born in 1924, he served in the Korean war before going into politics. He stood against Park Chun Hee in the 1971 presidential elections as the opposition New Democratic Party nominee. An outspoken critic of the government, he was kidnapped from Japan in 1973 and imprisoned for anti-government activities from 1976–78. Following the 1980 Kwangju uprising in his power base of Cholla, he was sentenced to death for plotting to overthrow the military government. International pressure led to the sentence being commuted to life in 1981, and he was released in 1982 in a general amnesty. After medical treatment in the USA, he returned to Seoul in 1985 where he was put under house arrest, his powers of oratory and his popularity undiminished. In 1983, he had issued a joint statement with the leader of the opposition Reunification Democratic Party, **Kim Young Sam**, promising a common struggle for democracy, but in 1987 he stood against him in the presidential elections as head of the PPD, splitting the opposition vote. In 1989 Kim was indicted in connection with the unauthorized

visit of a PPD representative to North Korea in 1988. In 1990 the PPD was excluded from the ruling-opposition party merger, which Kim called a *coup d'état*. Later that year, he offered to relinquish his leading role in the opposition, proposing a merger of the remaining opposition parties under collective leadership.

**KIM IL-SUNG.** *North Korea.* President and "Great Leader". Born in 1912, Kim – according to his official biography – organized the guerrilla resistance against the Japanese in 1932–35. Less flattering accounts say he was a Manchurian bandit leader "planted" by Soviet occupiers in 1945. In any event, he emerged from the Korean War as head of the Democratic People's Republic of Korea. President since 1972, he heads the Korean Workers' Party, the central people's committee and both party and state military commissions, and is supreme commander of the army. The subject of a massive personality cult, he is hailed as the originator of the *Chuche* ideal of socialist self-reliance.

**KIM JONG PIL, Brigadier-General.** *South Korea.* Co-leader of ruling Democratic Liberal Party (DLP). Born in 1926, he supported Park Chung Hee's 1961 coup and was head of the Korean Central Intelligence Agency from 1961–63 and later premier from 1971–75. Head of the opposition Democratic Republican Party from 1963, he resigned in the wake of a corruption scandal in 1980. Barred from politics for eight years, he headed the New Democratic Republican Party from 1987, and stood for the presidency that year. In 1990, he became joint president of the DLP, seeing in the merger with the ruling Democratic Justice Party an opportunity for further political advancement.

**KIM YONG-NAM.** *North Korea.* Vice-premier and foreign minister. Born in 1925, he worked in the Korean Workers' Party central committee's international department in the 1960s and 1970s before becoming vice-premier in 1983 and foreign minister in 1986. A former party secretary, he joined the politburo in 1977 and the parliament's standing committee in 1972.

**KIM YOUNG SAM.** *South Korea.* Co-leader of ruling Democratic Liberal Party (DLP). Born in 1927, he was a key opposition figure during Park Chung Hee's regime and was put under house arrest several times in the 1980s and banned from political activity. In 1985 he helped to set up the reformist New Korean Democratic Party, but left to head the breakaway

Reunification Democratic Party in 1987. He stood as the new party's candidate for the presidency that year, splitting the opposition vote. In 1990 he became executive chairman of the three-member leadership of the merged ruling DLP.

**KIMMITT, Robert.** *USA.* Under-secretary for political affairs in the State Department. He held several posts in **Ronald Reagan**'s administration, including executive secretary to the National Security Council (1983–85) and general counsel of the Treasury Department (1985–87). In 1988 he supervised background checks on prospective Republican vice-presidential candidates, a process that ended with the selection of **Dan Quayle**.

**KING, Bruce.** *USA.* Republican governor of New Mexico. Born in 1924, he was governor of the state from 1971–73, and from 1979–82, and returned to office with his victory in the 1990 election.

**KING, Tom.** *UK.* Defence secretary since 1989. King was born in 1933 and graduated from Cambridge University before going into business. He became an MP in 1970 and held a succession of spokesman posts in opposition, before being made a minister at the Department of the Environment in 1979. He entered the cabinet as secretary of state for the environment in 1983, but moved quickly to transport and then employment. Appointed Northern Ireland secretary in 1985, he skilfully presided over the Anglo-Irish agreement, and in June 1989 was brought back to London as defence secretary. A reputation for bluff common sense will be tested by the need to assess changes in the UK's defence priorities in the wake of German unification and the Gulf crisis.

**KINGIBE, Babagana.** *Nigeria.* Social Democratic Party (SDP) chairman. A northern businessman, he was elected chairman of the SDP, one of the two political parties set up by the government in 1989 to participate in the planned return to civilian rule in 1992, at its first congress in August 1990. The SDP won a narrow majority of local government posts contested in elections in December 1990, on a low turnout.

**KINNOCK, Neil.** *UK.* Leader of the Labour party. Born in 1942, he studied industrial relations and history, graduating with a third class degree from Cardiff University, and taught in the Workers' Educational Association before being elected to parliament (for Bedwellty, since 1983 Islwyn) in 1970. During the 1970s, he

established a reputation as one of the fiercest left-wing critics of the Labour governments of Harold Wilson and **James Callaghan**, and his outspokenness and his Welsh background led many to cast him in the role of another Aneurin Bevan. In 1979 he became opposition spokesman for education. After Labour's heavy defeat in the 1983 election, many in the party feared its right and left wings would break apart altogether: this worried many in the battle to succeed Michael Foot as leader. In the ensuing compromise, Kinnock was elected party leader by an overwhelming margin on the so-called "dream ticket" with **Roy Hattersley** as deputy. His declared aim was to modernize the party to make it electable. This of necessity involved nudging Labour back into the centre-left and making it less class-based. Kinnock has shown himself an adept party manager in this process, jettisoning hallowed but vote-losing policies – unilateralism, nationalization, subservience to the unions – and not shrinking from some ruthless purges of the hard left. The 1987 election was lost, but Labour clearly reasserted itself as the main opposition party. Kinnock is not regarded as one of the party's deepest thinkers, and has been criticized as stronger on rhetoric than substance – his speaking style inclines to the verbose and he has made a poor showing in some key debates in the House of Commons. But his willingness to delegate substantial decision-making powers to colleagues in the shadow cabinet, such as **John Smith** and **Gordon Brown,** has helped to broaden the party's credibility with the electorate. Ironically, however, **Margaret Thatcher**'s demise as leader of the Tories resulted in renewed questioning of Kinnock's suitability as leader.

**KIRKLAND, Lane.** *USA.* American Federation of Labor and Congress of Industrial Organizations (AFL-CIO) president. Elected president of the AFL-CIO in 1979, he has played a major role in shaping union policy since becoming the union confederation's secretary-treasurer in 1969. The son of a cotton buyer, Kirkland was born in 1922, and worked as a merchant navy officer and nautical scientist. After joining the AFL in 1948, he worked toward broadening the scope of union activity to include political issues. His programme as president has been to fight a declining membership and reaffiliate the United Automobile Workers and the Teamsters.

**KIRNER, Joan.** *Australia.* Premier of Victoria. Born in 1939 and an educationist by profession, she entered the state parliament in 1982. Associated with the "Socialist Left" faction of the Victoria state Labor Party, she succeeded to the premiership in August 1990.

**KIS, János.** *Hungary.* Opposition Free Democrat leader. A leading dissident philosopher, Kis, born in 1943, was expelled from the Hungarian Socialist Workers' Party (MSM) in 1973 for his outspoken opposition to János Kádár's regime. His intellectual force, rather than any political skill, made him a spiritual leader of the radical Alliance of Free Democrats (SzDSz) as it emerged in November 1988. During the campaign before the spring 1990 elections, on a television debate he scored points off rival **József Antall**, but came over less convincingly as a future premier, despite his personal affability. Leading the Free Democrats into opposition, and confirmed as party chairman in April 1990, he pressed at once for Hungary to shake off Warsaw Pact ties and to develop its European identity. On the key issue of economic transformation, he represents a social democratic strand in the Free Democrats in the face of pressures from ardent free marketeers.

**KISEKKA, Samson.** *Uganda.* Prime minister. A doctor of medicine, he became the chief spokesman of **Yoweri Museveni**'s National Resistance Movement (NRM) during its campaign to overthrow President Milton Obote. He was appointed prime minister after the NRM took power in January 1986, but was provided with three deputies in the reshuffle of February 1988 because of his poor health.

**KISSINGER, Henry.** *USA.* Foreign policy consultant, author and academic. Born in 1923 to a devout German-Jewish middle-class family which emigrated to New York in 1938, he served in World War II and participated in the military government of occupied Germany. Kissinger received his PhD from Harvard University and became a leading authority on international relations after the publication of his influential *Nuclear Weapons and Foreign Policy* in 1957. He was a Harvard professor before becoming assistant to the president for national security affairs (1967–75) and secretary of state (1973–77) in the administrations of Richard Nixon and Gerald Ford. He was credited with opening relations with China in 1972, and with negotiating the withdrawal of US troops from Vietnam, winning the Nobel peace prize in 1973. He was the main intellectual force behind John Kennedy's policy of "flexible response", and several major policy turnarounds during the Nixon administration. The original shuttle diplomatist, he played a crucial role in preparing the groundwork for the Camp David agreements between Egypt and Israel. Always considered too liberal by the political right, he has stayed on the political periphery since leaving government but has been a more visible participant in the political debate since the election of **George Bush**.

**KITANGAN, Datuk Seri Joseph Pairin.** *Malaysia.* Chief minister of Sabah. Kitangan is a member of the largely Christian Kadazan community, the largest ethnic group in the eastern state of Sabah. He became chief minister in 1985 after his newly-created opposition Sabah United Party (PBS) swept to victory in state elections. The re-election of the PBS for a third term in June 1990 was an endorsement of Kitangan's policy of firmly standing up to the federal government in Kuala Lumpur, reinforced by the PBS's defection to the opposition just before the October 1990 elections.

**KIYONGA, Crispus.** *Uganda.* Finance minister. After standing for parliament in the 1980 elections as a member of **Yoweri Museveni**'s Uganda Patriotic Movement, he joined Museveni in resistance to the Obote government. Appointed co-operatives and marketing minister in the first Museveni government in January 1985, he was made finance minister in November 1986. Diminutive but tough, Kiyonga is one of the most powerful ministers in the government.

**KI-ZERBO, Joseph.** *Burkina Faso.* Politician and academic. Born in 1922 and educated in France, Ki-Zerbo is an internationally respected historian who has been active on the radical left wing of the country's politics for much of its independent history. The leader of a succession of socialist parties and alliances in the 1970s, he stood unsuccessfully as a presidential candidate in 1978, later resigning his parliamentary seat to return to academic life. He resumed political activity as an exile in France in the mid-1980s as secretary-general of the banned Volta Progressive Front (FPV) and a thorn in the side of both the Sankara and **Blaise Compaoré** regimes.

**KJÆRSGAARD, Pia.** *Denmark.* Leader of the Progress Party (FP). Born in 1947, she has worked in an advertising agency and as a home help. She unexpectedly became a member for the right-wing anti-tax and anti-immigration FP in 1984, after the expulsion from the Folketing (parliament) of controversial party leader **Mogens Glistrup**. Within two years she had unseated the increasingly unpredictable Glistrup as leader, and has since re-established FP as the country's main "protest" party, feeding in particular on resentment against an influx of refugees from third world countries but moderating some of its other radical policies.

**KLAUS, Václav.** *Czechoslovakia.* Finance minister. Born in 1941 in Prague, he worked in the economic institute of the Czechoslovak Academy of Sciences during the 1960s, but was dismissed in 1970 during the "normalization" campaign after the Warsaw Pact invasion of 1968. Thereafter he worked at the Czechoslovak State Bank until 1988, when he joined the prognostic institute of the Academy of Sciences. A leading figure in Civic Forum during November 1989, he first became finance minister in the federal government of national accord in December that year, and was re-appointed after the June 1990 elections. Identified with the policy of rapid privatization and liberalization of the economy, he has risked seeming impatient when President **Václav Havel** has expressesd hesitation over the pace of such traumatic change. In October 1990 he was elected by an overwhelming majority as chairman of Civic Forum and is now tipped as a future federal prime minister and possible challenger to Havel as president.

**KNAPP, Jimmy.** *UK.* Trade unionist. Born in 1940, he worked as a railway signalman from 1955 until becoming a full-time divisional officer of the National Union of Railwaymen (NUR) in 1972. Amiable but also a formidable negotiator, he joined the union headquarters in 1981 and became general secretary in 1983.

**KOHL, Helmut.** *Germany.* Chancellor. Kohl will be seen as one of the most influential and underestimated politicians of the postwar generation. A Catholic, born in 1930 in Ludwigshafen, he studied law, politics and history, and became active within the Christian Democratic Union (CDU) at Land (state) level in Rhineland-Palatinate, chairing the party group in the regional parliament from 1963–69 and going on to a seven-year term as premier (1969–76). From this power base he was chosen to succeed Rainer Barzel as CDU federal chairman in 1973, and got his party's nomination as candidate for chancellor, the Christian Social Union (CSU) reluctantly conceding him the right to head the joint CDU/CSU ticket. His defeat in the 1976 election seemed to many to indicate that his hour had passed. But his political tenacity was

such that he was again nominated by the CDU as its candidate for chancellor in 1980. On this occasion, however, he was passed over when it was decided to run a more charismatic (if controversial) ticket headed by CSU leader Franz Josef Strauss. This backfired badly, but Kohl, shrewdly keeping himself at the reins as chairman of the CDU/CSU parliamentary group, became chancellor in 1982, when the Free Democratic Party (FDP) was tempted into switching coalition partners. He then won a convincing election victory early in 1983 and, with a slightly reduced majority, won again in 1987. Not an expert in foreign affairs, Kohl found himself at first having to defer to his FDP deputy chancellor and foreign minister **Hans-Dietrich Genscher,** who continued the policy of reconciliation with the Soviet bloc, including East Germany, as well as pushing for European integration. Kohl was long considered rather dull and accident-prone, and on several occasions he maladroitly offended foreign sensibilities. Unlike his predecessor, Helmut Schmidt, he does not speak English; he takes his holidays in Austria, and seems almost to cultivate his homely image. In opinion poll ratings before 1990 he lagged well behind Genscher, and even trailed several aspiring rivals in his own party as well as the main contenders for national leadership in the opposition Social Democratic Party (SPD). In 1989–90, however, his keen political instincts were revealed as he harnessed national sentiment to the CDU cause, pushing to encourage the rapidly developing momentum that won him election in December 1990 as the first postwar chancellor of a united Germany.

**KOIRALA, Girija Prasad.** *Nepal.* Nepali Congress Party (NCP) general secretary. The latest in the line of family members to hold leading positions in the NCP, he was one of those who advocated the controversial policy of participation in the 1987 non-party local elections. Reverting to the more familiar politics of civil disobedience, he was arrested briefly in December 1989 and again in February 1990, until the success of the "stir" agitations forced **King Birendra** to accept the need for fundamental reforms.

**KOIVISTO, Mauno.** *Finland.* President. Born in 1923, he worked as a teacher and studied sociology and philosophy before being appointed director of the Helsinki Workers' Savings Bank in 1959. Nine years later he was appointed governor of the Bank of Finland, a post he held until 1982 and in which he gained a reputation for calmness, competence and authority. A Social Democrat, he was finance minister from 1966–67 and in 1972, and prime minister in centre–left coalitions in 1968–70 and 1979–82. In 1981 he took over the presidency on an interim basis from the incapacitated Urho Kekkonen. The following year he was elected president – a post with considerable powers, particularly in the formulation of foreign policy and the appointment of prime ministers. Following precedent, he resigned from all party posts. Re-elected in 1988, he has largely continued the foreign policy set by Kekkonen, which rests on neutrality and friendly relations with the USSR. In domestic policy, however, he broke with tradition in 1987 by appointing a conservative prime minister, **Harri Holkeri**, thus effectively marginalizing the long-dominant Centre Party (KP).

**KOK, Wim.** *Netherlands.* Deputy prime minister and finance minister. Leader of the Labour Party (PvdA) since July 1986, he is credited with reshaping the party and persuading it to drop much of the ideological ballast of the 1970s and 1980s, particularly on defence and employment. Born in 1938, the son of a carpenter, he graduated from a prestigious business school and soon afterwards took up his first union job. He quickly rose through the ranks and in 1973 became the youngest-ever chairman of the Dutch Federation of Trade Unions (NVV) at the age of 35. He led the NVV into a merger with the Catholic Federation to form the Federation of Dutch Trade Unions (FNV), which he led until 1985. He proved himself an intelligent and sensible negotiator and a persuasive advocate of agreements negotiated with employers. He was elected to the Staten Generaal (parliament) in 1986, the anointed successor to veteran leader Joop den Uyl, who had unwisely insisted on leading the party into the elections of that year despite strong evidence that Kok's relaxed, business-like manner appealed more to voters. Kok in turn was criticized for a lack of charisma and passion during the 1989 elections, which did not produce the advances the PvdA had hoped for. Even so, coalition negotiations with the Christian Democrats proved relatively straightforward and in November 1989 he became deputy prime minister and finance minister in **Ruud Lubbers**'s third administration.

**KOLBIN, Gennady.** *USSR.* Senior government administrator. A Russian, born in 1927, Kolbin trained as an engineer, but became a full-time Communist Party official after 1959. He came to national prominence when his appointment in December 1986 to head the Communist Party in Kazakhstan, with a brief to clean up the corrupt administration of his sacked predecessor Dinmukhamed Kunayev, provoked nationalist riots in the capital, Alma-Ata. In 1989 he was elected by the USSR Supreme Soviet to chair the USSR People's Control Commission, a nationwide watchdog body intended to combat red tape, inefficiency and bad management.

**KOLINGBA, General André.** *Central African Republic.* President. Formerly armed forces chief of staff, he overthrew President David Dacko in 1981 in a bloodless coup, governing through a military committee for the next four years. He appointed a largely civilian cabinet in 1985 and further moved to legitimize his position with the creation of a new party, the Central African Democratic Rally (RDC) and the introduction of a new constitution in 1986; one-party elections to a new National Assembly followed a year later. Kolingba has won over opponents through the offer of government posts and has shown increasing willingness to tolerate criticism and active debate within the RDC.

**KOLLEK, Teddy.** *Israel.* Mayor of Jerusalem since 1965 and Labour stalwart. Born in Vienna in 1911, he presided over Jerusalem's "unification" in 1967, trying to give Arabs equal rights. He is renowned as a master fund-raiser on behalf of his city, carrying out an energetic campaign to invigorate its artistic and cultural life. An essentially secular man who presides over one of the world's most intensely religious cities, Kollek is well regarded by most Jerusalemites of all faiths, though the Palestinian *intifada* has tested his diplomatic skills to the limit.

**KOLLER, Arnold.** *Switzerland.* Justice and police minister. Born in Appenzell in 1923, he studied law and economics and gained a doctorate from Fribourg University in 1967. He lectured in law at St Gallen University and was appointed director of the European and International Institute there in 1971. A Catholic, he was president of the parliamentary group of the Christian Democratic People's Party (CVP) from 1980–84. Entering the government in 1987 as defence minister, he moved to the justice and police portfolio in 1989, after scandal had forced Elisabeth Kopp to stand down. Koller found himself in an unexpectedly controversial role as protesters took to the streets in March 1990 to denounce "state snooping".

**KOŁODZIEJCZYK, Vice-Admiral Piotr.**
*Poland.* Defence minister. Born in 1939, he was a naval officer before his appointment as defence minister in a July 1990 reshuffle of the Solidarity-led coalition government. Since he had been a member of the former ruling communist Polish United Workers' Party (PZPR), his appointment seemed partly at odds with **Tadeusz Mazowiecki**'s policy of clearing communists from the government, but also demonstrated the communists' previous dominance of the military command.

**KOMOTO, Toshio.** *Japan.* Liberal Democratic Party (LDP) politician and faction leader. Born in 1911 in Hyogo prefecture, he was first elected to the House of Representatives (lower house) in 1949, after he had successfully built up a shipping concern. This company was to provide the financial springboard for a political career which brought him his own faction within the ruling LDP, "inherited" from former prime minister Takeo Miki in 1980 and, on a number of occasions, saw him come close to the coveted presidency of the LDP. In 1989 he expressed his desire for the leadership of the party, but his advanced age, his lack of followers within the party, and the bankruptcy of his company (Sanko Kisen) in 1985 prevented him from making an effective challenge.

**KONAN-BÉDIÉ, Henri.** *Côte d'Ivoire.* National assembly speaker. Born in 1934, an economist by training, Konan-Bédié began his career in the French civil service. He was the first Ivorian ambassador to the USA and the UN from 1960–66, returning home to take up the finance portfolio which he held for 11 years. Since 1980, he has been speaker of the national assembly and thus, under the constitution, president in the event of President **Félix Houphouët-Boigny**'s death. It has been rumoured that the president plans officially to name Konan-Bédié, who is of the same Basulé ethnic group, as his successor. He remains the favourite to take over, although facing increasing competition both from within the ranks of the ruling party and from more radical figures outside it.

**KONDO, Motiji.** *Japan.* Agriculture, forestry and fisheries minister. Born in 1930, he is a veteran politician with a track record of involvement in agricultural affairs; he took up his present post in the December 1990 cabinet reshuffle.

**KOROTICH, Vitaly.** *USSR.* Editor of *Ogonek*, poet and writer. A Ukrainian, born in 1936, he studied medicine and was a practising physician until 1966, when he took over the editorship of the Ukrainian literary review *Radok.* Becoming editor-in-chief of the political review *Ogonek* in 1986, he overhauled the magazine's editorial style. *Ogonek*'s wholehearted embrace of *glasnost* and its radical pro-reform stance attracted readers, leading to a 17-fold increase in circulation to 4.5 million in 1990. As editor, Korotich has waged campaigns against corruption in Central Asia and privilege in the military elite. He was elected to the USSR Congress of People's Deputies in May 1989.

**KOSTIĆ, Branko.** *Yugoslavia.* Former president of Montenegro. Born in 1939 in Rvaši, he joined the communist party in 1957. He held party posts for 30 years before his election as president of the presidency of Montenegro in March 1989. In 1990 he served as chairman of the federal assembly's commission for implementing the Kosovo programme. Kostić failed to secure the party's nomination for the multi-party presidential elections of late 1990; the nominee, Momir Bulatovic, was elected on the second round.

**KOSTIĆ, Jugoslav.** *Yugoslavia.* President of Vojvodina. An ethnic Serb, appointed a member of the presidency of Vojvodina in February 1989, he was elected president in April 1989 and re-elected in December 1989.

**KOUCHNER, Bernard.** *France.* Government minister. Born in 1939, he became a doctor of medicine, founding in 1971 the humanitarian organization Médecins sans Frontières. In 1980, he went on to create Médecins du Monde to aid victims of famine and disaster in the third world. Indefatigably active in this field, notably in Vietnam and Latin America, Kouchner was a notable recruit to **Michel Rocard**'s government as junior minister for humanitarian action in 1988.

**KOZAKIEWICZ, Mikołaj.** *Poland.* Sejm speaker. A leading figure in the official peasant movement under communist rule, he owed his unopposed election as Sejm (parliament) speaker in July 1989 to a parliamentary tradition that the office should go to a deputy from the United Peasants' Party (now the Polish Peasant Party – PSL).

**KOZŁOWSKI, Krzysztof.** *Poland.* Interior minister. A well-known Catholic journalist who was editor of *Tygodnik Powszechny* and a Solidarity member, he was named deputy interior minister in March 1990 in a move indicating the gradual transformation of the police and security service to suit democratic conditions. He was responsible for overseeing the disbanding of the communist secret police and in May 1990 he took charge of a new security service, the office for protection of the state. He replaced the former communist Czesław Kiszczak as minister in a July 1990 cabinet reshuffle that was meant to remove the last representatives of the old order from the government.

**KRAAG, Johan.** *Suriname.* President. A veteran creole politician, Kraag was elected by the National Assembly as president following the December 1990 coup which toppled President Ramsewak Shankar. The limits of his influence were swiftly revealed when he re-appointed **Désiré Bouterse** as army commander-in-chief.

**KRASUCKI, Henri.** *France.* Trade union leader. Born of Polish extraction in 1924, he was naturalized in 1947. Trained as a machinist-fitter, he has been a member of the French Communist Party's central committee since 1956 and of its politburo since 1964. He became secretary-general of the communist-influenced General Confederation of Labour (CGT) in 1982. Faced with a declining membership, he played a key role in formulating the federation's response to industrial modernization and the introduction of new technology, giving these developments a guarded welcome and arguing that they should result in improved conditions and shorter working hours.

**KRAUSE, Günther.** *Germany.* Minister without portfolio. Rising star of the Christian Democratic Union (CDU) and a minister without portfolio in the post-unification cabinet, he was previously right-hand man to **Lothar de Maizière**, and responsible, as state secretary, for the negotiation of the unification treaty. Originally from Halle, he joined the CDU aged 21, in 1974, and went into an academic career in engineering and information science. An articulate and self-confident technocrat, and a reformer by conviction, he became more politically active as a CDU regional chairman with the fall of Erich Honecker's regime, and was elected to the Volkskammer (East German parliament) in March, where he became parliamentary whip before de Maizière picked him as state secretary. After unification he topped the poll in elections for the 10-member presidium of the merged CDU.

**KRAUSS RUSQUE, Enrique.** *Chile.* Interior minister. Born in 1932, Krauss studied law at the University of Chile. He worked for the National Congress until 1965, and was appointed under-secretary in the interior ministry in 1968. He was appointed interior minister in 1990.

**KRAVCHUK, Leonid.** USSR. Ukrainian president. Born in 1934, he was elected to the Ukrainian Communist Party leadership and put in charge of ideology in October 1989, succeeding **Stanislav Gurenko** as party second secretary in June 1990. He relinquished that post one month later when he was elected to replace Volodymyr Ivashko as chairman of the Ukrainian Supreme Soviet (*de facto* president) in a ballot boycotted by the influential nationalist opposition. He maintains a difficult balance between old-guard communists and the advocates of an independent Ukraine.

**KRIANGSAK CHAMANAN, General.** *Thailand.* Army officer and politician. Born in 1917, Kriangsak was a highly influential figure in Thai politics in the 1970s. He participated in two military coups in the mid-1970s and went on to serve as prime minister and supreme commander of the armed forces. He allowed a cautious return to parliamentary politics in 1979 but was replaced as prime minister the following year by Prem Tinsulanonda. With other leading military figures, Kriangsak was arrested for his alleged involvement in the abortive 1985 "Young Turk" coup. He was pardoned by **Chartchai Chunhawan** soon after the latter's appointment as prime minister in 1988.

**KRIEGER, Verena.** *Germany.* Green politician. One of the new generation of environmentalists, she was born in 1961 in Erlangen, and was a student and journalist before her election to the Bundestag as a deputy for The Greens (Die Grünen) in 1987.

**KRISTOL, William.** *USA.* Assistant to the vice-president, domestic policy. The son of Irving Kristol, the prominent conservative columnist, he is widely seen as one of the rising generation of American conservative intellectuals gathered around vice-president **Dan Quayle**, who took him on to his staff in May 1989, at the age of 36. A native of New York city, he holds a PhD in political science from Harvard University. Under **Ronald Reagan**, he was chief of staff and counsellor to secretary of education **William Bennett**.

**KRÓL, Henryk.** *Poland.* Silesian German leader. Born in 1948 and a veterinary surgeon by profession, he heads the Silesian German Minority Cultural Association, which has been galvanized by Poland's new democracy and German reunification into campaigning for the rights of Germans living in the territories ceded to Poland in 1945. Król unsuccessfully contested a February 1990 Senate by-election in Silesia's Opole region on a platform of improved German minority rights.

**KRYUCHKOV, General Vladimir.** *USSR.* KGB chairman. A Russian born in 1924, he started work aged 16 as an industrial labourer in his native Stalingrad (now Volgograd) and in Gorky. After World War II, in 1946, he began work with the Stalingrad prosecutor's office, at the same time taking a correspondence course in law (he graduated in 1949). In 1951 he began training for the diplomatic service, which he entered on graduation in 1954, and served at the embassy in Hungary during the 1956 uprising. The Soviet ambassador in Budapest at the time was Yury Andropov, subsequently KGB chief and ultimately Soviet leader, who remained Kryuchkov's patron throughout his career. Five years later he entered the Communist Party of the Soviet Union (CPSU) central committee apparatus, working under Andropov. By 1965 he had risen to the position of assistant to Andropov, who was central committee secretary with responsibility for the CPSU's relations with ruling communist parties. He joined the KGB in 1967, when Andropov did – progressing through the senior command to become deputy chairman in 1978 and chairman in 1988. In the climate of *glasnost* and democratization, he was responsible for efforts to improve public perceptions of the KGB and to give that much feared organization an image of integrity and accountability; his efforts included throwing open the doors of the KGB's notorious Lubyanka headquarters in Moscow to Soviet television cameras. He was a full member of the CPSU politburo from September 1989 until that body's restructuring (and effective downgrading) in July 1990. **Mikhail Gorbachev** (also an Andropov protégé) named him to the short-lived Presidential Council in March 1990. In December 1990, evidently alarmed at the strength of popular aspirations for national self-determination, especially in the Baltic states, Kryuchkov committed KGB troops to "act as a barrier against those forces which seek to push the country towards chaos".

**KUČAN, Milan.** *Yugoslavia.* President of Slovenia. Born in 1941, he obtained a law degree in 1963. From 1968–69 he was president of the Slovene Socialist Youth League, the communist party's official youth organization. From 1969–73 he served on the organization's

secretariat. From 1973–78 he was secretary of the Socialist Alliance for Slovenia, the party's umbrella organization. His next post was that of president of the Slovene national asssembly from 1978–82. In 1982 he became a member of the central committee of the Slovene party and in 1986 he was elected its president, a post he held until December 1989. During his three years in charge in Slovenia, he played a key role in pushing the party in the direction of social democracy, full political pluralism and the market economy. In April 1990 he defeated Jože Pučnik, candidate of the coalition Democratic Opposition of Slovenia (Demos), for the post of president of Slovenia. There was little indication in the early stages of his career that he would earn the title of Slovenia's **Alexander Dubček**. Kučan favours Slovenia's membership of a loose confederal Yugoslavia rather than outright secession, but the growth of separatist feeling in Slovenia reached the point that 95% voted in an end-1990 referendum in favour of secession unless a new federal structure was agreed with six months.

**KUCZYŃSKI, Waldemar.** *Poland.* Minister in charge of privatization. An economist, he was an adviser to Solidarity in the early 1980s and a deputy editor of the union's newspaper *Tygodnik Solidarność* (then edited by **Tadeusz Mazowiecki**). He spent the mid-1980s in academic work in France. When Mazowiecki became prime minister in 1989 he picked Kuczyński to head his advisory team. In September 1990 he brought him into the government as ownership transformation minister, with the job of pushing through privatization of state monopoly holdings in industry and services.

**KUKRIT PRAMOJ, Mom Rachawongse.** *Thailand.* Elder statesman. Kukrit Pramoj and his brother, Seni Pramoj, are members of a noble family of royal descent and both have played a major role in Thailand's political maturation. Born in 1911, Kukrit served in the legislature for 30 years before becoming prime minister in 1975–76; he was preceded, and followed, in the post by his brother. Kukrit founded the Social Action Party in 1976, resigned the post in 1985, and was re-appointed leader (on an interim basis) in 1990. His access to the leading political players, including **King Bhumibol**, has made him one of the most powerful figures behind the scenes.

**KUNIN, Madeleine.** *USA.* Former Democratic governor of Vermont. Born in Zürich in 1933, she and her family came to the USA as refugees from Nazism. A journalist and state legislator before securing two terms as lieutenant-governor, she then in 1984 became the fourth woman governor ever elected. A liberal who is concerned to balance growth with quality-of-life issues, she did not win in the 1990 gubernatorial elections, however, when her seat went to Republican **Dick Snelling**.

**KUPA, Mihály.** *Hungary.* Finance minister. Born in 1941, he was a professional economist brought into the government of **József Antall** in December 1990 after the departure of his radical predecessor **Ferenc Rabár**. His non-party technocratic credentials as a financial administrator included a distinction of possibly dubious popular appeal, in that he was credited with devising Hungary's (and Eastern Europe's) first income tax system.

**KUPTSOV, Valentin.** *USSR.* Senior Communist Party official. Born in 1936 and an engineer by training, he was a regional Communist Party of the Soviet Union (CPSU) leader in northern Russia before his appointment in April 1990 to head a new central committee department dealing with relations with the emerging political and social organizations. After the July 1990 CPSU congress these responsibilities were upgraded to a full secretariat portfolio.

**KUROKAWA, Takeshi.** *Japan.* Trade union leader. Born in 1928, he worked for Tokyo's subway company from 1946. He led the movement of private railway workers' unions and in 1980 became the chairman of the central executive committee of the Japan General Federation of Private Railway and Bus Workers' Unions (Shitetsu Soren). A popular and influential trade unionist, he became president of the General Council of Trade Unions of Japan (Sohyo) in 1983 and, since its dissolution, he has served as adviser to the Japanese Trade Union Confederation (Rengo), established in November 1989. He has also been president of Shitetsu Soren since 1988.

**KUROŃ, Jacek.** *Poland.* Labour and social policy minister. Born in 1934 in Lvov, he is an historian and publicist. He was a member of the ruling communist Polish United Workers' Party (PZPR) briefly in 1953 and again from 1956–64, when he was jailed for writing a critical open letter to party members. Over the next two decades he spent more than 10 years in prison for dissident activity. In early 1989 he was a member of the Solidarity team in the round-table talks. In September he was included in the Solidarity-led coalition government, his dissident credentials giving him considerable political stature.

**KWAŚNIEWSKI, Aleksander.** *Poland.* Social Democracy of the Polish Republic (SDRP) chairman. Born in 1954, he rose through the official Socialist Youth Union to serve as youth minister from 1985–87, and as head of the government's socio-political committee (with ministerial rank) in 1988–89. He worked pragmatically, advocating co-operation with Solidarity in the 1989 round-table talks, and took over as party chairman when the former ruling communist Polish United Workers' Party (PZPR) was reconstituted as the SDRP in January 1990.

# L

**LABORDA MARTÍN, Juan José.** *Spain.*
Senate president. Born in 1947 in Bilbao, he
joined the Spanish Socialist Workers' Party
(PSOE) in 1975, was elected a senator for Burgos
in 1977 and served on various Senate
committees. He became Senate president in
1989.

**LACALLE HERRERA, Luis Alberto.** *Uruguay.*
President. Born in 1941, Lacalle Herrera was
first elected a representative in 1972. On the
return to democratic rule in 1984 he became a
senator for the ruling National Party (Blancos)
and, representing the party's right wing, won
the 1989 presidential election. He promised
consensus politics to heal the wounds within
Uruguayan society and deal with the economy.

**LACAYO, Antonio.** *Nicaragua.* Minister of the
presidency. Born in 1947 and educated at MIT
in the USA, he is married to President **Violeta
Chamorro**'s daughter Cristiana. A businessman
with no previous political experience, Lacayo was
general manager of Grasas y Aceites, and helped
to run his mother-in-law's election campaign. As
a close adviser, he was appointed to the
important post of minister of the presidency
following Chamorro's victory in 1990.

**LACHMON, Jaggernath.** *Suriname.* Politician.
The elder statesman of Surinamese politics,
Lachmon was born in 1916 of parents of Asian
descent and he trained as a lawyer. He first
entered De Staten (parliament) in 1949 as leader
of the United Hindustani Party (later the
Progressive Reform Party – VHP), which he
founded to represent the Asian-descended
population. During the 1950s and 1960s he co-
operated with the National Party of Suriname
(NPS) in an inter-ethnic coalition, but until the
last minute opposed moves towards
independence in the 1970s. He joined the
negotiations for a return to civilian rule in 1987
and helped to form the Front for Democracy and
Development (FDO), which overwhelmingly
won the 1987 elections. He was then chosen as
the new assembly's chairman, a post swept away
in the December 1990 coup.

**LACINA, Ferdinand.** *Austria.* Finance
minister. Born in Vienna in 1942, he graduated
in commerce in 1965, and by 1973 had become
head of economic research in the Vienna
chamber of labour. A member of the Socialist
Party of Austria (SPÖ), he was appointed in
1978 to head the financial planning department
of the holding company of Austria's nationalized
industries. Chancellor Bruno Kreisky brought
the cool technocrat into government in 1980 as
cabinet secretary with special reference to
economic policy. In 1982 he became state
secretary responsible for development aid,
international technological co-operation and
OECD affairs; two years later he was appointed
transport minister, adding to this in 1985
responsibility for the public sector. In 1986 he
took over the finance portfolio.

**LAFONTAINE, Oskar.** *Germany.* Social
Democratic Party (SPD) politician. Born in 1943
in Saarlouis, his political base has always been
the Saarland, where he was mayor of Saarbrücken
for nine years before becoming Land (state)
premier in 1985. His track record there has
enabled him to claim success in defeating the
entrenched Christian Democrats, while keeping
the Greens at bay (in part by his willingness to
steal their environmentalist clothes). Colourful
and robust, he was chosen ahead of duller rivals
to head the SPD ticket for chancellor in 1990.
His selection suggested that the party saw the
need to win younger voters to an anti-nuclear,
environment-friendly "red-green" standard. As
the prospect of German unity came increasingly
to dominate all else on the political scene,
however, Lafontaine attracted controversy as well
as support by warning against over-hasty
commitments, and emphasizing the cost to West
Germany would pick up. His warnings were
almost silenced when a woman stabbed and
seriously wounded him at a political meeting in
April 1990, but he recovered to regain the
momentum of his campaign. After the election
defeat in December he declined the party
leadership, preferring to return to the Saarland.

**LAGOS ESCOBAR, Ricardo.** *Chile.* Education minister. Born in 1938, Lagos studied law at the University of Chile and economics at Duke University, USA. He was secretary-general of the University of Chile and supported the Salvador Allende government. He became actively involved in opposition to the military regime and was a member of the Democratic Alliance (AD), becoming its president in 1984. In 1987 he formed his own centrist party, the Party for Democracy (PPD), which joined the opposition coalition, gaining one cabinet post in **Patricio Aylwin**'s government in 1990.

**LAGUILLER, Arlette.** *France.* Trotskyist leader. Born in 1940 and a public-sector employee, she is a veteran of French presidential election contests (1974, 1981, 1988) and leading voice in the Trotskyist Workers' Struggle (LO) movement. A somewhat untypical member of the Workers' Strength trade union, in the 1988 presidential election she polled nearly 2% of the vote, while criticizing fellow Trotskyists who backed **Pierre Juquin**.

**LAHAD, Major-General Antoine.** *Lebanon.* Commander of the South Lebanon Army. A regular army officer, Lahad is a Maronite Christian and former follower of Camille Chamoun's National Liberal Party. He rose to be army commander of the Mountain region until his retirement in 1983. The following year, he took over command of the "Haddad militia", an unofficial Israeli-backed Christian unit formed by its eponymous leader in 1978, which effectively controls part of southern Lebanon. On Lahad's appointment, the militia was reorganized as the semi-official "South Lebanon Army". It is involved in frequent clashes with Hezbollah fighters, and has been accused of numerous atrocities against Shia villages.

**LAHAT, Shlomo.** *Israel.* Mayor of Tel Aviv since 1974. Born in 1927, he is Likud's counterpart to **Teddy Kollek** in Jerusalem. A populist, he has pushed through projects for museums, an opera house and beach development. He has a reputation as an energetic maverick, favouring the legalization of prostitution and, even more controversially for a Likud member, Israel's withdrawal from the occupied territories. The contrast between his brusque, direct approach, and Kollek's caution and urbanity, is often seen as a reflection of the differences between their two cities.

**LAHUD, General Emile.** *Lebanon.* Army commander. A Christian and a career army officer, Lahud was appointed commander in

November 1989 when President **Elias Hrawi** formally dismissed General Michel Aoun from the post. Lahud's mandate was to replace Aoun's "mutinous" army forces with his own united army command.

**LAIGNEL, André.** *France.* Government minister. Born in 1942 and a graduate in law and politics, he became a teacher of constitutional law in 1971. In the 1970s he emerged at level within the Socialist Party (PS), becoming a mayor and local councillor, and was first elected to the National Assembly in 1981. In 1988 he was appointed junior minister for vocational training. Identified as a strong supporter of **François Mitterrand**, he is considered a likely candidate for higher office.

**LAÍNO, Domingo.** *Paraguay.* Opposition leader. President of the Liberal Radical Party in the 1970s, he led a breakaway faction in 1977 to form the Authentic Liberal Radical Party (PLRA). He was deported in 1982, but returned in 1987 and although harrassed by the authorities he continued to oppose Alfredo Stroessner's regime. He unsuccessfully contested the presidential elections in May 1989, and questioned the legitimacy of **Andrés Rodríguez**'s victory.

**LAIRD, Gavin.** *UK.* Trade unionist. Born in 1933, he worked for the Singer company for many years before becoming a full-time official of (what is now) the Amalgamated Engineering Union (AEU). Its general secretary since 1982, he has been an articulate spokesman for the union's controversial "new-realist" policies.

**LAJOINIE, André.** *France.* Communist politician. Born in 1929 into a poor farming family, he joined the Communist Party (PCF) in 1948 and became party agricultural specialist. A politburo member since 1976 and a deputy in the National Assembly since 1978, he is head of the PCF group in the assembly and ran as the party's candidate in the 1988 presidential elections, but polled only 6.8%. Orthodox and loyal, he is seen as a potential caretaker successor to long-term party leader **Georges Marchais**.

**LAL, Devi.** *India.* Deputy prime minister, agriculture and tourism minister. Born in 1914 in the Chautala District of Haryana, he was a prominent political leader of the North Indian Jat peasant caste, and was elected to the state assembly in Punjab (which then included Haryana) as a Congress member in 1952. He became a supporter of Jat political leader Charan Singh and his Lok Dal party, serving as chief minister of Haryana in 1977–79 and again in

1987–89. After the Lok Dal split in 1987, Lal supported the wing of the party led by H.N. Bahugna, the Lok Dal (B). However, the following year he opposed Bahuguna to bring about the fusion of Lok Dal (B) with Janata Dal. He was elected to the Lok Sabha for the Janata Dal in November 1989, and was named deputy prime minister and agriculture minister in the National Front government. Lal proved to be an awkward member of the government, frequently expressing views at variance with those of his colleagues. His efforts to ensure the succession of his son, Om Prakash Chauthala, as Haryana chief minister caused a crisis in Janata Dal, which at one point threatened to bring down the government. After attacking the then prime minister **V.P. Singh** and accusing cabinet colleagues of corruption he was dismissed in March 1990, but went on to join the minority government formed by **Chandra Shekhar** in November.

**LALONDE, Brice**. *France*. Government minister and environmental campaigner. Born in 1946, he was a student leader at the Sorbonne in the 1960s and worked as a journalist. Initially the left-wing of the Unified Socialist party (PSU), he became an environmentalist. He rose to prominence in the 1970s as a successful leader of French Friends of the Earth, mounting a fringe campaign for the presidency in 1981, backed by environmentalists who supported his political stand. Subsequently at odds over tactics with fellow-ecologists, he maintained a high public profile, and his appointment in 1988, as junior minister for the environment, was something of a coup for **Michel Rocard**'s government – although it laid him open to attacks by colleagues who saw his acceptance of office as a sell-out. He created the Ecology Generation movement, and was promoted to the rank of minister-delegate in 1990.

**LA MALFA, Giorgio**. *Italy*. Italian Republican Party (PRI) leader. Born in 1939 in Milan, he graduated in law and political economy at Pavia University and also gained a degree in economics at Cambridge University, UK. He has taught at various Italian universities, and entered the Chamber of Deputies in 1972. He was budget minister in **Francesco Cossiga**'s second government, formed in April 1980, and he kept the post in **Amaldo Forlani**'s and **Giovanni Spadolini**'s governments which followed. When Spadolini became president of the Senate, La Malfa was elected unopposed to succeed him as party leader in September 1987. He is the son of long-serving PRI leader Ugo La Malfa, but has not won the wide public respect his father enjoyed.

**LAMASSOURE, Alain**. *France*. Right-wing politician. Born in 1944, he studied at the Institut d'Etudes Politiques and the Ecole Nationale d'Administration, then held public service jobs, notably at the Court of Accounts. He also acted as a technical adviser to **Valéry Giscard d'Estaing** in the 1970s. He was elected to parliament for the Union for French Democracy–Republican Party (UDF–PR) in 1986, and won a seat in the European Parliament in 1989 on Giscard's list. A highly intelligent and articulate UDF official spokesman and delegate-general of the Giscardian think-tank, Perspectives and Realities, Lamassoure supports Giscard's efforts to regain leadership of the French right.

**LAMBSDORFF, Otto**. *Germany*. Free Democratic Party (FDP) chairman. A leading FDP figure, the aristocratic Graf Lambsdorff saw his high-profile career come unstuck in 1984, when he was forced to resign as economics minister over the "Flick" political pay-offs affair. A Bonn court in 1986 dropped the main charge against him: that he was bribed to give tax concessions while a minister. However, he was found guilty and fined for having aided tax evasion by the FDP, when he had a local party job. Born in Aachen in 1926, he lost a leg in World War II but overcame this handicap with courage and skill. He studied law and politics at Bonn and Cologne universities, and built a successful career from 1955–71 in the credit and insurance business. A staunch free-market liberal, he was first elected to the Bundestag in 1972 and became a member of the FDP executive the same year. For 10 years (1968–78) he acted as treasurer for the FDP in North Rhine-Westphalia. As economics minister from 1977 in the SPD-led coalition government, he nonetheless remained a staunch critic of the political left and was one of the prime movers in the FDP's controversial decision in 1982 to change coalition partners and go into a government led by the Christian Democrats. Since his departure from government in 1984 he has remained prominent in the FDP, making a dramatic return to active politics in October 1988, when he was elected FDP chairman, in succession to **Martin Bangemann**, defeating **Irmgard Adam-Schwätzer**. He went on to play a major role in bringing together the liberals in both parts of Germany in 1989–90 and was overwhelmingly elected to chair the merged party in August 1990.

**LAMONT, Norman.** *UK.* Chancellor of the exchequer. Born in 1942 and educated at Cambridge University, Lamont was elected to parliament in 1972. He spent many years as a junior minister, becoming chief secretary to the Treasury in 1989. Respected for his cautious diplomacy, he is nonetheless ambitious. In 1990 he masterminded **John Major**'s leadership campaign and was rewarded with promotion to the new prime minister's old job.

**LANDSBERGIS, Vytautas.** *USSR.* Lithuanian supreme council chairman (*de facto* president) and nationalist leader. Born in 1932, Landsbergis pursued a career as a music professor, specializing in Lithuanian music. He became actively involved in politics in 1988, when the founding congress of the nationalist Popular Front (Sajudis) elected him chairman of its ruling council. After Sajudis-backed candidates scored a landslide victory in early 1990 elections, Lithuania's parliament elected Landsbergis as president. In the dispute with the Soviet authorities over Lithuania's March 1990 unilateral declaration of independence he has shown reluctance to compromise, leading to conflict with his more pragmatic prime minister, **Kazimiera Prunskiene.**

**LANE, Lord (Geoffrey Lane).** *UK.* Lawyer and judge. Born in 1918, he practised as a barrister until appointed a high court judge in 1966, an appeal court judge in 1974 and lord chief justice in 1980. Among the more controversial cases he has heard in recent years was the appeal of the "Birmingham Six", which he and two other judges dismissed in January 1987. He was knighted in 1966 and made a life peer in 1979. Keen on preserving the independence of the judiciary, he is less interested in sentencing reform, and holds strong views on what he regards as the deterioration of the moral fabric of society.

**LANG, Ian.** *UK.* Secretary of state for Scotland. Born in 1940, he was educated at Cambridge University, and entered parliament in 1979. He served briefly as a junior employment minister before taking on responsibility for Scottish industry and education in 1986. He was promoted to secretary of state in place of **Malcolm Rifkind** in **John Major**'s first cabinet in November 1990. He is a firm opponent of Scottish self-government.

**LANG, Jack.** *France.* Culture minister. Born in 1939 and a graduate in politics from the Institut d'Etudes Politiques, his career has revolved around theatre, culture, education and politics, initially in Nancy and later in Paris. A member of the Socialist Party (PS), he has been a local councillor in Paris since 1977, culture minister from 1981–86 and again since 1988, and a member of the National Assembly since 1986. A popular figure nationally, and a close friend of **François Mitterrand**, he dominated French public policy on cultural provision in the 1980s, helping to make such issues feature prominently, albeit controversially – especially as regards new plans in Paris – on the political platform of the PS.

**ŁAPICKI, Andrzej.** *Poland.* Solidarity activist. A leading actor and director, born in Riga (Latvia) in 1924, he was dismissed from the Polish actors' union in 1981 for supporting Solidarity. He was elected as a Solidarity deputy to the Sejm (parliament) in June 1989, and named as chairman of its committee for culture and mass media.

**LAPTEV, Ivan.** *USSR.* Soviet of the Union chairman. A journalist, born in 1936, he was formerly deputy editor of *Pravda* (1982–84) and editor-in-chief of the government newspaper *Izvestia* (1984–90). The latter became a champion of liberal reform policies under his editorship. In April 1990 Laptev replaced **Yevgeny Primakov** as chairman (speaker) of the Soviet of the Union, one of the two USSR Supreme Soviet chambers.

**LARAKI, Azzedine.** *Morocco.* Prime minister. Born in 1929 in Fez, he qualified as a doctor of medicine in Paris and remained in medical practice and teaching until his appointment as national education minister in 1977. He was appointed prime minister in September 1986 on the retirement of Karim Lamrani.

**LAROUCHE, Lyndon, Jr.** *USA.* Economist and politician. Born in 1922 in New York, LaRouche began his political career in 1968 as a Marxist, slowly moving towards the centre and then to the extreme right. His views encompass many forms of militant jingoism and conspiracy theory: anti-Soviet, anti-Zionist, and anti-gay. He collected a small but loyal support base, and ran for president between 1976 and 1988. In 1989, he and six associates were convicted of fraud and conspiracy involving $34m solicited by his organization, the national Democratic policy committee.

**LARSSON, Allan.** *Sweden.* Finance minister. Born in 1938, he has worked as a journalist, trade union official and as head of the influential

Labour-Market Board, where he earned the respect of both business and unions. A man with a low public profile, he was made finance minister in 1990 after the resignation of Kjell-Olof Feldt.

**LAUREL, Salvador Hidalgo (Doy).** *Philippines.* Vice-president and Nacionalista Party leader. Born in 1928 and educated at Yale University, he was a professor of law in the Philippines before entering politics during Ferdinand Marcos's regime, initially as a Liberal Party activist and subsequently as leader of the eight-party United Democratic Opposition (Unido – a largely conservative grouping.) Although of a more traditional political persuasion than **Cory Aquino**, he agreed to be her vice-presidential running mate in the 1986 "snap" election which prompted the downfall of Marcos. Appointed foreign secretary after Aquino's victory, he soon differed with her over peace talks with the communist New People's Army, to which he was implacably opposed. He resigned from the government in August 1988, complaining that Aquino had reneged on a promise to allow him to appoint one-third of the government. Although he retains the elected post of vice-president, he has gradually moved closer to other disaffected figures, such as **Juan Ponce Enrile**, and is widely seen as offering at least tacit support to anti-government sections of the military.

**LAURIEN, Hanna-Renate.** *Germany.* Christian Democratic Union (CDU) politician. She was a senator in charge of education in West Berlin from 1981–89, and held the rank of deputy mayor. Born in Danzig in 1928, she studied languages in Berlin, gained her doctorate in 1951, and embarked on a career in the school service and later in politics. She was state secretary for culture in the Rhineland-Palatinate from 1971–76, and minister there from 1976–81. She has also held posts in the CDU.

**LAURISTIN, Marju.** *USSR.* Estonian nationalist leader, deputy speaker of the Estonian supreme council. Born in 1940, the daughter of a prominent Estonian communist, she heads the journalism department at Tartu State University and is a leader of the Estonian Popular Front, formed in 1988. A champion of Estonia's independence, and widely respected for her moderate views, she left the Estonian Communist Party at the end of 1989 to chair the interim board of a new Estonian Social Democratic Party. After the Popular Front's March 1990 victory in the Estonian

parliamentary elections she was named deputy parliamentary speaker.

**LAVEROV, Nikolai.** *USSR.* Deputy prime minister. Born in 1929. A geologist and vice-president of the USSR Academy of Sciences, he was appointed in July 1989 as one of the 10 USSR deputy premiers and chairman of the State Committee for Science and Technology.

**LAWRENCE, Carmen.** *Australia.* Premier of Western Australia. Born in 1948 and a psychologist by profession, she became Labor state premier in February 1990 (the first woman to hold a state premiership). She has attracted particular attention because one of her fiercest political opponents is her brother, an anti-corruption campaigner concerned to probe the cosy relationship between the Labor state government and the buccaneering entrepreneurs who held the Western Australian financial stage in the 1980s.

**LAWSON, Nigel.** *UK.* Conservative politician and journalist. Born in 1932, he studied philosophy, politics and economics at Oxford University and then worked as a journalist for a number of newspapers and magazines, including the *Financial Times* and *The Spectator* (of which he was editor from 1966–70). Elected to parliament in 1974, he was made a junior Treasury minister in 1979 and energy minister in 1981. In 1983 he became chancellor of the exchequer, and presided over the economic boom of the mid-1980s. Strong-willed and intellectually self-confident, he found himself increasingly at odds with **Margaret Thatcher** over her refusal to let him take the pound into the EC Exchange Rate Mechanism (ERM) and her continued reliance on the advice of **Sir Alan Walters**, whose attitudes towards ERM in particular conflicted with Lawson's. Thatcher's failure to repudiate Walters provoked Lawson's resignation in 1989. He quickly accumulated a number of well-paid directorships and in 1990 announced that he would not stand at the next election.

**LE DUC ANH, General.** *Vietnam.* Defence minister and politburo member. He was the architect of Vietnam's successful invasion of Cambodia in late 1978. As a member of the politburo's "military" faction, he is reputed to have had misgivings about Vietnam's military withdrawal from Cambodia.

**LE QUANG DAO.** *Vietnam.* Chairman of the National Assembly. Born in 1921, He spent most of his career in the army's General Political Department. First elected a full member of the Communist Party central committee in 1972, he replaced Nguyen Huu Tho as chairman of the National Assembly in June 1987.

**LEACH, James (Jim).** *USA.* Republican congressman from Nebraska. Born in 1942, he was a foreign service officer and was elected to the House of Representatives in 1976. Personally and politically close to **George Bush**, he founded the Republican Mainstream Committee to counter the party's Reaganite image. An early critic of standards of probity in the savings and loan sector, he helped to toughen the legislation that sanctioned its bail-out. An expert on international debt issues, he is sympathetic to third-world needs.

**LEE, Allen.** *Hong Kong.* Politician and businessman. Born in 1940, he is a member of the Legislative Council and sits as an industrial nominee on the policy-making Executive Council. He is associated with the conservative business grouping, the Hong Kong Foundation.

**LEE, Martin (Chu-ming).** *Hong Kong.* Radical politician and lawyer. Born in 1938, he became a QC in 1979 and was elected to the Legislative Council in 1985. He served on the joint Chinese-Hong Kong basic law drafting committee until his suspension in November 1989 for pro-democracy activities: he is vice-chairman of the Hong Kong Alliance in Support of the Patriotic Democratic Movement in China. In 1990, Lee founded a liberal political party, the United Democrats of Hong Kong, to campaign for greater democracy. He has condemned the basic law, and accused the British government of appeasement in negotiations with China.

**LEE HSIEN LOONG, Brigadier-General (reserves).** *Singapore.* Deputy prime minister, industry and trade minister. Born in 1952, the son of **Lee Kuan Yew.** After gaining a degree at Cambridge he served in the Singapore Armed Services and rose to second in command before resigning in 1984 to enter parliament. He was appointed to the cabinet in 1985 and it was widely believed that he would be the country's next prime minister. However, his father announced in the late 1980s that he would prefer a "non-Lee" successor to avoid any suggestion of nepotism; in November 1990 he was appointed one of the two deputies to the new prime minister, **Goh Chok Tong.**

**LEE HUAN.** *Taiwan.* Former prime minister. Born in 1917 on the Chinese mainland, Lee did youth work before becoming education minister in 1984. As secretary-general of the ruling Kuomintang's (KMT's) central standing committee from 1987–89, the reformist Lee set about the "Taiwanization" of the KMT by bringing his protégés into the party. In 1989 he replaced Yu Kuo-hua, an unpopular ally of the former ruling Chiang family, as premier, and was at one time considered a challenger to President **Lee Teng-hui**, but was replaced a year later by **Hau Pei-tsun.**

**LEE KUAN YEW.** *Singapore.* Senior minister. Born in Singapore in 1923, he took a law degree at Cambridge before being called to the English Bar in 1950. He helped to found the People's Action Party in 1954 and five years later became Singapore's first prime minister. He was re-elected to the post seven times, most recently in 1988. Under Lee's firm, and his critics would say ruthless, leadership, Singapore was transformed from a tiny colonial outpost into one of the world's major economic success stories. In November 1990 Lee handed over to his deputy **Gok Chok Tong**, but he remains in the cabinet as senior minister and few doubt that he will continue to wield considerable influence.

**LEE SANG OCK.** *South Korea.* Foreign minister. Appointed in the December 1990 reshuffle, he replaced **Choi Ho Joong**, who moved to the new post of national unification. Lee's priorities would include relations with the USA and other Pacific Rim states. A career diplomat, he has no previous cabinet experience.

**LEE TENG-HUI.** *Taiwan.* President. Born in 1923, Lee is the first native-born president. Trained in rural economics, he was mayor of Taipei in 1978–81, and subsequently governor of Taiwan province. Vice-president from 1984, he became president in January 1988 after the death of Chiang Ching-kuo, as his chosen successor. He was overwhelmingly re-elected for a six-year term by the National Assembly in 1990. A Kuomintang reformist, Lee has made progress in political democratization. He has advocated "flexible diplomacy" in dealing with mainland China, and lifted restrictions on visits and trade.

**LEGUINA HERRÁN, Joaquín.** *Spain.* Madrid region premier. Born in 1941 in Santander, he joined the Spanish Socialist Workers' Party (PSOE) in 1977 from Socialist Convergence, and became the Socialist premier of the Madrid regional government in 1983. He was one of the few leading PSOE figures to remain on good terms with the Socialist General Workers' Union (UGT) during the late 1980s crisis in relations with the government over economic policy. In 1990 he became the figurehead for those urging greater internal democracy in the PSOE.

**LEHMAN, Ronald Frank, II**. *USA*. Assistant secretary, defence department. He was born in Napa, California in 1946 and was educated at Claremont Men's College in Southern California. He has worked in the National Security Council and the Pentagon since 1978. A specialist in arms control, he has been one of the senior negotiators on long-range arms reduction in the administrations of both **Ronald Reagan** and **George Bush**.

**LEHR, Ursula-Maria**. *Germany*. Youth, family, women and health minister. Born in 1930 and an academic psychologist, Lehr was director of Heidelberg University's Institute of Ageing, and was appointed to her present position in 1989.

**LEIGH-PEMBERTON, Robin**. *UK*. Governor of the Bank of England. Born in 1927 into a wealthy land-owning family, he trained and practised as a barrister until 1960 before moving into the corporate, insurance and, finally, banking sectors, becoming chairman of National Westminster Bank (one of the big four commercial banks) in 1977. Appointed governor of the Bank of England in 1983, he has on the whole been a loyal – some would say over-compliant – supporter of the Conservative government's financial policies. But many of those who were at first sceptical of his technical knowledge and expertise recanted when he was appointed for a second term of office in 1988. He has also emerged as a more independent figure through his public support for economic and monetary union within the EC.

**LEKHANYA, Major-General Justin Metsing**. *Lesotho*. Chairman of the military council. Head of the armed forces and leader of the January 1986 military coup that overthrew the prime minister, Chief Leabua Jonathan, Lekhanya holds several key portfolios. These include defence, internal security and agriculture, and his position as military council chairman makes him the country's *de facto* leader. The coup was precipitated by Jonathan's moves towards the Eastern bloc and increasingly strained relations with South Africa. Lekhanya has since reversed this policy, in particular moving Lesotho back into the South African sphere of influence. Following growing divisions within the military council and donor pressure to counter the country's deteriorating economic position, he announced major political and economic reform programmes in February 1990, instituted a major cabinet reshuffle, and suggested that **King Moshoeshoe** should take a "sabbatical" in exile.

In November 1990 he engineered the replacement of Moshoeshoe by the king's eldest son, **Letsie**. An assembly has been set up to draft a new constitution for a return to democratic rule by 1992.

**LEKOTA, Patrick "Terror"**. *South Africa*. United Democractic Front (UDF) leader. A former supporter of Black Consciousness who has switched to backing the non-racial African National Congress (ANC) charter stance, he was publicity secretary of the UDF before his arrest and eventual conviction, with **Popo Molefe** and others, in the marathon Delmas treason trial (1986–88). His release in December 1989 with Molefe and Murphy Morobe was a sign of changing government policy. Irrepressibly energetic and politically skilled, he is expected to win a place on the ANC's national executive. He has latterly distinguished himself in calming the conflict with Inkatha as the ANC's convener in Natal, and has since been transferred to the Orange Free State.

**LENIHAN, Brian**. *Ireland*. Former deputy prime minister. Born in 1930, he was a barrister until his election to parliament for Fianna Fáil in 1961. He has held the portfolios of justice, education, transport and power, foreign affairs, forestry and fisheries, agriculture and defence, and is one of the most experienced of Irish politicians; he was also deputy prime minister under **Charles Haughey** from 1987–90. In 1990 he was chosen by his party as its candidate for the state presidency and was widely expected to win. However, he became embroiled in a political controversy concerning alleged requests for political favours from the then president several years earlier. Although he strongly denied the charges, he was dismissed from both his ministerial posts a few days before the presidential election, which he lost to **Mary Robinson**.

**LÉOTARD, François**. *France*. Right-wing politician. Born in 1942, he was educated at the Institut d'Etudes Politiques and at the Ecole Nationale d'Administration. His early career was in the civil service, in the foreign affairs and urban planning ministries, and then in local government with the rank of sub-prefect. He was elected mayor of Fréjus in 1977 and entered the National Assembly the following year. From 1982–90 he was secretary-general of the Republican Party (PR), and served under **Jacques Chirac** as culture and communication minister (1986–88), emerging as a potential power-broker in the jockeying for position on the political right. Impatient of the "old guard" leadership and something of a showman, Léotard nurtures his own ambitions for high office.

**LE PEN, Jean-Marie.** *France.* National Front leader. Born in 1928 and a law graduate, he became France's youngest parliamentary deputy when he was returned as a follower of the right-wing populist Pierre Poujade in 1956. As politician and former paratrooper, he identified strongly with French settlers in Algeria, and with resentment over Charles de Gaulle's "betrayal" of their cause. Since 1972 he has been president of the extreme right-wing National Front (FN), raising it from the obscurity of the early 1970s to the point where it was impossible to ignore. Le Pen has a platform in the European Parliament, of which he has been a member since 1984, and between 1986 and 1988 he led a substantial FN contingent in the National Assembly, only to see it wiped out after the abolition of proportional representation. The elimination of the FN from parliament made it easier to treat Le Pen as a political pariah, but his defiant campaign in the 1988 presidential election marked his high point to date. His endorsement by 4m voters attracted worldwide attention and provided the basis for the continuing assertiveness of his political stance. Notably on the immigration issue, his violent, simplistic oratory stirs the passions of supporters and opponents alike.

**LE PENSEC, Louis.** *France.* Overseas departments and territories minister. Born in 1937 and a graduate in social sciences and company administration, he worked initially as a manager at Renault before, in the 1970s, turning to a university career as a lecturer in personnel management. Since 1971, he has been a successful candidate for the Socialist Party (PS) as a deputy, mayor and general councillor, becoming minister for the sea in 1981–83 and again, briefly, in 1988. Since June 1988, he has been overseas departments and territories minister, and official government spokesman since 1989.

**LESTOR, Joan.** *UK.* Labour politician. Born in 1931, she studied sociology, worked as a nursery school teacher from 1959–66 and became active in various organizations concerned with children's welfare. Elected to parliament (for Eton and Slough) in 1966, she held a series of junior ministerial posts from 1969 until she resigned from the government over spending cuts in 1976. She lost her seat in 1983, but was re-elected (for Eccles) in 1987. One of Labour's

old-guard left-wingers, she was often at odds with the party's new-style centrist politics under the leadership of **Neil Kinnock** and she lost her seat on the party's national executive in 1990.

**LETSIE III (Mohato Bereng Seeisa).** *Lesotho.* King. The eldest son of **King Moshoeshoe**, he was sworn in as Lesotho's new king in November 1990, at the age of 27, after the ruling military council, headed by Major-General **Justin Lekhanya**, had deposed his exiled father.

**LEVI, David.** *Israel.* Foreign minister, deputy prime minister and leading Sephardic (oriental Jewish) politician. Levi was 19 when he left his native Morocco for Israel in 1957. A construction worker by trade, he led the Likud grouping in the Histadrut labour federation. He entered the Knesset (parliament) as a Herut member in 1969, and joined the cabinet as absorption (of new immigrants) minister in the first Likud government of 1977. Despite teasing by political sophisticates of all hues for his humble origins and alleged lack of intellect, Levi became deputy prime minister under **Yitzhak Shamir** from 1981–84. A nationalist and affable champion of the *sephardim* and working class, he was the only minister to fight Likud's austerity measures in 1979. He was also the only Likud member of the inner cabinet to support withdrawal from Lebanon in 1984. In 1989 he, **Ariel Sharon** and **Yitzhak Moda'i** forced Shamir to toughen up his Palestinian elections plan, a course of action which eventually drove Labour from the government in March 1990. With little English and limited overseas experience, Levi seemed to many a poor choice as foreign minister in June 1990. Soon after he suffered a mild heart attack, but if his health permits this wily operator has every chance of remaining at the forefront of Israeli politics.

**LEVINE, Mel.** *USA.* Democratic congressman from California. Born in 1943, he was a lawyer and state assemblyman before being elected to the House of Representatives in 1982. A strongly pro-Israel member of the Middle East subcommittee, in 1989 he advocated US sanctions against foreign companies selling chemical weapons to Iran, Iraq, Libya and Syria. Co-founder of Rebuilding America, a think-tank on high technology, he advocates federal assistance to improve the international competitiveness of this sector of US industry.

**LEWIS, Jerry.** *USA.* Republican congressman from California. Born in 1934, he worked in insurance and was a state assemblyman before being elected to the House of Representatives in

1978. A thoughtful and skilful politician, in 1987 he became chairman of the House Republican Research Committee, a forum for policy ideas, but his pragmatism is in conflict with the new confrontational political style, represented by **Newt Gingrich**.

**LI GUIXIAN**. *China*. Governor of the People's Bank of China. Born in 1938 and educated in Moscow, Li held top provincial party and government posts before becoming governor of the main state bank in 1988. A Central Committee member since 1985, he became a state councillor in the 1988 leadership rejuvenation drive.

**LI PENG**. *China*. Premier. Born in Chengdu in 1928, Li studied at the Moscow Power Institute and then worked in the electrical power industry for 20 years, rising to head the powerful electric power ministry in 1981. The adopted son of the late premier Zhou Enlai, Li was elected to the Central Committee in 1982 and appointed vice-premier the following year as part of a drive to introduce young blood. In 1985, Li became head of the State Education Commission, joined both the Politburo and the Secretariat, and two years later became a member of the Politburo Standing Committee. In 1987 he succeeded **Zhao Ziyang** as premier, making himself unpopular with Zhao's young reformist advisers by instituting a massive economic retrenchment programme to counter spiralling inflation and over-spending. Li is close to **Chen Yun**, a conservative central planner and **Deng Xiaoping**'s most influential rival. Also a political conservative, he confirmed his hardline image in May 1989 by imposing martial law in Beijing and presiding over the crushing in June of the pro-democracy movement which had called for his resignation.

**LI RUIHUAN**. *China*. Member of the Chinese Communist Party Politburo Standing Committee. Born in 1935, Li was a trade unionist in Beijing before becoming site director for the construction of the Mao Memorial Hall in 1977. In 1979 he was named a national model worker. He moved to Tianjin in 1981 to become deputy mayor and the following year was promoted to mayor, a position he held until 1989. At the same time he held top party posts in the municipality. A member of the Central Committee from 1982, he joined the Politburo in 1987. Following the crushing of the pro-democracy movement in June 1989, he was further elevated to membership of the Secretariat and the Politburo Standing Committee, where

he is responsible for ideology, as a moderate counterbalance to conservatives such as **Li Peng** and **Yao Yilin**, perhaps because of his low-key approach towards demonstrators in Tianjin. Based on his experience in Tianjin, his views urging controlled reform ("like flying a kite"), while avoiding ideological extremes of left and right were given great prominence in late 1989, and reflect the pragmatism of **Deng Xiaoping**.

**LI TIEYING**. *China*. State councillor. Born in 1937, the son of a former wife of **Deng Xiaoping**, Li was a provincial party secretary before becoming electrical industry minister in 1985. In 1988 he became a state councillor in the leadership rejuvenation drive and moved to head the State Education Commission after a year in the State Commission for Economic Restructuring.

**LILLEY, Peter**. *UK*. Secretary of state for trade and industry since July 1990, and an MP since 1983. Born in 1943, the quiet economist was a surprise replacement for **Nicholas Ridley**. The seventh trade secretary in as many years and a member of the right-wing "No Turning Back" group, Lilley is known to hold similar views to Ridley's on Europe and free trade, despite having served as parliamentary private secretary to **Nigel Lawson** in the mid-1980s. In 1987 he became economic secretary to the Treasury, promoted to financial secretary in 1989.

**LILOV, Aleksandur**. *Bulgaria*. Leader of the Bulgarian Socialist Party (BSP). Born into a poor peasant family in Granichak in 1933, Lilov graduated in literature from Sofia University and the Academy of Social Sciences in Moscow. He served as a Communist Youth League official from 1947–60, before becoming a member of the National Assembly in 1962, under the name Alexander Petrovski. He then worked his way up through the party, to become a full member of the politburo in July 1974. A leading ideology expert, he was director of the Institute for Modern Social Theories from 1983–89 and in February 1990 became chairman of the BSP, formerly the Communist Party, two months later. A moderate reformer, he advocates "democratic socialism". He was re-elected as BSP chairman in September that year, despite criticism from radicals that he was at best lukewarm towards reform.

**LIM KENG YAIK, Dato**. *Malaysia*. Primary industries minister. Born in 1939, Lim was appointed as a senator in 1971 and soon afterwards entered the cabinet for a short period as special functions minister, a post that placed him in charge of the resettlement of Chinese villagers in the aftermath of the 1948–60 emergency. He has served as president of Gerakan, a ruling National Front component, since 1980. After his election to parliament in 1986 he was appointed primary industries minister, becoming one of the highest-ranking ethnic Chinese in the cabinet.

**LIM KIT SIANG**. *Malaysia*. Opposition leader. Born in 1941. Leader of the Chinese-dominated Democratic Action Party (DAP), Lim is one of the foremost critics of the **Mahathir Mohamad** government. He has been detained by the authorities on two occasions, in 1969 and 1987, after periods of racial tension between Malays and ethnic Chinese. Since the mid-1970s Lim has led the opposition in parliament.

**LING LIONG SIK, Dato**. *Malaysia*. Malaysian Chinese Association (MCA) president. Born in 1943. A trained medical doctor, Ling was elected as president of the MCA (the largest Chinese-based component party in the ruling National Front coalition) in 1986, replacing Tan Koon Swan. Ling is widely regarded as a moderate, and just before his election was appointed as transport minister.

**LINI, Father Walter**. *Vanuatu*. Prime minister. Born in 1942, he was ordained as an Anglican priest in 1970. As chief minister of what was then the New Hebrides he steered the country through its troubled passage to independence in 1980. As prime minister ever since, leading the largely anglophone and "Melanesian socialist" Vanuaaku Pati, Lini has pursued an adventurous and radical non-aligned foreign policy, including a flirtation with Libya. He called in troops from Papua New Guinea early on, to prevent the secession of Espiritu Santo, and was accused by the opposition of discouraging foreign investment and running an increasingly authoritarian regime. After his stroke in early 1987 there were attempts to oust him, including a "constitutional coup" in December 1988 involving the then president George Sokomanu. He survived this and strengthened his position, isolating the left-wing "pro-Libyan" party faction led by Barak Sope, and securing the election of **Fred Timakata** to the country's presidency in place of Sokomanu.

**LION, Robert**. *France*. Inspector-general of finance. Born in 1934 and a graduate of the Institut d'Etudes Politiques and of the Ecole Nationale d'Administration, he was decorated for wartime service and followed a career as a civil servant, principally as technical adviser and public housing administrator within government departments and state agencies. From 1981–82 he headed **Pierre Mauroy**'s private political office, and since 1982 has been director-general of the state-owned bank, Caisse de Dépôts et Consignations.

**LIVINGSTONE, Ken**. *UK*. Labour politician. Born in 1945, he trained as a teacher and also worked as a technician in a cancer research institute. First elected as a Labour councillor in 1971, he was a member of the Greater London Council (GLC) until its abolition in 1986 and was its leader for five years after Labour won London's local government elections in 1981."Red Ken" proved an inspirational figure for the left, presiding over an unashamedly socialist programme that included lowering public transport fares, stimulating co-operatives, and funding controversial cultural and minority activities. But his use of a local government position to espouse wider issues – such as national policy over Northern Ireland or nuclear defence – incensed **Margaret Thatcher**'s government and led directly to the abolition of the GLC. Since his election to parliament in 1987, his public profile and his influence have been much reduced.

**LONČAR, Budimir**. *Yugoslavia*. Foreign minister. Born in 1924, he joined Tito's partisans in 1941 and the communist party in 1943. A staff member first of the interior ministry and then, since 1949, of the foreign ministry, he has been Yugoslav ambassador to Indonesia, the USA and West Germany. In 1984 he was appointed deputy foreign minister and in 1988, federal minister. A moderate reformist, he is strongly in favour of Yugoslav access to and possible membership of the EC.

**LONGUET, Gérard**. *France*. Right-wing politician. Born in 1946 and a graduate in politics and administration from the Ecole Nationale d'Administration, he pursued a civil service career before becoming a county councillor, then a member of the National Assembly and, from 1979, of the European Parliament. He is one of the three principal figures (alongside **François Léotard** and **Alain Madelin**) in the Republican Party (PR), of which he was elected secretary-general in 1990. He won a reputation for "savage" liberalism during a relatively brief spell in **Jacques Chirac**'s government in 1986–88, in various ministerial posts.

**LÓPEZ MICHELSEN, Alfonso**. *Colombia*. Liberal politician. Born in 1913, the son of former president Alfonso López, he studied and practised law before being elected a member of the House of Representatives in 1960 for the Liberal Party. He was foreign minister between 1968 and 1970 and president from 1974–78. A consistent representative of the moderate wing of the party, his candidature in the 1982 presidential election split the vote and allowed the Conservatives to win.

**LÖSCHNAK, Franz.** *Austria.* Interior minister. Born in Vienna in 1940, he has a doctorate in law. A member of the national council of the Socialist Party of Austria (SPÖ), he began his career in the Vienna city administration. He served as minister in charge of the chancellor's office from 1985–87, and from 1987–89 as health and civil service minister. He was appointed interior minister in 1989.

**LOTT, Trent.** *USA.* Republican senator from Mississippi. Born in 1941, he practised law and was elected to the House of Representatives in 1972 and the Senate in 1988. Minority whip in the House, where he cultivated southern Democrats' support for **Ronald Reagan**'s administration, he has no leadership responsibilities in the Senate, but is a prominent spokesman on defence as an armed services committee member.

**LOUEKOSKI, Matti.** *Finland.* Finance minister. Born in 1941, he trained and practised as a lawyer, worked as a civil servant, and was appointed education minister in 1971. He was minister without portfolio in 1972, and justice minister from 1972–75. A Social Democrat, Louekoski returned to the cabinet in 1987 as justice minister, a post he held until 1989, and again in 1990. He was finance minister from 1989–90, and again since September 1990.

**LUBBERS, Ruud.** *Netherlands.* Prime minister. The pre-eminent and most popular Dutch politician of his generation, he became in June 1990 the longest-serving prime minister since the end of World War II. Born in 1939, the son of a wealthy Rotterdam industrialist, he studied economics at Rotterdam University, graduating in 1962, and then joined the family engineering firm, Hollandia Kloos. Within the Dutch Christian Employers' Federation (NCW) he handled wage negotiations in the engineering industry and revealed his talent for defusing potentially explosive situations with carefully crafted compromises. Originally on the left of the Catholic People's Party (KVP), one of the precursors of the Christian Democratic Appeal (CDA) formed in 1975, he was a surprise

appointment as economic affairs minister in the centre–left Joop den Uyl government in 1973. When he failed to secure a place in the cabinet formed by Dries van Agt in 1977, he turned his attention to parliamentary politics and was elected CDA parliamentary leader in 1978. When van Agt retired from politics in 1982, Lubbers became the Netherlands' youngest-ever prime minister at the age of 43, heading a centre–right CDA–People's Party for Freedom and Democracy (VVD) coalition. Leaving most of the arguing to his ministers and holding himself above the fray, he was able to maintain a high personal standing throughout the seven years of this coalition, despite the implementation of unpopular austerity policies aimed primarily at cutting public spending. Increasingly irritated by the VVD's more strident free-market policies, he tried to improve relations with the opposition Labour Party (PvdA), particularly after its veteran leader den Uyl had been replaced by the more pragmatic **Wim Kok** in 1986. After the early elections in 1989 – precipitated by a wrangle with the VVD over the financing of an ambitious environmental clean-up plan – he was able to form his third administration, a centre–left coalition with the PvdA.

**LUCHINSKY, Petru.** *USSR.* Former Moldavian Communist Party leader. Born in 1940. A full-time party official, he was named as first secretary in 1989 in place of the unpopular Semyon Grossu. He immediately set about trying to earn the goodwill of Moldavia's influential Popular Front by accepting party responsibility for political tensions in Moldavia centring on the nationalist issue. This, however, failed to earn him sufficient credibility to be elected chairman of the Moldavia Supreme Soviet in April 1990, the majority of the republic's parliament favouring **Mircha Snegur**. His party post earned him membership of the Communist Party of the Soviet Union politburo in July 1990.

**LUDZHEV, Dimitur.** *Bulgaria.* Deputy prime minister. Deputy premier in the transitional coalition government formed by **Dimitur Popov** in December 1990, he represents the Union of Democratic Forces (UDF) and exercises its right to share in supervision over the sensitive interior and defence portfolios.

**LUGAR, Richard.** *USA.* Republican senator from Indiana. Born in 1932, he was a Rhodes Scholar at Oxford University, and then worked in agribusiness and was mayor of Indianapolis, before being elected to the senate in 1976. An influential foreign relations committee chairman in 1985–86, he usually supported the administration of **Ronald Reagan** but denounced **Ferdinand Marcos**'s regime in the Philippines and backed sanctions against South Africa. He often works with the Democratic majority on the committee to counter **Jesse Helms**, who replaced him as its ranking Republican in 1987.

**LUJAN, Manuel.** *USA.* Secretary of the interior. Born in New Mexico in 1928, he had a successful career in insurance and then in 1969 was elected to the House of Representatives. Although he left no particular legislative imprint, he acquired a reputation for amiable diligence and for possessing an excellent grasp of the governmental process. In 1988 he was chosen as interior secretary by **George Bush**, becoming the second Hispanic in the cabinet. Although Lujan's voting record on environmental issues was conservative, following his appointment he characterized himself as an "environmentalist". As head of the principal conservation agency under the country's first self-proclaimed environmentalist president, Lujan has made every effort to purge the legacy of James G. Watt, his controversial predecessor in the early years of **Ronald Reagan**'s administration, for whom most environmentalists were members of a "left-wing cult". Nevertheless, the Department of the Interior has maintained many of the policies of the Reagan years, which were sympathetic to Western economic interests such as mining, ranching and oil development. Lujan himself has staunchly supported oil development on the country's outer continental shelf, attacking congressional bans on offshore drilling and angering legislators from coastal states.

**LUKANOV, Andrei.** *Bulgaria.* Vice-chairman of the Bulgarian Socialist Party (BSP), chairman of the parliamentary affairs committee. He was born in 1938 in the USSR. The son of former politburo member Karlo Lukanov, he graduated from the Moscow State Institute for International Relations and speaks seven languages. A member of the Communist Party (later the BSP) from 1965 and a member of the National Assembly from 1976, he became foreign economic relations minister in 1987. In 1989 he played a key role in the ousting of president Todor Zhivkov and in February 1990 he was appointed prime minister. Earthy and direct, Lukanov proved a skilled political operator and technocrat, advocating multi-party

democracy and a market economy. He resigned in November, however, unable to broaden the base of his government, unable to push through the market economic reform programme as protests paralysed the country, and unable to respond effectively to the continuing attacks on the BSP's associations with the former communist regime.

**LUKMAN, Alhaji Rilwanu.** *Nigeria.* Politician. Born in 1938 in Kaduna state, he trained as a mining engineer in the UK and Austria, returning to Nigeria to work as a mines inspector. He was chief executive of the state-owned Nigerian Mining Corporation from 1978 until he joined the government as mines, power and steel minister in 1984. The following year he was appointed petroleum resources minister, combining that job with the presidency of the Organization of the Petroleum Exporting Countries (Opec) from June 1986, a role in which he gained considerable international respect. In December 1989, he was appointed external affairs minister. He left the cabinet in the August 1990 reshuffle, amid speculation that he would be the future presidential candidate of the National Republican Convention, one of the two government-created political parties.

**LUKYANENKO, Levko.** *USSR.* Popular Ukrainian nationalist leader. Born in 1928, Lukyanenko was a contemporary of **Mikhail Gorbachev** at Moscow University's law faculty in the early 1950s, but subsequently spent a total of 26 years in prison for dissident activities in support of human rights and Ukrainian self-determination. In 1976 he was among the founders of a human rights monitoring group, the Ukrainian Helsinki Association, which in 1990 was reconstituted as the pro-independence Ukrainian Republican Party, with Lukyanenko as chairman. Elected in March 1990 to the Ukrainian parliament, he heads an opposition coalition.

**LUSHCHIKOV, Sergei.** *USSR.* Justice minister. He was brought into this post in December 1990 to replace **Veniamin Yakovlev**, who became chief state arbiter. Aged only 39, Lushchikov had previously been deputy chair of the parliamentary committee on legislation.

**LUTCHMEENARAIDOO, Seetanah Vishnu.** *Mauritius.* Former finance minister. Born in 1944 and educated in France, he was chief economist at the commerce and industry ministry from 1973–78. He managed a consulting firm for two years before joining the government as finance minister in 1983. Since then, his policy of promoting export-led growth has worked something of an economic miracle for Mauritius. He was appointed vice-premier in 1986, but was dismissed in August 1990 after opposing plans by the prime minister **Aneerood Jugnauth** to form an electoral pact with the opposition Mauritian Militant Movement (MMM).

**LUTZENBERGER, José**. *Brazil*. Environment secretary. Born in 1927, Lutzenberger trained as an agricultural chemist and sold pesticides before being converted to the ecological cause in the 1960s. He became a dedicated campaigner on environmental issues in Brazil and was awarded the "alternative Nobel prize" for ecology – the Right Livelihood Award– in 1988.

Unexpectedly appointed to the government in 1990, he proposes radical measures to protect Brazil's rainforests.

# M

**MABUS, Ray.** *USA.* Democratic governor of Mississippi. Born in 1948, he was a lawyer, and later a state auditor who crusaded against government corruption. He won election as a reform governor in 1986 and is seen as the representative of a new Mississippi that is suburban, middle class, economically conservative and socially liberal. He has proved adept at building bi-racial support.

**MABUZA, Enos.** *South Africa.* Chief minister of KaNgwane "homeland" and leader of the national Inyandza movement there. The first "homeland" leader to build an effective bridge to the African National Congress (ANC), whose Lusaka headquarters he visited in 1987, Mabuza has shown himself sufficiently sophisticated to preserve leeway for future negotiations, avoiding an outright merger with the ANC while clearly nailing his colours to its mast.

**MACCANICO, Antonio.** *Italy.* Public administrator. Born in 1924 in Avellino, he gained a law degree at Pisa University and entered the administrative service of the Chamber of Deputies. He became general secretary of the chamber in 1976 and from 1978 served as an efficient chief of staff to his close friend, President Sandro Pertini. From March 1987–April 1988 he served as president of the state-controlled merchant bank Mediobanca. In April 1988 he was appointed minister without portfolio responsible for regional affairs and institutional reforms in **Ciriaco De Mita**'s government and was re-appointed to that position in **Giulio Andreotti**'s administration. He is not affiliated to any party, but is considered to be in sympathy with the Italian Republican Party (PRI).

**McCARTHY, William.** *USA.* Trade union leader. He was elected president of the Teamsters' union – one of the nation's three largest – in 1988, one month after the federal government filed an unprecedented suit against the Teamsters' leadership under its Racketeering Influenced and Corrupt Organizations (Rico) laws. Born in 1919, he is known as a "tough

contract bargainer" and a right-leaning Democrat who often voted against the decisions of his colleagues. He has also been challenged by deregulation in the trucking industry, falling membership, and a call to reform the union's voting procedures.

**McCLURE, Fred.** *USA.* Chief congressional lobbyist. Born in 1955, he graduated from Texas A&M University. He was an executive at the Texas Air Corporation and then acted as **Ronald Reagan**'s special assistant for legislative affairs. Although McClure had no role in **George Bush**'s election campaign, he secured some of the victor's spoils, becoming the main liaison between the White House and Congress. He is a long-time associate of John Tower, the former senator who was Bush's first choice for defence secretary, but who failed to get Senate confirmation.

**McCOLLUM, Bill.** *USA.* Republican congressman from Florida. Born in 1944, he practised law and was elected to the House of Representatives in 1980. A flexible conservative, he is a bridge between older House Republicans and the more partisan young ones. He favours user-accountability penalties for drug abuse and a hard line on immigration policy.

**MacDONALD, Margo.** *UK.* Scottish nationalist politician. Born in 1944, she won a spectacular by-election victory for the Scottish National Party (SNP) in a Glasgow seat in 1973. Although her vigorous campaigning for the cause of Scottish self-determination brought her national exposure, she failed to hold her seat in the two 1974 general elections. In recent years she has worked as a television and radio presenter and reporter. She is married to SNP MP, **Jim Sillars**.

**McDOUGALL, Barbara.** *Canada.* Employment and immigration minister. Born in Toronto in 1937, she was educated at the University of Toronto and became a financial analyst. A tough, aggressive politician, she was elected to the House of Commons for the Progressive Conservative Party of Canada in 1984 and has held various portfolios including a two-month stint as minister with responsibility for the status of women. She is seen by some as a potential successor to **Brian Mulroney** as leader.

**MacGREGOR, John**. *UK*. Lord President of the Council (leader of the House of Commons) since 1990, MP since 1974. Born in Edinburgh in 1937, the unassuming but able MP for South Norfolk succeeded **Kenneth Baker** as secretary for education after serving as agriculture minister, inheriting sweeping education reforms centred on the new national curriculum and the powers for schools to opt out of local authority control. He began a process of simplifying the reforms before he was moved by **John Major** in November 1990.

**MACHUNGO, Mario Fernandes da Graça**. *Mozambique*. Prime minister. Born in 1940, he is an economist and has held various ministerial posts since independence, notably as planning minister from 1980–86. Initially a proponent of central planning, he was converted to market-oriented policies after successful experiments in Zambezia province, where he also served as governor from 1983–86. In July 1986 he was appointed the country's first prime minister by President Samora Machel and has since overseen the introduction of market economics at a national level.

**MACKAY, Lord (James Mackay)**. *UK*. Lord Chancellor since 1987. Born in 1927, he had a strict Scottish non-conformist religious upbringing. Intellectually distinguished, he first graduated in mathematics and philosophy from Edinburgh University and lectured in mathematics from 1948–50. He obtained a law degree from Edinburgh in 1955 and steadily rose through the legal ranks. After becoming Lord Chancellor in 1987, he proposed radical reforms of both branches of the legal profession which, despite his considerable personal charm, antagonized the judiciary and much of the legal establishment.

**McKENNA, Frank**. *Canada*. Premier of New Brunswick. He was born in 1948 in Apolaqui, New Brunswick, and was educated at St Francis Xavier University, New Brunswick, Queen's University and the University of New Brunswick. A lawyer, McKenna was elected to New Brunswick's legislative assembly in 1982 and was chosen as leader of the New Brunswick Liberal Party in 1985. His party won all the seats in the assembly in 1987 after a lengthy period of Conservative rule, and he became premier. He is best known for infusing life into the constitutional debate by being the first premier to refuse to sign the Meech Lake Accord on constitutional reform in 1990.

**McKERNAN, John (Jock)**. *USA*. Republican governor of Maine. Born in 1948, he was a lawyer, state legislator and US congressman (1982–86), before being elected governor in 1986. He has given priority to environmental protection and educational programme improvements. In November 1990, he came from behind to win re-election.

**MACKIEWICZ, Aleksander**. *Poland*. Democratic Party (SD) chairman and domestic trade minister. Born in 1944, he held managerial office in the post and telecommunications service and in industry. When the SD cast in its lot with Solidarity after the June 1989 elections (having been allied with the communist Polish United Workers' Party for 40 years), he was appointed domestic trade minister in the Solidarity-led coalition government, and took over as party leader soon afterwards. Under his leadership, part of the SD allied itself with the pro-**Lech Wałęsa** Centre Alliance against the prime minister, **Tadeusz Mazowiecki** in Solidarity's factional struggles in 1990.

**McKINNON, Don**. *New Zealand*. Deputy prime minister and external relations and trade minister. Born in 1939, he studied agriculture before becoming a real estate agent. He was elected to parliament in 1978, at his third attempt, and served as opposition spokesman on health and defence, before becoming deputy leader of the National Party in 1987. Appointed deputy prime minister and external relations and trade minister in November 1990, in the new National Party cabinet of **James Bolger**, he was known as a former supporter of the Anzus Pact defence agreement with the USA and Australia, now acknowledged by both government and opposition as effectively defunct.

**McKNIGHT, William**. *Canada*. National defence minister. Born in 1940 in Elrose, Saskatchewan, he was a farmer before entering politics. He was elected to the House of Commons in 1979, and held several ministerial positions before becoming Conservative defence minister in 1989. His major task in this post has been to cut spending.

**McLAUGHLIN, Audrey**. *Canada*. Leader of the New Democratic Party. She was born in 1936 in Dutton, Ontario and was educated at the University of Western Ontario and the University of Toronto. She owned a mink farm, taught, practised social work and founded a consultancy business, before entering politics in 1987, when she was elected New Democratic Party (NDP) member of the House of Commons for the single seat of Yukon. McLaughlin became the first woman national political leader when she won the NDP leadership in December 1989. Her lack of political experience means there is still a question mark over her abilities.

**McNAMARA, Kevin.** *UK.* Labour politician. Born in 1934, he studied law and taught history and law until his election to parliament in 1966. On the right of the party, he has specialized in defence issues and has been opposition spokesman on Northern Ireland since 1987.

**MacSHARRY, Ray.** *Ireland.* European commissioner for agriculture and rural development. Born in 1938, he worked for many years in local government in Sligo in west Ireland. Elected to parliament for the centre-right Fianna Fáil in 1969, he was agriculture minister from 1979–81 and finance minister in 1982 and from 1987–89. He was appointed an EC commissioner in 1989, responsible for agriculture, and the increasingly criticized common agriculture policy (CAP). His poor relations with **Frans Andriessen** have hampered their efforts in the General Agreement on Tariffs and Trade (Gatt) negotiations. MacSharry is thought to have ambitions to succeed **Charles Haughey** as Fianna Fáil leader.

**McWHERTER, Ned.** *USA.* Democratic governor of Tennessee. Born in 1930, he was a businessman and speaker of the state legislature before being elected governor in 1987. As governor he has concentrated on educational expenditure, transportation network improvements and job creation schemes.

**MADANI, Sheikh Abassi.** *Algeria.* Opposition leader. A veteran of the independence struggle, he was imprisoned by the French in 1954, and later became a professor of Islamic studies. Madani leads the main opposition party, the Islamic Salvation Front (FIS), which was legalized in September 1989. The FIS made impressive gains in the June 1990 local elections, and is the major challenge to the National Liberation Front (FLN). Despite his party's militant stance, Madani has promised to pursue its aims democratically, but in November 1990 called for a "holy war" if the government postponed the multi-party parliamentary elections scheduled for 1991.

**MADAR, Mohamed Hawadie.** *Somalia.* Prime minister. A cabinet veteran, having held the posts of public works, posts and telecommunications and national planning minister in the late 1970s and early 1980s, he was appointed prime minister in September 1990. The appointment of Madar, an Issaq from Hargeisa in the north, was seen as a conciliatory gesture to the rebel Somali National Movement (SNM), which controls most of north Somalia.

**MADELIN, Alain.** *France.* Right-wing politician. Born in 1946, he graduated in law, and built a political career in the 1970s as part of **Valéry Giscard d'Estaing**'s Independent Republican (RI) party and its successor, the Republican Party (PR). He has been a deputy in the National Assembly since 1978. As industry, posts and telecommunications and tourism minister in the privatizing right-wing government of 1986–88, he earned a reputation as a firm adherent of *laissez-faire* economics. Madelin was elected to the European Parliament in 1989.

**MADIGAN, Edward.** *USA.* Republican congressman from Illinois. Born in 1936, he was a businessman and state legislator before election to the House of Representatives in 1972. His pragmatic style was out of step with the growing partisanship of House Republicans who elected **Newt Gingrich** whip in 1989 in preference to him. An expert legislative tactician, he has left his imprint on major legislation, particularly the elimination of production controls from the 1985 farm bill.

**MAGARA, Eikichi.** *Japan.* Trade unionist. Born in 1929, he graduated from Waseda University in 1953 and served as a public servant in Niigata prefecture. Magara joined the National Council of Local and Municipal Government Workers' Unions (Jichiro) and became its secretary-general in 1975. He was secretary-general of the General Council of Trade Unions of Japan (Sohyo) from 1983 until its dissolution in November 1989, when he was appointed chairman of the board of directors of the Sohyo-Center, its provisional successor. One of Japan's veteran trade unionists, he has a reputation as a pragmatist, unwilling to provoke unnecessary confrontation.

**MAGNAGO, Silvius.** *Italy.* South Tyrol People's Party (SVP) politician. Born in 1914, he studied law at Bologna University. He served as an officer in the German army during World War II but was invalided out after losing a leg. From 1948–52 he was deputy mayor of Bolzano (Bozen), the principal town of Alto Adige. In 1948 he was also elected to the Alto Adige provincial council and remained a member for the next forty years; he was leader of the council. Since 1957 Magnago has been SVP president.

**MAHANTA, Prafulla Kumar.** *India.* Chief minister of Assam. Born in 1952, he has been chief minister of Assam since December 1985 and is leader of the regionalist Asom Gana Parishad.

**MAHATHIR MOHAMAD, Datuk Seri.** *Malaysia.* Prime minister. Mahathir's appointment as prime minister in 1981 was a watershed in Malaysian politics. Born in 1925, he was the first prime minister whose political career had not been personally shaped by British rule. He was also the first to be educated locally, rather than in the UK, and – as a medical graduate – also the first not to be a lawyer by profession. During the early stages of his political career, Mahathir showed rebellious tendencies. In 1969 his membership of the United Malays National Organization (UMNO) was suspended, and he lost his parliamentary seat, after he was accused of Malay chauvinism during the racial tensions surrounding the emergency of that year. He was readmitted to UMNO and parliament in the early 1970s and by 1976 he had risen to deputy prime minister. During his prime ministership he has adopted a forceful, and at times controversial, leadership style. In 1987 he only just survived an attempt by a rebel faction led by **Tengku Razaleigh Hamzah** to unseat him as UMNO president. Mahathir underwent major heart surgery in early 1989, prompting speculation over his political future. Nevertheless, he went on to secure a fourth term in the October 1990 elections.

**MAHDI, Sadiq el-.** *Sudan.* Former prime minister. Born in 1936, the great grandson of the religious leader who defeated General Gordon, he was educated at Oxford University. Leader of the Ansar religious sect and a member of one of Sudan's most powerful families, he became leader of the Umma Party in 1961 and served as prime minister in 1966–67. Arrested and charged with high treason after the coup of 1969, he spent much of the 1970s in exile, and in 1976 was sentenced to death *in absentia* for alleged involvement in an attempt to overthrow President Jaafar Nimeiri. After a reconciliation with Nimeiri he returned to Sudan in 1977 and joined the ruling party but was imprisoned again in 1983 for protesting against the introduction of Islamic law. Released the following year, he was elected prime minister in April 1986 at the head of a coalition government, the first of three he was to lead. Riven by divisions and under

pressure from Islamic fundamentalists, his governments proved incapable of tackling the country's economic problems or of ending the civil war in the south and he was overthrown by a military coup in June 1989. He was later released from detention but put under house arrest.

**MAHUAD WITT, Jamal.** *Ecuador.* Popular Democracy (DP) leader. Appointed labour minister in **Osvaldo Hurtado**'s cabinet in 1983, Mahuad succeeded him as leader of the Christian democratic DP. He was an unsuccessful candidate in the first round of the 1988 presidential elections. A DP member of the congress, he remains a potentially strong contender for the presidency.

**MAI CHI THO, Major-General.** *Vietnam.* Interior minister. Younger brother of veteran party leader, Le Duc Tho, he worked clandestinely in the South throughout the war and emerged after the communist victory in 1975 as a key figure in the political transformation of Saigon into Ho Chi Minh City. Appointed to the politburo in 1986, and interior minister the following year, he has become an increasingly vehement critic of political pluralism and spearheaded a crackdown on any form of dissidence.

**MAIJ, Hanja.** *Netherlands.* Transport and public works minister. Born in 1943, she trained as a nurse and later became a lecturer in health care. She was elected to the European Parliament in 1979 and became a vice-chairwoman of the Christian-Democratic European People's Party (EPP) in 1987. Maij was a surprise appointment in November 1989 as transport and public works minister in **Ruud Lubbers**'s third administration.

**MAJLUTA AZAR, Jacobo.** *Dominican Republic.* Opposition party leader. Born in 1934 of mixed Dominican and Lebanese parentage, Majluta was a businessman and served as finance minister in the 1963 **Juan Bosch** government. He was vice-president from 1978–82 and acted as president after the suicide of President Silvestre Guzmán in 1982. His determination to secure the Dominican Revolutionary Party (PRD) nomination for the presidency weakened the PRD and led him to form his own party, the Independent Revolutionary Party (PRI), for the 1990 elections.

**MAJOR, John.** *UK.* Prime minister since 1990, MP since 1979. Born in 1943, the son of a circus performer, Major was brought up in relative poverty. As a young man he was unemployed for several months and drifted between various non-descript jobs. He eventually entered the City with a job at Standard Chartered Bank, where he made rapid progress, and cut his political teeth in the hectic atmosphere of Lambeth borough council from 1968–71. He served in a number of junior ministerial posts before becoming chief secretary to the Treasury in 1987. In a sudden reshuffle, the relatively unknown Major replaced **Geoffrey Howe** as foreign secretary in July 1989, but had little time to make his mark before he was brought in to succeed **Nigel Lawson** as chancellor. Despite much nervousness in the financial markets over the outlook for sterling and the bleak forecasts of steadily rising inflation, Major achieved plaudits for his steady management of affairs and for a cautious "savers" budget in 1990. Major eventually succeeded where others had failed in persuading **Margaret Thatcher** to agree to sterling's entry into the European exchange rate mechanism (ERM) and the announcement was made, with what many thought was blatant political timing, just before the Conservative Party conference in 1990. He was Thatcher's preferred candidate in the leadership elections after she had stood down, but on winning was careful to emphasize that he was no "son of Thatcher". He is liked and respected both by party members and by those in opposition, and his unflappable diplomatic manner has already effected a distinct change in the tone of British political life.

**MAKHKAMOV, Kakhar**. *USSR*. President of Tadjikistan. Born in 1932, he worked as a mine engineer until 1961, when he became mayor of Leninabad, his home city. From there he moved into the republican government, becoming a deputy premier in 1965 and premier in 1982. Elected head of the Tadjik Communist Party in 1985, he offered his resignation in February 1990 at the height of nationalist unrest, but this was refused. He was elected chairman of the Tadjik Supreme Soviet (*de facto* president) in April 1990, retaining his party post, which earned him Communist Party of the Soviet Union politburo membership at the July 1990 party congress. After the switch to a system of executive presidency, he was elected to the new post in November 1990.

**MAKTOUM, Sheikh Maktoum bin Rashid al-**. *United Arab Emirates*. Ruler (amir) of Dubai. Born in 1943, he succeeded his father Sheikh Rashid bin Said al-Maktoum as ruler of Dubai, prime minister and vice-president of the United Arab Emirates in October 1990. He was prime minister from 1971–79 and deputy prime minister from 1979–1990. He is also the premier of the Council of Ministers which initiates federal draft laws including the budget, and draws up regulations for their implementation.

**MAKWETU, Clarence**. *South Africa*. Pan-Africanist Congress (PAC) president. A founder member of the PAC, he was elected vice-chairman after the organization was "unbanned" in February 1990. He became president in December, following the death in October of veteran leader Zephaniah Mothopeng.

**MALAN, General Magnus**. *South Africa*. Defence minister. Born in 1930, he was a career officer, rising to be chief of defence staff in 1976, and became defence minister in 1980. A close ally of former state president P.W. Botha and linchpin of the "securocrat" state that Botha built, he lacked the political finesse to secure the succession in early 1989, and then suffered when **F. W. de Klerk** set about dismantling the National Security Management System. Buffeted in 1990 by criticism of the security forces, and omitted from the government team when talks began with the African National Congress, he was bolstered by de Klerk in his refusal to resign over the Harms committee's report on security force assassination squads.

**MALECELA, John**. *Tanzania*. Prime minister. Born in 1934 and educated at Bombay and Cambridge universities, Malecela began his career in the civil and diplomatic services. He served as ambassador to the UN from 1964–68 and held his first ministerial post as the now-defunct East African Community's communications and social services minister from 1969–72. A series of posts in the Tanzanian government followed: minister of foreign affairs (1972–75), agriculture (1975–80), mines (1980–81) and transport and communications (1982–86). After a spell on the international scene, as a member of the Commonwealth Eminent Persons Group on South Africa and as vice-chairman of the Desert Locust Control Organization for Eastern Africa, he was appointed high commissioner in the UK in 1989 but was recalled to become prime minister in November 1990. Energetic and affable, he is well suited to the new climate of openness and pragmatism in Tanzanian politics.

**MALIETOA TANUMAFILI II, Susuga**. *Western Samoa*. Head of state (O le Ao o le Malo). Born in 1913 and educated in New Zealand, he became his country's joint head of state on independence in 1962, and has been sole head of state since April 1963, functioning as a constitutional monarch.

**MALLON, Seamus.** *UK.* Socialist and Irish nationalist politician. Born in 1936 in Northern Ireland, he trained and worked as a teacher. He was elected to a (still-born) Northern Ireland Assembly for the nationalist Social Democratic and Labour Party (SDLP) in 1973. Deputy party leader under **John Hume** since 1979, he became MP for Newry and Armagh in 1986.

**MALM, Stig.** *Sweden.* Trade union leader. Born in 1935, he trained as a toolmaker and became a full-time official of the Swedish metalworkers' union in 1967. In 1981 he was elected vice-president of the powerful Swedish Trade Union Confederation (LO) and two years later took over as president. An instinctive modernizer, he has not been afraid to question received wisdoms such as the LO's links with the Social Democrats or public-sector workers' right to strike.

**MAMALONI, Solomon.** *Solomon Islands.* Prime minister. Born in 1943, he completed his education in New Zealand before joining the colonial administrative service in the then British protectorate of the Solomon Islands. Elected to the assembly in 1970, he served as chief minister from 1974–77. He was then out of office until after the first post-independence elections in 1980 when he returned as leader of the centre-left People's Action Party (PAP). After the fall of the government led by Sir Peter Kenilorea he formed his own administration from 1981–84. He became prime minister again in 1989, this time heading the country's first single-party government, albeit none too secure in his grip over the party itself. In October 1990, he resigned dramatically as PAP leader in a daring manoeuvre that enabled him to form a "government of national unity" the following month, including Kenilorea as foreign minister.

**MAMAYUSUPOV, Mukhammadsadyk.** *USSR.* Grand Mufti of Central Asia, and thus spiritual leader of the USSR's largest Islamic community. Born in 1952, he was appointed in March 1989 after popular protest forced his predecessor's dismissal. Mamayusupov has quickly gained wide respect among Soviet Muslims for promoting Islamic education and securing the return of mosques from secular authorities.

**MAMMÌ, Oscar.** *Italy.* Posts and telecommunications minister and Italian Republican Party (PRI) politician. Born in 1926 in Rome, he entered the Chamber of Deputies in 1968. He was minister for parliamentary relations from 1983–87, then posts and telecommunications minister in the successive administrations of **Giovanni Goria, Ciriaco De Mita** and **Giulio Andreotti**. In this post he has introduced privatization to the post office and piloted through parliament the controversial "Mammì law", which tried to bring order to the jumble of television frequencies but also confirmed Silvio Berlusconi in his ownership of the three big national networks.

**MANAYENKOV, Yury.** *USSR.* Senior Communist Party official. A Russian born in 1936, he has a professional background in farm management, and has spent most of his career in the regional Communist Party of the Soviet Union (CPSU) apparatus (except for a brief period in 1981–82 as a political adviser in Afghanistan), reaching the office of regional party first secretary in Lipetsk, south of Moscow. He was elected to the CPSU secretariat in September 1989, and after the July 1990 party congress was given a new secretariat portfolio dealing with the CPSU's relations with the new Russian Communist Party.

**MANDELA, Nelson.** *South Africa.* African National Congress (ANC) deputy president. Born in 1918 to a noble Xhosa family in Umtata in the Transkei, a graduate of Fort Hare College and Witwatersrand University, he trained and worked as a lawyer, sharing his Johannesburg practice from 1952 with **Oliver Tambo**, while involving himself in the work of the ANC and becoming a national organizer. He was first arrested in 1956 and charged with treason under the Suppression of Communism Act, in distinguished company including ANC leader Albert Luthuli, Tambo, and **Walter Sisulu**. He was eventually acquitted on this charge and released in 1961, the year in which the ANC abandoned non-violence. He was arrested again in 1962 and sentenced to five years' imprisonment, then faced fresh treason charges after the authorities uncovered the "high command" of the ANC's military wing Umkhonto we Sizwe (Spear of the Nation) at Rivonia, Johannesburg, in July 1963. His powerful speech from the dock in April 1964 confirmed his status as the most important of ANC political prisoners; it included the denial that he was a communist, the admission that he had helped form Umkhonto and planned sabotage actions, and the affirmation that he was prepared to die for the idea of ending white domination. Sentenced to a life term, he went to Robben Island (later being transferred to Pollsmoor), but retained his aura of inborn authority even with his jailers, urging his fellow prisoners to retain their high ideals, and managing to turn his harsh confinement into a proving-ground for greatness. Revered as a near-divine figure by succeeding generations in the black townships, he made a powerful impression on fellow prisoners, and surprised the visiting Commonwealth Eminent Persons Group in 1986 by his grip on changing political developments. "Free Nelson Mandela" became an international rallying-song in the 1980s; his treatment became the touchstone of any South African government's seriousness about reform. By 1989 he could take tea with state presidents but apparently bided his own time, contriving to deny the regime a propaganda triumph until it delivered on the substance of change. His release in February 1990, the first of the global Mandela media events that he was able to attend in person, brought the attendant risk of anti-climax; could the man measure up to the myth? In the event he did only too well proving himself a statesman and showing by his views on the mixed economy that he was a man you could do business with. At the end of 1990, his health was just holding up to his punishing schedule of visits and his status remained undiminished, allowing him to compromise (as some in the ANC feared), while keeping his eyes firmly on the prize – a unitary state and majority rule.

**MANDELA, Winnie Nomzano.** *South Africa.* Born in 1936 in Pondoland, a relative of **Oliver Tambo,** she trained as a social worker before her marriage in 1958 to Tambo's law partner **Nelson Mandela,** 18 years her senior. He was arrested in 1960, and in prison awaiting trial when their second child was born. Two years later he was re-arrested and imprisoned, for the next 28 years. Banned herself almost continuously from 1962–86, with spells in prison without trial, she was otherwise kept out of circulation in remote Brandfort from 1977–85, a reproach to the government as she built her image as the African nationalist queen. Her return to Soweto in 1985 pitched her, unprepared, into the militant politics of township turmoil. Her image was tarnished by association with bully-boy gangs, radicalized rashly by her April 1986 support for the "necklace" killing of informers, and then spectacularly soured by her implication in the end-1989 killing of 14-year-old "Stompie"

Moeketsi. Fearing that legal charges could open many cans of worms, there were those who wanted to minimize her profile in the ANC. This had to be ruled out as she took the public stage alongside her newly released husband after February 1990; but her value as a symbol had become a card in her enemies' hand. To the surprise of many observers she was appointed head of the ANC's department of social welfare.

**MANDELSON, Peter.** *UK.* Labour politician. Born in 1953, he studied philosophy, politics and economics at Oxford University and worked for the British Youth Council and as a television producer before becoming director of campaigns and communications for the Labour Party (1985–90). He was credited with injecting a welcome note of professionalism into the party's 1987 election campaign, and was believed to have had considerable influence on the formulation of party policy. Widely tipped for senior party office, he epitomizes the "designer socialism" side of **Neil Kinnock**'s Labour Party. He secured selection as candidate for a safe Labour seat (Hartlepool) in 1989.

**MANGLAPUS, Raul.** *Philippines.* Foreign secretary. Born in 1918, he fought against the Japanese occupation and was a prisoner of war from 1942–44. He entered politics after World War II, specializing in foreign affairs, and became known as a fierce nationalist. Opposition to the growing corruption of the Marcos regime led him to seek political asylum in the USA in 1973. He formed the Movement for a Free Philippines in exile, and returned following the "people power" revolution which swept Marcos from power in 1986. He was appointed foreign secretary in the wake of **Salvador Laurel**'s resignation in September 1987. Known as a long-term opponent of US bases in the Philippines, he staged successful negotiations with the US administration in 1990 which were expected to conclude with an agreement for a phased closure of Subic Bay naval base, and the assertion of Philippine sovereignty over, but not control of, Clark air base by September 1991.

**MANIGAT, Leslie.** *Haiti.* Former president. Born in 1930, Manigat was educated at the Sorbonne, Paris. He served in the Haitian foreign ministry until jailed in 1961 and exiled in 1963. He opposed the Duvalier regime from exile, while also pursuing an academic career as a university lecturer in history and politics. He returned to Haiti after the fall of "Baby Doc" Duvalier in 1986 to found the National Democratic Progress Party. As the military-backed candidate he won the fraudulent January 1988 presidential elections, but was removed six months later after trying to assert his control over the army and was forced into exile.

**MANLEY, Michael.** *Jamaica.* Prime minister. Born in 1924, educated at the London School of Economics, and at first involved in trade union affairs, he succeeded his father, Norman Manley, as leader of the People's National Party (PNP). A charismatic speaker and leader, he led the PNP to victory in 1972 and then began pursuing "democratic socialism", moving the PNP to the left and stressing links with Cuba and other non-aligned countries. Defeated in 1980, he moderated his stance and won the election in 1989, but ill-health clouds his political future.

**MANN, Simranjit Singh.** *India.* Leader of Akali Dal faction. Born in 1945 in Simla, he is a former superintendent of police, who resigned after the assault on the Amritsar Golden Temple in 1984. He was arrested soon after Indira Gandhi's murder and accused of complicity in the assassination. In 1988, while still in prison, he was chosen as president of a new "Unified Akali Dal" created by senior Sikh priests in an attempt to unite the party. The new party in turn split into different groups, but Mann's faction did well in the 1989 union election, becoming the only section of Akali Dal to win seats from the Punjab, capturing six of the state's 13 constituencies. Mann contested the election from prison and was released after his victory. In October 1990 he resigned his parliamentary seat in protest over the extension of president's rule to Punjab. After the formation of the new union government the following month, he held talks with **Chandra Shekhar** in an effort to open a dialogue on the future of Punjab.

**MANUKYAN, Vazguen.** *USSR.* Armenian prime minister. Born in 1946, he was a lecturer in applied mathematics at Yerevan University until his election as republican premier in August 1990. Like the Armenian president, **Levon Ter-Petrosyan** (who nominated him for the premiership), Manukyan was a founder-member in 1988 of the Karabakh committee, campaigning for Armenian control over the disputed Nagorny Karabakh region of neighbouring Azerbaijan, and was jailed from December 1988 to May 1989. A leader of the Armenian National Movement, he favours Armenia's complete independence.

**MARA, Ratu Sir Kamisese.** *Fiji.* Prime minister. Born in 1920 and educated in Fiji, New Zealand, and at Oxford University and the London School of Economics, he joined the colonial service in 1950. Ten years later he founded the moderate nationalist Alliance Party and in 1965, led the Fijian delegation to the 1965 constitutional conference and became chief minister. Mara led the country to independence in 1970, dominating its politics as prime minister until the 1987 elections. The 1980s appeared to be a success story for the tall, aristocratic Mara, but he reacted with bitterness when the electorate voted the multi-racial opposition alliance into office in April 1987. He failed to condemn the two coups led by Major-General **Sitiveni Rabuka** later that year and became prime minister again. Responsible for piloting through the controversial constitutional changes to enshrine ethnic Fijian dominance, he has attempted to marginalize Rabuka and regain the political initiative with a bold programme for economic growth.

**MARAN, Murasoli.** *India.* Leading Tamil politician. Born in 1939 in Thirukuvalai, Tamil Nadu, he is a leading Tamil screenwriter and film director. He has been a member of either the lower or upper house of parliament for the Dravida Munnetra Kazhagam (DMK) since 1968, and was imprisoned by Indira Gandhi's administration during the emergency of 1975–77. He represented the DMK as urban development minister in the 1989–90 National Front government.

**MARCHAIS, Georges.** *France.* Communist leader. Born in 1920 into a mining family, he was a metalworker before becoming an official in the General Confederation of Labour (CGT), and he joined the Communist Party (PCF) in 1947. A member of the party politburo from 1959, he has dominated it since becoming secretary-general in 1970. He has been a member of the National Assembly since 1973, and was a member of the European Parliament from 1979–84. He stood for the French presidency in 1981, but it was **François Mitterrand** who emerged as the victorious standard-bearer of the briefly united left. Strongly associated with Stalinism, but later with Euro-communism in the 1970s, he has since struggled in vain to keep pace with the demand for a new image and direction on the left, and has watched his party decline in credibility and support. The tide of change unleashed by the collapse of communism in Eastern Europe in 1989 seemed to have left him an increasingly isolated survivor of the old guard, but his comrades re-elected him as party leader in December 1990.

**MARCHELLI, Paul.** *France.* Trade union leader. Born in 1933, he has worked as a technician, supervisor, company representative and managing director. In 1967, he joined the General Confederation of Executives trade union and became its deputy secretary-general in 1979, delegate-general in 1981 and president in 1984.

**MARGRETHE II.** *Denmark.* Queen. Born in 1940, she studied history, politics, law and economics at Danish, British and French universities. She married a French aristocrat, now Prince Henrik, in 1967. She succeeded to the throne on the death of her father, Frederik IX in 1972. A constitutional monarch with no significant executive functions, she has nevertheless been able to influence national affairs through her espousal of social, environmental and artistic causes. She has also gained a reputation as an illustrator, costume designer and translator.

**MARÍN GONZÁLEZ, Manuel.** *Spain.* European Commission vice-president and commissioner for co-operation and development and fisheries. Born in 1949, he studied in Spain, France and Belgium and was active in the anti-Franco student movement in the early 1970s. Elected to parliament for the Spanish Socialist Workers' Party (PSOE) in 1977, he ably handled the negotiations over Spain's entry to the EC in the mid-1980s. Marín González was appointed an EC commissioner in 1986, primarily responsible for social affairs and employment until 1989, and for co-operation and development and fisheries since then, having failed to get the budget post he had sought.

**MARKOVIĆ, Ante.** *Yugoslavia.* Prime minister. An ethnic Croat born in 1924 in Konjic, he joined Tito's partisans in 1941. After the war he graduated from Zagreb University and went on to work as an engineer, designer and then head of the test department at Croatia's largest engineering factory, Rade Končar in Zagreb, of which he was director-general from 1961–86. From 1982–86 he was prime minister of Croatia and in May 1986 he became the republic's president. Appointed prime minister of Yugoslavia in March 1989, Marković has pursued a dynamic economic policy, pegging the dinar to the Deutschmark and liberalizing imports. The resulting dramatic reduction in inflation boosted his popularity. Strongly in favour of a multi-party system, he launched a coalition in 1990 committed to economic reform – the Alliance of Reformist Forces of Yugoslavia – to run independently of the communists in elections. In his "state of the nation" address in November 1990 he adopted a combative attitude against the forces of disintegration, and was especially severe on Serbia's economic protectionism, reinforcing the belief that he saw his future increasingly as manager of an economic federation.

**MARSHALL, Thurgood.** *USA.* Associate justice of the Supreme Court. Born in 1908, he was educated at Lincoln and Howard universities and qualified as a lawyer in 1933. He was appointed director-general of the legal defence and education fund of the National Association for the Advancement of Colored People in 1940, a position he held until 1961 when he became an appeal court judge. He served as solicitor-general from 1965–67, before being appointed to the Supreme Court by President Lyndon Johnson. A staunch liberal, Marshall became the oldest of the court's members following the retirement of William Brennan in July 1990. He is the only black to have sat on the Supreme Court.

**MARTELLI, Claudio.** *Italy.* Deputy prime minister and Italian Socialist Party (PSI) politician. Born in 1943 in the province of Milan, he gained a degree in philosophy and in 1963 joined the Italian Republican Party (PRI). In 1967 he joined the Unified Socialist Party (PSU), going over to the PSI when the PSU split in 1969. He entered the Chamber of Deputies in 1979 and became joint deputy leader of the PSI in 1981 and deputy leader in 1982. In the government formed by **Giulio Andreotti** in July 1989, he was appointed deputy prime minister. He introduced controversial legislation regularizing the position of illegal immigrants which almost brought the government down but was approved in 1990. Although he is nominally the senior socialist in the administration, the arbiter of party policy is **Bettino Craxi**.

**MARTENS, Wilfried.** *Belgium.* Prime minister. Born in 1936, he practised law, was a senior adviser to several Christian Democratic prime ministers in the 1960s and also president of the youth wing of the Christian People's Party (CVP) from 1965–72. He had already proved his exceptional skill as a negotiator and conciliator by the time he was elected CVP leader in 1972, indispensable qualities in Belgium's fractious political world. He was drafted in as prime minister in 1979 with no previous ministerial experience, but resigned two years later when neither his Socialist coalition partners nor a large section of his own party proved willing to support his austerity programme. Elections later that year strengthened his position, however, and he formed a centre–right coalition. He has since emerged as the great survivor of Belgian politics, pushing through economic reforms while muddling through on the language question. It was a language dispute, the **José Happart** affair, that brought the coalition down in 1987. Elections later that year led to protracted negotiations that culminated in his leading a new centre–left coalition.

**MARTÍ ALANIS, Joan.** *Andorra.* Co-prince. In his capacity as bishop of Urgel (Seu d'Urgell), the Spanish episcopal see which extends into Andorra, he holds the position of co-prince with the French president, under a 700-year-old agreement. He has the power of veto over decisions taken by the General Council of the Valleys (parliament).

**MARTIN, James.** *USA.* Republican governor of North Carolina. Born in 1935, he was a chemistry professor before being elected to the House of Representatives in 1972 and as governor in 1984. He is conservative in national politics, but has been moderate at state level and had maintained strong support for education. His stand has led to a feud with North Carolina's conservative senator **Jesse Helms.**

**MARTIN, Lynn.** *USA.* Nominated by **George Bush** in December 1990 to succeed **Elizabeth Dole** as labour secretary, her confirmation would make her the only woman in the cabinet. She was the defeated Republican candidate in the November 1990 Illinois senate contest against the incumbent, **Paul Simon,** and was an Illinois member of the House of Representatives.

**MARTINEZ, Bob.** *USA.* Director of the Office of National Drug Control Policy. Born in 1934, he was a teacher and education administrator who became governor in 1986 after eight years as a highly successful mayor of Tampa. His tough stand on drugs was popular, but his governorship became embroiled in taxation controversy. His attempt to pressure the state legislature to adopt tough anti-abortion legislation proved disastrous. In November 1990 he lost his bid for re-election, but was then appointed to replace **William Bennett** to head the fight against drugs.

**MARTINI, Carlo Maria.** *Italy.* Archbishop of Milan. Born in 1927 in Turin, he joined the Jesuit order and was ordained in 1952. Appointed archbishop of Milan in December 1979, he was created a cardinal in 1983. He is a recognized biblical scholar and has served as vice-chancellor of the Jesuit-run Pontifical Gregorian University. As church leader in the country's economic capital he is assured of a wide audience for his views on social issues.

**MARTIN TOVAL, Eduardo.** *Spain.* Socialist politician. Born in 1942 in Malaga. A lawyer and a deputy for Barcelona, he is leader of the Socialist group in the Congress of Deputies.

**MASALIYEV, Absamat.** *USSR.* Former chairman of the Supreme Soviet of Kirghizia. Born in 1933, he is a career official in the Kirghiz Communist Party. First secretary since 1985, he became chairman of the Kirghiz Supreme Soviet (*de facto* republican president) in April 1990. His party post earned him membership of the Communist Party of the Soviet Union politburo in July 1990. In direct presidential elections in October he was eliminated after the first round as the party sought a way round a deadlocked poll, and **Askar Akayev** was then chosen as a compromise president.

**MASIRE, Quett.** *Botswana.* President. Born in 1925, a former teacher and journalist, he was a close associate of Botswana's founding president, Sir Seretse Khama, and served as vice-president from independence in 1966 until Khama's death in 1980. A popular and respected figure, he played a pivotal role during this period in Botswana's transformation from a country with few resources and prospects into Africa's fastest-growing economy. Khama's choice as successor, Masire was elected by secret parliamentary ballot to take over as head of state. He has preserved Botswana's traditions as a non-racial multi-party democracy and has taken an independent line in relations with South Africa.

**MASLYUKOV, Yury.** *USSR.* First deputy premier and former Presidential Council member. A Russian born in 1937 in Tadjikistan, he worked in engineering until the 1970s, when he was appointed a deputy defence minister responsible for military hardware. He was transferred to the State Planning Committee (Gosplan) in 1982 as a first deputy chairman; became a USSR deputy premier in 1985; and was promoted to first deputy premier and returned to Gosplan as chairman in February 1988. He was a member of the Communist Party of the Soviet Union politburo in 1988–90. **Mikhail Gorbachev** appointed him to the short-lived Presidential Council in March 1990.

**MASOL, Vitaly.** *USSR.* Former Ukrainian prime minister. An industrial manager by profession, born in 1928, he was elected premier in 1987 after eight years as head of the republic's

State Planning Committee. He faced a difficult re-election in June 1990, with some deputies in the Ukraine's turbulent new parliament blaming him for the republic's economic woes. In October 1990 he resigned after losing a motion of no confidence, in what was seen as a victory by nationalist student demonstrators; he was replaced the following month by Vitold Fokin.

**MASSUD, Ahmed Shah.** *Afghanistan.* *Mujaheddin* leader. Born in 1953, a Tadzhik, and an engineer by training, he took up the guerrilla struggle against the communist regime in 1975, and has been its most militarily successful leader. He dominated the resistance in the Panjshir valley region and scored signal successes against Soviet troops in the long war following their intervention in 1979, earning himself a fearsome reputation as the "Lion of Panjshir". In the fluid situation after the Soviet withdrawal in 1989, he had increasing contact with the Pakistani military, but faced the possibility of a split within his own Jamiat-e Islami faction, whose political leader Berhanuddin Rabbani appeared to lean towards the more vehement fundamentalism of his bitter rival **Gulbuddin Hekmatyar.** Charismatic and courageous, Massud's relatively secular orientation is more appealing to Western backers than some of his fiercely Islamic rivals.

**MATES, Michael.** *UK.* Conservative politician. Born in 1934, he served in the army from 1954–74, rising to the rank of lieutenant-colonel. Elected to parliament in 1974 (for Petersfield, later East Hampshire), he became chairman of the defence select committee in 1987 and is an influential backbencher on the left of the party. In the 1990 leadership contest he was a staunch supporter of **Michael Heseltine,** acting as his campaign manager.

**MATIBA, Kenneth.** *Kenya.* Former minister. A leading Kikuyu businessman, ex-chairman of Kenya Breweries, and former civil servant, he was first elected to parliament in the 1979 elections, when he defeated a cabinet minister. In 1983 he was appointed culture and social services minister, moving to works and housing in 1986, health in 1987 and transport and communications in 1988. After making allegations of vote-rigging in elections to posts in the ruling Kenya African National Union (KANU), he resigned from his cabinet post and was expelled from the party in December 1988. He has since emerged as a leading opponent of the one-party state; his calls for the return of a multi-party system were met with harassment and allegations of corruption and subversion against him by government supporters. In July 1990 he was detained without trial.

**MATSUI, Robert.** *USA.* Democratic congressman from California. Born in 1941 and interned with his Japanese-American family during World War II, he helped to enact the 1987 bill providing federal redress for surviving internees. After practising law, he was elected to the House of Representatives in 1978. An influential ways and means committee member, he supports tax code overhaul to benefit low-income families, but has vigorously defended Californian business, notably by crafting the 1988 trade bill amendment mandating retaliation against countries that restrict US telecommunications equipment exports.

**MATTHÄUS-MAIER, Ingrid.** *Germany.* Social Democratic Party (SPD) politician. Born in 1945, she became a judge, but then left the legal profession to enter politics, becoming chairman of the youth organization of the Free Democratic Party (FDP) and entering the Bundestag in 1976. Always on the left wing of the FDP, she switched to the SPD in 1982 after the FDP had changed coalition partners to throw in its lot with the Christian Democrats.

**MATTHEI AUBEL, Major-General Fernando.** *Chile.* Air force commander. Born in 1925, Matthei followed a career as an air force officer, rising to the rank of brigadier-general in 1975. He was appointed public health minister the following year, and in 1978 became air force representative on the military junta, with the rank of major-general. In 1986 he first openly expressed his willingness to seek a dialogue with political parties for a return to democratic rule after the expiry of President **Augusto Pinochet**'s term in 1989; among the senior military officers he has remained the strongest supporter of the democratization process . After **Patricio Aylwin**'s accession to power he was asked to remain as air force commander.

**MAUDE, Francis.** *UK.* Financial secretary to the Treasury, MP since 1983. Born in 1953, the son of a conservative politician, Baron Maude of Stratford-upon-Avon (a life peer), he was educated at Cambridge University and practised as a barrister before gaining office initially as under-secretary for corporate affairs. In 1989 he was made a minister of state at the Foreign and Commonwealth Office, specializing in the turbulent issues of Hong Kong and the "boat people". On the intellectual right of the party and a supporter of the "No Turning Back" group, he replaced **Peter Lilley** at the Treasury in July 1990.

**MAUROY, Pierre.** *France.* Socialist Party (PS) leader. Born in 1928, he became a technical-school teacher, rose within the old socialist party (SFIO), and has played a key role in the new PS since the late 1960s. Since 1973 he has been mayor of Lille and a member of the National Assembly. For most of the 1970s he was second only to **François Mitterrand** in the PS hierarchy and was the natural choice as prime minister after the election victory in 1981. His government associated itself initially with the left-wing demand for reform, but as its leader he suffered a loss of credibility over the subsequent *volte face*, and he was supplanted by **Laurent Fabius** as prime minister in 1984. His political standing improved again in 1988, when he defeated Fabius in the PS leadership contest, and he set about unifying the movement for future elections, while making himself something of a thorn in the flesh of **Michel Rocard**'s government by lobbying for more forthright implementation of party policy.

**MAWHINNEY, Brian.** *UK.* Deputy secretary of state at the Northern Ireland Office. Born in Ulster, he pursued an academic career, lecturing in theology in the UK and the USA, before entering parliament in 1979. He was appointed education minister for the province, where his loyalist background was seen as useful in defusing Protestant mistrust of London in the wake of the Anglo-Irish agreement. He then served as information minister, opening up contacts between nationalist and loyalist politicians, and was appointed to his present post in November 1990.

**MAYHEW, Sir Patrick.** *UK.* Attorney-general since 1987, MP since 1974. Born in 1929, Mayhew was an executive member of the Tory backbench "1922 Committee" before joining **Margaret Thatcher**'s first government. A patrician and distinguished figure, he is a moderate who disliked the Lord Chancellor's reform proposals for the legal profession.

**MAYOR ZARAGOZA, Federico.** *Spain.* Director-general of the UN Educational, Scientific and Cultural Organization (Unesco). Born in 1934, he trained as a biochemist and was a university professor until 1973. Chairman of the council for scientific research from 1974–78, he was also briefly a member of parliament for a centrist party and education minister in 1981–82. Known as a political moderate with a talent for reconciling opposing views, he was

elected director-general of Unesco in 1987 largely on the strength of his commitment to reforming the troubled organization. He has extensive experience of the workings of Unesco, since he was its deputy director-general in 1978–81 and a special adviser to his controversial predecessor, Amadou Mahtar M'Bow, in 1983–84.

**MAZANKOWSKI, Donald.** *Canada.* Deputy prime minister. Born in 1935 in Viking, Alberta, he was a businessman before being elected to the House of Commons for the Progressive Conservative Party of Canada in 1968. A veteran politician, "Maz" is well liked by all parties and is considered to be **Brian Mulroney**'s right-hand man.

**MAZOWIECKI, Tadeusz.** *Poland.* Former prime minister. Born in 1927, he graduated in law. He was dismissed from his first job in a publishing house in 1948 because of his "clericalism". He became active in the official Catholic Pax organization, editing a Catholic weekly in Wrocław, but conflict with the Pax leadership meant dismissal in 1954. Excluded from Pax in 1955, he became identified with independent Catholic circles; he was editor of the Catholic journal *Wiez* from 1958–81. He sat in the Sejm (parliament) from 1961 in the Znak group of Catholic deputies, but was barred from standing in the 1972 Sejm elections for having tried to establish a parliamentary investigation into the December 1970 killing of strikers in the Baltic ports. Associated with dissident causes during the 1970s, he acted as an adviser in August 1980 to the Gdansk strike committee led by **Lech Wałęsa** and helped negotiate the accords that allowed Solidarity's emergence. In 1981 he was founding editor of the Solidarity newspaper *Tygodnik Solidarność* (he took up the editorship again in May 1989). Following the December 1981 imposition of martial law he was interned for a year, but on release continued working with the Solidarity underground (being identified with the moderate Roman Catholic wing), and in early 1989 was a negotiator in round-table talks with the government. After the partly free June 1989 elections Mazowiecki's was among names put forward by Solidarity chairman Wałęsa to head a Solidarity-led coalition government. He was confirmed as prime minister by the Sejm in August, although at that time there were fears that his evident ill health might affect his performance. Despite his government's "shock therapy" to reform and revive the Polish economy, it was accused of hesitancy, and in mid-1990 it was undermined by a dispute with Wałęsa that was principally about Solidarity's future structure and Wałęsa's political ambitions. A Mazowiecki-Wałęsa rift split the veteran Solidarity leadership, with both men lining up to contest the November 1990 presidential elections. His pitch for the presidency ended in unexpectedly heavy defeat in the first round of the polls, when he came third behind Wałęsa and emigré businessman Stanisław Tymiński. Parliament accepted his resignation, and that of his government, following the elections (although the government continued in a caretaker capacity).

**M'BA ABESSOLE, Father Paul**. *Gabon*. Opposition leader. Born in 1939, he trained as a Catholic priest. He led the opposition National Rectification Movement (Morena) from exile in France from 1976 until his return home in May 1989. His statement soon after his return that he would participate in national politics strained relations within the Morena leadership. Morena subsequently split into three factions, with M'ba Abessole elected president of the larger "bûcheron" (foresters) faction. He refused an offer of a government post in May 1990, claiming that he had not been consulted about the composition of the government, and Morena-bûcheron emerged as the second largest party in parliament after the first multi-party elections in September and October 1990. M'ba Abessole is a member of the country's largest and most vocal ethnic group, the Fang.

**MBEKI, Thabo**. *South Africa*. African National Congress (ANC) director of international affairs. Born in 1942, he is the son of veteran ANC leader and long-term prisoner Govan Mbeki. He was educated to postgraduate level in economics at Sussex University and then at Moscow's Lenin School, and has emerged as the ANC's leading negotiator, taking over his present post after a period as information director. He is widely regarded as a likely future leader. An articulate and indispensable aide first to **Oliver Tambo** and latterly to **Nelson Mandela**, his prestige rose as the emphasis swung in 1989 from the military to the diplomatic struggle. He lacks **Chris Hani**'s guerrilla credibility, but his urbane style conveys a more reassuring image; in ideological terms his long-suspected membership of the South African Communist Party disguises a moderate on the social democratic wing.

**MEACHER, Michael**. *UK*. Labour politician. Born in 1939, he graduated from Oxford

University and then lectured in social administration. Elected to parliament in 1970, he held several junior ministerial posts from 1974 until Labour lost power in 1979. Originally on the left of the party (he was the left-wing candidate in the deputy leadership election of 1983), he has moved towards the centre while a member of the shadow cabinet, as spokesman on health and social security (1983–87), employment (1987–89) and most recently social security. His reputation was damaged, perhaps irretrievably, over an ill-judged and unsuccessful libel action against a newspaper which had ridiculed his claim to be the son of a farm labourer.

**MEČIAR, Vladimír**. *Czechoslovakia*. Prime minister of the Slovak republic. Born in 1942 in Zvolen in Slovakia, he graduated from secondary school in 1959 and worked for several years as a high-ranking functionary in the communist youth movement. After openly advocating proscribed reformist ideas Mečiar was recalled from his post in 1969 and expelled from the Communist Party of Czechoslovakia (KSČ) a year later. He worked as a welder in Dubnica steelworks while reading law at the law faculty of the Comenius University in Bratislava in 1973. Subsequently he worked as a company lawyer. After the "velvet revolution" of November 1989 he served as interior and environment minister of the Slovak republic.

**MEDEIROS, Antonio Carlos**. *Brazil*. Trade union leader. Medeiros became leader of the São Paulo Metalworkers' Union (the political rival to "Lula" Da Silva's São Bernardo Metalworkers' Union and the largest single trade union in Latin America) in succession to its long-serving leader, Joaquim dos Santos Andrade. Medeiros backed **Fernando Collor de Mello**'s campaign for the presidency in 1989–90, but later stated his refusal to support any anti-inflationary measures that would affect workers' incomes.

**MEDVEDEV, Roy**. *USSR*. Historian and former dissident. Born in 1925, he is the son of a Bolshevik executed under Stalin. He was dismissed from academic work and expelled from the Communist Party of the Soviet Union in 1969 for anti-Stalinist writings. His dissident works include *A Question of Madness*, an exposé of Soviet psychiatric abuses co-written with his twin brother Zhores, and the famous critical assessment of Stalinism, *Let History Judge*. In April 1989 he was elected to the USSR Congress of People's Deputies; in the same month his expulsion from the Communist Party of the

Soviet Union was declared unjustified and he was rehabilitated.

**MÉHAIGNERIE, Pierre**. *France*. Centrist politician. Born in 1939 and an agronomics graduate, he followed a career as a rural engineer and civil servant. Since 1973 he has sat in the National Assembly. He was junior minister, then minister, for agriculture, between 1976 and 1981, and infrastructure, housing, regional planning and transport minister from 1986–88. Since 1982, he has been president of the Centre of Social Democrats (CDS). In this role he upholds a centrist perspective in French politics, seeking to maintain a distinct identity against encroachment as the right rebuilds its own party structures. Since 1989 he has been president of the Union for French Democracy (UDF) group in the National Assembly.

**MELLOR, David**. *UK*. Chief secretary to the Treasury, MP since 1979. Born in 1949, he served as junior Home Office minister from 1983–87 before moving to the Foreign and Commonwealth Office, where he caused a minor sensation by after publicly upbraiding an Israeli army colonel during a visit to the Gaza Strip in 1988. As minister of state at the Home Office in 1988–90, Mellor's genial approachability helped to allay the suspicions of the media, put on their guard by deregulation measures in the Broadcasting Bill. He was briefly minister for the arts in 1990, but then was rewarded with a move to the Treasury after playing a key role in **John Major**'s leadership campaign.

**MENEGUELLI, Jair**. *Brazil*. Trade union leader. Actively involved in trade unionism, Meneguelli succeeded **"Lula" da Silva** as leader of the metalworkers' union in the São Paulo industrial centre of São Bernardo. He was elected leader of the Trade Union Confederation (CUT) on its formation in 1983.

**MENEM, Carlos Saúl**. *Argentina*. President. Born in 1935 of parents of Syrian descent, Menem, a Catholic convert, studied law at Córdoba University. He became active in politics for the Peronist party within his home state of La Rioja, and was elected governor in 1973. Imprisoned after the military coup in 1976, he was transferred to house arrest in 1978 and released in 1982. He was re-elected governor of La Rioja in 1983 and again in 1987. A flamboyant if diminutive figure, Menem has cultivated his macho and populist image, including his physical resemblance to a local 19th century leader, Juan Faundo Quiroga. This image has been augmented by that of his wife,

Zulema, who has compared herself to Eva Perón, although the marriage itself has broken up several times (most recently in 1990). Menem was chosen as Peronist presidential candidate in 1988 and won the elections the following year, taking office much sooner than expected after his predecessor Raúl Alfonsín stepped down. In office, he has proved to be more pragmatic than his rhetoric might suggest, restoring diplomatic relations with the UK, and pursuing a tough anti-inflationary policy, including sweeping privatizations of state enterprises, at the expense of alienating his traditional supporters in the Peronist trade unions. His popularity declined dramatically as inflation mounted and other economic problems multiplied. In August 1990 he was elected chairman of the Peronists, extending his control to both party and government. In December he survived a coup attempt by junior army ranks, and then pushed through the controversial release of former junta leaders imprisoned for their part in the "Dirty War" of the 1970s and 1980s.

**MENGISTU HAILE MARIAM, Lieutenant-Colonel**. *Ethiopia*. President. Born the son of a palace servant in 1937, he was educated at a military academy. He was a leader of the military coup that deposed Emperor Haile Selassie in 1974, emerging after a vicious power struggle as head of state in 1977 and beginning the transformation of Ethiopian society along Marxist lines. In 1984 he was appointed secretary-general of the newly formed Worker's Party of Ethiopia (renamed the Ethiopian Democratic Unity Party in 1990) and was confirmed as president of Ethiopia following a constitutional referendum in 1987. Mengistu has adapted and refined the imperial system of surveillance and control with ruthless efficiency and seems determined, despite the loss of Soviet backing and a string of military gains by rebel secessionist movements, to preserve Ethiopia's territory at whatever cost.

**MERBAH, Kasdi**. *Algeria*. Former prime minister. Born in 1928, a former independence fighter, Merbah was director of military security from 1962–78, organized the 1979 National Liberation Front (FLN) congress that confirmed **Chadli Bendjedid** as president and joined the cabinet in 1980. As agriculture minister from 1984–88 he oversaw the transformation of many large state farms into smaller private enterprises. He served briefly as health minister in 1988 before being appointed prime minister in November with a brief to push through reforms in response to the October riots. His failure to pursue reform with sufficient vigour led to his replacement in September 1989 by **Mouloud Hamrouche**. He resigned from the FLN in October 1990 to form his own party, the Algerian Movement for Justice and Democracy.

**MERIDOR, Dan**. *Israel*. Justice minister. Born in Israel in 1947, the suave and moderate Meridor trained in law and became a Likud MP in 1984. He joined the government as justice minister in 1988, and is tipped for higher office, but may find his moderate instincts in conflict with **Yitzhak Shamir**'s Likud administration.

**MERMAZ, Louis**. *France*. Government minister. Born in 1931 in Paris, a former teacher and lecturer in contemporary history, Mermaz has a long-standing political association with **François Mitterrand** and served as his campaign director for his unsuccessful bid for the presidency in 1965. Mayor of Vienne since 1971, he was first a member of the National Assembly in 1967–68 and has been a Socialist Party (PS) deputy for Isère continuously since 1973. Before his appointment as minister of agriculture and forestry in October 1990, his ministerial experience was limited to two brief spells in charge of transport (in 1981 and 1988), but his claim to a cabinet post was hard to ignore, with his credentials as a party heavyweight and Mitterrand associate, amid the contending PS factions. He had been president of the National Assembly in 1981–86, and was PS leader in the assembly from June 1988 until he joined the government.

**MESIĆ, Stjepan**. *Yugoslavia*. Vice-president. A prominent member of the right-of-centre Croat Democratic Union (HDZ), Mesić became prime minister of Croatia when the HDZ formed the republic's first non-communist government in May 1990. He was elected to the republic's presidency by the Croatian assembly in August, in succession to the communist, **Stipe Šuvar**, thereby also becoming federal vice-president, in accordance with the rotation principle. He was due to become Yugoslavia's first non-communist president for nearly 50 years in May 1991.

**MICHEL, James**. *Seychelles*. Finance minister. Michel has been a loyal member of President **Albert René**'s administration and, as deputy secretary-general of the sole party, the Seychelles People's Progressive Front, is a strong candidate to succeed him. He has recently appeared to desert his earlier staunch socialist line, calling for constructive dialogue between the party and the population as a whole.

**MICHEL, Robert**. *USA*. Republican congressman from Illinois and House Republican leader. Born in 1923, he was educated at Bradley University and was a congressional aide before election to the House of Representatives in 1956. Initially a typical Midwestern conservative, he became more pragmatic and an expert deal-maker. He is a master of legislative detail, a skill that also makes him very effective on the powerful appropriations committee, but he is less happy dealing with broader issues. Elected minority leader in 1981, he became indispensable to the Reagan administration through his capacity to win votes from conservative southern Democrats, but his influence faded somewhat as partisanship increased after 1982 and his scepticism about military aid to the Contras surfaced. Michel, who has never chaired a committee or subcommittee, is frustrated by his party's permanent minority status in the House. He opposes the confrontational approach of younger Republicans, who are taking over the junior leadership positions, but the election of the conciliatory **Tom Foley** as speaker of the House is expected to work to his advantage.

**MICHNIK, Adam**. *Poland*. Editor of *Gazeta Wyborcza*. An historian, he was arrested in 1968 and sentenced to three years' imprisonment for protesting against a ban on the staging of Mickiewicz's *Dziady*, but was amnestied in 1969. From the late 1970s he was active in the dissident Social Self-Defence Committee, which after 1980 was associated with Solidarity. Charged in 1982 with plotting to overthrow the state, but never tried, he was sentenced in June 1985 to three years' imprisonment for fomenting unrest; he was amnestied in mid-1986. In May 1989 he was named editor-in-chief of *Gazeta Wyborcza*, a new opposition daily that has become Poland's most widely-read newspaper. With **Władysław Frasyniuk** and **Zbigniew Bujak** he broke with Solidarity chairman **Lech Wałęsa** in July 1990, backing Prime Minister **Tadeusz Mazowiecki** and helping to set up the pro-Mazowiecki Citizens' Movement for Democratic Action (ROAD).

**MICKELSON, George**. *USA*. Republican governor of South Dakota. Born in 1941, he was a lawyer and state legislator, before becoming governor in 1987. He has sought to plough the state's fiscal surplus into economic development, placing special emphasis on education.

**MIENO, Yasushi**. *Japan*. Governor of the Bank of Japan. Born in 1924 in Oita prefecture, he graduated from the law faculty of Tokyo University and joined the Bank of Japan, in 1947. He became deputy governor in 1984 and governor, replacing Satoshi Sumita, in 1989.

**MIES, Herbert**. *Germany*. German Communist Party (DKP) leader. Born in Mannheim in 1930, he studied economics in Moscow and went on to become leader of the DKP. The party failed to achieve any electoral impact, despite receiving heavy subsidies from East Germany, and it became a casualty of the collapse of communism.

**MIFSUD BONNICI, Karmenu (Carmelo)**. *Malta*. Labour Party leader. Born in 1933, he comes from a politically active family (his brother has been a Nationalist Party MP since 1966 and his cousin Ugo is education minister). He himself studied law and specialized in trade union work, becoming deputy leader of the Maltese Labour Movement in 1980, and only then entering a full-time political career, with the encouragement of Labour leader and prime minister Dom Mintoff. He helped organize the party's controversial 1981 election victory, was co-opted into parliament and given ministerial office the following year, and groomed to succeed Mintoff, who resigned in December 1984. Under his less abrasive and non-confrontational leadership the Labour government resolved its long and bruising battle with the church over education, and improved its relations with Western countries. He accepted the election defeat of 1987 with good grace, describing it as "the most peaceful election in our history" and thus "an historic day for Malta", and he has continued to lead the Malta Labour Party in opposition, despite serious doubts over his health.

**MIGUEL, Lorenzo**. *Argentina*. Trade union leader. A champion of orthodox Peronism, he has led the powerful Metalworkers' Union (UOM) for over 20 years, also leading a semi-independent faction within the General Confederation of Labour (CGT). Generally regarded as more willing than other union leaders to reach an accommodation with the government, in July 1990 he launched a strike in protest at government restriction of wage increases to below the rate of inflation.

**MIKLOSKO, Jozef**. *Czechoslovakia*. Deputy premier. In the government formed in June 1990 and dominated by Civic Forum, he is the sole Christian Democrat. He is from Slovakia, where the Christian Democratic Movement is increasingly a force to be reckoned with, recording the highest proportion of the vote in the November 1990 local elections. His government brief includes responsibility for human rights, including information policy.

**MIKULSKI, Barbara**. *USA*. Democratic senator from Maryland. A second-generation Polish-American, born in 1936, she was a social worker and Baltimore councillor before election to the House of Representatives in 1976. She became one of only two women in the Senate in 1986. A strong supporter of minority and women's rights, she retains blue-collar support through her pro-labour stance and energy in helping constituents. She lacked committee influence in the House, but has gained this rapidly in the Senate on the appropriations and labour and human resources committees.

**MILLER, Bob**. *USA*. Democratic governor of Nevada. Born in 1945, he practised law and served as lieutenant-governor before taking over as acting governor in 1987 from Richard Bryan, who had gone on to the Senate in January 1990. He was elected in his own right in November 1988. His main concern is to encourage economic diversification and reduce Nevada's dependence on gambling.

**MILLER, George**. *USA*. Democratic congressman from California. Born in 1945, he practised law and was elected to the House of Representatives in 1974. Partisan and liberal, he is a strong conservationist and environmentalist. He is likely to succeed **Mo Udall** as chairman of the interior committee. Also interested in social issues, he chairs the select committee on children, youth and families.

**MILLER, Zell**. *USA*. Democratic governor of Georgia. Born in 1942, he was elected governor in 1990, and had previous state government experience as Georgia's secretary of state.

**MILLON, Charles**. *France*. Right-wing politician. Born in 1945 and trained in economics, he became mayor of his home town, Belley, in 1977. A National Assembly member since 1978, he played a key role in the 1988 presidential campaign of **Raymond Barre**, and has since hitched his star to ex-president **Valéry Giscard d'Estaing**'s aspirations to lead a centre-right revival in French politics.

**MILO, Ronni**. *Israel*. Minister for police. Born in Tel Aviv in 1949 and trained in law, Milo, Menachem Begin's son-in-law, has been a Likud MP since 1977. His early brashness has given way to maturity.

**MILOŠEVIĆ, Slobodan**. *Yugoslavia*. President of Serbia. Born in 1941, he began his career in local government, leaving the Belgrade city information service in 1969 to become deputy director of Tehnogas Enterprises, of which he was later director-general from 1973–78. He then became president of Beobanka in Belgrade, before becoming Belgrade communist party leader. In 1986 he was elected Serbian party leader and in 1988 was chiefly responsible for constitutional changes which brought Kosovo and Vojvodina back under Serbian control. In 1989 he became president of Serbia. In July 1990, he was also elected president of the Socialist Party of Serbia, the renamed communist party. Personally ambitious, Milošević has built up his image as the champion of the Serbs, successfully forcing their perceived grievances to the top of the political agenda. In the process, he has inflamed the fears of other nationalities of a Serbian attempt to turn Yugoslavia into Greater Serbia. Widely criticized for his rigid dogmatism, Milošević has retaliated through the dismissal of unsympathetic journalists and the silencing or emasculation of publications critical of him. In December 1990 his party effectively eclipsed the challenge from the right in Serbia's elections, unashamingly vying for the nationalist vote, and he himself won a landslide victory in the presidential poll against **Vuk Drasković**.

**MIODOWICZ, Alfred**. *Poland*. Trade union leader. Born in 1929, he worked as a furnaceman at the Nowa Huta steelworks. When Solidarity was banned he came to the fore in 1984 as chairman of the new official All-Poland Alliance of Trade Unions (OPZZ). He joined the ruling communist Polish United Workers' Party politburo in 1986, leading to accusations in some union quarters that he was compromising the OPZZ's professed independence. His pugnacious approach to the 1989 round-table talks appears to have reflected the OPZZ's understandable insecurity about its future once Solidarity was legalized again.

**MIRGHANI, Mohamed Osman el-**. *Sudan*. Leader of Democratic Unionist Party. A member of a leading Sudanese political and religious family, he heads the Democratic Unionist Party (DUP), which draws its support from the Khatmiya Muslim sect. The DUP, the second largest party in parliament after the 1986 elections, joined the coalition government formed by the prime minister, **Sadiq el-Mahdi**. In 1988 El-Mirghani became involved in efforts to end the civil war in the south, signing an agreement with Sudan People's Liberation Movement leader **John Garang** in November which included the abrogation of Islamic law.

El-Mahdi reluctantly agreed to adopt this agreement, but was prevented from doing so by the June 1989 coup. Six months after the coup, El-Mirghani was allowed to travel to London for medical treatment.

**MIRSAIDOV, Shakurulla**. *USSR*. Vice-president of Uzbekistan. Born in 1938, he managed during 25 years working in state economic planning to remain untainted by the widespread corruption which brought down many fellow Uzbek officials in the 1980s. Recently he was mayor of the Uzbek capital, Tashkent, for five years. He was named a deputy premier in 1989, and in March 1990 he was elected premier by a new Uzbek parliament. He moved in November to the new post of vice-president.

**MISUARI, Nur**. *Philippines*. President of the Muslim separatist Moro National Liberation Front (MNLF). He rose to prominence as a commander of the Mindanao-based MNLF in the early 1970s, and led the separatist delegation at the inconclusive 1975 talks with the government, held under the auspices of the Islamic Conference Organization. For much of the past two decades he has lived in exile in Saudi Arabia, and has at various times received support from both Libya and Iran. He controls a militia several thousand strong, but its effectiveness has been hampered by internal divisions, which have seen the emergence of a rival Egyptian-backed Moro Islamic Liberation Front under Hashim Salamat. While rejecting various government offers of autonomy, the separatists have at times made common cause with disaffected rightist army elements.

**MITCHELL, George**. *USA*. Democratic senator from Maine and Senate majority leader. Born in 1933, he was educated at Bowdoin College and Georgetown University, and capped his legal career with a judgeship. Appointed in May 1980 to take over Ed Muskie's Senate seat, he was returned to office in the 1982 election and has held the seat ever since, rising rapidly within party ranks to become majority leader in 1988. The son of a janitor, he identifies strongly with the Democratic party's working class roots and often took offence at the philosophy and style of **Ronald Reagan**'s administration. His combative role as chairman of the Democratic senatorial campaign committee in the victorious 1986 mid-term election belied his former reputation as a low-key partisan. His performance on the committee investigating the Iran-Contra affair, particularly his tough questioning of Oliver

North, and his nationally televised response for the Democrats to Reagan's statement on it brought further kudos. Mitchell, who feels that his party can get more mileage out of the Iran-Contra affair, would like to reopen investigations. He is a more liberal and activist Senate leader than his predecessor, **Robert Byrd**, but he moved quickly to establish good relations with powerful conservatives, such as **Lloyd Bentsen**. His style combines partisanship, coalition-building and mastery of detail, best evidenced by his handling of environmental issues, his main concern before 1988.

**MITCHELL, James**. *St Vincent and the Grenadines*. Prime minister. Born in 1931 on the island of Bequia, and trained as an agronomist, he was first elected to the House of Assembly in 1966. He resigned from the St Vincent Labour Party in 1972 and became premier as an independent by holding the balance of power. He later founded the New Democratic Party, which overwhelmingly won elections in 1984. Mitchell combines popular policies, such as land reform, with a centre-right stance stressing economic prudence and diversification.

**MITKOV, Vladimir**. *Yugoslavia*. President of Macedonia. Elected in April 1990 from among the existing communist-dominated collective republican presidency, he was to hold office only until Macedonia had held its multi-party elections; however, those elections, at the end of the year, produced a hung parliament.

**MITRA, Ramon**. *Philippines*. Speaker of the House of Representatives. A former chairman of the ruling alliance, Lakas ng Demokratikong Pilipino, and agriculture minister early in **Cory Aquino**'s presidency, he is associated with both the president's brother, José "Peping" Cojuangco and her estranged cousin **Eduardo Cojuangco**, Mitra is regarded as a strong contender in the 1992 presidential election.

**MITROVIĆ, Aleksandar**. *Yugoslavia*. Deputy premier. Elected vice-president of the presidency of Serbia in May 1988, he was released from this post in March 1989 to take up his appointment as federal deputy premier. In October 1990, some Serb deputies in the federal assembly demanded his dismissal because of his participation in a federal mission led by **Vasil Tupurkovski** which tried to mediate between the Croat government and certain Serb-populated districts in Croatia engaged in armed rebellion. He refused to resign.

**MITSOTAKIS, Constantine**. *Greece*. Prime minister. A Cretan, born in 1918, he is the

nephew of the liberal elder statesman Eleftherios Venizelos, a relationship that helped his entry into dynasty-dominated Greek politics. He studied law and economics in Athens but returned to Crete during the Nazi occupation. He was twice arrested and condemned to death but escaped execution. Since 1946, he has been one of the MPs representing Chania. He gained notoriety in 1964 when he joined with other liberal deputies in splitting away from the Centre Union government, a move that set off the chain of events leading to the colonels' dictatorship (1967–74). He escaped abroad to Paris where he was active in the opposition to the military regime. On his return he founded the New Liberal Party, but in 1978 joined New Democracy (ND), rising rapidly through the ranks to be elected its leader in 1984. After failing to secure an overall majority in three successive elections, he finally became prime minister in April 1990, since when he has been responsible for implementing a vigorous economic reform programme.

**MITTERRAND, Danielle**. *France*. Born Danielle Gouze in 1924, she married **François Mitterrand** in 1944. After the war (she was decorated for her resistance activities) she specialized in bookbinding and craft work, while playing an active supporting role in her husband's career, reminding him of socialist ideals amid the world of political compromises. An elegant but retiring person, she has come under criticism from the right in her role as "first lady", but has continued her involvement with human rights causes, the provision of local democracy and aid to disaster victims.

**MITTERRAND, François**. *France*. President. Born in 1916, he initially followed a career in law and journalism; later, he was to publish numerous books of essays and political reflections. Decorated for his wartime resistance role, he sat in the National Assembly in 1946–58 and the Senate in 1959–62, holding many ministerial posts, notably as interior minister (1954–55) and justice minister (1956–57) during the Algerian war. Under the Fifth Republic he has contested no fewer than five presidential elections, and was derided by his opponents as the "eternal loser" until he was third time lucky in 1981. At his first unsuccessful attempt, in 1965, he nevertheless campaigned impressively against Charles de Gaulle and built himself a base to lead the left in succeeding years as president of two umbrella groups, the Federation of the Democratic and

Socialist Left (FDGS) and the Convention of Republic Institutions (CIR). In 1971 he joined, and became leader of, the revamped Socialist Party (PS), drawing up in 1972 the common programme for government with the Communist Party (PCF), and losing only narrowly in the 1974 presidential campaign against **Valéry Giscard d'Estaing**. His success in revitalizing the socialist camp in the 1970s, and the progressive enlargement of the PS to make it the dominant party of the left, led to serious strains with the Communists, and it became impossible to conclude a common programme for parliamentary elections in 1978. In 1980, still committed to a united left strategy and touting a programme for fundamental change, Mitterrand declared his candidacy once again for the presidential elections of 1981. The socialist **Michel Rocard** withdrew in his favour, and the communist **Georges Marchais** was eliminated in the first round, leaving Mitterrand to defeat Giscard in the run-off, after a campaign in which he had remained free of the scandal that tarnished the image of the outgoing regime. The Communists were quickly brought into government, but by 1984 it seemed that the bold promises of change had led up an economic cul de sac. Sufficiently decisive to commit himself to a tricky U-turn, which many believed he had foreseen all along, Mitterrand survived, with a growing reputation for statesmanship and consensual politics. His own popularity was perhaps higher than his party's, but he did his image no harm in attempting "cohabitation" (1986–88) with a right-wing government and assembly majority. Nor was he above changing the electoral rules before calling legislative elections in 1988, at which the left recovered a majority. After his success in making his party the main single force in French politics, he has proved himself a pragmatist in power, continuing to command the centre field around which his would-be successors jockey for position. In person, he is cool and impassive and, despite his reputation for Machiavellian intrigue, he has gradually acquired an impressive presidential air. When the Gulf crisis flared up in late 1990, he first supported calls for a diplomatic settlement, while at the same time being careful to distance France from Iraq. However, the eventual decision to send French troops to the region underlined Mitterrand's commitment to the Atlantic alliance.

**MIYAMOTO, Kenji.** *Japan.* Japan Communist Party (JCP) leader . Born in 1908 in Yamaguchi prefecture, he graduated from the economics faculty of Tokyo Imperial University (now Tokyo University) and in 1931 became a member of the JCP, which was illegal during the pre-war period. He played an active part in the party and spent 12 years in prison. After World War II, Miyamoto made efforts to reconstruct the party. He became a leading member and served as secretary-general in 1958. First elected to the House of Councillors (upper house) in 1977, he became chairman of the JCP central committee in 1982. His influence both within and outside the party has declined in line with the eclipse of communism worldwide. Despite this, he retained the chair of the central committee at the party conference in 1990. Miyamoto's wife, Yuriko, was a famous writer of so-called "proletarian novels".

**MIYAZAWA, Kiichi.** *Japan.* Liberal Democratic Party (LDP) politician and faction leader. Born in 1919 in Hiroshima prefecture, he worked in the finance ministry before his election in 1953 as an LDP member of the House of Councillors (upper house), where he served two terms before winning a seat in the House of Representatives (lower house). Immensely experienced in government, he has held a string of cabinet posts dating back to 1962, including terms as chief cabinet secretary, foreign minister and (twice) finance minister. In 1986 he became leader of a party faction, and was seen as a likely contender for the party presidency, but was one of those tainted by involvement in the Recruit shares scandal, and had to resign as finance minister in December 1988. A fluent English speaker of undoubted intellectual capacity, his political views put him on the left of the party, but his influence may be diminished by jealousy of his abilities and by resistance to his rather stiff and formal manner.

**MLADENOV, Petar.** *Bulgaria.* Former president. Born into a peasant family in Toshevtsi in 1936, Mladenov studied at Sofia University and the Moscow State Institute of International Relations. He was active in the Communist Youth League before joining the party, and by the age of 34 he was a full member of the party central committee and a member of the National Assembly. He was foreign affairs minister from 1971–89, when he was instrumental in the November palace coup which ousted president Todor Zhivkov. Pro-reform, Mladenov took over as party leader and head of state. In April 1990 he was elected president of the new non-socialist republic, but resigned amid scandal three months later.

**MMUSI, Peter.** *Botswana.* Vice-president, finance and development planning minister. A veteran politician and member of the Botswana Democratic Party, of which he is chairman, he took over his present posts on **Quett Masire**'s accession to the presidency in 1980. His financial policy has been conservative, leading to criticism from those who would like to see Botswana's diamond wealth used more actively to create jobs and alternative engines of growth. Lacking Masire's popularity, he lost his parliamentary seat to opposition Botswana National Front leader Kenneth Koma after a contested vote in the 1984 elections, a victim of popular dissatisfaction at rising unemployment. Only the resignation of another MP and his subsequent assignment to one of four nominated seats enabled him to retain his posts. Since 1983 he has been chairman of the council of ministers of the Southern African Development Co-ordination Conference (SADCC).

**MOADA, Mohammed.** *Tunisia.* Opposition politician. He was elected as secretary-general of the centre-left Social Democratic Movement (MDS) in September 1989, in succession to Ahmed Mestiri, who had stepped down following the party's poor showing in the April 1989 elections. The MDS has lost support both to the ruling Constitutional Democratic Rally (RCD) and the Islamic fundamentalists.

**MOAKLEY, Joe.** *USA.* Democratic congressman from Massachusetts. Born in 1927, he was a lawyer, state legislator and Boston councillor before his election to the House of Representatives in 1972. An old-style Irish-American politico, his power base is the rules committee, the gateway for all House legislation, which he chairs. Though mainly interested in constituency matters, he has a liberal reputation on national security issues and was an early critic of the star wars programme.

**MOBUTU SESE SEKO, Marshal (Joseph Désiré).** *Zaïre.* President. Born in 1930, the son of a cook, he was educated at mission schools and later studied journalism in Brussels. He served as a non-commissioned officer in the Belgian colonial army from 1950–56 and then worked as a journalist for two years. As a key member of Patrice Lumumba's Congo National Movement (MNC) from 1957, he took part in the independence negotiations in Brussels in 1959. In June 1960 Lumumba appointed him chief of staff of the Congolese army, where he proved ruthlessly effective in suppressing an army mutiny. In September that year he intervened in the power struggle between Lumumba and Joseph Kasavubu, taking control with the backing of Belgium and the USA. Mobutu handed over power to a civilian government in August 1961 but intervened again in November 1965 in renewed conflict between President Kasavubu and the prime minister, Moïse Tshombe. This time Mobutu installed himself as head of state and, with the army firmly in control, outlawed most political activity and concentrated power in his own hands. A new party, the Popular Revolutionary Movement (MPR), formed in 1967, became the country's sole political organization and, under Mobutu's careful control, the means of preferment. Opposition has been suppressed or neutralized by the distribution of patronage; the president has been particularly careful to preserve the loyalty of the army and to prevent any rival from building a power base. In the early 1970s a campaign of Africanization was pursued: the country was renamed Zaïre, the capital Léopoldville became Kinshasa, and the president Africanized his name and ordered others to follow suit. The relative stability Mobutu has brought to Zaïre was most seriously challenged in 1977 and 1978, when remnants of Tshombe's army invaded the crucial copper-producing Shaba province in the south; on both occasions French and other foreign troops had to be brought in to put down the rebellion. Mobutu has cultivated close links with the West; the support of the USA has been particularly valuable in gaining Zaïre a sympathetic hearing from international financial organizations on its economic problems, including its enormous debt. A wily diplomat, Mobutu allowed his country to be used during the late 1980s as a conduit for US covert aid to the Angolan rebels but retained sufficient credibility to act as a mediator between the rebels and the Angolan government. His relationship with Belgium, the former colonial power, has been marked by frequent ruptures, sometimes provoked by the attacks of Zaïrean exiles in Belgium on his government's corruption or its human rights record, and sometimes by criticism in the Belgian media of Mobutu's extravagant lifestyle. Mobutu shows no signs of wishing to step down, despite doubts about his health. In 1990, aware, as always, of the direction in which the political wind was blowing, he announced moves to transform Zaïre into a multi-party democracy, with both presidential and multi-party legislative elections to be held in 1991. Mobutu was widely expected to stand for a further presidential term.

**MOCK, Alois.** *Austria.* Foreign minister. Born in 1934, he studied law at the universities of Vienna, Bologna, and Brussels. A member of the Austrian People's Party (ÖVP), he was its deputy leader from 1975–79 and party head for 10 years from 1979, but took much of the blame for the party's failure to dislodge the socialists from pre-eminence, and was replaced by **Josef Riegler** after the party's lacklustre performance in the 1989 regional elections. His first cabinet-level post was at education in 1969–70. After a long spell in opposition he became foreign minister in 1987. As minister he has committed himself deeply to seeking Austrian membership of the EC. He served as deputy chancellor from 1987–89, but was supplanted in this, as in the party leadership, by Riegler.

**MOCUMBI, Pascoal.** *Mozambique.* Foreign minister. A former health minister, in January 1987 he was appointed to foreign affairs, a portfolio formerly held by the new president, **Joaquim Chissano.** He was simultaneously appointed external relations secretary on the central committee secretariat of the ruling Front for the Liberation of Mozambique (Frelimo) and was elected to the Frelimo politburo in 1989.

**MOCZULSKI, Leszek.** *Poland.* Right-wing politician. He is chairman of the Confederation for an Independent Poland (KPN), which he set up in 1979. Having spent most of the Solidarity period in prison, Moczulski was twice imprisoned and then granted an amnesty between 1982 and 1986 for his anti-communist activities. He participated in the partly free June 1989 elections as an independent candidate, but lost to his Solidarity-sponsored rival. In 1989–90 he led the KPN to legitimacy as a fully fledged political party in Poland's new democracy. He was one of six candidates to gather the 100,000 signatures required to participate in the 1990 presidential elections, in which he finished last.

**MODA'I, Yitzhak.** *Israel.* Liberal MP and finance minister. Born in 1926, Moda'i has been rather a late political developer. He has led planning, finance, energy and justice ministries since 1978 and entered the inner cabinet in 1988. He won praise for helping to reduce inflation in 1985 but lacks significant popular support.

**MODROW, Hans.** *Germany.* Party of Democratic Socialism (PDS) politician. Born in

1928 at Jasenitz, he rose slowly through the ruling Socialist Unity Party (SED) but gained a popular reputation for honesty and open-mindedness as party secretary in Dresden. Brought into the politburo and made prime minister at the height of the convulsions of November 1989, he formed the grand coalition government pending the March 1990 elections. Elected to the Volkskammer (East German parliament) under the renamed PDS banner, he became one of the PDS members of the enlarged Bundestag after unification in October and was re-elected in December.

**MOGGIE ANAK IROK, Datuk Leo.** *Malaysia.* Works minister. Born in 1941, Moggie Anak Irok made his mark as a member of the Sarawak state cabinet in the 1970s. He entered the federal cabinet as energy, telecommunications and posts minister in 1979. He was given charge of works (a slight promotion) in June 1989. Leader of the Dayak nationalist Sarawak National Party, he is tipped to be the state's next chief minister and was re-elected in December.

**MOHORITA, Vasil.** *Czechoslovakia.* Chairman of the Communist Party of Czechoslovakia. Born in 1952 in Prague, educated at the Komsomol college in Moscow and a Communist Party member from the age of 18, he joined its central committee in 1988. Propelled forward as a new face after the "velvet revolution" of 1989, he became party first secretary in December of that year, and was the man who revealed that the 1968 Soviet invasion was acknowledged to have been "unjustified and mistaken". He has helped to maintain a credible position for the party in the new political era, with second place at the June 1990 elections and an improved share of the vote at local elections in November that year. In August 1990 he became party chairman on the retirement of Ladislav Adamec.

**MOHTASHAMI, Hojatoleslam Ali Akbar.** *Iran.* Radical politician. Born in Tehran in 1946, he worked in Ayatollah Khomeini's Paris office before the 1979 revolution, having studied under him in exile in Najaf, Iraq. Ambassador to Syria from 1982, he was interior minister from 1985 until dismissed by **Ali Akbar Hashemi Rafsanjani** in August 1989. He was elected to the Majlis (parliament) in late 1989 as a member for Tehran. A committed radical, he is a leader of the radical Council of Militant Clerics and consistently supports Lebanon's militant Shia Hezbollah (Party of God). A regular contributor to the *Kayhan* daily, he also has his own monthly, *Bayan*. He remains a focus of radical challenge to Rafsanjani's pragmatism.

**MOI, Daniel arap.** *Kenya*. President. Born in 1924, he began his career as a teacher, entering politics in 1957 as a nominated member of the pre-independence legislative council. In 1960 he left the Kenya African National Union (KANU), which had become the leading African political party, to form the Kenya African Democratic Union, which aimed to protect the interests of Kenya's smaller ethnic groups. In 1964 he agreed to dissolve the party and rejoin KANU. He was parliamentary secretary at the education ministry before becoming its minister in 1961. From 1962–64 he was local government minister, later moving to the home affairs ministry, a post he combined with that of vice-president from 1967 until succeeding to the presidency on the death of Jomo Kenyatta in 1978. A member of the small Kalenjin ethnic group, Moi was seen as a consensus successor to Kenyatta, reducing the political dominance and rivalry of the country's major ethnic groups, the Kikuyu and Luo. As president he has steadily consolidated his power through the extension of the role of KANU as the sole party, easing Kikuyu out of positions of influence and skilfully playing off potential rivals against each other. He has become increasingly intolerant of opposition, accusing critics of the one-party state of tribalism and subversion. Evidence of heavy-handed repression, notably the allegations of government involvement in the murder of foreign minister Robert Ouko in February 1990, has been a cause of growing concern among Kenya's allies.

**MOJADEDI, Sighatulla.** *Afghanistan*. *Mujaheddin* leader. President of the so-called "interim government" and a key figure among the more moderate of the Peshawar-based political leadership, he lacks military experience but is widely respected. He will enhance his credibility if he can help to forge a consensus among the powerful guerrilla commanders. Given the fractious dynamics of the Afghan resistance, this will remain an uphill struggle.

**MOKHEHLE, Ntsu.** *Lesotho*. Politician. Born in 1919, he founded modern politics in Lesotho by setting up the Basutoland African Congress (later the Basutho Congress Party – BCP) in 1952. Although he played a pivotal role in securing Lesotho's independence in 1966, he has spent most of the years since in exile. Arrested after the prime minister Chief Leabua Jonathan refused to accept the BCP's victory in the 1970

elections, he fled the country four years later. Although an early opponent of apartheid, he based himself in South Africa, setting up a guerrilla force that attempted to topple Jonathan. In 1989 he returned home after disbanding his guerrillas and in 1990 agreed to participate in the constitutional assembly set up by the military government to prepare the way for a return to democracy. A strong contender to be the next civilian prime minister, he is on record as favouring the ultimate merger of Lesotho with a post-apartheid South Africa.

**MOLEFE, Popo.** *South Africa*. United Democratic Front (UDF) leader. The secretary-general of the UDF, he was one of the defendants in the three-year Delmas treason trial, on charges arising from the September 1984 unrest in the Vaal triangle. Sentenced in December 1988, his release in late 1989 marked an important shift in the government's approach. He resumed his leading role in the UDF, and when the African National Congress (ANC) was unbanned he became its branch leader in the Alexandra township.

**MOLIN, Rune.** *Sweden*. Industry minister. Born in 1931, he was a bus conductor and shop assistant before becoming a full-time trade union official. In 1983 he became a deputy leader of the powerful Swedish Trade Union Confederation (LO). Benefiting from the strong links between the LO and the Swedish Social Democratic Labour Party (SAP), he was appointed industry minister in 1990, with a brief to supervise the phasing out of the nuclear energy programme.

**MÖLLEMANN, Jürgen.** *Germany*. Education and science minister. Born in Augsburg in 1945, he was a qualified teacher, and also ran his own public relations agency. A Christian Democrat before joining the Free Democratic Party in 1970, he was appointed education and science minister in 1987, having previously served as state secretary in the foreign ministry.

**MOLYNEAUX, James.** *UK*. Northern Irish unionist politician. Born in 1920, he was for years a partner in the family printing firm. Elected to parliament in 1970, he became leader of the Official Unionist Party (OUP) in 1979. Although he heads the dominant unionist formation in the province, he has frequently been overshadowed by the assertive **Ian Paisley**.

**MOMOH, Major-General Joseph Saidu.** *Sierra Leone*. President. Born in 1937, Momoh, like his predecessor Siaka Stevens, is from the northern Limba ethnic group. He received his military training in the Gold Coast (now Ghana), UK and Nigeria. He was commissioned in the Sierra Leone armed forces in 1963 and became a major-general in 1983. In 1973 he was appointed an MP and minister of state by President Stevens, whose chosen successor he became, taking over the presidency in November 1985. Momoh's position was strengthened by the failure of the 1987 coup attempt, which led to the trial and execution of first vice-president Francis Mishek Minah and to the eclipse of some members of the influential Lebanese trading community. His appointment of a new finance minister in November 1989 appeared to indicate a new determination to tackle severe economic problems and attack corruption.

**MOMPER, Walter.** *Germany.* Former mayor of West Berlin. He was born in Sulingen, Lower Saxony, in 1945 but grew up in Bremen. After studying politics, history and economics he worked for the West Berlin historical commission until 1986. He joined the Social Democratic Party (SPD) in 1969, rising through the Berlin young socialists, and was elected to the Berlin parliament in 1975. He chaired the SPD parliamentary group in Berlin from 1985–89, and has been chairman of the Berlin SPD since 1986 and a member of the West German SPD executive at federal level since 1988. In March 1989 Momper was elected, with Green support, as governing mayor of West Berlin, leading an SPD-Green coalition. With his academic background he did not seem ideally suited for what was to be such a high-profile role as the wall came down. He coped well with the limelight and showed administrative and political skills in framing the arrangements for a unified Berlin but lost the mayorship to his predecessor and long-standing rival **Eberhard Diepgen** in December 1990.

**MONGE ALVÁREZ, Luis Alberto.** *Costa Rica.* Former president. Born in 1925 and educated at the universities of Costa Rica and Geneva, Monge was among the founders of the National Liberation Party (PLN) in 1951. First elected to the Legislative Assembly in 1958, he was its president between 1970 and 1974. In 1982 he was elected president for the PLN. His presidency was marked by attempts to preserve the country's neutrality against pressure from the USA to join an anti-Sandinista alliance. He remains an influential figure within the PLN.

**MONTAZERI, Ayatollah Hossein Ali.** *Iran.* Former leader-designate. Born in Najafabad, Isfahan province, in 1922, Montazeri played an active part in anti-Shah politics, and in 1966 was imprisoned and subsequently tortured. After spending a period in Najaf with Ayatollah Khomeini, he returned to Iran and was again arrested and sentenced in 1975. On his release in 1978, he was appointed by Khomeini to the Council of the Islamic Revolution. Following the 1979 revolution, he became speaker of the first Assembly of Experts, charged with drafting the constitution. In 1985 the second Assembly of Experts chose him to succeed Khomeini as spiritual leader. Something of a moderate, in 1986 he instigated the release of all political prisoners no longer considered a threat to the regime, and later made a number of outspoken attacks on economic mismanagement and political oppression. Later, however, his career suffered a setback through his close association with Mehdi Hashemi, a radical maverick executed in 1987. His continuing outspokenness contributed to his dismissal by Khomeini as his successor in 1989 and he was confined to teaching in Qom. He is politically rather naive, but much admired for his sincerity.

**MONTGOMERY, Sonny.** *USA.* Democratic congressman from Mississippi. Born in 1920, he saw active service in World War II and Korea, then worked in insurance before election to the House of Representatives in 1966. A conservative, he has concentrated since 1985 on chairing the veterans affairs committee; the 1988 GI education bill carries his name.

**MOORE, Michael Kenneth (Mike).** *New Zealand.* Labour Party leader. Born in 1939, he was a social worker and printer before entering politics, becoming an MP at the age of 23, but suffering a spell of unemployment after losing his seat in 1975. Returning to parliament in 1978, he built his career on the left of the party, and was a cabinet minister from 1984 onwards, taking on the job of external relations and trade minister in 1988. An effective negotiator, energetic and with a colourful and convivial personality, he was sometimes criticized for being erratic and for failing to follow through on ideas and initiatives. The party turned to him as the prospect of electoral defeat loomed large in 1990, dropping him into the post of prime minister only weeks before the October poll, in place of Geoffrey Palmer. In opposition he faces the task of rebuilding a party still divided over former finance minister Roger Douglas's harsh prescription of austere liberal "Rogernomics".

**MORGAN, Peter.** *UK.* Business leader. Born in 1936, he studied history and then joined IBM.

He was appointed to the IBM board in 1980 and was director of corporate services when he left the company in 1989 to become director-general of the Institute of Directors, in succession to John Hoskyns.

**MORIYAMA, Mayumi.** *Japan.* Liberal Democratic Party (LDP) politician. While studying law at Tokyo University she married an LDP politician, the late Kinji Moriyama. After a long career in the labour ministry she was brought into the government at the age of 61, as one of two female members of the first **Toshiki Kaifu** cabinet form August 1989. Initially appointed director-general of the Environment Agency, she moved up after two weeks to become chief cabinet secretary (when Tokuo Yamashita resigned over a sex scandal), but encountered much prejudice within the party, where many believed that a woman could not successfully perform the tasks of the prime minister's "right-hand man". She lost her post in the February 1990 reshuffle, to fellow **Toshio Komoto** faction member **Misoji Sakamoto**, and left in no doubt about her angry reaction to this dismissal. Elected twice to the House of Councillors (upper house), she had to drop plans to stand in 1990 as an LDP candidate for the House of Representatives (lower house), in which her party has no female representation.

**MOSALA, Itumeleng.** *South Africa.* Azanian People's Organization (Azapo) president. A theology lecturer at Cape Town University and exponent of Black Consciousness, he was elected in March 1990 as Azapo president and has confirmed its hardline stance against negotiations with the white regime.

**MOSBACHER, Robert.** *USA.* Secretary of commerce. Mosbacher, one of four Texans appointed to the cabinet by **George Bush**, has a background similar to that of the president. Born in 1927 into a wealthy family in New York, he settled in Texas after World War II, and made a personal fortune as head of an energy development company with leases along the Gulf of Mexico coast. His career in the oil business proved even more lucrative than that of Bush – he amassed net wealth reportedly in excess of $200m, making him the wealthiest member of the cabinet. An old friend of President Bush, he served as finance chairman for his 1988 election campaign, raising more than $25m. A vigorous proponent of economic nationalism, Mosbacher supports the tough enforcement of US laws against allegedly unfair foreign trade practices, and favours relaxing anti-trust laws to allow US companies to co-operate in new technological areas in order to improve their international competitiveness. While admitting to "mixed feelings" about growing foreign investment in US real estate and industry, he believes in limiting foreign investment only when it threatens national security, deters US technological innovation or affects strategic sectors.

**MOSHOESHOE II, Motlotlehi (Constantine Bereng Seeiso).** *Lesotho.* Former king. Born in 1938, he was educated at Oxford University, succeeded as paramount chief of Basutoland in 1960 and became king of Lesotho at independence in 1966. His reign was turbulent, in part because of his reluctance to act as a political figurehead. His frequent clashes over constitutional issues with the prime minister, Chief Leabua Jonathan, reached a head in 1970 when Jonathan suspended the constitution after early results showed he had lost the general election to **Ntsu Mokhele**'s Basuto Congress Party. Moshoeshoe was forced into eight months' exile in Europe, being allowed to return only after signing an agreement not to participate in politics. His relationship with Jonathan's successor, Major-General **Justin Lekhanya**, was equally stormy and resulted in another period of forced exile, which began in March 1990. From his base in London he has called for the restoration of the 1966 constitution and an immediate return to civilian rule. He was officially deposed in November 1990.

**MOSTOVOI, Pavel.** *USSR.* Former deputy prime minister. Born in 1931, he was brought in from the Ukrainian government to take over in July 1989 as a USSR deputy premier and chairman of the USSR State Committee for Material and Technical Supply.

**MOTZFELDT, Jonathan.** *Denmark (Greenland).* Chief minister. Born in 1938, he became a Lutheran pastor, then co-founded the Forward party (Siumut) in 1977. As party leader, he became Greenland's first chief minister under the new autonomy statute when Siumut won the 1979 elections outright, and remained in office as leader of a left-wing coalition after his party lost overall control in the Landstring (parliament) in the election of 1984. In December 1990 he called new elections, scheduled for March 1991, after claims that cabinet ministers had misused public funds for entertaining party members.

**MOUREAUX, Philippe.** *Belgium.* Deputy prime minister, minister for the Brussels region.

Born in 1939, he studied history, becoming a professor at Brussels University. In the 1970s he was senior adviser to various Walloon Socialist Party (PS) ministers and in 1980 was appointed interior minister and in 1981 justice minister. Elected to parliament later that year, he took over as chief minister of the regional government of Wallonia, a post he held until 1985 and briefly again in 1988 before being appointed a deputy prime minister and minister for the Brussels region. In 1989 he was also put in charge of the reform of education in Wallonia.

**MOUSSA, Pierre.** *Congo.* Minister of state for plan and economy. The long-serving economic supremo of President **Sassou-Nguesso**'s government, Moussa appeared to yield overall responsibility for the government's market-oriented economic reforms to the prime minister, Alphonse Poati-Souchalaty, until the latter's resignation in December 1990. Moussa is associated with the radical-socialist M-22 faction of the ruling Congolese Labour Party (PCT).

**MOUZAOIR, Abdallah.** *Comoros.* Politician. A former foreign minister and a long-standing opponent of former president Ahmad Abdallah, Mouzaoir was imprisoned from 1982–84 before going into exile in France, where he founded the moderate Union for a Democratic Republic of Comoros. He returned to the Comoros in 1985 but was prevented from contesting the 1987 elections. In April 1990, following the overthrow of Abdallah, he was appointed special adviser for economic and financial affairs by President **Saïd Mohammed Djohar**.

**MOVSISYAN, Vladimir.** *USSR.* Former Armenian Communist Party leader. Born in 1933, he worked in agriculture before becoming a full-time party official in 1969, rising to first deputy premier in Armenia by 1984. He was elected Armenian Communist Party first secretary in April 1990 (the political instability created by Armenia's dispute with neighbouring Azerbaijan having unseated his two predecessors in the previous two years). In August 1990 he lost the Armenian presidential election to nationalist leader **Levon Ter-Petrosyan** and was replaced as party leader by Stepan Pogosyan.

**MOWLAM, Marjorie.** *UK.* Labour politician. Born in 1949, she studied social anthropology and went on to lecture and become a college administrator. Elected to parliament in 1987, she has published several books on disarmament issues, and was appointed to the opposition Treasury team, with special responsibility for City affairs, in 1990.

**MOYNIHAN, Colin.** *UK.* Parliamentary under-secretary in the Department of Energy since July 1990, MP since 1983. Born in 1955, the energetic Olympic medallist was sports minister from 1987–90, when he became the first holder of that portfolio to be offered another government job.

**MOYNIHAN, Daniel.** *USA.* Democratic senator from New York. Born in 1927, he was educated at New York's City College, Tufts University and Fletcher School of Law and Diplomacy, gaining a PhD in government. A specialist on work and the family in the welfare state, he was co-author of a controversial book, *Beyond the Melting Pot* (1965), which attributed social problems among blacks to unstable family structures. After a professorial career, he moved into federal administration in the mid-1960s and later drew up President Richard Nixon's Family Assistance Plan, which Congress rejected. Nixon made him ambassador to India and in 1975 Gerald Ford appointed him ambassador to the UN, where he was fervently pro-Israel. This stance helped gain him election as New York senator in 1976. A "neo-liberal" since the late 1960s, Moynihan rediscovered his old liberal loyalties in the 1980s as one of the foremost opponents of the welfare policy of **Ronald Reagan**'s administration. In 1981 he led the successful Senate fight against social security cutbacks and he authored the 1986 tax reform removing 6m low-income families from the rolls, a cause that reflected his concern to shift welfare away from service provision to income support. He also modified his trenchant anti-communism, opposing Reagan's Central American policy and urging arms reduction.

**MSUYA, Cleopa David.** *Tanzania.* Industry and trade minister. Born in 1931 and educated at Makerere University College in Uganda, he joined the civil service in 1956, working in community development and rising to hold the post of principal secretary in a series of ministries after 1964. He joined the cabinet as finance minister in 1972, becoming industries minister in 1975 and being appointed prime minister in 1980 after the resignation of Edward Sokoine for health reasons. When Sokoine returned to the post in 1983, Msuya again became finance minister. Given added responsibility for economic affairs and planning from 1985, he presided over the economic reforms implemented by new President **Ali Hassan Mwinyi**. In 1990 he handed over the finance portfolio to the rising star **Stephen Kibona** and moved to industry and trade.

**MSWATI III (Makhosetive).** *Swaziland.* King. Born in 1968, Prince Makhosetive, the second-youngest of the 70 or so sons of King Sobhuza II, was chosen as successor on his father's death in 1982. A power struggle within the royal family followed the old king's death, from which Makhosetive's mother Ntombi emerged the victor. She governed as queen regent while the prince completed his education at an English public school, after which he was crowned as Mswati III in April 1986. As king he has appeared as traditional and absolutist as his father. He has spent the first years of his reign clamping down on opposition and installing his supporters at all levels of the political hierarchy but faces growing agitation for democratic reform.

**MUBARAK, Mohammed Hosni.** *Egypt.* President. Born in 1928 in a village in lower (northern) Egypt, he joined the air force in 1950, training as a fighter pilot. He served as a bomber squadron commander in the Yemen civil war, and in 1967 after the war with Israel, he was appointed director of the air academy, with the task of rebuilding the air force. He became air chief of staff in 1969 and was overall military commander in chief from 1972–75, gaining some credit for the army's performance in the 1973 war (which is officially celebrated as a victory in Egypt). In 1975 he was appointed vice-president by President Anwar Sadat, with responsibility for the state security apparatus and for the organization of the ruling National Democratic Party after its foundation in 1978. He became president after Sadat's assassination in October 1981. Mubarak's low-key style contrasted strongly with the flamboyance of his predecessor, but he soon proved that he possessed authority, moving quickly to establish his position and put down the unrest that followed Sadat's death. He has overseen a gradual democratization of the country, with the 1984 elections being the freest for 35 years. He launched a popular anti-corruption drive that led to the departure of some Sadat cronies from the cabinet. His conciliatory and sensitive approach towards other Arab leaders led to Egypt's gradual return to the Arab fold. This culminated in the renewal of diplomatic relations by most Arab states in late 1987, albeit achieved at the price of a virtual freeze in relations with Israel. Mubarak's profile in pan-Arab affairs has been heightened still further by his role as leader of one of the Arab states that opposed Iraq's August 1990 annexation of Kuwait and sent troops to join the multinational force in Saudi Arabia.

**MUDENDA, Elijah Haatukali Kaiba.** *Zambia.* Politician. Born in 1927 and one of President **Kenneth Kaunda**'s loyal inner circle, he is a technocrat who became one of the ruling United National Independence Party's (Unip's) leading intellectuals. During his long political career he has held a variety of top government and party posts, including the agriculture, finance and foreign affairs portfolios during the 1960s. Prime minister from 1975–77, he now chairs the appointments and disciplinary committee of the Unip central committee.

**MUDGE, Dirk Frederik.** *Namibia.* Republican Party leader and chairman of opposition Democratic Turnhalle Alliance. Born in 1928, he was the first white politician in power to advocate a black majority government. In October 1977 he formed the Republican Party after leaving the ruling National Party, of which he was deputy chairman, when it insisted on maintaining apartheid in the proposed new constitution. A month later he participated in a walkout, on the same issue, at the Turnhalle constitutional conference, which led to the foundation of the Democratic Turnhalle Alliance (DTA), of which he was elected chairman. He was chairman of the ministers' council of the first national assembly from 1980 until it was abolished by the South African administrator-general three years later. During his tenure he supervised the Namibianization of the civil service and promoted the abolition of formal apartheid. He was finance and government affairs minister in the 1985–89 transitional government and was instrumental in the DTA's decision to act as a constructive parliamentary opposition after Swapo's victory in the November 1989 independence elections.

**MUFAMADI, Sydney.** *South Africa.* Confederation of South African Trade Unions (Cosatu) deputy general secretary. One of the few prominent leaders from the Venda ethnic group, he has championed the African National Congress (ANC) and the South African Communist Party in the labour movement, since his days with the General Allied Workers' Union.

**MUGABE, Robert Gabriel.** *Zimbabwe.* President. Born in 1924, he was a nationalist leader during the liberation war, becoming independent Zimbabwe's first prime minister in April 1980 and in December 1987 its first executive president. He is also first secretary and president of the ruling ZANU (PF) party. A highly educated, ascetic and disciplined politician, he has become one of Africa's foremost statesmen, a leader of the non-aligned movement and of the pro-sanctions anti-apartheid lobby. Part of his early career as a teacher was spent in Ghana, where he met his wife Sally Mugabe. Returning home in 1960 he became active in nationalist politics, first as a member of **Joshua Nkomo**'s ZAPU and then as founder and secretary-general of ZANU when it split from ZAPU. In 1964 he was arrested by the Ian Smith regime and spent the next 10 years in detention, together with many of his present cabinet colleagues, to whom he remains notably loyal. In 1975 he escaped to Mozambique to direct ZANU's armed struggle. He was elected president of ZANU in 1977 and as joint leader with Nkomo of the Patriotic Front negotiated Zimbabwe's independence at the 1979 Lancaster House conference. After his party's victory at the 1980 elections he confounded expectations of a rapid move to a socialist one-party state, keeping strictly to the terms of the Lancaster House accord and instituting policies which, while raising the living standards of the black majority, emphasized economic continuity and reconciliation with the white minority. The acclaim this won him was soured by the widening breach with Nkomo and especially the army's excesses against so-called ZAPU dissidents in Matabeleland in 1983–84. The rift was not bridged until the 1987 agreement to merge the two parties, formally achieved in December 1989. The agreement brought him closer to his goal of a one-party state, which he continues to champion despite growing popular criticism of the party leadership. Mugabe himself – although re-confirmed as president in the 1990 elections – has not escaped this. His initial reluctance to act against colleagues implicated in high-level corruption in 1988–89 undermined his moral authority and – although he is in no immediate political danger – left a lasting impression of him as isolated from the grassroots on which his popularity depends.

**MUGICA HERZOG, Enrique.** *Spain.* Justice minister. Born in 1932 in San Sebastián in the Basque country, and a graduate in law, he worked secretly as an opponent of the Franco regime, in the Spanish Communist Party and, from 1967, on the executive of the clandestine Spanish Socialist Workers' Party (PSOE). After the restoration of democracy he emerged as a senior member of the PSOE secretariat, on which

he served until 1987. He entered parliament as a deputy for Guipuzcoa in 1977, and became justice minister in 1988.

**MUKONG, Albert.** *Cameroon.* Writer and opposition politician. Born in 1935 in Bamenda, he is a long-standing government critic who represents Cameroon's sometimes restive anglophone minority. He is a leader of the Social Democratic Front, set up in 1989 to press for greater democracy. Detained without trial for six years by the Ahidjo government during the 1970s – an experience recounted in his book *Prisoner without a Crime* – and on several occasions since, Mukong was found not guilty of subversion in April 1990.

**MULRONEY, Brian.** *Canada.* Prime minister. Born in Baie Comeau, Quebec, in 1939, he was educated at St Francis Xavier University, Nova Scotia and Laval University, Quebec City. He then joined a prominent Montreal law firm and remained a partner until 1976 when he joined the Iron Ore Company of Canada. He served as a negotiator in labour disputes at the company, and has lectured on labour issues and labour law. An aspiring politician from an early age, Mulroney has been involved with the Progressive Conservative Party of Canada since 1956 when he was an elected delegate to the leadership convention at the age of 17. Twenty years later, he was himself a candidate when **Joe Clark** became Conservative leader in 1976. He persisted in his quest for power, and was elected Conservative leader in June 1983, winning a seat in the House of Commons in a by-election in a Nova Scotian constituency two months later. In the same year his book *Where I Stand* was published, containing a collection of his speeches and essays. Mulroney finally achieved his dream in the 1984 general election when the Conservatives inflicted the heaviest-ever defeat on the Liberals. Mulroney was re-elected in 1988, although not with the overwhelming majority he had received in 1984. His popularity was affected by numerous political scandals involving his ministers. He laid his political career on the line with the proposed constitutional reforms known as the Meech Lake Accord, which were intended to give more power to the provinces, particularly Quebec. When some provincial premiers failed to ratify the accord, Mulroney's credibility and his standing in the opinion polls dropped to unprecedented levels. Mulroney has been criticized by many for being a street politician, more interested in power than in running the country.

**MUNTASIR, Umar Mustafa al-.** *Libya.*
Planning and economy secretary. Born in Tripoli
in 1938, Al-Muntasir was educated at the
prestigious Victoria College in Alexandria,
studied business administration at the American
University of Beirut and worked as an
accountant for an oil company. Active in
revolutionary politics from an early age, he was
briefly imprisoned by the royalist regime in
1969 but released after **Muammar Qaddafi**
took power in September that year. He joined
the petroleum ministry and became director-
general of the Libyan National Oil Company in
1973, before entering the cabinet as heavy
industry secretary in 1979. His administrative
competence earned him the post of secretary of
the General People's Committee (cabinet) –
effectively prime minister – in 1987, but his
October 1990 appointment to the planning and
economy ministry amounted to a demotion,
although still allowing him scope to advocate
economic liberalization.

**MUNTEANU, Marian.** *Romania.* President of
the League of Students. Born in 1964, he studied
at Bucharest University. Ardently anti-
communist, he led the 1990 demonstrations
against the National Salvation Front in central
Bucharest. This turned into a mass occupation
which was ended by force. Arrested in the
resulting crackdown, he was released in August
after mass demonstrations in his support.

**MURATA, Keijiro.** *Japan.* Liberal Democratic
Party politician. Born in 1924, he studied law in
Kyoto and has represented an Aichi constituency
in the House of Representatives (lower house)
since 1969. Powerful in the construction lobby,
and a former chairman of the party's policy
research council, he headed the important
international trade and industry ministry in
1984–85.

**MURATA, Ryohei.** *Japan.* Ambassador to
USA. Born in 1929 in Kyoto prefecture, he
graduated from the law faculty of Kyoto
Imperial University (now Kyoto University) and
entered the foreign ministry. Murata became
first secretary at the Japanese embassy in
Washington in 1970. After serving as director-
general of the Economic Affairs Bureau, he was
appointed director-general for inspection in
1984. After a spell as ambassador to Australia in
1985, he became deputy and later vice-minister
of foreign affairs in 1987. Murata became
ambassador to the USA in 1989.

**MURDANI, General Leonardus Benjamin
(Benny).** *Indonesia.* Defence and security

minister. Born in 1932. A blunt-talking
Javanese Catholic, Murdani won his spurs at the
head of a paratroop unit against the Dutch in
Irian Jaya in 1962. He went on to serve in a
number of high-level military intelligence posts
before his appointment as the armed forces
commander in 1983. Five years later he was
shifted into the cabinet as defence minister.

**MURMANN, Klaus.** *Germany.* Federal
Association of Employers (BVA) president. Born
in 1932 in Dortmund, he studied in Bonn,
Harvard, the Sorbonne and Kiel, gaining a
doctorate in law in 1957. A Christian Democrat,
he practised law before joining the employers'
organization, the BVA, of which he became
president in 1986.

**MURR, Michel al-.** *Lebanon.* Deputy prime
minister and national defence minister. Murr
was appointed to the cabinet formed by **Umar
Karami** in December 1990. As a strong
supporter of the Syrian presence in Lebanon, his
appointment angered hard-line Phalangists.

**MURRAY, Lowell.** *Canada.* Government
leader in the Senate. Born in 1936, in New
Waterford, Nova Scotia, Murray was educated at
St. Francis Xavier and Queen's universities. He
has long been an adviser to the Progressive
Conservative Party of Canada and was appointed
to the Senate in 1979. In 1986 Murray was made
government leader in the Senate and minister of
state for federal-provincial relations. He was
**Brian Mulroney**'s key aide during the failed
Meech Lake Accord discussions of June 1990.

**MUSA, Alhaji Balarabe.** *Nigeria.* Politician.
Born in 1936, he was a teacher and accountant
before being elected governor of Kaduna state as
the candidate of the People's Redemption Party
(PRP) in the 1979 elections. In 1981 he was
impeached by the state house of assembly, in
which his political opponents had a majority, for
irregular conduct of state business and was
replaced as governor. Breaking away from the
PRP, Musa set up the People's Progressive Party,
but was prevented from contesting the 1983
elections because the party did not gain official
recognition. He was detained by Muhammadu
Buhari's government, but released after Major-
General **Ibrahim Babangida** took power in
1985. In May 1989 he tried to launch a new,
radical socialist party, the People's Liberation
Party, but was immediately charged with
contravening the government's ban on former
politicians; the charges were later dropped.

**MUSA HITAM, Datuk.** *Malaysia.* Envoy to
UN, former deputy prime minister. Born in

1934. Formerly education minister, Musa in 1981 defeated **Tengku Razaleigh Hamzah** in the contest to become deputy president of the United Malays National Organization (UMNO); he was at the same time appointed deputy prime minister and home affairs minister. After five years in the post, Musa resigned, citing "irreconcilable differences" with **Mahathir Mohamad**. The following year he joined Razaleigh in challenging Mahathir's leadership of the UMNO. However, in early 1988 Musa ended his alliance with Razaleigh and rejoined Mahathir's reconstituted UMNO. In reward, Musa was appointed as a special envoy to the UN, with ministerial status, effectively paving the way for his return to a full cabinet post.

**MUSEVENI, Yoweri.** *Uganda.* President. Born in 1944 and educated in Tanzania, he was involved in the radical youth wing of the Uganda People's Congress (UPC) in the 1960s, and worked briefly in the State Research Department at State House. He went into exile after the takeover by Idi Amin in 1971 and the following year took part in an unsuccessful invasion from Tanzania designed to restore Milton Obote to the presidency. Museveni was active in opposition to Amin from exile and was one of the leaders of the successful invasion that finally overthrew Amin in 1979. He became defence minister in the interim administration and vice-chairman of the military commission that ruled for a time after the ousting of President Godfrey Binaisa. By this time an opponent of Obote, Museveni stood against him in the 1980 presidential elections as candidate of the Uganda Patriotic Movement, a regrouping of the dissatisfied factions of the UPC. Denouncing the elections as a fraud, he began a guerrilla campaign that gained support as disillusion with Obote's government grew. The five-year campaign by Museveni's National Resistance Army culminated in the capture of Kampala in January 1986 and the installation of a government with Museveni as president. Although plagued by persistent violence in some parts of the country, Museveni has done much to restore some stability and security.

**MUSSGNUG, Martin.** *Germany.* National Democratic Party (NPD) chairman. Born in Heidelberg in 1936, he served as a member of the parliament of Baden-Württemberg for the far-right NPD from 1968–72, and was elected chairman of the NPD in 1971.

**MUTAFCHIEV, Iordan.** *Bulgaria.* Defence minister. Appointed in the Socialist-led government formed by **Andrei Lukanov** in September 1990, he was retained in the transitional coalition government formed by **Dimitur Popov** in December 1990.

**MUTALIBOV, Ayaz.** *USSR.* President of Azerbaijan. Born in 1938, he worked in Azerbaijan's oil industry until the late 1970s, when he became a full-time Communist Party official and subsequently a republican government minister. He was named Azerbaijan's deputy premier in 1982, and premier in January 1989. He was elected Azerbaijani Communist Party first secretary in January 1990, his predecessor having been sacked in disgrace because of the collapse of Soviet rule in Azerbaijan in the face of nationalist violence. Mutalibov combined the party leadership with the new post of president in May; the former office gave him Communist Party of the Soviet Union politburo membership in July 1990. In September-October 1990 his party won convincingly in elections to the republic's Supreme Soviet.

**MWINYI, Ali Hassan.** *Tanzania.* President. Born in 1925 on the mainland, Mwinyi was taken to Zanzibar as a child by his parents and was educated there. He was Zanzibar's permanent secretary for education from 1963–64 and held a series of public service appointments until 1970, when he was appointed minister of state. During the 1970s and early 1980s he held several ministerial portfolios. In 1984 he was elected president of Zanzibar and vice-president of Tanzania after the resignation of Aboud Jumbe. This made him the designated successor to Nyerere, who had announced his intention to step down the following year. The choice of Mwinyi was seen as a compromise between the claims of **Rashidi Kawawa**, secretary-general of the ruling Chama Cha Mapinduzi (CCM), and the then prime minister **Salim Ahmed Salim**, but since taking over the presidency in August 1985, Mwinyi has proved very much his own man. He immediately launched a campaign against corruption and inefficiency and has gradually consolidated his position by removing conservative ministers. His economic policies have continued to steer Tanzania away from state socialism and have helped to bring about a reconciliation with international lending agencies, often in the face of opposition from party old guard. In 1990 he was reconfirmed as president in the October election, in which he was sole candidate.

# N

NABABSINGH, Prem. *Mauritius*. First deputy prime minister, Mauritian Militant Movement (MMM) leader. A former ambassador to France and a minister in **Aneerood Jugnauth**'s first government in 1982, Nababsingh took over from **Paul Bérenger** as leader of the opposition MMM in the run-up to the 1987 elections in a bid to broaden the party's appeal with the island's Hindu population. After the forging of a new coalition between the MMM and Jugnauth's Mauritian Socialist Movement in September 1990, Nababsingh joined the government as deputy prime minister and health minister.

NADER, Ralph. *USA*. Political campaigner. A lobbyist and campaigner who has pressed for legislation dealing with consumer protection, he was born in 1934 to Lebanese immigrants and was educated at Harvard University. His first victory was the passage of the 1966 Traffic and Motor Vehicle Safety Act, which made him something of a folk hero among the US public. His group of like-minded attorneys, "Nader's Raiders", have been successful advocates of changes in the law on food safety, data protection, occupational health and automobile insurance.

NAGY, Ferenc József. *Hungary*. Agriculture minister and leader of the Independent Smallholders' Party. Born in 1923 and trained as an agricultural engineer, he was a small farmer (and former director of a pilot agricultural co-operative) before mobilizing for the spring 1990 election campaign. In May he became agricultural minister, one of the four cabinet posts exacted by his party for joining **József Antall**'s Hungarian Democratic Forum (MDF)-dominated coalition government; he had shown his political skills the previous month by securing the chairmanship of his party and effectively shutting out those who had preferred a pact with the Alliance of Free Democrats. The uneasy task of government, to be reconciled somehow with his party's sole electoral platform of restoring pre-communist property ownership, was made even more difficult by the party's

choice of the more demagogic József Torgyán as its parliamentary group leader.

NAHAYAN, Shaikh Zaid ibn Sultan al-. *United Arab Emirates*. President, ruler (amir) of Abu Dhabi. Born in about 1915 in Al-Ain, he has been ruler of Abu Dhabi since 1966, and he became president of the UAE on its formation in December 1971. Re-elected president in 1976, 1981 and 1986, he is the driving force behind Abu Dhabi's oil-financed transformation into a modern state. Although Shaikh Zaid has retained certain traditions such as national dress and the Majlis (consultative council) system, he has also brought the federation into the technological age; his wife, Shaikha Fatima ibn Mubarak, has played an important part in developing the status of UAE women.

NAIDOO, Jay. *South Africa*. Confederation of South African Trade Unions (Cosatu) general secretary. A prominent figure in the agitation of the Mass Democratic Movement for the lifting of the state of emergency, his position makes him a key figure in determining how the labour unions will feature in the negotiations on a new South Africa. He was arrested in late August 1990 and charged with kidnapping a police officer whom Cosatu had paraded at a news conference.

NAJDER, Zdzisław. *Poland*. Chairman of Solidarity's Central Citizens' Committee. A literary critic, he was sentenced to death in his absence by the martial law regime for taking over the directorship of Radio Free Europe's Polish Service. He returned to Poland in 1989 to head the network of grassroots organizations through which Solidarity fought and won the June 1989 national and May 1990 local elections.

NAJIBULLAH, Mohammed. *Afghanistan*. President. Born in 1947, a doctor by training and a member of the (communist) People's Democratic Party of Afghanistan (PDPA) since 1965, he was twice imprisoned for his political activities, before the communist take-over of 1978, and shortly afterwards he fled to the USSR as the party was riven by factionalism. Returning after the Soviet intervention in 1979, he was put in charge of the state security information service, joined the party politburo in 1981, and became party general secretary in 1986. His coming to power continued the fragile ascendancy within the PPDA of the Parcham (flag) faction, in its rivalry with the more hardline Khalq (masses) faction, although he is a Pashtun from the Pakistan border area, and most of his Parcham allies came from the Dari-speaking urban intelligentsia. He holds the presidency on a seven-year term, having been elected by the Loya Jirga (national gathering of leaders) in November 1987. Since the completion of the Soviet withdrawal in February 1989, he has confounded the prediction that he would last six months at most. Adroitly fostering the divisions in the *mujaheddin* by suggesting his willingness to compromise, and going so far as to promise political pluralism without a leading role for the PDPA, he remains shrewdly aware that he needs to keep the USSR behind him. To this end he plays up the danger of Soviet Central Asia being inflamed by a militant Islamic Afghanistan to the south.

**NAKAJIMA, Hiroshi.** *Japan.* Director-general of World Health Organization (WHO). Born in 1928, he trained as a doctor and then carried out medical research in France and Japan. He joined WHO in 1973 as a senior adviser on drug policies. Devoted to medicine rather than diplomacy, he was nevertheless appointed WHO director-general in 1988, at the time Japan's only representative at the highest level within intergovernmental organizations.

**NAKAO, Eiichi.** *Japan.* International trade and industry minister. Born in 1930, he entered the House of Representatives (lower house) in 1967 and has served as chair of the Liberal Democratic Party (LDP) executive council and national organizing committee. He was director-general of the Economic Planning Agency in the **Noboru Takeshita** government from 1987–88, and was brought back to the cabinet by **Toshiki Kaifu** in the December 1990 reshuffle. Charged with putting Japan's case at the deadlocked General Agreement on Tariffs and Trade (Gatt) talks, he was expected to prove less accommodating than his predecessor Kabun Moto over US demands to reduce protection for the rice-growing industry.

**NAKASONE, Yasuhiro.** *Japan.* Former prime minister. Born in 1918 in Gunma prefecture, he graduated from the law faculty of Tokyo Imperial University (now Tokyo University) and

started work within the interior ministry. First elected to the House of Representatives (lower house) for the Liberal Democratic Party (LDP) in 1947, he entered the cabinet as director-general of science and technology under Nobusuke Kishi in 1959. Originally a member of the Kinsho Kono faction, he established his own faction after Kono's death. He was appointed transport minister in 1967 and director-general of the Defence Agency in 1970, both under Eisaku Sato, and subsequently took over as international trade and industry minister. Nakasone successively held various important LDP posts, including chairman of the general council and secretary-general. In spite of his implication in the Lockheed scandal, he stood for the LDP presidency in 1978, unsuccessfully on this occasion. Four years later he won the post, and took over as prime minister. During his three terms as prime minister he visited 29 foreign countries in a strenuous effort to improve Japan's image abroad, notably in the USA. Declaring his wish to be seen as a "president-like prime minister", he also established many private advisory bodies. He resigned from the premiership and party leadership in 1987, nominating **Noboru Takeshita** as his successor. He remained a powerful politician within the party, but was implicated in the Recruit scandal, which led to him being called by the budget committee of the House of Representatives as a witness in 1989 and to his resignation from LDP.

**NAKAYAMA, Taro.** *Japan.* Foreign minister. A qualified doctor and specialist in paediatrics, he was born in 1924 in Osaka prefecture, and comes from a highly political background; his mother Masa was Japan's first female cabinet minister. He entered the prefectural assembly in 1955, the House of Councillors (upper house) in 1968, and the House of Representatives (lower house) in 1986. He served in Zenko Suzuki's cabinet as director-general of the Management and Co-ordination Agency, and plays an important role in formulating government policy in the medicine and technology fields. He has also been active in the formation of Liberal Democratic Party policy groups cutting across factional lines. **Toshiki Kaifu** made him foreign minister in August 1989 and retained him after the December 1990 cabinet reshuffle, despite opposition from the **Shintaro Abe** faction.

**NALLET, Henri.** *France.* Justice minister. Born in 1939 and a graduate in law and politics, he held posts with Catholic student, peasant and farming organizations before becoming a government adviser on agricultural matters. Elected to parliament in 1986 for the Socialist Party (PS) and a mayor since 1989, he was agriculture minister in 1985–86, a sensitive job to which he was re-appointed in 1988. In October 1990 he replaced **Pierre Arpaillange** as keeper of the seals (Garde des Seaux) and justice minister.

**NAMALIU, Rabbie**. *Papua New Guinea*. Prime minister. Born in 1947, he was a notable historian, studying in Australia and California and then teaching at the University of Papua New Guinea before taking up government posts as a protégé of **Michael Somare**. He entered parliament in 1982 and became foreign minister, then primary industry minister (1984–85), and took on in 1988 the post of prime minister as well as leadership of the Pangu Pati, something of a poisoned chalice as he faces repeated challenges and votes of confidence in the unstable ebb and flow of party allegiances. He has swallowed a sharp dose of IMF austerity medicine and re-introduced the death penalty to contend with growing violence. He has had to face up to the Bougainville secessionists, ordering in the troops before giving Somare the job of sorting out a negotiated solution. Energetic, persistent and intelligent rather than charismatic, he has shown himself in Pacific regional affairs to be a strong advocate of co-operation among island states, even at the risk of sharpening the conflict with the developed countries (Australia and New Zealand) in the South Pacific Forum.

**NAMBOODIRIPAD, E.M.** *India*. General secretary of Communist Party of India (Marxist). Born in 1909, he became involved in left-wing politics from an early age, and in 1938 was secretary of the Kerala unit of the Communist Party. He was a member of the state assembly for Madras (which then included Kerala) in 1939–40, and elected to the central committee of the Communist Party in 1941 and the politburo in 1950, becoming general secretary in 1962. Although generally regarded as a "centrist" in the factional disputes that divided the party in the 1960s, he supported the left-leaning CPI(M) when the party split in 1964, and has been its general secretary since 1977. He was first elected to the Kerala state assembly in 1957 and served as the state's chief minister in 1957–59, heading the first Communist government in the country's history. He occupied the same position in 1967–69.

**NAPOLITANO, Giorgio**. *Italy*. Italian Communist Party (PCI) politician. Born in 1925 in Naples, he gained a law degree. In 1945 he joined the PCI, later becoming a leading member of the central committee, and taking on responsibilities as parliamentary group leader (until 1984) and then foreign affairs spokesman. He has played a leading role in making contacts between the PCI and West European socialist parties. Identifying with the old guard, he led opposition to the nomination of the reform-minded **Achille Occhetto** as deputy general secretary in 1987, but was eventually persuaded not to vote against the appointment. He has sat in the Chamber of Deputies since 1953.

**NARONG WONGWAN**. *Thailand*. Agriculture minister. Born in 1925, Narong leads the Solidarity Party, Thailand's main opposition grouping which was formed in 1989 by the merger of four parties. Narong's son, Anusorn Wongwan, entered the House of Representatives as a Solidarity deputy in mid-1990. Narong became agriculture minister when Solidarity joined the ruling coalition in December 1990.

**NĂSTASE, Adrian**. *Romania*. Foreign minister. Born in Bucharest in 1950, he graduated in law from Bucharest University in 1973 and completed a doctorate in 1978, specializing in international law, on which he has published many works. He is vice-president of the Romanian Association of International Law and International Relations and an associate member of the International Institute for Human Rights in Strasbourg. A history of mild dissent under the Ceauşescu regime helped him to become established as a member of the National Salvation Front during the revolution, and he was elected to parliament in May 1990.

**NATHAN, Abie**. *Israel*. Prominent peace activist. Born in India in 1926, Nathan is renowned for his (illegal) contacts with the Palestine Liberation Organization (PLO); he was jailed for six months for having had a meeting with the PLO in October 1989 but met **Yasser Arafat** again a month after his release. He runs a pirate radio station, the Voice of Peace, broadcasting from a ship off Tel Aviv.

**NATTA, Alessandro**. *Italy*. Italian Communist Party (PCI) politician. Born in 1918 in Imperia, he gained a degree in letters at Pisa University in 1941 and was elected to the Chamber of Deputies in 1948. After the death of Enrico Berlinguer, Natta was elected general secretary of the PCI in June 1984, and continued his predecessor's policy of bringing the PCI closer to the other democratic left-wing parties. He resigned in June 1988 after a heart attack, and was succeeded by his deputy **Achille Occhetto**, with whose reform of the party he has been out of sympathy.

**NAVARRO WOLFF, Antonio.** *Colombia.* Politician and former guerrilla leader. Born in 1949, he was a leader of the left-wing April 19 Movement (M-19) guerrillas, now a political party. He lost a leg in an assassination attempt in 1985. He returned from exile in 1989 and became a presidential candidate after the murder of the previous Democratic Alliance–April 19 Movement candidate, coming third and helping to break the traditional mould of Colombian politics. Appointed health minister, he resigned almost at once to head his party's slate for constituent assembly elections, in which it won 19 seats, becoming the effective third force in Colombian politics.

**NAYEF IBN ABDUL-AZIZ, Prince.** *Saudi Arabia.* Interior minister. Born in Riyadh in 1933, he was the city's governor before moving on through various security posts to become interior minister in 1975, with additional responsibility for the kingdom's special security forces. Like **King Fahd** he is one of the favoured "Sudairi Seven" brothers. Nayef is tough and sometimes outspoken. After the incident in July 1987 when over 400 pilgrims, mostly Iranian, were killed by Saudi police after demonstrations in Mecca, Nayef openly called for the downfall of the Iranian regime.

**NAZARBAYEV, Nursultan.** *USSR.* President of Kazakhstan. Born in 1940, a metallurgical engineer by profession, he became a full-time Communist Party official in 1977. He was elected Kazakhstan's prime minister in 1984, survived the clean-up of the republic's administration begun in late 1986 by **Gennady Kolbin**, and replaced Kolbin as Kazakh Communist Party leader in June 1989; in July 1990 that post gave him Communist Party of the Soviet Union politburo membership. He was elected chairman of the Kazakh Supreme Soviet (*de facto* president) in February 1990. In April he was elected to the new post of executive president. In December 1990 he took an unexpected stand alongside **Boris Yeltsin**, arguing that the republics rather than the centre should determine the distribution of powers under a new union treaty.

**NAZER, Shaikh Hisham.** *Saudi Arabia.* Oil minister. Born in 1932, an ebullient, urbane and charming Saudi commoner, he took two degrees at the University of California. Director-general of the Central Planning Organization since 1968, Nazer launched the first five-year plan in 1970, acutely aware of the kingdom's inadequate bureaucracy, primitive infrastructure and shortage of skilled manpower. In late 1975 he was made planning minister. Although Nazer voted for restraint after the 1973–74 oil boom, he did so with caution, so beholden had he become to the then crown prince **Fahd**, even earning himself the nickname *Hisham abdul-Fahd* (Hisham, slave of Fahd). In October 1986 he replaced veteran oil minister Ahmad Zaki Yamani, after reports of growing tension between the king and Yamani over the latter's support for price cuts and production increases.

**NDAW, Abdoul Azizi.** *Senegal.* Political secretary of Socialist Party (PS). A member of Senegal's national assembly (parliament) since 1983, he was elected the assembly's president in December 1988, after the resignation of Daouda Sow. In March 1990, he was picked by President **Abdou Diouf** to replace French-born Jean Collin as political secretary of the ruling PS, number two in the party hierarchy.

**NE WIN.** *Myanmar (Burma).* "Strongman" of the regime. Born in 1911, he is one of the few surviving "30 Comrades", members of a group of young nationalists who founded the army during the Japanese occupation in the early 1940s. In 1962, as head of the army, Ne Win moved against the prime minister, U Nu, and installed a military government. He went on to rule Burma with an iron fist, dragging the country into isolation and economic and political ruin. Massive nationwide demonstrations in 1988 forced him to step into the background, but most commentators are agreed that he remains the supreme source of political power.

**NEAOUTYNE, Paul.** *France (New Caledonia).* Kanak leader. Elected in April 1990 to the presidency of the Kanak Socialist National Liberation Front (FLNKS), he faces the challenge of filling the void left by the assassination of Jean-Marie Tjibaou. His task is made more difficult still by the opposition of Yann Ureguei's radical anti-colonialist United Front for Kanak Liberation (FULK) party to the Matignon accord. Neaoutyne leads the Palika party, which is one of the smaller FLNKS components.

**NECKER, Tyll.** *Germany.* Federal Association of German Industry (BDI) president. A graduate in economics and a successful manufacturer of cleaning machines, he has done much to modernize the BDI and increase its political influence since he became its president in 1987.

**NEGROPONTE, John.** *USA.* Ambassador to Mexico. Born in London in 1939, he graduated from Yale University and made a career in foreign affairs, participating in the Paris peace talks with North Vietnam and serving on the National Security Council from 1970. He was ambassador to Honduras from 1981–85 and a presidential adviser on national security affairs between 1985 and 1987. His appointment as ambassador to Mexico in 1989 caused some controversy because of his close ties to the Central Intelligence Agency (CIA), suggesting to some that **George Bush** saw Mexico as a security risk. The Senate delayed confirmation for several weeks, amid its probing of the Iran-Contra affair, while looking into Negroponte's role in schemes to help the contras by channelling more aid to Honduras.

**NEHRU, Arun Kumar.** *India.* Leading Janata Dal politician. Born in 1944 in Lucknow, a businessman and cousin of **Rajiv Gandhi**, he was persuaded to leave the business world for politics when Gandhi assumed the premiership in 1984. He became a general secretary of Congress (I) and was appointed as minister of state for power in 1985 and subsequently for internal security. He was one of the prime minister's principal strategists until his sudden dismissal from office in 1986. He was expelled from Congress in 1987 because of his criticisms of the party leadership and joined **V.P. Singh** in the creation of Jan Morcha, which later merged into Janata Dal. He served as commerce minister in the 1989–90 National Front government.

**NEIERTZ, Véronique.** *France.* Junior minister for consumer affairs. Born in 1942, she studied commerce before taking up a university post. She was elected to the Socialist Party (PS) executive in 1979, with special interests in women's issues and international affairs. Since 1981 she has held a seat in the National Assembly, and was party parliamentary spokeswoman in 1983–86. She has been in her present post since 1988.

**NELSON, Ben.** *USA.* Republican governor of Nebraska. A trained lawyer, he was born in 1941 and was elected governor in 1990, when he defeated Republican incumbent Kay Orr.

**NEWMAN, Constance.** *USA.* Office of Personnel Management (OPM) director. From humble beginnings as a typist in the Department of the Interior in 1962, she rose to high-ranking positions in the administrations of Richard Nixon and Gerald Ford, notably as assistant secretary for housing and urban development. She was appointed in 1989 to head the OPM, a post regarded as one of the most difficult in Washington. She supervises over 2m civil servants, and is set to spearhead the recruitment of minorities.

**NEWTON, Antony.** *UK.* Secretary of state for social security since 1989, MP since 1974. Born in 1937, he was a keen member of the Tory Bow Group and later worked at the party's Central Office. He served as a whip and in several positions within the Department of Health and Social Security.

**NGUYEN CO THACH.** *Vietnam.* Foreign minister. Born in 1923, Thach took part in the Paris peace negotiations of the early 1970s. He became foreign minister in early 1980 and was promoted to deputy prime minister in 1986. Throughout the 1980s the urbane Thach has constituted the public face of the secretive Hanoi leadership and has ably represented his country in complex international negotiations on Cambodia and the "boat people" issue.

**NGUYEN DONG SY, General.** *Vietnam.* Deputy prime minister and politburo member. General Nguyen played a prominent role in the military campaign to conquer the South in 1975. He was transport and communications minister from 1982–86, when he was promoted to his present positions.

**NGUYEN DUC TAM.** *Vietnam.* Politburo and secretariat member since 1982 when he also took over the influential position of head of the party's organization committee from veteran leader Le Duc Tho, to whom he is said to be related.

**NGUYEN THANH BINH.** *Vietnam.* Politburo member. Appointed to the politburo in 1986, when he also became "Mayor of Hanoi" for two years, Binh is now often used as a troubleshooter by general secretary **Nguyen Van Linh**.

**NGUYEN VAN LINH.** *Vietnam.* Party general secretary. Born in 1913 in Hanoi, he was sent south by the party in 1939 and worked there clandestinely until 1975 when he emerged as a key figure in the political transformation of Saigon into Ho Chi Minh City. He entered the politburo the following year but was dropped in 1982 after opposing rigid socialist economic policies in the South. He regained his position in 1986 when he was also appointed party general secretary to spearhead a nationwide policy of economic renovation known as *Doi Moi*. But he ran into opposition from party diehards when he launched a vigorous personal campaign against bureaucracy and has now firmly identified himself with the hardliners in opposing political pluralism. Suffering from poor health, Linh was expected to retire at the next party congress in 1991.

**NGUZA KARL I BOND.** *Zaïre.* Opposition politician. One of the great survivors of Zaïrean politics, he was born in 1938 in Shaba province and studied international relations in Belgium. He worked as a radio announcer in Lubumbashi and Kinshasa before embarking on a diplomatic career in 1964, first under his uncle Moïse Tshombe and, from 1965, under the second republic of President **Mobutu Sese Seko**. After government and diplomatic postings he was appointed foreign minister in 1972, a post he held until 1974 and for three later periods (1976–77, 1979–80 and 1988–90). His relationship with President Mobutu has not always been amicable, however; in 1977, after the Shaba invasion, he was accused of treason and sentenced to death. Subsequently pardoned, he was given his old job back and in 1980 appointed prime minister. In 1981, after attacking Mobutu for corruption, he resigned and went into exile in Belgium. A second rapprochement in 1985 led to his appointment as ambassador to the USA, followed by a return to the foreign ministry three years later. In May 1990 he left the government, announcing in August that he would stand as a candidate in the presidential elections due in 1991. He also formed his own party, the Federal Union of Independent Republicans of Zaïre.

**NISHANOV, Rafik.** *USSR.* Soviet of Nationalities chairman. Born in 1926, he was a career Communist Party official, but a succession of ambassadorial appointments in the 1970s and early 1980s enabled him to avoid being tainted by the official corruption then endemic in Uzbekistan. He returned home as republican foreign minister in 1985; from 1986–88 he was Uzbekistan's head of state; and in January 1988 he was named Uzbek Communist Party leader, after corruption investigations toppled his predecessor. His election in June 1989 as chairman (speaker) of the Soviet of Nationalities (one of the two USSR Supreme Soviet chambers) made him one of the highest-ranking officials from Central Asia.

**NISHIOKA, Takeo.** *Japan.* Liberal Democratic Party (LDP) general council chairman. Born in 1936 in a political family where both parents were members of parliament, he followed in their footsteps, representing a Nagasaki constituency for the LDP. On the right of the party, and with a particular interest in educational issues, he was a founder member of the New Liberal Club splinter group in 1976 but rejoined the LDP, well before most of his dissident colleagues, in 1980. **Noboru Takeshita** gave him the post of education minister in 1988. After the general election in February 1990 he was named as chairman of the LDP's general council, as part of the party changes which reflected the increasing influence of his younger generation. He retained his post after the December 1990 cabinet reshuffle, despite pressure for change from the faction of **Kiichi Miyazawa**.

**NIYAZOV, Saparmurad.** *USSR.* President of Turkmenia. Born in 1940, he headed the Communist Party organization in Ashkhabad (the Turkmen capital) before being transferred to Communist Party of the Soviet Union (CPSU) personnel work in Moscow in 1984. Returning to Turkmenia in March 1985 as prime minister, he was appointed the following December as Turkmen Communist Party first secretary, his predecessor having been dismissed in a purge of corrupt or incompetent Turkmen officials. Niyazov was elected chairman of the Turkmen Supreme Soviet (*de facto* republican president) in January 1990; he retained his party post, which gave him CPSU politburo membership in July 1990. An old-style Communist whose republic has been less affected than any other by *glasnost* and *perestroika*, he was returned unopposed under a new system of direct elections to the Turkmen presidency in October 1990. The following month his deputy Sakhat Muradov took over the chairmanship of the Supreme Soviet.

**NKOMO, Joshua Mqabukonyongolo.** *Zimbabwe.* Vice-president. Born in 1917, founder and president of ZAPU and one of the leaders of the independence war, he is Zimbabwe's longest-serving nationalist politician. He began his political career in earnest in 1952, when he became president of the (Southern Rhodesian) African National Congress and later its successors, the National Democratic Party and ZAPU. ZAPU was banned in 1963 and he spent much of the next decade under restriction or detention by the Rhodesian government. After his involvement in the failed constitutional talks of 1976, he based himself in Lusaka directing ZAPU's military and diplomatic activities. In 1979 he was co-leader with **Robert Mugabe** of the Patriotic Front at the Lancaster House independence negotiations. After his party's heavy defeat in the 1980 elections, Nkomo turned down the ceremonial post of president to remain in active politics. He was appointed home affairs minister in the first post-independence cabinet, then minister without portfolio. The uneasy alliance between PF-ZAPU and ZANU (PF) collapsed in 1982 when Nkomo was sacked from the cabinet after the alleged discovery of weapons on two of his farms. Subsequent ZANU (PF) attacks on his party forced him into temporary exile and culminated in the army excesses in Matabeleland in 1983–84. Negotiations to end the rift began in 1986, leading to the December 1987 agreement to merge the two parties and Nkomo's return to the cabinet as senior minister without portfolio. He spent the next two years exercising his considerable political skills, building a working relationship with Mugabe and persuading his supporters that the merger was more than a shotgun wedding. In April 1990 Nkomo was appointed one of two national vice-presidents.

**NOBILI, Franco.** *Italy.* Industrial manager. Born in 1925 in Rome, he pursued a career in management in the construction industry, joining Cogefar Costruzioni Generali, the largest Italian private-sector construction enterprise, in 1959 and rising to become managing director and chairman. In November 1989 he was appointed chairman of the largest state holding company IRI (Istituto per la Ricostruzione Industriale) in succession to **Romano Prodi.** Nobili is a friend of **Giulio Andreotti.**

**NOIR, Michel.** *France.* Former Gaullist politician. Born in 1944 and a graduate in politics from the Institut d'Etudes Politiques, he had a career in private industry and marketing before rising to national prominence as a Gaullist Rally for the Republic (RPR) member of parliament since 1978, party officer and minister-delegate for urban affairs, housing, regional planning and transport in **Jacques Chirac**'s government of 1986–88. Mayor of Lyon since 1989, Noir has emerged as a popular critic of the divisive party structures and lack of unified sense of purpose on the right. He left the RPR in December 1990.

**NOOITMEER, Rufus.** *Suriname.* Leader of the Front for Democracy and Development faction in the National Assembly, Nooitmeer is widely tipped to be the future leader of the National Party of Suriname.

**NORI, Andrew.** *Solomon Islands.* Opposition leader. A law graduate from Papua New Guinea

University, he entered parliament in 1984 and formed the National Front for Progress the following year. He gained cabinet experience in the government of Sir Peter Kenilorea in 1986 and the government of Ezekiel Alebua which followed at the end of that year. In 1989, when the People's Alliance Party under **Solomon Mamaloni** returned to power, Nori took on the leadership of the opposition coalition, proving a vociferous critic of the government and particularly of what he saw as its divisive federalist proposals. His power base is in Malaita, the most populous island, but he represents a new generation of political leaders who have built a career outside traditional village-based power structures.

**NORIEGA MORENA, Manuel Antonio.** *Panama.* Former commander-in-chief of Panama Defence Forces and head of state. Born in 1938, Noriega joined the Panama Defence Forces (PDF), rising to become head of intelligence in 1970. By this time he was also working as an agent for the US Central Intelligence Agency (CIA). Within two years of the death in 1981 of General Omar Torrijos he had become effective ruler of Panama, although sheltering behind the facade of civilian figurehead presidents. His involvement in gun running, drug smuggling and money laundering led to the imposition of US economic sanctions aimed at forcing his removal, which he resisted. He eventually gave himself up after US troops invaded Panama in December 1989 and he was taken to Florida for trial on drugs charges.

**NOUMAZALAY, Ambroise.** *Congo.* Congolese Labour Party (PCT) secretary-general. Noumazalay was appointed to the post of secretary-general at the end of the PCT's fourth extraordinary congress in December 1990, which followed the resignation of prime minister Alphonse Poaty-Souchalaty.

**NOURBAKHSH, Mohsen.** *Iran.* Economy and finance minister. Born in Isfahan in 1948, Nourbakhsh read economics at Tehran University and gained a doctorate at the University of California. A student activist in the USA before the revolution, he returned to Iran in 1979 to work for the Islamic guidance ministry and teach economics at the Computer College and National University of Iran. He was deputy economy and finance minister and governor of the central bank for several years, resigning the latter post over differences with former prime minister Mir Hossein Moussavi. **Ali Akbar Hashemi Rafsanjani** appointed him economy and finance minister in 1989, with a mandate to reform Iran's chaotic foreign exchange market. He is in favour of controlling the money supply and boosting industrial production in line with Rafsanjani's free-market policies.

**NOURI, Abdollah.** *Iran.* Interior minister. Born in Isfahan in 1949, Nouri taught theology before the revolution. Member of parliament for Isfahan, he replaced **Ali Akbar Mohtashami** in 1989 as minister of the interior. He is close to the radicals and **Ahmad Khomeini**, though obviously trusted by **Ali Akbar Hashemi Rafsanjani** who has put him in charge of the National Security Council. His rapid rise to prominence came through his work as Khomeini's representative to the Islamic Revolution Guards Corps and as a member of the parliamentary plan and budget committee.

**NOZUE, Chimpei.** *Japan.* Politician. Born in 1932, he rose to national notice as a writer for television, entered the House of Councillors (upper house) in 1971 as an independent, and later joined the New Liberal Club, the Liberal Democratic Party (LDP) offshoot which rejoined the parent party in 1986. By this time, however, he had gone his own way again, setting up the Tax Party and exercising a strong influence over government policy in this sphere. In October 1990 the Tax Party was merged back into the LDP.

**NUJOMA, Sam (Shafilshuna Samuel).** *Namibia.* President. Born in 1929 in northern Namibia, he worked as a clerk before joining the Ovamboland People's Organization (OPO) and became its president in 1959. He retained the post, which he still holds, when OPO was reconstituted a year later as the South West Africa People's Organization (Swapo). He set up Swapo's provisional headquarters in Dar es Salaam, Tanzania, in 1961 and committed the organization to armed struggle five years later when the International Court of Justice rejected a Swapo complaint against South Africa. After gaining recognition for Swapo at the UN in 1972, he led the party at successive rounds of negotiations on Namibian independence over the following 17 years. He returned to Namibia in September 1989, after 23 years in exile, to lead Swapo's campaign for the November independence elections. After Swapo's victory he was unanimously elected Namibia's first executive president by the national assembly in February 1990 and was sworn in as head of state the following month.

**NÚÑEZ MUÑOZ, Ricardo.** *Chile.* Moderate socialist politician. Leader of the moderate faction of the Socialist Party (PSCh), Núñez was the president of the Chilean Socialist Bloc alliance which supported protests against the **Augusto Pinochet** regime in 1983–85, and was a founder member of the broad-based Democratic Alliance.

**NUNN, Sam.** *USA.* Democratic senator from Georgia. Born in 1938, he was educated at Georgia Institute of Technology and Emory University, farmed and practised law, served as state legislator, and was elected senator in 1972. Nunn played an unaccustomed role in 1989 when leading the Democratic assault that prevented John Tower's nomination as defence secretary, the first occasion that any new president was denied his choice of cabinet member. This became a messy partisan brawl and hurt his image as an independent operator: his supporters were dubbed the "Nunnpartisans" by **Robert Dole**. Armed services committee chairman since 1987, Nunn's expertise on new weapons systems and overall defence strategy is generally recognised. Though supportive of the defence build-up of **Ronald Reagan**'s administration, he criticized its over-reliance on nuclear weapons at the expense of conventional forces. He strongly supports nuclear arms control, but wants increased incentives for military service, fearing that volunteer recruitment will not be able to meet US military manpower needs. He confounded expectations by declining to seek the Democratic presidential nomination in 1988. Whether he could have won the nomination is debatable, since he is far more conservative than the party mainstream on social and economic issues. His influence on the party is nevertheless great and he expressed strong reservations on the administration's military policy after the Iraqi invasion of Kuwait.

**NYERERE, Julius Kambarage.** *Tanzania.* Former president. The most influential African political thinker of his generation, he was born in 1922 in Butiama on Lake Victoria, the son of a local chief. He was educated at local schools and at Makerere College (now University) in Uganda, where he received a diploma in education in 1945. After teaching for four years at a Catholic school in Tabora, he won a scholarship to study British history and politics at Edinburgh University, where, he later said, he "evolved the whole of my political philosophy". He also developed a deep interest in literature, and was later to translate *Julius Caesar* and *The Merchant of Venice* into Swahili. Returning home to teach, he became active in politics, becoming president of the Tanganyika Africa Association in 1953 and remodelling it as the Tanganyika African National Union (TANU) the following year. He became a popular national figure as leader of the campaign for independence and after TANU's election victory in 1960 he became chief minister and, at independence in December 1961, prime minister. In January 1962, however, he stepped down to concentrate on party work and was elected the first president of the republic of Tanganyika in October 1962. In 1964 the united republic of Tanzania was formed with Zanzibar, with Nyerere as president. Nyerere continued to develop his self-help philosophy of *ujamaa* ("togetherness"); the Arusha declaration of 1967 stressed egalitarianism and self-reliance, to be achieved through an African brand of socialism, and nationalization of key economic sectors. The implementation of these policies did not always meet their ideals, however. Despite great advances in social welfare, collective agricultural schemes failed to win wide acceptance and there was evidence of growing corruption and mismanagement in industry. In 1977 an attempt at a new start was made with the merger of TANU and the Afro-Shirazi Party of Zanzibar to form a new ruling party, Chama Cha Mapinduzi (CCM). Nyerere's sincerity and popularity was never in doubt, however, and he was re-elected four times, announcing in 1980, the last occasion, that he would stand down at the end of his five-year term. Nyerere had won widespread international respect for his persuasive championing of third-world causes, advocating the establishment of a new international economic order that would give developing countries true independence and equality with their industrialized trading partners. In 1985 he handed over to **Ali Hassan Mwinyi** but retained the CCM chairman until August 1990, when this was also passed on to Mwinyi. As chairman of the South Commission, Nyerere has continued to foster third-world causes, his charisma undimmed.

# O

**OBANDO Y BRAVO, Miguel.** *Nicaragua.*
Cardinal Archbishop of Managua. Born in 1926,
he was ordained into the Salesian order in 1958
was appointed archbishop of Managua in 1970.
A strong critic of Anastasio Somoza's regime, he
later clashed with the Sandinistas over the role of
the church and curbs on the opposition and
freedom of the press. He became a cardinal in
1985.

**OBASANJO, General Olusegun.** *Nigeria.*
Former head of state. Born in 1937 in Abeokuta,
he joined the Nigerian army in 1958 and had
risen to the rank of lieutenant-colonel by the
outbreak of the civil war in 1967, in which he
led a marine commando division. In January
1970, he accepted the surrender of the Biafran
forces. Appointed chief of staff in 1975, he took
over as head of state after the assassination of
General Murtala Muhammed the following year,
continuing the policy of returning the country to
civilian rule. In 1979 he handed over on
schedule to the elected civilian president, **Shehu
Shagari**, and devoted himself to farming and a
role as an elder statesman. He has been a
trenchant critic of the economic policies of
**Ibrahim Babangida**'s government and recently
expressed support for a one-party state as the
only workable form of civilian government for
Nigeria. He has also achieved international
stature, notably as a member of the
Commonwealth Eminent Persons Group on
South Africa in 1985.

**OBEID, Atef Mohammed.** *Egypt.* Cabinet
affairs and administrative development minister.
Educated at the universities of Cairo and Illinois,
he was a professor of business administration in
Cairo before joining the government in 1985 as
cabinet affairs and administrative development
minister. He has been a key figure in the
government's negotiations with the IMF, and is
widely seen as one of the more enthusiastic
advocates of economic reform.

**OBENG, P.V.** *Ghana.* Head of government. A
former businessman from the Ashanti region,
Obeng has headed the Committee of Secretaries

since the **Jerry Rawlings** government took
power in 1982, effectively filling the role of
prime minister. With **Kwesi Botchwey** he has
been a leader of the economic reformers in the
government.

**OBEY, David.** *USA.* Democratic congressman
from Wisconsin. A powerful congressional
leader, he heads the House of Representatives
appropriations subcommittee on foreign
relations (which makes recommendations on
foreign aid, and has given him a platform for
condemning corrupt and brutal third-world
regimes) and the joint economic committee. He
was born in Oklahoma in 1938 and won his
congressional seat at the age of 24. He has carved
out a reputation for backing unpopular
legislation and for promoting traditional
Democratic economic interests.

**OBIANG NGUEMA MBASOGO,
Lieutenant-Colonel Teodoro.** *Equatorial
Guinea.* President. Born in 1942 in Río Muni,
Equatorial Guinea's mainland territory, he
trained at a military academy in Spain from
1963–65 and then joined Equatorial Guinea's
territorial guards, becoming military governor of
Bioko (Fernando Póo) in 1968. As deputy
defence minister in the government of his uncle,
Francisco Macías Nguema, he led a palace coup
in October 1979 after which the former head of
state was executed for "genocide". Although
Obiang Nguema has made some progress in
restoring constitutional government, he has
failed to end the political domination of his
Mongomo clan and Fang ethnic group; two coup
attempts, in 1983 and 1986, are thought to have
originated in family squabbles. He has expertly
managed relations with Spain, the former
colonial power, and with France, to maximize
the flow of aid, taking Equatorial Guinea into
the franc zone in an effort to end its isolation as
Africa's only Spanish-speaking country.

**OCAMPO, Saturnino.** *Philippines.* Communist
Party of the Philippines (CPP) secretary-general.
A former journalist, he is a life-long communist
activist who was imprisoned several times under

the Marcos regime. As spokesman of the National Democratic Front, the political arm of the New People's Army guerrillas, he held inconclusive negotiations with **Cory Aquino**'s government during 1986–87, before returning to a clandestine existence. In April 1988, he replaced Rafael Baylosis as secretary-general of the CPP at a time when the party faced crisis as a result of the arrest of many of its leading figures. In an effort to boost the flagging fortunes of the armed struggle, Ocampo has endorsed attacks on US servicemen and interests. His arrest, together with that of his wife, Carolina "Bobby" Malay, in July 1990, further weakened the communist position.

**OCCHETTO, Achille**. *Italy*. Italian Communist Party (PCI) leader. Born in 1936 in Turin, to a well-off family, he is rare among Italian political leaders in that he is not a university graduate. He entered the Chamber of Deputies in 1976. In June 1988 he became general secretary of the PCI, having served only a one-year apprenticeship as deputy before **Alessandro Natta** stepped down because of ill health. Occhetto initiated a major review of party structure and policy, gaining approval at an extraordinary congress of the PCI in March 1990 for proposals to work towards a relaunch of the party in consultation with the non-communist left and under a different name, the Democratic Party of the Left (PDS), which was to be put to the party congress in January 1991. Occhetto has aimed to bring the PCI, consistently the second largest party in Italian parliaments, closer to other democratic socialist parties, to create a plausible left-wing alternative to Christian Democrat-led coalition governments.

**OCHIRBAT, Gombojavyn**. *Mongolia*. Mongolian People's Revolutionary Party (MPRP) general secretary. Born in 1929, he studied Russian language and literature at Moscow State University, graduating in 1985. He worked as an editor and lecturer and from 1972–82 was chairman of the Central Council of Mongolian Trade Unions. In 1990, after two years in Prague on the editorial board of *World Marxist Review*, he replaced Jambyn Batmonh as party leader and joined the politburo. Although he has stated his commitment to the transition to a market economy, he is regarded as one of the more cautious advocates of reform in the MPRP leadership.

**OCHIRBAT, Punsalmaagiyn**. *Mongolia*. President. Born in 1942, he studied geology at Leningrad University and began his career in the mining industry. He was made deputy fuel and power minister in 1972 and minister four years later. In 1987 he became external economic relations minister. He was elected president and ex-officio head of the armed forces in September 1990, after briefly heading the presidium of the People's Great Hural (upper house) until the office was abolished.

**O'CONNOR, Sandra Day**. *USA*. Supreme Court associate justice. Born in Texas in 1930, she practised law in Arizona before serving in the state legislature from 1969–75. She then served as a state Superior and Appeal Court judge until 1981 when she became the first woman to be appointed to the US Supreme Court. Although O'Connor has tended to vote with the conservatives within the nine-member court, her attitude towards abortion has been ambiguous. She is sometimes spoken of as a potential vice-presidential candidate.

**OGATA, Sadaka**. *Japan*. UN high commissioner for refugees since 1990. Born in 1927, she was formerly dean of the faculty of foreign studies at Tokyo's Sophia University, and had served as a diplomat in Japan's UN mission in 1976–78. Later she chaired the executive board of the UN Children's Fund (Unicef), before being appointed to the UN's Human Rights Commission, travelling to investigate alleged violations in Burma and elsewhere. She is the first woman ever to head a major UN agency.

**OGI, Adolf**. *Switzerland*. Transport and energy minister. Born in 1942, the son of a mountain guide and ski instructor, he held several leading positions with the Swiss Ski Federation from 1964–83. A long-standing member of the Christian Democratic People's Party (CVP), he then held the office of party president from 1984–87. In the following year he joined the cabinet as transport and energy minister.

**OHUCHI, Keigo**. *Japan*. Democratic Socialist Party (DSP) chairman. Born in 1930 in Tokyo and a graduate in law, he first entered the House of Representatives (lower house) in 1976. Highly influential in formulating the policies of the DSP, and dubbed "prince of the DSP", he helped to shift the party to the right while in office as its secretary-general (from 1985), and succeeded Nagasue Eiichi as its chairman after the electoral reverse of February 1990.

**O'KENNEDY, Michael**. *Ireland*. Agriculture minister. Born in 1936, he trained as a lawyer. Elected to parliament for Fianna Fáil in 1969, he was minister without portfolio in 1972–73 and has since held the transport (1973), foreign affairs (1977–79) and finance (1979–81) portfolios. In 1981–82 he was briefly EC commissioner for agriculture. As agriculture minister since 1987, he is a firm friend of the Irish farmer and has exhorted the current EC agriculture commissioner, **Ray MacSharry**, a former colleague in the Fianna Fáil party, not to ditch the interests of this powerful lobby in the General Agreement on Tariffs and Trade (Gatt) talks.

**OLARTE CULLEN, Lorenzo.** *Spain.* Canaries premier. Born in 1932, he founded the Canaries Union which merged into the Union of the Democratic Centre (UCD), and later joined the Democratic and Social Centre (CDS). He was a parliamentary deputy and a member of the Canaries parliament before becoming premier of the Canaries government in 1988.

**OLAV V.** *Norway.* King. Born in 1903, he was given the old Norwegian name Olav two years later as a symbol of his father's commitment to Norway. (Haakon, a Danish prince, had ascended the Norwegian throne after the dissolution of the union between Sweden and Norway.) Olav became an outstanding athlete, excelling in particular as a yachtsman, and gained stature during World War II, when he joined his father and the government in exile in London. His uncomplicated personal style has struck a chord with Norwegians.

**OLIVER, Daniel.** *USA.* Federal Trade Commission (FTC) chairman. Born in 1939, he is a lawyer who has served the government in the education and agriculture departments. He became chairman of the FTC in **Ronald Reagan**'s second term. Federal deregulation has somewhat limited the scope of Oliver's authority and he has been criticized by state attorneys-general for failing to enforce consumer protection laws.

**O'MALLEY, Desmond.** *Ireland.* Industry minister. Born in 1939, he trained as a solicitor and practised law until his election to parliament for Fianna Fáil in 1968. He was justice minister from 1970–73 and industry minister from 1977–81 and again in 1982. A long-standing feud with party leader **Charles Haughey**, rooted in personal antipathy, rivalry for the leadership and policy differences, boiled over in 1985, and he was expelled from the party. He formed the Progressive Democrats (PD), which enjoyed considerable success in the 1987 elections, due in no small part to his personal popularity, but lost more than half its seats in 1989. Two years later he returned to government, once again as

industry minister, when Fianna Fáil failed to gain an absolute majority and needed PD support.

**OMAR, Dato Abu Hassan Bin Haj.** *Malaysia.* Foreign minister. Born in 1940, he worked in the civil service before being elected to parliament, and to the supreme council of the United Malays National Organization, in 1978. He entered the cabinet in 1984 as welfare services minister and was promoted to foreign minister three years later.

**OMAR GUELLEH, Ismail.** *Djibouti.* Security chief and head of presidential cabinet. Nephew of President **Hassan Gouled**, and a strong candidate to succeed him, he was promoted to assistant secretary-general of the ruling Popular Rally for Progress in November 1988.

**OMINAMI PASCUAL, Carlos.** *Chile.* Economy minister. Born in 1951, he is an economist whose appointment at the beginning of 1990, as one of five Socialist Party (PSCh) members in the new civilian regime, was the cause of some concern in business circles.

**O'NEILL, Martin.** *UK.* Labour politician. Born in 1945, he studied economics and worked as a teacher before being elected to parliament in 1979. He was unexpectedly promoted to defence spokesman in 1988 and has helped shape Labour's new mainstream defence policy.

**ONG TENG CHEONG.** *Singapore.* Deputy prime minister. Born in 1936, Ong trained as an architect. He entered parliament in 1972 and held a number of cabinet posts before his appointment as second deputy prime minister in 1985. During the 1980s he also served as secretary-general of the National Trades Union Congress and chairman of the ruling People's Action Party executive committee.

**ONOFRE JARPA, Sergio.** *Chile.* Opposition politician. Born in 1921, Onofre Jarpa was a businessman before becoming involved in politics as leader of his own party, National Action (AN) in 1963. He joined the conservative anti-Salvador Allende alliance in 1972 and was elected a senator in 1973. A supporter of the military coup that year, he held a series of diplomatic posts and was interior minister from 1983–85. Often regarded as a possible civilian successor to President **Augusto Pinochet**, Onofre Jarpa became the centre of the grouping of right-wing parties that formed National Renovation (RN), but later withdrew as their candidate for the 1990 presidential elections.

**OREJA AGUIRRE, Marcelino.** *Spain.* Right-wing politician. Born in 1935, a career diplomat, he resigned as under-secretary for information in 1974, to become involved in the efforts to form political associations in the last months of the Franco era. He was foreign minister under **Adolfo Suárez** from 1976–80 and the government's representative in the Basque region from 1980–82. He was appointed a senator in 1977 and became secretary-general of the Council of Europe in 1984, resigning in 1989 to win election to the European Parliament at the head of the Popular Party (PP) list.

**ORTEGA SAAVEDRA, Daniel.** *Nicaragua.* Opposition leader. Born in 1945, he began studying at the University of Central America, but dropped out to join the Sandinista National Liberation Front (FSLN) in 1963. In 1967 he was captured while leading an urban resistance campaign. He was imprisoned until 1974 when his release was obtained after FSLN guerrillas had seized hostages at a Christmas party. After training in Cuba he returned to Nicaragua to resume the armed struggle. In alliance with his brother **Humberto Ortega**, he formed the third of the main FSLN tendencies, the *tercerista*, which advocated widening the struggle against the regime of Anastasio Somoza to appeal to as wide a section of society as possible. He became one of the nine "commanders" when the three tendencies joined to form a unified command structure in 1978. Ortega also became the co-ordinator of the five-member junta set up just before Somoza's overthrow. The Reagan administration's shift in policy towards Nicaragua, with the imposition of economic sanctions and the arming of the "Contras". This helped push Ortega towards seeking support from Cuba and other socialist countries. When the Patriotic Revolutionary Front was disbanded in 1984, Ortega became effective head of state of the FSLN regime, as co-ordinator of the three-member junta and the government council. He was elected president in 1984, a position formalized in 1987 by the new constitution. Unexpectedly defeated in the 1990 presidential contest, he handed over power to **Violeta Chamorro**, remaining as leader of the opposition.

**ORTEGA SAAVEDRA, Humberto.** *Nicaragua.* Army commander. The younger brother of **Daniel Ortega**, he followed his brother in joining the Sandinista National Liberation Front (FSLN). He was one of the nine commanders of the FSLN appointed in 1978. After the fall of Somoza he was made defence minister and army commander. On the adoption of traditional ranks in 1986 he was appointed a general. In 1990 he was retained as army commander by **Violeta Chamorro**, despite the protests of many of her supporters, and resigned from the FSLN leadership.

**OSIPYAN, Yury.** *USSR.* Scientist and former Presidential Council member. An Armenian born in Moscow in 1931, he is a leading solid-state physicist, head of the Moscow Physical Technical Institute and a vice-president of the USSR Academy of Sciences. The USSR Congress of People's Deputies elected him chairman of its vote-counting commission in 1989, and he was named a member of **Mikhail Gorbachev**'s short-lived Presidential Council in March 1990. He is reputed to be a liberal.

**OSMAN, Ahmed.** *Morocco.* Speaker of parliament. Brother-in-law and long-time ally of **King Hassan**, he was born in 1930 and – although from a poor family – was educated at the royal school. He trained as a lawyer in Paris and joined the royal cabinet in 1956 as its legal head. He held a series of ministerial and ambassadorial posts during the 1960s and was brought in to negotiate with the opposition following the assassination attempt on King Hassan in 1971. The following year he became prime minister, a post he held for seven years. Since 1978, Osman has been leader of the National Rally of Independents (RNI), the second largest party in parliament, and since 1984 has been speaker of parliament. In 1989, he was elected first president of the consultative council of the Arab Maghreb Union.

**OTUMFUO NANA OPUKU WARE II.** *Ghana.* Asantehene (paramount chief of Asante). Born in 1919, he is widely seen as a modernizing influence among Ghana's traditional leaders. He trained as a barrister in London and became first president of the African Civil Aviation Commission in 1969. He was due to take up the post of ambassador to Italy in 1970 when he was elected Asantehene on the death of his uncle, Prempe II.

**OUATTARA, Alassane Darmane.** *Côte d'Ivoire.* Prime minister, economy and finance minister. Born in 1942 of parents from Burkina Faso, and educated in the USA, he spent five years as an economist with the IMF before joining the West African Central Bank (BCEAO) in 1973, rising to the post of deputy governor in 1983. In 1984 he returned to the IMF as director of the Africa department and was appointed BCEAO governor in January 1989. Dubbed the "Zorro of international finance" by one journalist, he was called back to Abidjan by President **Félix Houphouët-Boigny** in May 1990 as a "super-minister" charged with tackling the country's economic crisis, although he retains his BCEAO position. In November 1990 he was appointed prime minister, and re-appointed at the head of a new cabinet after the first multi-party elections later that month. He promised a government that would bring a "clean air of incorruptibility " to Ivorian politics.

**OWEN, David**. *UK*. Social Democratic politician. Born in 1938, he trained as a medical doctor. Elected to parliament in 1966, he held a series of junior ministerial posts from 1967–70 and from 1974 until 1977, when at the age of 39 he was a surprise appointment as foreign secretary, a post he held until Labour lost power in 1979. As the party moved to the left in opposition, he became one of the "gang of four" which split to form the Social Democratic Party (SDP). He took over from **Roy Jenkins** as SDP leader in 1983. Though widely respected as a knowledgeable and authoritative commentator on foreign affairs, his political style is often attacked as arrogant and overbearing: it has won him few political friends. He was the only one of the four architects of the SDP to reject a merger with the Liberals after their electoral alliance failed to break the mould of traditional British politics in the 1987 elections. Increasingly forlorn, the rump SDP disbanded in 1990, leaving Owen with no obvious political future.

**ØYANGEN, Gunhild**. *Norway*. Agriculture minister . Born in 1947, she graduated from Trondheim University and worked as a teacher and then as a farmer. She has been active in the Norwegian Labour Party (DNA), both at municipal and national level, becoming a member of the executive board and also the Labour committee on agriculture. Øyangen was agriculture minister from 1986 until 1989 when she was elected to the Storting (parliament). She was made agriculture minister again, in 1990, in **Gro Harlem Brundtland**'s minority Labour government.

**ÖZAL, Turgut**. *Turkey*. President. Turkey's prime minister from 1983–89, he took over the post of president in November 1989 from General Kenan Evren, who had ruled the country since the military coup of 1980. Widely acknowledged as the architect of Turkey's economic reform and of its international rehabilitation during the period of martial law, Özal has been known to describe himself as a

monetarist. He launched Turkey's so far unsuccessful attempt to join the EC, and has been a firm backer of Turkey's Nato membership. Born in 1927 in Malataya in south-east Turkey, he has a degree in electrical engineering and he studied economics in the USA. After working in various national and international planning agencies, he was chief economic adviser first to the government of **Süleyman Demirel**, until the 1980 coup, and then to the military government of General Evren. Although forced to resign in 1982 over the Kastelli banking scandal, he was quickly back in the political arena, forming the Motherland Party (Anap) from a heterogeneous mixture of political groupings, and becoming prime minister in 1983 after leading it to a convincing win in elections in 1983. Özal has shown signs of seeking a strengthening of presidential powers; the 1982 Constitution does stipulate that the president should have an executive role, but he has come under fire for an allegedly autocratic manner. The persistence of Turkey's economic woes has added to his problems, and in 1988 he survived an assassination attempt by an extreme right-winger.

**OZAWA, Ichiro**. *Japan*. Liberal Democratic party (LDP) secretary-general. Born in 1942 in Iwate prefecture, he graduated from Keio University and entered the National Diet (parliament) for the LDP in 1969, following his father, Saeki. He was appointed home affairs minister under **Yasuhiro Nakasone** in 1985. Although close to former prime minister Kakuei Tanaka, he played a leading role in starting the Soseikai group (the vehicle by which **Noboru Takeshita** took over the Tanaka faction) and aroused Tanaka's anger. After the LDP's crushing defeat in the 1989 election, Ozawa took over from Tanaka as secretary-general; at 47, he is the youngest person to assume the post. His considerable political acumen was seen by many as a key factor in enabling the LDP to win a comfortable majority in the 1990 general election. Within the Takeshita faction, Ozawa and **Ryutaro Hashimoto** compete against each other for the future presidency of the LDP, in what has become known as the "Ichi-Ryu War". Ozawa's widespread popularity within the party is seen as standing him in good stead in any leadership contest, and he retained his post when the prime minister, **Toshiki Kaifu**, reshuffled the cabinet in December 1990.

# P

**PAASIO, Pertti.** *Finland.* Deputy prime minister and foreign minister. Born in 1939, the son of 1960s prime minister Rafael Paasio, he studied political science and then worked in local government in his native Turku. He was elected to the Eduskunta (parliament) for the Finnish Social Democratic Party (SDP) in 1975. Paasio succeeded **Kalevi Sorsa** as party leader in 1987, and as deputy prime minister and foreign minister two years later.

**PACKWOOD, Robert (Bob).** *USA.* Republican senator from Oregon. Born in 1932, he was a lawyer and state legislator before being elected senator in 1968. As finance committee chairman in 1985–86, he piloted into law the 1986 tax code reform. Constituency interests make him a strong free trader and advocate of deregulation.

**PAENIU, Bikenibeu.** *Tuvalu.* Prime minister. A representative of the younger generation in Tuvalu's non-party political system, he became prime minister in October 1989 at the age of 33. Elections the previous month had shown a swing against his predecessor, **Tomasi Puapua**. He declared his intention to reduce dependence on aid and took control of foreign affairs and economic planning himself.

**PAISLEY, Ian.** *UK.* Northern Irish unionist politician. Born in 1926, he studied theology and was ordained a Presbyterian minister in 1946. In 1951 he founded the Free Presbyterian Church of Ulster and is still its moderator. When the civil-rights movement began to demand an end to economic and political discrimination against the Catholic minority in the province in the late 1960s, he rose to prominence as the voice of those Protestants most implacably opposed to change. He was first elected to parliament for North Antrim in 1970 and founded the Democratic Unionist Party (DUP) in 1972 as a more populist and assertive alternative to the Official Unionist Party (OUP). Owing much to his rhetorical skills, he established himself as the most popular Unionist politician (universally known as "the Big Man"),

while the party was able to erode the OUP's traditional dominance. He denounced the 1985 Anglo-Irish Agreement, which gave the Irish government consultative rights in the province's affairs, in characteristically forceful terms. In recent years he has indicated a readiness to compromise with Westminster as the price of re-establishing some form of local political authority in Northern Ireland. But his rejection of the Nationalist platform remains implacable.

**PALENQUE, Carlos.** *Bolivia.* Mayor of La Paz. Born in 1944, Palenque became a household name as a radio and television broadcaster, presenting highly popular programmes that criticized bureaucracy and political leaders. In 1989 he entered politics by forming his own party, the Conscience of the Homeland (Condepa) and later that year was elected mayor of La Paz.

**PÁLSSON, Thorsteinn.** *Iceland.* Right-wing politician. Born in 1947, he studied law and worked as a journalist before joining the employers' federation. He became leader of the Independence Party (Sjálfstaedisflokkurinn) in 1983 and the country's youngest-ever prime minister in 1987 at the head of a centre–right coalition. He resigned the following year when his coalition partners refused to support his austerity policies.

**PANČEVSKI, Milan.** *Yugoslavia.* Communist party president. Born in Debar in 1935, he graduated from the Higher School of Political Sciences in Belgrade. A party member since 1957, he held a series of posts at regional and republican level in the party and its umbrella organization, the Socialist Alliance, before becoming Macedonia's member of the collective state presidency in 1984. In May 1989 he became president of the Yugoslav communist party. After the party's collapse at its unfinished congress in January 1990, Pančevski sided with the hardliners seeking to keep the rump going, especially in the Yugoslav army. In the autumn of 1990, his political stance was sharply criticized by Macedonia's party leadership.

**PANDAY, Basdeo.** *Trinidad and Tobago.* Opposition politician. Born of East Indian parents in 1934, he became head of the main sugar workers' union. He led the union-backed United Labour Front formed in 1975, which merged into the National Alliance for Reconstruction in 1976. Appointed foreign minister, he was dismissed from the cabinet in 1987 and expelled from the party after disagreements with the prime minister, **Arthur Robinson.**

**PANDOLFI, Filippo Maria.** *Italy.* European Commission vice-president and commissioner for research and science, telecommunications and information technology. Born in 1927 in Bergamo, he studied philosophy and worked as a company director before being elected to parliament for the Christian Democrats (DC) in 1968. He held a range of economic and financial portfolios from 1976 until 1983, when he became agriculture minister. He was appointed EC commissioner responsible for science, research, telecommunications and information technology in 1989, but has kept a very low profile in Brussels.

**PANETTA, Leon.** *USA.* Democratic congressman from California. Born in 1938, he was a lawyer and former Republican who was elected to the House of Representatives in 1976. He typifies the new breed of socially liberal, fiscally conservative Democrats. After becoming budget committee chairman in 1989, he criticized **George Bush**'s first budget for demanding expenditure cuts but placing the onus on Congress of deciding where they should be made. He insists that the budget deficit must be reduced through a bipartisan approach.

**PANNELLA, Marco.** *Italy.* Radical Party (PR) politician. Born in 1930 in Teramo, in Abruzzo region, he obtained a law degree and became a journalist. He was one of the founders of the PR, following the split in the Italian Liberal Party (PLI) in 1955. From 1962–67 he served as the secretary of the PR and from 1966–74 as secretary of the Italian Divorce League (LID). In 1973 he became editor of the PR newspaper *Liberazione.* He was elected to the Chamber of Deputies for the first time in 1976 and has been re-elected on each subsequent occasion, although he has twice resigned his seat by way of protest. Even though his own views have not necessarily prevailed, Pannella has had considerable success, through unorthodox and often dramatic methods, including civil disobedience and hunger strike, in ensuring full public debate,

sometimes forcing referenda, for numerous social issues, such as divorce, abortion, homosexual rights, conscientious objection and votes at 18. He has been a member of the European Parliament since 1979.

**PAPANDREOU, Andreas.** *Greece.* Former prime minister. Born in 1919, he was arrested by the Metaxas dictatorship in 1939 while studying law, but was allowed to go to the USA to continue his studies. He took US citizenship and became an economics professor. Returning to Greece in 1959, he entered politics in the Centre Union party in 1964. When his father, George Papandreou, became prime minister that year, Andreas was given ministerial appointments over the heads of more senior men, a move that eventually contributed to the break-up of the party. In 1967, he was imprisoned by the military dictatorship (1967–74), but freed after the intervention of the US ambassador. Going into exile, he formed the Panhellenic Resistance Movement (PAK) which was committed to the overthrow of the dictatorship. Following the restoration of democracy, PAK became the Panhellenic Socialist Movement (Pasok). Papandreou painstakingly built up the party until in 1981 it won the general election, ending nearly half a century of conservative domination of Greek public life. During his tenure as prime minister (1981–89) he overcame the image of Greece as a US client state and a docile EC member. Papandreou's years of office were marred by poor economic performance, however, and his term ended after newspaper articles linked his name with a bank embezzlement scandal. Although these allegations were not substantiated, his authority within Pasok had been seriously eroded by the end of 1990. He had also undergone a serious heart operation.

**PAPANDREOU, Vasso.** *Greece.* European commissioner for social affairs and employment, education and training. Born in 1944, she studied and then lectured in the UK. She was an energetic director of Greece's national small businesses organization from 1981–85 and was then industry and commerce minister in the Socialist government of **Andreas Papandreou** (no relation). She was appointed to the EC Commission, its youngest member, in 1989. Responsible for social affairs and health issues, she has pushed for new Europe-wide measures (including the Social Charter) on job creation, training, and workers' and women's rights.

**PARIZEAU, Jacques.** *Canada.* Leader of the Quebec Party. Born in Montreal in 1930, he was educated in Montreal, Paris and at the London School of Economics and was a professor for over 20 years. One of the founding fathers of the Quebec Party (PQ) and the separatist movement in Quebec, Parizeau was elected to the provincial national assembly in 1976 and served as finance minister to René Lévesque but resigned from this post in 1984. He returned as PQ leader in 1988 and has breathed new life into the separatist movement in Quebec.

**PARK JUN BYUNG**. *South Korea*. Politician. Born in 1933, he is a retired general and ally of Chun Doo Hwan responsible for the ruthless military crackdown in Kwangju in 1980. Despite protests, in 1988 he was appointed secretary-general of the Democratic Justice Party until the party merger in 1990.

**PARK TAE JOON**. *South Korea*. Co-leader of ruling Democratic Liberal Party (DLP). Born in 1927 and related by marriage to former president Chun Doo Hwan, he headed the Democratic Justice Party until the merger with two opposition parties into the DLP, of which he became joint leader. Park also heads the state-owned Pohong Iron and Steel Company.

**PARKIN, Sara**. *UK*. Green politician. Born in 1946, she trained and worked as a nurse. She was the Green Party's international liaison secretary from 1983–90 and was co-secretary of the European Greens from 1985–90. She shot to prominence after the party's spectacular showing in the 1989 elections to the European Parliament, and is now one of its leading public figures. Firmly on the "pragmatic" wing of the party, she has alienated some of the more radical members, describing them as "parasites".

**PARKINSON, Cecil**. *UK*. Former cabinet minister and Conservative Party chairman. The debonair Parkinson was the darling of grass-roots Tories and tipped for the top until his widely publicized extramarital affair with Sarah Keays forced him out of office in 1983. A railwayman's son born in 1932 and educated at Cambridge, he was elected MP in 1970 after a successful business career. To many people's surprise he was appointed trade minister by **Margaret Thatcher** in 1979. As party chairman from 1981–83 he was credited with the Tories' election success. He returned from the wilderness in 1987 as energy secretary, and in 1989 inherited the transport ministry from the long-suffering Paul Channon, and with it a welter of problems of underinvestment, overcrowding and accidents. The problems that beset the privatization of electricity were largely laid at his door and may

have destroyed any lingering chance he may have had of becoming chancellor. Parkinson remained popular with the Conservative rank and file, but resigned from the cabinet after **John Major** became party leader.

**PASQUA, Charles**. *France*. Gaullist politician. Born in Grasse in 1927, Pasqua studied law and worked in private business before being elected to the National Assembly as a Union for French Democracy (UDF) deputy in 1968. For two years from 1974 he was secretary-general of the party. He became a senator representing Hauts de Seine in 1977, and since 1981 he has been president of the Gaullist Rally for the Republic (RPR) in the Senate. He was interior minister from 1981–86. In 1990 he and fellow-Gaullist **Philippe Séguin** formed an alliance aimed at regenerating the French right

**PASTRANA BORRERO, Misael**. *Colombia*. Conservative politician. Born in 1923, he studied law and served as a judge, civil servant and diplomat before entering politics for the Conservative Party (now the Social Conservative Party – PSC). He achieved ministerial status in 1960 and was interior minister from 1966–68. He was president from 1970–74 and continues to exercise influence as a leader of the Conservative Party.

**PATASSÉ, Ange**. *Central African Republic*. Opposition leader. Born in 1937, Patassé worked as an agricultural officer before holding a series of ministerial posts under Jean-Bédel Bokassa in the 1960s and 1970s, serving as prime minister from 1976–78. He was detained after Bokassa's fall and, since 1982, when he was involved in an unsuccessful coup attempt, has lived in exile, active in opposition to **André Kolingba's** regime.

**PATNAIK, Biju**. *India*. Chief minister of Orissa. Born in Orissa in 1916, he served as the Congress chief minister in 1961–63, resigning under the "Kamaraj Plan" (separation of government and party posts) to devote himself to party work. He later broke with Congress and was elected to the Rajya Sabha (upper house) in 1971 and to the Lok Sabha (lower house) in 1977. He was steel and mines minister in the Janata government of 1977–79. After the break-up of the Janata coalition he joined the rump Janata Party, becoming a member of Janata Dal after the Janata Party fused with it in 1988 and leading the party to victory in the Orissa state elections of February 1990.

**PATTEN, Christopher (Chris)**. *UK*. Chancellor of the Duchy of Lancaster and

Conservative Party chairman since November 1990, MP since 1970. Born in 1944, he served a long apprenticeship as head of the Tory research department. As overseas development minister in 1986–89, he developed a reputation as a "listener", accessible to pressure groups. In the wake of **Margaret Thatcher**'s conversion to the green cause, Patten's appointment as environment secretary, his first cabinet post, seemed a political masterstroke. With a deserved reputation for sensitivity, his determination to take the green lobby seriously contrasted with the dismissiveness of his predecessor, **Nicholas Ridley**. Respected for his astuteness, niceness and his integrity – as a practising Catholic he has consistently opposed abortion – his chances of reaching the top were possibly dashed by the election of one of his own generation of high-flyers, **John Major**, as party leader. However, his public relations skills and popularity were recognized by Major who appointed him party chairman in November 1990, with responsibility for ensuring a Conservative victory at the next election.

**PATTEN, John**. *UK*. Minister of state at the Home Office since 1987, MP since 1983. Born in 1945, Patten, a former Oxford University don, entered parliament after learning his trade on Oxford city council. He is viewed as competent and sharp-minded and retains a fluent and entertaining academic style. He was housing minister from 1985–87.

**PATTERSON, Percival**. *Jamaica*. Deputy prime minister. Loyal deputy to People's National Party leader **Michael Manley**, he was a minister in the 1972–80 government and helped to reorganize the party after its 1980 defeat. In 1989 he was appointed deputy prime minister and also holds the production, development and planning portfolio.

**PAVLOV, Valentin**. *USSR*. Finance minister. Born in 1937, he rose through the finance ministry, State Planning Committee (Gosplan) and State Pricing Committee. He was appointed finance minister in 1989 and his tenure in the post has been marked by rapid growth in the money supply and in the Soviet budget deficit.

**PAWAR, Sharad**. *India*. Chief minister of Maharashtra. Born in Poona in 1940, he was elected to the state assembly for Congress in 1967 and held a series of state ministerial posts before becoming chief minister from 1978–80. He broke with Congress (I) in 1979 to support the Congress (U) of Devraj Urs, and formed Congress (S) in 1981. He rejoined Congress (I) in

1986 and was named chief minister in 1988. He led the party to victory in the February 1990 elections, making him one of only three Congress chief ministers of major states.

**PAYE, Jean-Claude**. *France*. Secretary-general of the Organisation for Economic Co-operation and Development (OECD). Born in 1934, he studied law, politics and public administration before joining the civil service in 1961. He progressed smoothly into the upper echelons, while remaining discreetly behind the scenes, acting as adviser to several ministers, European commissioners and a prime minister (the centrist **Raymond Barre**, from 1976–79). In 1979 he became head of economic and financial affairs at the foreign ministry and president of the OECD executive committee. He was appointed secretary-general in 1984.

**PAZ ZAMORA, Jaime**. *Bolivia*. President. Born in 1939, the nephew of President Víctor Paz Estenssoro, and educated at the Catholic University of Louvain, Belgium, Paz Zamora founded the Revolutionary Leftist Movement (MIR) in 1971. After a brief imprisonment and exile, he returned to Bolivia in 1979. He was elected vice-president in 1980, serving until 1985, even after the withdrawal of the MIR from the ruling coalition. During the 1980 election campaign he survived a plane crash that was seen by some as an assassination attempt. His politics have proved more pragmatic than revolutionary. After the inconclusive presidential elections in 1989 he reached an accommodation with the right-wing Nationalist Democratic Action (ADN) that allowed him to assume the presidency. In late 1990 he was threatened with impeachment by the opposition National Revolutionary Movement (MNR) after a conflict with the Supreme Court over the constitutionality of a tax increase.

**PEASE, Henry**. *Peru*. Left-wing politician. Born in 1946, and a respected but uncharismatic university lecturer, Pease stood unsuccessfully as candidate of the United Left (IU) coalition in the 1990 presidential elections. His campaign became briefly controversial after he was shot by police during a disturbance at a political rally in February that year.

**PEDERSEN, Thor**. *Denmark*. Interior and Nordic affairs minister. Born in 1945, he studied political science and subsequently became managing director of a construction company. Elected to the Folketing (parliament) for the Liberals (Venstre) in 1984, he became housing minister in 1986 and interior minister in 1987, adding the Nordic affairs portfolio the following year.

**PELL, Claiborne.** *USA.* Democratic senator from Rhode Island. Born in 1918, he was a financier and was elected senator in 1960. His greatest legislative achievement is the "Pell grants" programme for low and middle income college students. In 1987 he became foreign relations committee chairman, but his low-key leadership style has limited his effectiveness. He strongly favours arms control and has a special interest in international maritime law.

**PELLETIER, Jacques.** *France.* Co-operation and development minister. Born in 1936 and a graduate of the Institut d'Etudes Politiques and of the Ecole Nationale d'Administration, he had a career in the civil service, rising to the rank of inspector-general of finance in 1986. A member of the Radical Party within the Giscardian Union for French Democracy (UDF), he nevertheless responded to overtures from the left and helped **Michel Rocard** to broaden the basis of his 1988 government, taking on the post of co-operation and development minister.

**PEÑA GÓMEZ, José Francisco.** *Dominican Republic.* Opposition party leader. Born in 1937 of parents of Haitian descent and trained as a lawyer, he became secretary-general of the Dominican Revolutionary Party (PRD) in 1963. Popular among the urban poor, he became mayor of Santo Domingo in 1982, but finished a poor third as PRD presidential candidate in 1990.

**PENG CHONG.** *China.* Secretary-general of the National People's Congress Standing Committee. Born in 1909, Peng held top party and government posts in Shanghai and was a member of the politburo and Secretariat until 1982. He headed the parliament's law committee from 1983, and took up his present post in 1988.

**PEREIRA, Arístides Maria.** *Cape Verde.* President. Born in 1923, the son of a Catholic priest, Pereira helped found the independence movement in Portuguese West Africa in 1956, becoming its leader when Amílcar Cabral was assassinated by the Portuguese secret service in 1972. A modest, fatherly figure, he has led his country since independence in 1975, laying the foundations for genuine participatory democracy within a one-party state and in July 1990 relinquishing his position as secretary-general of the ruling African Party for the Independence of Cape Verde (PAICV) as a step towards the introduction of a multi-party system. He is the

acknowledged elder statesman of the five lusophone African countries.

**PERES, Shimon.** *Israel.* Leader of the opposition Labour party and former prime minister. Born Shimon Persky in Poland in 1923, Peres came to Palestine in 1934. He soon rose to prominence in the HaNoar HaOved Socialist Zionist Youth Movement. He headed the naval division of the defence ministry in 1948, and was director-general of the ministry from 1953–55. A protégé of David Ben-Gurion, Peres helped to mould the Mapai government of 1959–65, but left to found the Rafi Party with his mentor in 1965. Back in the Labour fold in 1968, he became minister for communications in 1970, information in 1974, and was defence minister from 1974–77. Thwarted by **Yitzhak Rabin** for the top party post in 1974, he was blamed by some for plotting Rabin's downfall in 1977. Peres at last succeeded Rabin, and led Labour in opposition to Menachem Begin's Likud government until 1984, lambasting it for mismanaging the economy and the Lebanese campaign. But he could not win an absolute majority in the 1984 elections, and reluctantly joined a Likud-Labour coalition, serving as prime minister until 1986 and deputy prime minister and foreign minister under **Yitzhak Shamir** until 1988. The two men increasingly came into conflict over Peres's advocacy of talking to moderate Palestinians as a prelude to exchanging "land for peace". In 1988 he signed the London agreement with **King Hussein** of Jordan on procedure for negotiations but he again failed to sway the nation in the 1988 elections, fought in the tense atmosphere of the *intifada* and growing international criticism of Israel. Peres served as finance minister in the resulting coalition until March 1990, when Labour-Likud differences over the speed of the "peace process" led to its collapse. His efforts to weld together a new coalition of Labour, religious and left-wing parties ended in failure, despite having commanded an anti-Likud majority in parliament sufficient to topple the government. The years of uneasy coalition with Shamir appear to be over at last, and Peres now leads a purer opposition to the most right-wing government Israel has known. His reputation for missing opportunities is hard to shrug off; he now faces another round of contests challenging his party leadership.

**PÉREZ DE CUÉLLAR, Javier.** *Peru.* UN secretary-general. Born in 1920, he studied law and joined the foreign ministry in 1940. After 20 years as a junior diplomat and three years as a

20 years as a junior diplomat and three years as a senior administrator in the foreign ministry he gained his first ambassadorship in 1964. He was ambassador to the UN in 1971–75 (representing Peru on the Security Council in 1973–74), served as the UN secretary-general's personal representative to Cyprus (1975–77) and Afghanistan (1981), and was appointed under-secretary-general for political affairs in 1979. Two years later, he was elected secretary-general in a close contest, defeating **Salim Ahmed Salim** of Tanzania. A soft-spoken, patrician diplomat, known for his discretion and diligence rather than dynamism, he is fond of quoting the French saying *"Le ton fait la chanson"* ("It's the tune that makes the song" – as opposed to the amount of noise made by the singer) and of pointing out that it is much easier for governments to make concessions to the UN than to each other. His first term had an inauspicious start when he tried in vain to mediate between the UK and Argentina after the latter's occupation of the Falkland Islands in 1982. Two months later, Israeli troops brushed aside the UN peace-keeping force stationed in southern Lebanon. He was luckier in his second five-year term, which he won unopposed in 1986. He achieved his greatest personal success in 1988 when he was able to announce a ceasefire in the war between Iran and Iraq. It marked the most unlikely in a series of breakthroughs achieved with the help of the UN in intractable regional conflicts in Afghanistan, Cambodia, Namibia, Cyprus and the Western Sahara, culminating in the united stance against Iraq in the wake of its invasion of Kuwait. The self-deprecating Pérez de Cuéllar would no doubt be the first to admit that the improved relationship between the superpowers made the restoration of the UN's authority possible, but inevitably the enhanced prestige of the world organization has reflected favourably on its senior representative.

**PÉREZ RODRÍGUEZ, Carlos Andrés.** *Venezuela.* President. Born in 1922, the son of a coffee-grower, Pérez was first elected to the legislature in 1946 for the social democratic Democratic Action (AD). A close associate of President Rómulo Betancourt, he served as interior minister in the early 1960s, when he conducted a forceful campaign against left-wing rebels. Elected president in 1974, he oversaw the rapid growth of the Venezuelan economy brought about by rising oil prices. He gained popularity by nationalizing the petroleum and iron ore industries, but by the end of his term had become unpopular. A charismatic leader and speaker, with strong trade union backing, Pérez won the AD presidential nomination in 1987 and was elected president for a second term the following year. Strained economic circumstances forced Pérez to go to the IMF for a support package, which provoked rioting after the prices of staple goods had been raised.

**PETERLE, Lojze.** *Yugoslavia.* Prime minister of Slovenia. As leader of the Christian Democrats, he controlled the largest single element of the coalition Democratic Opposition of Slovenia (Demos), and became prime minister after the coalition's April 1990 election victory in the republic. In the forefront of demands for virtually complete autonomy, he had moved with the tide of Slovene feeling by the end of 1990, proposing the referendum by which backed secession if a new federal structure was not agreed within six months.

**PETERS, Winston.** *New Zealand.* Maori affairs minister. The only prominent Maori in the National Party, Peters has the education (a law and politics degree), the charisma and the debating skills to outshine his party's leader and prime minister, **James Bolger**, and is often viewed as a future premier. He is somewhat isolated, however, as a maverick opponent of the currently dominant philosophy of monetarist liberal economics, advocating instead an increase in public spending and intervention to stimulate growth.

**PETERSEN, Gert.** *Denmark.* Leader of the Socialist People's Party. Born in 1927, he has worked as a journalist, editor and writer on the future of socialism. Initially a hardline member of the Communist Party, he left the party at the time of the Hungarian uprising in 1956. He was a founding member of the Socialist People's Party (SF) in 1959, and has been its leader since 1974. He was elected to the Folketing (parliament) in 1966 and proved himself an eloquent advocate of his party's anti-Nato and anti-EC stance.

**PETERSEN, Niels Helveg.** *Denmark.* Radical Liberal politician. Born in 1939, he was first elected to the Folketing (parliament) for the Radical Liberals (RV) in 1966, and became party leader in 1978, on his return from a three-year stint in Brussels as *chef de cabinet* to the Danish EC commissioner Finn Gundelach. From 1982–88 he played kingmaker in Danish politics, leading a party that gave external support to the centre–right minority coalition on economic issues while usually supporting the left-wing opposition on foreign policy and defence issues. He was appointed economic affairs minister in a new centre–right coalition in 1988, and was replaced as party leader by **Marianne Jelved**. He lost his economic affairs portfolio to **Anders Fogh Rasmussen** in December 1990.

**PETKOFF MALEO, Teodoro.** *Venezuela.* Left-wing politician. A former guerrilla, Petkoff is leader of the leftist Movement towards Socialism (MAS), formed in 1971 in a split with the Communist Party. Petkoff contested the 1988 presidential election, but gained few votes.

**PETKOV, Krustyu.** *Bulgaria.* Trade unionist. A bureau member of the Central Council of Bulgarian Trade Unions since April 1987, Petkov became the council's chairman in December 1989. He remained chairman when the council was reconstituted as the Confederation of Independent Trade Unions, one of the two principal trade union organizations in Bulgaria, in February 1990. His decision to join **Konstantin Trenchev**'s Podkrepa-led general strike in November 1990 helped to bring down **Andrei Lukanov**'s government.

**PHOUMI VONGVICHIT.** *Laos.* Acting president. Born in 1910, he joined the anti-French resistance in 1945 and served publicly as the trusted lieutenant of **Souphanouvong** throughout the war. He was appointed education and religion minister in 1975.

**PHOUNE SIPASEUTH.** *Laos.* Foreign minister. Born in 1920. A veteran party member and experienced public negotiator during the war, he was a natural choice as foreign minister after the communist victory in 1975, but his workload was reduced after he suffered a serious heart attack four years later.

**PICKERING, Thomas.** *USA.* Ambassador to the UN. Born in 1931 in New Jersey, he is a career diplomat, who joined the State Department in 1959. He held the sensitive post of ambassador to Israel from 1985–88, at a time when the US administration was becoming increasingly critical of Israel's treatment of the Palestinians. He has also been ambassador to El Salvador, Nigeria and Jordan. The appointment of such a high-ranking diplomat to the UN in 1989 was seen as a show of support for the organization, even though **George Bush** denied him the cabinet seat that had gone with this post under **Ronald Reagan**.

**PIERRET, Christian.** *France.* Socialist politician. Born in 1946 and a graduate of the Ecole Nationale d'Administration, he followed an administrative and political career. He has been active within the Socialist Party (PS), as first secretary of the Paris federation (1974–76), a member of the national committee in 1975 and of the executive since 1981. Since 1978, he has held a seat in the National Assembly, specializing in economic and planning matters. Close to **Laurent Fabius**, he is the PS's national secretary responsible for local government and ecology.

**PINDLING, Sir Lynden.** *Bahamas.* Prime minister. Born in 1930, a British-trained barrister, he first won an elected seat in 1956. As leader of the Progressive Liberal Party he championed the rights of black Bahamians. He became premier in 1967 and led the country to independence from the UK in 1973. He remains popular, despite allegations concerning his substantial income and extravagant lifestyle during investigations in 1983–84 into corruption linked to the drug trade.

**PINHEIRO, João de Deus.** *Portugal.* Foreign minister. Born in 1919, he made a career in the legal profession, served as a judge, and was attorney-general from 1974–77 and justice minister from 1974–76. He served as education and culture minister from 1985–87, when he was appointed foreign minister.

**PININFARINA, Sergio.** *Italy.* Industrialist. Born in 1926 in Turin, he gained a degree in mechanical engineering at Turin Polytechnic in 1950 and in 1951 entered his father's firm, Carrozzeria Pininfarina. He became president of the company when his father died in 1966, and successfully expanded the business. From 1979–88 he was a member of the European Parliament, adhering to the liberal and democratic group. In May 1988 he became chairman of Confindustria, the private sector industrialists' association, which lobbies with government on behalf of employers' interests. He has also been involved in a series of meetings with trade unions that for a time raised hopes of a less confrontational approach to industrial relations.

**PINOCHET UGARTE, General Augusto.** *Chile.* Army commander. Born in 1915, Pinochet followed a career in the army, rising to become commander of the second army division in 1968 and garrison commander in Santiago in 1971, with the rank of general in 1972. He became the army's representative on the military junta after the 1973 coup, but soon came to dominate the other members, declaring himself president in 1974. With Congress dissolved and a state of siege declared, Pinochet ruled by decree. His regime was widely condemned for its harrassment of political opponents, censorship, and violations of human rights. In economic affairs he was responsible for introducing the monetarist policies formulated by the "Chicago Boys" which gave Chile a temporary economic boom. He relaxed the repression during the 1980s, but showed no signs of wishing to give up power in 1989, as provided for in the 1980 constitution, and suggested – amid growing discontent – that his term should instead be renewed until 1997. He survived an assassination attempt in 1986 and re-imposed the state of emergency, but later agreed to the legalization of political parties. In 1988 he acceded to opponents' demands for a plebiscite over whether he should stand again as president; he was duly defeated by a concerted opposition. His defeat was made more bitter by the opposition election victory the following year. One condition of the transfer of power was the security of his position as army commander, from which he continues to exercise substantial influence.

**PINTE, Etienne.** *France.* Gaullist politician. Born in 1939 and a graduate in politics (IEP) and law, he began his career in the 1960s within ministerial teams attached to the ex-Gaullist minister, Alain Peyrefitte. Since 1973 he has been a member of the National Assembly and belongs to the Gaullist Rally for the Republic (RPR). Since 1977, he has been deputy mayor of Versailles.

**PINTO DA COSTA, Manuel.** *São Tomé and Príncipe.* President. Born in 1937, he is an East German-trained economist. He founded the Movement for the Liberation of São Tomé and Príncipe in 1972, coming to power with the collapse of Portuguese colonial rule in 1975. He has dominated the islands' politics since, surviving coup attempts and concentrating power in the hands of his family. Since 1985, his initial Marxist line has been replaced by an attempt to woo Western donors with economic reforms and the introduction of multi-party democracy. In November 1990 he announced that he would not contest the presidential elections due in March 1991.

**PINTON, Michel.** *France.* Right-wing politician. Born in 1937, he studied at the Ecole Polytechnique, and his early career was as a mathematician within the state aviation industry. A member of the Giscardian Union for French Democracy (UDF), he became delegate-

general in 1978 and secretary-general in 1981. Subsequently, he became UDF national delegate for "evaluation and prospects".

**PIRES, General Pedro Verona Rodrigues.** *Cape Verde.* Prime minister and defence minister. Born in 1934, he studied medicine before joining the struggle against Portuguese colonial rule. He led the negotiations that won independence for Cape Verde and Guinea-Bissau in 1975. He has been prime minister since independence. In July 1990, he also took on the defence portfolio and was elected secretary-general of the ruling African Party for the Independence of Cape Verde (PAICV) in succession to President **Arístides Pereira**. Pires and the PAICV faced a challenge from the newly formed Movement for Democracy in the first multi-party elections in January 1991.

**PITHART, Petr.** *Czechoslovakia.* Prime minister of the Czech republic. Born in 1941 in Kladno, he was a lecturer in law at Charles University, Prague during the 1960s, and edited *Literarni Noviny* in the late 1960s. Forced to leave these posts in 1970, he worked subsequently in various menial posts, and was a signatory of the dissident Charter 77. After the founding of Civic Forum in November 1989 he became spokesman of its co-ordination centre. Following the success of the "velvet revolution", he became premier of the Czech republic in February 1990, and was re-appointed after the June elections.

**PLEŞU, Andrei Gabriel.** *Romania.* Culture minister. A former dissident, he was born in Bucharest in 1948 and graduated in fine arts with a doctorate in history. A writer, he was placed under house arrest for his criticism of the Ceauşescu regime, and has proved a popular culture minister, a post he has held since the 1989 revolution.

**POCATERRA, Roberto.** *Venezuela.* Finance minister. A former president of the state industrial bank, he was financial adviser to **Carlos Andrés Pérez** during the 1988 election campaign. He was appointed finance minister in 1989 and has played an important role in negotiations with the IMF and with other countries over Venezuela's foreign debt.

**POGOSYAN, Stepan.** *USSR.* First secretary of the Armenian Communist Party. He was elected to this post in late November 1990, replacing **Vladimir Movsisyan**. Pogosyan, aged 58 when he became party leader, was an historian with a record of communist youth work and government service in the press and broadcasting sphere.

**POHER, Alain.** *France.* Senate president. Born in 1909, and decorated after World War II for his resistance work, he was a post-war junior minister and identified with Christian democratic centrist politics. He played a major part in the process of European integration, notably as a member of the European Coal & Steel Community assembly and as president in the European Parliament from 1966–69. Since 1968 he has been re-elected no fewer than seven times as president of the Senate, confirming in this role his reputation as an opponent of fundamental reform; in 1969 he stood in as acting president of France after Charles de Gaulle's dramatic resignation. Seeking to capitalize on the status this gave him in the public eye – partly as a plain man of common sense and suburban probity in contrast to de Gaulle's grandeur – he stood as a candidate in the ensuing election, polling creditably but nevertheless having to concede that Georges Pompidou had inherited the support of the right. In 1974 he was again briefly acting president after Pompidou's death in office.

**PÖHL, Karl Otto.** *Germany.* Bundesbank chairman. One of a remarkable breed of Social Democratic economic experts, he was born in Hanover in 1929 and worked as an economic journalist before entering the government apparatus in Bonn, first in the economics ministry, then as a state secretary in the finance ministry under Helmut Schmidt in 1972. Schmidt pushed him forward and he was appointed deputy chairman of the Bundesbank in 1977, taking over in 1980 as chairman and thus becoming one of the world's most influential financial figures. The constraints on his exercise of power within Germany, where the Bundesbank must work in consensus with the various political, regional and economic interests, were demonstrated in 1990 over the pace of German unification. Pöhl found himself taken aback by **Helmut Kohl**'s rush for unity, and clashed with the chancellor over the generosity of the terms for East Germany, fearing that they would impose too heavy a burden on West Germany. He nevertheless looks set to continue in office until 1996, and is emerging, with finance minister **Theo Waigel**, as a voice of restraint against rapid moves to European economic and monetary union.

**POL POT.** *Cambodia.* Khmer Rouge leader. Born as Saloth Sar in 1928, he studied in Paris where he joined a "Marxist Circle" of Khmer students led by **Ieng Sary**. Joining the Communist party politburo in 1960, he became general secretary two years later after the incumbent had mysteriously vanished. In 1963 he and Sary disappeared from Phnom Penh after an anti-leftist crackdown by **Prince Norodom Sihanouk**. He resurfaced, as Pol Pot, only in 1976 when he was named prime minister of the Khmer Rouge regime, a year after it assumed power. During his premiership he embarked on a series of brutal purges to ensure the continued dominance of his faction. He remained as Khmer Rouge military commander after his government had been driven from Phnom Penh in 1979, but gradually resigned official posts after 1985. Many regard his "retirement" as little more than a public-relations exercise and reports suggest that he has played a major part in recent Khmer Rouge military operations.

**POLOZKOV, Ivan.** *USSR.* Russian Communist Party leader. Born in 1935, he was a collective farm worker who rose the ranks to serve from 1985–90 as regional Communist Party of the Soviet Union (CPSU) first secretary in Krasnodar (south Russia), where he gained notoriety for closing down private co-operative businesses that had been permitted under **Mikhail Gorbachev**'s *perestroika*. He emerged in 1990 as a leader of the CPSU's neo-conservatives, arguing that the country's current crisis stemmed from failures in the national leadership. In May 1990 he was defeated by **Boris Yeltsin** for the presidency of Russia, but in the following month the conservative-dominated founding congress of the Russian Federation Communist Party elected him first secretary. This post earned him CPSU politburo membership at the July 1990 Congress. Since the retirement of Yegor Ligachev, Polozkov has become the *bête noire* of the reformist wing, the archetypal party hack; he represents those who think they have most to lose from radical reform.

**PONS IRAZAZÁBAL, Félix.** *Spain.* President of the Cortes. Born in 1942 in Majorca, he has held the largely ceremonial posts of president of the Congress of Deputies (lower house) and of the Cortes (parliament) since 1986, and was re-elected in 1989. A lawyer, he joined the Spanish Socialist Workers' Party (PSOE) in 1975, was elected a deputy for the Balearics in 1977, and became minister for regional and local government in 1985.

**POOS, Jacques.** *Luxembourg.* Deputy prime minister, foreign minister. Born in 1935, he studied economics and has worked as a researcher, managing director of a daily newspaper and banker. Elected to parliament for the Luxembourg Socialist Workers' Party (LSAP/POSL) in 1974, he became its deputy leader in 1982. He was finance minister from 1976–79 and became deputy prime minister and foreign minister in 1984.

**POPEREN, Jean.** *France.* Minister for relations with parliament. Born in 1925, Poperen studied literature and history before taking up a university lecturing post. Politically, he moved from the Communist Party (PCF) through the Unified Socialist Party (PSU) and the Federation of the Democratic and Socialist Left (FDGS) in the 1960s, to the higher echelons of the current Socialist Party (PS), where he was effectively number two for most of the 1980s. Appointed minister for relations with parliament in 1988, Poperen is identified with unity on the left and service to the party; he is not one of the obvious PS heavyweights, but cannot be discounted in the party leadership stakes.

**POPOV, Dimitur.** *Bulgaria.* Prime minister. A compromise choice to lead the transitional government formed in December 1990 pending fresh elections. Proposed by President **Zhelyu Zhelev**, he was accepted by all the main political forces in the country. Born in 1927, Popov had no government experience. He was a lawyer who specialized in criminal and transport law and from 1971–90 he was a judge. He was not a member of the Communist Party. His final legal post was Chairman of the Sofia Municipal Court. Popov came to the attention of both the public and politicians as secretary of the Central Electoral Commission, which oversaw the elections of June 1990. His impartial handling of the job won him widespread respect.

**POPOV, Gavriil.** *USSR.* Mayor of Moscow. Born in 1936, of Greek descent, he was professor of economics at Moscow State University and editor of the review *Voprosi Ekonomiki* (Questions of Economics) before his April 1990 election as mayor. A leading radical, in July 1989 he joined **Boris Yeltsin**, **Yury Afanasyev** and the late Andrei Sakharov in heading the Inter-Regional Group, the first parliamentary opposition faction in the USSR Congress of People's Deputies. He emerged as leader of the "Democratic Russia" bloc of reformist groups which wrested control of Moscow city council from the Communist Party in the March 1990 elections. He left the party following the July 1990 congress.

**PORRITT, Jonathon.** *UK.* Environmentalist campaigner and politician. Born in 1950, he was educated at Eton College and then studied modern languages and was a teacher from 1975–84. He contested numerous local, general and European elections for the Ecology Party (renamed the Green Party in 1985) between 1979 and 1985, and chaired the party from 1979–80 and 1982–84. He served as director of Friends of the Earth from 1984–90, presiding over a massive increase in membership which accompanied growing national interest in green issues. Bright and articulate, he has become one of the country's most persuasive environmentalist campaigners. He left Friends of the Earth in 1990 to concentrate on writing and broadcast journalism.

**PORTER, Lady (Shirley Porter).** *UK.* Conservative local government politician. Born in 1930, the heiress to her father's Tesco supermarkets empire, she was elected to London's Westminster city council, the country's richest borough, in 1974, becoming its leader in 1983. Energetic, plain-speaking and often in the headlines, she has become a darling of the Conservative right for her value-for-money approach to local government, but has attracted much criticism – notably for approving the decision to sell three cemeteries to a private company for less than the price of a cup of tea.

**PORTILLO, Michael.** *UK.* Minister for local government and inner cities, MP since 1984. Born in 1953 to a Spanish father and Scottish mother, he was one of the Tory party's fastest-rising stars. As a member of **Chris Patten**'s team at the environment his role was to provide a hard edge to the reform of the unpopular poll tax. He kept his job when **John Major** became prime minister.

**POWELL, Sir Charles.** *UK.* Private secretary to the prime minister since 1983, under-secretary since 1987. Born in 1941, the former diplomat steadily accumulated power within 10 Downing Street as private secretary to **Margaret Thatcher** and exerted an influence over public life that appeared to go well beyond the sphere of foreign affairs. As a civil servant, his contribution was never publicly acknowledged but he was one of the key players in the Thatcher administration, more powerful than many cabinet members. He was knighted in the Thatcher resignation honours list and stayed on to help **John Major** but was expected to leave government service for business before long.

**POWELL, General Colin.** *USA.* Joint chiefs of staff chairman. Born in New York in 1937, the son of Jamaican immigrants, he joined the army in 1958 after graduating from university. He has worked in the defence department since 1979 and has been a close associate of former defence secretary Frank Carlucci, but prefers service in the field. Between 1987 and 1989 Powell was instrumental in rebuilding the National Security Council which had been demoralized by the Iran-Contra affair and the heavy involvement in it of the then National Security Adviser Vice-Admiral John Poindexter. Powell's promotion in 1989 to chairman of the joint chiefs of staff by **George Bush** made him the youngest holder of that office as well as the first black incumbent. The Gulf crisis that erupted in 1990 gave him a high profile and his calm authority was widely respected.

**POZSGAY, Imre.** *Hungary.* Former Hungarian Socialist Party parliamentary leader and pre-eminent reform communist. Born in 1933 and a career party official in the Hungarian Socialist Workers' Party (MSM), Pozsgay was identified as reform-minded from the early 1970s, and particularly as culture minister in 1975–82. Resisting János Kádár's efforts to marginalize him, he was instrumental in commissioning the influential 1987 "Change and Reform" document which helped open the floodgates, with its advocacy of fundamental political as well as economic change. After Kádár's departure he was brought back into the government. He joined the four-member MSM presidium, and consistently outmanoeuvred his more conservative colleagues. In October 1989 he stood at the height of his popularity, a skilled and polished communicator who had guided the party through the round-table talks, reappraisal of 1956, acceptance of multi-party democracy, and "rebirth" as the Hungarian Socialist Party (MSP). Within six months, however, he was yesterday's man, as his chance of election to the presidency disappeared.

**PRABHAKARAN, Vellupillai.** *Sri Lanka.* Military leader of Tamil separatist Liberation Tigers of Tamil Eelam. After spending 18 months in hiding before the withdrawal of Indian troops in March 1990, he emerged to offer the prospect of a political solution. He proved insufficiently flexible to reach a compromise with the **Ranasinghe Premadasa** government, and relaunched the bloody Tamil armed struggle in mid-year.

**PRADHAN, Sahana.** *Nepal.* Industry and commerce minister. A leading member of the long-banned Communist Party of Nepal, she is prominent in the United Left Front coalition. She became industry and commerce minister in the government of **Krishna Prasad Bhattarai** in April 1990.

**PRAMARN ADIREKSARN, Major-General.** *Thailand.* Interior minister. Born in 1914, Pramarn was appointed to head the powerful interior ministry in 1988 by his brother-in-law, **Chartchai Chunhawan.** One of Chartchai's main rivals within the Chart Thai Party, Pramarn was demoted to industry minister in early 1990 after he had been involved in a long quarrel with the popular mayor of Bangkok, **Chamlong Srimaung** but returned to the interior ministry in December 1990.

**PRAMUAL SABHAVASU.** *Thailand.* Industry minister. Born in 1927. Prime minister **Chartchai Chunhawan** brought his Chart Thai colleague Pramual into his first cabinet in 1988 to head the finance ministry. Under Pramual's stewardship the Thai economy flourished, but during early 1990 he was one of a number of ministers attacked by the opposition over their alleged involvement in financial scandals. He was expected to lose his cabinet place, but in August Chartchai appointed him deputy prime minister. In December he was demoted to industry minister.

**PRANDINI, Giovanni.** *Italy.* Christian Democrat Party (DC) politician. Born in 1940 in the province of Brescia, he gained a degree in economics and commerce at the Catholic University of Milan. He entered the Chamber of Deputies in 1972 and became a senator in 1983. His first cabinet appointment was as merchant navy minister in July 1987. In July 1989 he was appointed public works minister.

**PRAWIRO, Dr Radius.** *Indonesia.* Co-ordinating minister for economy, finance, industry and development supervision. Born in 1928, a Dutch-educated economist, Prawiro has been a key member of **Suharto's** government since 1966, serving as governor of Bank Indonesia and trade and finance minister before taking up his current post as the country's economic supremo in 1988.

**PREGL, Živko.** *Yugoslavia.* Deputy premier. Born in 1947 in Ljubljana, he joined the communist party in 1965. After graduating in economics, he built a career within the party and in March 1989 was appointed federal deputy premier in charge of the economy. A sharp-minded technocrat, he has been the architect of sweeping economic reforms and is a key player in pushing forward constitutional changes to introduce full political pluralism.

President. Born in 1924 and educated in Colombo, he began his political career in the trade union movement and the Ceylon Labour Party. He moved over to the United National Party (UNP) in 1956 and has represented central Colombo in parliament since 1960. A specialist in local government, he held this portfolio in the UNP government from 1968–70, and again when the UNP returned to office in 1977, when he also took on the housing portfolio, on which he was to build much of his growing prestige. The party's deputy leader from 1976, he was given the largely ceremonial job of prime minister from 1978, the first holder of this office not to come from the country's social elite. He used the job astutely to position himself for the succession to Junius Jayawardene as president when the old man stood down in 1988. He took a political risk, which paid off, by marking himself out as the leading government critic of the decision to invite in Indian troops, a desperate measure which signally failed to advance any solution in the Tamil secessionist war. In late 1988 he conducted a successful presidential election campaign against **Sirimavo Bandaranaike**, afterwards sidelining his erstwhile rivals in the formation of a new government. Despite the devastation of the civil war, he has managed to engineer some optimism about economic growth prospects, allowing him to entertain the possibility of seeking a second term in office.

**PRESCOTT, John**. *UK*. Labour politician. Born in 1938, he worked as a steward on the Cunard shipping line for ten years before studying economics and politics at Ruskin College and Hull University. He was briefly a full-time official of the National Union of Seamen (NUS) before being elected to parliament in 1970. He entered the shadow cabinet in 1983, and has been spokesman on transport (1983–84 and since 1988), employment (1984–87) and energy (1987–88). A plain-speaking and pugnacious politician, his outspoken attacks on government transport policy in the wake of one major disaster after another in the late 1980s made him one of the more effective opposition spokesmen. But a fiery temperament has occasionally produced clashes with his own colleagues as well as Tory opponents and his relations with the Labour leadership have often been strained.

**PRICE, George**. *Belize*. Prime minister. Born in 1919, he helped found Belize's first political party, the People's United Party (PUP) in 1950 and was first elected to the Legislative Council in

1954. He became leader of the movement for independence, serving successively as first minister, premier and then as prime minister at independence in 1981. He lost his seat in the 1984 elections, but was returned to power in 1989. Charismatic but somewhat ascetic, Price has a reputation for incorruptibility and has achieved the status of "father of the nation".

**PRIMAKOV, Yevgeny**. *USSR*. Former Presidential Council member and Gulf crisis envoy. A Russian born in 1929, he was originally a journalist, working notably as *Pravda*'s Middle East correspondent in the late 1960s. After 1970 he worked in the Academy of Sciences, holding senior posts including director of the Institute of World Economy and International Relations. Elected in June 1989 as chairman of the Soviet of the Union (one of two USSR Supreme Soviet chambers), he relinquished that post upon his appointment in March 1990 to **Mikhail Gorbachev**'s short-lived Presidential Council. From September 1989 to July 1990 he was a candidate Communist Party of the Soviet Union politburo member. In late 1990 he acted as special envoy in the Gulf crisis.

**PRODEV, Stefan**. *Bulgaria*. Journalist. A Communist Party member, Prodev was dismissed as editor-in-chief of the noted cultural journal, *Narodna Kultura*, in November 1988, for his association with the unoffical Club for the Support of Glasnost and Perestroika in Bulgaria, of which he was a founder-member. He was reinstated a year later, after the ousting of president Todor Zhivkov. In January 1990 he was elected president of the National Union of Journalists, and a month later, aged 62, he was appointed editor-in-chief of the party paper.

**PRODI, Romano**. *Italy*. Former chairman of Istituto per la Ricostruzione Industriale (IRI). Born in 1939 in the province of Reggio Emilia, he obtained a degree in economics and commerce at the Catholic University of Milan and subsequently studied at the London School of Economics. He embarked upon a career in teaching, becoming professor of industrial economics at Bologna University. From November 1978 to March 1979 Prodi served as trade and industry minister under **Giulio Andreotti**; appointed as a non-party extra-parliamentary expert, he has subsequently been identified with the Christian Democrats. In November 1982 he was appointed chairman of IRI, the largest state holding company, a post he held until October 1989. During his period of held until October 1989. During his period of office, he resisted undue political pressure and succeeded in bringing IRI back into operational profit. He was responsible for increasing private-sector participation in IRI and for the disposal of some of its subsidiaries, notably the controversial sale of Alfa Romeo to Fiat in January 1987. His tenure coincided almost exactly with that of **Franco Reviglio** at ENI and the period is sometimes referred to as the era of the professors.

**PROKOFYEV, Yury.** *USSR.* Senior Communist Party official. A Russian born in 1939, he has held office in the Moscow city administration since 1968, mostly in the city Communist Party apparatus, but with a brief spell as secretary to the city council from 1986–88 (while **Boris Yeltsin** was city party first secretary). Despite the political embarrassment of failing to win election to the USSR Congress of People's Deputies in March 1989, he was named Moscow city party first secretary the following November, and was elected to the Communist Party of the Soviet Union politburo after the July 1990 congress. He has a reputation as a moderate.

**PRONK, Jan.** *Netherlands.* Development co-operation minister. Born in 1940, he studied economics under Jan Tinbergen, and traces, from this formative influence, his strong interest in the problems of developing countries. Elected to the Staten Generaal (parliament) in 1971, he was development co-operation minister from 1973–77. In 1980 he was appointed deputy secretary-general of Unctad. He returned to domestic politics six years later and chaired the Labour Party (PvdA) committee that planned the revision of the party's policies in a more pragmatic direction. He was put in charge of the development co-operation portfolio for a second time when the PvdA returned to government in coalition with the Christian Democrats in November 1989.

**PRUNSKIENE, Kazimiera.** *USSR.* Lithuanian prime minister. An economist, born in 1943, she was one of many Lithuanian communists who joined the nationalist Popular Front (Sajudis) on its foundation in 1988. An academic before becoming deputy premier in 1989, she was elected Lithuania's premier (and left the Communist Party) after the landslide Sajudis

victory in the February 1990 Lithuanian elections, which was followed by the republic's unilateral declaration of independence. Tough but more pragmatic than Lithuanian President **Vytautas Landsbergis**, her willingness to compromise on conditions for negotiations with the Soviet authorities angered hardline nationalists.

**PUAPUA, Dr Tomasi.** *Tuvalu.* Former prime minister. Born in 1938, he trained in medicine in Fiji and New Zealand. A keen sportsman, he and Toaripi Lauti (the first prime minister on Tuvalu's independence in 1978) have dominated the politics of the tiny island. Puapua held office as prime minister from 1981 until his defeat at a general election in September 1989, when he was succeeded by a member of the new generation, **Bikenibeu Paeniu.**

**PUGO, Boris.** *USSR.* Interior minister. A Latvian born in Moscow in 1937, he trained as an engineer but became a Komsomol official in 1961, progressing to a party career. He transferred to the KGB in 1976, rising to the post of Latvian KGB chief (1980–84), with the rank of major-general. He was Latvian Communist Party first secretary from 1984–88. In September 1988, he was appointed chairman of the Communist Party of the Soviet Union (CPSU) control committee (responsible for internal party affairs, and renamed the central control commission in 1990). From 1989–90 he was a candidate CPSU politburo member. A hardliner, he was appointed interior minister in place of **Vadim Bakatin** in December 1990.

**PUJOL I SOLEY, Jordi.** *Spain.* Catalonia premier. Born in 1930 in Barcelona, he trained as a doctor, but went on to become a banker. In the 1950s he served two years of a seven-year prison sentence for singing the banned Catalan anthem in the presence of members of the Franco government. He founded Convergence and Union (CiU) in 1976, became its secretary-general, and was elected to the Cortes (parliament) in 1977. In 1980 he led his party to victory in elections to the Catalan parliament and became premier of the Generalitat or Catalan government. He renewed his mandate, with increased majorities, in 1984 and 1988 and is the undisputed leader of Catalonia. Politically conservative, he is also deeply committed to Catalan nationalism.

# Q

**QABOOS IBN SAID, Sultan.** *Oman.* Ruler. Born in Muscat in 1940, Qaboos staged a palace coup in 1970 to succeed his father Said ibn Taymour, who had kept his country in medieval darkness. His first acts were to abolish restrictions on smoking in public as well as lifting bans on singing and the wearing of spectacles. For the first five years of his reign he concentrated on defeating the Marxist-led rebellion in the southern province of Dhofar. Since then, with unstinting British support, he has raced his rugged nation into the 20th century. In November 1990, he announced plans for the creation of a consultative council to widen public participation in "the responsibilities of the fatherland".

**QADDAFI, Colonel Muammar Abu Meniar al-.** *Libya.* Head of state. Born in 1942 near Sirte into a bedouin family, his precocious politicking led to his expulsion from high school. He studied history at Benghazi University in 1960–61 and received his military training at the Libyan military academy. Commissioned into the Libyan army as a signals officer in 1965, he attended a short signals course in the UK in 1966–67. Inspired by Egyptian President Gamal Abdel Nasser's Arab nationalism, he formed a Libyan version of the Free Officers' Movement, and overthrew the ailing King Idris in an almost bloodless coup in 1969. Moving quickly to consolidate his position, he established a socialist republic headed by a Revolution Command Council in which he initially held the posts of prime minister and defence minister. In 1972, however, he handed over the prime ministership to his trusted associate **Abdel-Salam Jalloud**. At about this time he developed his revolutionary philosophy, the "Third Universal Theory", an alternative to "capitalist materialism and communist atheism" and expounded it in the three volumes of his *Green Book* published between 1976 and 1979. It consisted of a heady mix of socialism, Islam and bedouin wisdom, and its development was accompanied by a transformation of the political structure, with

the establishment of the General People's Congress and proclamation of the "state of the masses", the Socialist People's Libyan Arab Jamahiriya, in 1976. Qaddafi stepped down from his official posts in 1979, preferring to be known simply as "leader of the revolution" and leaving political authority officially vested in a complex structure of people's committees. However, there has never been any doubt about who determines the direction of policy or of the penalties for those who oppose it. The transformation of society was fuelled by Libya's oil earnings and considerable advances in social welfare and education were achieved. But the collapse of the oil market in the mid-1980s led to shortages and other economic difficulties and damaged Qaddafi's popularity. His response was the announcement in 1988 of measures to liberalize the economy and promises of political reforms. His espousal of Arab unity and attempts to export revolution have made him an awkward neighbour, prone to announcing plans for immediate union with startled other Arab states. Since 1989 Libya has been a member, with four other North African states, of the Arab Maghreb Union (UMA), but Qaddafi chafes at the slow pace of regional integration. His support for radical groups and attacks on exiled opponents have earned him the distrust and enmity of the West, but he has generally been more effective at rhetoric than action. Although his prestige was dented by the US bombing raids of 1986 and the defeat of his forces in Chad the following year, Qaddafi retains faith in his vision, hailing the collapse of communism in Eastern Europe in 1989 as evidence of wide acceptance of his Third Universal Theory and continuing to exhort Libyans to abandon materialism and return to simple bedouin ways. Qaddafi's response in late 1990 to the Gulf crisis revealed his continuing distrust of the USA but also included a call to Iraq to withdraw from Kuwait.

**QASEM, Marwan al-.** *Jordan.* Foreign minister. Born in 1938, he studied at various US universities. He joined the Jordanian foreign ministry and became chief of the Royal Hashemite Court before replacing Taher al-Masri as deputy prime minister and foreign minister in December 1988.

**QIAN QICHEN.** *China.* Foreign minister. Born in 1928 in Tianjin, Qian worked as a diplomat in the USSR and Africa before moving to head the information department of the foreign ministry in 1977 where he rose to become minister in 1988. A member of the Central Committee from 1985, Qian was special envoy in the 1983–87 Sino-Soviet consultations which led to the resumption of relations in 1989. He should be given the credit for the improvement in China's international image since the military crackdown on the pro-democracy movement in June 1989.

**QIAO SHI.** *China.* Member of the Chinese Communist Party (CCP) Politburo Standing Committee. Born in about 1924, Qiao worked in the steel industry and probably held a senior intelligence position. He headed the Central Committee's international liaison department before joining the Secretariat and Politburo in 1985, and its Standing Committee in 1987. Vice-premier from 1986–88, he became head of the leading group for rectifying party style at central level in 1986, and secretary of the central Discipline Inspection Commission in 1987. He headed the central party school from 1989, after being tipped to succeed **Zhao Ziyang** as CCP general secretary.

**QIN JIWEI.** *China.* Defence minister. Born in 1912, Qin held military and party posts in Yunnan before becoming commander of the Chengdu Military Region in 1974. Rivalry with **Yang Shangkun** led to Qin relinquishing command of the powerful Beijing Military Region in 1987 after seven years. A member of the Central Committee from 1977, he joined the Politburo in 1982 and in 1988 became a state councillor and defence minister. Reportedly reluctant to use military force to crush the pro-democracy movement in June 1989, he has nevertheless remained a member of the state Central Military Commission.

**QOMI, Ayatollah Ahmad Azeri.** *Iran* . Conservative cleric and member of parliament. Born in the holy city of Qom in 1925, Qomi represents his home city and serves on the parliament's key economy and finance committee. He is also a member of the second

Assembly of Experts. Arrested twice under the Shah, he was a member of the Teachers' Association of the Qom Theological Seminaries. The proprietor of the conservative newspaper *Resalat*, Qomi has challenged economic radicals within the establishment, and is openly critical of their alleged financial misdeeds. He is the most articulate of the conservatives who kept their ties with Ayatollah Khomeini.

**QUAYLE, James Danforth (Dan).** *USA.* Vice-president. Born in 1947, he was educated at DePauw and Indiana universities. In 1974 he entered his family's multi-million-dollar newspaper and publishing business, where he worked as an associate publisher until 1977 when he was elected to the House of Representatives as a conservative Republican. In 1980 he became a senator from Indiana, and was re-elected in 1986. Quayle's unremarkable congressional career was disrupted in 1988 when **George Bush** confounded all speculation by choosing him as vice-presidential running mate. The choice was believed to have been motivated by the hope that his youth and good looks would attract the support of women and younger voters. His selection provoked immediate accusations that he had avoided serving in Vietnam by securing a posting in the Lousiana national guard, and during the campaign he made a poor showing in a television debate with Democratic nominee for vice-president, **Lloyd Bentsen.** Although he has kept a low profile since taking office in 1989 and has been subject to intensive training in public relations, Quayle has made numerous ill-conceived comments and has continued to provide a rich source of humour for comedians and political commentators alike. He is nonetheless a possible future presidential candidate.

**QUILÈS, Paul.** *France.* Minister of posts, telecommunications and space. Born in 1942, he graduated from the Ecole Polytechnique and began an engineering career. Politically, he moved up the hierarchy of the Socialist Party (PS) as an organizer and an energy specialist, winning a seat in parliament for the first time in 1978 and holding ministerial office from 1983–85 as, successively, housing and urban affairs, transport, and defence minister. In 1988 he became posts, telecommunications and space minister, with modernization high on his agenda.

# R

**RABIN, Yitzhak.** *Israel.* Former Labour prime minister. Born in Israel in 1922, Rabin commanded a brigade of the Palmach (proto-Israeli army) in 1943–44. Commander of the Northern Command from 1956–59, Israeli Defence Forces chief of staff Rabin was the architect of victory in the six-day war in 1967 and was rewarded with the ambassadorship to the USA from 1968–73. After Golda Meir's resignation in 1974, Rabin defeated his arch-rival, the more politically experienced **Shimon Peres**, to take the premiership and lead the Labour party. Faced with the task of tackling inflation and patching up national prestige after near-defeat in the 1973 war, Rabin fell prey to a scandal arising from his wife's technical breach of foreign currency regulations and resigned in 1977 on the eve of an election which let in Likud for the first time. In 1984 he returned to office as defence minister in the Likud-Labour coalition, and gained a new reputation as a hardliner after his crackdown on the Palestinian uprising after 1987. In opposition again, Rabin has designs on the Labour leadership, but with the Israeli electorate growing disillusioned with the old guard, his chances may be receding.

**RABUKA, Major-General Sitiveni.** *Fiji.* Army commander. Born in 1948 and a career army officer, he staged a dramatic coup in May 1987 to restore the political dominance of ethnic Fijians, following the election victory of Timoci Bavadra's multi-racial left-wing coalition. After arresting the government in the parliament building, he initially handed the reins of government to **Penaia Ganilau**'s interim administration, claiming he would return to barracks, but staged a second coup in September, making himself interim head of state. Relinquishing power to a civilian administration again three months later to counteract growing international isolation, he remained in government as home affairs minister, until the prime minister, **Kamisese Mara** made him choose in January 1990 between the army and the cabinet. Exploiting his strongman image, he has made no secret of his desire to become prime minister himself by winning elections in 1991 or 1992 under the new constitutional arrangements which protect ethnic Fijian hegemony. A commoner, he has increasingly been seen as an uncomfortable rival of Mara and Ganilau, and their long-dominant chiefly families.

**RAE, Bob.** *Canada.* Premier of Ontario. Born in Ottawa in 1948, he was educated at Toronto University, where he received a law degree, and at Oxford University. He worked in a housing and legal aid clinic in London before returning to Canada, where he was first elected to the House of Commons in 1978. Rae served as a member of the federal parliament until 1980, and was elected leader of the New Democratic Party in Ontario in 1982, when he also won a seat in the provincial legislative assembly. Rae fashioned a coalition government in Ontario when, in 1985, he joined with Liberal leader David Peterson to overthrow the Conservatives, after 42 years of provincial rule. After a Liberal victory in 1987, he came back to win a majority in the provincial elections of September 1990 and become Ontario's first socialist premier.

**RAFIDAH AZIZ, Dato' Seri.** *Malaysia.* International trade and industry minister. Born in 1943, she is one of only two women in the cabinet. She took charge of the powerful trade and industry portfolio in 1987, breaking new ground for a woman in a predominantly Muslim country. After the October 1990 elections, this portfolio was split in two, with Rafidah Aziz retaining responsibility for international trade, enhancing her standing by taking on the task of creating a Malaysian "MITI", on the Japanese model. She had previously served as public enterprises minister since 1980 and heads Wanita UMNO, the powerful women's wing of the dominant Malay party.

**RAFSANJANI, Hojatoleslam Ali Akbar Hashemi.** *Iran.* President. Born in 1934 in the south-eastern desert region at Rafsanjan, near Kerman, Rafsanjani's parents were pistachio-nut farmers. He supported Ayatollah Khomeini after the latter's exile in 1963 and remained loyal to the cause, despite becoming a wealthy property speculator in the 1970s, operating through a company called Dezh-Saz (Castle Builders). He suffered imprisonment under the Shah in 1963, 1967, 1970, 1972 and 1975. After the revolution in 1979 he helped to found the dominant Islamic Republican Party, and built up the strength of the Islamic Revolution Guards Corps to neutralize any threat of a coup from the regular army. In 1980 he was elected speaker of the Majlis (parliament). Appointed acting commander-in-chief in 1988, he surprised many by helping to persuade the hitherto inflexible Khomeini to "drink poison" by agreeing to end the war with Iraq. Of charming demeanour, Rafsanjani is capable of both ruthlessness and pragmatic compromise. Although he represents the moderates who favour improved relations with the West, he has at times had to toe the radical line. However, he was the key figure in the release of hostages in Beirut in 1990 and, after the earthquake in June of that year, confounded hardliners with his announcement that Iran would welcome foreign aid from the West. Such attitudes strike a chord with most Iranians, weary of the deprivations brought about by a decade's defiance of the "Great Satan". The Gulf crisis brought Rafsanjani both a satisfactory peace settlement with Iraq and growing attention from Western and Arab states seeking to use Iran as a counterweight to the power of **Saddam Hussain**.

**RAHMAT, Datuk Mohamad**. *Malaysia*. Information minister and secretary-general of the United Malays National Organization (UMNO). Born in 1938, Rahmat served as information minister for four years before his appointment in 1982 as ambassador to Indonesia, with full cabinet status. He resigned in the mid-1980s, but **Mahathir Mohamad** brought him back into the cabinet as information minister in 1987 after a number of anti-Mahathir ministers had been purged.

**RAINIER III, Prince**. *Monaco*. Head of state. Born in 1923, son of the Comte de Polignac, he fought in the French resistance during World War II and gained a commission in the French army. He was educated at the University of Montpellier and the Ecole Libre des Sciences Politiques in Paris. On the death of his grandfather, Prince Louis II, in May 1949, he became the 26th ruler of the Grimaldi dynasty, which has reigned in Monaco since 1297. His

marriage in 1956 to the film star Grace Kelly, who died in a car accident in 1982, provided the chroniclers of fashionable society with a "fairytale princess" story.

**RAKOTONIRINA, Manandafy**. *Madagascar*. Opposition politician. A university lecturer in sociology, he is leader of the Party of Proletarian Power (MFM), founded in 1972 as a radical left-wing student organization. Increasingly a party of the centre, the MFM has moved from supporting President **Didier Ratsiraka**'s regime to become its principal opponent. Rakotonirina took second place in the 1989 presidential elections.

**RALLIS, George**. *Greece*. New Democracy (ND) politician. Born in 1918 into one of Greece's oldest political families, he practised law before entering parliament for the Populist Party in 1950. As public order minister in 1967, he was the only cabinet minister able to maintain contact with King Constantine at the time of the coup d'état; he counselled first active and then, when this proved impossible, passive opposition to the military dictatorship. Rallis was arrested on several occasions under the colonels' regime and for a time was sent into internal exile. After 1974, he served in ND governments variously as minister of education, economy and foreign affairs before succeeding **Constantine Karamanlis** as prime minister in May 1980. After ND's defeat at the hands of the Panhellenic Socialist Movement (Pasok) in the 1981 elections, he lost the party leadership. Highly respected for his integrity and dignity, he remains an MP but devotes much of his time to writing. A patrician figure, he has been suggested as a possible successor to Karamanlis as president.

**RAMADHAN, Taha Yassin**. *Iraq*. First deputy prime minister. Born in Mosul in 1939, he worked as a bank cashier until 1980. As first deputy prime minister and head of the Ba'th militia, a key post, he is widely considered to be President **Saddam Hussain**'s number two. A hardliner who was dedicated to all-out war with Iran, he has been deeply sceptical about attempts at political liberalization within Iraq.

**RAMAHATRA, Lieutenant-Colonel Victor**. *Madagascar*. Prime minister. A French-trained military engineer, born in 1945, he joined the government in 1982 as public works minister. He became head of government in 1988.

**RAMAPHOSA, Cyril**. *South Africa*. Politician and trade unionist. Born in 1953 in Johannesburg, his studies were interrupted by the upheavals of the mid-1970s, in which he was a key student organizer. Imprisoned for spells of 11 months and six months, he finally qualified in law in 1981, and the following year became general secretary of the powerful National Union of Mineworkers. Believed to be a South African Communist Party member, and seen by many as a future leader of the African National Congress (ANC), he is widely respected for his astuteness and intelligence. He has a strong power base in the local politics of Soweto, and was a member of the "Soweto People's Delegation" which finally obtained concessions sufficient to warrant calling off the three-year rent strike there in October 1989. Valuable as a counter-weight in what **Winnie Mandela** increasingly treated as her local fief, he was the guiding hand in the **Nelson Mandela** reception committee. He was constantly at Mandela's side after his release in February 1990, until ceding this role to **Zwelakhe Sisulu**, taking a lower profile himself while increasing his familiarity with other strands in the ANC.

**RAMGOOLAM, Nuvin**. *Mauritius*. Mauritius Labour Party (MLP) leader. The son of Mauritius's first prime minister and former MLP leader Sir Seewoosagur Ramgoolam, he took over from Satcam Boolell as party leader after the departure of the MLP from the governing coalition with **Aneerood Jugnauth**'s Mauritian Socialist Movement in August 1990. Seen by many as sharing his father's political abilities and principles, he was expected to use the Ramgoolam name to win back former MLP supporters.

**RAMOS, General Fidel**. *Philippines*. Defence secretary and armed forces deputy commander-in-chief. Born in 1928, he was educated at Illinois University and the elite West Point military academy in the USA. He enjoyed a glowing army career, serving in Korea and Vietnam, and was appointed deputy chief of staff in 1981 and chief of staff in 1986. Despite being Ferdinand Marcos's second cousin, he joined **Juan Ponce Enrile** in supporting **Cory Aquino**'s "people power" revolt following the 1986 elections. In contrast with Enrile and other army colleagues, Ramos has remained loyal to the Aquino regime and, despite his sympathy for the grievances of rebellious soldiers, professes total commitment to constitutional process. He is considered a likely contender for Aquino's blessing as a presidential candidate in 1992.

**RANGEL, Charles**. *USA*. Democratic congressman from New York. Born in 1930, he

was a lawyer and state assemblyman before election to the House of Representatives in 1970. Probably the most pragmatic of the senior black congressmen, he aspired to party leadership but failed in his 1987 bid to become whip. Chairman of the select committee on narcotics since 1983, he has advocated a wide range of strong drug control measures.

**RASPUTIN, Valentin**. *USSR*. Writer and former Presidential Council member. Born in 1937, he worked as a journalist in his native East Siberia before becoming a full-time novelist and poet in 1966. He is well known for environmentalist activities, particularly in the campaign to save Siberia's Lake Baikal. The way in which he has championed Russian traditions and national identity has provoked charges of conservatism and even anti-semitism. He was elected as the only non-communist member of **Mikhail Gorbachev**'s short-lived Presidential Council in March 1990.

**RAŢIU, Ion**. *Romania*. A leader of the Christian Democratic National Peasants' Party (CDNPP) and member of the Assembly of Deputies. Born in Turda, Transylvania, in 1917, he studied law, then sought asylum in the UK in 1940. He worked at the Romanian legation in London, where his uncle was ambassador. At the end of World War II he set up a shipping company and married Elisabeth Pilkington of the English glass-manufacturing family. From the mid-1970s onwards he devoted himself to politics, founding the World Union of Free Romanians in 1984. Returning to Bucharest in January 1990, he became a leader of the CDNPP and ran for president in the May 1990 elections, coming a poor third with less than 5% of the votes.

**RATSIRAKA, Admiral Didier**. *Madagascar*. President. Born in 1936 into a leading Malagasy political family, he was a French-trained naval officer who served as naval attaché in Paris from 1970–72 and as foreign affairs minister in the government of Gabriel Ramanantsoa from 1972–75, when he negotiated the withdrawal of Madagascar from the franc zone and the departure of French troops from the island. He emerged as head of state in 1975 after a period of anarchy following the resignation of Ramanantsoa. Initially a radical socialist, he established a revolutionary party, publishing his own "Red Book" and receiving support from the USSR and from North Korea, which provides his bodyguard. In recent years, Ratsiraka has shifted ground, winning the praise of Western donors for market-oriented economic reforms. Despite a fragile power base, centring on his wife's family (which has built up extensive commercial interests), the navy and the eastern port city of Toamasina, Ratsiraka has brought relative stability to the country. But his failure to deliver economic recovery despite years of painful austerity has led to mounting, although divided, opposition, finding new expression since the formal restoration of full multi-party politics in 1990.

**RAU, Johannes.** *Germany.* Social Democratic Party (SPD) politician and premier of North Rhine-Westphalia. Born in Wuppertal in 1931, the son of a parson, he worked as a book dealer and journalist before going into politics. Initially a member of the pacifist, neutralist All-German People's Party (GVP), he joined the SPD when the GVP was dissolved in 1957, and was elected at the age of 27 as a deputy in the North Rhine-Westphalia parliament. Briefly mayor of Wuppertal, and appointed to the Land (state) government in 1970 (as scientific research minister), he became premier in 1978 and has held on to this office ever since. A steady rise through the SPD party hierarchy took him to the rank of deputy chairman in 1982, but the highlight of his career came at the SPD conference in August 1986, when he was unanimously chosen as the party's candidate for the federal chancellorship. The SPD's showing in the 1987 elections was disappointing, however, with the party's share of the vote declining, and in 1990 the SPD chose the younger, more charismatic **Oskar Lafontaine.**

**RAUSCH, Jean-Marie.** *France.* Foreign trade minister. Born in 1929, he has successfully blended a career in private industry and public service with political office. Since 1971, he has won elections as a general councillor, regional councillor, mayor and senator, sitting in the Senate as a centrist and specializing in scientific and technical questions. Elected president of the Association of Mayors of Large French Towns in 1983, he was appointed foreign trade minister in 1988.

**RAUTI, Giuseppe (Pino).** *Italy.* Italian Social Movement–National Right (MSI–DN) leader. Born in 1926 in the province of Cosenza, he served in Mussolini's armed forces. Later, after gaining a degree in law, he became a journalist. From 1948–56 he was youth leader of the MSI, and founded the extreme right-wing Ordine Nuovo (New Order) movement, banned in November 1973. A member of the Chamber of Deputies since 1976, he was narrowly defeated

by **Gianfranco Fini** in December 1987 in election for party secretary, but this result was reversed in Rauti's favour in January 1990, against a background of violence between supporters of the two contenders.

**RAWLINGS, Flight-Lieutenant Jerry.** *Ghana.* Head of state. Born in Accra in 1947, son of a Scottish father and a Ghanaian mother, he was commissioned as a pilot in the air force in 1969 and promoted to flight lieutenant in 1978. In May 1979 he was detained after leading a mutiny of junior officers against the then military government, but was freed by his supporters a few weeks later to lead a successful coup. Under pressure from the coup's rank and file he allowed the execution of eight senior officers (including three former heads of state) and carried out a "house-cleaning" of corrupt officials, politicians and businesspeople. Rawlings handed over power to an elected civilian government, led by Hilla Limann, but soon grew critical of its corruption and inefficiency. In December 1981, with considerable popular support, he took power again at the head of the Provisional National Defence Council. Rawlings's rule has been characterized by a combination of revolutionary rhetoric and pragmatic economic reforms that have made Ghana a model for the kind of policies advocated by institutions such as the IMF. Conscious of his reputation for "saying the wrong things but doing the right ones", Rawlings appears to be genuinely motivated by a desire to improve the lot of ordinary Ghanaians, but has also proved intolerant of dissent and capable of ruthless action against opponents. He is more popular among southerners than in the north, which has been traditionally neglected by Accra. Increasingly under pressure because of the growing unpopularity of economic austerity policies and signs of unrest within the armed forces, his true power base, he faces a choice between conceding to demands for greater democracy or repressing dissent.

**RAZALEIGH HAMZAH, Tengku Tan Sri Datuk.** *Malaysia.* Opposition politician. Born in 1936, Razaleigh served as a member of the Kelantan state assembly during the 1960s. Before his appointment as finance minister in 1976 he headed Bank Bumiputra, Pernas and the state-run oil company, Petronas. Razaleigh moved to trade and industry in 1984 but three years later he was dismissed from the cabinet after he and his supporters (the so-called "Team B" dissidents) challenged prime minister

**Mahathir Mohamad** for the leadership of the United Malays National Organization (UMNO). In 1989 Razaleigh formed a new party, Semangat '46, but the defeat of the coalition he put together to oppose the government in the October 1990 elections was a severe blow to his political hopes.

**REAGAN, Ronald.** *USA.* Former US president and governor of California. Born in Illinois in 1911, he pursued a moderately successful career as a film actor, starring in numerous B movies. A speech made on behalf of conservative presidential candidate Barry Goldwater thrust him into the political limelight, and he spent two terms (1966–75) as governor of California. As governor, Reagan was unable to control inflation or limit the role of government, as he had promised to do, but made lasting reforms in state welfare. Elected president in 1980 on a wave of frustration at **Jimmy Carter**'s inability to release US hostages in Iran, Reagan presided over an unprecedented military build-up. He pursued a more aggressive foreign policy line than his predecessor in office, refusing to back down on the star wars programme and pursuing the "Reagan doctrine", which emphasized the arming and support of anti-communist guerrillas, especially in Nicaragua and Afghanistan. His "Reaganomics", involving widespread deregulation of industry, succeeded to some extent in cutting inflation and boosting the economy, but his "hands-off" presidential style led to considerable infighting in the administration and some illegal behaviour by those he trusted to run things, such as in the Iran-Contra scandal. Although an immensely popular president, Reagan's public image has been substantially eroded since leaving office.

**REDDY, Marri Chenna.** *India.* Congress (I) politician and chief minister of Andhra Pradesh. Born in Andhra Pradesh in 1919, he was a member of the Hyderabad provincial parliament in 1950 and of the Hyderabad assembly from 1952–67, holding several state ministerial offices. Elected to the Rajya Sabha (upper house) in 1967, he served as steel minister in 1967–68. He was appointed governor of Uttar Pradesh in 1974. Returning to state politics in 1977, he was elected to the Andhra Pradesh assembly and appointed chief minister from 1977–80. In 1982 he served briefly as governor of the Punjab. After Congress's victory in the Andhra Pradesh state election in November 1989, he was appointed chief minister, making him one of only three Congress chief ministers of major states. The

continuing communal unrest over the Ayodhya mosque dispute, which contributed to the fall of the national government in November also led to his resignation the following month, as he proved unable to deal with rioting in Hyderabad.

**REDONDO URBIETA, Nicolás.** *Spain.* Trade Union leader. Born in 1927 in Baracaldo in the Basque region, he was a worker in the metallurgical industry from the age of 15, and became a youth activist in the General Workers' Union (UGT) and the Spanish Socialist Workers' Party (PSOE) in the Basque region. He resigned from the PSOE executive in 1984, gave up his seat as a PSOE deputy in 1987 and became one of the government's harshest critics. He has been secretary-general of the UGT since 1976, and in 1988 he masterminded Spain's first general strike since 1934.

**REDWOOD, John.** *UK.* Corporate affairs minister. Born in 1951, he was educated at Oxford University, where he became a fellow of All Souls, and then became an investment adviser in the City of London. A keen supporter of **Margaret Thatcher**, he headed her policy unit in 1984–85. Elected to parliament in 1987, he was made a junior trade and industry minister in 1989 and was promoted to corporate affairs minister by **John Major** in November 1990.

**REES-MOGG, Lord (William Rees-Mogg).** *UK.* Journalist and publisher. Born in 1928, he was educated at Oxford University and then worked for the *Financial Times* (1952–60, a period in which he twice stood unsuccessfully for parliament), *The Sunday Times* (1960–67) and was editor of *The Times* from 1967–81. He was chairman of the Arts Council from 1982–89 and was appointed head of the new Broadcasting Standards Council in 1988. He was knighted in 1981 and created a life peer in 1988. As one of the "great and good" his views are widely sought and on social issues such as broadcasting standards attract much comment.

**REHNQUIST, William.** *USA.* Chief justice of the Supreme Court. Born in Wisconsin in 1924, he was educated at Stanford and Harvard universities. After working briefly as a clerk for Justice Robert Jackson of the Supreme Court in 1952–53, he practised law for 16 years in Phoenix. A right-wing Republican who supported Barry Goldwater's 1964 presidential campaign, he became assistant attorney-general in charge of the Justice Department's office of legal counsel in 1969. He held the post until 1971 when he was appointed to the Supreme

Court, one of four justices selected by President Richard Nixon to create a conservative majority on the nine-member court. An opponent of judicial activism and an advocate of a "strict construction" of the intent of the founders of the constitution, Rehnquist soon proved himself to be the court's most consistent conservative. In 1986 **Ronald Reagan** provoked a storm of criticism by appointing him as chief justice when Warren Burger resigned. During the Senate confirmation hearings which followed, allegations against Rehnquist included political extremism, opposition to measures designed to combat racial discrimination, and a lack of candour. The Senate eventually confirmed Rehnquist's appointment by 65 votes to 33. Despite an effective rearguard action by the aged liberal caucus, the Rehnquist Supreme Court has tended to roll back some of the precedents established in its more liberal past. The scope and effectiveness of affirmative action programmes and anti-discrimination legislation has been reduced, and, in July 1989, the court began reinterpreting *Roe v. Wade*, the 1973 ruling which had established a woman's constitutional right to abortion.

**REILLY, William.** *USA.* Administrator, Environmental Protection Agency (EPA). A graduate of Yale, Harvard, and Columbia universities, Reilly was appointed to head the EPA by **George Bush** in 1989. He has made a career of building a consensus between environmentalists and industry. He served as president of the Wildlife Fund and the Conservation Fund, as well as on the Presidential Council on Environmental Quality. He has been an outspoken critic of the inadequacies of clean-up efforts following the Alaska oil-spill, but has been criticized for the vagueness of the government's response to the greenhouse effect. Some observers have suggested that the president prefers the advice of **John Sununu**, White House chief of staff, on environmental matters.

**RENÉ, France Albert.** *Seychelles.* President. Born in 1935, the former barrister was prime minister in Seychelles' first independent government, headed by James Mancham, whom he overthrew in 1977. Creation of a socialist party, the Seychelles People's Progressive Front (SPPF), and establishment of a one-party state followed. René subsequently concentrated power in his own hands, as president, SPPF secretary-general and armed forces commander, as well as usually holding several key ministerial posts. His exiled opponents have made several attempts to

unseat him, most notably in the attempted invasion by a group of mercenaries in 1981, but their activities have appeared to be on the wane since 1986 and René has shown more willingness to delegate responsibility within his government and allow more private-sector and foreign involvement in the economy. He remains committed to the principle of a one-party socialist state, but in late 1990 hinted at the possibility of a referendum on the issue.

**RENGER, Annemarie.** *Germany.* Social Democratic Party (SPD) politician. One of the most successful of the postwar generation of women politicians, she was born in Leipzig in 1919. She trained in publishing, then worked as a typist until 1945. The war left her a widow with a small son. Her work as secretary to Kurt Schumacher, the SPD leader until his death in 1952, was a key factor in her election to the Bundestag in 1953. She has remained a member ever since, serving as president of the parliament (1972–76) and then as a vice-president.

**RENON, Gérard.** *France.* Government minister. Born in 1940, and a graduate of the Ecole Polytechnique, he qualified as a mining engineer, subsequently serving as adviser to state agencies on energy, technical and industrial matters. In the mid-1980s he headed the Atomic Energy Commission and sat on the national Economic and Social Council. In 1988 he was appointed junior minister for the prevention of major technological and natural disasters.

**RENTON, Timothy.** *UK.* Minister for the arts, MP since 1974. Born in 1932 and educated at Eton and Oxford University, Renton took over from **David Waddington** as government chief whip after earlier stints at the Foreign and Home Offices, and replaced **David Mellor** as arts minister in the November 1990 reshuffle.

**RESAMPA, André.** *Madagascar.* Opposition leader. A veteran politician, he was secretary-general of the Social Democratic Party (PSD), founded in 1956, and interior minister in the first government of independent Madagascar, from 1960–71. He was an effective electoral manager on the PSD's behalf during this first period of multi-party democracy. In 1971 he fell out with President Philibert Tsirinana and was accused of trying to overthrow the government; Resampa was briefly exiled to an offshore island but the two men were later reconciled and worked to restore the PSD's position during the period of virtual anarchy in the early 1970s. The PSD was banned after President **Didier Ratsiraka** took power and Resampa became associated with the centre-right National Unity Party (Vonjy). After the reintroduction of a multi-party system in early 1990, Resampa returned to prominence as secretary-general of a reformed PSD.

**REVENKO, Grigory.** *USSR.* Ukrainian official and former Presidential Council member. Born in 1936, he worked in industry before becoming a full-time Komsomol official in the 1960s and subsequently a Communist Party official. He was appointed regional party leader in Kiev in 1985. Generally regarded as a conservative (like most senior Ukrainian communists), he was appointed by **Mikhail Gorbachev** as a member of the short-lived Presidential Council in March 1990.

**REVIGLIO, Franco.** *Italy.* Former chairman of Ente Nazionale Idrocarburi (ENI). Born in 1935 in Turin, he obtained a law degree at Turin University in 1959 and began a career as a university teacher, becoming the university's professor of financial science. In 1979 he was elected to the Chamber of Deputies, and held the post of finance minister from 1979–81, initially as a non-party member of the cabinet and subsequently affiliated to the Italian Socialist Party (PSI). Following the resignation of Umberto Colombo, in February 1983 Reviglio was appointed chairman of the second largest state holding company, the energy conglomerate ENI and served in the post until October 1989. Intelligent and prickly, he resisted political pressure and succeeded in bringing ENI back into profit and reducing its debt.

**REYSHAHRI, Hojatoleslam Mohammad Mohammadi.** *Iran.* Prominent justice. Born in Rey, south of Tehran, in 1946, Reyshahri's Islamic militancy landed him several prison terms under the Shah. After the 1979 revolution he became president of the Islamic revolutionary courts and military tribunals in several Iranian towns, including Tehran. A hardline ally of **Ali Akbar Mohtashami**, Reyshahri was dropped in 1989 as intelligence minister, a post he had held since 1984, and was appointed state prosecutor.

**REZEK, Francisco.** *Brazil.* Foreign minister. Born in 1944, he studied law at the Sorbonne, Paris, and rose to become Brazil's youngest Supreme Court judge. He also served as president of the superior electoral tribunal which oversaw the 1990 elections. Little known outside the legal world, he was an unexpected choice for the post of foreign minister, being the last cabinet minister appointed by **Fernando Collor de Mello.**

**RIBIČIČ, Ciril.** *Yugoslavia.* Slovene party leader. In January 1990, he led the Slovenian delegation to the communist party congress, at which it announced its withdrawal from the federal party. He was subsequently elected president of the presidium of the central committee of the new Slovene party, the Party of Democratic Renewal. A supporter of pluralism and devolution of power to the republics, he does not favour Slovenian secession from Yugoslavia but, rather, Slovene membership of a loose Yugoslav confederation.

**RICE, Norman.** *USA.* Mayor of Seattle. Born in 1943, he had a varied career in television news editing, local government and banking before becoming black mayor of a predominantly white city. Typical of new-breed black mayors he was elected because of his ability not his race, and his politics are moderate.

**RICHARD, Alain.** *France.* Socialist politician. Born in 1945, he gained a degree in literature and then graduated from the Institut d'Etudes Politiques and the Ecole Nationale d'Administration, before starting his career in public administration, notably at the Council of State. He moved from the Unified Socialist Party (PSU) to the Socialist Party (PS) in 1975, winning office as a local councillor, mayor and deputy. In the 1980s he was secretary, then vice-president, of the PS group in the National Assembly; he is a close ally of **Michel Rocard**, and is a recognized specialist in local government issues.

**RICHARDS, Ann.** *USA.* Democratic governor of Texas. Born in 1933 and a former state treasurer, she came through a dirty primary campaign in 1990 – she was accused of having been an illegal drug user – to defeat the rich and macho businessman Clayton Williams in the November gubernatorial election.

**RICHARDSON, Jo.** *UK.* Labour politician. Born in 1923, she was secretary of the once-influential left-wing Tribune Group within the Labour Party from 1948–78, and chaired it from 1978–79. Elected to parliament for an east London seat in 1974, she has been a prominent campaigner for women's rights and the party's spokeswoman on women's issues since 1983.

**RICHARDSON, Ruth.** *New Zealand.* Finance minister. Appointed to the National Party cabinet formed by **James Bolger** in November 1990, she is the most prominent among the party's new generation of tough and determined right-wingers. Born in 1951, a lawyer from a wealthy farming background, she was elected to parliament in 1981 and appointed opposition finance spokesman in 1987. She espouses the "Rogernomics" path of economic liberalization, especially the deregulation of wages, pioneered by Roger Douglas, finance minister in the former Labour government.

**RICO, Aldo.** *Argentina.* Army officer. As commander of the 18th infantry regiment, Rico led rebellions in 1987 protesting against the trials of junior officers for actions carried out during the military regime. In October 1989 he was pardoned and dismissed from the army, but continued to campaign on the soldiers' behalf.

**RIDLEY, Nicholas.** *UK.* Former secretary of state for trade and industry in 1989–90, MP since 1959. Born into an old Northumbrian family in 1929, he was transport secretary from 1983–86 and environment secretary until 1989, hence part-architect of the controversial poll tax. The chain-smoking Ridley's brash disdain for environmental anxieties was something of a liability at a time when the government was keen to promote a green image. As trade secretary, he inherited awkward rows over the Harrods affair, British Aerospace's takeover of Rover and insider trading in the Guinness scandal. Described as a Thatcherite before **Margaret Thatcher**, Ridley finally shot his bolt with indiscreet but widely reported remarks to the effect that Germany was planning to "take over Europe". Fiercely loyal to Thatcher, he was always prepared to voice opinions she could not be seen to say publicly.

**RIEGLE, Don.** *USA.* Democratic senator from Michigan. Born in 1938, he worked in business before his election to the House of Representatives in 1966 (as a Republican until 1972) and senator (as a Democrat) in 1976. A highly partisan liberal, he was very active in fighting the welfare cuts of **Ronald Reagan**'s administration and is zealous in defending constituency interests, mainly the automobile industry and its workers. Banking committee chairman since 1989, he has shown unexpected consensus-building skills, particularly in getting bipartisan agreement on a savings and loan sector bail-out bill. However, he came under scrutiny for his relations with Charles Keating, head of a failed thrift.

**RIEGLER, Josef.** *Austria.* Deputy chancellor. Born in Judenburg in 1938, to a farming family, he graduated in agriculture and was executive secretary of the Austrian peasant farmers' federation until 1987. A member of the conservative Austrian People's Party (ÖVP), he

replaced **Alois Mock** as its leader in 1989, after the party's poor performance in regional elections. His government career began with his appointment as agriculture and forestry minister in 1987, a post he held until 1989, when he became minister for the constitution and federalism. In the same year Riegler also took over the deputy chancellorship. Although committed to seeking membership of the EC, Riegler was more cautious than Mock. The heavy defeat of the ÖVP in the election of October 1990 weakened his position as party leader, although he retained cabinet office as deputy chancellor and minister of federation and administrative reform.

**RIESENHUBER, Heinz.** *Germany.* Research and technology minister. Born in Frankfurt-am-Main in 1935, he went into the chemicals industry after gaining his doctorate in 1965. He made his way in politics through the youth wing of the Christian Democratic Union, securing election to the Bundestag in 1976, and was appointed research and technology minister in 1982.

**RIFKIND, Malcolm.** *UK.* Secretary of state for transport since November 1990. Born in Edinburgh in 1946, Rifkind entered parliament in 1974 and by 1976 was opposition spokesman on Scotland. After four years in the Foreign and Commonwealth Office, specializing in overseas aid and the Commonwealth, he returned to Scotland as secretary of state with the unenviable task of imposing the poll tax on a Labour-dominated country. **John Major** moved him to transport, an area of increasing public concern, where his undoubted political skills will be tested.

**RIGOUT, Marcel.** *France.* Communist politician. Born in 1928, he started out as a metalworker and then as a journalist. He sat in the National Assembly for the Communist Party (PCF) from 1967–88 and held office as professional training minister in **Pierre Mauroy**'s socialist administration in 1981–84. Subsequently he became conspicuous within the PCF as one of the leading so-called "reconstructors", anxious to reform the party from the inside and unhappy with the leadership of the old-style **Georges Marchais**.

**RÍOS MONTT, Efraín.** *Guatemala.* Former president. Born in 1927, Ríos Montt served as an army officer, rising to army chief of staff with the rank of general. He was the unsuccessful presidential candidate of the Christian Democrat-led National Opposition Front (FNO) coalition in 1974. He then served as military attaché in Madrid and later as director of the military academy. After a military coup by junior officers in March 1982 he was a member of a three-man junta, later assuming full powers as president. Although at first thought to favour reform, his administration soon became overshadowed by his fervent adherence to a fundamentalist Protestant sect (in a traditionally Catholic country) and the conduct of a military campaign against the Indian population in which thousands died. Overthrown in a coup in August 1983, he was exiled. He returned to contest the 1990 presidential election but was prevented by the courts from standing because he had taken part in a military coup, his support passing to **Jorge Serrano**.

**RIPA DI MEANA, Carlo.** *Italy*. European commissioner for the environment, nuclear safety and civil protection. Born in 1929, he worked as a journalist for communist newspapers until he left the Italian Communist Party (PCI) in 1957. He then worked in publishing, served as a regional councillor for the Italian Socialist Party (PSI), held various influential cultural posts and became a member of the European Parliament. He was appointed an EC commissioner in 1985, responsible for culture and tourism. A debonair, confident self-publicist, he has come into his own since his shift in 1989 to environment, traditionally a backwater but now very much a high-profile posting. Advertising his eco-credentials by wearing bright, green-rimmed glasses, he has been the powerhouse behind a series of wide-ranging directives, and a counterweight to the traditional industrial bias of the Commission's structural funds.

**RITZEN, Jo.** *Netherlands*. Education minister. Born in 1945, he was appointed professor of public-sector economics at Rotterdam's Erasmus University in 1983. An internationally respected expert on the relationship between educational policy and economic growth, he advised the Labour Party (PvdA) on employment issues in the early 1980s. He was appointed education minister when the PvdA returned to government in coalition with the Christian Democrats in November 1989.

**RIVERA BRYAN, Brooklyn.** *Nicaragua*. Minister for the Atlantic coast. Born in 1952 of Miskito Indian descent, he studied mathematics at Managua University. He was elected co-ordinator general of the Misurasata organization in 1980 and joined the Democratic revolutionary Alliance-Nicaraguan Democratic Movement

(ARDE-MDN) "Contra" front in 1982 to wage a military campaign against Sandinista policies towards the Indian population. After **Violeta Chamorro**'s election victory in 1990 he was given ministerial responsibility for the Atlantic coast.

**RIVERA Y DAMAS, Arturo.** *El Salvador*. Archbishop of San Salvador. Born in 1923, Rivera was ordained in 1953 and appointed a bishop in 1977. In 1983 he succeeded his old friend Oscar Romero (murdered in 1980 but not immediately replaced by the Vatican) as archbishop. He has consistently used his position and integrity to mediate between the government and left-wing groups.

**RIVIELLO BAZÁN, Antonio.** *Mexico*. Defence minister. Born in 1926, he pursued a military career, rising to the rank of brigadier-general in 1973. He then served as general inspector of the army and military attaché to Spain before becoming commander of the first army corps in 1988.

**RO JAI BONG.** *South Korea*. Prime minister. Born in 1936, a former university professor with little government experience before becoming President **Roh Tae Woo**'s chief aide, he was appointed prime minister in December 1990. His appointment coincided with a growing interest in improving relations with North Korea. He announced that his priorities would be the establishment of "social discipline as well as law and order and progress in inter-Korea dialogue".

**ROBAINA GONZÁLEZ, Roberto.** *Cuba*. Union of Young Communists (UJC) secretary. Born in 1959, his open and frank manner is popular among the young, especially those disillusioned by the "Old Guard". In 1990 he was elected an alternate member of the party political bureau.

**ROBB, Charles (Chuck).** *USA*. Democratic senator from Virginia. Born in 1939, he was a marine corps officer and lawyer, served as governor, and was elected senator in 1988. A fiscal conservative, he established the Democratic Leadership Council, a largely southern body intent on giving the national party a centrist identity. This has met with limited success. He generally follows the party leadership line in the Senate. Ambitious for higher office, he has to live down revelations that as governor he unwittingly socialized with businessmen under investigation for drug trafficking. His wife, Lynda Byrd, is former president Lyndon Johnson's daughter.

**ROBERTS, Barbara.** *USA.* Democratic governor of Oregon. Born in 1936 and a former secretary of state in the Democratic state administration, her victory in the 1990 gubernatorial election made her Oregon's first woman governor.

**ROBERTSON, Pat.** *USA.* TV evangelist. Born in Virginia in 1930, he is a trained lawyer and baptist minister. He rose to prominence in the late 1960s as the founder of the Christian Broadcasting Network (CBN) and as the host of his own evangelical television programme. He also has political aspirations, surprising many when, as a prospective Republican presidential nominee, he defeated **George Bush** in Michigan and Iowa caucuses. In 1990 he turned his attention to censorship, campaigning against federal funding for the National Endowment for the Arts on the ground that it supports "sodomy, child pornography, and attacks on Jesus Christ".

**ROBINSON, Mary.** *Ireland.* President. An unexpected victor in the November 1990 elections, her effectiveness on the campaign trail enabled her to take advantage of the discomfort of her main opponent, **Brian Lenihan**, who had been dismissed from his ministerial posts, following a political controversy. Nominated by Labour and also supported by the small Workers' Party, she was nevertheless a member of neither. Born in 1944 and a member of the Senate for 20 years, elected by the graduates of Trinity College Dublin, she had stood twice for Labour in elections for the Dáil (parliament), but left the party in 1985, when it backed the Anglo-Irish agreement, since she felt this took insufficient account of Northern Unionist views. She softened her image for the campaign for the presidency, but deployed her track record as an astute civil rights lawyer and activist on social issues, who had fought for the decriminalization of homosexuality, for the right of inheritance for illegitimate children, and against the constitutional prohibition of information on abortion. She was thought to be vulnerable to the charge of anti-family radicalism; however, she brushed aside the attempt to label her as pro-abortion, polling remarkably well among women even in rural areas that were expected to be the heartland of traditionalism. She offered herself as a modern president, independent of the government of the day. After her victory she declared that the women of Ireland had rocked the system, not just the cradle.

**ROBINSON, Peter.** *UK.* Northern Irish Unionist politician. Born in 1948, he has been active in unionist politics since his youth. He was appointed general secretary of **Ian Paisley**'s Democratic Unionist Party (DUP) in 1975 and became its deputy leader in 1980. MP for Belfast East since 1979, he has recently been at odds (not yet too publicly) with his mentor over how to end the political deadlock in the province.

**ROBINSON, Raymond (Ray).** *Trinidad and Tobago.* Prime minister. Born in 1926, he was educated at Oxford University and trained as a barrister. In 1961 he was appointed finance minister in the People's National Movement government, rising to become deputy leader and foreign minister, but in 1968 a disagreement over the Black Power movement led to his resignation. He then concentrated on his native Tobago, becoming chairman of the Tobago House of Assembly in 1980. He was chosen to lead the combination of opposition parties that merged into the National Alliance for Reconstruction in 1986, but criticism of his style of leadership has led to serious divisions within the party. In July 1990, he was wounded and held hostage during an unsuccessful coup attempt by a Black Muslim group.

**ROCA I JUNYENT, Miguel.** *Spain.* Catalonia politician. Born in 1940 in France, he is leader and spokesman of the Catalan group in the Congress of Deputies (lower house) and secretary-general of the Democratic Convergence of Catalonia.

**ROCARD, Michel.** *France.* Prime minister. Born in 1930 and educated at the Ecole Nationale d'Administration and Institut d'Etudes Politiques, his first national political role was as national secretary of the socialist students' association in 1953–55. He went on to a civil service career as one of the elite of inspectors of finance. Confident, articulate and at that time politically well to the left, he led the small Unified Socialist Party (PSU) from 1967–73 and gained much public exposure in the student-led upheavals of 1968, but in the 1969 presidential election he won only 3.7% of the vote. By 1974 he had come to support the union of the left, backing **François Mitterrand** for the presidency and, in the following year, merging his PSU faction into the revamped Socialist Party (PS). There he gradually performed a *volte-face*, establishing himself as the leader of the social democratic wing, but the prospect of an open contest for the party's soul, pitting Rocard against his leftist rival **Jean-Pierre Chevènement** as potential presidential candidates, was averted when Mitterrand declared his own candidacy for 1981. In government from 1981, he was first minister of state for planning, then agriculture minister, but resigned in protest in 1985 when the government of **Laurent Fabius** introduced proportional representation (a decision soon to be reversed). He soon re-established a reasonable *modus vivendi* with Mitterrand, supporting him through the "cohabitation" period of right-wing government, and returning after the 1988 elections to head a PS-led government with the emphasis very much on consensus. Under fire from the left for putting sound financial management before social justice, his government has confirmed the opening towards the political centre. He was put in an uncomfortable position in November 1990 when a demonstration by *lycée* students, demanding higher public spending on education, elicited declarations of sympathy from Mitterrand. Rocard, while clearly a front-rank candidate for the presidential succession, has had the tact on occasion to leave the limelight to Mitterrand.

**ROCKEFELLER, John, IV.** *USA.* Democratic senator from West Virginia. Born in 1937, he maintains family traditions of public service, having been state legislator and governor before his 1984 election to the Senate. A passionate defender of his state's coal industry, he also serves its large elderly population as chairman of the medicare and long-term care subcommittee. He spent millions on his own election campaign.

**RODRÍGUEZ FANDEO, Miguel Antonio.** *Venezuela.* Planning and co-ordination minister. An associate of President **Carlos Andrés Pérez**, he was appointed planning minister in 1989 and leads the cabinet team attempting to deal with Venezuela's economic problems.

**RODRÍGUEZ PEDOTTI, Andrés.** *Paraguay.* President. Born in 1923, Rodríguez joined the military academy and became a career soldier, rising to the rank of colonel and commander of the premier first cavalry division in 1961. Promoted to full general in 1970, he became second-in-command to President Alfredo Stroessner. Critics accused him of collaborating with the regime to acquire vast wealth and land. He led the coup that replaced Stroessner in February 1989 and was elected president as candidate of the ruling conservative Colorado Party in May 1989.

**RODRÍGUEZ RODRÍGUEZ, Carlos Rafael.** *Cuba.* Vice-president. Born in 1913, Rodríguez studied economics at Havana University. He joined the Cuban Communist Party (PCC) in

1932 and remains one of the few pre-revolution communists to fare well under **Fidel Castro**. In the early years of the Castro regime he edited the PCC newspaper *Hoy*, and from 1962–64 he headed the agrarian reform institute.

**RODRÍGUEZ SAHAGÚN, Agustín.** *Spain.* Mayor of Madrid. Born in 1932 in Avila and trained in law and business management, he was vice-president of the employers' organization, the CEOE, until his appointment by **Adolfo Suárez** as industry and energy minister in 1978. He served as defence minister from 1979–81. A deputy for Avila and president of the Union of the Democratic Centre (UCD) until its disintegration, he is now spokesman for the Democratic and Social Centre (CDS) and became mayor of Madrid in June 1989.

**ROE, Robert.** *USA.* Democratic congressman from New Jersey. Born in 1924, he was a construction company owner and local government representative before his election to the House of Representatives in 1969. Chairman of the science and technology committee since 1987, he fervently supports space exploration and bigger science budgets. He is also recognized as the dominant member of the public works committee.

**ROEMER, Buddy.** *USA.* Democratic governor of Louisiana. Born in 1943, he was a business executive and US congressman (1981–88), before being elected governor in 1988 on a populist platform critical of Louisiana's entrenched political elite. Under the "Roemer Revolution" he has cut spending in a drive to balance the state budget. He has concentrated on education, environmental protection, and economic diversification, seeking to reduce dependence on oil and natural gas.

**ROGNONI, Virginio.** *Italy.* Defence minister and Christian Democrat party (DC) politician. Born in 1924 in the province of Milan, he gained a law degree and subsequently taught law at Pavia University. He has been elected to the Chamber of Deputies at every general election since 1968 and is on the left of the DC. Rognoni first attained cabinet rank as interior minister in June 1978 and remained in this post until the June 1983 general election. From August 1986–June 1987 he held office as justice minister. In August 1990 he returned to the cabinet as defence minister.

**ROH TAE WOO.** *South Korea.* President. Born in 1932, he attended military college and served in the Korean war. His army career culminated in control of the Defence Security Command, the military intelligence network which also monitors dissent, and he retired from the army in 1981 as a four-star general after supporting Chun Doo Hwan's military coup following the crushing of the Kwangju uprising in 1980. He became minister of state for national security and foreign affairs, followed by spells as sports and home affairs minister. In this last post, the opposition called for his resignation over police violence. Roh took over as head of the ruling Democratic Justice Party (DJP) in 1985, and in 1988 became Chun Doo Hwan's chosen successor as president. After an unexpected reconciliation with the opposition over the Kwangju uprising, in 1990 he announced the merger of the DJP and two major opposition parties, creating the Democratic Liberal Party (DLP), which consequently held two-thirds of the seats in the National Assembly and effectively divided the opposition. Since taking power, Roh has developed his "nordpolitik" in foreign affairs, establishing ties with the USSR. He has also matched **Kim Il-sung**'s proposals for reunification of the divided Koreas, Roh cultivates a populist image, favouring less power for the president and greater liberalization, but because of internal opposition in the enlarged ruling party he has had to shelve plans for a cabinet system of government.

**ROJAS SAAVEDRA, Patricio.** *Chile.* Defence minister. Born in 1934, he joined the Christian Democratic Party (PDC) and, as a close associate of **Patricio Aylwin**, participated in the PDC administration of the late 1960s. After many years working for international agencies, Rojas returned to politics in the late 1980s and was appointed defence minister in March 1990. In this sensitive position he has attempted to deal firmly with the army and its commander, former president **Augusto Pinochet**.

**ROLDÓS AGUILERA, León.** *Ecuador.* People, Change and Democracy-Popular Roldosista Party (PCD) leader. The brother of former president Jaime Roldós, he was elected vice-president on the death of his brother in an aircraft accident in 1981, but broke with President **Osvaldo Hurtado** in 1982 and withdrew his support. He helped form the PCD to uphold his brother's policies, but since the mid-1980s the party has lost much of its popular support.

**ROLLINS, Edward, Jr.** *USA.* National Republican Congressional Committee (NRCC) co-chairman. Born in Boston in 1943 with a working class, Irish Catholic background, he

became a loyal Reaganite in the 1960s. He directed **Ronald Reagan**'s presidential campaign in 1984, and has earned a reputation as an able and shrewd operator. As head of the NRCC, his main aim is to end Democratic control of the House of Representatives. He found himself at loggerheads with **George Bush** over the budget crisis in the run-up to the November 1990 mid-term elections, urging the party's congressional candidates "to run away from the budget package" to improve their poll prospects. He had previously been criticized for the highly partisan campaign against former speaker Jim Wright.

**ROMAN, Petre.** *Romania.* Prime minister. Born in Bucharest in 1946, the son of Valter Roman, a veteran communist, he went to Bucharest Polytechnic before studying from 1971–74 in Toulouse, where he completed his doctorate. He was professor of fluid mechanics and head of the hydraulics department at Bucharest Polytechnic at the outbreak of revolution. Despite being a long-standing Romanian Communist Party member, he soon became involved in the uprising, and was named interim prime minister by the newly established National Salvation Front (NSF) after the overthrow of the Ceauşescu regime. His conformist past attracted strident criticism from those suspicious of persisting communist influence in the government, but he succeeded in steering the NSF to electoral victory in May 1990, albeit amid some allegations of electoral irregularities.

**ROMER, Roy.** *USA.* Democratic governor of Colorado. Born in 1928, he was a lawyer, businessman and state legislator before becoming state treasurer from 1977–86. He was elected governor in 1986 and has followed policies of economic development, environmental protection and educational expansion.

**ROMERO HERRERA, Carlos.** *Spain.* Agriculture, fisheries and food minister. Born in 1941 in Zamora province. Previously a civil servant, he has been agriculture, fisheries and food minister since December 1982. In 1986 he entered parliament as a Spanish Socialist Workers' Party (PSOE) deputy.

**ROMITA, Pier Luigi.** *Italy.* Minister for co-ordination of EC policy and Italian Democratic Socialist Party (PSDI) politician. Born in 1924 in Turin, he gained a degree at Rome University and became professor of agricultural hydraulics at Milan University in 1963. He has sat in the Chamber of Deputies since 1958. Having held a number of junior ministerial positions, he was minister without portfolio with responsibility for scientific and technological research from 1972–73 and held that post again in later administrations. From 1976–78 he served as secretary of the PSDI. He was appointed minister for the regions in July 1983, becoming budget minister a year later, a post he held until April 1987. Romita was appointed minister for the co-ordination of EC policy in July 1989.

**ROMMEL, Manfred.** *Germany.* Mayor of Stuttgart. A native of Stuttgart and its successful mayor since 1974, he was born in 1928, the son of General Erwin Rommel. He is popular well beyond the ranks of his own Christian Democratic Union and has succeeded in promoting his city as a financial and cultural centre. He has nevertheless been somewhat eclipsed in state politics in Baden-Württemberg by **Lothar Späth**, the state premier since 1978.

**ROSTENKOWSKI, Dan.** *USA.* Democratic congressman from Illinois. Born in 1928, he attended Loyola University, and was an insurance executive and state legislator before being elected to the House of Representatives in 1958. Initially he had the reputation of being an old-style Chicago machine politician, more interested in exercising power than making policy, but in 1981 opted to become ways and means committee chairman in preference to rising up the ladder of party leadership from his then position as chief deputy whip. In 1986, he piloted tax reform legislation through a reluctant Congress. His committee has also produced landmark laws on social security, trade and medicare. This represented a turnaround from 1981–82, when Rostenkowski had problems within the weak and divided committee that he inherited and was constantly outmanoeuvred by **Ronald Reagan**'s administration and its allies. Since then ways and means has virtually become his personal machine and he attributes his success to horse-trading skills learnt in Chicago city politics.

**ROTH, Wolfgang.** *Germany.* Social Democratic Party (SPD) politician. Born in 1941, he launched his career in the SPD via student activity. Chairman of the students' union at the Free University of Berlin in 1964, he emerged as a level head in the turbulent early 1970s as chairman of the young socialists (1972–74). Before being elected to the Bundestag in 1976 he worked as a local government adviser and is now a deputy chairman of the SPD parliamentary group in the Bundestag.

**ROYBAL, Edward.** *USA.* Democratic congressman from California. Born in 1916, he was a social worker, public health official and Los Angeles councillor, before his election to the House of Representatives in 1962. A liberal, who chairs the select committee on ageing, he lacks the horse-trading zeal to get many of his plans enacted. He is recognized as a spokesman for Mexican-Americans, and has a particular interest in immigration issues.

**RUBERTI, Antonio.** *Italy.* Minister without portfolio. Born in 1927 in the province of Caserta, he did research in electrotechnical engineering, was appointed professor of automatic control systems at Rome University in 1965, and became professor of the theory of systems and dean of the faculty of engineering in 1973. From 1976–87 he was the university's vice-chancellor. He is not an elected member of parliament, but was appointed to the cabinet in July 1987 as minister without portfolio responsible for scientific research and universities.

**RUBIAL CAVIA, Ramón.** *Spain.* Spanish Socialist Workers' Party (PSOE) president. Born in 1906 in Bilbao, he was a worker in the metallurgical industry, and was imprisoned in 1934 and from 1937–56 for political and trade union activities. He was a vice-president of the Senate, and president of the Basque General Council in 1978–79. He has been president of the PSOE and of the socialist General Workers' Union (UGT) since 1977, resigning from the former in 1979 and then returning to the post in a clear identification with party leader **Felipe González**'s mainstream socialist stance.

**RUBIKS, Alfred.** *USSR.* Latvian Communist Party leader. Born in 1935 and an engineer by profession, he held senior posts in the Latvian Komsomol and in the party apparatus in Riga (Latvia's capital) until 1984, when he was appointed the city's mayor. A hardliner, he was elected Latvian Communist Party first secretary at the April 1990 congress during which a large minority walked out to form an independent party.

**RUDA, José Maria.** *Argentina.* President of the International Court of Justice (ICJ). Born in 1924, he trained as a lawyer and worked for the office of legal affairs at the UN secretariat from 1951–55. He alternated political and academic appointments in Argentina with representing his country at the UN. Appointed to the ICJ in 1973, he earned respect for his objectivity and was elected president in 1988.

**RUDDOCK, Joan.** *UK.* Labour politician. Born in 1943, she graduated from London University and then worked for numerous pressure groups and organizations concerned with housing, unemployment, citizens' advice and disarmament. She was chairwoman of the Campaign for Nuclear Disarmament (CND) from 1981–85, at the time of the cruise missile debate which brought a massive growth in membership. She was elected to parliament for a London seat in 1987. She is a close friend of Glenys Kinnock, wife of the Labour leader, **Neil Kinnock.**

**RUDING, Onno.** *Netherlands.* Economist, banker and Christian Democratic politician. Born in 1939, he held important posts in several banks and the IMF before being appointed finance minister in 1982. His imposition of tight austerity measures, coupled with a certain personal brusqueness, probably cost him his job in 1989, when the Christian Democrats opted for a softer image. After failing to secure the presidency of the new European Bank for Reconstruction and Development, which went to **Jacques Attali,** he was appointed in 1990 chairman of the Dutch Christian Employers' Federation (NCW).

**RUDMAN, Warren.** *USA.* Republican senator from New Hampshire. Born in 1930, he practised law and was state attorney-general before his 1980 election as senator. His career took off in 1985 when he co-authored the Gramm-Rudman-Hollings deficit reduction law. He was vice-chairman of the select committee investigating the Iran-Contra affair and is active in shaping anti-drugs legislation.

**RUFFOLO, Giorgio.** *Italy.* Environment minister and Italian Socialist Party (PSI) politician. Born in 1926, he was lecturer in economic planning at Florence University, then worked for Banca Nazionale del Lavoro and as chairman of the state-owned investment company for southern Italy, Finanziaria Meridionale (FIME). Acting as a consultant to the PSI, he was involved in drawing up the economic plans that were a feature of the 1960s and 1970s. He entered the Chamber of Deputies in 1983 and the Senate in 1987, and since July 1987 has been environment minister, his well-intentioned efforts repeatedly hampered by opposition from vested interests.

**RUGGIERO, Renato.** *Italy.* Foreign trade minister and Italian Socialist Party (PSI) politician. Born in 1930 in Naples, he graduated in law and served as a diplomat in Moscow, Washington, Belgrade and elsewhere; from 1980–84 he was Italy's permanent representative to the EC. He moved from the post of secretary-general in the foreign ministry in July 1987 to become foreign trade minister. Effective and energetic, he is widely respected by the diplomatic community in Rome.

**RÜHE, Volker.** *Germany.* Christian Democratic Union (CDU) secretary-general and conservative rising star of the party's younger generation. Born in 1942, he sat in the Hamburg parliament before entering the Bundestag in 1976, where he became noted for his expertise in foreign affairs, relations between the two Germanies and security issues, and for his eloquence and cool pragmatism. Passed over for the job of defence minister in April 1988, he had been a deputy leader of the CDU/Christian Social Union parliamentary party for seven years before Chancellor **Helmut Kohl** put him forward in July 1989 for the post of party secretary-general, the job held for 12 years by left-leaning **Heiner Geissler**. The CDU congress's endorsement of Rühe, who has a reputation as a loyal Kohl supporter, marked the chancellor's reassertion of his control over the party.

**RUMBOLD, Angela.** *UK.* Minister of state at the Home Office since July 1990, and MP since 1982. A right-winger and founder of the "No Turning Back" group of Thatcherite Tories, she was previously minister of state for education from 1986. Outside parliament she chairs the Women's National Commission and was a founder of a child welfare hospital charity.

**RUPEL, Dimitrij.** *Yugoslavia.* Slovene politician and foreign minister. A former philosophy lecturer and writer, he was the founder of *Nova Revija* (New Review), Slovenia's most important cultural magazine and a vehicle for promoting pluralism. He is the president and driving force of the Slovene Democratic League, formed in January 1989. He is pro-democracy, advocates free-market liberalism and closer links with western Europe, and is a supporter of Slovene independence. In May 1990 he was appointed Slovenia's foreign minister.

**RUPÉREZ RUBIO, Francisco Javier.** *Spain.* Diplomat and conservative politician. Born in 1941 in Madrid. A diplomat and deputy for Cuenca, he was kidnapped by the Basque nationalist ETA and held prisoner for a month in 1979. He was the Union of the Democratic Centre's (UCD's) secretary for international relations before taking on the presidency of the Popular Democratic Party (PDP) and becoming vice-president of the European Christian Democratic Union. In 1989 he merged his minority PDP with the main conservative party, the Popular Party (PP). He was Spain's ambassador to the EC in 1980–82 and to Nato in 1982–83.

**RUSTAM, General Supardjo**. *Indonesia*. Co-ordinating minister for public welfare. Born in 1926, Rustam served as a military attache before being appointed head of the foreign ministry's Asia-Pacific directorate in the late 1960s. He was appointed as governor of Central Java in 1974 and nine years later **Suharto** brought him into the cabinet as home affairs minister. He was promoted to his current position in 1988.

**RÜÜTEL, Arnold**. *USSR*. Chairman of the Supreme Council of Estonia. Born in 1928, an agronomist by training, he was a first deputy premier of Estonia prior to his April 1983 election as chairman of the Estonian Supreme Soviet presidium (*de facto* president). In 1988–89 he was among the majority of Estonian communists who declared sympathy with the aims of the pro-independence Popular Front. The nationalist-dominated Estonian parliament elected in March 1990 re-elected him as head of state (the post was restyled as chairman of the Estonian Supreme Council). He has since been at the forefront in negotiating with Moscow the conditions for restoring Estonia's independence.

**RYABEV, Lev**. *USSR*. Deputy prime minister. Born in 1933, he was promoted in 1986 from first deputy minister to minister of medium machine building, and in July 1989 was elected a USSR deputy premier and chairman of the Bureau for the Fuel and Energy Complex. He has since struggled with a series of crises in his sector, including miners' strikes, a collapse in the oil industry's infrastructure, and continuing nuclear power problems after the Chernobyl disaster.

**RYCHETSKÝ, Pavel**. *Czechoslovakia*. Deputy premier. Brought into the government in June 1990, he is responsible for legislative affairs. He was designated "unaffiliated" at the time he joined the cabinet, but has increasingly identified with the more liberal wing of Civic Forum in effort to resist its conversion into a right-of-centre party led by **Václav Klaus**. With **Jiří Dienstbier** he was a prime mover in setting up the Civic Forum Liberal Club.

**RYDER, Richard**. *UK*. Parliamentary secretary to the Treasury and chief whip. Born in 1949, he served as **Margaret Thatcher**'s political secretary in 1975–81, before entering parliament

in 1983, after spells of work for Tory novelist Jeffrey Archer and the *Daily Telegraph* newspaper. He was later parliamentary economic secretary at the treasury. He is characterized by allies and opponents alike as shrewd and discreet.

**RYRIE, Sir William**. *UK*. Executive vice-president of International Financial Corporation (IFC). Born in 1928, he studied history and joined the then colonial service. He transferred to the Treasury in 1963, where he reached the top grade. His appointment to the Overseas Development Administration in 1982 was widely seen as a downward move, precipitated by his lack of enthusiasm for the monetarist policies that had become fashionable. He was appointed chief executive of the IFC, the World Bank affiliate devoted to private-sector development, two years later.

**RYZKHOV, Nikolai**. *USSR*. Prime minister. Born in the Donetsk region of the east Ukraine in 1929, he began his career in 1950 as a shift foreman at the Uralmash heavy engineering complex in Sverdlovsk and, after graduating in 1959 as an engineer, rose to become chief engineer in 1965 and director-general in 1971. He was appointed USSR first deputy minister of heavy and transport engineering in 1975, and in late 1979 as first deputy chairman of the USSR State Planning Committee (Gosplan). Like **Mikhail Gorbachev** he owed a rapid rise within the Communist Party of the Soviet Union (CPSU) hierarchy largely to Yury Andropov, and came to be considered one of the closest Gorbachev associates. As CPSU leader, Andropov appointed him central committee secretary responsible for the economy in November 1982, and in April 1985 he was one of the first appointees to the politburo made by Gorbachev following his assumption of the CPSU leadership. (Ryzhkov left the politburo in July 1990 when that body was restructured.) He was appointed chairman of the USSR council of ministers (prime minister) in September 1985. A general perception of him as a somewhat colourless technocrat was radically altered when his visits to the scene of the December 1988 Armenian earthquake and personal supervision of rescue operations raised his public profile and enhanced his popularity. He was re-appointed prime minister in July 1989. Generally seen as a decent man who is not up to his job, Ryzhkov has been a victim of the stubborn resistance of the Soviet economy to respond to the half-hearted reform efforts carried out by his government. As the economy sank deeper into crisis, and especially after attempts in December 1989 and May 1990 by Ryzhkov and his ministers to produce a reform programme had been judged inadequate, there was a growing chorus on the streets, in burgeoning strike committees, and in the chambers of the republican and USSR Supreme Soviets calling for him to resign. In August–September 1990 his authority was seriously undermined when Gorbachev and Russian Federation leader **Boris Yeltsin** sponsored a commission to draft radical market reforms, presented to the USSR Supreme Soviet by **Stanislav Shatalin** in competition with Ryzhkov's more cautious proposals. Nevertheless, Gorbachev appeared deeply reluctant to jettison Ryzhkov, until the prime minister's heart attack at the end of 1990 left the president with no alternative.

# S

SA'ADAH, George. *Lebanon.* Christian leader. Born into a well-established Christian family, Sa'adah rose through the Phalangist Party to become party president in June 1986, when he defeated Elie Karamah, whose tenure had been marked by violent clashes between pro- and anti-Syrian elements. Sa'adah aligned himself broadly with the pro-Syrian faction, coming into conflict with the party's militia leader, **Samir Geagea**. He played an important role in the Taif negotiations of September 1989.

SABAH, Shaikh Ali al-Khalifa al-Adhibi al-. *Kuwait.* Finance minister. Born in Kuwait in 1945 and educated in Cairo, San Francisco and London, Shaikh Ali has served successively as oil and finance minister since 1978. His latest spell as finance minister began in June 1990, when he also became chairman of the Kuwait Investment Authority. He was replaced by Rashid Salim al-Amiri as oil minister. Shaikh Ali had been a leading proponent of maintaining low oil prices to encourage demand. The Iraqi invasion of Kuwait in August 1990 forced him to flee to Saudi Arabia, where he remained a member of the government in exile.

SABAH, Shaikh Jabir al-Ahmad al-Jabir al-. *Kuwait.* Ruler (amir). Born in Kuwait in 1926, Shaikh Jabir was educated at Kuwait's Al-Mubarakiya School and with private tutors. After holding a number of ministerial posts, he became prime minister in 1965 and heir apparent the following year. In December 1977 he succeeded his uncle Shaikh Salem as amir. In the wake of growing parliamentary criticism, he suspended Kuwait's National Assembly in 1986 but was generally considered to be in harmony with Kuwait's progressives, allowing demonstrations in favour of the Assembly's restoration to take place in mid-1990. However, the Iraqi invasion of Kuwait in August 1990 forced him to flee into exile in Saudi Arabia.

SABAH, Shaikh Saad al-Abdullah al-Salim al-. *Kuwait.* Crown prince and prime minister. Born in Kuwait in 1924, Shaikh Saad is the eldest son of a former amir, Abdullah al Salem al-Sabah (1950–65). After training at the UK's Hendon Police College (1952–54), he returned to Kuwait to become assistant director of police and entered the cabinet in 1962. In 1978 he became crown prince and prime minister. Responding to calls for the re-establishment of Kuwait's National Assembly in early 1990, he reassured critics that the amir was committed in principle to popular participation in public life. The Iraqi invasion of Kuwait in August 1990 forced him to flee to Saudi Arabia, where he remained a member of the government in exile.

SABAH, Shaikh Sabah al-Ahmad al-Jabir al-. *Kuwait.* Foreign minister. Born in 1929, Shaikh Sabah was educated at Kuwait's al-Mubarakiya School. He first entered the cabinet in 1962 and became foreign minister the following year. He has held the additional post of deputy prime minister since 1978. The Iraqi invasion of Kuwait in August 1990 forced him to flee to Saudi Arabia, where he remained a member of the government in exile.

SADDAM HUSSAIN. *Iraq.* President. Born in 1937 in Takrit in northern Baghdad province, Saddam Hussain joined the Arab Ba'th Socialist Party in 1957. Two years later he was sentenced to death for the attempted assassination of General Abdel-Karim Qasim, the founder in 1958 of the Iraqi republic. He played a prominent part in the revolution of 1968 and became vice-president of the Revolutionary Command Council in 1969. On the "retirement" of fellow Takriti, President Ahmad Hasan al-Bakr, he became sole president in 1979. Saddam's attack on Iran in the following year led to a bloody war which ended when Iran, starved of arms and ammunition, was forced to sue for peace in 1988. Saddam has brooked no opposition, carrying out systematic purges within the ruling elite and waging a near-genocidal policy of oppression against the Kurdish minority. For much of the 1980s Saddam was regarded by the West and conservative Arab states as a bulwark against revolutionary Iran; the ruthlessness of his regime became more widely recognized after the revelation of his use of chemical weapons against Iraqi Kurdish villages in 1988 and the execution in March 1990 of a British-based journalist, Farzad Bazoft. Once peace with Iran seemed secure, he horrified the international community in August 1990 by invading and annexing his former ally, Kuwait. The reaction of the UN to the aggression was almost unprecedented in its forcefulness and coherence.

**SADIK, Nafis.** *Pakistan.* Executive director of UN Population Fund (formerly known as the UN Fund for Population Activities – UNFPA). Born in 1929, she trained as a gynaecologist and obstetrician and worked in the USA and Pakistan until she was put in charge of Pakistan's family planning programme in 1964. She began working for UNFPA in 1973, and was appointed assistant executive director in 1977 and executive director in 1987.

**SÁENZ DE COSCULLUELA, Javier.** *Spain.* Public works minister. Born in 1944 in Logrono, a labour lawyer and an active opponent of the Franco regime, he joined the Spanish Socialist Workers' Party (PSOE) in the early 1970s and was detained several times. He was the PSOE's secretary-general in La Rioja and was elected to its executive in 1981. He has been public works minister since 1986.

**SAHLIN, Mona.** *Sweden.* Labour minister. Born in 1957, she was active in the Social Democratic Labour Party (SAP) from the age of 16, and elected a member of the Riksdag (parliament) at 25. Very much a rising star, not afraid to speak her mind and go beyond received socialist wisdom, she was appointed labour minister in 1990.

**SAIBOU, Brigadier Ali.** *Niger.* President. Born in 1940, the former chief of staff and trusted ally of President Seyni Kountché, Saibou took over on Kountché's death in November 1987 in what initially appeared to be a transitional appointment. His previous political experience was limited to a short spell as rural development minister before his appointment as chief of staff after the 1974 coup that brought Kountché to power. Saibou was careful to consolidate his position, however, shifting potential rivals to less powerful posts. He has proved more flexible and accommodating than his austere predecessor and has laid the foundations for a more democratic society.

**SAID, Sayyid Fahad ibn Mahmoud al-.** *Oman.* Deputy prime minister. Born in 1944, a member of the ruling family, he studied in Cairo, Paris

and the Netherlands, and was appointed director of the foreign ministry in 1971. In 1980 he was appointed deputy prime minister for legal affairs.

**SAID, Sayyid Fahr ibn Taymour al-.** *Oman.* Deputy prime minister. Born in 1928, he is the brother of the late Sultan Said ibn Taymour. He studied at a military academy in British-ruled India before joining the Muscat Infantry and later served in the sultanate's defence department. In 1974 he was appointed interior minister and in May 1979 deputy prime minister for security and defence.

**SAITOTI, George.** *Kenya.* Vice-president and finance minister. The former head of the mathematics department at Nairobi University and an ex-chairman of Kenya Commercial Bank, he was appointed finance and planning minister in October 1983 and simultaneously nominated to a seat in parliament by President **Daniel arap Moi.** Saitoti is a Masai, and his appointment as vice-president in May 1989 following the downfall of Josephat Karanja marked a break with the tradition of appointing a Kikuyu, the country's largest ethnic group, to the post and represented a considerable political gamble on Moi's part. It also marked the beginning of the transformation of Saitoti from a loyal if rather colourless technocrat into a leading spokesman for the government's resistance to political and economic reforms.

**SAKAMOTO, Misoji.** *Japan.* Chief cabinet secretary. Born in 1923 in Ishikawa prefecture, he was elected to the House of Representatives (lower house) as a Liberal Democratic Party (LDP) member in 1967, and later held office as labour minister in **Yasuhiro Nakasone**'s government. A close associate of former prime minister **Takeo Miki**, he did not share his admiration of **Toshiki Kaifu**, and in the 1989 LDP leadership contest backed the rival candidacy of his faction leader **Toshio Komoto** until the last moment. It was on Komoto's insistence that Kaifu, himself a member of Komoto's faction, appointed Sakamoto to the important post of chief cabinet secretary in the February 1990 post-election reshuffle. Sakomoto enjoys a reputation within his party as a "clean" politician, although he had been one of the many to profit in 1986 from the shares of the subsequently discredited Recruit-Cosmos operation.

**SALEH, Ali Abdullah.** *Yemen.* President. Born in about 1942, a member of the Hashed tribe in North Yemen, he joined the army and played a key role in the 1974 coup, becoming security chief for Taiz province until mid-1978. He was elected president in July of that year after the assassination of his predecessor Ahmad al-Ghashmi. After weathering a South Yemen-backed rebellion, he worked hard to achieve union with the south, containing the effects of Aden's civil war in early 1986. He was appointed president of the united state on its formation in May 1990.

**SALEH, Brigadier-General Zubeir Mohammed.** *Sudan.* Deputy prime minister. A hardline Islamic fundamentalist and vice-chairman of the ruling Revolution Command Council, he is regarded by many as one of the major instigators of the June 1989 military coup.

**SALIM, Salim Ahmed.** *Tanzania.* Secretary-general of Organization of African Unity (OAU). Born in 1942 in Zanzibar, he studied in the USA and India and joined the diplomatic service of the newly unified republic of Tanzania in 1964. He held various key ambassadorships and was permanent representative to the UN (1970–80), foreign minister (1980–84), prime minister (1984–85) and defence minister (1986–89). Intelligent and debonair, he was twice strongly tipped for higher office but narrowly lost out: in 1981 he was the Non-Aligned Movement's candidate for the post of UN secretary-general, and in 1985 he was considered a strong contender to take over from **Julius Nyerere** as president of Tanzania. He became OAU secretary-general in 1989.

**SALINAS DE GORTARI, Carlos.** *Mexico.* President. Born in 1948 into a political family (his father was a senator and former minister), Salinas studied economics and political science at the National University of Mexico and at Harvard University. His keen intellect and skill as an economist, together with family connections, helped his career in the finance ministry, where he rose to become general director of economic and social planning. He was appointed budget and planning minister in 1982. He soon became a close associate and adviser to President Miguel de la Madrid (who had been his law professor at university), and was strongly influential in managing the direction of Mexican economic policy. He was also responsible for bringing young technocrats, such as **Pedro Aspe Armella** and **Víctor Camacho Solís**, into the ministry to help formulate and administer the adjustment policies that led to a massive devaluation of the peso and IMF-backed

liberalization of the economy. Although widely viewed within the ruling Institutional Revolutionary Party (PRI) as a technocrat, with little popular appeal, particularly among the trade unions, the backing of de la Madrid ensured his selection as as presidential candidate in 1987. He was elected by the slimmest of absolute majorities in 1988, the lowest share of the vote achieved by a PRI candidate. He made clear that he would continue to reform Mexico's ailing economy.

**SALMOND, Alexander.** *UK.* Scottish National Party (SNP) leader. Born in 1954, he graduated in economics from St Andrew's University, where he first became involved with the SNP, and subsequently pursued careers in banking and the civil service. He was first elected to parliament in 1987 as MP for Banff and Buchan. Regarded as a left-winger within the party, he served as energy, treasury and fisheries spokesman before winning the contest to succeed Gordon Wilson as party leader in September 1990, scoring an unexpectedly convincing victory over Margaret Ewing. His emergence as leader underscored the SNP's determination to gain votes at the expense of the Labour Party.

**SALOLAINEN, Pertti.** *Finland.* Foreign trade minister. Born in 1940, he worked as a television journalist in Finland and as a foreign correspondent before joining the Finnish Employers' Confederation (STK) in 1969. A member of the national executive of the conservative National Coalition Party (Kokoomus) since 1969, he was appointed foreign trade minister when the party returned to government in 1987, for the first time in 21 years.

**SAMAK SUNDARAVEJ.** *Thailand.* Communications minister. A veteran politician and originally a member of the Democrat Party, he split away after the October 1976 coup to form his own party, the Thai Citizens' Party (Prachakorn Thai). At the same time he served as interior minister in the right-wing government set up after the coup. A forceful public speaker, Samak is rarely out of the political limelight. His party joined the ruling coalition in December 1990 and Samak was appointed communications minister.

**SAMARAS, Antonis.** *Greece.* New Democracy (ND) politician. Born in 1951, Samaras is considered a high flyer in the conservative ND party. A graduate of the Harvard Business School, he has been an MP since the age of 26. He served briefly, and rather unimpressively, as

finance minister during the 1989
ND–Synaspismos coalition, after which he
became foreign minister. His youth and
ambition have him marked out as potential party
leadership material.

**SAMPAIO, Jorge**. *Portugal*. Socialist Party (PS)
leader. Born in 1941 in Lisbon, he is a lawyer by
profession. He was elected secretary-general of
the PS in January 1989, and has been credited
with restoring the credibility of the party
leadership after three years in the doldrums
following its electoral defeat in 1987. Local
elections in December 1989 gave him an
important power base as mayor of the capital,
Lisbon, while he also took personal plaudits for
the PS's improved performance, a revival
attributed in part to its new pragmatism.

**SAMY VELLU, Datuk Seri S**. *Malaysia*.
Energy, telecommunications and posts minister.
Born in 1936, Samy Vellu has been Malaysia's
most prominent ethnic Indian politician since
1979, when he replaced Tan Sri V.
Manickavasagam as president of the Malaysian
Indian Congress and as works minister. In mid-
1989 he was appointed to his present post, a
portfolio which is set to take on a much higher
profile in view of the government's electricity
privatization plans.

**SÁNCHEZ DE LOZADA BUSTAMANTE,
Gonzalo**. *Bolivia*. Opposition politician. Born in
1931 into a land-owning family, Sánchez was a
successful mining entrepreneur. As planning
minister from 1985 he was responsible for an
austerity package designed to cure Bolivia's
hyper-inflation. As the presidential candidate of
the Nationalist Revolutionary Movement
(MNR), he won the first round of the
inconclusive 1989 elections.

**SANDIFORD, Erskine**. *Barbados*. Prime
minister. Born in 1937, he was a school teacher
and college lecturer in Barbados and Jamaica
before becoming a cabinet minister in 1967. A
loyal member of the Democratic Labour Party,
he rose to be deputy to the party leader Errol
Barrow. As deputy prime minister he succeeded
automatically on Barrow's sudden death in 1987,
ensuring a smooth transfer of power.

**SANGUINETTI CAIROLO, Julio Maria**.
*Uruguay*. Former president. Born in 1936,
Sanguinetti studied law at Montevideo
University and practised as a lawyer until being
elected to the Chamber of Deputies in 1962. He
held ministerial posts between 1969 and 1973.
He became secretary-general of the Colorado
Party after its legalization by the military regime

and was elected president of Uruguay in 1985.
He helped manage the transition to democratic
rule, gaining a reputation as a moderate
reformer, although sometimes accused of
allowing the military to escape responsibility for
their actions during the previous regime.

**SANTER, Jacques**. *Luxembourg*. Prime minister.
Born in 1937, he practised law before becoming
a senior official of the Christian Social Party
(CVP/PSC) in 1966. He was elected party
general secretary in 1972, and leader in 1974,
when he was also first elected to parliament. He
was finance minister, labour and social security
minister from 1979 and became prime minister
of a centre-left coalition in 1984.

**SANTO, Akiki**. *Japan*. Science and Technology
Agency director-general (minister of state). Born
in 1942, she became well known as an actress
and television presenter, and was identified with
the faction of **Noboru Takeshita** in the ruling
Liberal Democratic Party. In December 1990
**Toshiki Kaifu** appointed her to his cabinet, the
only woman in the top echelons of government.

**SAOUMA, Edouard**. *Lebanon*. Director-general
of the UN Food and Agriculture Organization
(FAO). Born in 1926, he trained as an
agricultural engineer and worked as a researcher,
becoming head of the national institute of
agricultural research in 1957. He joined the
FAO in 1962, first as a regional representative
and then at the Rome headquarters. He was
elected director-general in 1976. Initially well-
regarded, his performance in the post – he is now
in his third six-year term – has become
increasingly autocratic and controversial.
Western countries led an unsuccessful attempt to
unseat him in 1987.

**SAPUNXHIU, Riza**. *Yugoslavia*. Kosovo's
member of the collective state presidency. Born
in 1925 in Peć, he graduated in economics from
Belgrade University. An Albanian, and a banker
by profession, he joined the communist party in
1945 and held a series of party posts prior to his
election as member of the collective state
presidency for Kosovo.

**SARBANES, Paul**. *USA*. Democratic senator
from Maryland. Born in 1933, he was a lawyer
and state legislator before his election to the
House of Representatives in 1970 and to the
Senate in 1976. A member of the foreign
relations committee and chairman of the
international finance subcommittee, he has taken
particular interest in third world issues.

**SARCINELLI, Mario**. *Italy*. Senior civil
servant. Born in 1934 in Foggia, he graduated in

law and worked at the Banca d'Italia. While deputy general manager of the central bank he helped to expose the Banco Ambrosiano scandal in 1979. This resulted in his arrest and detention for two weeks on trumped-up charges. He has been director-general of the Treasury since 1982. During 1987 he briefly held the post of foreign trade minister. In March 1991 he was to take up the post of senior vice-president of the European Bank for Reconstruction and Development.

**SARRE, Georges.** *France.* Government minister. Born in 1935, he worked initially as a postal inspector. His political involvement on the socialist left led to his being a co-founder, with **Jean-Pierre Chevènement**, in 1965 of the Centre for Socialist Studies, Research and Education (CERES), which subsequently became the active left-wing think-tank of the Socialist Party (PS). National secretary of the PS from 1971–75, Sarre led the party in Paris and entered the National Assembly in 1981. In 1988 he became junior minister for transport.

**SARTORIUS ALVÁREZ DE LAS ASTURIAS BOHORQUES, Nicolás.** *Spain.* Communist politician. Born in 1938 in San Sebastian, and a militant trade unionist opponent of the Franco regime, he was sentenced to 19 years for illegal association as a member of the Communist Workers' Commissions following the infamous "trial 1001" of December 1973, but was pardoned by King **Juan Carlos** in 1975. A lawyer, he is deputy secretary-general of the Communist Party of Spain (PCE) and vice-president of the United Left (IU) coalition.

**SASSOU-NGUESSO, General Denis.** *Congo.* President. Born in 1943 and a career soldier, he became Congo's leader in February 1979 when the ruling party, the Marxist-oriented Congolese Labour Party (PCT), deposed his predecessor Colonel Joachim Yhombi-Opango. He has established strong personal control of policy, pursuing a pragmatic line that accommodated close links with the USSR alongside use of Western multinationals to develop oil resources. His government has in recent years adopted market-oriented economic policies, setting aside the earlier socialist ideology, although not without opposition from within the PCT. Economic liberalization has yet to be accompanied by any loosening of party control over political life, although the clear-headed president has insisted that the PCT learn from events in Eastern Europe and broaden its popular support. Sassou-Nguesso has gained international stature – and the friendship of the USA – from his role as mediator in several African conflicts, both during his period as OAU chairman from 1986–87 and after.

**SATO, Megumu.** *Japan.* Justice minister. Born in 1924, and a member of the House of Representatives (lower house) since 1969, he was appointed to his present position in the December 1990 cabinet reshuffle. He previously held cabinet office as posts and telecommunications minister in the **Yasuhiro Nakasone** government from 1984–85.

**SAUD AL-FAISAL, Prince.** *Saudi Arabia.* Foreign minister. Born in Riyadh in 1943, and educated at Princeton University, he is eloquent and effective in presenting Saudi interests to the West. Saud is the eldest of the five sons of King Faisal by his last wife Iffat. Like his four brothers, he is a modernist who believes, to a large extent, in economic liberalisation. He was appointed foreign minister in 1975.

**SAUTTER, Christian.** *France.* Adviser to the president. Born in 1940 and a graduate of the Institut d'Etudes Politiques and Ecole Polytechnique, he became a civil servant with an emphasis on planning. In 1981–82 he was technical adviser in the general secretariat of **François Mitterrand**, and became inspector-general of finance, in 1985. He has been deputy secretary-general to Mitterrand from 1982–85 and since 1988.

**SAVIMBI, Jonas.** *Angola.* Nationalist leader. Born in 1934, he is a far better-known figure than President **José Eduardo dos Santos**. A veteran nationalist, he founded the National Union for the Total Independence of Angola (UNITA), of which he is president, in 1966. He led UNITA in the guerrilla war against the Portuguese, although he was also prepared to ally with the Portuguese against rival guerrilla forces on occasion. After the Portuguese withdrawal in 1975, he proclaimed himself president of the People's Democratic Republic of Angola, in opposition to the socialist Angolan People's Liberation Movement (MPLA) government. He has since fought to overthrow the MPLA and establish a multi-party capitalist-oriented democracy. Initially his operations were concentrated in the heartland of UNITA support in the centre and southeast of the country, co-ordinated from his "capital" at Jamba in Kuando Kubango province. After 1981, with South African military and logistical support and covert aid from the USA, operations extended to most of the country, causing serious disruption to the economy and massive displacements of the population. The reorientation of South African policy since 1988, leading to its withdrawal first from Angola and then, in 1989, to agreement on Namibian independence and the ending of direct support for Savimbi, has increased the importance of US support for UNITA. The MPLA was also under pressure, from a reforming Soviet government and a deteriorating economy, and in June 1989 the two sides came together in Zaïre to agree a ceasefire and moves towards national reconciliation. The ceasefire collapsed, but negotiations continue.

**SAVISAAR, Edgar.** *USSR.* Estonian prime minister. Born in 1949, he is an economist and leader of the nationalist Estonian Popular Front, formed in 1988. He was named Estonia's deputy premier and State Planning Committee chairman in July 1989, when he promised rapid moves towards economic independence. He then became premier after the Popular Front's March 1990 victory in the republic's Supreme Soviet elections. One of the more radical Popular Front leaders, he left the Communist Party in January 1990, and is prominent in the Congress of Estonia, a revival of the parliament of pre-war independent Estonia set up in parallel to the Supreme Soviet.

**SAW MAUNG.** *Myanmar (Burma).* Prime minister and State Law and Order Restoration Council (SLORC) chairman. Born in 1929. After months of anti-government riots in 1988 the armed forces, led by Saw Maung, took control of the country. Saw Maung was appointed chairman of SLORC, the military junta, and prime minister. However, real power within the junta rests with first secretary and military intelligence chief, **Khin Nyunt**, who enjoys the patronage of "strongman" **Ne Win**.

**SAWYER, Amos.** *Liberia.* Interim president. Born in 1945, he studied in Liberia and the USA and became a professor of political science at the University of Liberia. A lifelong campaigner for democracy, he played an active role in the Movement for Justice in Africa, supporting liberation movements in southern Africa. From 1981–83 he chaired the commission drafting a new constitution, adopted by referendum in 1984. In August 1984 he founded the Liberian People's Party (LPP) but was almost immediately detained, accused by the government of President Samuel Doe of masterminding a "communist plot". He was released from prison two months later after student demonstrations in his support had been brutally repressed, but was banned from politics.

The following year, after the LPP had been banned from contesting the elections, Sawyer moved to a teaching post in the USA, where in 1988 he set up a lobbying group, the Association for Constitutional Democracy in Liberia. In August 1990 he was chosen as head of the interim government formed in exile, but remains a president without power, dependent on the presence of the west African peacekeeping force.

**SAYEED, Mufti Mohammed.** *India.* Janata Dal politician. A long-standing leader of Congress in Kashmir, he was a member of the Jammu and Kashmir assembly from 1962–72, of the state legislative council from 1972–77, and president of the state Congress (I) unit from 1975–87. Elected to the Rajya Sabha (upper house) in 1986, he was tourism minister under **Rajiv Gandhi** in 1986–87. He resigned from Congress over its policies in Kashmir, joining Jan Morcha and later Janata Dal. He was elected to the Lok Sabha (lower house) for Janata Dal from an Uttar Pradesh constituency in 1989, and served in the 1989–90 National Front government as home affairs minister.

**SCALIA, Antonin.** *USA.* Supreme Court associate justice. Born in New Jersey in 1936, he held a variety of academic and government posts before becoming a judge in the US Court of Appeals (DC District) in 1982. **Ronald Reagan** appointed him to the Supreme Court in 1986, where he acquired the reputation of an intellectual but sometimes partisan conservative who favoured a narrow interpretation of the constitution.

**SCARGILL, Arthur.** *UK.* Trade unionist. Born in 1938, he worked as a miner from the age of 15. He became president of the Yorkshire region of the National Union of Mineworkers (NUM) in 1973 and president of the national union in 1981. A *bête noire* for the right, he had for years a strong following on the far left of the Labour Party, where his Marxist oratory and appeal to traditional working-class solidarity was much appreciated. The failure of the 1984–85 national miners' strike, however, was a personal defeat that marked the beginning of a long decline. His power base within the coal industry has been steadily eroded – not least by allegations of financial skulduggery during and after the 1984–85 strike – and he has been reduced to a marginal figure in national politics.

**SCHAEFER, William.** *USA.* Democratic governor of Maryland. Born in 1921, he was a lawyer who served colourfully as mayor of

Baltimore from 1971–86, winning national praise for his record on urban rejuvenation. Elected governor in 1986, he has been active in persuading business to stay in the state, and has raised gasoline taxes to combat a budget deficit.

**SCHÄUBLE, Wolfgang.** *Germany.* Interior minister. As interior minister he was a key figure in the West German Christian Democratic Union (CDU), playing a central role in the German unity negotiations. Born in Freiburg in 1942, he studied law and economics, gained his doctorate, and joined the tax inspectorate of Baden-Württemberg in 1971. From 1978–84 he worked as a lawyer. He started his political activities in 1961 when he joined the youth wing of the CDU. He was first elected to the Bundestag in 1972, served as chairman of the CDU sports committee from 1976–84, and was in charge of running the joint CDU/Christian Social Union parliamentary group from 1981–84. In 1984 he was appointed minister for special tasks and head of the chancellor's office, and brought into the cabinet. A close adviser to **Helmut Kohl**, he was promoted to his current post in 1989. He was paralysed in an assassination attempt in October 1990, but returned to his ministry, working from a wheelchair.

**SCHILTZ, Hugo.** *Belgium.* Deputy prime minister, budget and science policy minister. Born in 1927, he followed an academic career before being elected to parliament for the People's Union (VU) in 1965. As budget and finance minister for the Flanders region (1981–85) he proved himself an able administrator. When the VU joined the centre-left government in 1988 he was appointed a deputy prime minister and minister for the budget and science policy.

**SCHLÜTER, Poul.** *Denmark.* Prime minister.Born in 1929, he was politically active from an early age, chairing the Conservative People's Party (KF) youth wing in his home town of Tønder in southern Jutland at the age of 15, and the national party youth organization at 22. A lawyer by training, he was elected to the Folketing (parliament) in 1964, became the party's policy spokesman in 1971, and was elected party leader in 1974. In 1982, heading a four-party centre-right minority coalition, he became the first Conservative prime minister for 81 years, and embarked on a major overhaul of Denmark's debt-burdened economy and shaky public finances. Unable to rely on his Radical Liberal partners for support on foreign policy

and defence issues, he displayed a talent for getting out of tight corners. He also showed political courage in calling snap elections in 1984, 1987, 1988 and 1990, seeking a mandate for economic and defence policies, as well as going over parliament's head by calling and winning a referendum on the Single European Act in 1986.

**SCHMALZ-JACOBSEN, Cornelia.** *Germany.* Free Democratic Party (FDP) politician. Born in 1934, she studied music and languages before taking up a career as a journalist in Munich. She served as senator for youth and family affairs in West Berlin from 1985–89.

**SCHMID, Peter.** *Switzerland.* Green Party of Switzerland (GPS) president. An Italian-speaker from the minority region of Tessin, he is president of the expanding GPS and aims to capitalize on growing concern within the country over the despoliation of the alpine environment and the controversy surrounding Switzerland's nuclear power programme. He is also a member of the national parliament.

**SCHÖNHUBER, Franz.** *Germany.* Republican Party leader. Born in 1923, the son of a Bavarian butcher, he served in the Waffen SS during World War II. His book about his wartime experiences led to his dismissal as presenter of a popular chat-show on Bavarian television and in late 1983 he formed a right-wing party, the Republicans, with Franz Handlos and Ekkehart Voigt, both prominent members of Bavaria's ruling Christian Social Union (CSU). The new party attacked the CSU for going soft on communism and demanded restrictions on foreigners working or seeking asylum in West Germany. It also took a predictably hard line on law and order, advocated a neutral, united Germany with its own nuclear weapons, and opposed further European integration. In interviews Schönhuber has distanced himself from the Third Reich and from neo-Nazis in West Germany. His party had its first success in the West Berlin elections of 1989 (winning 7.5% of the vote) and in the European elections (with 7.1%) the same year. Since then it has fallen away in the polls, and did very badly in the two big Land (state) elections of May 1990. Schönhuber responded by resigning the party leadership, but was reinstated later that year.

**SCHÜSSEL, Wolfgang.** *Austria.* Economic affairs minister. Born in Vienna in 1945, he studied law at Vienna University, receiving his doctorate in 1968. In the same year, Schüssel became secretary of the parliamentary Austrian

People's Party (ÖVP). In 1975 he was appointed secretary-general of the Austrian Economic Federation, a subsidiary of the ÖVP, and he held this post until he joined the government as economic affairs minister in April 1989. Schüssel was elected to a seat in parliament in 1979, representing the ÖVP. In 1987 he became leader of the group of Economic Federation parliamentary delegates within the parliamentary ÖVP and deputy chairman of the parliamentary party. He also serves as deputy chairman of the parliamentary finance committee and has been a firmer advocate of privatization and deregulation than some of his fellow party members.

**SCHWARZ-SCHILLING, Christian.** *Germany.* Posts and telecommunications minister. Born in Austria in 1930, he gained a doctorate in Asian studies in Munich before going into business and becoming managing director of a factory making batteries. He was a Christian Democratic Union member of the Hesse parliament before entering the Bundestag in 1976, and was appointed posts and telecommunications minister in 1982.

**SCOON, Sir Paul.** *Grenada.* Governor-general. Born in 1935, he was a school teacher before becoming a senior civil servant. He was deputy director of the Commonwealth Foundation from 1973 until his appointment as governor-general in 1978. After the 1983 coup he issued a call for outside intervention, duly answered in the form of the US invasion, and then used his position as the remaining legitimate authority to supervise the return to democratic government.

**SCOTT, Nicholas.** *UK.* Conservative politician. Born in 1933, he made a political career in local government before being elected MP for Paddington in 1966 and Chelsea in 1974. He has held several junior ministerial posts, including minister of state for social security, but as one of the original "wets" (opposed to **Margaret Thatcher**'s more radical policies) he was by-passed by her for more senior appointments.

**SCOTTI, Vincenzo.** *Italy.* Interior minister and leder of the Christian Democrat (DC) group in parliament. Born in 1933 in Naples, he studied law and was involved in a Catholic youth movement in Naples, later working for the DC trade union federation, CISL. After ten years in the civil service, he was elected as a member of parliament for a Naples constituency. Since the late 1970s he has held various ministerial portfolios, including employment and social security, EC affairs, and culture and heritage. In

October 1990 he became interior minister after the resignation of Antonio Gava, who had been criticized for his failure to deal with organized crime, particularly that of the Camorra, the Naples version of the Mafia.

**SCOWCROFT, Brent.** *USA.* Assistant to the president for national security affairs. Born into a Mormon family in Utah in 1925, he graduated from West Point military academy in 1947. He joined the air force and flew fighters until he damaged his spine in a forced landing; the two years of recuperation meant that he missed service in the Korean war. He then earned a doctorate from Columbia University and in 1953 returned to West Point to teach Russian history. In 1959 he became assistant air attaché at the US embassy in Belgrade, returning to the USA in 1961 to teach political science at the US Air Force Academy, Colorado. After other air force and defence posts he became military aide to secretary of state **Henry Kissinger** in 1972. From 1975–77 he was assistant to the president for national security affairs (having served as deputy assistant since 1973), forging a close relationship with the then CIA director **George Bush**. After leaving the White House and retiring from the military, Scowcroft worked for Kissinger's international consultancy firm and served as chairman of a presidential panel on strategic missile basing. A strong supporter of the Midgetman single-warhead mobile missile, Scowcroft was highly critical of the plan during **Ronald Reagan**'s administration to place 10-warhead MX missiles on railway tracks. He was appointed to his current post when George Bush became president in 1989.

**SEAGA, Edward.** *Jamaica.* Opposition leader. Born in 1930 of parents of Lebanese origin and educated at Harvard University, he was a minister in Jamaica Labour Party (JLP) governments between 1962 and 1972. As JLP leader he won the 1980 elections and pursued a policy of restoring links with the USA and promoting free enterprise until his defeat in the 1989 elections.

**SÉGUIN, Philippe.** *France.* Gaullist politician. Born in 1943, he graduated in literature and politics and studied at the Ecole Nationale d'Administration, and he has been a lecturer in politics and an *auditeur* at the Court of Accounts. In the 1970s he became an adviser to government, notably to the prime minister, **Raymond Barre**. Since 1978, he has sat in the National Assembly as a Gaullist Rally for the Republic (RPR) member, and since 1983 he has been mayor of Epinal. As social affairs and employment minister in **Jacques Chirac**'s "cohabitation" government of 1986–88 he won a reputation for competent, articulate management, consensus and leadership potential. Since 1988 he has been openly critical of lack of direction in the RPR, and in 1990 he formed a much-publicized alliance with Gaullist strongman **Charles Pasqua** to reform and restructure the French right. Notably cool on European integration, he is the main force behind the RPR's growing antipathy to monetary union.

**SEGURADO, José Antonio.** *Spain.* Conservative politician. Born in 1938 in Barcelona. A business executive and a founder of the employers' organization CEOE, from 1986 he was secretary-general of the Liberal Party which he incorporated into the Popular Party (PP) in March 1989.

**SEIN WINN.** *Myanmar (Burma).* Leader of opposition "National Coalition Government of the Union of Burma". A cousin of National League for Democracy (NLD) leader **Aung San Suu Kyi**, he and seven other opposition MPs set up their shadow government at Manerplaw, on the Thai border, in December 1990. Although the majority of its members were from the NLD, Sein Winn himself was a member of the Party for National Democracy.

**SEINELDIN, Mohammed Alí.** *Argentina.* Army officer. Born in 1934 of Lebanese Druze parentage, he joined the army, rising to the rank of major during the 1970s, when he had links with extreme right-wing organizations. A veteran of the Falklands war, Seineldin, by then a colonel, served as an adviser to Panama's **Manuel Noriega**, before secretly returning to Argentina to lead a revolt in December 1988 by middle-ranking and junior army officers protesting about conditions and the threat of trials for human rights abuses during the 1970s. Pardoned by **Carlos Menem**, he was forcibly retired in late 1989, but remains technically part of the army reserve and is active on the right wing of the Peronist party. Re-arrested in October 1990 for bypassing the military chain of command to write to Menem about discontent in the armed forces, he was the focus of a further army revolt in December.

**SEITERS, Rudolf.** *Germany.* Head of chancellery. Appointed minister without portfolio and head of the chancellor's office in 1989, he figured prominently in the negotiations on German unity. Born in Osnabrück in 1937, he studied law and went into local government, was elected to the Bundestag in 1969 and held various Christian Democratic Union posts during the party's long years in opposition up to 1982.

**SEKERAMAYI, Sydney Tigere.** *Zimbabwe.* Politician. Born in 1944, a doctor of medicine by training and a member of the ZANU (PF) central committee, he has been in government since independence. Lands, resettlement and rural development minister in the first post-independence cabinet, he became minister of state for defence in 1982 and subsequently health minister, a portfolio he held until January 1988 when he was appointed minister of state with responsibility for national security.

**SEKHONYANA, Chief Evaristus Retselisitsoe.** *Lesotho.* Finance minister. Born in 1937, a leading figure in Lesotho's politics, he has made the transition from the government of former prime minister Chief Leabua Jonathan, in which he served as minister of finance, foreign affairs, planning, economic affairs and commerce and industry, as well as chairman of the ruling Basutho National Party, to that of Major-General **Justin Lekhanya**, who ousted Jonathan in 1986. Initially joining Lekhanya's cabinet as agriculture, co-operatives and marketing minister, he moved to the finance ministry in March 1988.

**SEMERDZHIEV, Colonel-General Atanas.** *Bulgaria.* Vice-president. Born in 1924 in the district of Pazardhik, Semerdzhiev became a Communist Party member in 1939 and joined a partisan detachment in 1941. He graduated from miliary staff academies in the USSR after World War II and went on to become the chief of general staff of the Bulgarian army from 1962–89. A full member of the party central committee from 1966, he became a member of the National Assembly in 1981. He is pro-reform and spent a brief period as interior minister before being appointed vice-president of Bulgaria in August 1990.

**SEMPRÚN MAURA, Jorge.** *Spain.* Culture minister. Born in 1923 in Madrid. A novelist and scriptwriter – author of the screenplay of Konstantinos Costa-Gavras's *Z* (1989), among others – he went into exile in France after the civil war, fought in the French resistance and spent time in Buchenwald concentration camp in 1943. He was expelled from the Spanish Communist Party (PCE) in 1965 as a "deviationist". He was appointed culture minister in August 1988.

**SEREGNI MOSQUERA, Líber**. *Uruguay*. Left-wing politician. Born in 1916, a retired general and Colorado Party member, Seregni was imprisoned during military rule in 1973–74 and 1976–84. In 1971 he had been presidential candidate for Broad Front (FA), a coalition of leftist parties, and was their candidate again in 1989, but came fourth.

**SERRA PUCHE, Jaime**. *Mexico*. Trade and industry ministry. Born in 1951 and educated in political science at the National Autonomous University of Mexico and at Yale University in the USA, he became an adviser to the finance minister in 1979. After a period as director of the Centre for Economic Studies, he was under-secretary for finance between 1986 and 1988 before being appointed trade and industry minister.

**SERRA SERRA, Narcís**. *Spain*. Defence minister. Born in 1943 in Barcelona, and a member of the Catalan Socialist Party, he held ministerial office in the Catalan regional government before becoming mayor of Barcelona in 1979. Appointed to the central government as defence minister in 1982, he has been a deputy for Barcelona since 1986.

**SERRANO ELIAS, Jorge**. *Guatemala*. Presidential candidate. Candidate of the Solidarity Action Movement (MAS) in the November 1990 elections, he came second in the first round but was expected to pick up right-wing votes in the run-off in January 1991. An industrial engineer and property developer, born in 1945, he has degrees in economics from Stockholm University and education from Stanford University in the USA. He served as president of the council of state under President **Efraín Ríos Montt**, whose evangelical Protestant convictions he shares. Serrano promised if elected to finalize a peace agreement with left-wing guerrillas and to forge a "social pact" between workers, government and business.

**SEVERIN, Adrian**. *Romania*. Deputy premier and minister for reform and relations with parliament. Born in Bucharest in 1954, he has a first degree and doctorate in law from Bucharest University. A legal consultant and member of the Romanian Association of International Law and International Relations, he served on the International Trade Arbitration Court of the Romanian Chamber of Trade and Industry. Together with **Petre Roman** and **Ion Iliescu**, he succeeded in making the relatively smooth transition from a privileged position under the Ceauşescu regime to high office in the post-revolutionary interim government of the National Salvation Front (NSF), becoming state secretary for privatization. He was elected to the Assembly of Deputies on a NSF ticket in the May 1990 elections.

**SHAGARI, Alhaji Shehu Usman Aliu**. *Nigeria*. Former president. Born in 1925, he worked as a teacher before entering politics as a member of parliament in the mid-1950s. Ministerial posts followed, and a period in local government, until he was plucked from relative obscurity to stand as candidate of the National Party of Nigeria in the 1979 presidential elections. As head of the first civilian government for 13 years, he came to be regarded as the clean figurehead of a corrupt administration. Deposed by the military in 1983, he remained in detention or under restriction for the next five years. Although banned, like other former politicians, from active participation in politics, Shagari was reported to be influential in the attempt to launch a new party, the Nigerian National Congress, in 1989.

**SHAHAL, Moshe**. *Israel*. Labour MP, former energy minister and prominent lawyer. Shahal was born in Iraq in 1934 and has been in the Knesset (parliament) since 1969. One of the few leading Sephardic (oriental Jewish) politicians in the Labour Party, Shahal was a member of the inner cabinet in the coalition government before March 1990.

**SHAMIR, Yitzhak**. *Israel*. Prime minister and Likud party leader. Born Yitzhak Yazernitsky in Poland in 1915, he came to Palestine at the age of 20 and soon joined Irgun, the right-wing Zionist underground. In 1941 he helped to found the more extreme Lehi ("Stern Gang"), soon becoming its effective leader. The British arrested him for allegedly directing a spate of assassinations, but he escaped and went to France. After Israeli independence he temporarily withdrew from politics and ran a chain of cinemas, before being absorbed back into the mainstream, working in Mossad (Israeli intelligence) from 1955–65. Shamir joined Herut only in 1970, and became a member of parliament in 1973. Cautious, loyal and hardworking, he was the prime minister Menachem Begin's choice as Knesset (parliament) speaker in 1977. Though at the time he opposed Begin's 1978 Camp David accords with Egypt, he was later given the job of foreign minister after Moshe Dayan resigned in 1979. Shamir was the surprise successor to Begin in 1983. Some said this unglamorous man was a compromise choice, others that he would take a tougher stance on the Palestinian issue. In the event, widespread disenchantment with the Lebanese war and an ailing economy deprived Shamir of total victory in the 1984 polls. He was forced into coalition with **Shimon Peres**'s Labour party, serving as foreign minister until 1986 and prime minister thereafter. The 1988 election, fought with the Palestinian *intifada* as a backdrop, was equally inconclusive, but Shamir retained the premiership in another coalition. The following year, he bowed to pressure from his right wing to curtail plans for Palestinian local elections. In March 1990 the coalition at last split over whether to accept the US Secretary of State **James Baker**'s suggestions for peace talks with the Palestinians. After three months of unprecedented horsetrading, Shamir fashioned a Likud-led right-wing coalition in early June, although some suggested that he would have preferred a new alliance with Labour to soften the impact of hardliners such as **Ariel Sharon** and **David Levi**. Shamir has proved he is a political survivor but, as one of the world's oldest premiers, his years at the centre of Israeli politics may be drawing to a close.

**SHAMUYARIRA, Nathan Mawirakuwa.** *Zimbabwe.* Foreign minister. Born in 1930, he is a leading member of the government and ZANU (PF) politburo, where his early career as a journalist has been utilized in his role as secretary for publicity and information. A founder member of ZANU, he spent the 1970s combining an academic career at Dar es Salaam University with active involvement in the liberation war, during which he founded his own liberation movement, Frolizi, before returning to the ZANU fold. He held the information portfolio, subsequently expanded to include posts and telecommunications, from independence until January 1988, when he was appointed foreign minister. An early proponent of reconciliation, he later became known for his fiery attacks on Western dealings with South Africa. However, he has proved a successful and surprisingly diplomatic foreign minister, doing much to rebuild relations with the USA in particular.

**SHARIF, Mian Mohammad Nawaz.** *Pakistan.* Prime minister. A successful industrialist, he identifies strongly with Lahore in the Punjab, where he was born in 1948, and in November 1990 became the first Pakistani prime minister

from a business background. A protégé of General Zia ul-Haq, who reversed Zulfiqar Ali Bhutto's decision to nationalize his family's Ittehaq Industries group, he was and remains a convinced proponent of economic deregulation. He was prominent as an opponent of **Benazir Bhutto**'s government in his role as chief minister in the Punjab, and emerged within months of her dismissal in August 1990 to brush aside rivals' claims and succeed her as prime minister. Commanding considerable support in the army and the top echelons of the administration, he also won the endorsement of the Muslim League, the largest component of the conservative Islamic Democratic Alliance (IDA), which came together to defeat Bhutto's Pakistan People's Party at the October 1990 elections. He has a reputation for being authoritarian and manipulative but may need to be more conciliatory in his dealings with other figures in the ideologically disparate IDA.

**SHARON, Ariel.** *Israel.* Housing minister. Born in 1928 on a *moshav* (agricultural settlement), Sharon rose to prominence in the army. He founded the elite counter-insurgency Unit 101 in the 1950s, but his reprisal against the Arab village of Qbiya in 1956 shocked many because of its high level of civilian casualties. Seen variously as fearless or foolhardy, Sharon has always had contempt for political niceties. He led the paratroops in the 1956 Suez war, and was a divisional commander in Sinai in the 1967 war. In 1973 he saved Israel's honour by breaching the Suez Canal in an otherwise depressing conflict. That year, after leaving the army, he helped to found the right-wing Likud party with Menachem Begin and became an MP. As agriculture minister from 1977–81, Sharon encouraged new Jewish settlements in the occupied territories, and as defence minister from 1981–83 he master-minded Israel's invasion of Lebanon. Forced to resign over the Sabra and Chatila massacre scandal, Sharon returned in 1984 as trade and industry minister. Pugnacious as ever, he antagonized Arabs by buying a home in the heart of Jerusalem's Old City Muslim Quarter.His adamant rejection of the US Secretary of State **James Baker**'s peace proposals helped to sink the second Likud-Labour coalition in March 1990. As housing minister Sharon is also responsible for settling Soviet Jewish immigrants, a task for which he is arguably just the right man. With **David Levi** and **Moshe Arens** he is a contender for the Likud leadership.

SHATALIN, Stanislav. *USSR*. Economist and former Presidential Council member. A Russian born in 1934, he is an economic theoretician with the Academy of Sciences. He champions market economic reforms, and openly calls himself a social democrat, although he is a Communist Party member. He was appointed to the short-lived Presidential Council by **Mikhail Gorbachev** in March 1990. In August 1990 he was charged by Gorbachev and **Boris Yeltsin** with drawing up the so-called "presidential" or "500-days" programme for radical economic reform. Amid the deepening crisis he suffered a serious heart attack in late 1990 and has since been dropped from Gorbachev's team.

SHENIN, Oleg. *USSR*. Senior Communist Party official. A Russian, born in 1937, he worked as an engineer in an aluminium plant in Krasnoyarsk, East Siberia, before becoming a Communist Party official in the Krasnoyarsk region in 1974, reaching the post of party first secretary in 1987. He also served as a political adviser in Afghanistan in the early 1980s. He was elected to the Communist Party of the Soviet Union politburo and secretariat (with responsibility for personnel) in July 1990.

SHEPHARD, Gillian. *UK*. Minister of state at the Treasury. Born in 1940, she was educated at Oxford University and entered parliament in 1987. She was quickly made a junior social security minister, where she supported the retention of child benefit, contrary to the wishes of some of her Conservative Party colleagues. She became minister of state at the Treasury in November 1990.

SHEVARDNADZE, Eduard. *USSR*. Former foreign minister. A Georgian, born in 1928, he spent his early career as a Komsomol official, rising to first secretary of the Georgian Komsomol in 1957. From there he moved in 1961 into the Georgian Communist Party district apparatus. He became first deputy interior minister of Georgia in 1964, and minister the following year. In July 1972 he was appointed party leader in Tbilisi after the Communist Party of the Soviet Union (CPSU) central committee had criticized the Georgian capital's party organization. Two months later he was appointed Georgian Communist Party first secretary; he immediately made his mark by attacking Georgia's sluggish economic performance and the corruption encouraged by his predecessor. In his 13 years as party leader he battled widespread corruption and organized crime with a purge of officials and thousands of

arrests. His tough approach also extended to nationalists and other dissidents. He was appointed a candidate CPSU politburo member in November 1978, at the same time as **Mikhail Gorbachev** joined the CPSU leadership as agriculture secretary – although their association dates from Gorbachev's time as a party official in Stavropol, just over the Caucasus mountains from Georgia. He was appointed a full politburo member in July 1985, the first Georgian to reach that body since Stalin's death in 1953. The same month he was named foreign minister, replacing Andrei Gromyko. At the time his limited experience of foreign affairs and foreign travel seemed a disadvantage, but it was noted that by putting a trusted associate in the post Gorbachev, CPSU leader for just four months, stood to gain close personal control over foreign policy, which had become virtually a one-man show during Gromyko's long tenure. The Gorbachev-Shevardnadze tandem in diplomacy then proceeded to carry through a worldwide foreign policy offensive whose "new thinking" has brought the end of the Cold War with the West, rapprochement with former ideological adversaries such as China, and has allowed Eastern Europe to democratize and break free of the Soviet sphere. Often accompanied on trips abroad by his wife Nanuli, Shevardnadze also presented a more amiable image than the dour Gromyko. In March 1990 he was included in Gorbachev's short-lived Presidential Council and in July 1990 he left the politburo. Alongside **Aleksandr Yakovlev**, he was considered Gorbachev's closest ally in the leadership. His resignation in December 1990 came in a dramatic speech warning that "dictatorship is coming"; it was seen as a severe blow to the reformists in the crisis-torn government, and dented confidence internationally as the West became apprehensive about the direction of Soviet policy.

SHIH CHI-YANG. *Taiwan*. Vice-premier. Born in 1935 and a lawyer by profession, Shih is a member of the ruling Kuomintang's central standing committee and was vice-minister of education in 1976–80 before moving to the justice ministry, where he was promoted to minister in 1984–88. Subsequently made vice-premier of the Executive Yuan (parliament) and deputy to the prime minister, he also heads the mainland affairs committee.

SHORT, Clare. *UK*. Labour politician. Born in 1946, she studied politics at Leeds University and worked as a civil servant until 1976. She was a director of pressure groups on race issues and youth unemployment before being elected to parliament for Birmingham Ladywood in 1983. She has been a junior spokeswoman on employment issues, also taking a strong stand on women's rights.

**SHUKLA, Vidya Charan.** *India.* External affairs minister. Born in 1929 in Raipur, he made a career as a Congress (I) politician after leaving university. First entering the Lok Sabha (lower house) as a member for Uttar Pradesh in 1957, he has held the seat ever since, except briefly from 1977–80. In 1987, however, he was expelled from the Congress (I), whereupon he formed the Jan Morcha (People's Party) before joining up with the Janata Dal for the 1989 elections. Identified as a supporter of **Chandra Shekhar**, he joined the latter's dissident group (Janata Dal–S) in bringing down **V.P. Singh**'s government in November 1990, and was rewarded with appointment to the foreign affairs post. Unlike many of his cabinet colleagues, he had considerable previous experience in central government, having first become a deputy minister under Indira Gandhi in 1966; he had held a series of ministerial posts prior to 1977, including that of information and broadcasting (1974–77), and was civil supplies minister from 1980–81. A keen sportsman, he has been president since June 1990 of the Indian Olympic Association.

**SHUKRI, Ibrahim.** *Egypt.* Opposition leader. One of the longest-serving figures in Egyptian politics, he was born in 1916 into a landowning family and joined the extreme right-wing Young Egypt (Misr el-Fahat) nationalist movement in 1935. He became its secretary-general in 1946 and in the following year vice-president of the Socialist Party, into which Young Egypt had transformed itself. He later became president of the new party, a post he held until 1953. In 1952 he was imprisoned briefly for his opposition to the monarchy but was released after the Free Officers' coup later that year. After a period of quiescence managing his family estate, he returned to active politics in 1962, joining the ruling Arab Socialist Union and being elected to the People's Assembly two years later. After four years in parliament he was appointed governor of Wadi el-Gadeed, a post he held until 1976. In 1977 President Anwar Sadat appointed him agriculture and agrarian reform minister, reflecting his landowning background and a long-standing interest in land reform. In the following year, however, he left the

government to become chairman of the Socialist Labour Party (SLP), set up with Sadat's encouragement to act as a "loyal opposition" in parliament. Unsurprisingly, it performed well at the 1979 elections, becoming the principal opposition to the ruling National Democratic Party. It suffered a major setback in the (freer) 1984 elections, failing to win a single seat. Before the 1987 elections, Shukri entered into a controversial alliance with the Liberal Socialist Party, which was widely seen as a "Trojan Horse" arrangement designed to allow Muslim fundamentalists to gain entry to parliament. Before the vote the SLP's offices were raided by police and Shukri appeared to have resumed his role as a leading opponent of Egypt's rulers. But splits in the SLP over policy towards the 1990 Iraqi invasion of Kuwait – culminating in Shukri's boycott of the November 1990 elections – may have led to his political marginalization.

**SIBOMANA, Adrien.** *Burundi.* Prime minister. A member of Burundi's underprivileged Hutu majority, Sibomana was appointed by President **Pierre Buyoya** in October 1988 as part of his efforts to achieve ethnic reconciliation. Continuing opposition from the dominant Tutsi community led him and other Hutu members of the government to threaten resignation in November 1989. Sibomana was a former provincial governor and vice-president of the now-dissolved National Assembly under the regime of Jean-Baptiste Bagaza.

**SIGUA, Tengiz.** *USSR.* Georgian premier. A member of the Round Table, which in alliance with the Free Georgia group had ensured a decisive victory for the Georgian nationalists in the elections in the republic in October–November 1990, he was named as the republic's new premier on November 15, the day after the election of Round Table leader **Zviad Gamsakhurdia** as president of Georgia. Sigua, aged 56 when he became premier, was a scientist and director of the metallurgy institute of Georgia's academy of sciences; his nationalist credentials were supported by his chairmanship of the All-Georgia Rusteveli Society.

**SIHANOUK, Prince Norodom.** *Cambodia.* Head of the anti-Vietnamese resistance coalition. Born into the Khmer royal family in 1922. The French authorities unexpectedly placed Sihanouk on the throne in 1941, apparently believing that he would be easily manipulated, which proved a monumental miscalculation. He secured Cambodian independence in 1953 and two years later he formed his own political movement,

Sangkum. He then abdicated in favour of his father to remove any constitutional restraints on his political ambitions. During the 1950s and early 1960s he managed to control Cambodia's internal political machinery through the Sangkum. At first Sihanouk avoided entanglement in the Vietnam war, but he became increasingly vulnerable and in March 1970 he was deposed by a group of pro-USA rightists, led by his prime minister, Lon Nol. He formed a Beijing-based alliance with the Khmers Rouges in 1970, but on his return to Cambodia in late 1975, was held a virtual prisoner by **Pol Pot**'s new government. He was rescued from Phnom Penh by the Chinese in early 1979, just before the Vietnamese invasion, and eventually agreed to head a resistance coalition including the Khmers Rouges cobbled together in 1982. Since then, the prince has applied his considerable, if eccentric, diplomatic skills towards eradicating Vietnamese domination of his country and establishing a new broad-based government.

**SIŁA-NOWICKI, Władysław**. *Poland*. Head of the Christian Democratic Labour Party. A lawyer championing human rights, he was a legal adviser to Solidarity in the early 1980s, but was accused of deserting the opposition cause in December 1986 when he joined a "consultative council" formed by President **Wojciech Jaruzelski**. He was elected chairman of the Christian Democratic Labour Party on its (unofficial) revival in February 1989 (it had been banned in 1946), and re-elected in April 1990. The party faces tough competition for the Christian Democratic vote from **Wiesław Chrzanowski**'s Christian-National Union.

**SILAYEV, Ivan**. *USSR*. Russian Federation prime minister. Born in 1930, he worked as an engineer in Gorky before being appointed as deputy USSR aircraft industry minister in 1974. In the early 1980s he was variously machine tool and instrument making minister and aircraft industry minister, and in 1985 was appointed a USSR deputy premier, with responsibility after 1986 for the government's new Machine Building Bureau. Regarded as a moderate reformer, he was backed by **Boris Yeltsin** in the June 1990 Russian premiership election only after beating the candidate favoured by Yeltsin.

**SILLARI, Enn-Arno**. *USSR*. Former Estonian Communist Party leader. Born in 1943, he was successively a local party leader and speaker of the Estonian parliament before being elected as Estonian Communist Party first secretary in

March 1990, sharing the leadership with party chairman **Vaino Vaelaes**. Although considered more in favour of party and state independence than Vaelaes, Sillari was chosen in July 1990 to take up the party's seat on the Communist Party of the Soviet Union politburo. In December 1990 he was replaced by Lembit Annus.

**SILLARS, Jim**. *UK*. Scottish nationalist politician. Born in 1937, he worked as a trade union official before being elected to parliament for the Labour Party in 1970. In 1976 he was one of the co-founders of the Scottish Labour Party, which took a stronger line on devolution for Scotland. He lost his seat in 1979 and subsequently joined the Scottish National Party (SNP). In 1988 he won a spectacular by-election victory over Labour in the Glasgow seat of Govan (the seat held briefly by his wife, Margo MacDonald, in 1973–74).

**SILVA CIMMA, Enrique**. *Chile*. Foreign minister. A lawyer, and former president of the constitutional tribunal, Silva became a leader of the moderate wing of the Radical Party (PR) in exile in Mexico and its president in 1983. He was appointed foreign minister in March 1990.

**SIMMONDS, Kennedy**. *St Kitts and Nevis*. Prime minister. Born in 1936, he studied medicine and practised on his native island of St Kitts. A founder member of the People's Action Movement, he became prime minister in a coalition government with the Nevis Reformation Party in 1980. He then led the state to independence from the UK in 1983 with a controversial federal constitution that gave wide autonomy to Nevis.

**SIN, Cardinal Jaime**. *Philippines*. Head of the Catholic church. Born in 1928, he became archbishop of Manila in 1974 and a cardinal two years later. During the closing years of the Ferdinand Marcos regime, Sin repeatedly spoke out against government repression. He played a key role in **Cory Aquino**'s rise to power, openly endorsing her and mobilising "people power". While taking an orthodox Catholic line on such issues as contraception, he has not shrunk from making controversial political statements. Although he has remained one of Aquino's strongest supporters, he has also criticized the administration for failing to carry out much-needed social reforms.

**SINGH, Ajit**. *India*. Janata Dal general secretary. He is the son of the late Charan Singh, a political leader of the North Indian peasantry and founder of Lok Dal. Educated in the USA as a computer engineer, he lived there for 17 years before returning to India to enter politics after his father became incapacitated. He became general secretary and then president of Lok Dal in 1987. Opposition to his leadership led to a split in the party, and he led his faction – Lok Dal (A) – into a merger with the Janata Party in 1988, becoming Janata president. After the fusion of the Janata Party with Janata Dal he became general secretary of the latter and served as industries minister in the 1989–90 National Front government.

**SINGH, Ganesh Man.** *Nepal.* Opposition leader. A veteran leader of the Nepali Congress Party, the septuagenarian Singh opposed the idea of participation in non-party local elections in 1987, holding out for more meaningful democratic reforms. Briefly arrested in December 1989, and again detained under house arrest the following February, he was a prominent figure in the "stir", the agitation which forced **King Birendra** to promise in early 1990 that multi-party democracy would be introduced.

**SINGH, V.P. (Vishwanath Pratap).** *India.* Former prime minister. Born in 1931 in Allahabad, he became actively involved in politics in his thirties, and served in the Uttar Pradesh state assembly from 1969–71, when he was elected to the Lok Sabha (lower house). He became deputy commerce minister in 1974–76 and was promoted to full minister in 1976–77. After Congress returned to power, he was despatched to the chief ministership of Uttar Pradesh in 1980 with the brief of cracking down on the state's crime wave. Unable to achieve this, he resigned in 1982. He was appointed to the Rajya Sabha (upper house) in 1983, becoming commerce and supply minister, and elected to the Lok Sabha in 1984. Appointed finance minister by **Rajiv Gandhi** the same year, he gained a reputation for honesty and toughness by vigorously enforcing corporate tax rules, mounting raids on company offices and threatening to cut off defaulters from state aid. In 1986 he was shifted to the defence ministry, in a move that was seen as the result of pressure from the business community. Here he initiated an investigation into allegations of corruption in the granting of a major defence contract to the Swedish company Bofors. His enthusiasm for rooting out corruption was viewed with unease by some government colleagues. He resigned as defence minister after coming under attack from his own party for employing an American detective firm. He soon became a focus for opposition to Gandhi's leadership, resulting in

his expulsion from the party in 1987. He then set up Jan Morcha – originally projected as a "forum" for Congress dissenters – and gradually moved into the centre stage of opposition politics, highlighting the issue of corruption. In August 1988 Jan Morcha took part in the creation of the National Front alliance of union-wide and regionalist opposition parties, and later merged with several centrist groups to form Janata Dal. This managed to deprive Congress of its parliamentary majority in the November 1989 elections, and the National Front formed a government with Singh as prime minister, relying on parliamentary support from the right-wing Bharatiya Janata Party (BJP) and from the Communist Party of India (Marxist). Singh's administration attempted to develop a clean and consultative style of government, but was plagued by internal factionalism, a weak parliamentary position, and the eruption of several violent political and social crises. The withdrawal of support by the BJP led to Singh's defeat on a vote of confidence in November 1990 and he was succeeded by his adversary within the now divided Janata Dal, **Chandra Shekhar.**

**SINHA, Yaswant.** *India.* Finance minister. Brought into the cabinet in November 1990, he had previously been a government official, and was a close aide to the prime minister, **Chandra Shekhar.**

**SINIORA, Hanna.** *Palestinian.* Leading moderate. Palestinian editor of the Jerusalem *Al-Fajr* newspaper, Siniora represents the Palestinian moderates who favour direct talks with the Israelis. He met **Shimon Peres** in 1987 and in July 1989 held talks in the USA with **George Bush** and Jewish leaders.

**SINNER, George.** *USA.* Democratic governor of North Dakota. Born in 1928, he was a farmer, agribusinessman and state legislator before being elected governor in 1984. Though failing to secure tax increases, he has been energetic in restoring state fiscal integrity.

**SISON, Jose Maria (alias Amado Guerrero).** *Philippines.* Chairman of the central committee of the outlawed Communist Party of the Philippines. A leader of the communist New People's Army, he enjoys considerable personal popularity. Released when **Cory Aquino** came to power in 1986 after nine years in prison, he formed the People's Party (Partido ng Bayan) in order to be able to participate in the 1987 congressional elections. The party failed to capitalize on widespread enthusiasm among the urban poor, however, leaving Sison as more of a respected "elder statesman" of the Filipino left than an active force in the country's politics. He now lives in exile in the Netherlands, and has published a book, *The Philippine Revolution: The Leader's View*.

**SISULU, Walter.** *South Africa.* Veteran African National Congress (ANC) leader. The ANC's secretary-general in the period after World War II, he was a close friend and sometime mentor to **Nelson Mandela**, a cousin of his first wife, Sisulu was sentenced with Mandela to life imprisonment at the 1964 Rivonia treason trial, and held with him in Robben Island. Released with a group of long-term political prisoners in October 1989, and reunited with his activist wife Albertina, he was a dignified spokesman in the continuing campaign to free Mandela. In March 1990 he was re-elected to the ANC's national executive, and in May he joined the negotiating team for the first talks with the government in Cape Town.

**SISULU, Zwelakhe.** *South Africa.* Journalist and politician. Born into an anti-apartheid family of impeccable credentials, with his father **Walter Sisulu** a long-term African National Congress (ANC) political prisoner, and his mother Albertina later to become a figurehead for the United Democratic Front, Zwelakhe made his own mark as a journalist, editing the radical *New Nation* and becoming the focus of human rights campaign efforts when he was imprisoned for two years to December 1988. Released under restrictions designed to stop him working on the paper, he returned to national prominence as "minder" to **Nelson Mandela** in mid-1990, travelling with him and seeking to control his punishing schedule of meetings and star appearances.

**SIYAD BARRE, Major-General Mohammed.** *Somalia.* President. Born in 1921, Siyad Barre received military training in Rome and held senior posts in the Somali police force during the 1950s. In 1960 he was appointed deputy commandant of the national army, with the rank of colonel, rising to commander-in-chief of the armed forces in 1966. From this position he led a successful coup after the assassination of President Abdirashid Ali Shermake in 1969. With support from the Soviet Union, Siyad Barre adopted socialist policies, while also cultivating links with Arab states. Deteriorating relations with Ethiopia resulted in Somalia launching an invasion of the disputed Ogaden region in 1977; initially successful, the Somali forces were beaten back after the USSR switched

its support to the Ethiopian side. Although responsible for improvements in social welfare in his early years in power, Siyad Barre became increasingly unpopular and isolated during the 1980s, concentrating power and privilege in the hands of his immediate family and fellow members of the small Marehan clan, and brutally repressing opposition. The president's strategy of "divide and rule" has led to the virtual disintegration of Somalia, with rebel movements active and successful in large areas of the country and the economy in ruins. At the end of 1990, with rebel and government forces confronting each other in the streets of Mogadishu, Siyad Barre's downfall seemed a matter of weeks away.

**SKAUGE, Arne.** *Norway.* Conservative politician and former finance minister. Born in 1948, he graduated as an economist in 1971 and then worked in local government. Elected a member of the Storting (parliament) for the Conservatives (Høyre) in 1977, he was appointed minister of trade and shipping (a particularly important post in Norway) and Nordic co-operation in 1981 and became state secretary in the prime minister's office in 1984. In 1986 he was appointed finance minister, but had to clear his desk later in the year when the centre-right coalition was defeated in the Storting. He held the same post again when the coalition held power from 1989–90.

**SKINNER, Dennis.** *UK.* Labour politician. Born in 1932, he worked as a miner and studied at Ruskin College, Oxford, before being elected to parliament in 1970. On the far left of the party, the "Beast of Bolsover" is a hard-hitting orator of the old class-struggle school, but is also widely respected for his parliamentary skills, and for his personal frugality.

**SKINNER, Samuel (Sam).** *USA.* Secretary of transportation. A former federal prosecutor, he was head of north-eastern Illinois's transport authority, the nation's second largest, before being appointed to his current post in 1989.

**SKUBISZEWSKI, Professor Krzysztof.** *Poland.* Foreign minister. Born in 1926, he studied law in France and the USA, holding teaching posts in international law at Harvard and Columbia universities and in Geneva and Oxford. He was the only independent in the Solidarity-led coalition government formed in September 1989. One of the most popular government ministers, he has pursued a foreign policy designed to cement Poland's independence and maintain good relations with Germany and the USSR.

SLABBERT, Frederik van Zyl. *South Africa*. Liberal opposition figure. Born in 1940, he was a sociology lecturer from 1964–74, when he entered parliament, becoming leader of the liberal opposition Progressive Federal Party in 1979. Recognized as one of the country's foremost political brains, he eventually became disillusioned with white parliamentary politics, resigned in 1986, and now devotes his considerable energies to his work with the Institute for a Democratic Alternative in South Africa (Idasa). He led the Afrikaner delegation to the milestone July 1987 talks with the African National Congress (ANC) in Dakar, and is increasingly in evidence as a "facilitator", with access to all the parties as they feel for the way forward across the minefield of constitutional negotiations.

SLOVO, Joe. *South Africa*. South African Communist Party (SACP) general secretary and principal white member of the African National Congress (ANC) leadership. Perhaps the most potent hate symbol for conservative Afrikanerdom, Slovo was stigmatized as the evil genius of the guerrilla war. He was identified as its hardline Marxist theoretician, and as a key strategist in his pre-1987 role as Maputo-based chief of staff of the military wing Umkhonto we Sizwe (Spear of the Nation). Born in 1926 in Lithuania, he was called to the Johannesburg bar in 1951 after finishing his studies at Witwatersrand University. His involvement in radical politics led him into exile and the armed struggle, after a long spell in London where he was at the London School of Economics in the mid-1960s. The first white on the ANC's national executive, his undeviating pro-Soviet line made him one of the last Brezhnev apologists. Succeeding to the SACP leadership in 1987, he relinquished his Umkhonto role to **Chris Hani**. His eventual reappraisal, published in late 1989 as *Has Socialism Failed?*, committed the SACP to multi-party democracy. In the new era from 1990, the unbanned party revealed part of its leadership for the first time in mid-year; its influence, and Slovo's, would depend on the continuance of its symbiotic links with the ANC. Enormously popular in the townships, but obviously no leadership contender in the ANC, he lowered his initial high profile as the government sought to engineer his removal from the negotiating team. His 23-year marriage and ideological partnership with Ruth First ended when she was killed by South African agents in Maputo in 1982.

SMIRNOV-OSTASHVILI, Konstantin. *USSR*. Pamyat leader. Born in 1926, he leads a faction of Pamyat, an organization set up in 1980 ostensibly to preserve Russian culture and historical monuments, but which increasingly stands accused of neo-fascism and anti-semitism. He went on trial in Moscow in July 1990 on charges of inciting racial hatred, and was sentenced in October to two years in prison.

SMITH, Andrew. *UK*. Labour politician. Born in 1951, he graduated from Oxford University and worked as a full-time officer of a co-operative society. He was elected to the local council in Oxford in 1976 and to parliament for Oxford East in 1987.

SMITH, John. *UK*. Labour politician. Born in 1938, he studied law and practised as a barrister, being appointed Queen's Counsel in 1963. Elected to parliament in 1970, he held a series of junior ministerial posts until being appointed secretary of state for trade in 1978. In opposition he has been Labour spokesman on trade, prices and consumer protection (1979–82), energy (1982–83), employment (1983–84), trade and industry (1984–87), and economic affairs (since 1987). Avuncular, articulate and persuasive, he has played a crucial role in moderating Labour's economic policies and, with his junior colleague, **Gordon Brown**, has done much to diminish the electorate's misgivings about a Labour government's ability to control public spending. He has sought to win the confidence of the financial sector, holding a series of lunchtime meetings (dubbed the "prawn cocktail offensive") with leading City analysts. Very much on the right of the party, he is often mentioned as a possible future leader.

SMITH, Sir Cyril. *UK*. Liberal Democrat politician. Born in 1928, he worked as a Liberal and Labour Party agent and founded his own spring manufacturing firm before being elected to parliament for the Liberals for his native Rochdale in 1972. A rumbustious maverick of extraordinarily substantial physique, he has been one of the Liberals' and Liberal Democrats' most popular MPs. He was knighted in 1988.

SMOLE, Jože. *Yugoslavia*. Slovene politician. Born in 1927 in Ljubljana, he became a communist party member in 1943. A partisan and Communist Youth League activist during World War II, he went on to become editor of *Borba*, the communist party daily. He also served as *chef de cabinet* to President Tito. In 1975 he was appointed ambassador to the USSR. Active in Slovene communist party politics throughout the 1980s, he backed the Slovene walkout from the federal party congress in January 1990, and the declaration of an independent Slovene party, the Party of Democratic Renewal. He is in favour of a market economy and is an outspoken reformist.

**SNEGUR, Mircha.** *USSR.* President of Moldavia. Born in 1939, he worked as an agronomist before becoming a Communist Party official in the early 1980s. In July 1989 he was elected chairman of the Moldavian Supreme Soviet presidium (*de facto* Moldavian president), and re-elected in April 1990 when the post was restyled as chairman of the Moldavian Supreme Soviet. An advocate of Moldavian sovereignty and full economic independence, his victory in the April 1990 election over Communist Party leader **Petru Luchinsky** reflected the strength of his support among nationalists in Moldavia's parliament. In September the Moldavian Supreme Soviet created a new post of executive president, to which he was elected unopposed.

**SNELLING, Richard (Dick).** *USA.* Republican governor of Vermont. Born in 1927 and with a successful background in business, he held representative office at state level for the first time in the late 1950s, and was Vermont's Republican governor from 1977–84. His 1990 gubernatorial campaign emphasized a businesslike approach, with the promise to take a firmer grip on state government and finances than his environmentally-minded Democrat predecessor **Madeleine Kunin**.

**SOARES, Mário.** *Portugal.* President. Born in 1924 in Lisbon, he is very much the familiar face of the older generation in Portuguese democratic politics. He remains identified with a *soarista* left wing in the Socialist Party (PS), although he resigned his post as party secretary-general in an attempt to rise above the fray of party politics when he became president in 1986. A lawyer, he first came to public attention as an opposition candidate in the 1965 and 1969 legislative elections under the Salazar dictatorship. He was repeatedly arrested for his political activities and married in prison while still a student. He was deported for several months in 1968, then spent four years in exile in France from 1970–74, founding the PS and becoming its secretary-general in 1973. He returned home after the 1974 revolution to take up what he clearly saw as his rightful role as one of Portugal's leading political figures. As foreign minister from 1974–75 he conducted the negotiations leading to swift independence for Portugal's overseas

territories. Briefly minister without portfolio in 1975, and a deputy in the constituent and legislative assemblies, he was appointed prime minister in 1976; he was twice reappointed, in 1978 and, after a break, in 1983, but his government fell in 1985. His party lost badly in the ensuing elections, but he won in the presidential elections the following year by securing the reluctant endorsement of the Communist Party in the second round.

**SOBCHAK, Anatoly.** *USSR.* Mayor of Leningrad. A lawyer, born in 1938, Sobchak emerged in 1989–90 as one of the most forceful, influential and popular leaders of the radical Inter-Regional Group in the USSR Supreme Soviet. When the Democratic Elections '90 bloc of reformist groups wrested control of the Leningrad city council from the Communist Party of the Soviet Union (CPSU) in elections in March 1990, Sobchak was recognized as the only figure capable of uniting the bloc's factions, and was persuaded to fight a May city council by-election in order to stand for the post of mayor. He left the CPSU after the July 1990 party congress, having joined only in 1988; the briefness of his stint in the party distinguishes him from nearly all other prominent reformers. He performs well on television and may use Leningrad as a platform for national ambitions.

**SODANO, Angelo.** *Vatican.* Secretary of state. Born in 1927, he spent 10 years as apostolic nuncio in Latin America before becoming Vatican "foreign minister". He succeeded Agostino Casaroli as secretary of state in December 1990, and was himself succeeded at foreign affairs by Jean-Louis Tauran.

**SOGLO, Nicéphore.** *Benin.* Prime minister. A respected former finance ministry official and World Bank representative, Soglo was installed as head of an interim government after the "civilian coup d'état" of March 1990, with a brief to reform the ravaged economy and prepare for multi-party democracy.

**SOISSON, Jean-Pierre.** *France.* Labour minister. Born in 1934, he graduated in law and then studied at the Institut d'Etudes Politiques and the Ecole Nationale d'Administration, subsequently following a career as university lecturer, technical adviser to government and centrist politician. Since 1968, with only brief interruptions, he has held a seat in the National Assembly. In the 1970s he occupied junior ministerial positions, specializing in vocational training, and was promoted to youth, sport and leisure minister in 1978–81 under **Valéry**

Giscard d'Estaing's presidency. When **Michel Rocard** was assembling his 1988 government, Soisson agreed to join the cabinet as labour minister. With **François Mitterrand**'s apparent approval he founded "United France" in 1990 to promote consensus politics.

**SOKOLOV, Yefrem.** *USSR.* Former Byelorussian Communist Party leader. Born in 1927, he became a full-time party official in 1958. Since his appointment as Byelorussian Communist Party first secretary in February 1987 the republic's leadership has retained its reputation as one of the most conservative in the USSR. He was replaced in December 1990 by Anatolii Malofeev.

**SOLANA MADARIAGA, Javier.** *Spain.* Education and science minister. Born in 1942 in Madrid, Solana has been a member of the Spanish Socialist Workers' Party (PSOE) executive since 1976, and was appointed culture minister in December 1982, becoming government spokesman in 1986. In 1988 he became education and science minister.

**SOLANA MORALES, Fernando.** *Mexico.* Foreign minister. Born in 1931 and educated at the National Autonomous University of Mexico, Solana worked as a university lecturer until 1976. He served as minister of commerce and then of education between 1977 and 1982. He was president of the National Bank of Mexico before being appointed foreign minister by **Carlos Salinas** in 1988.

**SOLARZ, Stephen.** *USA.* Democratic congressman from New York. Born in 1940, he was a public official and state assemblyman before his 1974 election to the House of Representatives. A high-profile foreign relations committee member, who chairs the Asian and Pacific affairs subcommittee, he is often publicly critical of governments with poor human rights records. He is also well known as one of Israel's strongest US supporters.

**SOLCHAGA CATALÁN, Carlos.** *Spain.* Economy and finance minister. Born in 1944 in Tafalla, Navarra, a former member of the central bank's research department and a university lecturer in economic sciences, Solchaga joined the Spanish Socialist Workers' Party (PSOE) in 1974. He was appointed industry minister in 1982 and became economy and finance minister in 1985. A leading member of the right wing of the PSOE, his strict monetarist policies have drawn fire from the trade unions.

**SOLHEIM, Erik.** *Norway.* Leader of the Socialist Left Party. Born in 1955, he was elected leader

of the youth wing of the Socialist Left Party (SV) in 1977 while studying history and sociology. He became SV general secretary in 1981 and party leader in 1987. He was elected a member of the Storting (parliament) in 1989.

**SOMARE, Michael.** *Papua New Guinea.* Foreign minister. Born in 1936, a teacher, journalist and civil servant, he and other young civil servants set up in 1967 the centre-left Pangu Pati, which became the dominant formation in pre-independence politics. Somare as its leader was chief minister from 1972, then prime minister for five years from independence in 1975. After two years in opposition he was again prime minister from 1982–85, and was again ousted after losing his majority in parliament. Since Pangu's return to government in 1988 he has been foreign minister, taking the credit for finding a formula to deal with Bougainville secessionists in mid-1990.

**SON SANN.** *Cambodia.* Leader of a non-communist resistance faction. Born in 1911, Son Sann held posts in both pre- and post-independence Cambodia, including a short period as prime minister in 1967. He exiled himself to Paris after Lon Nol took charge in 1970 and nine years later established the Khmer People's National Liberation Front (KPNLF) opposed to the pro-Vietnamese regime. Since 1982 he has acted as nominal prime minister in the resistance coalition headed by **Prince Norodom Sihanouk**, despite long-standing mutual suspicion between the two men. Son Sann has also quarrelled publicly with some of his own faction's military commanders.

**SONG PING.** *China.* Member of the Chinese Communist Party Politburo Standing Committee. Born in 1917, Song headed the State Planning Commission in 1983–87. A former state councillor and head of the Central Committee's organization department in 1987–90, he rose to his present post in June 1989 after backing **Li Peng** in the crackdown on the pro-democracy movement.

**SOONG, James (Chu-yul).** *Taiwan.* Secretary-general of the Kuomintang central standing committee. Born in 1942, Soong was personal secretary to the president from 1978. He took up his present position in 1989, succeeding **Lee Huan** after two years as his deputy. A prominent businessman, Soong is a close associate of President **Lee Teng-hui**.

**SORSA, Kalevi.** *Finland.* Speaker of parliament. Born in 1930, he worked first as a journalist and editor, then spent ten years at the UN

Educational, Scientific and Cultural Organization (Unesco) in Paris and in Finland, until his election in 1969 as general secretary of the Finnish Social Democratic Party (SDP). He entered the Eduskunta (parliament) the following year, and was elected party leader in 1975. By this time he had already established himself as one of the country's dominant political figures. He was foreign minister on three occasions (1972, 1975–76, 1987–89) and prime minister on another three (1972–75, 1977–79, 1982–87). In both positions he did much behind-the-scenes work to keep alive the flagging arms control and disarmament process, developing good contacts with the Soviet leadership in particular. In 1987 he announced his resignation as party leader, and in 1989 he made way for the new leader, **Pertti Paasio**, at the foreign ministry. Elected speaker of parliament in compensation, he was also offered a senior post in the Bank of Finland, an ideal opportunity to stand aside from political in-fighting and cultivate a statesmanlike image in preparation for running for the presidency in 1994.

**SOUPHANOUVONG**. *Laos*. President. Born in 1909 as a junior member of the royal family, he qualified as a highway construction engineer in France and returned to work in Vietnam. In 1945, after the Japanese surrender, he went home with his Vietnamese wife to join the anti-French government set up by one of his half-brothers, but soon identified himself with the communist cause and became known as "The Red Prince". As public front man of the Pathet Lao throughout the war, he was ideally suited to become head of state when the monarchy was abolished in 1975, but in old age he has become increasingly a figurehead.

**SOUTER, David**. *USA*. Supreme Court associate justice. Born in 1940, he studied law at Harvard University before serving as attorney-general of New Hampshire. He was appointed to the New Hampshire Supreme Court in 1983 and in 1990 he became a federal appeals court judge. In July 1990 he became **George Bush**'s first nomination to the Supreme Court following the resignation of Justice William Brennan, a renowned liberal.

**SOYINKA, Wole**. *Nigeria*. Playwright, poet and novelist. One of Nigeria's leading writers, awarded the Nobel prize for literature in 1986, he is a vociferous and influential critic of government abuses. Born in 1934 in Abeokuta, he was educated at Ibadan University and Leeds

University in the UK and began his theatre career working at the Royal Court Theatre in London. His first play, *The Lion and the Jewel*, was published in 1959. His political activities led to his detention from 1967–69; his account of this experience was published as *The Man Died* in 1972. Since 1976 he has been head of the department of dramatic arts at Ife University and has used his international standing to voice his criticisms of Nigeria's political and military leaders, attacking the growing religious divisions in Nigerian society.

**SPADOLINI, Giovanni**. *Italy*. Senate president and Italian Republican Party (PRI) politician. Born in Florence in 1925, he was professor of modern history at Florence University and edited two daily newspapers, the Bologna-based independent *Il Resto del Carlino* from 1955–68, and the Milan-based national *Corriere della Sera* from 1968–72. He was elected to the Senate in 1972, and held cabinet office as national heritage minister in the 1974–76 administration of Aldo Moro, and as education minister in March-June 1979. As leader of the PRI (from September 1979), he was invited to form a government after **Arnaldo Forlani**'s resignation following the P-2 (secret masonic lodge) revelations in May 1981. Spadolini's five-party coalition, the first since 1948 not headed by a Christian Democrat, lasted from June 1981 to November 1982. In the subsequent **Bettino Craxi** government Spadolini was defence minister, but precipitated a crisis which almost brought the government down in October 1985, criticizing Craxi for the decision to release the Achille Lauro cruise ship hijack leader Abu Abbas and complaining that he had not been sufficiently consulted. Following the general election of June 1987, Spadolini was elected president of the Senate. Coming late to politics after an academic career (he is an authority on the Italian Risorgimento), he has a professorial and somewhat humourless air.

**SPÄTH, Lothar**. *Germany*. Baden-Württemberg premier. Popular as Christian Democratic Union premier of Baden-Württemberg since 1978, he was long seen as **Helmut Kohl**'s arch rival in the party and as a future contender for the chancellorship. Born in 1937, he started his career in the finance department of Bietigheim, where he was elected mayor in 1967. His housing policy won favourable notice, and he was invited to join the board of the Neue Heimat building society, later notorious for alleged corruption. Späth, however, a member of the Land (state) parliament since 1968, had resigned from Neue Heimat in 1974 to devote more time to politics. In recent years he has gained a reputation as an enthusiast for the introduction of modern technology.

**SPICER, Michael.** *UK.* Conservative politician. Born in 1943, he studied economics, worked for the Conservative Party (1966–70) and then set up his own computer software company. Elected to parliament in 1974, he has held a series of junior ministerial posts since 1979. From 1981–84, as a party vice-chairman, he played a key role in running the party headquarters and organizing the 1983 election campaign. He was made housing minister in early 1990 but lost the post in **John Major**'s reshuffle later that year.

**SPITAELS, Guy.** *Belgium.* Walloon Socialist Party (PS) president. Born in 1931, he studied politics and law and became a university professor. He was elected to the Senate for the PS in 1977. He has held various ministerial posts, including deputy prime minister, and was elected president of the PS in 1981 and of the Confederation of European Socialist Parties (CSPEC) in 1989. Known for his strident support of French-language interests and his didactic manner, he has shown himself to be a pragmatic socialist.

**SPRING, Dick.** *Ireland.* Labour politician. Born in 1950, he trained as a lawyer and had already made a name as an international rugby player when he was elected to parliament in 1981 (inheriting a seat held by his father for 37 years). Thrust into the party leadership the following year when his predecessor defected to the centrist Fine Gael, he has been credited with slowing the party's slide from popular favour. He was deputy prime minister (1982–87) and minister for the environment (1982–83) and energy (1983–87) in what was at times an unhappy coalition with Fine Gael. He was instrumental in ensuring that his party selected **Mary Robinson** as Labour's 1990 presidential candidate.

**SSEMEGORERE, Paul Kawanga.** *Uganda.* Second deputy prime minister and foreign minister. Leader of the largely Baganda Democratic Party (DP), he has been an important figure in Uganda's turbulent politics for the past two decades. A member of the interim government set up after the overthrow of Idi Amin in 1979, he was the DP's candidate in the 1980 presidential elections. Ssemegorere remained in the country as leader of the opposition after Milton Obote's victory but joined the government of **Yoweri Museveni** as interior minister after Museveni captured

Kampala in 1986. In 1988 he was named one of three deputy prime ministers and given the foreign affairs portfolio.

**STALS, Chris.** *South Africa.* South African Reserve Bank governor. The top South African treasury official before his mid-1989 appointment to head the central bank, Stals marks a decided switch away from the political decision-making of his higher-profile predecessor Gerhard de Kock. Criticized by some for stifling the economy's potential for growth at a sensitive time, he has insisted on tight monetary controls to eliminate inflation, and can claim credit for bringing the runaway foreign debt under closer control.

**STĂNCULESCU, Colonel-General Victor Atanasie.** *Romania.* National defence minister. Born in 1928 in Tecuci, Galaţi county, he studied international economic relations at the Military Academy and General Staff Academy. A professional soldier, he prospered under the Ceauşescu regime, rising to the post of first deputy defence minister. Despite this close association with the fallen dictator, he became minister of the economy in the interim government.

**STANOVNIK, Janez.** *Yugoslavia.* Former president of Slovenia. Born in Ljubljana in 1922, he read law at Ljubljana University and studied at the Institute for Social Sciences in Belgrade. Active in the resistance movement during World War II, he later entered the civil service before becoming economic counsellor to the Yugoslav permanent mission in New York. A leading academic within Yugoslavia, he held various UN posts before becoming UN under-secretary-general in 1982. A member of the Slovene presidency since 1984, he served as president from 1988 to April 1990. He is pro-democracy and a supporter of Slovenia's full autonomy within Yugoslavia.

**STARKOV, Vladislav.** *USSR.* Newspaper editor. A Russian born in 1940, he began his career in journalism in 1973, did stints with Moscow Radio and leading publishing houses, and in 1980 became editor of the weekly *Argumenty i Fakty.* Thriving in the atmosphere of *glasnost*, his editorial policy made the newspaper a best-seller, reputedly with the highest circulation of any in the world. In October 1989 he was accused by **Mikhail Gorbachev** of going too far in publishing a controversial popularity poll of parliamentary deputies but, with the backing of his staff, he withstood official pressure to resign.

**STEEG, Helga**. *Germany.* Executive director of the International Energy Agency (IEA). Born in 1927 in Bonn, she studied at Bonn and Lausanne universities before joining the West German Finance Ministry in 1954, becoming head of its foreign trade department in 1973. Apart from a spell at the World Bank in 1965–67, she spent her whole career at the ministry until her appointment as executive director of the Paris-based IEA in 1984.

**STEEL, Sir David**. *UK.* Liberal Democrat politician. Born in 1938, he worked as a journalist and broadcaster in Scotland after completing his law studies. He won a by-election for the Liberal Party and entered parliament as its youngest member in 1965. In 1967 he sponsored the private member's bill liberalizing the law on abortion. The Liberal chief whip from 1970, he was elected party leader in 1976. Under his purposeful but temperate leadership, the Liberals made electoral gains in the 1980s, but Steel's own position was weakened by the (largely inaccurate) public perception of him as the junior partner in the "the two Davids" alliance with **David Owen**'s Social Democrats. Steel resigned as leader in 1988 after the alliance failed to achieve an electoral breakthrough. A strong supporter of the subsequent merger of the two parties, he became foreign affairs spokesman of the new Social and Liberal Democrats. He was knighted in 1990.

**STEFANOPOULOS, Konstantinos**. *Greece.* Democratic Renewal (Diana) leader. Born in 1926 in Patras, he practised law before entering parliament for the National Radical Union in 1964. A member of each parliament since the restoration of democracy in 1974, he was successively interior minister and minister of social services in the first New Democracy (ND) government from 1974–77 and was minister to the prime minister from 1977–80 in the second. After losing to **Constantine Mitsotakis** in the party leadership election in 1984, he broke away in 1985 together with nine other deputies to form Diana. He describes himself as "a wet conservative" and has argued that the state should not be involved in entrepreneurship but should concentrate on the provision of education and social services. In the April 1990 election he was defeated. He pledged the support of the party's only deputy to ND, enabling the latter to form a government, only to see this MP (Theodoros Katsikis) cross the floor and join the ruling party.

**STEIGER, Janet**. *USA.* Federal Trade Commission chairwoman. Steiger replaced the more conservative Daniel Oliver in 1989, at the age of 49. The wife of late Wisconsin representative William Steiger, she was appointed to the postal commission during **Jimmy Carter**'s administration and became its chairwoman under that of **Ronald Reagan**. She has shown a willingness to use the commission's powers on issues such as exaggerated promotional claims for dietary products.

**STEKELENBURG, Johan**. *Netherlands.* Trade unionist. Born in 1942, he has been a trade union official all his working life, first with the socialist metalworkers' union and then with the Federation of Dutch Trade Unions (FNV), the main trade union federation, of which he has been president since 1988.

**STELMACHOWSKI, Andrzej**. *Poland.* Senate speaker. A lawyer and academic, born in 1925, he was an adviser to Solidarity and Rural Solidarity throughout the 1980s, including the martial law period when he worked with the Solidarity underground. From 1987–90, as head of the Warsaw Catholic Intelligentsia Club, he helped to initiate the round-table talks. He was elected Senate speaker in July 1989 following Solidarity's almost clean sweep in the free Senate elections.

**STEPHENS, Stan**. *USA.* Republican governor of Montana. Born in 1929, he is a former radio broadcaster, cable television company executive and state senator. His 1988 election as governor ended 20 years of Democratic rule, and owed much to the ailing economy, whose revitalization is his main concern.

**STEVENS, John Paul**. *USA.* Associate justice of the Supreme Court. Born in 1920, he studied at Chicago and Northwestern universities before serving in the US navy from 1942–45. After private practice, he served as an appeal court judge from 1970–75, and was then appointed to the Supreme Court by Gerald Ford. Stevens is the youngest of the dwindling liberals on the nine-member court.

**STEVENS, Ted**. *USA.* Republican senator from Alaska. Born in 1923, he was a lawyer and state legislator before being appointed to the Senate in 1968, and was elected in his own right in 1970. He is an accomplished deal-maker who rose to become whip in 1981 and aspires to succeed **Robert Dole**, who narrowly beat him in 1984, as Republican leader. Constituency interests occupy much of his time and he is an advocate of oil exploration on federally protected land.

**STICH, Otto.** *Switzerland.* Finance and customs minister. Born in Dornach in 1927, he has a doctorate in education from Basle University. After a spell in teaching he was elected mayor of Dornach in 1957 and retained this position until 1965. After his resignation he held various leading positions in the Swiss Co-op. A Social Democrat Party (SPS) member, he has been finance and customs minister since 1984.

**STIRN, Olivier.** *France.* Centrist politician. Born in 1936 and a graduate in politics from the Institut d'Etudes Politiques, he followed a career in the prefectoral and government administration. Since 1968, with one brief interruption, he has sat in the National Assembly, and in the 1970s he occupied several junior ministerial posts. Politically he identified with the centre ground, founding several groupings to promote social democratic principles, and in 1984 he recognized the extent to which the socialist-led government had changed course, and left the opposition Union for French Democracy (UDF) to align himself with the Socialist Party (PS). In 1988 he accepted a post as minister for overseas departments and territories, then for tourism, only to resign amid controversy over alleged improprieties in 1990.

**STOLÉRU, Lionel.** *France.* Government minister. Born in 1937 and a graduate of the Ecole Polytechnique, Stoléru completed a doctorate in economics at Stanford University in the USA before beginning a career in public administration, specializing in economic and technical matters. From 1969–76 he advised **Valéry Giscard d'Estaing**, before becoming junior minister for manual labour and immigration from 1976–81. In 1988, still a member of the Giscardian Union for French Democracy (UDF), he became junior minister for planning, directly responsible to the prime minister, **Michel Rocard**.

**STOLPE, Manfred.** *Germany.* Brandenburg premier. A member of the Social Democratic Party (SPD) only since the spring of 1990, Stolpe was chosen, at the age of 54, to lead the party list in its only winnable Land (state) election in what had been East Germany in October. Modest but authoritative in manner, he won popular approval for his non-adversarial approach on political issues, although after the election he was adamantly against a "grand coalition" arrangement with his Christian Democratic Union rival **Peter-Michael Diestel**. Born in Stettin, he studied in Berlin and combines vivid memories of the division of the city (he was pursuing legal studies in the west when the wall went up in 1961) with a strong loyalty to those he chose to return to work with in the east. Under the Erich Honecker regime he was active primarily in the Berlin-Brandenburg Protestant church, promoting its concerns for human rights and peace, environmental and social issues.

**STOLTENBERG, Gerhard.** *Germany.* Defence minister. With a reputation for cool and objective decision-making, he has often been seen as a Christian Democratic Union (CDU) contender for the chancellorship. Born in Kiel in 1928, the son of a parson, he served in the final days of World War II as an "anti-aircraft helper" and was taken prisoner by the British. He gained a doctorate in social sciences in 1954, and embarked on an academic career but was soon drawn into full-time politics, entering the Schleswig-Holstein parliament in 1954 and the Bundestag in 1957. From 1957–61 he was chairman of the CDU youth wing. He rejected Konrad Adenauer's offer of the defence ministry, but took up Ludwig Erhard's offer of the science ministry in 1965. When the CDU/Christian Social Union lost power in 1969 he spent a year with Krupp, but then returned to regional politics and was premier of Schleswig-Holstein from 1971. The return of a CDU/CSU government at federal level saw him back in the cabinet, with a seven-year period as finance minister before he took up his current post.

**STOLTENBERG, Thorvald.** *Norway.* Foreign minister. Born in 1931, he studied international relations and joined the foreign service in 1959. He held several junior posts in Labour governments of the 1970s and was minister of defence from 1979–81 and of foreign affairs from 1987 until Labour lost power two years later. After a brief stint as ambassador to the UN, he was appointed UN high commissioner for refugees in 1990, but in November that year resigned to join the new Labour government as foreign minister. He is an uncomplicated politician in the traditional Scandinavian mould – down-to-earth and consensus-seeking.

**STRAUSS-KAHN, Dominique.** *France.* Socialist politician. Born in 1949, he graduated in law and commercial studies, studied at the Institut d'Etudes Politiques and gained a doctorate in economics, before following a career in university teaching, research and public administration. Within the Socialist Party (PS), he entered the central committee in 1983 and secretariat in 1984. Since 1986, he has sat in the National Assembly, where he is president of the important finance committee and generally seen as a candidate for higher political office.

**STRAW, Jack.** *UK.* Labour politician. Born in 1946, he studied law and was a radical president of the National Union of Students from 1969–71. Called to the bar in 1972, he also acted as special adviser to several ministers, worked as a broadcaster and was active in local government in the 1970s. Elected to parliament in 1979 he joined the shadow cabinet in 1987 and became opposition spokesman on education, his main political interest since his student days.

**STREIBL, Max.** *Germany.* Bavaria premier. Premier since 1988, after almost 20 years in the Land (state) government at ministerial level, he was born in 1932, grew up in his parents' hotel, and worked there and then in the Bavarian civil service until 1960. He was general secretary of the youth wing of the Christian Social Union (CSU) from 1961–67 and CSU general secretary from 1967–70.

**STROYEV, Yegor.** *USSR.* Senior Communist Party official. A Russian born in 1937, he worked as an agricultural engineer until the mid-1970s, when he was given responsibility for agrarian affairs in the regional party organization in Orel, near Moscow. He was named party leader in Orel region in 1985. He joined the Communist Party of the Soviet Union (CPSU) secretariat in September 1989, reporting to Yegor Ligachev on agricultural affairs. Regarded as more pragmatic than Ligachev on matters such as the revival of private farming, Stroyev was elected to the politburo after the July 1990 CPSU congress, taking over Ligachev's secretariat agricultural portfolio.

**SUAREZ, Xavier.** *USA.* Mayor of Miami. Born in 1949, he was a lawyer who became mayor in 1985 with the support of Miami's large Cuban-American population. Drug control dominates his agenda, but constituency concerns make him more interested in foreign affairs than most other mayors and he firmly supports a strong US stance against Cuba.

**SUÁREZ GONZÁLEZ, Adolfo.** *Spain.* Former prime minister. Born in Cebreros (Avila province) in 1932, he pursued a career in the National Movement, then Spain's only legal political party, for nearly 20 years under Franco and became its under-secretary. Picked by King **Juan Carlos** to replace the Francoist veteran Carlos Arias Navarro as prime minister in July 1976, Suárez surprised all by rapidly

dismantling the system he had previously served. He lifted bans on political parties, freed political prisoners and called the first free elections in Spain for more than 40 years in June 1977. Suárez won the elections at the head of the Union of the Democratic Centre (UCD), a coalition of non-socialist parties, and he steered through a new constitution that recognized wide-ranging regional autonomy and which remains the cornerstone of Spain's post-Franco democracy. Suárez's bold reformism sparked widespread opposition in conservative circles and forced his resignation as premier in January 1981, shortly before pro-Franco officers staged an abortive military coup. In 1982 he founded a new progressive party, the Democratic and Social Centre (CDS) but he has been unable to regain the popularity and power he exerted in the latter half of the 1970s.

**SUBROTO.** *Indonesia.* Secretary-general of Organization of the Petroleum Exporting Countries (Opec). Born in 1928, he studied economics in Indonesia and the USA and then lectured in international economics. He became a minister in 1971 and from 1978 he was energy minister. As Indonesia's representative to Opec, he proved himself the strife-ridden organization's best mediator and peace-maker. He was appointed secretary-general in 1988.

**SUCHINDA KRAPRAYOON, General.** *Thailand.* Army commander-in-chief. Suchinda was promoted to the top army post in March 1990 after serving less than a year as deputy army commander. He had been groomed for the post by his predecessor, **Chaovalit Yongchaiyut**, who left the post to enter the cabinet. Suchinda is leader of the class five graduates of Chulachomklao Royal Military Academy, a group known to have close links with Chaovalit's class one contemporaries.

**SUDHARMONO, Lieutenant-General.** *Indonesia.* Vice-president. Born in 1927, an army lawyer by profession, Sudharmono has served as **Suharto**'s right-hand man since 1966. He wielded considerable power as secretary of state (1973–88) and chairman of the government-sponsored Golkar party (1983–88). Vice-president since 1988, his election was controversial as he very nearly had to face a challenge from opposition leader Jailani Naro. In any bid to succeed Suharto he would be severely hampered by lack of support in the military.

**SUDOMO, Admiral.** *Indonesia.* Co-ordinating minister for political affairs and security. Born in 1926, Sudomo is one of **Suharto**'s "inner core" of supporters. Suharto appointed him to head the navy in 1969 and in 1978 he was promoted to command Kopkamtib, the powerful agency for domestic security and intelligence. He entered the cabinet as manpower minister in 1983, and five years later was promoted to his current position where he wields overall charge of a number of crucial ministries, including home and foreign affairs.

**SUHARTO, General.** *Indonesia.* President. Born into a Javanese farming family in 1921, Suharto joined the Netherlands East Indies Army in 1940 and went on to hold a guerrilla command in the war of independence against the Dutch after World War II. He became a career army officer after independence in 1949 and was deputy chief of the army when he was given command in 1962 of the campaign to wrest Irian Jaya from the Dutch. The following year he took command of the Strategic Reserve, a low-profile mobile striking force. Hitherto virtually unknown to the Indonesian people, he gained prominence as leader of the troops who retook control of vital points in Jakarta in the aftermath of the abortive October 1965 coup. He quickly manoeuvred aside President Sukarno, who was seen as being sympathetic to the communists, and in 1968 was formally elected president. Since the beginning of his fifth presidential term in March 1988, speculation has been rife over his possible retirement in 1993. All agree, however, that behind Suharto's public persona of simplicity lurks a shrewd political mind; the succession is likely to take place on his terms. Under Suharto's "New Order" regime, the army has emerged as the nation's dominant political institution and a fluid military "inner core" constitutes the power base for the president's continuing rule.

**SULEIMENOV, Olzhaz.** *USSR.* Environmental activist. The foremost living writer in the Kazakh language and head of the Kazakhstan Writers' Union, he became politically active in February 1989 when he organized protests against nuclear tests in the Semipalatinsk region of north-east Kazakhstan.

**SULLIVAN, Louis.** *USA.* Secretary of health and human services. Born in Atlanta in 1933, he was educated at Boston University, before becoming a fellow in pathology at Massachusetts General Hospital. Thereafter he held a series of academic medical posts, returning to Atlanta in 1975 to become dean and subsequently president of the School of Medicine at Morehouse College. In late 1988 he became the first black to be selected for the cabinet by president-elect **George Bush**, and was confirmed in office in March 1989. During his confirmation hearings before the Senate, Sullivan was widely characterized as amiable and anxious to please but reluctant to make clear his stance, on contentious issues such as abortion and federal funding of foetal research. Since taking office, however, he has antagonized the powerful tobacco lobby through uncompromising opposition to smoking and outspoken criticism of the targeting of minority groups by tobacco companies.

**SULLIVAN, Michael (Mike).** *USA.* Democratic governor of Wyoming. Born in 1939, he was a lawyer with no political experience until his 1986 election as governor. Diversification of the state economy is his main concern, and he is strongly supportive of state higher education.

**SULTAN, Fouad Abdel Latif.** *Egypt.* Tourism and civil aviation minister. Born in 1931 and educated at Cairo University, he worked for the Central Bank of Egypt for 21 years before being seconded to the IMF to work in North Yemen from 1971–74. On his return he headed the Misr-Iran Development Bank, joining the cabinet in 1985 with responsibility for tourism, one of Egypt's major sources of foreign exchange. His success in attracting private investment for tourism and hotel projects has led to him being given responsibility for the day-to-day running of the government's privatization programme.

**SULTAN IBN ABDUL-AZIZ, Prince.** *Saudi Arabia.* Second deputy prime minister. Born in Riyadh in 1924, he is one of the elite "Sudairi Seven" brothers. On the day after the assassination of King Faisal in 1975 and the confirmation of his brother **Fahd** as king, Sultan was appointed second deputy prime minister. More important, perhaps, he has been defence and aviation minister since 1962. He had originally joined the cabinet in 1953 as agriculture minister, helping to settle Saudi Arabia's nomads on modern farms.

**SUNDLUN, Bruce.** *USA.* Democratic governor of Rhode Island. Born in 1920, he made his money in the broadcasting business before turning his attention to political office. His successful 1990 campaign against incumbent governor Edward DiPrete, made great play of the fact that he had never held political office.

**SUNDSTEIN, Jøgvan.** *Denmark (Faroe Islands).* Chief minister. Born in 1933, he worked as an accountant in the Faroe Islands and metropolitan

Denmark, before being elected to the Løgting (local parliament) for the People's Party (Fkfl) in 1970. Elected its leader in 1980, he was chief minister of a centre-right coalition from 1988–90.

**SUNGURLU, Mahmut.** *Turkey.* Justice minister. Born in 1936, he practised law before entering parliament in 1983. One of the "technocrats" brought in after the retirement of the generals from Turkish politics, he was appointed justice minister in September 1986, and since 1988 has been deputy chairman of the ruling Motherland Party (Anap). As justice minister, Sungurlu has taken the brunt of international criticism of Turkey's human rights record. His blunt style has sometimes caused offence.

**SUNUNU, John H.** *USA.* White House chief of staff. Born in Cuba in 1939, of Lebanese and Greek extraction, he studied engineering at MIT, where he obtained a doctorate in 1966. After working as an engineer and as an associate professor of mechanical engineering at Tufts University, he served an undistinguished term in the New Hampshire House of Representatives from 1973–75, followed by unsuccessful campaigns for the state senate, the state's elected executive council and the US Senate. In 1982 he was elected state governor after a hard-fought campaign in which he attacked high public expenditure and promised to balance the state budget without imposing a state income tax or a general sales tax. He was subsequently re-elected for two terms. Although abrasive and unorthodox, Sununu displayed impressive intellectual ability and raw determination, moving quickly to erase a $33m deficit by speeding up revenue collections and raising taxes, while upholding his election pledge on taxation. In 1988 he managed **George Bush**'s presidential campaign, and was rewarded by being chosen as the new president's chief of staff, although some thought him too forceful and impetuous for a post requiring a combination of diplomatic skills, self-effacement and patience. After an unhappy start – compounded by his misreading of the mood of the Senate over its rejection of the appointment of John Tower as defence secretary – he has built a reputation as one of the most influential of Bush's aides.

**SUOMINEN, Ilkka.** *Finland.* Trade and industry minister. Born in 1939, he worked in the family engineering firm until he was elected leader of the conservative National Coalition Party (Kokoomus) in 1979, succeeding **Harri**

Holkeri. A member of the Eduskunta (parliament) from 1970–75 and since 1983, he led his party to its best-ever election performance in 1987, but was denied the premiership because President **Mauno Koivisto** opted for the more widely respected Holkeri. He was appointed trade and industry minister in the new left-right coalition.

**SÜSSMUTH, Rita.** *Germany.* Bundestag president. A moderate and eloquent Christian Democrat who is seen as a possible candidate for the chancellorship, she was born in Wuppertal in 1937, pursued an academic career and became professor of education at Dortmund university, a post she left in 1982. She turned to politics late, joining the Christian Democrats only in 1981. In 1985 she was appointed youth, family and health minister, and took on the additional portfolio of women's affairs the following year. In 1989 she was elected president of the Bundestag, and she has repeatedly led polls on the popularity of leading Christian Democrats. She was re-elected as Bundestag president at the first session of the all-German parliament in December 1990.

**SUTRISNO, General Try.** *Indonesia.* Armed forces commander in chief. Born in 1935, Sutrisno is a Javanese Muslim and a leading member of the "academy" generation of officers, those professionally trained in the 1960s who are increasingly taking over from older "guerrilla" officers from the independence period. He served as President **Suharto**'s personal adjutant in the 1970s and rose rapidly through the ranks, replacing **Benny Murdani** as armed forces chief in 1988. Sutrisno, whose leisure interests include martial arts and weightlifting, is widely tipped as a possible successor to Suharto.

**ŠUVAR, Stipe.** *Yugoslavia.* Former member for Croatia of the collective state presidency. Born in 1936, he holds a doctorate in law and is a professor of sociology at Zagreb University. A former editor of *Naše Teme* (Our Times), the Croatian theoretical party journal, and long-time and highly unpopular Croatian education minister, he served as president of the federal party presidium from June 1988 to May 1989. He was elected in May 1989 to the collective state presidency as the member for Croatia but replaced in August 1990 by former Croatian prime minister **Stjepan Mesić**. He is a hardliner but also a political infighter with an abrasive style. He resigned from the Croatian party in October 1990 on the grounds that it had abandoned socialism.

**SUZUKI, Shunichi.** *Japan.* Governor of Tokyo. Born in 1910, he graduated from the law faculty of Tokyo Imperial University (now Tokyo University) and entered the interior ministry in 1933. Later, he successively held the important posts of vice-minister of home affairs, vice-director of the cabinet secretariat and vice-governor of Tokyo. Suzuki was first elected as governor of Tokyo in 1979, and has held the office since. He undertook a largely successful overhaul of the capital's financial structure and, in spite of his advanced age, said he would stand again in early 1991.

**ŚWIĘCICKI, Marcin.** *Poland.* Foreign economic co-operation minister. An economist, born in 1947, he was an economic planning adviser to successive communist Polish United Workers' Party (PZPR)-led governments from 1972. He was one of four PZPR ministers appointed to the Solidarity-led coalition government formed in September 1989, and was the only one left in place after a July 1990 cabinet reshuffle, making him the old regime's last survivor in the government.

**SYRYJCZYK, Tadeusz.** *Poland.* Industry minister. Born in 1948, he is an engineer by profession, and worked from 1985–89 as a lecturer at Kraków's University of Mining and Metallurgy. He was active in the Solidarity movement and was interned for seven months after the declaration of martial law. In 1986 he set up his own highly successful computer company. He is a founder of the Kraków Industrial Society, a private group espousing free-market economics. A Solidarity member, he was appointed to the Solidarity-led government formed in September 1989.

**SYSE, Jan P.** *Norway.* Leader of the Conservatives and former prime minister. Born in 1930, he completed a law degree in 1957 and held a senior post in a shipping company during the 1960s. A former leader of the youth wing of the Conservatives (Høyre), he chaired the party's influential Oslo branch from 1974–82. Elected a member of the Storting (parliament) in 1973, he held the industry portfolio from 1983–85 and then served as leader of the parliamentary group before being elected party leader in succession to Kaare Willoch in 1988. He became prime minister in 1989 at the head of a minority centre-right coalition, but was unable to hold it together in late 1990 when the Centre Party rebelled against his increasingly pro-European stance.

# T

TABAI, Ieremia. *Kiribati*. President. Born in 1950 and educated mainly in New Zealand, he entered the House of Assembly at the age of 24 and rapidly made himself the dominant figure in the politics of what was then the British-ruled Gilbert Islands, successively as leader of the opposition, chief minister, and first president of independent Kiribati from 1979, serving also as foreign minister. As he approached the end of his current term of office in 1991, even his supporters accepted that a further term would be unconstitutional, and he is widely touted as the next leader of the South Pacific Forum.

TABONE, Vincent. *Malta*. President. Born in 1913 and trained in ophthalmics, he has been a member of the centre-right Nationalist Party (NP) since 1961. In the nine years of NP government from 1962 he served the party as its secretary-general. He entered parliament on the tide of the NP's success in the post-independence elections of 1966, and briefly held ministerial office under the then prime minister, Borg Oliver. In opposition from 1972–87 he continued in party posts, as first deputy leader and then as NP president. When **Edward Fenech Adami** led the NP to electoral success in 1987, he made Tabone his foreign minister, a key appointment in confirming Malta's neutral but European identity rather than the radical non-aligned posture of the Dom Mintoff years. His election to the presidency in April 1989 was pushed through the House of Representatives with the support of NP members only, and the Labour Party members (wanting the post for their former leader Mintoff) boycotted the swearing-in ceremony.

TAGAWA, Seiichi. *Japan*. Progressive Party leader. Born in 1918, he worked as a journalist on the prestigious *Asahi Shimbun* newspaper, and was first elected to the House of Representatives (lower house) in 1960 on the Liberal Democratic Party (LDP) list. As part of a group of party dissidents critical of "political and spiritual corruption", he left to form the New Liberal Club in 1976. When this group joined the LDP

in a coalition government under **Yasuhiro Nakasone** in 1983, Tagawa as its leader became home affairs minister. Setting himself against the dominant New Liberal Club current, which favoured re-amalgamation into the LDP, he formed the Progressive Party, effectively a one-man band, in January 1987. He remains a critic of "money politics", opposes any change in the constitution and any re-emergence of a military role for Japan, and takes a special interest in promoting improved relations with China.

TAIB MAHMUD, Tan Sri Datuk Haji Abdul. *Malaysia*. Chief minister of Sarawak. Taib Mahmud was born in 1936. After serving as minister of defence, information, primary industries and federal territories, he was appointed chief minister of Sarawak in 1981, replacing his uncle Tun Abdul Rahman Yaqub. As an ethnic Melanu, Taib Mahmud's right to head the Sarawak state government has been challenged by Dayak nationalists.

TAKESHITA, Noboru. *Japan*. Liberal Democratic Party (LDP) politician and faction leader. Born in Shimane prefecture in 1924, he graduated from the faculty of commerce at Waseda University in 1947. He became a teacher of English, but in 1951 was elected to the prefectural assembly. Seven years later, he became a member of the House of Representatives (lower house) for the LDP. Appointed chief cabinet secretary under Eisaku Sato in 1972, he became construction minister in 1976. After serving briefly as finance minister in 1979, he was re-appointed in 1982, holding the post for four years. Takeshita had been a member of the Sato faction but followed Kakuei Tanaka (prime minister from 1972–74) when he took over the faction. In 1968, Takeshita's eldest daughter married a son of **Shin Kanemaru**, a very powerful LDP member. This union was to help Takeshita in his own plot to wrest control of the Tanaka faction. In 1985, he formed the Soseikai, a grouping of Tanaka faction members which he claimed was a study group, but in practice was a crypto-faction. After Tanaka's stroke, an increasing number of faction members rallied to Takeshita, and by April 1986 he had effectively taken over the Tanaka faction. In 1986, he became secretary-general of the party, a post that is seen as a stepping-stone to the party presidency. This position he duly attained in October the following year, when he was nominated by outgoing leader **Yasuhiro Nakasone**, and took over the prime ministership the following month. One of Takeshita's strengths was his ability to bring together conflicting opinions; he was not noted for strong personal views on points of policy. However, despite his political acumen and large following, a disastrous showing in the opinion polls following revelations about the Recruit scandal led to him being ousted from the premiership in 1989. He remains a powerful and influential LDP figure.

**TALABANI, Jalal.** *Iraq.* Kurdish rebel leader. Arch-rival of Mulla Mustafa Barzani, leader of the Iraqi Kurdish Democratic Party (KDP), he formed the Patriotic Union of Kurdistan (PUK) in 1976. In November 1986 the PUK and the KDP agreed to unify their efforts but the PUK's attempt to negotiate with the Iraqis failed. An amnesty offered by the Ba'th to all Kurds inside and outside Iraq in 1988 significantly excluded Talabani. In November 1989 he said that the PUK would take "our urban guerrilla war to Arab cities" but added reassuringly that sensible Kurds would neither resort to terrorism nor take the war outside Iraq's frontiers. The PUK is supported by Iraq's main Arab enemy, Syria. He took a cautious approach when the Gulf crisis erupted in 1990, declining to align his Kurdish following with the western alliance against Iraq but taking the PUK into an anti-**Saddam Hussain** front formed with other exiled Iraqi opposition groups.

**TALEB, Youssef Sabry Abu.** *Egypt.* Defence minister, deputy prime minister. A career army officer and former governor of Cairo, he was appointed defence minister in August 1989 on the demotion of Field-Marshal **Mohammed Abu Ghazala**.

**TALHI, Jadallah Azouz al-.** *Libya.* Strategic industries secretary. Industry minister from 1972–77, he was appointed secretary of the General People's Committee (*de facto* prime minister) in March 1979, a post he held until 1984 and regained in 1986. He returned to the cabinet as foreign secretary in February 1987. More pragmatic than some of his predecessors, Al-Talhi played a leading role in negotiations to

settle Libya's territorial dispute with Chad over the Aozou strip. In October 1990, after differences with **Muammar Qaddafi** over the Gulf crisis, he moved to take charge of strategic industries, with responsibility for oil refining, petrochemicals and iron and steel.

**TAMBO, Oliver.** *South Africa.* African National Congress (ANC) president. Born in 1917, graduate of Fort Hare College, he became a teacher and then a solicitor, in partnership with **Nelson Mandela** during the 1950s. He was deputy ANC president from 1958–67 (having escaped to London in 1960), seeing many of his colleagues condemned to life prison terms, and acted as the ANC's leader in exile. An old-fashioned Christian socialist with a detached leadership style and a reputation for simple honesty, he has been ANC president since 1967, but increasingly his role has been confined to that of esteemed figurehead, the more so as illness sapped his energies. He returned to South Africa for the first time in 30 years to attend the ANC's December 1990 conference.

**TANDLER, Gerold.** *Germany.* Christian Social Union (CSU) politician. Born in 1936 in the Sudetenland, he worked for 27 years in a Bavarian bank, rising through the CSU to become its secretary-general from 1971–78 and from 1983–88. In the intervening period he was Bavaria's interior minister and chairman of the CSU group in the regional parliament.

**TANER, Güneş.** *Turkey.* Minister of state. An economist, he spent 11 years at the US bank Citibank before entering parliament in his mid-40s in 1987, having also been vice-chairman of the ruling Motherland Party (Anap) from 1984–87 and economic adviser to then prime minister, **Turgut Özal** for two years. Appointed in 1987 as a minister of state with responsibility for banking, the treasury and – most important – the government's privatization programme, he favours a rapid end to the country's transitional and interventionist economic policies, and the liberalization of the economy. He stood unsuccessfully for the premiership in October 1989, losing to Yıldırım Akbulut.

**TAPIE, Bernard.** *France.* Businessman and politician. Born in 1943, he is a self-made multi-millionaire who has become one of France's most famous faces. In 1986, he became managing director of football club Olympique de Marseille, guiding it to great success. Simultaneously, his high public profile enabled him, in 1988, to win a parliamentary seat with Socialist Party (PS) encouragement, making anti-National Front politics and job creation his priorities. Business success complemented political and sporting laurels; in 1990 he acquired a majority share in sports goods company Adidas.

**TAŞAR, Mustafa.** *Turkey.* Minister of state. A nationalist, once seen as one of the bigger thorns in President **Turgut Özal**'s side, he was brought into **Yıldırım Akbulut**'s government as a minister of state. He was secretary-general of the ruling Motherland Party (Anap) until 1987, but resigned after a dispute with **Mehmet Keçeciler** and now leads his own nationalist grouping within the party.

**TASCA, Catherine.** *France.* Communications minister. Born in 1942 and a graduate of the Institut d'Etudes Politiques and the Ecole Nationale d'Administration, she worked initially as a civil servant, specializing in theatre and the arts. In 1968 she joined the Unified Socialist Party (PSU), alongside **Michel Rocard**, and in the 1980s she advised **François Mitterrand** on cultural matters. In 1986, she joined **Jacques Chirac**'s new broadcasting body (the CNCL) as a token left-wing appointee. She became communications minister in 1988, answerable to culture minister **Jack Lang**.

**TAUFA'AHAU, Tupou IV.** *Tonga.* King. Born in 1918, Australian-educated and with a long career as premier while crown prince from 1949–65, he then succeeded his mother as monarch. He prides himself on his educational achievements on the island, where the political system remains dominated by the nobility, but where he has allowed a gradual widening of participation, marked by elections in 1990.

**TAYA, Colonel Maaouya Ould Sid'Ahmed.** *Mauritania.* President. Born in Atar in 1941, he trained at a French military academy. He served in the Saharan War against the Polisario Front from 1976–79 and was army chief of staff from 1980–81. After a spell as prime minister and defence minister (1981–84), he returned to the post of army chief of staff. In December 1984 he successfully led a bloodless coup against Mohamed Khouna Ould Haidallah, replacing him as president and chairman of the Military Committee for National Salvation (CMSN). He also holds the posts of prime minister and defence minister. His efforts towards political and economic reform have been threatened since the late 1980s by growing tension between the Moorish and black communities.

**TAYLOR, Charles.** *Liberia.* Rebel leader. Born in 1948, son of a Liberian mother and an American father, he was a student in the USA, where he became active in the Union of Liberian Associations in the Americas, agitating against the government of president William Tolbert. He returned home after the 1980 coup to head the government procurement agency, later becoming assistant commerce minister, but fled the country in 1984 to escape corruption charges, which he claims were fabricated. He escaped while awaiting extradition from the USA in 1985, and re-emerged as head of a previously unknown rebel group, the National Patriotic Front of Liberia, which crossed the border from Côte d'Ivoire on Christmas Eve 1989. By September 1990, Taylor's forces were in control of nine-tenths of the country and had achieved their aim, the overthrow and death of President Samuel Doe. However, they faced a formidable coalition of interests, including the rival rebel faction led by Prince Yormie Johnson, Liberian exiles, the peacekeeping force organized by the Economic Community of West African States (Ecowas), and the USA, who were determined to prevent Taylor consolidating his position as self-proclaimed head of state. Taylor signed the Bamako ceasefire agreement with the leaders of rival factions in November 1990, but remained opposed to the Ecowas-installed government of **Amos Sawyer**.

**TEBBIT, Norman.** *UK.* Former employment secretary and Conservative party chairman. He personifies the rugged populist basis of Thatcherism. Born in 1931 in Enfield, on the outskirts of London, he was educated at state schools and had careers in journalism, the Royal Air Force and advertising before working as a civil airline pilot until 1970, making a name as an aggressive negotiator in the pilots' union. He was elected to parliament in 1970. Unpopular with Tory worthies, he found a welcome from Thatcherite radicals. As employment secretary, he inflamed liberal sensibilities by telling the jobless to "get on their bikes" and look for work. He succeeded **Cecil Parkinson** as trade and industry secretary from 1983–85, and became parliament's arch-Labour-baiter. He amplified this role when as Tory party chairman he led the successful election campaign in 1987. A victim of the IRA's bomb attack on a Brighton hotel during the Conservative party conference in 1984, Tebbit recovered to serve as Chancellor of the Duchy of Lancaster from 1985–87. He withdrew from the political frontline to care for his wife, disabled in the Brighton bombing. Having gathered a clutch of lucrative company directorships, Tebbit continued to take an active role in politics as a forceful proponent of Thatcherism. From the backbenches he embarrassed the government in 1990 by attacking plans to absorb Hong Kong refugees. After a brief public flirtation with the idea of becoming **Margaret Thatcher**'s successor, Tebbit became a satellite television presenter in 1989. He supported Thatcher to the last in the leadership contest and was vociferous in advocating the continuation of her policies.

**TEKERE, Edgar Zivanai.** *Zimbabwe.* Politician. Born in 1937, he is a volatile populist who has moved from being a leader of ZANU (PF) to become one of its leading opponents. After 10 years in detention with other nationalist leaders he escaped in 1975 to Mozambique, where he helped rebuild ZANU's political and military fortunes. Appointed party secretary-general in 1977, he was briefly a cabinet minister in 1980. His tenure was cut short by accusations, of which he was acquitted, of his involvement in the murder of a white farmer. He later became party chairman for Manicaland province, his birthplace and political power base, and began outspoken criticism of the one-party state and top-level corruption. In October 1988 he was expelled from ZANU (PF) and six months later formed the Zimbabwe Unity Movement (ZUM). ZUM won only two seats in the 1990 elections but its potential as a focus of opposition was underlined by ZANU (PF)'s vitriolic election campaign against it.

**TEMBO, John Zenas Unapake.** *Malawi.* Ruling party politician. Born in 1932, he is a member of the central executive of the ruling Malawi Congress Party (MCP), is close to President **Hastings Banda** and is considered a likely successor. Tembo was a member of parliament from 1964–70, during which period he also held the finance and trade portfolios. From 1970–84 he was governor of the Reserve Bank of Malawi. In the late 1970s there were rumours that he would be appointed prime minister as a means of designating him successor. However, he was not popular with the army, unlike his rival Dick Matenje, the last MCP secretary-general, who died in mysterious circumstances, officially reported as a car crash, in 1983. After Matenje's death, Tembo took a low political profile, resurfacing after 1986 to carry out successful shuttle diplomacy to resolve the crisis in relations with Zimbabwe. He has been working behind the scenes to consolidate his political position, but his unpopularity and that of his niece, **Mama Kadzamira,** may prove

an obstacle.

**TER BEEK, Relus.** *Netherlands.* Defence minister. Born in 1944, he entered the Staten Generaal (parliament) in 1971 and went on to establish himself as the leading defence and foreign affairs expert in the Labour Party (PvdA). He became head of the parliamentary committee on foreign affairs in 1982. On the left of the party in the 1970s and a strong proponent of the PvdA's anti-nuclear defence policy in the 1980s, he subsequently stressed the need to find a national consensus on defence. He was appointed defence minister when the PvdA returned to government in coalition with the Christian Democrats in November 1989.

**TER-PETROSYAN, Levon.** *USSR.* President of Armenia. Born in 1945, he established his credentials as a radical nationalist in the Karabakh Committee, campaigning for Armenian control of the Nagorny Karabakh region of neighbouring Azerbaijan, for which he was imprisoned from December 1988 to May 1989. A leader of the pro-independence Armenian National Movement, formed in November 1989, he was chosen by the newly elected Armenian Supreme Soviet as its chairman (*de facto* republican president) in August 1990 in preference to **Vladimir Movsisyan,** the then Armenian Communist Party leader.

**TERRE'BLANCHE, Eugene.** *South Africa.* Afrikaner Resistance Movement (AWB) leader. Born in 1943, a farmer and a former policeman and bodyguard to J.B. Vorster, the charismatic Terre'blanche has cultivated the militaristic "man on horseback" image to present himself as a neo-fascist saviour of the Afrikaner *volk.* His AWB, with its quasi-nazi paraphernalia, was founded in 1973 and rose from obscurity in the 1980s with the growing popularity of the notion that white extremists would stake all to defend a *Boerevolkstaat.* He claims a powerful measure of support among the police, and may be an unexpected and probably disruptive fringe participant in constitutional negotiations. His notoriety reached new heights in December 1988, when police discovered him breaking into the Boer War monument at Pardekraal under cover of darkness with a glamorous woman journalist who had written of being "impaled on his blowtorch eyes". Critics seized this opportunity to attack him for loose living and womanizing, although he denied any improper liaison.

**TESFAYE DINKA.** *Ethiopia.* Foreign minister. A long-serving member of the government, he was appointed commerce minister in September 1977, moving to the industry ministry in 1981 and serving as finance minister from 1983–87. On the introduction of civilian rule in September 1987 he was appointed a member of the state council and deputy prime minister. He became foreign affairs minister in November 1989.

**TETELBOIM, Volodia.** *Chile.* Chilean Communist Party (PCCh) leader. Born in 1916, he was elected PCCh general secretary in 1989 to replace veteran leader Luis Corvalán. Tetelboim expressed his support for the anti-**Augusto Pinochet** alliance, even though the PCCh was not legalized, but since the restoration of democratic rule he has maintained the distance between the communists and the parties in government.

**THANI, Shaikh Hamad ibn Khalifa al-.** *Qatar.* Crown prince. Born in 1950, he is the eldest son of the ruler, **Shaikh Khalifa**. Educated in Qatar to secondary school level, he graduated from the UK's Sandhurst Military Academy in 1971. In 1977 he became crown prince and defence minister. He has set up the Qatari air force and navy as well as various specialist army units.

**THANI, Shaikh Khalifa ibn Hamad al-.** *Qatar.* Amir (ruler). Born in 1932, Sandhurst-educated Shaikh Khalifa deposed his cousin Shaikh Ahmad Bin-Ali al-Thani in 1972, following the British withdrawal and the declaration of Qatari independence in the previous September. He takes an authoritarian stance and most matters are decided by his decree after consultations with members of the royal family. Although the council of ministers, which he heads, can initiate legislation, it usually leaves this to the Amir. The advisory council, which he appoints, can comment on proposed legislation but has no power to initiate changes.

**THATCHER, Margaret.** *UK.* Former prime minister. Britain's first woman prime minister and the leader of its longest uninterrupted post-war government. She was the architect of a radical conservatism which favours a maximum role for private enterprise and the free market and the scaling down of government bureaucracy and the welfare state. Born Margaret Roberts, daughter of a grocer, in the small Lincolnshire town of Grantham in 1925, her first contacts with political life were through her father, who was an alderman. She has often cited him as her first and most lasting influence. After studying

chemistry at Oxford University and training as a barrister, she was elected to parliament in 1959 as Conservative MP for Finchley, in north London – a seat she has held ever since. After holding a number of junior ministerial posts from 1961, she was brought into the cabinet in 1970 as secretary of state for education and science in **Edward Heath**'s government. She soon gained a reputation as a fiscal hardliner, and was dubbed "Maggie Thatcher, Milk Snatcher", after her decision to end the provision of free milk to schoolchildren. By 1975, her radical brand of hardline conservatism appealed to enough Tory MPs to gain her a surprise victory over Heath in the party leadership contest. She became prime minister in 1979, when the Conservatives defeated Labour with a manifesto promising to curb union power and to lower inflation. Embarking on a broadly monetarist strategy, her new government cut back public spending virtually across the board and passed a succession of laws which effectively emasculated the unions. Up to a point, the strategy worked: inflation fell, strikes went out of fashion and the economy prospered – but at a cost. Rising unemployment combined with cuts in welfare benefits fuelled widespread accusations that the prime minister "lacked compassion". Outside parliament, some of Thatcherism's strongest critics were to be found in the Church of England – once known as "the Tory party at prayer". Re-elected in 1983 after the Falklands war, her government embarked on a long series of privatizations of state utilities. A fiercely anti-communist "Iron Lady" on foreign affairs, she was a close friend and ally of US president **Ronald Reagan**, displaying little enthusiasm for European integration. Re-elected for a third term, with a reduced majority, in 1987, her celebrations of 10 years in Downing Street were marred by growing public dissatisfaction with government policies, and her unashamedly robust, even abrasive style continued to alienate the public as well as some of her Tory colleagues. December of that year witnessed the first formal challenge, however nominal, to her leadership of the party. The European elections of June 1989 saw the Tory vote collapse. Her stridently voiced opposition to further British integration into the EC ran counter to the views of most of her cabinet, and provoked the resignations of the chancellor, **Nigel Lawson**, in 1989 and deputy prime minister, **Sir Geoffrey Howe**, in 1990. The latter's departure prompted a leadership challenge by her long-time rival **Michael**

Heseltine. Although gaining more votes, Thatcher narrowly failed to win the requisite majority for outright victory on the first ballot, and she was persuaded by senior Tories to stand down rather than face possible defeat. She will be remembered as one of the most resolute and influential British leaders this century, whose convictions changed the tenor of public debate – and added a new term to the political lexicon.

**THIERSE, Wolfgang.** *Germany.* Social Democratic Party (SPD) deputy chairman. Successor to the leadership of the SPD in East Germany after the resignations of Ibrahim Böhme in February and Markus Meckel in May 1990, he took his party into the merger with the West German SPD in September with no illusions about the low ebb it had reached. As deputy chairman of the merged party, he called for a campaign which would show it to be the true political representative of workers' interests. A strong theme of Thierse's is that the inhabitants of the former East Germany should not be treated like citizens of a defeated country.

**THOMAS, Clarence.** *USA.* Judge, US Circuit District Court of Appeals, Washington, D.C. Born in Savannah, Georgia, in 1948 and rose from poverty to earn a law degree from Yale University in 1974. He was appointed in 1989, and is seen as a potential successor to Supreme Court Justice **Thurgood Marshall**, the only black member of the court. From 1982 to his appointment, as judge, he was chairman of the Equal Opportunities Commission. As federal appeals judge, he promises to "follow Supreme Court precedent", and not to establish law on his own.

**THOMAS, Dafydd Elis.** *UK.* Welsh nationalist politician. Born in 1946, he studied and then taught Welsh studies. He was elected to parliament for the Welsh nationalist party Plaid Cymru in 1974. Since becoming leader in 1984 he has steered the party on a broadly left-of-centre line.

**THOMPSON, James.** *USA.* Former Republican governor of Illinois. Born in 1936, he was a state attorney, law professor and US attorney before being elected governor in 1976. Conservative on fiscal matters and liberal on social issues, Thompson is widely regarded as a possible US attorney-general in **George Bush**'s administration, and may yet gain appointment to the Supreme Court. He was to retire as governor in January 1991, giving way to party colleague **Jim Elgar**, who won the November 1990 gubernatorial election.

**THOMPSON, Tommy.** *USA.* Republican governor of Wisconsin. Born in 1941, he was a lawyer and state legislator, before his fervently conservative successful 1986 gubernatorial campaign to oust the incumbent liberal. Against a background of a Democrat-controlled state legislature, he has been pragmatic as governor, refraining from cutting social programmes.

**THONDAMAN, Savumyamoorthy (Solomon).** *Sri Lanka.* Tourism and rural development minister. A trade unionist and leader of the Ceylon Workers' Congress, he represents "Indian Tamils" – those brought in during the 19th century as tea plantation workers. His party was a founder member of the moderate Tamil United Liberation Front in 1976 and he won a seat in parliament in 1977, joining the government two years later as rural industrial development minister. He has held a cabinet post ever since, moving to the tourism and rural development portfolio in March 1990.

**TIAN JIYUN.** *China.* Vice-premier. Tian held provincial finance posts and was deputy secretary-general of the State Council in 1981–83, before becoming vice-premier. The youngest of the three post-holders (he was born in 1929), he is in charge of forest-fire and flood prevention, and has had a politburo seat since 1987.

**TIMAKATA, Fred.** *Vanuatu.* President. Born in 1936 in the Shepard Islands, he was elected to the post-independence parliament as a member of the ruling and primarily anglophone Vanuaaku Pati, becoming deputy prime minister and home affairs minister, and then holding office as speaker from 1985–88. In this capacity he came under particular criticism from the primarily francophone opposition, which in 1986 mounted a boycott of parliament in protest at his alleged misuse of standing orders and favouritism towards his own party. He became health minister in the cabinet formed in December 1988 by **Walter Lini**, and in January 1989 was chosen as president, following the arrest of George Sokomanu for his attempt to oust Lini.

**TINDEMANS, Leo.** *Belgium.* Flemish Christian Democratic politician and MEP. Born in 1922, his election to parliament for the Christian People's Party (CVP) in 1961 marked the beginning of a career that made him one of the country's dominant political figures. He first entered the cabinet in 1968 and from 1974–78 was prime minister of two broad-based administrations that agreed in principle a new federal arrangement splitting Belgium into Dutch-speaking Flanders, French-speaking Wallonia and bilingual Brussels. Ostracized by his previous coalition partners, he had to pass the premiership to his party colleague **Wilfried Martens**, but returned as foreign minister in 1981. He left national politics in 1989 to head the CVP faction of the European Parliament.

**TIZARD, Dame Catherine Anne (Kath).** *New Zealand.* Governor-general. Born in 1931, she graduated from the University of Auckland, where she subsequently worked for several years as a senior tutor of zoology. She served as an Auckland city councillor from 1971–83 and as the city's first woman mayor from 1983–90, initially for Labour and then as an independent. She was appointed the country's first woman governor-general in 1990.

**TLASS, General Mustafa.** *Syria.* Defence minister. Born in 1932 in Rastan City, Tlass studied at the military and law colleges and Voroshilov Academy in Moscow before becoming an active member of the Ba'th Arab Socialist Party. Having held many senior posts, he helped to install President **Hafez al-Assad** in the "correctional movement" of 1970 and became defence minister and deputy prime minister two years later. He played a key role in defeating the bid for power by the president's brother, Rifaat, in 1984, and later commented that "anyone who says 'No' to Assad will be a head shorter".

**TODD, Ron.** *UK.* Trade unionist. Born in 1927, he worked at Ford Motors from 1954 until he became a full-time official of the Transport and General Workers' Union (TGWU) in 1962. Working his way up from regional officer to regional secretary and national organizer, he was elected general secretary of the country's largest union in 1985. Fervently left-wing and a believer in traditional working-class solidarity, he has maintained a careful ambivalence about the need for the union movement to accommodate the new labour laws of the 1980s.

**TOFILAU ETI ALESANA.** *Western Samoa.* Prime minister. Tofilau leads the Human Rights Protection Party, a loose grouping whose basis is in family and local allegiances rather than any ideological ties. Prime minister from 1983–85 and again since the February 1988 elections, he retains the foreign affairs and numerous other portfolios, although after undergoing heart surgery he did transfer some responsibilities to cabinet colleagues in September 1989.

**TÖKEŞ, László.** *Romania.* Reformed Church bishop of Oradea and honorary president of the Hungarian Democratic Union of Romania. Born in Transylvania in 1937, he followed his father into the priesthood of the protestant Reformed Church. A courageous and outspoken critic of Nicolae Ceauşescu, it was his forced removal from his Timişoara parish that sparked the demonstrations that led to the overthrow of the communist dictatorship. Appointed a member of the Provisional National Unity Council, he became increasingly critical of the National Salvation Front's failure to address the grievances of the ethnic Hungarian minority.

**TOLBA, Mostafa.** *Egypt.* Executive director of UN Environment Programme (Unep). Born in 1922, he studied in Egypt and the UK and lectured in microbiology until 1959. He was then successively head of Egypt's science council, a junior minister and president of the academy of scientific research. One of the country's best-known scientists, energetic and an able administrator, he was appointed Unep deputy executive director when it was set up in 1973, and became director two years later. Although his public utterances occasionally drift dangerously close to hyperbole, few doubt his personal commitment to achieving global environmental security.

**TOMOV, Aleksandur.** *Bulgaria.* Deputy premier. Leader of the radical Movement for Democratic Socialism (Demos) faction of the Bulgarian Socialist Party (BSP), he was an important figure in the opposition to the re-election of **Aleksandur Lilov** as BSP chairman at the September 1990 congress. An unsuccessful candidate for the chairmanship, he was the only clearly identifiable radical reformer elected to the party council. In December, however, he became the highest-ranking BSP member of the coalition government formed pending fresh elections. Holding the rank of deputy premier, he was also to exercise for the party its share in the overseeing of the defence and interior ministries.

**TÖPFER, Klaus.** *Germany.* Environment minister. Appointed in 1987 as environment, nature conservation and nuclear safety minister, he has seen East Germany's environmental problems rise dramatically to the top of his agenda. Born in Lower Silesia in 1938, he studied economics, became head of the planning department in Saarbrücken, and worked as state secretary in the federal social and health affairs ministry from 1985–87. In January 1990 he sought to become premier of the Saarland in the state elections, but was crushed by the Social Democratic Party incumbent, **Oskar Lafontaine**.

**TOUR, Abdulrahman**. *Somalia*. President of Somali National Movement (SNM). Tour replaced Ahmed Mohammed Silyanyo as president of the SNM, the rebel group which has won control of much of northern Somalia, at its congress in March 1990. He was Somalia's first ambassador to Ethiopia after independence and a former governor of Hargeisa province.

**TRAORÉ, Moussa**. *Mali*. President. Born in 1936, Traoré was trained as a soldier in France and served in the French army until Mali's independence in 1960. In 1968, when a lieutenant, he led the coup that deposed Mali's first president, Modibo Keita, becoming president the following year. Infighting among the military continued for some time, but since 1973 Traoré has kept a tight grip on power, as head of the ruling Military Committee for National Liberation, head of government and secretary-general of the only party, the moribund Democratic Union of Malian People (UDPM). His position is secured by cultivation of interest groups; opposition has been weak, although he has faced challenges from within the army and growing unrest as Mali remained one of the few African states untouched by the tide of political change in 1990. Mali's former close links with the USSR have been replaced by developing relations with France and the USA, fostered by the economic adjustment policies pursued since 1981.

**TRENCHEV, Konstantin**. *Bulgaria*. Founder and chairman of the Podkrepa (Support) trade union. Working initially underground, and then (after the fall of the communist regime) as an affiliate of the main opposition coalition the Union of Democratic Forces (UDF), Podkrepa was a powerful force in bringing the country to a state of effective paralysis in opposition to the policies of the former communist Bulgarian Socialist Party government. Trenchev himself was not only an outspoken critic of the socialists, but an opponent of UDF involvement in coalition talks, and was reputedly instrumental in securing the downfall of **Petar Beron**, the UDF leader. In August 1990 he was accused of inciting anti-socialist demonstrators to set fire to party headquarters in Sofia; a police investigation was started. Despite his active opposition to a coalition government, he has since collaborated with it and agreed to a

moratorium on stikes. He is an ardent monarchist.

**TRENTIN, Bruno**. *Italy*. Trade unionist. Born in 1926 in France, he obtained a law degree and, having fought in the resistance during World War II, in 1949 he joined the staff of the Italian General Confederation of Labour (CGIL), Italy's largest labour organization. He served as a Rome councillor from 1960–73 and as a member of the Chamber of Deputies from 1962–72, representing the Italian Communist Party (PCI), to which he had belonged since 1950. From 1962 he was secretary-general of the metalworkers' federation. In October 1988, Trentin was appointed general secretary of CGIL.

**TREURNICHT, Andries**. *South Africa*. Conservative Party leader. Born in 1921, he was a minister in the Dutch Reformed Church from 1946–60, then editor of the church's newspaper before first winning election to parliament as a National Party candidate in 1971. The party's powerful Transvaal leader, and chairman of the influential Broederbond secret society of Afrikaner intellectuals, he led a group of right-wingers who opposed the perceived liberalizing of apartheid under P.W. Botha. In 1982 he split off to form the Conservative Party, eclipsing the older far-right Reconstituted National Party (HNP) and triumphing at the 1987 white elections, when his party emerged as the second largest and he became official opposition leader. Recruiting the diehards who reject **F. W. de Klerk**'s road to a constitutional settlement with the black majority, he and his lieutenant Koos van der Merwe now stand as the country's leading right-wingers, confident that Afrikaners would support him in a general election against those he stigmatizes as traitors to the *volk*.

**TRICHET, Jean-Claude**. *France*. Treasury director. Born in 1942 he has degrees in civil engineering and economics and is also a graduate of the Institut d'Etudes Politiques and of the Ecole Nationale d'Administration. By profession a finance inspector, he advised **Valéry Giscard d'Estaing**'s political staff in 1978 and in 1986 was appointed chief of staff (*directeur de cabinet*) to **Edouard Balladur, Jacques Chirac**'s economics and finance minister, subsequently becoming director of the Treasury during **Michel Rocard**'s premiership.

**TROVOADA, Miguel dos Anjos da Cunha**. *São Tomé and Príncipe*. Opposition leader. A pioneer of opposition to Portuguese colonial rule, founder of the Committee for the Liberation of São Tomé and Príncipe in 1960,

Trovoada was the country's first prime minister at independence in 1975. Accused of involvement in an alleged coup attempt against President **Manuel Pinto da Costa** in 1979 he was imprisoned without trial before being allowed to go into exile in France in 1981. Still very popular at home, he returned in May 1990 and announced his intention to stand as an independent in the March 1991 presidential elections.

**TRULY, Richard.** *USA.* Administrator of National Aeronautics and Space Administration (Nasa). Born in 1937 he served as a naval fighter pilot before becoming a Nasa astronaut in 1969. He was appointed director of the space shuttle programme in 1986, shortly after the Challenger disaster, and in 1989 became head of Nasa. Since his appointment he has faced considerable criticism over continuing difficulties with the programme and problems with the Hubble space telescope.

**TRUMPINGTON, Baroness.** *UK.* Minister of state at the Ministry of Agriculture, Fisheries and Food. A Tory stalwart, she was born in 1922, and saw war service with the Women's Land Army. Created a life peer in 1980, she represented the government in the House of Lords on a range of subjects before taking on agriculture in 1987. She was formerly mayor of Cambridge.

**TSHISEKEDI WA MULUMBA, Etienne.** *Zaïre.* Opposition leader. A long-standing opponent of President **Mobutu Sese Seko** and advocate of multi-party democracy, Tshisekedi leads the best-known opposition party, the Union for Democracy and Social Progress (UDPS), established in 1982. The UPDS succeeded in remaining active in Zaïre and abroad during the years in which it was banned. Tshisekedi was released from two years' house arrest in April 1990 and in September announced that he would stand in the 1991 presidential elections.

**TSIKATA, Captain Kojo.** *Ghana.* Government number two. A retired army officer who was at one time former president Kwame Nkrumah's representative with the Angolan People's Liberation Movement (MPLA), he is a close friend and colleague of **Jerry Rawlings** and helped organize the 1979 coup that first brought him to power. Tsikata represents the hardline left wing of the ruling Provisional National Defence Council (PNDC), on which he has responsibility for foreign affairs and security. He first came to prominence in 1975 when he was

imprisoned in connection with a plot by members of the Ewe ethnic group to overthrow the then military government but was released in 1978. Appointed head of security in the second Rawlings government in 1982 with PNDC membership, he rebuilt the Bureau of National Investigations along political lines, stressing loyalty to the PNDC. Tsikata has shown increasing unease with Ghana's recent adoption of free-market capitalism.

**TSUCHIYA, Yoshihiko.** *Japan.* Speaker of House of Councillors (upper house). Born in 1926 in Saitama prefecture, he graduated from Chuo University and served as a member of the Saitama prefectural assembly before entering the House of Councillors in 1965. He was appointed director-general of the Environment Agency under Masayoshi Ohira in 1979. He became speaker of the House of Councillors in 1988, following Masaaki Fujita.

**TUDJMAN, Franjo.** *Yugoslavia.* President of Croatia. Born in 1922 in northern Croatia, he joined Tito's partisans in 1941. After 1945 he studied at the Higher Military Academy in Belgrade and subsequently worked for the federal defence ministry and the Yugoslav army general staff. In 1961 he left the army with the rank of major-general to take up the running of the Institute for the History of the Working Class Movement in Zagreb. In 1963 he became professor of history at the political science faculty of Zagreb University. In 1965 he obtained a doctorate in history. Two years later he was sacked from the institute for signing a declaration demanding that Croat be recognized as the official language of Croatia. He was also expelled from the communist party. In 1972 he was sentenced to two years' imprisonment for "counter-revolutionary activity". He was again sentenced to three years in 1981. Tudjman in 1989 founded the Croat Democratic Union, a mass right-of-centre party, which in 1990 won an overwhelming victory in Croatia's first free election since 1945. He was then elected president of the presidency of Croatia. In office, he has pursued a pro-market economic policy and is strongly in favour of Croatia's association with and eventual entry into the EC. He supports Croatia's membership of a loose, confederal Yugoslavia.

**TUPURKOVSKI, Vasil.** *Yugoslavia.* Macedonia's member of the collective state presidency. Born in 1951 in Skopje, Macedonia, he obtained a doctorate of law in 1976 and is now professor of international law at Skopje

University. He became a party member in 1972 and rose rapidly, to become a member of the presidium of the central committee of the Yugoslav communist party in 1986. In 1989 he was elected at a direct election as Macedonia's member of the collective state presidency.

**TURABI, Hassan Abdullah el-**. *Sudan*. Leader of National Islamic Front (NIF). Born in 1930, a graduate of Khartoum University, with a doctorate of law from the Sorbonne, he is leader of the fundamentalist NIF. A law lecturer in Khartoum, he became a member of the Constituent Assembly in 1965 and was appointed attorney-general by President Jaafar Nimeiri in 1979, paving the way for the introduction of Islamic law in 1983. He also served as presidential adviser on legal and foreign affairs until his dismissal in 1985. El-Turabi took the NIF, formed after a split in the Muslim Brotherhood in the mid-1980s, into a coalition government led by **Sadiq el-Mahdi**, his brother-in-law, in May 1988, with the post of justice minister. He was appointed deputy prime minister and foreign minister following the withdrawal of the Democratic Unionist Party from the coalition in December 1988. His party was excluded, however, from the broad-based coalition formed in March 1989, after pressure from the army to reduce the fundamentalist influence in government. The June 1989 coup, however, placed the reins of power in the hands of El-Turabi's supporters and in March 1990 he admitted that his party had been behind the coup and was directing the implementation of an Islamic programme by the government.

**TURBAY AYALA, Julio César**. *Colombia*. Liberal politician. One of the elder statesmen of the Liberal Party, he was born in 1916 and first elected to the House of Representatives in 1943. He was first made a minister (for mines and energy) in 1957, and was foreign minister from 1958–61. He was successively ambassador to the

UN, UK and USA between 1967 and 1976 and served as president from 1978–82.

**TUTU, Archbishop Desmond**. *South Africa*. Archbishop of Cape Town. Born in 1931, he studied at the University of South Africa, at a theological college and at London University, and was a schoolmaster before becoming an Anglican priest in 1960. He rose to be Bishop of Johannesburg in 1984 and Archbishop of Cape Town since 1986. By this time he had made an international impression as a dedicated anti-apartheid campaigner, articulating the moral outrage of committed Christians as secretary-general of the South African Council of Churches from 1979–84. Awarded the Nobel peace prize in 1984, Tutu was again to the forefront of the protest against the state of emergency in the late 1980s and, with **Allan Boesak**, led the "march for peace" to the Cape Town parliament on the day before **F. W. de Klerk**'s election as state president in September 1989. He remains active in local politics, and was on the "Soweto People's Delegation" which eventually secured concessions to end the three-year rent strike. One of the foremost exponents of non-violence, he has ceded the limelight of late to **Nelson Mandela**, and has praised the political courage of de Klerk's bold reform programme.

**TYMIŃSKI, Stanisław**. *Poland*. Presidential candidate. Born in 1948, he emigrated as a young man, making a successful business career in Canada with interests also in Peru (and citizenship of both those countries). He led the fringe Libertarian Party of Canada, but returned to Poland for the presidential election in November 1990. His campaign featured scathing attacks on alleged government economic mismanagement and extravagant promises about what his business acumen could achieve for Poland. His appeal to the disaffected carried him into the second round run-off, in which he was heavily defeated by Lech Wałęsa.

# U

**UBALDINI, Saúl Edolver**. *Argentina*. Trade union leader. Born in 1938, Ubaldini was a long-standing leader of the brewery workers' union. In 1980 he was appointed secretary-general of the General Confederation of Workers (CGT), the hardline wing of the labour movement. When the CGT splits were healed in 1983 he became joint general secretary, later assuming sole leadership. An active Peronist, his brand of populist Catholicism and socialism has led to him being dubbed the "**Lech Wałęsa** of the River Plate". In 1989 he began to oppose the policies of President **Carlos Menem**, but lost his post as secretary-general in the faction-ridden CGT, although remaining leader of the most powerful group of organized labour.

**UDALL, Morris (Mo)**. *USA*. Democratic congressman from Arizona. Born in 1922, Udall was educated at the University of Arizona, practised law and became county attorney. Elected to the House of Representatives in 1961, he was frustrated in his quest for party leadership posts in the early 1970s, but made a creditable bid for the presidential nomination in 1976, running as a liberal, when he effectively came second to **Jimmy Carter**. As chairman of the interior committee since 1977, he has been active on environmental issues, seeing through laws controlling strip mining, protecting Alaska's wilderness, expanding federal wilderness land, and raising the liability of commercial nuclear reactor operators. Also active on the post office committee, he piloted the Carter administration's civil service reform legislation. Diagnosis of Parkinson's disease probably prevented him running for the presidential nomination in 1984 and the speakership in 1986, and looks like forcing his retirement from Congress.

**UNGO, Guillermo Manuel**. *El Salvador*. Left-wing leader. A lawyer and university professor, born in 1931, Ungo has led the socialist National Revolutionary Movement (MNR) since it was founded in 1965. He was José Napoleón Duarte's vice-presidential running mate in 1972. In 1979 he joined the military-civilian junta, but resigned in 1980 because of its drift to the right. Forced into exile, he joined with others to form the Revolutionary Democratic Front (FDR) as the political arm of the Farabundo Martí National Liberation Front (FMLN) guerrilla movement and became its president in late 1980. He returned to El Salvador in 1988 to campaign as presidential candidate of the left-wing Democratic Convergence (CD).

**UNNIKRISHNAN, K.P.** *India*. Congress (S) politician. Born in 1936 in Coimbatore and originally an activist in the socialist movement, he joined Congress and became a member of its leadership in 1962. He was first elected to the Lok Sabha (lower house) in 1971. He left Congress (I) in 1979 for Congress (U), later to become Congress (S), which he represented in the 1989–90 National Front government as surface transport and communications minister.

**UPENDRA, P.** *India*. Telugu Desam (TD) general secretary. Born in 1936 in Andhra Pradesh, a journalist by training, he joined the regionalist TD party in 1982 and became its general secretary in 1983. He represented the TD in the 1989–90 National Front government as information and broadcasting minister.

**URRUTIKOETXEA BENGOETXEA, José Antonio**. *Spain*. Basque nationalist leader. Born in Miravilles in the Basque region in 1950, he became involved with the Basque nationalist movement ETA while studying engineering at Deusto University. He was implicated in the murder of Admiral Carrero Blanco in Madrid in 1973, subsequently fleeing to France. He joined ETA's executive in 1975 and was later put in charge of the organization's international apparatus. Known in the organization as Josu Ternera, and regarded as a hardline opponent of talks with the Spanish government, he became ETA's leader after the arrest of Santiago Arrospide in September 1987. He himself was arrested in Bayonne, France, in January 1989.

**URSU, Doru Viorel.** *Romania.* Interior minister. Born in Dobreta-Turnu Severin in 1953, he studied law at Bucharest University and became a prosecutor and military judge. As president of the military tribunal in Bucharest, he presided over the first part of the trial in Sibiu of Nicu Ceauşescu, before being appointed interior minister in June 1990, following the violent suppression of the student-led protest movement.

# V

VAELAES, Vaino. *USSR*. Estonian Communist Party leader. Born in 1931, he was a party official who transferred to the diplomatic service in 1975, serving as ambassador to Jamaica, Venezuela and Nicaragua, before returning to Estonia as Communist Party first secretary in June 1988. At the March 1990 Estonian Party congress (when it was decided in principle to seek independence from the Communist Party of the Soviet Union), Vaelaes was elected to the new post of party chairman.

VAJPAYEE, Atal Behari. *India.* Member of Rajya Sabha (upper house) and general secretary of the Bharatiya Janata Party (BJP). Born in 1926, in Gwalior, Madhya Pradesh, he was imprisoned during the Quit India agitation of 1942. In 1951 he became a founder-member of the Hindu communalist Bharatiya Jan Sangh, serving as its president from 1968–73. He was elected to the Lok Sabha (lower house) in 1957 and has served continuously in either the Lok Sabha or the Rajya Sabha ever since. His opposition to Indira Gandhi led to a spell of imprisonment during the emergency of 1975–77. The Jan Sangh fused with other opposition parties into the Janata Party in 1977 and Vajpayee served as external affairs minister in the Janata government of 1977–79. After the break-up of the Janata coalition the Jan Sangh reformed as the BJP, with Vajpayee as its first president. In 1986 he became its general secretary.

VALEŠ, Václav. *Czechoslovakia.* Deputy premier. Brought back to the government at the age of 68 by his former dissident friend **Václav Havel** in April 1990, and retained in the June post-election reshuffle, he had been deputy premier in 1969, before the purges that followed the fall of **Alexander Dubček** really took hold. He is an expert economist, with the brief of overseeing economic reform, and is classified as an unaffiliated member of the government, although as a founder-member of Charter 77 he is identified with other former dissidents such as Havel and **Jiří Dienstbier**.

VALLEJO ARCO, Andrés. *Ecuador.* Government and justice minister. A member of the Democratic Left (ID), Vallejo was president of Congress during the 1984–88 **Febres Cordero** presidency and was appointed government and justice minister in 1988. He was responsible for the negotiations with guerrilla groups that brought to an end their armed struggle.

VAN DEN BROEK, Hans. *Netherlands.* Foreign minister. Born in 1936, he studied law at Utrecht University and then practised in Rotterdam from 1965–68 before joining the synthetic-fibre company Enka. Active in local government in the early 1970s, he was elected to the Staten Generaal (parliament) in 1976. He was appointed a state secretary (junior minister) for foreign affairs in 1981 and foreign minister in **Ruud Lubbers**'s first administration in 1982. A committed European and Atlanticist, his first two terms in the post were dogged by criticism that he blindly followed the lines laid down by the larger Nato and EC countries and failed to develop initiatives of his own. In the 1980s he argued strongly for deployment of Cruise missiles, a stance which caused considerable unease even within the Christian Democrats (and actually brought him into conflict with the then defence minister, Jacob de Reiter, a party colleague). Stung by allegations of inactivity, he has adopted a higher profile, particularly since his confirmation in the post in November 1989 in Lubbers's third administration.

VAN DER MERWE, Stoffel. *South Africa.* Minister in the office of the state president in charge of information. Born in 1939, a career diplomat from 1962 and an MP since 1981, he took up his present job in 1988 after two years as Pik Botha's deputy. One of the new **F. W. de Klerk** generation, his appeal is to younger educated Afrikaners, and he is on the government's inner negotiating team for the crucial forthcoming constitutional talks.

VAN DER VLIES, B.J. *Netherlands.* Fundamentalist Calvinist politician. Born in

1942, he studied engineering and worked in the education service before being elected to the Staten Generaal (parliament) in 1981 for the Political Reformed Party (SGP) which, though small, enjoys consistent electoral support in some rural areas. He has led the party's parliamentary group since 1987.

**VAN-DÚNEM, Pedro de Castro dos Santos (Loy).** *Angola.* Foreign minister. A rising star of the ruling Angolan People's Liberation Movement (MPLA) and long-standing member of the politburo, Van-Dúnem is a leader of the reforming wing of the party. A Soviet-trained economist, he was petroleum and energy minister until 1986, when in a reshuffle aimed at reducing hardline opposition to economic reform he was made one of three "super" ministers and was given added responsibility for the entire productive sector. Since 1988 he has been increasingly involved in negotiations to end the civil war; in 1989 this role was confirmed when he replaced the more conservative Afonso Van-Dúnem as foreign minister.

**VAN HEERDEN, Neil.** *South Africa.* Director-general of the foreign affairs department. He is credited with masterminding **Pik Botha**'s diplomatic breakthroughs, in the Angola and Namibia settlements in particular. The son of a senior army officer, he enjoys cordial relations with the military hierarchy, and is widely expected to use his skills to good effect in higher office.

**VAN LEDE, Cees.** *Netherlands.* Industrialist. Born in 1942, he studied law and worked briefly for the Shell group before joining management consultant McKinsey. In 1976 he became director of a large construction firm. In 1984 he was elected president of the Federation of Dutch Industries (VNO), the main employers' organization.

**VAN MIERLO, Hans.** *Netherlands.* Left-of-centre politician. Born in 1931, he was one of the founding members of the mould-breaking Democrats 66 (D66), whose main planks were decentralization of decision-making and, later, environmentalism. Elected to the Staten Generaal (parliament) in 1967, he has led the party from 1967–73 and again since 1986. From 1981–82 he was briefly defence minister in a centre–left coalition, and from 1983–86 was a member of the First Chamber (upper house of parliament) for D66.

**VANDER JAGT, Guy.** *USA.* Republican congressman from Minnesota. Born in 1931, he was a lawyer and state legislator before election

to the House of Representatives in 1966. As chairman of the House Republican Campaign Committee, he won plaudits for the party's strong showing in 1980 and was nearly elected minority leader as a result. Later Republican defeats deflated his reputation.

**VANDER ZALM, William.** *Canada.* Premier of British Columbia. Born in 1934 in Noordwykerhout, The Netherlands, Vander Zalm attended school there and finished his education in British Columbia (BC). Active in local politics, he was elected to the provincial legislative assembly for the right-wing Social Credit Party in 1975. He left politics for business in 1983, setting up a "Fantasy Garden World" theme park in Richmond, BC. He returned to provincial politics in 1986 as party leader and was elected premier in the same year.

**VARGAS LLOSA, Mario.** *Peru.* Opposition politician. Born in Bolivia in 1936 and educated in Lima and Madrid, Vargas Llosa began his career as a journalist and broadcaster. Since his first book, *Los Jefes*, was published in 1958 he has acquired an international reputation as a writer and novelist, living abroad for much of the time. He stood as presidential candidate for the right-wing Democratic Front (Fredemo) coalition in the 1990 elections. Although ahead in the polls in the early stages, his policies failed to appeal suffficiently beyond the middle classes and he was defeated by **Alberto Fujimori**.

**VASSILIOU, George.** *Cyprus.* President. Born in 1931 in Famagusta, he is the son of two medical professionals. His father helped the communist insurgents during the Greek civil war and after their defeat the family was in exile in Eastern Europe, where Vassiliou gained a doctorate in economics at Budapest University. He supported the reform movement crushed by the Soviet invasion of Hungary in 1956, and then fled to London, where he worked as an economist and market researcher. Returning to Cyprus after independence he established Middle East Marketing Research Bureau, a consulting firm that flourished during the oil crises of the 1970s, making him a millionaire. In February 1988, he was elected president of the republic as an independent but with the tacit backing of the communist Progressive Party of the Working People (Akel). During 1989–90, he took part in over 100 hours of face-to-face negotiations with Turkish Cypriot leader **Rauf Denktas**, but failed to secure the federal settlement he sought for the divided island.

**VAUZELLE, Michel.** *France.* Socialist politician. Born in 1944 and a graduate of the Institut d'Etudes Politiques, he initially worked as a lawyer and as a civil servant. A member of the Socialist Party (PS), he became a deputy mayor from 1977–83, and was recognized in the party as an influential voice, particularly on judicial affairs. In 1981 he was appointed deputy director of **François Mitterrand**'s presidential staff office and official presidential spokesman until 1986, when he was elected to the National Assembly; he presides over the assembly's important foreign affairs committee. In the Gulf crisis that flared up in 1990 he became *de facto* envoy for Mitterrand.

**VEIGA, Carlos.** *Cape Verde.* Movement for Democracy (MPD) leader. A former public prosecutor, born in 1949, Veiga leads the MPD, set up in February 1990 to contest the country's first ever multi-party elections in 1991.

**VEIL, Simone.** *France.* Centrist liberal politician. Born in 1927, and a graduate of the Institut d'Etudes Politiques, she was persecuted by the Nazis for being a Jew, and later worked as an attaché to the justice ministry. Given her opportunity to make her own mark from 1974, as **Valéry Giscard d'Estaing**'s health minister, she pushed through controversial legislation liberalizing abortion and has retained a high political profile since then, ranking as France's most popular woman politician. Since 1979 her main political activity has been at the European level. She led successful campaigns in the 1979 and 1984 European Parliament elections, was elected president of the parliament at Strasbourg in 1979, and president of the Liberal group there from 1984. In the 1989 European election, however, she suffered from the division between her liberal centrist group and Giscard's united right-wing list.

**VELAYATI, Ali Akbar.** *Iran.* Foreign minister. Born in Tehran in 1945, Velayati taught as an associate professor at the hygiene sciences college before the 1979 revolution, and has also studied in the USA. After holding various junior ministerial posts in the health field, he became foreign minister in December 1981. One of the regime's leading moderates, Velayati has skilfully kept Iranian windows open to the outside world. He was retained as foreign minister when **Ali Akbar Hashemi Rafsanjani** became president in 1989 and shares the latter's wish for closer ties with the West.

**VELÁZQUEZ SÁNCHEZ, Fidel.** *Mexico.* Trade unionist. Born in 1900, "Don Fidel" is Mexico's longest-serving and most powerful union leader. He helped to found the Confederation of Mexican Workers (CTM) and became its secretary-general in 1941. He had two spells as a senator in the 1940s and 1950s. His loyalty to the ruling Institutional Revolutionary Party (PRI) has helped to ensure that organized labour has made no effective challenge to the party's monopoly of power.

**VENKATARAMAN, Ramaswamy.** *India.* President. Born in 1910 in Madras state, he trained as a lawyer, and was imprisoned during the Quit India agitation of 1942–44. He was a member of the provisional parliament of 1950–52 and served in the Lok Sabha (lower house) from 1952–57. He then entered state politics in the Madras legislative council, becoming state industry and labour minister, a position he held until 1967 when he was appointed to the national planning commission. He was a member of the Indian delegation to the UN General Assembly from 1953–61. He returned to the Lok Sabha in 1977 serving as union finance minister in 1980–82 and defence minister from 1982–84. He became vice-president of India in 1984. Towards the end of his term of office, President Zail Singh became embroiled in a dispute with **Rajiv Gandhi**, alleging that he was not properly consulted on state affairs. Congress decided not to support Singh for a second term and named Venkataraman as its candidate, believing him to be a loyal and pliant supporter of the Congress leadership. Venkataraman took office in July 1987 and proved to be an independent figure, defending the president's prerogatives. He appeared to have found no difficulty in working with a non-Congress government after November 1989. When **V.P. Singh**'s government was brought down in November 1990, he first invited Gandhi to form a government, turning to **Chandra Shekhar** when Gandhi declined.

**VIEIRA, General João Bernardo.** *Guinea-Bissau.* President. Born in 1939, Vieira is a veteran of the guerrilla war that led to independence from Portugal in 1975. In 1980, when prime minister, he deposed the country's first president, Luiz Cabral, accusing him of economic mismanagement. The coup, which came at a time of food shortages, was initially popular, reflecting resentment amongst Guineans of the Cape Verdean mixed-race elite, including Cabral, who had dominated the administration and the two countries' joint ruling party, the African Party for the Independence of Guinea and Cape Verde (PAIGC). The coup led to a rift with Cape Verde, and Vieira's rule has since been marred by factional disputes and a series of attempted or alleged coups. By 1990, however, Vieira appeared to feel sufficiently secure to contemplate cautious political liberalization.

**VIERA-GALLO QUESNAY, José Antonio.** *Chile.* President of the Chamber of Deputies. Born in 1943, Viera-Gallo studied law at the Catholic University and pursued an academic career. He was a member of the Socialist Party (PSCh) and under-secretary of justice in the Salvador Allende administration. He was elected as a socialist deputy in the 1989 elections and chosen by the chamber as its president.

**VIGOUROUX, Robert.** *France.* Mayor of Marseilles. Born in 1923 and a hospital surgeon by profession, he has occupied a prominent position in Marseilles politics, initially as a county councillor and then, from 1971–86, as deputy mayor to the redoubtable Gaston Defferre. Following Defferre's death in 1986, Vigouroux became mayor, in what was seen as a caretaker role. However, in 1989 he retained the job, running controversially and defiantly against the official candidate of his own Socialist Party (PS). In the process he enhanced his reputation as a capable practitioner of broad consensus-style politics. In the same year he became a senator. In November 1990 he founded a new body to promote consensus politics, with himself as its president.

**VILJOEN, Gerrit.** *South Africa.* Constitutional development minister. Born in 1926, and educated as a classicist at the universities of Cambridge, Leiden and the Sorbonne, he was a university professor, and chairman of the secret but highly influential Afrikaner grouping, the Broederbond, from 1974 until he was chosen to go to Namibia as administrator-general in 1979. Recalled the following year, he was national education minister for four years, then took on co-operation and development, until **F. W. de Klerk** promoted him in September 1989 to the key job in charge of constitutional development. He ranks with **Kobie Coetsee** as de Klerk's closest cabinet confidant, and will figure as the government's leading negotiator in the constitutional conference.

**VILLALOBOS, Joaquín.** *El Salvador.* Guerrilla leader. Born in 1951, Villalobos became the principal left-wing guerrilla leader in 1983 as commander of the People's Revolutionary Army (ERP) and one of the leaders of the Farabundo Martí National Liberation Front (FMLN).

**VILLIGER, Kaspar.** *Switzerland.* Defence minister. Born in Pfeffikon in 1941, he graduated in engineering from Zürich technical university. After serving in the cantonal parliament he moved into national politics as a member of the Radical Democratic Party (FDP). He became defence minister in 1989.

**VISENTINI, Bruno.** *Italy.* Businessman and Italian Republican Party (PRI) politician. Born in 1914 in Treviso, he graduated in law, was a member of the board of state holding company IRI (Istituto per la Ricostruzione Industriale) from 1948–72, and chairman of Ing. C Olivetti & C from 1964–74. He rejoined Olivetti in 1976 and served as either vice-chairman or chairman until 1983, with a brief interruption when he held government office in 1979. Elected to the Chamber of Deputies in 1972, he moved to the Senate in 1976, becoming president of the PRI in September 1979. He was also a member of the European Parliament from 1979–84. At various times since November 1974, he has held cabinet office, notably as finance minister from 1983–87. He has a reputation for financial rectitude and has been outspoken in his criticism of government over-spending. Since 1987, he has been chairman of Carlo De Benedetti's holding company CIR (Compagnie Industriali Riunite) and honorary chairman of Olivetti. Visentini has been active in campaigning for the preservation of Venice.

**VIZZINI, Carlo.** *Italy.* Merchant navy minister and Italian Democratic Socialist Party (PSDI) politician. Born in 1947 in Palermo, he graduated in law and was elected to the Chamber of Deputies in 1976. Deputy secretary of the PSDI from 1980–88, he first attained cabinet rank as minister for the regions from 1984–87. Subsequently, he held office as culture minister and in July 1989 was appointed merchant navy minister.

**VLLASI, Azem.** *Yugoslavia.* Leading Kosovo politician. Born in 1948, he is an ethnic Albanian from Kosovo. He has held a series of senior communist party posts in Kosovo, including president of the Kosovo party presidium from 1986–87 and was a central committee member from 1982–86 and again from May 1988 to February 1989. In March 1989 he was detained, following civil disturbances in Kosovo, and a month later was expelled from the party for allegedly contributing to intra-national divisions in

Kosovo. After over a year in jail on charges of counter-revolution, he was acquitted and released in April 1990.

**VLOK, Adriaan.** *South Africa.* Law and order minister. Born in 1937, he was a career civil servant, with a spell in J.B. Vorster's private office, until he won election as a National Party MP in 1974. Promoted from deputy to full minister of law and order in 1986, he has been convincing in his loyalty to the government, and prepared to take a tough line on security issues. He has spoken strongly of a police crackdown on Afrikaner Resistance Movement (AWB) neo-fascist infiltration of the security forces, but African National Congress critics remain to be convinced of his good faith, especially in view of his September 1990 talks with conservative **Andries Treurnicht** and old-style right-winger Jaap Marais of the Reconstituted National Party (HNP).

**VO CHI CONG.** *Vietnam.* President. Born in central Vietnam in 1912, Cong played a major role in the revolutionary struggle south of the 17th parallel. After re-unification in 1976 he entered the politburo and was appointed deputy prime minister. Despite rumours that he would replace the veteran Pham Van Dong as premier in mid-1987, he was instead appointed to the largely ceremonial post of president.

**VO NGUYEN GIAP, General.** *Vietnam.* Deputy prime minister and supreme military tactician. He taught French history in Hanoi until disappearing in the early 1940s to join Ho Chin Minh. He was appointed interior minister in 1945, but during the war against the French, Giap established himself as Ho's supreme military leader. His political influence was greatly enhanced by his tactical triumph at Dien Bien Phu in 1954. As defence minister, he played a major role in North Vietnam's success in the war against the USA, but he was inexplicably replaced in 1980 and dropped from the politburo in 1982. He remains, however, the most active and charismatic figure within the old-guard leadership; his visit to Beijing in September 1990 marked a great improvement in relations with Vietnam's old rival.

**VO VAN KIET.** *Vietnam.* Senior deputy prime minister and politburo member. Born in South Vietnam in 1922, Kiet played a prominent role in the Communist Party's southern nerve-centre (COSVN) during the war against the USA. His career runs parallel to that of **Nguyen Van Linh.** Appointed chairman of the State Planning Commission in 1982, Kiet pioneered Vietnam's

economic restructuring and became acting prime minister in March 1988. However, in June, northern deputies outnumbered Kiet's southern supporters in a National Assembly vote to select a new premier and Kiet was replaced by the conservative **Do Muoi.**

**VOGEL, Hans-Jochen.** *Germany.* Social Democratic Party (SPD) chairman. Born in Göttingen in 1926, he gained his doctorate in law in 1952 and was elected as SPD mayor of Munich in 1960. Having risen to prominence so rapidly, he was marked out as a future party leader, but ran into damaging conflicts with left-wingers in the local party, and resigned as mayor in 1972. He went to Bonn and into the federal government, first as planning, construction and urban building minister, and then for seven years as justice minister. In 1981 his career suffered a setback when he lost an election in West Berlin (to **Richard von Weizsäcker**), after the SPD had asked him to take on the job of mayor in an effort to save the party there from disintegration. The SPD executive kept faith with Vogel, choosing him to challenge **Helmut Kohl** for the chancellorship in 1983, but his defeat left the party little option but to turn to other candidates for 1987 and 1990 (first **Johannes Rau,** then **Oskar Lafontaine**). He was to step down as SPD chairman in May 1991 but was confirmed as chairman of the SPD's parliamentary leader in December 1990. Vogel's younger brother Bernhard used to be the Christian Democratic Union premier of the Rhineland-Palatinate, and the two remain close.

**VOINOVICH, George.** *USA.* Republican governor of Ohio. Born in 1936, he built his political career in Cleveland, becoming mayor of the city and taking credit for an impressive revival in its economic fortunes. From this power base, and with a reputation as a pragmatist, he was his party's unopposed choice to wrest the governorship from the Democrats in 1990. Holding to a firm pro-life stance on the emotive abortion issue, he was an unexpectedly easy winner of the election.

**VOLLMER, Antje.** *Germany.* Green politician. Born in 1943, Vollmer holds a doctorate in theology and worked as a parson in Berlin before entering the Bundestag in 1983 as one of the first wave of Green deputies.

**VON WEIZSÄCKER, Richard.** *Germany.* President. Before his election as president in 1984, he had been Christian Democratic Union governing mayor of West Berlin, where he had defeated **Hans-Jochen Vogel** in 1981. It is testimony to his success in presenting a non-partisan image that von Weizsäcker won Vogel's support and the backing of the opposition Social Democratic Party when he stood for the presidency. Born in 1920 in Stuttgart, he was the son of a leading diplomat who was sentenced for war crimes at the Nuremberg trials in 1945. He reached the rank of captain in the wartime army and then studied law at Oxford, Grenoble and Tübingen universities, gaining his doctorate in 1955. Admired for his work for reconciliation with Germany's eastern neighbours, he is generally respected and regarded as a successful president.

**VORONIN, Lev.** *USSR.* Former first deputy prime minister. A Russian born in 1928, he worked in the mining and heavy engineering industries in the Urals until 1968, when he was appointed head of planning and production administration in the USSR defence industry ministry. He was named deputy defence industry minister in 1979, first deputy chairman of the State Planning Committee (Gosplan) in 1980, then deputy premier and chairman of the USSR State Committee for Material and Technical Supply in 1985. In July 1989 he was promoted to be one of three first deputy premiers, and given the portfolio for "general questions".

**VORONTSOV, Nikolai.** *USSR.* Environment minister. A doctor of biology, born in 1934, he was reportedly a reluctant appointee in 1989 to chair the new State Environmental Protection Committee, responsible for trying to reverse the USSR's ecological catastrophe. His status as a non-communist (the first ever to serve in the USSR government) may help him to win the support and co-operation of the proliferating environmentalist groups. He has argued that vested economic interests pose his greatest problem.

**VOSCHERAU, Henning.** *Germany.* Mayor of Hamburg. A native of Hamburg, its mayor since 1988 and head of the senate there, he is pledged to wage war on the city's serious drugs problem. Born in 1941, he was first elected to the Hamburg parliament in 1974, and chaired the local Social Democratic Party parliamentary group from 1982–87.

**VRANITZKY, Franz.** *Austria.* Chancellor. Born in Vienna in 1937, he has a doctorate in commerce. A member of the Socialist Party of Austria (SPÖ), he was elected party chairman in 1988. Vranitzky held senior posts at various banks including the central bank, and Kreditanstalt-Bankverein, the country's biggest bank, whose deputy chairman he became in 1976. Subsequently he became chairman of Österreichische Länderbank in 1981. His ministerial career began in 1984 when he was appointed finance minister. He was sworn in as Austria's chancellor in 1986. He has enjoyed a reputation as a clean member of a political establishment bedevilled by scandals and his party has successfully emphasized his personal popularity to divert attention from these. At the October 1990 elections Vranitzky – normally a man of great caution – nailed his colours to the mast with a declaration that he would not contemplate sharing power with **Jörg Haider**'s right-wing Freedom Party. The election result reinforced his standing, with the Socialists retaining their pre-eminent position. Of partly Czech origin, his priorities include rebuilding the historic links in central Europe, while pursuing EC membership and dismantling some of the cumbersome apparatus of state economic management.

**VULKOV, Viktor.** *Bulgaria.* Deputy premier and foreign minister. Leader of the Bulgarian Agrarian People's Union (BZNS, which had been the junior partner in the communist-dominated Fatherland Front until 1989), Vulkov opposed a merger with the main opposition coalition Union of Democratic Forces (UDF) and led his party as a separate formation in the June 1990 elections, when it won 16 seats. In July 1990 he came within three votes of election as the country's president, with the support of the Bulgarian Socialist Party (BSP), but then withdrew and **Zhelyu Zhelev** was elected with BSP and UDF support. When the BZNS joined the transitional coalition government formed by **Dimitur Popov** in December 1990, Vulkov became a deputy premier and foreign minister, while the agriculture portfolio went to his party colleague Boris Spirov.

# W

WADDINGTON, Lord (David Waddington). *UK*. Lord Privy Seal and leader of the House of Lords, MP since 1974. Born in 1929, he was called to the Bar in 1951, and after junior ministerial office at employment and the Home Office, he was catapulted into the home secretary's job in 1989, when **Douglas Hurd** replaced **John Major** at the Foreign and Commonwealth Office. During his first short term in office he had already had to deal with prison unrest and with the damaging legal and political consequences of police corruption, in the wake of successful appeals by those wrongly convicted in the 1970s of IRA terrorist crimes. He was moved from the Home Office and created a life peer by John Major in 1990.

WADE, Abdoulaye. *Senegal*. Opposition politician. Born in 1927. A lawyer of international standing, he was a loyal supporter of President Léopold Senghor until persuaded to form an opposition party, the Democratic Party of Senegal (PDS), as part of the constitutional reforms of 1973 which introduced a limited multi-party system. In opposition, Wade became a strident critic of government corruption and state socialism, winning increasing support in urban areas and in the disaffected southern Casamance region. Wade has been his party's presidential candidate in three elections; in the wake of the 1988 elections, when widespread rioting greeted the announcement of the results, he was arrested on charges of threatening national security and given a one-year suspended sentence. Wade's supporters continue to claim that he was the real victor in the 1988 elections and he remains President **Abdou Diouf**'s most formidable opponent.

WAECHTER, Antoine. *France*. Ecologist and Green politician. Born in 1949 and a doctor of biology, he is an ecological engineer and consultant by profession. A veteran of many local, regional and national ecologist campaigns, he became a regional councillor in 1986, and spokesman for the Greens, winning the party over (in opposition to the **Brice Lalonde** line) to

his political strategy of refusing to be aligned (or co-opted) either by the left or the right. In 1988, he achieved an honourable 3.8% in the presidential election, subsequently leading the Greens to local and European election successes in 1989, when he became a member of the European Parliament and a leader of the Green group within the parliament.

WAHONO, Lieutenant-General. *Indonesia*. Chairman of Golkar. Born in 1925, a career soldier turned bureaucrat, Wahono was appointed chairman of the government-sponsored party Golkar in 1988. A solid and unambitious figure, Wahono is known to be close to **Suharto**, having served under his military command in the 1960s.

WAIGEL, Theo. *Germany*. Finance minister and Christian Social Union (CSU) leader. Born in 1939, he obtained a doctorate in law and worked as a lawyer in the Bavarian state service before entering the Bundestag in 1972, becoming CSU spokesman on economic affairs. He served as chairman of the CSU group in the Bundestag from 1982 and took over as party leader after the death of Franz Josef Strauss in 1988. As finance minister since 1989 he played a key role in the delicate negotiations with East Germany over monetary and social union, and has emerged alongside Bundesbank governor **Karl Otto Pöhl** as a voice of caution about the costs of European economic union.

WAIHEE, John, III. *USA*. Democratic governor of Hawaii. Born in 1926, he was a lawyer, community administrator and state legislator, before his election as lieutenant governor in 1982. Elected in 1986, he became the first governor of native Hawaiian ancestry. He has continued his predecessors' policies of supporting land development.

WAJED, Sheikh Hasina. *Bangladesh*. Awami League leader. She inherited leadership of the moderate socialist and secular Awami League on the overthrow and murder in 1975 of her father, prime minister Sheikh Mujibur Rahman. The league was the principal party of opposition to the government of Bangladesh Nationalist Party (BNP) leader president Ziaur Rahman. When Lieutenant-General **Hussein Mohammed Ershad** seized power in 1982, the league became the focus of one opposition alliance, and the BNP (led by Ziaur Rahman's widow **Begum Khaleda Zia**) became the core of another, in the extra-parliamentary campaign for the restoration of democracy. She came under intense pressure from Dhaka student demonstrators to sink her differences with Begum Zia in the interest of opposition unity. Rejecting the use of violence, she has been unpredictable in her tactics, flirting with the possibility of participation before swinging back to rejectionism and courting arrest when the anti-government campaign last peaked in November 1987. Recriminations between her and Begum Zia provoked her public charge in April 1989 that her rival had been involved in the assassination of her father, and Begum Zia's counter-charge alleging Hasina's involvement in the death of her husband in 1981. After Ershad's fall in December 1990, she announced her candidacy for the February elections, promising to remain true to her father's ideals.

**WAKEHAM, John**. *UK.* Secretary of state for energy since 1989, MP since 1974. A dependable party man and skilful politician, Wakeham was born in 1932 and trained as an accountant. After several junior ministerial posts he became chief whip in 1983, but suffered personal tragedy when his wife Roberta was killed in the IRA's Brighton bombing of 1984. Appointed Lord Privy Seal and leader of the House of Commons in 1987, he succeeded **Cecil Parkinson** at energy two years later, inheriting the difficult task of electricity privatization.

**WALDE, Eberhard Matthias**. *Germany.* Green politician. Born in 1949, he trained as a motor mechanic. A founder member of the Greens in Lower Saxony, he has been business manager of the party since 1982.

**WALDEGRAVE, William**. *UK.* Secretary of state for health since November 1990, MP since 1979. Born in 1946, the son of Earl Waldegrave, he is a moderate and highly intelligent "one nation" Tory. Educated at Eton College and Oxford University, he joined the Downing Street political staff in **Edward Heath**'s last year in power and served in education and environment posts from 1983–88.

**WALDHEIM, Kurt**. *Austria.* President. Born in 1918, he was UN secretary-general from 1972–81. On his return to Austria his "elder statesman" image helped him win election in 1986 as the first post-war non-socialist president. In this role, however, he has been a controversial figure, and internationally isolated because of persistent allegations that he had been involved in Nazi war crimes during service in the German army as an intelligence corps lieutenant in Yugoslavia. An international committee set up to investigate his war record found no evidence of complicity, but felt he had known more than he admitted. As a young man Waldheim studied at the consular academy in Vienna, gained a doctorate in law from Vienna University in 1944, and began a diplomatic career after the war, with postings including Canada and a term as permanent representative to the UN. He was foreign minister from 1966–70, and narrowly failed to win the presidency as the Austrian People's Party (ÖVP) candidate in 1971. Returning to the UN as Austria's permanent representative, he was chosen, as the candidate favoured by the Western powers and against strong opposition, to succeed U Thant as UN secretary-general. He faced a third-world challenge to his re-election in 1976, and was blocked by a Chinese veto when he sought a third term at the end of 1981. He went on to a professorship in diplomacy at Georgetown University in Washington DC, prior to his return to Austrian politics.

**WAŁĘSA, Lech**. *Poland.* President. Born in 1943 into a peasant family, he began work as an electrician for a collective farm administration in his native Włocławek province. Returning briefly to that work after military service (1963–65), in 1967 he moved to Gdańsk and became an electrician in the Lenin shipyard. When workers' protests erupted in the Baltic ports in December 1970 he headed a workshop strike committee. In 1976, an outburst against conditions in the shipyard at a trade union meeting cost him his job. He found work in a machine repair shop, but in 1979 was sacked for participating in anniversary commemorations of the 1970 protests. When a strike was called in the Lenin shipyard in August 1980 he joined the strikers and became head of the Gdańsk "inter-factory committee". At the end of August he signed with government leaders the "Gdańsk accords", which allowed free trade unions and the right to strike. Solidarity was created in September, with Wałęsa as chairman of the national co-ordinating commission. These events made him a political figure of national and international standing. By the time of

Solidarity's first delegate conference in September 1981, when Wałęsa was elected union chairman, tensions within Solidarity and strains in relations with the government were severe; when the Solidarity leadership in December proposed a referendum on ending communist rule the authorities declared martial law. Wałęsa was detained for 11 months. Early in 1983 he returned to work at the Lenin shipyard. In October 1983 he was awarded the Nobel peace prize for championing workers' rights, but was denied an exit visa to receive it in person in Oslo. While Solidarity was underground he remained titular head, and in October 1987 he resumed an active leadership role as chairman of a national executive commission. When industrial unrest in 1988 forced the government to seek accommodation with the opposition he negotiated the convening of round-table talks. Early in 1989 these produced Solidarity's re-legalization and democratic reforms. After the partly free June 1989 elections, he persuaded parties previously allied to the communist Polish United Workers' Party to defect to a Solidarity-led coalition government, ending communist rule. He sponsored **Tadeusz Mazowiecki** for prime minister, but by mid-1990 he was at odds with Mazowiecki's government over economic policy and Solidarity's future structure. His declared presidential ambitions also caused a rift with other veteran Solidarity leaders who accused him of behaving "like a Caesar". He nevertheless gained a landslide victory in the presidential elections in December 1990, defeating emigré businessman **Stanisław Tymiński**, who had come second in the first round. Wałęsa's campaign was based on accelerating the reform programme to combat social unrest. After his election, Wałęsa resigned as leader of Solidarity.

**WALI, Yusuf Amin**. *Egypt*. Agriculture and land reclamation minister, deputy prime minister. First appointed to the cabinet as agriculture minister in the major reshuffle of January 1982 that followed Anwar Sadat's assassination, the avuncular Wali is a long-term advocate of economic reform. This fact, combined with his unswerving loyalty, has guaranteed him a steady rise through the government and ruling party hierarchies. Appointed to the National Democratic Party political bureau in October 1984, he became its secretary-general in September 1985, when he was also elevated to one of the four new posts of deputy prime minister. In November 1986 his

portfolio was changed to include land reclamation – a key plank of Egypt's agricultural strategy that is assuming growing political importance as population pressures become even more acute.

**WALKER, Robert**. *USA*. Republican congressman from Pennsylvania. Born in 1942, he was a school teacher and congressional aide before being elected to the House of Representatives in 1976. A conservative who takes a confrontational partisan line, he is a close ally of **Newt Gingrich** and he can often be found on the House floor, in front of the TV cameras. He was appointed deputy whip in 1989. Drug control is his main legislative interest.

**WALLMANN, Walter**. *Germany*. Hesse premier. Christian Democratic Union premier of Hesse since 1987, he is the dominant figure in local politics, having risen to prominence as mayor of Frankfurt in 1977–86. Born in 1932, he studied law and politics before beginning a legal career. His one brief spell in federal government, in 1986–87, was notable because he was the country's first cabinet-level minister for the environment, nature protection and nuclear safety.

**WALTERS, Sir Alan**. *UK*. Monetarist radical and **Margaret Thatcher**'s chief economic adviser from 1981–84 and again in 1989. Born in 1926, he opposes Britain's membership of the European exchange-rate mechanism (ERM) and believes that sterling should be allowed to find its own level. His thinly veiled criticism of **Nigel Lawson**'s policy of shadowing the Deutschmark and Lawson's advocacy of ERM membership came to a head with the resignation of both men in 1989.

**WALTERS, David**. *USA*. Democratic governor of Oklahoma. Born in 1936 and a successful businessman, he won the governorship in 1990.

**WAN LI**. *China*. Chairman of National People's Congress Standing Committee. Born in 1916, Wan's background is in urban construction. A former vice-premier, he is also a Politburo member. In May 1989 pro-democracy activists called on Wan as a moderate and head of the parliament to dissolve the government. In the end, he decided – under pressure, many say – to back the subsequent military crackdown.

**WANG BINGQIAN**. *China*. State counsellor. Born in 1925, Wang worked his way up in the finance ministry to become minister in 1980, and a World Bank governor in 1986. A state counsellor since 1983, he heads various government financial bodies and is honorary chairman of the China Investment Bank.

**WANG FANG.** *China.* State counsellor. Born in 1920, Wang held internal security posts in Zhejiang, becoming provincial party secretary in 1983. Retiring from the Central Committee in 1987, he joined the Central Advisory Commission and became public security minister and party chief in the People's Armed Police. In 1988, he became state counsellor in charge of legal affairs. In December 1990 he was replaced as public security minister by former vice-minister Tao Siju, apparently accused of having allowed the 1989 demonstrations to get out of hand.

**WANG ZHEN.** *China.* Vice-president. Born in 1908, Wang is a conservative hardline general who made his name in land reclamation in the border regions. A former Politburo member, he retired from the Central Committee in 1985 to become vice-chairman of the Central Advisory Commission, before becoming vice-president in 1988.

**WANGCHUK, Jigme Singye.** *Bhutan.* King (Druk Gyalpo or Dragon king). Born in 1955 and educated in Darjeeling and in the UK, he was named as crown prince in March 1972 and succeeded to the throne four months later. Although pursuing the same brand of benevolent reformism as his modern-minded father, he has taken a strong line against the recent growth of political opposition, principally among ethnic Nepalese in the outlawed Bhutan People's Party. In mid-1988, seeking to rally the ruling Buddhist Drukpa tribe behind his traditional authority, he imposed a "code of conduct" directed against the Nepalese language and customs.

**WARNKE, Jürgen.** *Germany.* Economic co-operation minister and leading member of the Christian Social Union. Born in Berlin in 1932, he became a lawyer and worked for the Bavarian chemical industry association before going into politics. He entered the Bundestag in 1969 and has been in the cabinet since 1987, first as transport minister (1987–89) and then as economic co-operation minister. He is also a member of the synod of the Evangelical church.

**WATANABE, Michio.** *Japan.* Liberal Democratic Party (LDP) politician and faction leader. Born in 1923 in Tochigi prefecture, he graduated from Tokyo University of Commerce (now Hitotsubashi University) and served as a member of the Tochigo prefectural assembly for two years. Watanabe was first elected to the

House of Representatives (lower house) for the LDP in 1963 and entered the cabinet as health and welfare minister under Takeo Fukuda in 1976. Later, he successively held various posts such as agriculture, forestry and fisheries minister under Masayoshi Ohira in 1978, finance minister under Zenko Suzuki in 1980, and international trade and industry minister under **Yasuhiro Nakasone** in 1985. He belonged to the Nakasone faction, but was also leader of the Onchikai policy research group, which counted among its members key figures from other factions. Appointed chairman of the LDP policy affairs research council in 1987, he is regarded as a potential president of the party. He became the leader of the former Nakasone faction in 1990. His lively, sometimes controversial speeches, delivered in a strong regional accent, have helped to ensure for him a high public profile. Something of a populist, he stresses the need for politics that can be easily understood by the public.

**WATANJAR, Aslam.** *Afghanistan.* Defence minister. Appointed defence minister after the involvement of his predecessor Shahnawaz Tanai in the abortive March 1990 coup attempt, he had previously been internal affairs minister. He is a leading member of the Khalq (masses) faction of the ruling People's Democratic Party of Afghanistan (PDPA); his appointment appeared to counter claims that the coup attempt was a Khalq-inspired strike against the rival Parcham-dominated regime of **Mohammed Najibullah.**

**WATHELET, Melchior.** *Belgium.* Deputy prime minister and justice minister. Born in 1949, he was elected to parliament for the Social Christian Party (PSC) in 1977 and became Wallonian chief minister in 1985. In Wallonia, he showed considerable flair and energy in promoting the restructuring of the region's industrial base. He was brought into the national government in 1988 as a deputy prime minister and justice minister.

**WATKINS, James.** *USA.* Secretary of energy. Born in California in 1927, he pursued a career in the navy, specializing in nuclear technology and reaching the rank of admiral. He was in naval service when called to the energy department by **George Bush** in 1989.

**WAXMAN, Henry.** *USA.* Democratic congressman from California. Born in 1939, he was a lawyer and state legislator before being elected to the House of Representatives in 1974. Liberal in outlook, he is a consensus-builder who

accepts that social programmes must be tailored
to fiscal limitations. Chairman of the health and
environment subcommittee since 1979, he has
been active in expanding health care
programmes and takes a tough stand on acid
rain. In 1988 he helped to pilot the first
comprehensive AIDS bill into law.

**WEATHERILL, Bernard.** *UK.* Speaker of the
House of Commons since 1987, MP since 1964.
Born in 1920, Weatherill entered politics after
military service, was deputy chief whip in 1973,
and chairman of the ways and means committee
from 1979–83. Decisive but fair-minded, he is
known for his jovial ripostes and occasional
exasperation in trying to bring order to a
sometimes unruly House. He supported the
decision to televise proceedings in 1989,
commending it to viewers as "the best show in
town".

**WEBER, Vin.** *USA.* Republican congressman
from Minnesota. Born in 1952, he worked in
publishing and was elected to the House of
Representatives in 1980. A conservative who
supports calls for a more confrontational
partisanship, he was elected secretary of the
Republican Conference in 1989. More flexible
than his allies **Newt Gingrich** and **Robert
Walker**, he also opposed the administration of
**Ronald Reagan** on some foreign policy issues.

**WEBSTER, William.** *USA.* Director of the
Central Intelligence Agency. Born in 1924, he
practised law after graduating from Washington
University Law School. After serving as a judge
in the US Court of Appeals from 1973–78, he
was appointed director of the Federal Bureau of
Investigation in 1978 following the death of J.
Edgar Hoover. As head of the FBI, Webster was
generally credited with having improved its
relationship with the CIA (the former being
responsible for domestic intelligence work and
the latter for intelligence operations undertaken
abroad), thereby neutralizing one of the more
acrimonious legacies of the Hoover years. When
William Casey resigned as director of the CIA in
February 1987 his deputy, Robert Gates, who
had been acting director since Casey developed a
brain tumour in late 1986, was chosen as his
replacement. Congressional dissatisfaction with
the role of Casey and Gates in the emerging
Iran-Contra scandal, however, meant that the
nomination of Gates was withdrawn in favour of
Webster. In 1989 Webster was retained within
**George Bush**'s administration.

**WEDERMEIER, Klaus.** *Germany.* Mayor of
Bremen. Social Democratic Party mayor of

Bremen and president of the senate there since
1985, he was born in 1944 and was first elected
to the Bremen parliament in 1971.

**WEE KIM WEE.** *Singapore.* President. Born in
1915, Wee worked as a journalist and a
diplomat before being elected by parliament to
the largely ceremonial post of president in 1985.
He was re-elected for a second term in 1989.

**WEICKER, Lowell.** *USA.* Independent
governor of Connecticut. Born in 1931, he was a
Republican member of the House from 1969–71
and then a senator from 1971–89, but in 1990
he was elected governor as an independent. In
the Senate he enjoyed a reputation as a liberal,
was a member of the subcommittee investigating
the Watergate affair in 1973, and chaired the
small business committee. His 1990
gubernatorial campaign stressed his enthusiasm
for involving more ordinary people in
government.

**WEISS, Konrad.** *Germany.* Bundestag member
and former East German dissident. A
documentary film-maker, he was part of the
Democracy Now movement which subsequently
merged into Alliance '90. Seen as an authentic
spokesperson of East Germany's autumn 1989
popular dissident movement, he became one of
the Alliance '90 representatives in the all-
German Bundestag after the December 1990
parliamentary elections.

**WELD, William.** *USA.* Republican governor of
Massachusetts. Born in 1945, he benefited from
the support of liberal voters who had previously
backed **Michael Dukakis**, but found it hard to
swallow the right-wing opinions of Democrat
candidate John Silber in 1990.

**WELLS, Clyde.** *Canada.* Premier of
Newfoundland and Labrador. Born in 1937 in
Buchans Junction, Newfoundland, Wells was
educated at Memorial University, Newfoundland
and Dalhousie University Law School. He was
first elected to Newfoundland's legislature in
1966, resigned in 1971 and returned as leader of
the Liberal Party of Newfoundland and Labrador
in 1987. After being defeated in the 1989
provincial election, Wells won a seat in a by-
election and overthrew the Conservatives the
same year. He is best known for his stand on
principle against the Meech Lake Accord
constitutional reforms.

**WEN JIABAO.** *China.* Alternate member of the
Chinese Communist Party (CCP) Secretariat.
Born in 1942, Wen was a geological researcher
before being vice-minister of geology and
mining from 1983–85. Director of the CCP's

Central General Office, he joined the Secretariat in 1987. A moderate, Wen is an ally of former party leader **Zhao Ziyang**.

**WERNER, Lars**. *Sweden*. Leader of the Left Party-Communists. Born in 1935, he trained and worked as a bricklayer before becoming a trade union official. A member of the Riksdag (parliament) for the small Left Party-Communists (VpK) since 1965, he became deputy party leader in 1967 and leader in 1975. Under his tenure the VpK, which has traditionally followed a fairly independent line, has ditched much of its still considerable ideological ballast, particularly since the advent of *perestroika* and the demise of communism in Eastern Europe.

**WESTERBERG, Bengt**. *Sweden*. Leader of the Liberal Party. Born in 1943, he studied economics and then held various appointments in Stockholm's local government, including head of the transport commission. He was elected leader of the Liberal Party (FP) in 1983 and entered the Riksdag (parliament) the following year. Sharp and businesslike, he comes over well on television and led his party to one of the most remarkable electoral performances in modern Swedish politics in the 1985 elections, when it more than doubled its vote. If the three non-socialist parties were to form a government, he would be the most likely candidate for the premiership.

**WHITE, Byron Raymond**. *USA*. Supreme Court associate justice. Born in Colorado in 1917, he served as a Naval Intelligence officer during World War II. A Yale graduate and one-time professional footballer, White was appointed to the Supreme Court in 1962. Although generally considered a conservative, he has been responsible for the crucial swing vote in many of the Court's five-to-four majority rulings; in the 1989–90 session – which produced 20 conservative and 10 liberal victories by a single vote – White was among the majority in almost every case.

**WHITELAW, Lord (William Whitelaw)**. *UK*. Conservative politician. Born in 1918, he was educated at Cambridge University and managed his Cumbrian farm until his election to parliament (for Penrith) in 1955. Having held junior ministerial office from 1962–64, he became chief opposition whip in 1964 and leader of the house in 1970, during which time he established his credentials within the party as a mediator and fixer. As secretary of state for Northern Ireland (1972–73) he probably came

closer than any British minister has since in forging a constitutional settlement for the province. He narrowly lost to **Margaret Thatcher** in the 1975 leadership election, and as deputy leader became one of her closest advisers and the eminence grise of her government, despite the fact that, as an old-style patrician Tory, his views were closer to the "wet" consensus policies of her predecessor, **Edward Heath**. He served as home secretary from 1979–83, before being made a viscount and becoming leader of the House of Lords. In 1988 ill-health forced him to retire from active politics but he has remained an influential Tory "elder statesman".

**WHITMIRE, Kathryn**. *USA*. Democrat mayor of Houston. Born in 1946 in Houston, Texas, she trained as an accountant and has been in city government since 1977; she was first elected mayor in 1982. She is credited with achievements in urban planning and management, in a city which suffers from high levels of pollution, unemployment and crime. When she first took office, she appointed a black chief of police, and when the position became vacant again in 1990, she brought in a woman, the first to head a city police force in the USA. However, she is also criticized for having raised taxes, and for her management of the lengthy economic crisis caused by the crash in oil prices of 1982. Whitmire was re-elected to a fifth two-year term in November 1989.

**WHITTEN, Jamie**. *USA*. Democratic congressman from Mississippi. Born in 1910, he was a teacher and lawyer before being elected to the House of Representatives in 1941. He is known as the "permanent secretary of agriculture" because of his four-decade tenure of the agricultural appropriations subcommittee. As chairman of the appropriations committee since 1978, he has sided more often with the spenders than the economizers.

**WIDDECOMBE, Ann**. *UK*. Conservative Party MP. Born in 1947, she was educated at a convent school and elected to parliament in 1987, where she made her mark as an impassioned advocate of the anti-abortion lobby. She is national patron of the Life organization, which campaigns on this issue.

**WIJERATNE, Ranjan**. *Sri Lanka*. Plantation industries minister and minister of state for defence. A tea plantation owner and general secretary of the ruling United National Party, he was brought into the cabinet by **Ranasinghe Premadasa** in February 1989, initially in the foreign affairs post (which he gave up to Harold Herath in a reshuffle the following March), but more importantly to be the hard man in security matters. In this respect he operates nominally as minister of state for defence, with the defence portfolio still in Premadasa's hands; the innocuous-sounding portfolio of plantation industries is what formally entitles him to a cabinet seat. He was responsible for the ruthless police operation to eliminate the threat from the Sinhalese extremist People's Liberation Front (JVP) in the south, and gained further notoriety for proposing the evacuation of a million people from a broad area of northern Sri Lanka to allow for an unimpeded military onslaught on Tamil separatists.

**WIJETUNGA, Dingiri (D.B)**. *Sri Lanka*. Prime minister and finance minister. A United National Party stalwart and member of the government from 1977–88, latterly as finance minister, he was chosen as prime minister when **Ranasinghe Premadasa** moved up to the presidency in late 1988. His appointment to this largely ceremonial post (with which he combined continuing responsibility for finance) was widely seen as a way of preventing Premadasa's younger rivals from using it to build up a claim on the presidential succession. Premadasa's satisfaction with Wijetunga's low-key performance was reflected in his decision in March 1990 to renew the appointment, rather than rotating the job as he had previously suggested.

**WILDER, Douglas**. *USA*. Democratic governor of Virginia. Born in 1931, he was educated at Virginia Union and Howard universities, was a lawyer and law professor, and in 1969 became the first black since the 1870s to be elected to the state senate. In 1985 he became the first black lieutenant governor elected in the South and in 1989 the first black elected governor of a state. He picked up many votes in the suburbs and cities whose population has grown through migration from outside the state, but did poorly in rural areas, where native Virginians still predominate. Wilder did not campaign on traditional black issues, but emphasized his fiscal moderation and his new-found support for the death penalty and right-to-work legislation. Although it was thought that a pro-abortion stance would hurt him, this actually attracted middle-class suburbanites. He is a possible future vice-presidential nominee.

**WILHELM, Hans-Otto**. *Germany*. Christian Democratic Union (CDU) politician.

Environment and health minister in the Land government of the Rhineland-Palatinate since 1987, he was born in 1940 and was first elected to the regional parliament in 1974.

**WILLETTS, David**. *UK*. Economist. Born in 1956, he studied philosophy, politics and economics and then joined the Treasury in 1978. A bright and enthusiastic supporter of **Margaret Thatcher**, he moved from the Treasury to the Downing Street policy unit in 1984 and became director of the Centre of Policy Studies (CPS), in effect the Conservative Party's think-tank, in 1986. A protégé of **Nigel Lawson**, for whom he worked as private secretary at the Treasury, he found he had divided loyalties when Lawson resigned as chancellor. He has been selected to stand for parliament as Tory candidate for a Hampshire constituency at the next general election.

**WILLIS, Norman**. *UK*. Trade unionist. Born in 1933, he began working for the Transport and General Workers' Union (TGWU) at the age of 16. For 11 years from 1959 he was the personal assistant to the general secretary and from 1970–74 was national secretary in charge of research and education. He moved to the Trades Union Congress (TUC) in 1974 and surprised many by being elected general secretary in 1984. As such, he has for the most part aligned himself with the "new realists" of the union movement, who are prepared to accept some of the Conservative government's industrial relations legislation. With his avuncular, conciliatory style, he has had some success in holding the TUC together at a time of crisis and falling membership in the union movement.

**WILLIS, Ralph**. *Australia*. Finance minister. Born in Melbourne in 1938, he followed a familiar Labor Party path to parliament via a career as a trade union official. He was elected to the House of Representatives for the Victoria seat of Gellibrand in 1972. During Labor's period in opposition from 1975–83, he was shadow spokesman for economic affairs and the treasury. In **Bob Hawke**'s first government, he became employment and industrial relations minister, a post he held until 1989 when he moved to transport and communications. He became finance minister after the March 1990 election when transport and communications, having assumed greater significance with the projected re-organization of telecommunications, was taken over by the more heavyweight **Kim Beazley**. Willis has a maverick reputation in Australian Labor Party politics; although ideologically close to both Hawke and treasurer **Paul Keating** on the right of the party, he has differed from them publicly on a number of occasions.

**WILSON, Sir David.** *Hong Kong.* Governor. Born in 1935 and a career diplomat, he became governor and commander-in-chief of Hong Kong in 1987. In June 1989, he unsuccessfully proposed that UK citizenship be extended to all Hong Kong citizens. He has also introduced plans for a bill of rights for the colony.

**WILSON, Des.** *UK.* Political campaigner. Born in 1941, he worked as a journalist and broadcaster in his native New Zealand and in the UK until 1967, when he became head of Shelter, an organization campaigning for the homeless. He has since devoted his organizing and fund-raising skills to several pressure groups, including the Campaign for Freedom of Information and Friends of the Earth, and (since 1988) the Liberal Democrats. He has also found time to write a racy novel.

**WILSON, Gordon.** *UK.* Scottish Nationalist politician. Born in 1938, he trained as a solicitor. He held senior office in the Scottish National Party (SNP) from 1963 until 1990, first as national secretary, then vice-chairman (1972–74), deputy leader (1974–79) and leader, until his resignation in September 1990. From 1974–87 he was MP for Dundee West. Quiet-spoken and diplomatic, he succeeded in papering over party schisms to maintain the SNP as a radical, pro-independence movement.

**WILSON, Michael.** *Canada.* Finance minister. Born in Toronto in 1937 and educated at the University of Toronto, he was a businessman before entering politics. He was elected to the House of Commons for the Progressive Conservative Party of Canada in 1979 and has been minister of finance since 1984. Wilson has always been considered a "hard rock" in **Brian Mulroney**'s government, and had a reputation for being "clean" when the Conservatives were plagued by scandal. His solid image was tarnished in 1989 when his entire budget was leaked.

**WILSON, Pete.** *USA.* Republican governor of California. Born in 1933, he was a lawyer and state legislator, and from 1971–83 a well-respected and successful mayor of San Diego. He was elected to the Senate in 1982 and has been a strong defender of state farming and business interests, notably promoting the strategic defence initiative, which will greatly benefit California industry. In 1990, he ran for governor,

winning a crucial election that will affect congressional redistricting in the 1990s.

**WINA, Arthur.** *Zambia.* Movement for Multi-Party Democracy (MMD) interim committee chairman. A veteran politician, a former finance minister and member of the central committee of the ruling United National Independence Party (Unip), Wina has become one of the leaders of the opposition to President **Kenneth Kaunda**'s one-party rule. In July 1990 he was elected chairman of the newly launched MMD, which planned to transform itself into a political party in the wake of Kaunda's decision in October 1990 to permit a return to political pluralism.

**WINGTI, Paias.** *Papua New Guinea.* Opposition leader. Born in 1951, he emerged as a rising young leader in the centre-left Pangu Pati in the early 1980s. He briefly took on the post of deputy prime minister in 1984, but led a mass defection to form the centre-right People's Democratic Movement in March 1985 and to bring down **Michael Somare**'s government in a vote of no confidence later the same year. Prime minister from November 1985, he survived an electoral setback in 1987 and reconstructed a coalition to remain in power, but lost a vote of no confidence in July 1988. He has sustained a campaign to bring down the **Rabbie Namaliu** government, although sharing a broadly non-partisan approach on the Bougainville secessionist crisis.

**WIRTH, Timothy.** *USA.* Democratic senator from Colorado. Born in 1939, he was an education official, before being elected to the House of Representatives in 1974 and to the Senate in 1986. A pragmatist who does not identify with any party faction, he has become the Senate's foremost expert on global warming.

**WÖRNER, Manfred.** *Germany.* Nato secretary-general. Born in 1934, he trained and practised as a lawyer until his election to parliament for the Christian Democratic Union (CDU) in 1965. Early in his parliamentary career he gained a reputation as a combative right-winger with a knack for self-publicity. A former air-force pilot, he was the CDU's defence spokesman for most of the 1970s and was appointed defence minister when the party returned to power in 1982. He survived a scandal the following year over his hasty dismissal of a general on the basis of surveillance reports alleging, incorrectly, that the officer had frequented homosexual bars. In 1988 he was appointed Nato secretary-general in succession to **Lord Carrington**, taking over the reins just before the effective collapse of the Warsaw Pact threw the organization into an extended period of soul-searching and role-seeking.

**WORRALL, Denis.** *South Africa.* Opposition liberal leader. Born in 1935, he graduated in political science and taught afterwards at colleges including Cornell University and University of California at Los Angeles in the USA. Founder of the *New Nation* in 1967 and its editor for seven years, he then entered the upper house of parliament as a National Party senator for Cape Town. An MP from 1977–83, he was subsequently ambassador to Australia and the UK. In 1987 he threw his hat into the political ring as a liberal opponent of the regime, returning from London to contest a seat in the 1987 elections and falling just short of victory against his former party. From 1988 he led a new Independent Movement, but in February 1989 he merged this new grouping into a broader Democratic Party, with himself, **Zach de Beer** and Wynand Malan as its ruling triumvirate. He subsequently declined to stand for the sole leadership of the party, which went to de Beer, but remains an MP in the House of Assembly (white parliament).

**WU XUEQIAN.** *China.* Vice-Premier. Born in 1908, Wu worked in party youth organizations and is a veteran of the 1934–35 Long March. After 1949, he became a career diplomat specializing in Soviet and Eastern European affairs. Foreign minister from 1982–88, Wu was then appointed to his present post. A Politburo member since 1985, he heads the leading party group on foreign affairs. His son was the Radio Beijing official who authorized the English-language broadcast which condemned the June 1989 military crackdown and who was given a three-year prison sentence for his action.

**WUER KAIXI.** *China.* Dissident student leader. Born in 1968, the charismatic ethnic Uygur student in Beijing led negotiations with the premier, **Li Peng** while on hunger strike during the 1989 pro-democracy protests. After the crackdown, he escaped to the West, where he is a leader of the exiled Federation for a Democratic China.

# Y

YA'AKOBI, Gad. *Israel.* Labour MP since 1969 and former communications and transport minister. Born in Israel in 1935. His skills as an economist were put to the test when he held the economics and planning portfolio from 1984–88. He is a contender for the Labour leadership.

YADAV, Mulayam Singh. *India.* Chief minister of Uttar Pradesh. Born in the state in 1939, he was first elected to the state assembly in 1967, and has successively been president of the UP Lok Dal, Lok Dal (B), and the UP Janata Dal. He secured the chief minister's post through the support of former agriculture minister **Devi Lal** after Janata Dal won the November 1989 state election.

YAKOVLEV, Aleksandr. *USSR.* Former Presidential Council member. A Russian born into a peasant family in 1923, he saw active service in World War II, and after 1946 he held various posts in the Communist Party of the Soviet Union (CPSU) propaganda apparatus and as a journalist and lecturer (he has a doctorate in history). Yakovlev got himself into hot water by criticizing Russian nationalists and was sent into "exile" in 1973 as ambassador to Canada, where he met **Mikhail Gorbachev** during the latter's visit in 1983. Returning to Moscow later that year, he became director of the USSR Academy of Sciences Institute of World Economy and International Relations. In July 1985 he was named head of the CPSU central committee propaganda department, and in March 1986 was elevated to central committee secretary responsible for propaganda and the media. In this post he was responsible for appointing a number of liberals as editors of key journals. In September 1988 he was reassigned in the secretariat to the international policy portfolio. He joined the politburo as a candidate member in January 1987 and a full member in July. In March 1990 he was appointed by Gorbachev to the short-lived Presidential Council. Long identified as a leading liberal – "the godfather of *glasnost*" – he was pilloried at the July 1990

CPSU congress by party conservatives forming a majority of delegates, finding himself accused, alongside Vadim Medvedev, of allowing party ideological work to collapse. He was not even proposed for re-election to the central committee and since then appears to have lost much of his former influence with Gorbachev.

YAKOVLEV, Veniamin. *USSR.* Chief state arbiter. Born in 1932 and a doctor of juridical sciences, he was director of the National Research Institute of State-Building and Law-Making before his election in July 1989 as USSR justice minister. He was chosen for his keen advocacy of overhauling the Soviet legal system, and because of his unblemished record. In December 1990, however, he was transferred to the post of chief state arbiter, and replaced as justice minister by Sergei Lushchikov.

YAMAGUCHI, Tsuruo. *Japan.* Japan Socialist Party (JSP) secretary-general. Born in 1925, he began a career as a secondary school teacher in Gunma after graduating from technical college. Active in trade union affairs on behalf of his teaching colleagues, he also sat in the local prefectural assembly before entering the House of Representatives (lower house) on the JSP list in 1960. On the right wing of the party, he has been its secretary-general since 1986, backing the moderate line of the more high-profile party chairwoman **Takako Doi**.

YANAYEV, Gennady. *USSR.* Vice-president. A Russian born in 1937, he became active in politics after a career in agriculture, heading the USSR Committee for Youth Organizations from 1968–80 and then working as deputy chairman of the USSR Friendship Societies Union. He joined the leadership of the Central Council of Trade Unions in 1986 and was elected chairman in April 1990, but relinquished that post the following July upon his election to the Communist Party of the Soviet Union politburo and secretariat, where commentators identified him as the leading conservative. He took over the secretariat international affairs portfolio from **Aleksandr Yakovlev**. He was described as an "old-style leader" by radical deputies who opposed his election to the new post of vice-president at the December 1990 Congress of People's Deputies. The nominee of **Mikhail Gorbachev**, he was elected on the second round, and only after Gorbachev had effectively made the choice into a vote of confidence in his own leadership.

**YANG BAIBING.** *China.* Member of the party and state Central Military Commissions. Born in 1919, a half brother of **Yang Shangkun**, Yang is linked with **Deng Xiaoping** from the latter's time on political commissar in 1948–54 of the 2nd Field Army. Yang was political commissar of the Beijing Military Region before heading the army's political department in 1987. A member of the state Central Military Commission from 1988, he succeeded his elder brother as secretary-general of the party's equivalent top military organ in 1989, when he also joined the Secretariat.

**YANG RUDAI.** *China.* Politburo member. Born in 1926, Yang is a moderate associate of **Zhao Ziyang**. He worked under Zhao in Sichuan and became provincial party secretary and concurrently political commissar in the Chengdu Military Region in 1983. Elected to the Central Committee in 1982, he joined the Politburo in 1987.

**YANG SHANGKUN.** *China.* President. Born in 1907, Yang held central party posts before being imprisoned for ten years during the Cultural Revolution (1966–76) as a "top party capitalist-roader". Rehabilitated in 1978, he worked in Guangdong before he rejoined the Central Committee in 1982 and was appointed to the Politburo. A Long March veteran, Yang rose to become first vice-chairman of both the party and state Central Military Commissions in 1989 and April 1990 respectively. President since 1988 and considered a hardliner, Yang has placed his relatives in senior military positions, and sees himself as a successor to his long-term associate **Deng Xiaoping**.

**YAO YILIN.** *China.* Member of the Politburo Standing Committee. Yao was born in 1915 in Jiangxi, and his early career was in finance, trade and economic planning. He rose to become commerce minister in 1960–67, before being denounced as a "counter-revolutionary revisionist". He subsequently returned to the ministry for a year before becoming a vice-premier in 1979 and moving to head the fourth machine building ministry. A member of the Central Committee from 1977, he served in the Secretariat in 1980–88, and was a member of the Politburo from 1985, before joining its Standing Committee in 1987. A conservative economist, Yao follows the views of **Chen Yun**, the major proponent of central planning, and has said that he would not be concerned if the western industrial nations decided not to invest in China. He has twice headed the powerful State Planning Commission, once in 1980–83, and again in 1988. Yao's replacement as planning chief in November 1989 by the more moderate **Zou Jiahua** seemed to be a sign that the market reforms might be reasserted.

**YARD, Molly.** *USA.* President of the National Organization for Women (NOW), and civil liberties campaigner. She was born in China to Methodist missionaries in 1912, and has been active in women's and civil rights since the 1930s, when she was a protégé of Eleanor Roosevelt. As president of NOW, she takes a "grass roots" approach to her job, and is working for the appointment of women at all levels of government.

**YARIN, Veniamin.** *USSR.* Former Presidential Council member. A metalworker from Nizhny Tagil in the Urals, born in 1940, he is a leader of the United Workers' Front, an unofficial blue-collar organization strongly critical of market economic reforms, which was set up in July 1989. A deputy to the USSR Supreme Soviet, he was one of the more surprising appointees to **Mikhail Gorbachev**'s short-lived Presidential Council in March 1990.

**YAZDI, Ayatollah Muhammad.** *Iran.* Head of judiciary. A leading conservative cleric, with close ties to **Ayatollah Khamenei**, Yazdi was appointed head of the judiciary in September 1989. Born in Qom in 1931, he taught theology before the 1979 revolution. In 1980 he was elected to the Majlis (parliament), where he served as head of the powerful legal and judicial affairs committee and as deputy speaker until his defeat in the 1988 elections.

**YAZOV, Marshal Dmitry.** *USSR.* Defence minister. A Russian born in 1923 in West Siberia, he was a Red Army commander in World War II, and subsequently became a career army officer. From 1980 he was successively commander of the Central Asian and Far Eastern military districts. Appointed a deputy defence minister in charge of personnel in January 1987, he was elevated to minister the following May as part of the shake-up of the military hierarchy that followed the embarrassing affair of Mathias Rust (a West German amateur pilot who managed to fly unchallenged to Moscow's Red Square). The promotion of Yazov, considered at the time a relatively minor figure in the military leadership, surprised observers; many concluded that he had been hand-picked by **Mikhail Gorbachev**. He has since, however, frequently been identified as leaning towards the conservative wing of the Communist Party leadership (he was a Communist Party of the Soviet Union non-voting politburo member from 1987–90), and has even been compelled publicly to deny rumours that he threatened to carry out a military coup against Gorbachev. Nevertheless, the military hierarchy is clearly unnerved by the effects of Gorbachev's reforms as it faces a reduced military budget, serious draft and discipline problems, and the collapse of the Warsaw Pact alliance; Yazov's promotion from general to marshal in April 1990 was interpreted by some as a morale-boosting concession by Gorbachev to a restless Red Army command; the previous month, Yazov had been appointed by Gorbachev to his short-lived Presidential Council.

**YE XUANPING**. *China*. Governor of Guangdong. Born in 1925, Ye is the son of the late Marshal Ye Jianying, and this has protected him politically. He is an engineer by profession, and as governor since 1985 he has made use of the economic reforms to turn his native province of Guangdong into a boom region.

**YELTSIN, Boris**. *USSR*. Chairman of the Supreme Soviet of the Russian Federation. Born into a labourer's family in 1931 in the Sverdlovsk region, he worked as a construction engineer after graduating in 1955. He joined the Communist Party of the Soviet Union (CPSU) in 1961, and became a full-time party official in Sverdlovsk in 1968, rising to head the regional apparatus in 1976. After **Mikhail Gorbachev** became CPSU leader in 1985, Yeltsin was brought to Moscow in April to head the central committee construction department, and promoted in July to the central committee secretariat. In December 1985 he was put in charge of the Moscow city party organization and soon afterwards named a candidate politburo member. His radical populist approach to the Moscow job, which included eschewing his official car to experience crowded public transport, incognito visits to sparsely-stocked shops, and public denunciation of poor housing (testing the limits of the new *glasnost* policy), earned him popularity with Muscovites but hostility from party conservatives. In October

1987 at a central committee meeting he traded insults with leading conservative Yegor Ligachev and other politburo colleagues whom he accused of frustrating reform, and in the following month was dismissed as Moscow party boss, his conduct and leadership style personally criticized by Gorbachev. He was given a junior ministerial post and dropped from the politburo. In March 1989 he staged an unprecedented comeback with a landslide election victory to represent Moscow in the new Congress of People's Deputies, his populist appeal drawing large crowds to his election rallies. In July 1989 he was a founder of the Inter-Regional Group, the first parliamentary opposition faction. In March 1990 he was elected to the Congress of People's Deputies of the Russian Federation (the largest Soviet republic), and in May that body elected him chairman of the Russian Federation Supreme Soviet (*de facto* president). Claiming the need to be non-partisan in that post, he dramatically announced his resignation from the CPSU at the July 1990 congress. His election to the leadership of the Russian republic raised the prospect of his using it as a power base from which to challenge Gorbachev, whom he had often criticized for attempting half-baked reforms. Instead, Gorbachev in August 1990 sought an alliance with Yeltsin on economic reform, and they achieved a temporary personal reconciliation. Yeltsin's performance as leader of the Russian Federation, including a radical declaration of sovereignty and proposals for a 500-day dash to a market economy, has confounded criticism that he was a populist without policies.

**YEO, Timothy**. *UK*. Under-secretary of state at the department of the environment. Born in 1945, he was elected to parliament in 1983, and served as **Douglas Hurd**'s parliamentary private secretary from 1988. Despite strongly supporting Hurd's bid for the party leadership in November 1990, he was appointed to his first government post by Hurd's successful rival for the premiership, **John Major**.

**YEUTTER, Clayton**. *USA*. Secretary of agriculture. Born in 1930, the son of a poor German immigrant, he was educated at the University of Nebraska before joining the US Air Force in 1952. He left the service in 1957 and ran the family farm in central Nebraska. He also obtained a law degree in 1963 and a doctorate in agricultural economics in 1966. He served as an assistant secretary of agriculture from 1970–75 and deputy special trade representative from 1975–77, before leaving government to become president of the Chicago Mercantile Exchange, the world's second-largest futures market, a post he held from 1978–85. In 1985 he once again entered government as **Ronald Reagan**'s trade representative, making free trade in agriculture one of the primary US goals in international negotiations. Despite a childhood aspiration to be the country's agriculture secretary, by 1988 Yeutter claimed that his years in government had cured him of the ambition and that he wanted to return to the private sector. Nevertheless, he was persuaded by **George Bush** to accept the agriculture post in 1989. Although hard-working, with seemingly inexhaustible reserves of energy and optimism, Yeutter's relationship with the agriculture committees of the House and the Senate has not been easy, not least because his intense opposition to agricultural protectionism is at odds with some of the interests represented in Congress.

**YILMAZ, Mesut.** *Turkey*. Politician. Born in 1947, he was a "technocrat" in the first government of **Turgut Özal** in 1983, becoming a minister of state in 1983 and serving as culture and tourism minister from 1986–87 before taking on the foreign affairs portfolio. He has been regarded as one of the leading contenders in the struggle for political supremacy, and is sometimes tipped as a potential prime minister. However, he was forced out of the foreign ministry in February 1990 after a bout of infighting, and is unlikely to return as long as **Yıldırım Akbulut** heads the government. He later announced his intention of challenging Akbulut for the chairmanship of the ruling Motherland Party (Anap) at the party convention in early 1991.

**YNSFRÁN, Edgar.** *Paraguay*. Colorado Party vice-president. Born in 1920, and a noted historian and lawyer, Ynsfrán was interior minister from 1957–66. He then led a dissident faction within the ruling Colorado Party, and after Alfredo Stroessner's fall became first vice-president. In 1990 he was accused of repression during his term as a minister by a tribunal investigating Stroessner's regime.

**YON HYONG-MUK.** *North Korea*. Premier. Born in 1925, he is married to **Kim Il-sung**'s cousin. He joined the Korean Workers' Party central committee in 1970, but was demoted in 1977 after criticism from Kim Il-sung. His

rehabilitation in 1979 owed much to **Kim Chong-il**, to whom he is adviser on economics, science and technology. A reformist technocrat, he became premier in 1988. Yon is the sixth-ranking member of the politburo, and was party secretary from 1986–88. In September 1990 he began a historic series of meetings with his South Korean counterpart **Kang Young Hoon**.

**YOUNG, Andrew.** *USA*. Democratic politician. Born in 1932, he was a civil rights activist and close ally of Martin Luther King in the 1960s. A Georgia Democratic congressman in the early 1970s, he became UN ambassador in 1977 but was dismissed for talking with Palestine Liberation Organization representatives, after which he acknowledged that he was "not a very diplomatic diplomat". As Atlanta's mayor from 1982–89, he focused on working with business and making Atlanta an international financial centre. He ran for the Democratic gubernatorial nomination in 1990, but lost the run-off primary.

**YOUNG, Coleman.** *USA*. Mayor of Detroit. Born in 1918, he was a Michigan state senator and became Detroit's first black mayor in 1973. He sought to revive the city's economy by promoting the redevelopment of the downtown business district, but this has not resolved deep-rooted problems. Detroit has lost more population than any other big US city in the last 20 years.

**YOUNG, Don.** *USA*. Republican congressman from Alaska. Born in 1933, he had a varied career, including teaching and fur trapping, before being elected to the House of Representatives in 1973 after serving as a local councillor and state legislator. As ranking Republican on the interior committee, he has sought to open up Alaska's protected lands for development, arguing that the state should not be denied jobs because of the environmental concerns of "the lower 48" (the other US mainland states).

**YOUNG, Sir George.** *UK*. Housing and planning minister. Born in 1941 and a hereditary baronet, Young is on the moderate "wet" wing of the Conservative Party. His opposition to several Thatcherite policies, notably the poll tax, led him to be dismissed as environment under-secretary. He returned to the department in November 1990 under **John Major**, however, charged with finding solutions to the growing problem of homelessness.

# Z

**ZAHIR SHAH, Mohammad.** *Afghanistan.* Former king. Born in 1914, he was educated in Kabul and in France. He came to the throne in 1933 and during the 1930s concluded a mutual assistance pact with the USSR, but after World War II moved increasingly close to the USA. His resistance to then prime minister Mohammad Daoud's moves towards democratization in the 1960s led to Daoud's resignation. Zahir permitted two token elections to an impotent national assembly in 1965 and 1969, in part as a sop to US concerns, but his unwillingness to countenance further reforms provoked Daoud's 1973 coup. The Soviet invasion of 1979 had the unwitting effect of restoring some popular interest in the monarchy. In the chaotic conditions left by the Soviet withdrawal, Zahir's nationalist credentials make him a key figure with the potential to legitimize a post-communist regime in the eyes of the fiercely anti-foreigner Afghani people. He has quietly exploited these conditions, declaring his willingness to return to serve his country.

**ZALDÍVAR LARRIAN, Andrés.** *Chile.* Christian Democratic Party leader. Born in 1936, Zaldívar was educated at the University of Chile and served as a Christian Democratic Party (PDC) minister in 1968–69. He was elected a senator in 1973, became president of the PDC in 1977, but was expelled from Chile in 1980. In 1987 he was elected vice-president of the PDC and assumed the presidency of the party after **Patricio Aylwin** had been chosen as presidential candidate; he won a senatorial seat in the 1989 elections.

**ZAMORA, Rubén.** *El Salvador.* Left-wing leader. As a member of the Christian Democratic Party (PDC), Zamora joined the military-civilian government in 1979 as minister of the presidency, but resigned in 1980 and broke away from the PDC to form the Social Christian People's Movement (MPSC). In 1980 the MPSC joined the Revolutionary Democratic Front (FDR) and Zamora became one of its leaders. He spent most of the following years in exile,

returning to El Salvador in 1987 to play a leading role in the Democratic Convergence (CD) coalition.

**ZAPATERO GÓMEZ, Virgilio.** *Spain.* Parliamentary relations minister. Born in 1946 in Cisneros de Campos in Palencia province, a former teacher and law lecturer with published work on Marxism and legal theory, he joined the Spanish Socialist Workers' Party (PSOE) in 1970. He has sat in parliament since 1977 as a deputy for Cuenca and has been parliamentary relations minister and secretary to the government since 1986.

**ZASLAVSKAYA, Tatyana.** *USSR.* Radical economist. Born in 1927. As a senior economic theoretician with the USSR Academy of Sciences Siberian Division, based in Novosibirsk, she was one of the first to formulate the ideas for economic reform that later constituted **Mikhail Gorbachev**'s *perestroika.* In March 1988 she was appointed to head the first Soviet public opinion research centre, a major development in the application of *glasnost.* Elected in 1989 to the USSR Congress of People's Deputies, she is a member of the radical Inter-Regional Group.

**ZAWAWI, Qais Abdel-Moneim al-.** *Oman.* Deputy prime minister. Born in Muscat in 1935, he belongs to one of Muscat's longest established merchant families. During the reign of Said ibn Taymour, he lived abroad like many of the Omani intelligentsia, although he returned to run the family business on his father's death in 1966. In 1973 **Sultan Qaboos** chose him as minister of state for foreign affairs and in 1974 he was appointed vice-chairman of the development council, co-ordinating Oman's five-year plans. He was closely involved in setting up the six-nation Gulf Co-operation Council in 1981, and was promoted to deputy prime minister for financial and economic affairs in 1982.

**ZEKAN, Branko.** *Yugoslavia.* Finance minister. Born in 1939, he is a Croat and was the manager of a large Croatian insurance corporation before his appointment as federal finance minister in

March 1989. He is in favour of economic reform.

**ZELENOVIĆ, Dragutin**. *Yugoslavia.*
Vojvodina's member of the collective state
presidency. A member of the communist party
in Vojvodina, he was elected in May 1989 for a
five-year term.

**ZHAO ZIYANG.** *China.* Former Chinese
Communist Party (CCP) general secretary. Born
in 1918, the son of a landlord in Henan, Zhao
worked as a senior official in Henan and
Guangdong during the 1950s and early 1960s.
In 1967, he was branded as an agent of Liu
Shaoqi and paraded in a dunce's cap through
Guangzhou. He returned to work in Guangdong
in 1973, before being transferred to Sichuan in
1976 as party secretary. There he pioneered
agricultural and industrial reforms that were
subsequently introduced nationwide. A member
of the Central Committee from 1973, he joined
the Politburo in 1977 as an alternate member. In
1980 he replaced Mao Zedong's chosen successor
Hua Guofeng as premier and began to
implement **Deng Xiaoping's** modernization
programme. Groomed as Deng's successor, he
replaced Hu Yaobang as CCP general secretary
after the latter's disgrace in 1987 and was
elevated to become first vice-chairman of the
powerful party Central Military Commission. As
party general secretary, Zhao headed the political
reform movement to separate party and state set
forth at the 13th party congress in September
1987. In 1988 he yielded the premiership to **Li
Peng** when his reformist policies came in for
heavy criticism as inflation threatened the
successes of the past decade. His influence in the
leadership continued to wane, and in June 1989
he was stripped of all his posts for instigating
the "counter-revolutionary rebellion" and
attempting to split the party, and placed "under
investigation", although he was not expelled
from the CCP.

**ZHELEV, Zhelyu**. *Bulgaria.* President. Born in
1935, Zhelev studied philosophy at Sofia
University. In 1965 he was expelled from the
Bulgarian Communist Party because of his
doctoral thesis, which disputed Lenin's theory of
matter. After a period of unemployment he
began work as a sociologist in 1972 and in 1975
his thesis was finally accepted and he joined the
Institute of Culture in Sofia. He achieved some
notoriety in 1982 with a book entitled *Fascism*,
on the nature of totalitarianism, which was
promptly banned. In 1989 he emerged as a
prominent opposition leader, heading the main
opposition coalition Union of Democratic Forces

(UDF). In August 1990 Zhelev was elected by
the National Assembly to replace **Petar
Mladenov** as the country's president, thereby
becoming Bulgaria's first non-communist head
of state. He is a quietly-spoken but popular
politician; it was on his initiative that the
agreement was eventually reached for a coalition
government, formed in December 1990,
pending fresh elections.

**ZHOU NAN.** *China.* Head of the Xinhua News
Agency Hong Kong branch. The *de facto* Chinese
ambassador to Hong Kong, Zhou was born in
1927 and is a career diplomat. Assistant foreign
minister from 1984 until he took up his present
post in 1990, he is a tougher negotiator than his
urbane predecessor Xu Jiatun.

**ZIA, Begum Khaleda**. *Bangladesh.* Bangladesh
Nationalist Party (BNP) leader. Leader since
1982 of the Islamic centrist BNP and
determined opponent of the regime of former
president **Hussein Mohammed Ershad**, she is
the widow of president Ziaur Rahman, BNP
founder and president until his death in an
attempted coup the year before Ershad's 1982
takeover. Personal recriminations hindered co-
operation in the campaign for the restoration of
democracy between her and her rival opposition
leader **Sheikh Hasina Wajed**. After Ershad's
overthrow in December 1990, Zia prepared to
contest the elections scheduled for 1991.

**ZILK, Helmut**. *Austria.* Mayor of Vienna. Born
in Vienna in 1927, he studied philosophy,
German and education. After teaching, and
lecturing in education, he embarked on a career
in broadcasting and served as programme
director of the state broadcasting service from
1967–74. A member of the Socialist Party of
Austria (SPÖ), he served on Vienna city council
before joining the government as education and
culture minister in 1983. He became mayor of
Vienna in 1984. He is politically unorthodox
and very popular.

**ZIMMERMANN, Friedrich**. *Germany.*
Christian Social Union (CSU) politician. Born in
Munich in 1925, he gained a doctorate in 1950
and took up a legal career. Having joined the
CSU in 1948, he was its general secretary from
1956–63 and is credited with having put its
organization on a professional basis, greatly
expanding the membership. First elected to the
Bundestag in 1957, he chaired the CSU group
from 1976–82, emerging as a close associate of
his controversial party leader Franz Josef Strauss
and as an opponent of **Helmut Kohl** in the
Christian Democratic camp. As interior minister

from 1982–89 he cracked down hard on protest demonstrations, advocating a tougher line on most security issues and on those seeking political asylum. He was moved to the transport ministry in 1989 but did not stand for the Bundestag in the December 1990 elections.

**ZOU JIAHUA.** *China.* Head of the State Planning Commission. Born in 1926, Zou is the son-in-law of the late Marshal Ye Jianying. After a career in heavy industry, he successively headed the ordnance industry ministry, the State Machine Building Industry Commission and the machine building and electronics industry ministry. He replaced **Yao Yilin** as minister in charge of the State Planning Commission in November 1989. His appointment reflected a shift away from the centralized economic model espoused by Yao.

**ZUBI, Mahmoud.** *Syria.* Prime minister. An agronomist by training, Zubi was speaker of the People's Assembly (parliament) from 1981 until appointed prime minister in late 1987. His appointment appeared to reflect President **Hafez al-Assad**'s wish to improve Syria's agricultural performance.

**ZULU, Alexander Grey.** *Zambia.* United National Independence Party (Unip) secretary-general. Born in 1924, this former co-operative society manager has been a leading light in Zambian politics for more than 25 years, holding a series of ministerial posts in the 1960s and 1970s. Secretary-general of the ruling Unip since 1985, he is the acknowledged leader of the inner circle of loyalists to President **Kenneth Kaunda**. As Unip secretary-general, a post he also held from 1973–79, he is constitutionally Kaunda's successor. An advocate of scientific socialism, he has led the faction within the party opposing moves since the mid-1980s to reduce the state's hold on the economy. He has also been one of the most vociferous, and vitriolic, opponents of the movement that emerged in mid-1990 calling for the return of multi-party democracy. Kaunda's September 1990 decision to call multi-party elections presaged the end of Zulu's political career.

**Alliance '90 (Germany):** The opposition group Bundnis-90, which originated as an alliance of New Forum, Democracy Now and the Peace and Human Rights Initiative for the March 1990 East German elections. Alliance '90 contested the December 1990 all-German elections in the east of the country and won eight seats in alliance with the Greens.

**Althingi (Iceland):** Parliament, consisting of an upper and a lower house.

**Amal (Lebanon):** Hope, less commonly the Movement of the Deprived, a Lebanese Shia organization with a powerful militia, led by **Nabih Berri.**

**Anzus Pact:** The trilateral Australia, New Zealand and US security agreement dating from 1951, effectively defunct since New Zealand's adoption in 1985 of a nuclear-free policy.

**April revolution (Portugal):** the bloodless coup of April 25, 1974, which overthrew the Caetano regime and opened the way for the eventual establishment of liberal democratic government.

**Assembly of Experts (Iran):** The elective body set up in 1979 and charged with appointing the country's spiritual leader (*vali faqih*) and interpreting its constitution; the most recent elections to the Assembly of Experts were in October 1990.

**Azad Kashmir:** That part of Kashmir north of the "line of control" which is effectively administered as part of Pakistan; the name means "Free Kashmir".

*Boerevolkstaat* **(South Africa):** A separate state for the Afrikaner or Boer people, the response of some right-wingers to the perceived threat of majority rule in South Africa.

**Broederbond (South Africa):** The influential secret society of Afrikaner intellectuals.

**Bundesrat (Germany):** The upper house or Federal Council of the federal German parliament, comprising representatives of the component states or Länder.

**Bundestag (Germany):** The lower house or Federal Diet of the federal German parliament, directly elected and acting as the main legislative chamber.

**Central Advisory Commission (China):** A party body created in 1982 at the 12th party congress, consisting of senior party members of at least 40 years' standing.

*Chuche* **(North Korea):** The official ideology of socialist self-reliance, which is presented as **Kim Il-sung**'s distinctive contribution to political philosophy.

**Cortes (Spain):** Bicameral parliament comprising the Congress of Deputies and the Senate.

**Dáil (Ireland):** In full the Dáil Éireann, the lower house of the Irish parliament or Oireachtas, the upper house being the Senate (Seanad Éireann).

**Diet (Japan):** The bicameral parliament comprising the House of Representatives, the main legislative body, and the upper House of Councillors.

**Eminent Persons Group:** The group of distinguished figures, led by former Australian prime minister **Malcolm Fraser** and former Nigerian head of state **Olusegun Obasanjo,** sent by the Commonwealth Secretariat to South Africa in 1985 to examine the possibilities of establishing a dialogue between the government and anti-apartheid movements. Its visit was cut short when South African forces raided Zimbabwe, Zambia and Botswana on May 19, 1986.

**Fatah (Palestine):** The Arabic word which can be translated as "victory", taken as the title of the Al-Fatah group formed by Palestinian students including **Yasser Arafat** in the 1950s; it is a reverse acronym of the organization's full title Tahir al-Hatani al-Falastani or Movement for the National Liberation of Palestine. The largest guerrilla movement, Al-Fatah, has been a leading faction within the Palestine Liberation Organization (PLO) since Arafat became PLO leader in 1969.

**Federation Council (USSR):** A new body set up in March 1990 and comprising the chairmen of the supreme soviets in each of the union republics (i.e. the presidents of the republics). In December 1990 the council was expanded to include the USSR vice-president and the presidents of the 20 autonomous republics. Initially a consultative body, it was given executive responsibilities in December 1990 for co-ordinating the work of the centre and of the republics, as well as for ensuring observance of the union treaty and dealing with inter-republic disputes.

**Fianna Fáil (Ireland):** Literally "Soldiers of Destiny" but more commonly rendered in English as the Republican Party, the dominant force in Irish politics for much of the post-1945 period.

**Fine Gael (Ireland):** Literally "tribe of Gaels" but more commonly rendered in English as the United Ireland Party, a Christian democratic formation which has led several governments as an alternative to Fianna Fáil rule in the post-

1945 period.

**Frelimo (Mozambique):** Frente de libertação de Moçambique (Front for the Liberation of Mozambique), which led armed resistance to Portuguese rule from 1964–74 and has been the ruling party since the country's independence in 1975.

**Front-line states:** So called by reference to the confrontation with the apartheid regime of South Africa, the group consists of Angola, Botswana, Mozambique, Tanzania, Zambia and Zimbabwe, with the addition of Namibia since its independence in March 1990.

**Gatt:** see **Uruguay Round.**

**General People's Committee (Libya):** The government structure, effectively the cabinet, whose secretary-general is effectively the prime minister

**General People's Congress (GPC–Libya):** The top tier of the government structure, whose 1,112 members supposedly hold executive powers but in practice work through a general secretariat.

**Gramm-Rudman-Hollings deficit reduction law (USA):** The Balanced Budget and Emergency Deficit Control Act, passed in 1985 and amended in 1987, which provides a framework for the gradual reduction of the US budget deficit, leading to its elimination in 1993. The legislation triggers automatic across-the-board spending cuts if its deficit reduction targets are not met.

**Guildford Four (UK):** Three Irish men and an English woman sentenced to life imprisonment in 1975 in connection with the Guildford and Woolwich pub bombings the previous year. The four were freed in October 1989 after the Court of Appeal quashed their convictions, which had been based on uncorroborated confessions. The appeal court heard that police officers who gave evidence at the 1975 trial had altered interview notes and given false evidence.

**Gulf Co-operation Council (GCC):** The organization that brings together six Gulf states (Bahrain, Kuwait, Oman, Qatar, Saudi Arabia and the United Arab Emirates) for the purpose of policy co-ordination.

**Hezbollah (Lebanon):** The Party of God, a militant radical Shia organization with Iranian links.

**Inkatha (South Africa):** The movement led by Chief Mangosuthu Buthelezi, whose support is based primarily among his fellow ethnic Zulus.

*intifada* **(Palestine):** The Palestinian uprising in the occupied territories of the West Bank and Gaza, which broke out in December 1987.

**Komeito (Japan):** Founded originally as the political wing of a Buddhist organization, the Soka Gakkai, its name is often rendered in English as the Clean Government Party.

**Knesset (Israel):** The unicameral 120-member parliament.

**Kopkamtib (Indonesia):** The agency for domestic security and intelligence.

**Kuomintang (Taiwan):** The Nationalist Party of China, founded originally in 1894 and the dominant force in Taiwanese politics since the Chinese communist revolution of 1949.

**Land (Germany):** The component states (plural Länder) in the federal system, each with its own parliament (in most cases called the Landtag) and Land government headed by a minister-president (premier).

**Likud (Israel):** The right-of-centre "alliance of alliances" which forms the basis of the current government led by **Yitzhak Shamir.**

**Majlis (Iran etc):** The Islamic Consultative Assembly or Majlis-e- Shura e Islami, which in Iran is directly elected and has the right of approval of all ministerial appointments.

**Meech Lake Accord (Canada):** An agreement, reached in 1987, by which Quebec accepted provincial status in return for a clause recognizing its position as a "distinct society" because of its largely francophone population; previously Quebec had refused to accept the constitution repatriated from the UK in 1982. Other provinces, however, objected to the special status given to Quebec; the failure of Manitoba and Newfoundland to ratify it by the deadline of June 23, 1990 led to the collapse of the accord and growing pressure for Quebec to secede.

**Mujaheddin (Afghanistan):** Generic term, meaning holy warriors, used by a number of Islamic groups and most commonly applied as a blanket term for those fighting against the Soviet-backed communist regime in Afghanistan; some groups incorporate the word in a more specific title.

**National People's Congress (NPC):** China's parliament, with almost 3,000 members, whose Standing Committee functions as the permanent legislative body between NPC sessions.

**Palestine National Council (PNC):** The Palestinian "parliament-in-exile" which in November 1988 declared Palestine to be a sovereign state.

*panchayat* **(Nepal):** The system of "non-party democracy" introduced in Nepal and enshrined in its 1962 constitution, finally overturned by opposition pressure in 1990.

**Pathet Lao:** the military arm of the communist-led Laotian Patriotic Front in the civil war in 1963-73.

**Polisario Front (Morocco/Western Sahara):** The organization fighting against Moroccan forces for independence in Western Sahara. Led by **Mohammed Abdelaziz**, its full title means Popular Front for the Liberation of Saguia el Hamra and Rio de Oro. It was established in 1973, and took up armed struggle in 1975 after the Moroccan and Mauritanian governments had arranged to divide the former Spanish territory between them. In 1976 Polisario proclaimed a Sahrawi Arab Democratic Republic.

**Presidential Council (USSR):** A consultative body of presidential appointees, set up in March 1990. No provision was made for such a body in the constitutional arrangements approved by the Congress of Deputies in December 1990, although a new Security Council was to be created, on which the defence, interior and foreign ministers and the KGB chief would sit *ex officio*, together with "top scholars, specialists and public figures".

**Sejm (Poland):** Prior to 1989, the unicameral parliament, but since then the 460-seat lower house, elected (together with the new 100-seat Senate) in June 1989.

**Shia:** The "partisans" of Ali, the prophet Mohammad's cousin, and his successors. Shia Muslims account for about 10% of all Muslims and form the majority of the population in Iran. Iraq has a Shia majority among its Arab population and important Shia communities also exist in Yemen, Syria, Lebanon and the Arab Gulf states.

**Sinn Féin (Ireland):** Often described as the political wing of the Irish Republican Army, the name was first used by the nationalist party founded originally in 1905, and means "Ourselves Alone"; only the Provisional Sinn Féin retains the name today, the Workers' Party having dropped the prefix Sinn Féin in 1982.

**South Pacific Forum:** Regional organization set up in 1971, with Australia and New Zealand included in its membership.

**Swapo (Namibia):** The South West Africa People's Organization, the Namibian liberation movement led by **Sam Nujoma**, whose 30-year struggle effectively ended with the establishment of an independent Namibia in 1990.

**Taif peace agreement (Lebanon):** The agreement on national reconciliation accepted by the Lebanese National Assembly, meeting in Taif, Saudi Arabia, on October 22, 1989. The agreement, prepared by an Arab League committee headed by Saudi Arabia's **King Fahd**, Morocco's **King Hassan** and Algeria's President **Chadli Bendjedid**, provided for a redistribution of political power between the country's Muslim communities and the long-dominant Maronite Christians, the disarming of the country's militias and establishment of Lebanese government control throughout the country, backed initially by Syrian forces.

**Tweede Kamer (Netherlands):** The lower house of the Dutch parliament and its main legislative chamber.

**UMA:** Union du Maghreb Arabe (Arab Maghreb Union), a five-country regional grouping formed in 1989 by Algeria, Libya, Mauritania, Morocco and Tunisia.

**Unita (Angola):** The Angolan rebel National Union for the Total Independence of Angola or União Naçional para a Independência Total de Angola, established in 1966 and led by **Jonas Savimbi**, which since Angolan independence in 1975 has sustained a protracted civil war against the regime set up by its erstwhile rival, the marxist MPLA.

**Uruguay Round:** The round of multinational trade negotiations under way since 1986 under the General Agreement on Tariffs and Trade (Gatt); the Uruguay Round was suspended after failing to meet its deadline for agreement in December 1990, but resumed in early 1991.

*Vali faqih* **(Iran):** The spiritual leader, who exercises overall authority; the president is the chief executive.

*verligte* **(South Africa):** Literally "enlightened" in Afrikaans, and a term applied to those Afrikaners disposed towards liberal reform of the apartheid system; the converse term "verkrampte" is sometimes applied to more reactionary ultra-conservatives.

**Volkskammer (Germany):** The unicameral parliament in the former East Germany, to which multi-party elections were held in March 1990 prior to German unification.

**Xinhua (China):** the Chinese official news agency, the New China News Agency

**ZANU (PF – Zimbabwe):** The name adopted by the party formed by the merger of ZAPU into ZANU in December 1987, and signifying the retention of the Patriotic Front designation, under which they had co- ordinated their guerrilla struggle before independence.

**ZANU (Zimbabwe):** The Zimbabwe African

National Union, first formed in 1963 as a breakaway from ZAPU. Under **Robert Mugabe**'s leadership it proved itself the dominant partner in the Patriotic Front and was the leading force in the post-independence government.

**ZAPU (Zimbabwe):** The Zimbabwe African People's Union, formed in 1961 and led by **Joshua Nkomo**, which together with ZAPU constituted the Patriotic Front alliance in the struggle for liberation. Overshadowed by the more powerful ZANU in the post-independence period, it formally ceased to exist when it merged itself into the new unified ruling party structure of ZANU-PF in December 1987.

**AD (Chile):** Alianza Democrática (Democratic Alliance).

**AD (Venezuela):** Acción Democrática (Democratic Action).

**ADN (Bolivia):** Acción Democrática Nacionalista (Nationalist Democratic Action).

**ADOC (Panama):** Alianza Democrática de Oposición Civilista (Democratic Civil Opposition Alliance).

**AKEL (Cyprus):** Anorthotiko Komma Ergazomenou Laou (Progressive Party of the Working People).

**AL (Germany):** Alternative Liste (Alternative List).

**AN (Chile):** Acción Nacional (National Action).

**ANAP (Turkey):** Anavatan Partisi (Motherland Party).

**AP (Spain):** Alianza Popular (Popular Alliance).

**APRA (Peru):** Alianza Popular Revoluncionaria Americana (American Popular Revolutionary Alliance).

**ARDE – MDN (Nicaragua):** Alianza Revolucionaria Democrática – Movimiento Democrático Nicaragüense (Democratic Revolutionary Alliance – Nicaraguan Democratic Movement).

**Arena (El Salvador):** Alianza Republicana Nacionalista (Nationalist Republican Alliance).

**AWB (South Africa):** Afrikaner Weerstandsbeweging (Afrikaner Resistance Movement).

**BCEAO (West Africa):** Banque centrale des états de l'afrique de l'ouest (West African Central Bank).

**BDI (Germany):** Bundersverband der Deutschen Industrie (Federal Association of German Industry).

**BVA (Germany):** Bundesvereinigung der Deutsche Arbeitgeberverbände (Federal Association of German Employers).

**BZNS (Bulgaria):** Bulgarsky Zemedelsky Naroden Soyuz (Bulgarian Agrarian People's Union).

**CCM Chama Cha Mapinduzi (Tanzania):** the ruling Revolutionary Party, formed in 1977.

**CD (El Salvador):** Convergencia Democrática (Democratic Convergence).

**CD (Mexico):** Corriente Democrática (Democratic Current).

**CDA (Netherlands):** Christen-Democratisch Appel (Christian Democratic Appeal).

**CDR (Chad):** Conseil démocratique révolutionnaire (Democratic Revolutionary Council).

**CDS (France):** Centre des démocrates sociaux (Centre of Social Democrats).

**CDS (Portugal):** Partido do Centro Democrático Social (Democratic Social Centre).

**CDS (Spain):** Centro Democratico y Social (Democratic and Social Centre).

**CDU (Germany):** Christlich Demokratische Union (Christian Democratic Union).

**CEOE (Spain):** Confederación Española de Organizaciones Empresariales (Spanish Confederation of Employers' Organizations).

**CFDT (France):** Confédération française démocratique du travail (French Democratic Labour Federation).

**CGIL (Italy):** Confederazione Generale Italiano del Lavoro (Italian General Confederation of Labour).

**CGT (Argentina):** Confederación General del Trabajo (General Confederation of Labour).

**CGT (France):** Confédération générale du travail (General Confederation of Labour).

**CMRN (Guinea):** Comité militaire de redressement national (Military Committee for National Recovery).

**CMSN (Mauritania):** Comité militaire de salut national (Military Committee for National Salvation).

**CNIP (France):** Centre national des indépendants et paysans (National centre of independents and peasants).

**Condepa (Bolivia):** Conciencia de Patria (Conscience of the Homeland).

**COPEI (Venezuela):** Comité de Organización Politica Electoral Independiente (Organizing Committee for Independent Electoral Policy).

**CPD (Chile):** Concertación de los Partidos de la Democracia (Coalition for Democracy).

**CPN (Netherlands):** Communistische Partij van Nederland (Communist Party of the Netherlands).

**CSU (Germany):** Christlich Soziale Union (Christian Social Union).

**CTM (Mexico):** Confederación de Trabajadores de México (Confederation of Mexican Workers).

**CTV (Venezuela):** Confederación de Trabajadores de Venezuela (Workers' Confederation of Venezuela).

**CUT (Brazil):** Central Unica dos Trabalhadores (Trade Union Confederation).

**CVP (Belgium):** Christelijke Volkspartei (Christian People's Party).

**CVP (Switzerland):** Christlichdemokratische Volkspartei der Schweiz/Parti démocrate-chrétien suisse (Christian Democratic People's Party).

**CVP/PCS (Luxembourg):** Parti chrétien social

(Social Christian Party).

**D66 (Netherlands):** Democraten 66 (Democrats 66).

**DC (Italy):** Partito della Democrazia Cristiana (Christian Democratic Party).

**DGB (Germany):** Deutscher Gewerkschaftsbund (German Trade Union Federation).

**DKP (Germany):** Deutsche Kommunistische Partei (German Communist Party).

**DNA (Norway):** Det Norsk Arbeiderparti (Norwegian Labour Party).

**DP (Ecuador):** Democracia Popular (People's Democracy).

**DSP (Turkey):** Democratik Sol Parti (Democratic Left Party).

**DSU (Germany):** Deutsche Soziale Union (German Social Union).

**EA (Spain):** Eusko Alkartasuna (Basque Solidarity).

**ERP (El Salvador):** Ejército Revolucionario Popular (People's Revolutionary Army).

**ETA (Spain):** Euskadi ta Askatasuna (Basque Homeland and Liberty).

**FA (Uruguay):** Frente Amplio (Broad Front).

**FAN (El Salvador):** Frente Amplio Nacional (Broad National Front).

**FDN (Mexico):** Frente Democrático Nacional (National Democratic Front).

**FDO (Suriname):** Front voor Demokratie en Ontwikkeling (Front for Democracy and Development).

**FDP (Germany):** Freie Demokratische Partei (Free Democratic Party).

**FDP (Switzerland):** Freisinnig-Demokratischen Parti der Schweiz/Parti radical-démocratique suisse (Radical Democratic Party of Switzerland).

**FDR (El Salvador):** Frente Democrático Revolucionario (Revolutionary Democratic Front).

**FFS (Algeria):** Front des forces socialistes (Socialist Forces Front).

**FIS (Algeria):** Front islamique de salut (Islamic Salvation Front).

**FK (Denmark):** Fœlles Krus (Common Course).

**FLN (Algeria):** Front de libération nationale (National Liberation Front).

**FLNKS (France – New Caledonia):** Front de libération nationale kanake socialiste (Kanak Socialist National Liberation Front).

**FMLN (El Salvador):** Farbundo Martí de Liberación Nacional (Farabundo Martí National Liberation Front).

**FN (France):** Front national (National Front).

**FNV (Netherlands):** Federatie Nederlandse Vakbeweging (Federation of Dutch Trade Unions).

**FP (Denmark):** Fremskridtspartiet (Progress Party).

**FP (Norway):** Fremskrittspartiet (Progress Party).

**FP (Sweden):** Folkpartiet (Liberal Party).

**FPI (Côte d'Ivoire):** Front populaire ivoirien (Ivorian Popular Front).

**FPÖ (Austria):** Freiheitliche Partei Österreichs (Freedom Party of Austria).

**FSLN (Nicaragua):** Frente Sandinista de Liberación Nacional (Sandinista National Liberation Front).

**FULK (France - New Caledonia):** Front uni de libération kanake (United Front for Kanak Liberation).

**GPS (Switzerland):** Grüne Partei der Schweiz/Parti écologiste suisse (Green Party of Switzerland).

**GUNT (Chad):** Gouvernement d'union nationale de transition (Transitional Government of National Unity).

**HB (Spain):** Herri Batasuna (United People).

**HNP (South Africa):** Herstigte Nasionale Party (Reconstituted National Party).

**ID (Ecuador):** Izquierda Democrática (Democratic Left).

**INI (Spain):** Instituto Nacional de Industria (National Institute of Industry).

**IU (Peru, Spain):** Izquierda Unida (United Left).

**KF (Denmark):** Det Konservative Folkeparti (Conservative People's Party).

**KKE (Greece):** Kommunistiko Komma Elladas (Communist Party of Greece).

**KP (Finland):** Keskustapuolue (Centre Party).

**KSČ (Czechoslovakia):** Komunistická strana Československa (Communist Party of Czechoslovakia).

**KVP (Netherlands):** Katholischevolkspartij (Catholic People's Party).

**LO (France):** Lutte ouvrière (Workers' Struggle).

**LO (Sweden):** Landsorganisationen i Sverige (Swedish Trade Union Confederation).

**LSAP/POSL (Luxembourg):** Parti ouvrier socialiste luxembourgeois (Luxembourg Socialist Workers' Party).

**M-19 (Colombia):** Movimiento 19 de Abril (19 April Movement).

**MAS (Venezuela):** Movimento al Socialismo (Movement towards Socialism).

**MD (France):** Mouvement de démocrates (Movement of Democrats).

**MDA (Algeria):** Mouvement pour la démocratie en Algérie (Movement for Democracy in Algeria).

**MDF (Hungary):** Magyar Demokratic Fórum (Hungarian Democratic Forum).

**MDS (Tunisia):** Mouvement des démocrates socialistes (Social Democratic Movement).

**MFM (Madagascar):** Mpitolana ho amin'ny Fanjakana ny Madinika (Party for Proletarian Power).

**MIDH (Haiti):** Mouvement pour l'instauration de la démocratie en Haïti (Movement for the Installation of Democracy in Haiti).

**MIT (USA):** Massachusetts Institute of Technology.

**MIR (Bolivia):** Movimiento de la Izquierda Revolucionaria (Revolutionary Leftist Movement).

**MMM (Mauritius):** Mouvement militant mauricien (Mauritian Militant Movement).

**MNC (Zaire):** Mouvement national congolais (Congo National Movement).

**MNR (Bolivia):** Movimiento Nacionalista Revolucionaria (Nationalist Revolutionary Movement).

**Molirena (Panama):** Movimiento Liberal Republicano Nacionalista (National Republican Liberal Movement).

**Morena (Gabon):** Mouvement de redressement national (National Rectification Movement).

**MPD (Cape Verde):** Movimento para Democracia (Movement for Democracy).

**MPLA (Angola):** Movimento Popular de Libertação de Angola (Angolan People's Liberation Movement).

**MPR (Zaïre):** Mouvement populaire de la révolution (Popular Revolutionary Movement).

**MPSC (El Salvador):** Movimiento Popular Social Cristiano (Social Christian People's Movement).

**MRG (France):** Mouvement des radicaux de gauche (Movement of Left-Wing Radicals).

**MRND (Rwanda):** Mouvement révolutionnaire national pour le développement (National Revolutionary Movement for Development).

**MSI – DN (Italy):** Movimento Sociale Italiano – Destra Nazionale (Italian Social Movement – National Right).

**MSM (Hungary):** Magyar Szocialista Munkáspárt (Hungarian Socialist Workers' Party).

**MSM (Mauritius):** Mouvement socialiste mauricien (Mauritian Socialist Movement).

**MSP (Hungary):** Magyar Szocialista Párt (Hungarian Socialist Party).

**MTI (Tunisia):** Mouvement de la tendance islamique (Islamic Tendency Movement).

**NCW (Netherlands):** Nederlands Christelijk Werkgeversverbond (Dutch Christian Employers' Federation).

**ND (Greece):** Nea Demokratia (New Democracy).

**NE (Uruguay):** Nuevo Espacio (New Space).

**NPD (Germany):** Nationaldemokratische Partei Deutschlands (National Democratic Party of Germany).

**NPS (Suriname):** Nationale Partij Suriname (National Party of Suriname).

**NRI (Morocco):** Rassemblement national des indépendents (National Rally of Independents).

**OAU:** Organization of African Unity.

**OECD:** Organisation for Economic Co-operation and Development.

**OPZZ (Poland):** Ogólnopolskie Poruzmienie Zwiazków Zawodowych (All Poland Alliance of Trade Unions).

**ÖVP (Austria):** Österreichische Volkspartei (Austrian People's Party).

**PAD (Spain):** Partido de Acción Democrática (Democratic Action Party).

**PAICV (Cape Verde):** Partido Africano da Independência de Cabo Verde (African Party for the Independence of Cape Verde).

**PAN (Mexico):** Partido Acción Nacional (National Action Party).

**Panpra (Haiti):** Parti nationaliste progressiste révolutionnaire (Progressive Nationalist Revolutionary Party).

**PAR (Spain):** Partido Aragonés Regionalista (Aragonese Regionalist Party).

**Pasok (Greece):** Panellinion Socialistikou Kinema (Panhellenic Socialist Movement).

**PCC (Cuba):** Partido Comunista de Cuba (Cuban Communist Party).

**PCCh (Chile):** Partido Comunista de Chile (Chilean Communist Party).

**PCD (Ecuador):** Pueblo, Cambio y Democracia– Popular Roldosista (People, Change and Democracy–Popular Roldosista Party).

**PCE (Spain):** Partido Comunista de España (Spanish Communist Party).

**PCF (France):** Parti communiste français (French Communist Party).

**PCI (Italy):** Partito Comunista Italiano (Italian Communist Party).

**PCP (Portugal):** Partido Comunista Português (Portuguese Communist Party).

**PCPE (Spain):** Partido Comunista de los Pueblos de España (Communist Party of the Peoples of Spain).

**PCR (Romania):** Partidul Comunist Român (Romanian Communist Party).

**PCS (El Salvador):** Partido Comunista Salvadoreño (Communist Party of El Salvador).

**PCT (Congo):** Parti congolais du travail (Congolese Labour Party).

**PDC (Argentina, Chile, Ecuador, El Salvador, Panama):** Partido Democráta Cristiano (Christian Democratic Party).

**PDCG (Guatemala):** Partido Democracia Cristiana Guatemalteca (Guatemalan Christian Democratic Party).

**PDCH (Haiti):** Parti démocratique chrétien d'Haïti (Haitian Christian Democratic Party).

**PDCI (Côte d'Ivoire):** Parti démocratique de la Côte d'Ivoire (Ivorian Democratic Party).

**PDP (Spain):** Partido Demócrata Popular (Popular Democratic Party).

**PDS (Germany):** Partei des Demokratischen Sozialismus (Party of Democratic Socialism).

**PDS (Italy):** Partito Democratico della Sinistra (Democratic Party of the Left).

**PDS (Senegal):** Parti démocratique sénégalaise (Democratic Party of Senegal).

**PDT (Brazil):** Partido Democrático Trabalhista (Democratic Labour Party).

**PGP (Uruguay):** Partido por el Gobierno del Pueblo (Party for the Government of the People).

**PIP (Puerto Rico):** Partido Independentista Puertorriqueño (Puerto Rico Independence Party).

**PLD (Dominican Republic):** Partido de la Liberación Dominicana (Dominican Liberation Party).

**PLI (Italy):** Partito Liberale Italiano (Italian Liberal Party).

**PLI (Nicaragua):** Partido Liberal Independiente (Independent Liberal Party).

**PLN (Costa Rica):** Partido de Liberación Nacional (National Liberation Party).

**PLRA (Paraguay):** Partido Liberal Radical Auténtico (Authentic Radical Liberal Party).

**PMDB (Brazil):** Partido do Movimento Democrático Brasileiro (Brazilian Democratic Movement).

**PMSD (Mauritius):** Parti mauricien social démocrate (Mauritius Social Democratic Party).

**PN (Honduras):** Partido Nacional (National Party).

**PNP (Puerto Rico):** Partido Nuevo Progresista (New Progressive Party).

**PNV (Spain):** Partido Nacionalista Vasco (Basque Nationalist Party).

**PP (Spain):** Partido Popular (Popular Party).

**PPA (Panama):** Partido Panameñista Auténtico (Authentic Panameñista Party).

**PPD (Chile):** Partido por la Democracia (Party for Democracy).

**PPR (Netherlands):** Politieke Partij Radikalen (Radical Political Party).

**PQ (Canada):** Parti québécois (Quebec Party).

**PR (Chile):** Partido Radical (Radical Party).

**PR (Dominican Republic):** Partido Reformista (Reformist Party).

**PR (France):** Parti républicain (Republican Party).

**PRD (Dominican Republic):** Partido Revolucionario Dominicano (Dominican Revolutionary Party).

**PRD (Mexico):** Partido de la Revolución Democrática (Party of the Democratic Revolution).

**PRE (Ecuador):** Partido Roldosista Ecuatorano (Ecuadorian Roldosista Party).

**PRI (Dominican Republic):** Partido Revolucionario Independiente (Independent Revolutionary Party).

**PRI (Italy):** Partito Repubblicano Italiano (Italian Republican Party).

**PRI (Mexico):** Partido Revolucionario Institucional (Institutional Revolutionary Party).

**PRL (Belgium):** Parti réformateur libéral (Liberal Reform Party).

**PRSC (Dominican Republic):** Partido Reformista Social Cristiano (Social Christian Reformist Party).

**PS (Belgium, France, Senegal):** Parti socialiste (Socialist Party).

**PS (Portugal):** Partido Socialista (Socialist Party).

**PSC (Belgium):** Parti social chrétien (Christian Social Party).

**PSC (Colombia):** Partido Social Conservador (Social Conservative Party).

**PSC (Ecuador):** Partido Social Cristiano (Social Christian Party).

**PSCh (Chile):** Partido Socialista de Chile (Socialist Party).

**PSD (Madagascar):** Parti social démocrate (Social Democratic Party).

**PSD (Portugal):** Partido Social Democrata (Social Democratic Party).

**PSDB (Brazil):** Partido da Social Democracia Brasileira (Brazilian Social Democratic Party).

**PSDI (Italy):** Partito Socialista Democratico Italiano (Italian Democratic Socialist Party).

**PSE–PSOE (Spain):** Partido Socialista de Euskadi (Basque Socialist Party).

**PSI (Italy):** Partito Socialista Italiano (Italian Socialist Party).

PSL (Poland): Polskie Stronnictwo Ludowe (Polish Peasant Party).

PSM (Mauritius): Parti socialiste mauricien (Mauritius Socialist Party).

PSOE (Spain): Partido Socialista Obrero Español (Spanish Socialist Workers' Party).

PSP (Netherlands): Pacifistisch Socialistiche Partij (Pacifist Socialist Party).

PSP (Spain): Partido Socialista Popular (Popular Socialist Party).

PSU (France): Parti socialiste unifié (Unified Socialist Party).

PT (Brazil): Partido dos Trabalhadores (Workers' Party).

PTE–UC (Spain): Partido de los Trabajadores de España – Unidad Comunista (Workers' Party of Spain – Communist Unity).

PUSC (Costa Rica): Partido Unidad Social Cristiana (United Social Christian Party).

PUSD (Poland): Polska Unia Socjaldemokratyczna (Polish Social Democratic Union).

PvdA (Netherlands): Partij van der Arbeid (Labour Party).

PZPR (Poland): Polska Zjednoczona Partia Robotnica (Polish United Workers' Party).

RCD (Tunisia): Rassemblement constitutionnel démocratique (Constitutional Democratic Rally).

RI (France): Républicains indépendants (Independent Republicans).

RN (Chile): Renovación Nacional (National Renovation).

RN (Nicaragua): Resistencia Nicaragüense (National Resistance).

RPR (France): Rassemblement pour la république (Rally for the Republic).

RPT (Togo): Rassemblement du peuple Togolais (Togolese People's Rally).

RV (Denmark): Det Radikale Venstre (Radical Liberal Party).

SAP (Sweden): Socialdemokratiska Arbetarepartiet (Social Democratic Labour Party).

SD (Poland): Stronnictwo Demokratyczne (Democratic Party).

SDP (Finland): Suomen Sosialidemokraatinen Puolue (Finnish Social Democratic Party).

SED (Germany): Sozialistische Einheitspartei Deutschlands (Socialist Unity Party).

SF (Denmark): Socialistisk Folkeparti (Socialist People's Party).

SGP (Netherlands): Staatkundig Gereformeerde Partij (Political Reformed Party).

SHP (Turkey): Sosyal Demokrat Halkçi Parti (Social Democratic Populist Party).

SP (Belgium): Socialistische Partij (Socialist Party).

SPD (Germany): Sozialdemokratische Partei Deutschlands (Social Democratic Party of Germany).

SPÖ (Austria): Sozialistische Partei Österreichs (Socialist Party of Austria).

SPS (Switzerland): Sozialdemokratische Partei der Schweiz/Parti socialiste suisse (Social Democratic Party of Switzerland).

STK (Finland): Suomen Työnantajain Keskusliitto (Finnish Employers' Confederation).

UC (Morocco): Union constitutionelle (Constitutional Union).

UCD (Spain): Unión de Centro Democrático (Union of the Democratic Centre).

UCN (Guatemala): Unión del Centro Nacional (National Centrist Union).

UCR (Argentina): Unión Cívica Radical (Radical Civil Union).

UDF (France): Union pour la démocratie française (Union for French Democracy).

UDPM (Mali): Union démocratique de peuple malien (Democratic Union of Malian People).

UDPS (Zaïre): Union pour la démocratie et le progrès social (Union for Democracy and Social Progress).

UGT (Spain): Unión General de Trabajadores (General Workers' Union).

UNFP (Morocco): Union national des forces populaires (National Union of Popular Forces).

UNO (Nicaragua): Unión Nacional de Opositora (National Opposition Union).

UPF (France): Union pour la France (Union for France).

USFP (Morocco): Union socialiste des forces populaires (Socialist Union of Popular Forces).

VHP (Suriname): Vooruitstrevende Hervormings Partij (Progressive Reform Party).

VNO (Netherlands): Verbond van Nederlandse Ondernemingen (Federation of Dutch Industries).

Vonjy (Madagascar): Vonjy Iray Tsy Mivaky (National Unity Party).

VpK (Sweden): Vänsterpartiet– Kommunisterne (Left Party–Communists).

VU (Belgium): Volksunie (People's Unity).

VVD (Netherlands): Volkspartij voor Vrijheid en Democratie (People's Party for Freedom and Democracy).

ZSL (Poland): Zjednoczone Stronnictwo Ludowe (United Peasants' Party).

# Index